Philippe Lionnet
Finding a Path for China's Rise

Global and Colonial History | Volume 12

Editorial

Since national histories have been discredited as the only legitimate way to write history, global history has been gaining momentum. Global history, however, is not merely "history outside Europe"; and global is more than "around the world". Global history means historiography that tries to overcome Eurocentric perspectives and to focus on global complexity and interrelations. Thus, global historians tend to study topics such as colonialism, migration, trade, international cooperation, slavery, tourism, imperialism, globalization, knowledge transfers, etc.
The book series **Global and Colonial History** offers a common forum to discuss cutting-edge research on these issues. We consider colonial and imperial history to be a central part of global history because it is exemplary of this historiography as a history of interrelations and because it challenges past and present power structures and hegemonic discourses on a methodological level.

Philippe Lionnet, born in 1986, completed his doctorate in history at the University of Bern after receiving masters degrees from the Universities of Basel (MA) and Zurich (LLM). His research included visits to Beijing, Hong Kong, Pittsburgh and London. He works as a foreign economic policy advisor for the Swiss Federal Administration.

Philippe Lionnet

Finding a Path for China's Rise

The Socialist State and the World Economy, 1970-1978

[transcript]

Based on the author's dissertation submitted at the Faculty of Humanities at the University of Bern to obtain the degree of Doctor of Philosophy (PhD).
Accepted by Prof. Dr. Christian Gerlach and Prof. Dr. Lorenz Lüthi (McGill University, Montreal, Canada) on behalf of the Faculty.

Bibliographic information published by the Deutsche Nationalbibliothek
The Deutsche Nationalbibliothek lists this publication in the Deutsche Nationalbibliografie; detailed bibliographic data are available in the Internet at http://dnb.d-nb.de

Cover layout: Maria Arndt, Bielefeld
Cover illustration: Photography by Philippe Lionnet (Factory 798, Beijing, 2016)
Printed by: Majuskel Medienproduktion GmbH, Wetzlar
https://doi.org/10.14361/9783839464229
Print-ISBN 978-3-8376-6422-5
PDF-ISBN 978-3-8394-6422-9
ISSN of series: 2701-0309
eISSN of series: 2702-9328

Printed on permanent acid-free text paper.

For François, Kyllikki and Pia-Andrea,
who let me hit the road with them in the little red bus
and taught me almost everything I know.

Contents

Acknowledgements

As it tends to be the case with every project taking several years to complete, there are countless people who contributed decisively to this one. Many, I guess, without noticing. My advisor Christian Gerlach with both his relentless academic rigor and encouragement has guided my journey, far beyond this book. The late Mayling Birney, Felix Wemheuer and Lorenz Lüthi have given me valuable advice and criticism along the way. Dear friends and my beloved family – in Switzerland as well as Suomi – have supported me throughout. Thank you for sticking with me, even if there always seemed to be at least one project too many.

The People's Republic of China during the long 1970s

The economic reforms post 1978 (the so-called Reform Era[1]) in the People's Republic of China (PRC)[2], under the political leadership of the Chinese Communist Party (CCP) led by Deng Xiaoping, are widely considered to be of global historic importance as they paved the way for enormous economic growth and the subsequent rise from poverty of millions. According to Chinese data, per capita consumption rose by a factor of 3.62 for all households from 1978 to 1990. While growth was and still is unevenly distributed between regions as well as urban versus rural households, this is an unprecedented achievement.[3]

Moreover, the reforms are credited with opening the now second largest global economy[4] to the world, paving the way for its institutional integration in the political and legal systems of international markets shaped by the industrialised West after the Second World War. For example, China is currently a member state of all Bretton Woods-Institutions – the IMF, World Bank (WB) – as well as the World Trade Organization (WTO). It also has a working relationship with the Organisation for Economic Cooperation and Development (OECD), the organisation of democratic market economies. On the other hand, China has founded its own multilateral institutions, such as the Asian Infrastructure Investment Bank (AIIB) in 2016, and is pushing an enormous investment framework, the "Belt and Road-Initiative". Despite more recent tendencies towards a at least declared intention to "decouple" some of its economy from the US- and EU-markets as

1 Brandt Loren, Rawski Thomas G. (eds.), China's Great Economic Transformation, New York 2008.

2 While the People's Republic of China is the official designation of the state in control of the "Chinese Mainland", if the country is meant, I will refer to it as "China" throughout this book. People's Republic (PRC) is used for the political apparatus or stylistic reasons. It is well understood that this in no way implies a specific opinion of the author on the legal and political status of the Republic of China/Taiwan.

3 Chow Gregory C., China's Economic Transformation, third edition, Chichester 2015, pp. 162 f.

4 China is the second-largest economy in the world and the fastest-growing trillion-dollar economy. According to estimates from the International Money Fund's (IMF) latest World Economic Outlook, the country will account for 18.8 percent of the world's GDP based on purchasing power parity (PPP). That's up from just 8.1 percent two decade ago, when both the United States and the EU were miles ahead of China's economic output.China is about to become a twenty trillion USD economy by 2024. See: International Monetary Fund, World Economic Outlook Database. Available at: https://www.imf.org/en/Publications/WEO/weo-database/2022/April. Last accessed on 12 August 2022.

well as certain cross-border value chains: China remains a global economic power. In fact, its success and the methods to achieve it are driving current policies in the West that include remarkable government intervention, i. e. subsidies for the development and production of semiconductors. The rise of China has influenced economic policy in even the most successful market-oriented economies.

Marking historical turning points, the measures taken in the course of the Reform and Opening programmes (*gaige gaifang*) shifted scholarly attention to the undoubtedly important economic and – to a much lesser extent, political – progress that occurred after 1979. For decades since, China's impressive economic growth has overshadowed that of other emerging economies. While there have been fluctuations, the average growth rate of China's annual real gross domestic product (GDP) stands at 9.5 percent between 1979 and 2018.[5] While current restrictive policies both related to the COVID-19 pandemic in China and a revival of export controls imposed particularly by the United States have dampened the already slowing growth dynamic in recent years, the macroeconomic success story of China is difficult to overestimate in a historical perspective. Since 1979, on average, China has been able to double the size of its enormous economy in real terms every eight years.

It has done so also with foreign capital. The Indian businessman RAGHAV BAHL described his own experience with enthusiastic foreign investors after the sharp devaluation of the Indian rupee, and the abolishment of the *Licence Raj* in 1991.[6] While this bold step had resulted in a sharp spike in economic growth, political turmoil caused by a pronounced inequality in the distribution of the gains from liberalisation followed. But even so, the results yielded did not compare favourably with China's growth:

> "After decades of invisibility, it [India] had managed to create a blip on the western radar, but China was the sexy one. Exploratory droplets of western capital had fallen into India, but that was meagre compared to the torrential pouring into China. I remember what one of my legendary foreign investor friends told me around that time: 'China's got a real J-curve of growth. It's the classic hockey stick. Demand simply takes off after a couple of years, whether it's demand for cars or internet connections or refrigerators. You guys [India] are darn slow, mate. Your J-curve is just so f-l-a-a-a-t [sic!]. It stays horizontal for years and years and years, and just when you are about to give up, it shows a small upturn. Just why does your consumer take so long to change his habits? Why is he so brutal about paying low prices? Just why do you guys take so bloody long to decide about anything?"[7]

The "hockey stick" described here refers to the graphical depiction of Chinese *nominal* GDP – already in the early 1990s, China's real GDP growth rate did fluctuate, albeit

5 International Monetary Fund, World Economic Outlook Database.

6 AGHION PHILIPPE, BURGESS ROBIN, REDDING STEPHEN, ZILIBOTTI FABRIZIO, The Unequal Effects of Liberalization: Evidence from Dismantling the License Raj in India, Swiss National Centre of Competence in Research on Financial Valuation and Risk Management (Finrisk), Working Paper No. 426, September 2007. Available at: http://www.nccr-finrisk.uzh.ch/media/pdf/wp/WP426_A2.pdf. Last accessed on 1 April 2022.

7 BAHL RAGHAV, Superpower? The Amazing Race Between China's Hare and India's Tortoise, Allen Lane 2010, p. 9.

around a very high eight to ten percent. In any case, the steady rise of the curve had its effect on investors and politicians in industrialised countries. Alongside the similarly famous exponential graph indicating the concentration of carbon dioxide in Earth's atmosphere, it is arguably the depiction of numerical data that has most influenced discourses on globalisation in the late 20th and early 21st centuries.[8]

The effect of this economic rise on the perception of the China in the West is equally impressive, in particular compared with its staus a century earlier. As the New York Daily Tribune, a predecessor of the New York Times, known for its opposition to slavery, printed on the 29th of September 1854:

> "The Chinese are uncivilized, unclean, and filthy beyond all conception, without any of the higher domestic or social relations; lustful and sensual in their dispositions; every female is a prostitute of the basest order."[9]

In the early 1970s, during the period this book covers, China and its people seemed to have "changed color" as suggested by ELMAR SCHENKEL.[10] It implied a kind of graduation from the dubious status of "yellow peril" to the not much more flattering "red menace".[11] That the same people subsequently became one of the main driving forces behind the international capitalist economy is a phenomenon almost equally impressive as the economic progress on which this "evolution" is based. Until the recent turn towards a rather defensive geopolitical stance, the positive attitude towards the PRC in industrialised nations seemed almost universal at times: consumers enjoyed affordable prices of manufactured goods, investors saw potential for capital gains and producers saw opportunities for industrial production as well as competitive inputs to their value chains.[12]

Taking the starting point for China's rise in the 20th century into account makes it even more remarkable. Using GDP as a yardstick, China was among the poorest countries in the world in 1978.[13] Its real (adjusted for purchasing power) *per capita* GDP stood

---

8 Both phenomena arguably correlate, as the importance of China's role in global climate change mitigation is frequently emphasised. For an interdisciplinary discussion of the issue, see: SONG LIGANG, WOO WING THYE (eds.), China's Dilemma: Economic Growth, the Environment and Climate Change, Canberra 2008.

9 LEE GREGORY, Chinese Migrants and the "Infundation" Metaphor: Risk, Representation, Repression: Constructing and Manipulating Fear of the Chinese Other, Framing Risk: Hazard Perceptions as a Crucial Factor in Imagining East Asia, East Asia Net Workshop Paper, June 2007, p. 3.

10 SCHENKEL ELMAR, Unterwegs nach Xanadu, Begegnungen zwischen Ost und West, Frankfurt am Main 2021, p. 197.

11 A term which framed China mostly as an expansionist military aggressor, similar to the Soviet Union. See: GOH EVELYN, Constructing the U.S. Rapprochement with China 1961–1974, New York 2005, pp. 20 ff.

12 For a classic treatise on the process of marketisation and (partial) opening to foreign investment, see: COASE RONALD, WANG NING, How China became Capitalist, Houndmills 2012. With regard to the conditions offered to foreign businesses – still limited through negative lists for sectoral investments and joint-venture-obligations for portfolio investments, see: KROEBER ARTHUR R., China's Economy, What everyone needs to know, Oxford 2016.

13 ZHU XIAODONG, Understanding China´s Growth: Past, Present, and Future, in: Journal of Economic Perspectives, Vol. 26, No. 4, Fall 2012, pp. 103–124. In recent years, Chinese growth has faced a steady moderation, amounting to 6.567 percent in 2018. The World Bank, GDP growth – China,

at one-fortieth of the US level and one-tenth of the Brazilian level. Since then and until 2012, it grew at an average rate exceeding eight percent per year as well.[14] This transformation from one of the world's poorest to a highly successful industrialised economy is directly linked to adjustments made to relevant policies and particulary the embrace of international trade and investment after 1979. Today, both of the latter are the foundation of a common narrative about Chinese economic development. As a Swiss business guide for investors and entrepreneurs published in 2016 put it: "The history of China's economic rise is the history of a trading nation".[15]

Of course, this rise did not occur in a historical void. It was a product of circumstances and context in both China and the rest of the world. There was no blueprint, no pre-conceived plan to achieve what China did. Rather, experimentation allowed for the development of policies and – as I suggest, more important – their constant adjustment. This ability to learn from successes and failures allowed for relatively constant improvements, until circumstances changed again. It also included grave mistakes and excesses, causing horrendous loss and suffering.

This book examines the economic reform's recent prehistory, namely the history of Chinese economic policy during what ODD ARNE WESTAD and others have referred to as the Long 1970s.[16] It is based on a study of the political economy of socialist China, its industrialisation under what CHRIS BRAMALL called Late Maoism[17], and the relationship between its changing industrialisation paradigms and the early stages of the post-Bretton Woods world economy.[18] The primary research interest is the industrialisation

available at: https://data.worldbank.org/indicator/NY.GDP.MKTP.KD.ZG?locations=CN. Last accessed on 1 April 2020.

14 The Wall Street Journal named China together with Germany and Japan as such, implying that the course of the global economic development directly correlates with their internal conjunctural development. The Wall Street Journal, Global Economic Powerhouses Stuck in Low Gear, 14 November 2019. Interestingly enough, the Cambridge dictionary uses the term in the exemplary sentences "*Germany is an economic powerhouse*" and "*Analysts still believe that China and India will become the economic powerhouses of the world*". Available at: https://dictionary.cambridge.org/dictionary/english/powerhouse. Last accessed on 3 July 2022.

15 RUDOLF JOACHIM, TESTER ELISABETH, China – der nächste Horizont, Ein Kompass für Anleger und Unternehmer, Zürich 2016, p. 27.

16 As suggested by ODD ARNE WESTAD, ranging from 1969 to 1982 "*or thereabouts*". See: WESTAD ODD ARNE, The Great Transformation, China in the Long 1970s, in: FERGUSON NIALL, MAIER CHARLES S., MANELA EREZ, SARGENT DANIEL J., The Shock of the Global, The 1970s in Perspective, Harvard 2011, p. 65.

17 As proposed by CHRIS BRAMALL for the years following the official end of the Cultural Revolution in 1972, as well as by FREDERICK C. TEIWES and WARREN SUN as the "late Maoist era". See: BRAMALL CHRIS, The Last of the Romantics? Maoist Economic Development in Retrospect, in: The China Quarterly, No. 187, September 2006, p. 691; and TEIWES FREDERICK C., SUN WARREN, The End of the Maoist Era, Chinese Politics During the Twilight of the Cultural Revolution, 1972–1976, New York 2007.

18 Beginning with the unilateral termination of the guaranteed convertibility of the US-Dollar to gold on 15 August 1971, after unsuccessful attempts at modifying the system through improved international economic policy coordination between member states. See: TRUMAN EDWIN M., The End of the Bretton Woods International Monetary System, Peterson Institute for International Economics Working Paper, October 2017.

paradigm at work in China prior to Reform and Opening and, in particular, the continuities found therein. It is focused on the question how both internal and foreign economic policies, formulated within a distinctly socialist frame of reference, show political attempts to tackle specific challenges as well as contradictions within the Chinese economy – based on less paradigmatic adjustments than those occurring after 1978. I argue that to fully appreciate this shift, taking both China's position in the world economy from a transnational perspective – by which I specifically mean international economic exchanges with the non-socialist industrialised nations of the "West" including Japan – as well as the role of secular trends such as technological progress into account is crucial.

The period covered by this book falls into interesting, albeit to some extent confusing times. The 1970s are today perceived not only as a time of crisis and insecurity both within and outside China – in the words of HENRY KISSINGER, "Years of upheaval"[19] – but also as one of considerable economic and social development. While these seemingly contradictory tendencies were very unevenly distributed among societies around the globe, the degree of overall global interconnectedness had grown to an arguably unprecedented degree, further increasing rapidly, driven by structural shifts in the industrialised economies. The West has been described as transitioning from the second wave of economic and social development, as coined by futurist ALVIN TOFFLER, to the beginnings of a third wave during that period.[20] This transition consisted of a further shift away from the paradigms and basic innovations of industrialisation, fundamentally shaped by mass manufacturing of goods, towards a more services-oriented economic structure. In the most advanced economies, this shift was marked particularly by progress in information and communication technology.

As DEEPAK NAYYAR stated, the period also saw a political transition from a first phase of globalisation, peaking before the First World War in 1913/1914, to a second. Increasingly, capital movements reacting to freely floating exchange and interest rates and driven by investors searching for ever higher capital gains influenced markets and governments.[21] Also, from the perspective of long-term economic development as described in the work of NIKOLAI KONDRATTIEFF[22] and SOLOMOS SOLOMOU[23], a process of technological rollout of basic innovations that had been introduced around the turn of

19 Which, from his perspective as US Secretary of State, was certainly plausible, as the ending of the Vietnam War, the Middle East War of 1973 and the Oil Embargo, the Watergate scandal and the abrupt end of the Nixon presidency indicate. See: KISSINGER HENRY, Years of Upheaval, New York, London, Toronto, Sydney, 2011.

20 An argument developed over two seminal books, still inspiring a remarkable quantity of research and public opinion. TOFFLER ALVIN, The Third Wave, New York 1980; and Toffler Alvin, Future Shock, New York 1970.

21 NAYYAR DEEPAK, Globalization, history and development: a tale of two centuries, in: Cambridge Journal of Economics, Vol. 30, No. 1, January 2006, pp. 137–159.

22 See in particular: KONDRATIEFF NIKOLAI, HÄNDELER ERIK (ed.), Die langen Wellen der Konjunktur, second edition, Moers 2016.

23 Note that the postwar boom of 1950–1973 in the West appears to fall within the time band of an upswing of a long Kondratieff wave, in combination with processes of catching up under different conditions from the high-growth path of the world economy, during the years 1890–1929. SOLOMOU SOLOMOS, Phases of Economic Growth 1850–1973: Kondratieff Waves and Kuznets Swings, Cambridge, New York and Melbourne 1990, pp. 161 ff.

the century approached its end. This was particularly the case in Europe[24] and resulted in a state in which these old ways of production stagnated in advanced economies and new ways had not yet been established to replace them. Economic growth was structurally constrained.

While these long-term perspectives may well be and have been criticised for their rather broad-brush synthesis of very complex societal processes, the manifestations of material progress until the beginning of the 1970s are undeniable – particularly, where international economic exchanges are concerned. Transportation and communications networks continued expanding and became increasingly capable of moving people, goods, capital and information between the industrialised centres around the globe[25] at unprecedented speeds, reducing transaction costs. On the one hand, in the industrialised nation-states of the West, the lives of broad segments of their population seemed rich with new possibilities and individual freedoms, enabled by the continued rise of the consumer society and its promises of affordable abundance.

The material side of these promises depended on the nexus between highly standardised industrial mass-production allowing for economies of scale and thus low consumer-prices – and oil as a cheap source of energy to fuel both production and consumption.[26] Therefore, on the other hand, new worries and obstacles seemed to be imposed on politicians, producers and consumers alike. *Limits to growth* appeared as one of the dominant formulas summarising the *Zeitgeist* of the time. The best-known contemporary document illustrating such limits is the eponymous report on the findings of a study based on a computer simulation of exponential economic growth that – another innovation – took the important constraint of a finite availability of resources into account.[27]

Thus, another defining attribute of the decade was a state of what might be described as *generalised crisis*, which, in industrialised economies, stood in strong contrast to the optimism of the previous decades. It encompassed a number of phenomena, the strong perception and memory of which was decided by their consequences for people's daily lives. The "world energy crisis", also referred to as the *double-crisis*, as it came with inflation, is perhaps the best-remembered in the West as well as in the oil-producing and -exporting countries. Generally, the term refers to actual and perceived shortages in the supply of oil, resulting in significant price increases peaking twice in 1973 and again in 1979. The causes are (at least) both political – namely the consequences of the Yom-Kippur War of 1973 between Isreal and a coalition of Arab states led by Egypt and Syria, the oil-embargo enacted by the Organization of Arab Petroleum Exporting Countries (the Arab members of the Organization of Petroleum Exporting Countries, OPEC) and the Iranian Revolution of 1979 – as well as economic.

---

24 As suggested in EICHENGREEN BARRY, The European Economy since 1945, Coordinated Capitalism and beyond, Princeton and Oxford 2008, pp. 252–263.

25 HARVEY DAVID, Spaces of Capitalism, A Theory of Uneven Geographical Development, London 2019.

26 PFISTER CHRISTIAN, Das 1950er Syndrom, Der Weg in die Konsumgesellschaft, second edition, Bern, Stuttgart und Wien 1996.

27 MEADOWS DONELLA H., MEADOWS DENNIS L., RANDERS JORGEN, BEHRENS WILLIAM W. III., The Limits to Growth, A Report for the Club of Rome's Project on the Predicament of Mankind, New York 1972.

Concurrently, the "world food crisis" hit lesser developed countries severely, leading to hunger and starvation. The unresolved debate on the international marketisation of food, notably grain, is another legacy of the "long 1970s". PETER TIMMER suggested that at least two lessons can be drawn from the decade-long response to the world food crisis, demonstrating the issues created by interdependent markets. First, international food price volatility proved to be a very serious problem. Second, current food prices are a poor guide to long-run opportunity costs, precisely because they can be extremely unstable. Investments to raise agricultural productivity, by their very nature, have only long-run payoffs.[28] Furthermore, the "world currency crisis" and several manifestations of economic crisis brought another challenge: "stagflation". The omnipresent term described the simultaneous occurrence of slow economic growth and relatively high rates of inflation, coined to describe the 1973–1975 recessions in the West (in that case except Japan).

Whether the occurrence of stagflation was mainly caused by the external shocks linked to energy supply is subject to ongoing and extensive debate among both historians and economists. In any case, the political reaction was robust. An important landmark can be defined as the announcement of a "new economic policy" by US-president Richard Nixon on the 15th of August 1971. Prices and wages were frozen by presidential executive order for a period of 90 days to counteract inflation and the convertibility of the US Dollar to gold was suspended for foreign central banks. Also, trade-related measures were applied to counteract inflation: the imposition of a temporary import tax surcharge was intended to induce trade partners in Western Europe as well as Japan to make adjustments to the exchange rates of their currencies vis-à-vis the dollar.

Not nearly all of this was new. It is noteworthy that the international monetary crisis was only the most marked in a series of (international) monetary crises that occurred almost annually since the mid-1960s.[29] From the perspective of economic history, one of the most important consequences appears to be a crisis of Keynesian economics which were perceived to be unable to explain stagflation. It supported and encouraged politically influential critiques such as the monetarist approach. Arguably, the crises also had systemic consequences that led to diverse changes in political patterns as governments tried to react to the economic downturn. For instance, the status and form of the European welfare state[30], the organisation of north–south relations[31], and the rise of policy bundles that continue to be referred to as "neoliberalism" with many variations.

The workable definition of the term – at least for the author – remains unclear. It is frequently used in scientific as well as political debate to refer to the rise of certain eco-

---

28 TIMMER PETER, Reflections on food crises past, in: Food Policy, Nr. 35, 2010, pp. 1–11.

29 Also known as the *International Monetary Crisis*. See: JOHNSON HARRY G., The International Monetary Crisis of 1971, in: The Journal of Business, Vol. 46, No. 1, January 1973, pp. 11–23.

30 For an overview on related policy-cycles, see: ABRAHAMSON PETER, European Welfare States: Neoliberal Retrenchment, Developmental Reinforcement or Plural Evolutions, in: KYUNG-SUP C., FINE B., WEISS L. (eds.), Developmental Politics in Transition, International political Economy Series, London 2012, pp. 92–113.

31 RADICE HUGO, The Developmental State under Global Neoliberalism, in: Third World Quarterly, Vol. 29, No. 6, 2008, pp. 1153–1174.

nomic policy paradigms, most notably monetarism and supply-side economics,[32] since roughly the mid-1970s. It is also used to refer to an economic system in which the conceptualisation of social relations as "free" markets is increasingly extended to both the public and personal spheres, along with a perceived transformation of the state from a provider of public services and welfare to a promoter of markets and competition, limiting the power of organized labour to enable this shift. Accordingly, neoliberalism is associated with policies like cutting trade tariffs and non-tariff barriers (NTB) as well as the liberalisation of the cross-border movement of capital and, to a certain extent, labour markets. While such policies were re-discovered during the 1980s and 1990s, the political and cultural shifts in the 1970s are much more complex.

Most notably in Western Europe, the early 1970s marked the beginning of the end for a long period of increasing wealth across the board, driven by the fastest economic growth in history between 1945 and 1975. In more dramatic terms, the "Trentes Glorieuses", as coined by the French economist Jean Fourastié, ended, as did the German "Wirtschaftswunder".[33] The end of these allegedly glorious and miraculous times also implied the vanishing of the economic and cultural optimism of earlier decades. Promises of growth suddenly appeared to be both *unsustainable* as well as quite unreliable, subject to forces beyond political and individual control. The "General Social Survey", a periodic assessment of American citizens' moods and values, shows a 10 percent decline from 1976 to 2006 of the population who believe other people can "generally be trusted". The same survey also demonstrates declining trust in public institutions, although frequently related to specific events such as the Watergate scandal. From the 1970s until today, trust seems to have declined with regard to the press (24 to 11 percent), education (36 to 28 percent), banks (35 percent to 31 percent), corporations (26 to 17 percent), and even organized religion (35 to 25 percent).[34]

Regardless of these rather bleak tendencies, not everybody was entirely unhappy with the state of affairs. Particularly for the political left, the crises appeared to offer empirical evidence for theories of political economy. They seemingly demonstrated the perilous risks that the increasing international synchronisation of industrial cycles – a consequence of the "two unbundlings" of internationalisation in industrial production and the

---

32 Maybe this lack of conceptual clarity is a feature of the historically complex origins of the ideology, as Thomas Biebricher has suggested quoting Brian Singer's 1995 gangster movie "The usual suspects": "*The greatest trick the devil ever pulled was convincing the world he didn't exist*". See: Biebricher Thomas, Neoliberalismus, Hamburg 2012.

33 Crafts Nicholas and Toniolo Gianni, A Restructured Economy: From the Oil Crisis to the Financial Crisis, 1973–2009, in: Crafts Nicholas and Toniolo Gianni (eds.), The Oxford Handbook of postwar European History, Oxford 2012, pp. 406–422; and Herrmann Ulrike, Kein Kapitalismus ist auch keine Lösung, second edition, Frankfurt am Main 2019, pp. 210 ff.

34 MacKay Demerjian Louisa (ed.), The Age of Dystopia: One Genre, Our Fears and Our Future, Newcastle upon Tyne 2016, p. 3, FN i.

services industry[35] – entailed. Not only for capitalist economies, but also the developing countries that found themselves economically connected to them.

As ERNEST MANDEL suggested, the "first general recession of the international capitalist economy since the Second World War" culminated in 1974 and 1975. Different from earlier recessions occurring in national economies – perhaps with some spill over effects on neighbouring countries or important trade partners – it was not limited through the boundaries between national economies. Quite in the contrary, processes of international synchronization of conjuncture movements, be it with regard to industrial or credit cycles, spread and appeared to worsen the economic impact of crises of overproduction inherent to the capitalist mode of production.[36]

In fact, such spill over was indeed not limited to the industrialised countries of the West and their former colonies. But did this hold true to societies that saw themselves as separate from the "international capitalist economy"? After all, the socialist world and its political-economic system[37] had been described by Soviet leaders as constituting one of two *parallel* world markets.[38] Perceiving it as a real alternative to the varieties of capitalism existing in the West,[39] the Great Soviet Encyclopedia defined this "socialist world system" as"a social, economic and political community of free sovereign states developing toward socialism and communism and united by common interests and goals and by the bonds of international socialist solidarity" – also encompassing the socialist states of Vietnam, North Korea, Cuba and Mongolia.[40] But was this alternative system insulated from the economic turmoil shaking the rest of the world?

35 What RICHARD BALDWIN has referred to as the *two unbundlings*: The first unbundling being characterized by industrialization and rapid growth in today's developed economies, a widening of the income-divide between North and South, booming trade and migration, and local production agglomeration. Key features of the second unbundling included a surge towards industrialization in the emerging economies and the reduction in income dispersion between these economies and the industrialized ones. Global value chains (GVC) also emerged in the second unbundling, with all the complexities involved in networked trade, investment, services and innovation. The third unbundling, which the developed world is encountering today, is conceptualized primarily as the possibility to provide (digital) services remotely. See: BALDWIN RICHARD, The Great Convergence: Information Technology and the New Globalization, Cambridge and London 2016.

36 MANDEL ERNEST, Die Krise, Weltwirtschaft 1974–1986, Hamburg 1987.

37 Often defined as the Soviet Union and its Eastern European satellite-states, which from an analytical perspective certainly makes sense due to the (at least broadly) similar predominant economic and political paradigms. For innovative perspectives on these countries, see ROBERTSON JAMES M., The Socialist World in the Second Age of Globalization: An Alternative History?, in Markets, Globalization & Development Review, Vol. 3, No, 2, Article 5.

38 STALIN JOSEPH, Economic Problems of Socialism in the USSR, New York 1952, p. 26.

39 Both with regard to the organization of social relations *including* the economy. For an excellent narrative on the perception and effects of the era of *soviet optimism*, see: SPUFFORD FRANCIS, Red Plenty: Inside the Fifties' Soviet Dream, London 2010.

40 China was excluded for reasons elaborated on below. See: KRANCBERG SIGMUND, The Socialist World System: Alliance or Instrument of Domination?, in: Studies in Soviet Thought, Vol. 30, No. 1, July 1985, pp. 55.

By the early 1970s, the Soviet Union, the flagship state of the socialist world in both symbolic and descriptive terms, had left the post-war heroism of the Stalinist era[41] as well as the competitive ambitions of the Khrushchev years[42] behind. The rapid growth before 1970 was mostly attributed to exceptional growth of the capital stock, a marked increase in employment and the expansion of cultivated acreage. Over the years, these reserves of quantitative growth had been depleted. Estimates of Soviet productivity growth in earlier years matched those of East Asian economies such as South Korea and Taiwan during their boom years – the so-called "Tiger States".[43] Now, things slowed down remarkably. In the course of the 1960s, the Soviet economy had entered what ROBERT C. ALLEN termed the *Soviet Climacteric*. It was neither comfortable nor a cause for optimism: While the Soviet GDP had quite steadily grown in excess of 5 percent per year from 1928 to 1970, the annual rate dropped to 3.7 percent in the years 1970–1975, then to 2.6 percent in 1975–1980, hitting two percent in 1980–1985. One interpretation was that the political leadership had opted for moderate policies, favouring stability and thus the preservation of privileges over progress at any price.

Parts of the Soviet political elites publicly acknowledged this tendency towards slower growth and stagnating productivity. Nevertheless, attempts to improve the notoriously complicated bureaucratic system of centralised economic planning by introducing market-based elements – as proposed by the former chairman of *Gosplan* (1959–1960) and later prime minister (after 1964) Alexey Nikolayevich Kosygin together with the economist Evsei Grigorievich Liberman in 1965 – were abandoned. This lack of pragmatism was largely due to the political threat that relying on market forces for the allocation, organisation and management of resources in the economy represented to the established political rule and its ideological basis. The rationale behind these attempts was manifold and included the struggles against the substantial slowdown of growth, declining capital and labour productivity, increasing labour shortages, growing consumer expectations, as well as the under- or misutilisation of resources. Interestingly, these "Limited Market Relations Socialist Models" went back to Liberman's macroeconomic studies, which again drew heavily on neoclassical economics practiced in the western academic world. Those models, too, were instruments for understanding and optimising economic efficiency albeit under market conditions.[44] While the political approaches differed, the issues were still quite similar in both "worlds".

41 Leaving after it an industrialized country, but for an immeasurable price. As ROBERT CONQUEST noted: "Stalinism is one way of industrialization, just as cannibalism is one way of attaining a high protein diet". See: CONQUEST ROBERT, The Great Terror, New York 1968, p. 495; and KORT MICHAEL, The Soviet Colossus, New York 2010, p. 280.

42 Besides *De-Stalinization*, the economic achievements of the Khrushchev-era do deserve merit. The terror by the secret police was at least diminished, the Gulag was dissolved and the general standard of living was raised. And – and this is not self-evident – his cabinet did not start a nuclear war during the Cuban Missile Crisis. See KORT 2010, pp. 314 f.

43 ALLEN ROBERT C., From Farm to Factory, A Reinterpretation of the Soviet Industrial Revolution, Woodstock 2003, p. 189.

44 MARANGOS JOHN, Consistency and Viability of the Liberman-Kosygin Reforms: The Limited Market Relations Socialist Model, in: MARANGOS JOHN (ed.), Consistency and Viability of Socialist Economic Systems, New York 2013, pp. 93–105. For a perspective on Eastern Europe including exchanges between Yugoslav and Hungarian economist with their colleagues in the west, see: BOCK-

Embracing a more consumer-oriented "socialist way of life" despite persisting economic challenges in the Soviet Union was, to a notable extent, made possible through trade with the West. While, as an example, US exports to the Soviet Union totalled only about 100 million USD in 1970, they grew to more than 3.8 billion USD until 1979. Even when the Soviet invasion of Afghanistan halted trade abruptly as the US enacted sanctions, the Soviet Union continued to be the single largest buyer of grain from the US through to 1985.[45] In parallel, it seemed that the internationalist ideological mission of the socialist revolution's homeland was gradually dismantled. The demonstration of the interventionist Brezhnev Doctrine by the 1968 military intervention in Czechoslovakia underlined this: Along with asserting the dominant position of the Soviet Union within the socialist world, it violently suppressed initiatives seeking to establish "socialism with a human face" initiated by the Czech government under Alexander Dubcek.

Why were those initiatives perceived to be a threat by the Soviet Union? Besides lifting political repression such as media censorship, the bundle of measures and experiments envisaged was aiming particularly for significant economic policy reform. As far as it was able to unfold, the Czech approach suggested to keep collective property of the means of production as well as economic planning as its main pillars, while introducing elements of a market economy such as the free formation of prices guided through indirect regulation and taxation combined with targeted public investment and subsidies in key sectors determined by the government. Also, worker's participation in management decisions taken at enterprise-level as they had been practiced in Yugoslavia appeared as an integral element.[46] Not unlike the approach proposed by Kosygin and Liberman, the Czech reform ideas sought to fix the inherent shortcomings of a planned economy without abandoning political control over production and markets altogether.

Despite these shortcomings, as it was underlined at every occasion by the Soviet leadership, the Soviet socialist system seemed at least to deliver on the promise of economic stability as opposed to "anarchic" fluctuations of less controlled markets. This argument became more prominent in the face of the international crises manifesting themselves in capitalist countries. In 1976, considering the situation in which the economies of the West found themselves, the German Democratic Republic (GDR)-based economist HANS-JOACHIM HÖHME took a rather defensive stance:

> "In view of [these] unambiguous economic facts and their, for the majority of the population in the capitalist countries very noticeable consequences, even the lobbyists and ideologists of monopoly capitalism cannot deny the existence and seriousness of the current crisis. Even more, they are trying to distract from [its] capitalist character [...]. Of course, the socialist countries are connected to the capitalist part of the world economy by manifold economic relations. The capitalist crisis therefore also leads to changed foreign economic conditions for the socialist community of states [...]. The attempt, to

---

MAN JOHANNA, Markets in the Name of Socialism, The Left-Wing Origins of Neoliberalism, Stanford 2011.

45 Central Intelligence Agency (CIA) Report, USSR: The Role of Foreign Trade in the Economy, 1 July 1985, General CIA Records Collection, Document Nr. CIA-RDP08S01350R000200500001-0.

46 KOSTA JIŘÍ, Die tschechoslowakische Wirtschaftsreform der sechziger Jahre, in: LEIPOLD HELMUT (ed.), Sozialistische Marktwirtschaften, Munich 1975, pp. 50 ff.

> deduce [from these developments] that the crisis is a "worldwide" phenomenon is lead ad absurdum by few economic facts from the [experience of] the last five years."[47]

In hindsight, the idea of two economically separate world markets or world systems that interacted only via narrow and politically controlled exchanges of commodities does not hold true as an absolute. The increasing foreign debt of the Soviet Union and Eastern European states, caused by a persistent trade deficit, was an element of synchronisation that linked the two systems together.[48] Also, the galloping international inflation during the mid-1970s that followed the abolition of relatively fixed exchange rates in the West contributed to an increase of these liabilities and limited the *marge de manoeuvre* for economic policies. Arguably, these effects contributed decisively to the economic decline of the socialist world system.[49]

Furthermore, there were significant spill overs of the crises in both directions and beyond: The large-scale Soviet purchases of grain from the USA and other producers, as CHRISTIAN GERLACH has shown[50], contributed to an "economic tsunami"[51] on international grain markets in 1972. The devastating effects on the supply situation in the poorest countries demonstrated another important aspect of the intertwining of the economic systems: the consequences were carried particularly by those who were not able to pay the inflated prices neither out of their own pockets or on credit.

These effects also affected the other major socialist state, even if it stood outside both the international capitalist economy and the socialist world system built around the Soviet Union: China.

The socialist state between two worlds

The PRC, the largest socialist country in terms of population, was caught between a rock and a hard place in the early 1970s. Having severed most ties[52] with its once most important and reliable Soviet ally over the past decade, the still relatively young state found

---

47 Translation by the author. See: HÖHME HANS-JOACHIM, Charakter und Besonderheiten der gegenwärtigen kapitalistischen Wirtschaftskrise, in: Krise der kapitalistischen Weltwirtschaft 1974/76, IPW-Forschungshefte, Vol. 11, No. 2, 1976, pp. 10 f.

48 On the increase of Soviet debt until 1977 and the role of the non-convertible ruble, see: BIRMAN IGOR, The Financial Crisis in the USSR, in: Soviet Studies, Vol. 32, No. 1, January 1980, pp. 84–105.

49 An innovative perspective on the end of the Bretton Woods financial infrastructure and the active role of the Soviet Union has been contributed here: SANCHEZ-SIBONY OSCAR, Energie, die Sowjetunion und der Kampf um Kapital nach dem Zusammenbruch des Bretton-Woods-Systems, in: WEMHEUER FELIX (ed.), Jahrbuch für Historische Kommunismusforschung 2020, Berlin 2020, pp. 193–208.

50 GERLACH CHRISTIAN, Die Welternährungskrise 1972–1975, in: Geschichte und Gesellschaft, Vol. 31, Nr. 4, October-December 2005, pp. 546–585.

51 SCHERTZ LYLE P., Present shock – food prices, draft, 25.6.1973, FAO, RG 9. Quoted from GERLACH 2005, p. 547.

52 As LORENZ LÜTHI has shown, both Sino-Soviet military cooperation as well as contacts within (communist) party relations continued until the mid-1960s. See: LÜTHI LORENZ, The Sino-Soviet Split, Cold War in the Communist World, Woodstock 2008.

itself in the position of a pariah in the international orders of both systems. That its remaining closest ally was the People's Republic of Albania is a case in point. This weak international position was also induced by the fact that the collapse of both party and state authorities in the wake of the Cultural Revolution in 1966 included a massive reduction of the Chinese diplomatic corps. This severely limited the ability of the socialist state to act beyond its borders. By late 1966, even socialist countries that had taken rather pro-Chinese positions during the Sino-Soviet Split such as North Vietnam and North Korea had turned away from China.[53]

China's approach to economic policy was modelled along the lines of the Soviet blueprint[54] after the somewhat more experimental initial years of *New Democracy* (1949–1954).[55] It had achieved a degree of basic industrialisation, recognised even by some of the harshest critics of its political leadership. Still, it remained an agricultural society that struggled to reliably provide its fast-growing population with basic commodities. Throughout the 1950s, 1960s and 1970s, food remained rationed particularly in cities. Estimates on the basis of China's statistical yearbooks indicate that the average level of consumption in urban areas in the 1970s did not rise substantially over 2300 calories per capita per day. While such estimates are to be handled carefully as both historical production and population data are not comparable to current data in terms of reliability, the alimentary situation was certainly far from comfortable.[56]

This serious constraint made the effective financing of the massive investments required to follow the Soviet industry-centred path of development with comparable speed and success even more difficult. The emphasis on politically controlled institutional organisation – collectivisation – over targeted investment in agriculture added to a dire situation with regard to the low productivity of the sector. The matter was particularly serious as agriculture still accounted for well over three-quarters of total employment and half of the state's budgetary revenue during the 1970s.[57]

Moreover, the Chinese society, economy and political system had undergone decades of massive, often violent and rapid experimentation. The overly ambitious big push poli-

---

53 LÜTHI 2020, p. 131.

54 At least with regard to industrial planning. For a general overview, see: DILLON MICHAEL, China, A Modern History, New York 2012, pp.284 ff.

55 China was not founded as a socialist state, but as a "new democracy", based on an alliance between the working class, peasants, the petite bourgeoisie and the national bourgeoisie, as Mao described it in his tractate *On the democratic dictatorship of the people* in 1969. The approach was quite open, as the development of private capitalism in China as a complement to State Owned Enterprises was explicitly welcomed. See: WEMHEUER FELIX, Mao Zedong, Reinbek bei Hamburg 2009, pp. 74 ff.

56 HUANG JIKUN, OTSUKA KEIJIRO, ROZELLE SCOTT, Agriculture in China's Development, Past disappointments, Recent Successes and Future Challenges, in: BRANDT LOREN, RAWSKI THOMAS G. (eds.), China's Great Economic Transformation, New York 2008, pp. 471 f.

57 ASH ROBERT, Squeezing the Peasants: Grain Extraction, Food Consumption and Rural Living Standards in Mao's China, in: The China Quarterly, No. 188, The History of the PRC (1949–1976), December 2006, p. 960.

cies[58] of the Great Leap Forward (1957–1961) had caused the deaths of millions[59] while achieving little immediate[60] results. Nevertheless, despite being largely policy-induced, the catastrophe did not end socialist rule. The leadership showed a strong ability to adapt, including with regard to the interpretation of their ideological basis. A return to unified "rational economic planning," along with the decentralisation of various tasks to the provincial level and below combined with an emphasis on labour discipline and control quite successfully stabilised the Chinese economy after the catastrophe.[61] The importance of agricultural production – which in practice meant the ability of the economy to provide sufficient food for everyone as well as raw materials for industrial production – was not as blatantly neglected for the sake of accumulation for industrial investment as it had been in earlier years.[62]

The comparably successful years of readjustment and stabilisation in the early 1960s (1961–1965) demonstrated that state-led economic planning was able to consolidate the economy and advance industrial development in China, albeit at a relatively moderate pace.[63] Nevertheless, these efforts came under considerable pressure before they could play out their potential. The turmoil of the Cultural Revolution, leading to the brink of civil war[64], challenged relatively successful experiments on grounds of political ortho-

58 A term coined by BARRY NAUGHTON to describe investment-heavy policy-bundles to achieve industry-centered economic development. See: NAUGHTON BARRY, The Socialist Era, 1949–1978: Big Push Industrialization and Policy Instability, in: NAUGHTON BARRY (ed.), The Chinese economy, transitions and growth, Cambridge Mass and London 2007, pp. 55–84.

59 With estimates ranging from about 18 to 45 million direct and indirect casualties.

60 On the other hand, several authors have argued that the policies enacted during the Great Leap Forward did have some positive effects, albeit at a horrendous price. For an overview on the Chinese debate on the legacy during *Reform and Opening*, see: JOSEPH WILLIAM A., A Tragedy of Good Intentions: Post-Mao Views of the Great Leap Forward, in: Modern China, Vol. 12, No. 4, October 1986, pp. 419–457. ROBERT WEIL and others have noted that amidst the great losses, some lasting accomplishments like in particular the creation of a basis for rural industrialization and the opening of possibilities in particular for the rural population which would have been unimaginable under imperial rule. See: WEIL ROBERT, Red Cat, White Cat, China and the Contradictions of "Market Socialism", New York 1996, pp. 231 f.

61 For a comprehensive overview, see: PERKINS DWIGHT D., The Economic Transformation of China, Singapore 2015, pp. 16 ff., 84 ff. and 137 ff.

62 As DWIGHT H. PERKINS has argued, basically through the solving of the "incentive-problem" by changing the basic accounting unit from the Commune (4000–5000 households) to the Production Team (twenty to thirty households), see: PERKINS 2015, p. 16. FELIX WEMHEUER has emphasized improvements in the supply system as well as the role of some grain imports. See: WEMHEUER FELIX, A Social History of Maoist China, Conflict and Change, 1949–1976, Singapore 2019, pp. 164 ff. When reference is made to heavy industry, the production of "goods to make other goods" is meant: industrial raw materials such as steel and petrochemical compounds as well as industrial tools and machinery not intended for consumption by households.

63 According to official statistics, death rates fell rapidly in 1962 while grain production was still lower that it had been in 1959. FELIX WEMHEUER has argued, that China did not produce its way out of the famine by increasing yields, but rather by rebalancing the supply system. See: Ibid., pp. 164 ff.

64 With some of the worst confrontations taking place in Qinghai province in February 1966, where clashes between the People's Liberation Army (PLA) and "rebels" caused more than a hundred casualties. See: DIKÖTTER FRANK, The Cultural Revolution, A People's History 1962–1976, Croydon 2016, pp. 134 f.

doxy. The discrediting of hierarchies established on the basis of specialised labour and cadre status as well as the limited access to higher education were at the core of the movement, seemingly undermining efforts to consolidate and further develop a modern industrialised economy in the PRC. The upheaval had particularly affected the basis of progress, research and education: While some institutions of higher learning reopened in the fall of 1970 and enrolled their first students since 1966, approaches had changed. In addition to changes in the selection procedures for students (more class-conscious), the length of education (shorter) and the substance (more "practicable", less academic), political control on what could be taught to whom was tightened.[65]

The Chinese people had achieved a lot, but the political struggle within China had been relentless and exhausting. In addition, pressure on agricultural production remained high as a consequence of low yields and a growing population and the threat of war loomed over the PRC. A bitter irony of history underlined the position of China between two worlds: It was not only the "imperialists" of the West and the former Japanese arch-enemies that threatened the state but first and foremost the socialist neighbour to the north. The conflict with the Soviet Union had manifested itself in the skirmishes along the Ussuri river between March and September 1969 and at the Chinese-Soviet border in Xinjiang in August of the same year. While it has been disputed how acute the military threat of a Soviet invasion really was, the Chinese leadership was alarmed.

The perceived immediate threat legitimised the course of the Third Front-strategy, relocating industries to the interior of the country at a massive scale in order to protect them from military attacks.[66] Between 1964 and 1980, China devoted nearly forty percent of its capital construction budget to the implementation of this defense strategy, building more than a thousand industrial projects.[67] China once again needed to rely on itself. As the promises of the Great Leap Forward had not materialised and the Cultural Revolution had escalated to the brink of civil war, the socialist state appeared to be in a deep and relentless crisis. In hindsight, opening up towards export-led foreign trade and investment as well as adjusting economic policy towards what has been referred to as "capitalism with Chinese characteristics"[68] appears to be one of only a few alternatives.

Nevertheless, Chinese history throughout the 1970s is nuanced and complex. Despite its declared, perceived and partly real paradigm of "self-reliance"[69] and political disruptions, the economy of the PRC did not falter or stagnate during those years. Although not yet fully appreciated in discourses on China[70], both industrial and agricultural production continued to improve in many aspects before 1978. This tendency did not encom-

---

65 Chang Parris H., The Cultural Revolution and Chinese higher education: Change and Controversy, in: The Journal of General Education, Vol. 26, No. 3, Fall 1974, pp. 187–194.

66 Naughton Barry, The Third Front: Defence Industrialization in the Chinese Interior, in: The China Quarterly, No. 115, September 1988, pp. 351–386.

67 Meyskens Covell, Third Front Railroads and Industrial Modernity in Late Maoist China, in: Twentieth-Century China, Vol. 40, No. 3, October 2015, p. 238–239.

68 Yasheng Huang, Capitalism with Chinese characteristics, Cambridge 2008.

69 While it frequently appears in literature, the term *autarky* appears to be a description from the outside. *Self-reliance*, on the other hand, is frequent in Chinese publications and sources, its changing meaning inside China as well as in its foreign relations is addressed further on.

70 But suggested by e. g. Westad 2010.

pass the whole country – comparable in size to the United States – from the outset, but took place steadily and well-anchored in the political history of the PRC. Despite what was perceived as a bitter factional struggle within the Chinese communist movement, the basic idea that socialism *in China* had economic modernisation at its core was never abandoned.

Led by an awareness to preserve both the level of production achieved during the early 1960s and the Marxist–Leninist as well as Maoist[71] basis of the socialist state, increasing its economic efficiency and pushing industrial development remained among its *raisons d'être* and an important basis of its legitimation. There is little to no evidence confirming western narratives prevalent during the 1960s and 1970s around a Chinese development-path, which did *not* have industrialization via the construction of heavy industry as its core economic objective.[72] *How* economic modernisation along these lines could be achieved was, however, violently disputed.

Policy experimentation and compromise before 1979

When long-term planning was re-established in early 1975 and existing technologies were rolled out, self-reliant China started to look outside and sought ways to catch up and participate actively in the next wave of the technological progress. Within the Chinese socialist state, the general industrialisation paradigm established in the early to mid-1960s relied on independent or, perhaps more precisely, *non-interdependent* economic development. In short, the financing of investment was based on the accumulation of capital stemming from the procurement of agricultural products at fixed prices, combined with a general suppression of wages and consumption through rationing. This basic paradigm of economic policy that had its roots in the Soviet experience as much as in the factual circumstances of China continued, but persisting issues continued to be addressed with incremental adjustments throughout the 1970s.

---

71 In an interview with an Egyptian journalist published in early 1973, Zhou Enlai explained why the portrait of Stalin was still carried alongside the portraits of Marx and Engels. His answer pointed out the military achievements of the Soviet leader who's violent rule had caused him to fall out from the group of socialist leading figures that could be referred to as part of the ideological basis of socialist movements and parties in many countries: "The Soviet Union remained for a long time the only power fighting against fascism in Europe. The German army penetrated deep until it reached Stalingrad, Moscow and Leningrad. The losses of this German army, however, were high. The war on the Eastern Front was exhausting its strength, and it finally played the leading role in [...] final defeat. All Europeans admit this. We have discussed it with them. The Americans do not deny it. Thus, we appreciate Stalin's role." Joint Publications Research Service, Haykal "Frankly Speaking" article: "The Red East – A Long Discussion with Chou En-lai", Cairo Al-Ahram, Original in Arabic, 23 02 1873, p. 4, accessed through Readex.

72 Despite being framed differently by observers in the West, most importantly during this period when agricultural work in developing countries appear to have caused a lot of romantic framing. For a critique of the "agrarian myth", see: BRASS TOM, The Agrarian Myth, the "new" populism and the "new right", in: The Journal of Peasant Studies, Vol. 24, No. 4, pp. 201–245 as well as FROLIC, B. MICHAEL, Reflections on the Chinese Model of Development, in: Social Forces, Vol. 57, No. 2, December 1978, pp. 384–418.

I propose that such experiments and adjustments could be found in the areas of productive relations (such as technical hierarchies, legal rules, wage and price policies and labour discipline), the management of technological advancement and its material basis (the promotion of technological innovation, intra-industrial cooperation and austerity to improve efficiency), and lastly the financing of the process as well as the distribution of surplus. They were discussed quite publicly, experimented with and implemented at regional levels before they were dropped, adapted or more widely adopted. Adjustments of the internal workings were combined with attempts to increase and improve the use of foreign sources for the promotion of industrial development. They encompassed an expansion of foreign trade, both with regard to the actual exchanges and the structures required, and increasingly ambitious (i. e. expensive) objectives concerning the import of readymade capital goods and technology *as such* – blueprints to develop and build machines, not the machines as such – from advanced economies.

An underlying hypothesis is that the readiness for trying paradigmatic shifts from a socialist economic model was not given within the Chinese leadership in Beijing. In that regard, it is remarkable that while the Reform and Opening program eventually led to more fundamental changes such as the systematic abolition of the socialist welfare state, the initial measures after the Third Plenary of December 1978 were much more modest. First, industrial enterprises were formally allowed to retain a part of their profits as an incentive. Second, the open-door policy went beyond the opening to international trade occurred during the decade by allowing foreign direct investment in four designated Special Economic Zones in the south-east. Third, household farming was formally authorized.[73] All three of these cornerstones were not entirely new, as this book underlines.

For the period before these changes, long-standing political rhetoric both within and outside of China has established a *dualist* perspective on Chinese politics during the decade. It is based on the assumption of a struggle between two distinct political positions, thereby distinguishing the various opposing categories of political ideas. This creates the image of two camps such as "rightist" and "leftist" forces, struggling for ideological hegemony, of which one prevails. In agreement with a number of authors whose work is discussed below, I suggest that the paradigmatic shifts that eventually did happen were much more gradual and slower in reality. It is true that measures such as the use of bonus payments and extensive salary differentiation to increase worker productivity were publicly critizised on all levels of government and the CCP. At the same time, the Chinese leadership under the late Mao and his successor Hua Guofeng as well as their political legacy allowed for flexibilities and a certain degree of deviation from declared ideals to keep the economy afloat and pursue the underlying objective of industrial advancement. Brantly Womack has suggested with a nod to the leadership of Deng Xiaoping that ideology was relevant as an edge of a path, not a tightrope:

> "Deng encouraged a pragmatic, collective leadership in which policy success should be judged on economic accomplishments rather than ideological correctness. Ideology

---

73 Rawski Thomas G., China's Economy after Fifty Years: Retrospect and Prospect, in: International Journal, Vol. 55, No. 1, Winter 1999/2000, p. 64.

> defined the boundary of the permissible – one must not overtly challenge Marxism-Leninism-Mao Zedong Thought – but not its broad middle."[74]

This "middle" existed before 1978 and was important for the compromises and experiments I refer to throughout this book. Contravening currents in Marxist–Leninist economic theory as well as the more or less ambiguous comments on the economy by Mao himself allowed for adjustments within an existing frame of reference that were partly tolerated, partly sought. By establishing this category, the analysis in this book further suggests that a rather dialectical view of the organisation and running of the Chinese economy to determine the intended direction of economic policy between 1970 and 1978 is more helpful than a focus on a concurrent dualism of dogmas along the lines of Cold War historiography. This flexibility as well as the experiments and compromises it allows for generate a number of "heterodox remedies" in Chinese economic policy, which existed in economies with markedly different ideological frames of reference.[75] This is the case within China and its provinces and cities as well as its relations with the rest of the world, most notably – in terms of Maoist international relations theory[76] – the "capitalist industrial nations in search of their own independence" in the "intermediate zone" between the two "imperialist superpowers". It was *inter alia* specified in speeches given by Mao in 1963 and 1964:

> "In my view there are two intermediate zones: the first, Asia, Africa and Latin America and the second, Europe. Japan and Canada are not happy with the United States. The six-nation Common Market, represented by De Gaulle, is made up of powerful capitalist countries. Japan in the East is a powerful capitalist country. They are unhappy with the U.S. and the Soviet Union."[77]

Besides seeking ways to improve its economic system inside China, the political leadership of the socialist state that found itself in an intermediate zone between two worlds embraced this status ideologically and – perhaps in the most important and groundbreaking of experiments it undertook – reached out to others to drive its own moderni-

---

74 WOMACK BRANTLY (ed.), China's Rise in Historical Perspective, Plymouth 2010, p. 12.

75 The term "heterodox remedies" has been used by BARRY EICHENGREEN in his seminal study of the European continental economy and its historical development after the Second World War – used by several states when experimenting with policies including e. g., increased state intervention to counter rising unemployment and slowing growth, thereby relying and being influenced by existing institutions and structures. See: EICHENGREEN 2007, in particular pp. 47 ff.

76 While this term might be daring, it helps clarify a mistake which can be encountered quite often still today, in both public debate and scholarship. The concept as presented by the Chinese delegation at the United Nations in 1974 is different from the classification of nations brought forward by ALFRED SAUVY in 1952. For SAUVY, the second world was the *"communist block"*, whereas in the Chinese view, it was the *non-imperialist* part of the world outside Africa, Latin America and continental Asia (notably Japan, Europe and Canada). See: KEYFITZ NATHAN, Alfred Sauvy, in: Population and Development Review, Vol. 16, No. 4, December 1990, pp. 727–733.

77 Mao Zedong, 'There Are Two Intermediate Zones', September, 1963, History and Public Policy Program Digital Archive, Mao Zedong on Diplomacy (Beijing 1998), pp. 387–389. Available at: http://digitalarchive.wilsoncenter.org/document/121207, last accessed on 15 April 2020.

sation. This book seeks to shed light on this important chapter of the history of today's world economy that continues to shape it.

Literature review: The Reform Era and its prehistory

Literature on China and its economy is extensive and cannot be summarised or discussed here in its entirety. Focusing on the most relevant fields and sub-fields of research for this study, the contributions I highlight in this chapter are intended to represent the main strands of work that touch on the 1970s Chinese economic policy as well as contributions from disciplines other than historical science that informed my work.

As many recent studies on economic development focus on the quantitative macroeconomic developments and processes of marketisation and integration in international economic relations after the *end of Maoism* – the end of Mao's life, that coincided with important ideological changes – the years 1978 or 1979 as starting points of substantial economic reform are well-established waymarks. Former developments, except the core oscillation points such as the Great Leap Forward, the Cultural Revolution and related campaigns, are often treated in summary form, referring to the economic shortcomings in contrast with the successes of Reform and Opening. Examples are the contributions by RICHARD EVANS[78], BARRY NAUGHTON[79], NICHOLAS D. KRISTOF[80], RONALD COASE and NING WANG[81], MICHAEL DILLON[82] and ZHENG SONG, KJETIL STORESLETTEN and FABRIZIO ZILIBOTTI[83].

GREGORY C. CHOW[84], ALAN GELB, GARY JEFFERSON AND INDERJIT SINGH[85], JÜRGEN OSTERHAMMEL[86], MICHAEL ELLMAN[87], as well as YAN WANG and YUDONG YAO[88] include earlier years but mostly concentrate on quantitative analysis using the figures to prove or illustrate the effects of the post-1978 reforms as a contrast to the prior macroeconomic situation.

As an example, from the *Introduction to the Chinese Economy* by RONGXING GUO:

---

78 EVANS RICHARD, Deng Xiaoping and the Making of Modern China, London 1993.

79 NAUGHTON BARRY, Growing Out of the Plan: Chinese Economic Reform, 1978–1993, Cambridge 1995.

80 KRISTOF NICHOLAS D., Rise of China, New York 1993.

81 COASE RONALD, WANG NING, How China became Capitalist, Houndmills 2012.

82 DILLON MICHAEL, China, A Modern History, New York 2012.

83 ZHENG SONG, STORESLETTEN KJETIL, ZILIBOTTI FABRIZIO, Growing Like China, in: American Economic Review, Vol. 101, February 2011, pp. 196–233.

84 CHOW GREGORY C., China's Economic Transformation, third edition, Chichester 2015.

85 GELB ALAN, JEFFERSON GARY, SINGH INDERJIT, Can Communist Economies Transform Incrementally? The Experience of China, in: NBER Macroeconomics Annual, Vol. 8, 1993, pp. 87–150.

86 OSTERHAMMEL JÜRGEN, China und die Weltgesellschaft, Vom 18. Jahrhundert bis in unsere Zeit, Munich 1989.

87 ELLMAN MICHAEL, Economic Reform in China, in: International Affairs, Vol. 62, No. 3, Summer 1986, pp. 423–442.

88 WANG YAN, YAO YUDONG, Sources of China's Economic Growth, 1952–99, Incorporating Human Capital Accumulation, The World Bank, Policy Research Working Paper 2650, July 2001.

> "In the reform era since 1978, China has been one of the world's fastest growing economies. Between 1978 and 2008, China's real GDP grew at an average annual rate of almost 10 percent. [...] the Chinese model has been generally regarded as having achieved the most successful transformation of all of the former Soviet-type economies in terms of the improvement of economic performance."[89]

Overarching national histories even set 1978 as the year of the "birth of modern China", e. g., KONRAD SEITZ[90]. Nevertheless, there are nuances with regard to the shift. KAI VOGELSANG[91] set the "beginning of a new era" in 1977, as the year the Cultural Revolution actually ended and the ideological basis of the Chinese state moved away from many important tenets. The Chinese economy before 1978 is often reduced to its apparent underdevelopment, inefficiency and underlying political principles of *autarky* when analysed at all, establishing an overall negative attitude towards foreign influences. Where the existence of positive factors such as the establishment of preconditions for economic growth are recognised, their influence on production is seen as negligible or overshadowed by political quarrels. Quantitative indices are strongly emphasised, while developments of the economic policies in China are not. THOMAS G. RAWSKI and LOREN BRANDT[92] summarised their extensive and decades-long work on the Chinese economy and explained the stagnation of macroeconomic indices during the 1970s as due to wrong economic policies, weak institutions, vast misdirection of resources and overall poor incentives, all the while claiming that despite a positive attitude of China's leaders towards material progress, considerations of national defence and ideology trumped economics.

While western economists were mostly focusing on defining the shortcomings of the socialist economic system and determining why some aspects appeared to be working despite them, their extensive data is useful for critical analysis today. For the period prior to 1978, DWIGHT H. PERKINS' insights into the workings of the Chinese economy over several decades are indispensable sources of both precise economic analysis and broadly aggregated official and estimated quantitative data. Among the 21 books and over a hundred essays on the economic history of China since the early 1960s that he authored, co-authored or edited, his collection of essays on the *Economic Transformation of China*[93] is particularly noteworthy for its broad coverage and depth, combining the core of his research as well as new insights gained in the process, in one volume. In my view, his earlier analysis on *Rural Small Scale Industries* in China is among the few studies from the West that have granted adequate seriousness to the analysis of the expansion of decentralised rural industries and their noteworthy effects on production quantities and diversity as well as the expansion of technical knowledge and shaping of social norms, allowing for industrial work in China[94]. His work as an editor has brought together dis-

89 GUO RONGXING, An Introduction to the Chinese Economy, The Driving Forces behind Modern Day China, Singapore 2010, p.11.

90 SEITZ KONRAD, China, Eine Weltmacht kehrt zurück, fifth edition, Munich 2006.

91 VOGELSANG KAI, Geschichte Chinas, Stuttgart 2013.

92 BRANDT LOREN, RAWSKI THOMAS G. (eds.), China's Great Economic Transformation, New York 2008.

93 PERKINS DWIGHT D., The Economic Transformation of China, Singapore 2015.

94 PERKINS DWIGHT D., Rural Small-Scale Industry in the People's Republic of China, Berkeley, Los Angeles and London 1977.

tinctive contemporary experts on the Chinese economy, which – as the focus of scholarly debate shifted quickly away from the *Maoist years* after 1978 – is of great value for any retrospective[95].

An overview of the Chinese industrialisation paradigm is provided in a volume edited by NEVILLE MAXWELL[96], which is based on the relatively scarce data that's available from his own work and those of JOHN G. GURLEY, STEPHEN P. ANDORS and ROLAND BERGER, covering what was known in the West at the time. Geographers, economists and political scientists who conducted area studies (e. g., the handbook by HAROLD C. HINTON[97]) contributed to a general source of factual knowledge on 1970s China. Another author important for this book is CHRIS BRAMALL, whose extensive analysis of rural industrialisation in China is a key read on the topic[98]. The *learning hypothesis* he formulated pioneered critical thinking based on the perception of continuities rather than the strict distinction of separate periods in the economic history of China. In a ground-breaking recent contribution[99], he argued that regional centres of industrial development were decisive, *Jiangsu* being such a "growth pole" in the late Maoist era with its record resembling that of Lancashire and Yorkshire in the early years of Britain's industrial revolution. This holds the intriguing possibility that a Chinese economic take-off, diffusing from the Yangtze Delta, could potentially have occurred even without the post-1978 policy changes.

A seminal analysis of the Chinese economic system and its development prior to 1978 from the perspective of socialist economists was published by economists JAN MEYER and JIRI KOSTA[100]; this is an insightful work involving comparisons with other socialist economies that both authors are familiar with. Influential Chinese economist XUE MUQIAO'S[101] retrospective account of Chinese Socialism provides valuable indications of what the Chinese debates on economic policies focused on and the theoretical changes envisaged. With regard to the actual implementation of economic policies, the view on fundamental changes and long-term prospects by CHENG CHU-YUAN[102] lends both a highly useful phasing of development cycles as well as a conceptualisation of "policy oscillation" – a term and idea that I build on in the second Chapter. The events of the Cultural Revolution as well as some of their economic impacts have been reconstructed in specific works, for instance, by YICHING WU[103] and FRANK DIKÖTTER[104]. While not within the focus of these contributions, the relatively moderate impact of the turmoil on the economy is recognised by these authors. Looking at aspects of everyday life and

---

95 See e. g. PERKINS DWIGHT D., China's Modern Economy in Historical Perspective, Stanford 1975.

96 MAXWELL NEVILLE (ed.), China's Road to Development, second edition, Amsterdam 1979.

97 HINTON HAROLD C., The People's Republic of China: A Handbook, Dawson 1979.

98 BRAMALL CHRIS, The Industrialization of Rural China, Oxford and New York 2007; and Bramall Chris, Chinese Economic Development, London and New York 2009.

99 BRAMALL CHRIS, A Late Maoist Industrial Revolution? Economic Growth in Jiangsu Province (1966–1978), in: The China Quarterly, Vol. 240, December 2019, pp. 1039–1065.

100 MEYER JAN, KOSTA JIRI, Volksrepublik China, Ökonomisches System und wirtschaftliche Entwicklung, Frankfurt am Main and Cologne 1976.

101 XUE MUQIAO, Sozialismus in China, Erfolge, Fehlschläge, Reformperspektiven, Hamburg 1982.

102 CHENG CHU-YUAN, China's Economic Development, 1950–2014, London 2014.

103 WU YICHING, The Cultural Revolution at the Margins, Cambridge and London 2014.

104 DIKÖTTER FRANK, The Cultural Revolution, A People's History, 1962–1976, London 2016.

societal organisation, away from leadership politics, FELIX WEMHEUER[105] provides a balanced and concise analysis of Chinese social history under Maoism (1949–1976) that has informed many parts of this book – in addition to his critical biography of Mao Zedong[106]. Other particular aspects of pre-1978 development have been explored by MARTIN K. WHYTE[107] who, in addition to his many contributions regarding China's economy and society, brought forth the argument that small and medium-sized non-state enterprises were crucial for economic stability and even growth before 1978 and, most importantly, highlighted that the connection between imperfect socialist institutions and strong economic growth in the People's Republic strongly contrasts with current mainstream development paradigms. A similar argument was made by NICHOLAS LARDY[108].

Analyses of elite politics have dominated the field of China Studies for decades. More recent publications by EZRA VOGEL[109], ORVILLE SCHELL and JOHN DELURY[110], JOHN KEAY[111], JONATHAN FENBY[112], and the above-mentioned KONRAD SEITZ have outlined disputes among the political elites within and outside the CCP regarding the economic and political courses of the PRC. They also provide insights into the discourses on reforms and policy adjustments towards international opening and economic growth pre-1978. In particular, VOGEL has contributed a uniquely comprehensive biography of Deng Xiaoping, based on extensive and original source work, which also contains a detailed account of the struggle between the factions during the 1970s on the future course of economic development and the *"pragmatic"* economic thought of Deng.

While some studies (e. g. by MAURICE MEISNER[113]) strongly emphasise the role of Deng Xiaoping as the impersonation and principal source of economic reform within the CCP, and especially the standing committee of the politburo, FREDERICK C. TEIWES and WARREN SUN[114] have published detailed studies on the role of other party cadres, notably Hua Guofeng, as initiators of modernisation. Their underlying hypothesis of a *shift*

---

105 WEMHEUER FELIX, A Social History of Maoist China, Conflict and Change, 1949–1976, Singapore 2019.

106 WEMHEUER FELIX, Mao Zedong, Reinbek bei Hamburg 2009.

107 WHYTE MARTIN K., Sub-optimal Institutions but Superior Growth: The Puzzle of China's Economic Boom, in: China's Economic Dynamics: A Beijing Consensus in the Making?, London 2014, pp. 15–47.

108 LARDY NICHOLAS, Markets over Mao: The Rise of Private Business in China, Washington D.C. 2014.

109 VOGEL EZRA F., Deng Xiaoping and the Transformation of China, Cambridge and London 2013.

110 SCHELL ORVILLE, DELURY JOHN, Wealth and Power, China's Long March to the Twenty-First Century, New York 2013.

111 KEAY JOHN, China: A History, London 2009.

112 FENBY JONATHAN, Tiger Head, Snake Tails, New York 2012.

113 MEISNER MAURICE, Mao's China and After, third edition, New York 1999.

114 TEIWES FREDERICK C., SUN WARREN, The Tragedy of Lin Biao: Riding the Tiger During the Cultural Revolution, London 1996; TEIWES FREDERICK C., SUN WARREN, The End of the Maoist Era, Chinese Politics During the Twilight of the Cultural Revolution, 1972–1976, Armonk and London 2008; TEIWES FREDERICK C., SUN WARREN, Paradoxes of Post-Mao Rural Reform: Initial Steps Toward a New Chinese Countryside, 1976–1981, New York 2016; TEIWES FREDERICK C., SUN WARREN, The First Tiananmen Incident Revisited: Elite Politics and Crisis Management at the End of the Maoist Era, in: Pacific Affairs, Vol. 77, No. 2, Summer 2004, pp. 211–235; and TEIWES FREDERICK C., SUN WARREN, China's New Economic Policy under Hua Guofeng: Party Consensus and Party Myths, in: The China Journal, Vol. 66, July 2011, pp. 1–23.

away from Maoism before the end of Maoism is shared in this book. Further, their research demonstrating that Mao Zedong was "in command" of the majority of important policy decisions until his death lends an important assumption for this study and emphasises Mao Zedong Thought as a guideline for economic policymaking as well as the notions of the political *limits of the possible*, notably in foreign trade, which were present before 1978. A similar view has been brought forth earlier by JONATHAN D. SPENCE[115], who highlighted the compromising position of Hua Guofeng and defended the Dazhai production brigade as a relevant example of successful economic performance under a socialist paradigm. A similar perspective was shared by PETER NOLAN and ROBERT ASH[116], who established continuities between the post-Mao *interregnum* (1976–1978) and the reform programs of Deng Xiaoping, emphasising positive factors for economic growth within the economic system of the PRC pre-1978, as compared to the Soviet Union, but dismissed them by referring to the "declining growth momentum" between 1970 and 1976.

The notion of a moderate balancing line in the Chinese leadership has been reflected in biographical studies, especially of Zhou Enlai (e. g. by GAO WENQIAN, where Zhou is referred to as "a man of both sides"[117]). DAVID BACHMAN[118] on the other hand included the perspectives of less well-known actors within the Central Committee of the CCP, while leaving aside questions of the actual real-world effects of attempts at economic policy adjustments prior to 1978. CARSTEN KAVEN[119] conducted an innovative analysis of the political factions and their positions in the immediate run-up to the 1978 reforms, which concentrates on the political struggle within the PRC, while summarising the reasons for the economic reform pressure leading to political struggle as a combination of low productivity, outdated capital stock and a general stagnation in living standards under the planned economy, which was unable to fulfil growing production-goals.

Based on extensive data on the volume and kind of traded goods, ERNEST MANDEL[120] recognised increases in foreign trade exchanges between 1972 and 1977 and interpreted them as signs of changes occurring under Mao. He showed that a certain opening of the Chinese economy had already taken place before 1978. Further, he stated – correctly, in my view – that it became increasingly difficult for China to stay isolated from spillover effects caused by the transnational crises of the 1970s international capitalist economy. Contemporary studies released during the 1970s cover economic developments in the PRC in greater detail. Besides regular articles on annual developments in journals such as the China Quarterly, the Far Eastern Economic Review and others, numerous scholarly articles were published on various aspects of the Chinese economy in the 1970s. Notable

115 SPENCE JONATHAN D., The Search for Modern China, New York 1990.

116 NOLAN PETER, ASH ROBERT, China's Economy on the Eve of Reform, in: The China Quarterly, No. 144, 1995, pp. 980–998.

117 WENQIAN GAO, Zhou Enlai, The Last Perfect Revolutionary, New York 2007, pp. 131–148.

118 BACHMAN DAVID, Differing Visions of China's Post-Mao Economy: The Ideas of Chen Yun, Deng Xiaoping, and Zhao Ziyang, in: Asian Survey, Vol. 26, No. 3, March 1986, pp. 292–321.

119 KAVEN CARSTEN, Die Durchsetzung der Reformpolitik in China: Analyse eines Ereignisses, Berlin 2008.

120 MANDEL ERNEST, Die Krise, Weltwirtschaft 1974–1986, Hamburg 1987.

examples are MICHAEL D. EILAND[121] and RALPH POWELL[122] discussing the significance of the military in the Chinese economy, and LIANG-SHING FAN[123] discussing foreign trade and policy. In her – unfortunately unpublished – Master's thesis finished in 2011, ESTHER EGLI[124] has traced qualitative changes in particular reflected in the revised constitutions of the 1970s. Her pioneering work has also inspired this book.

More comprehensive contemporary analyses were presented by LLOYD G. REYNOLDS[125] and COLIN CLARK[126], who shared a strong focus on agricultural development, notably food production, and an economist's perspective on China as a developing country. GABOR HIDASI[127] contributed a series of three articles about various developments before and during 1978, trying to examine the economic output and estimate the growth based on the scarce figures available at the time, combined with Soviet scientific publications and reports. This provided a mixed assessment of the economic development prospects, which were ultimately made obsolete by the events after 1978. Generally, the contributions concentrating on the interpretation and interrelation of macroeconomic data show a rather fragmented picture of economic development in the PRC before 1978 while covering the later years in much greater detail (especially after the release of new and retrospective official data in 1984). In a study on the development prospects in China, ALEXANDER ECKSTEIN[128] argued that the economic policies of the 1950s and 1960s had been shaped through "highly abnormal" circumstances and that "the groundwork for a new course" was being laid. He concluded the following in the early 1970s:

> "There seems to be a return to economic rationality, to some kind of an economic calculus [...]. At the same time, management of the economy appears to be more decentralized, with considerable emphasis being placed on the development of small-scale industry representing features which have come more strongly to the fore in the 1960s.

---

121 EILAND MICHAEL D., Military Modernization and China's Economy, in: Asian Survey, Vol. 17, No. 12, December 1977, pp. 1143–1157.

122 POWELL RALPH L., Soldiers in the Chinese Economy, in: Asian Survey, Vol. 11, No. 8, August 1971, pp. 742–760.

123 FAN LIANG-SHING, The Economy and Foreign Trade of China, in: Law and Contemporary Problems, Vol. 38, No. 2, Trade with China, Summer-Autumn 1973, pp. 249–259.

124 EGLI ESTHER, Die wirtschaftlichen Veränderungen zwischen 1972–1978 in China, Politische und wirtschaftliche Vorbereitungen auf die Reformen von 1978, Master's thesis at the Institute of History, University of Bern, 2011 (unpublished).

125 REYNOLDS LLOYD G., China as a Less Developed Economy, in: The American Economic Review, Vol. 65, No. 3, June 1975, pp. 418–428.

126 CLARK COLIN, Economic Development in Communist China, in: Journal of Political Economy, Vol. 84, No. 2, April 1976, pp. 239–264.

127 HIDASI GABOR (both the following), China's Economy in the early 1970s, in: Acta Oeconomica, Vol. 9, No. 1, 1972, pp. 81–94; China's Economy in the mid-1970s and its Development Perspective, in: Acta Oeconomica, Vol. 14, No. 4, 1975, pp. 355–381.

128 ECKSTEIN ALEXANDER, Economic Development Prospects and Problems in China, in: The Annals of the American Academy of Political and Social Science, Vol. 402, No. 1, 1972, pp. 107–116; and ECKSTEIN ALEXANDER, Sino-American Trade Prospects and Policy, in: The American Economic Review, Vol. 64, No. 2, May 1974, pp. 294–299.

As a result, the Chinese economy seems to be in the early stages of a new wave of expansion."[129]

In retrospect, this perspective is plausible and has helped interpret the tendencies of the time with respect to the contemporary research on China's economy. An insightful and, at the time, unique analysis on Chinese agricultural modernisation was provided by ON KIT TAM[130], who mentions adjustments to agricultural planning and the Chinese development-paradigm, both of which – in his view – went beyond a mere optimisation of existing irrigation and production chains. Notably, TAM attributed the early 1970s limited independent use of surplus for investments outside the plan as an important distinctive element of the Chinese approach.

DAVID ZWEIG[131] investigated the implementation of agricultural reforms through local elites in Dazhai and applied an approach rooted in the comparative study of policy implementation. While the political decision-shaping processes and struggles between the supposed factions have been considered to a great extent, the approaches of the 1970s appear to rather dilute the processes of economic policy-implementation and adjustment. Possible alliances or compromises between different actors and *"wings"* within the Chinese leadership might have obscured experiments in economic policies and the search for an approach based on an adjusted socialist economy. On the other hand, ROBERT WEIL[132], with his still innovative views on the contradictions of what he refers to as "Market Socialism", contributed additional analytical nuance regarding the *limits of the possible* during the late Maoist years. In a critical analysis of the shifts in Chinese economic policies, he noted the problems caused by the dualist classification of Deng Xiaoping as a "pragmatist" with the "follies of an old man [Mao Zedong]". Futhermore, he emphasised the importance of taking into account the "dialectical whole" of the socialist era, including the pre-1978 years. In addition, taking modern public discourse as a starting point, he concluded, akin to CHRIS BRAMALL, that even if assessed based on their immediate outcomes, evident economic aberrations such as the Great Leap Forward had indirect effects that were of some importance for economic development. WEIL also stated that the breaking of social barriers allowed for industrial production methods that were unimaginable under the pre-liberation regime. He also acknowledged that the "middle way" in-between the "two-line struggle" helps understand actual policy decisions, instead of the abstract aims of political factions. He noted:

"Thus, the official attempt to divide Mao into "good" preliberation leader and "bad" post-triumph radical, not unlike the similar efforts in recent decades to oppose the "young" and "old" Marx, rests on separating what is unified. It can only be accomplished

---

129 ECKSTEIN 1972, p. 116.

130 ON KIT TAM, China's Agricultural Modernization, The Socialist Mechanization Scheme, London, Sydney, Dover and New Hampshire 1985.

131 ZWEIG DAVID, Agrarian Radicalism in China, 1968–1981, Cambridge 1989; and Zweig David, "Developmental Communities" on China's Coast: The Impact of Trade, Investment, and Transnational Alliances, in: Comparative Politics, Vol. 27, No. 3, April 1995, pp. 253–274.

132 WEIL ROBERT, Red Cat, White Cat, China and the Contradictions of "Market Socialism", New York 1996.

by a one-sided exaggeration of certain aspects, whose importance is inflated without a fundamental grasp of the dialectical whole."[133]

A similar argument was been brought forward by LOUIS T. SIGEL[134], who dismissed the scheme of "*two* [political] *roads*" in his critique of what he called "the myth of the capitalist road" and proposed the definition and application of an "objective standard for socialism".[135] In his critique of SIGEL's approach, MICHAEL SULLIVAN[136] relativised the concept of the "objective standard" by highlighting the risk of such a construction turning out to be misleading and "positivist", while underlining that a critique of general labels within the diversity of socialist economic policies, as proposed by SIGEL, is necessary.

Notably, after 1978, as in WEIL's approach, the classification of the Chinese economic policy paradigm proved difficult to fit into the socialism–capitalism dualism prevalent during and after the Cold War. Critical terms included "market communism", "market socialism", "market Leninism" and "state (monopoly) capitalism". MINXIN PEI and others even referred to the post-1978 years as "China's capitalist revolution"[137]. TOBIAS TEN BRINK[138] approached the issue by analysing the paradoxes of current "Chinese capitalism" and pre-1978 policies as an important part of its formation. Other approaches, notably since the late 1990s, have sought to establish links between *neoliberal* economic ideology and the policy-decisions in post-1978 China. DAVID HARVEY[139] famously described the Chinese economic reforms as both a "*strange case*" and an outcome of a "particular kind of neo-liberalism interdigitated with authoritarian centralized control"[140], which he again defined through the aim of achieving class restoration, thus counteracting economically egalitarian policies enacted during the socialist era. In principle, the reference to neoliberalism as an analytical category for the post-1978 Chinese economic policies is

133 Ibid., p. 223.

134 SIGEL LOUIS T., On the "Two Roads" and Following Our Own Path: The Myth of the "Capitalist Road", in: The Australian Journal of Chinese Affairs, No. 7, 1982, pp. 55–83.

135 His findings demonstrate the difficulties that arise with the attempt to clearly and exhaustively define socialism and socialist policies, as referred to in Chapter II. See: SIGEL LOUIS T., On the "Two Roads" and Following Our Own Path: The Myth of the "Capitalist Road", in: The Australian Journal of Chinese Affairs, No. 7, 1982, pp. 55–83.

136 SULLIVAN MICHAEL, Louis T. Sigel and "Two Line Struggle Analysis": The Myth of the Objective Standard of Socialism, in: The Australian Journal of Chinese Affairs, Vol. 8, July 1982, pp. 65–74.

137 See e. g. PEI MINXIN, From Reform to Revolution The Demise of Communism in China and the Soviet Union, Harvard 1998, pp. 85 ff.

138 TEN BRINK TOBIAS, China's Kapitalismus, Entstehung, Verlauf, Paradoxien, Frankfurt and New York 2013.

139 HARVEY DAVID, A Brief History of Neoliberalism, New York 2005.

140 Ibid., p. 120.

supported namely by scholars of international relations theory, such as YAQING QIN[141] and anthropologists like LISA HOFFMAN[142] and HAIRONG YAN[143].

Although the importance of differentiation from comparisons with the "western" *neoliberalism* originating in the USA and Great Britain is consistently emphasised, the usefulness of the concept for an understanding of Chinese economic policies has been criticised by scholars such as DONALD M. NONINI[144] and WANG HUI[145]. Both basically dismissed its validity by emphasising the oligarchic character of the system as well as the increasingly emerging focus on the solution to social issues instead of the mere promotion of markets. Geographer FULONG WU[146] synthesised different perspectives on the neoliberal character of Chinese reforms, in particular, in the urban sphere, by naming "the lack of development opportunity and investment space for economic growth that prevailed at the end of the 1970s"[147] as the political-economic origin of the reforms. He also added a transnational element in concluding that the prevalence of the market mechanism can be understood only as a reaction to the industrialised world – namely, the success of the newly industrialising East Asian economies, the so-called *tiger states*, providing a highly visible model for China in its immediate neighbourhood. According to WU, the Chinese leadership's sensible answer to the challenges of economic development was to focus on the benefits to be derived from a market-oriented economy and linkages to globalisation through export-oriented development. From a historical perspective, however, it remains unclear why the paradigm shift within the leadership of the PRC occurred in 1978 and why undoubtedly relevant factors such as economic stagnation, the success of other economies under different models, and falling or low living standards did not lead to a shift during an earlier stage.

The year 1978 as a historical watershed is frequently considered as given, or explained with very general factors and influences, such as a general turn towards economic reason or pragmatism of sorts. As it has been indicated by several authors, the economy of the PRC pre-1978 was not isolated from foreign markets and investments; therefore, decisions concerning economic policies cannot be fully understood through a perspective reduced to internal processes but must be analysed in the wider context of the world

141 QIN YAQING, Why is There No Chinese International Relations Theory?, in: International Relations of the Asia-Pacific, Vol. 7, No. 3, 2007, pp. 313–340.

142 HOFFMAN LISA (both of the following), Autonomous choices and patriotic professionalism: On governmentality in late-socialist China, in: Economy and Society, Vol. 35, No. 4, 2006, pp. 550–570; Urban Modeling and Contemporary Technologies of City-Building in China: The Production of Regimes of Green Urbanism, in: ROY ANANYA, ONG AIHWA, Worlding Cities: Asian Experiments and the Art of being Global, Hoboken 2011, pp. 55–76.

143 YAN HAIRONG, Neoliberal Governmentality and Neohumanism: Organizing Suzhi/Value Flow through Labor Recruitment Networks, in: Cultural Anthropology, Vol. 18, No. 4, pp. 493–523.

144 NONINI DONALD M., Is China Becoming Neoliberal, in: Critique of Anthropology, Vol. 28, No. 2, 2008, pp. 145–176.

145 WANG HUI, The Historical Origin of Chinese "Neoliberalism": Another Discussion on the Ideological Situation in Contemporary Mainland China and the Issue of Modernity, in: Chinese Economy, Vol. 36, No. 4, pp. 3–42.

146 WU FULONG, How neoliberal is China's Reform: The Origins of Change during transition, in: Eurasian Geography and Economics, Vol. 51, No. 5, 2010, pp. 619–631.

147 Ibid., p. 622.

economy in the 1970s, taking into account the significant shifts in energy prices with manifold consequences as well as the different strategies that move away from Keynesian or socialist economic models to counter adverse effects. Linkages to the concept of neoliberalism though bea the risk of ahistoricism.

However, the application of a more or less specific bundle of different policies and recommendations – in order to analyse developments and policies in the PRC – has not provided much insight, and the core question still remains unanswered. If neoliberalism is a viable analytical concept, why did partly comparable reform attempts occur in China during the same period as readjustments took place in the United States, Great Britain, Chile, Brazil, Uruguay and Argentina after 1973? Why were neoliberal ideas adopted but not socialist concepts of economic adjustment that were developed, for instance, in Hungary[148], the GDR[149], Poland[150], Yugoslavia[151] and the Soviet Union[152]? More recent studies have focused on the importance of the transnational exchange of ideas, accounting for the origins of emerging within the socialist world and the West. As an example, outside China, Johanna Bockman[153] argued that exchanges of ideas occurred between both Hungarian and Yugoslav economists and their colleagues in the West. This led to the development of models which allowed for the quick adaptation of market-economy elements after the end of the socialist regimes, which in turn influenced neoliberal ideas during the 1980s and 1990s.

The argument that economists of Eastern European origin, such as Włodimierz Brus, Janos Kornai and Ota Sik, had decisive influence on debates among Chinese

148 Under Janos Kadar, referred to as Goulash-Communism, *Kadarism* or the Hungarian Thaw. For a case-study, see: Swain Nigel, Hungary, The Rise and Fall of Feasible Socialism, New York 1992.

149 The quite technically sophisticated "new economic system of planning and management" was developed and tested in 1969/1970, which was at its core based on the ideals of the Kosygin/Liberman-program in the Soviet Union. It focused thus on improvements of relatively rigid and detailed planning. See: Hamel Hannelore, Sozialistische Marktwirtschaft in der DDR, Hinwendung und Abkehr, in: Leipold Helmut (ed.), Sozialistische Marktwirtschaften, Munich 1975, pp. 72–103.

150 Perhaps the example of economic policy reform within a socialist paradigm that is most related to trade and international markets. The rise of foreign as well as internal debt became the primary challenge for the polish model of heavily subsidised household consumption. See: Peters Florian, "Rette sich, wer kann", Die wirtschaftlichen Reformanläufe der polnischen Kommunisten in den 1980er-Jahren, in: Wemheuer (ed.) 2020, pp. 105–119.

151 Most famous for its implementation of self-management by the workers in state-owned enterprises, the Yugoslav approach also liberalised certain prices and allowed for private property as well as market-transactions. See: Estrin Saul, Yugoslavia: The Case of Self-Managing Market Socialism, in: Journal of Economic Perspectives, Vol. 5, No. 4, Fall 1991, pp. 187–194.

152 Besides the specific monographs cited below, see: Hewett Edbert Anscar, Economic Reform in the Soviet Union, in: The Brookings Review, Vol. 2, No. 3, Spring 1984, pp. 8–11, for a commentary on the main challenges for the adjustments under Yuri Andropov and Konstantin Chernenko, and for an overview on the reform cycles in Eastern Europe versus China after 1978: Wemheuer Felix, Über den "Marktsozialismus" hinaus: Ein Vergleich der chinesischen Reform und Öffnung mit den Reformzyklen in Osteuropa seit den 1960er-Jahren, in: Wemheuer (ed.) 2020, pp. 15–36.

153 Bockman Johanna, Markets in the Name of Socialism, The Left-Wing Origins of Neoliberalism, Stanford 2011.

economists during the 1980s was made by JULIAN GEWIRTZ[154]. He also referred to the influence of experts working for international economic organisations, such as the World Bank. Most recently, a contribution by SUSANNE WEIGELIN-SCHWIEDRZIK and LIU HONG[155] demonstrated that the leadership of the CCP was actively interested in such exchanges while searching for new economic paradigms. For the comparison and understanding of different approaches of economic policy reforms in Eastern Europe, the volume edited by HELMUT LEIPOLD[156] is particularly noteworthy. In his introduction to a collection of essays by renowned experts, such as THOMAS EGER, JIRI KOSTA, HANNELORE HAMEL and KURT WESSELY, as well as in the contribution by REINHARD PETERHOFF, the volume provides a theoretical interpretation of the different attempts that are still of unique value today.

Another important strand of scholarly work revolves around economic developments in the PRC before 1978 by embedding the developments in wider discussions on socialist economic policy and "communism". A comprehensive and immensely readable book on the world history of communism, authored by DAVID PRIESTLAND[157] is an important stepping stone for work on the topic. LORENZ LÜTHI'S[158] contribution regarding the *Sino-Soviet Split* contextualised many of the ideological differences between the Soviet Union and the PRC, which also concerned economic policy. His recent follow-up on the global nature of the Cold War(s)[159] challenges conventional notions of *dualism* during the era and beyond the level of inter-state relations as well as the importance of the re-emerging international relations with China and their theoretical re-conceptualisations. The history of Chinese foreign relations has been subject of a ground-breaking general analysis by JOHN W. GARVER[160], who – from an arguably realist theoretical point of view – analysed Chinese international relations before 1978 as a strategy to prevent Soviet encirclement, while establishing the beginning of the *opening to the world* in the same year. The analysis of the Sino-Soviet relations with regard to the different models of socialism and development paradigms, and the debates among political and academic elites by GILBERT ROZMAN[161] illustrates the potential of Soviet sources for research on China and the intensity of mutual surveillance and analysis of the respective policies of the other country during the 1970s. Several authors have made attempts to fit China's case into models of economic transition, notably via comparisons to Eastern European states or Russia.

Literature on the "significant others" to China with regard to the socialist industrialisation paradigm has analysed economic policies and their implementation in

154 GEWIRTZ JULIAN B., Unlikely Partners, Chinese Reformers, Western Economists, and the Making of Global China, Cambridge 2017.

155 WEIGELIN-SCHWIEDRZIK SUSANNE, LIU HONG, Vergessene Partner im Reformprozess: Der Dialog der VR China mit reform-kommunistischen Strömungen in Osteuropa (1977–1987), in: Wemheuer (ed.) 2020, pp. 37–54.

156 LEIPOLD HELMUT (ed.), Sozialistische Marktwirtschaften, Munich 1975.

157 PRIESTLAND DAVID, Weltgeschichte des Kommunismus, Munich 2009.

158 LÜTHI LORENZ, The Sino-Soviet Split, Cold War in the Communist World, Woodstock 2008.

159 LÜTHI LORENZ, Cold Wars, Asia, the Middle East, Europe, Cambridge 2020.

160 GARVER JOHN M., China's Quest, The History of the Foreign Relations of the People's Republic of China, New York 2016.

161 ROZMAN GILBERT, The Chinese Debate on Soviet Socialism, 1978–1985, Princeton 1987.

depth. Important examples are MICHAEL KORT's[162] seminal work on the Soviet Union as the *Soviet Colossus*, the focused analysis of shifts within the Soviet pattern by ROBERT C. ALLEN[163] and the contribution on Central and Eastern Europe after 1944 by IVAN T. BEREND[164], providing a similar analysis on shifts in economic policies. Economic thought in the Soviet Union, namely the constant adaptation of the Marxist theoretical basis to suit the political and economic needs, was of particular interest during and after the collapse of the system. PEKKA SUTELA[165] established continuities of the reformist program under Gorbachev and thus demonstrated the flexibility of ideological concepts. Important contributions to economic policy reforms in the Soviet Union and Eastern Europe have been provided by, for instance, BERNARD CHAVANCE et al.[166], MARIE LAVIGNE[167] and BARRY EICHENGREEN[168], without making direct references to developments in the PRC but outlining the development and applications of different approaches on economic policy within the socialist world. The connection between the 1973 oil crisis and Soviet economic development has been analysed by MARK HARRISON[169] and DAVID KOTZ and FRED WEIR[170]. HARRISON argued that growth halted abruptly for a long period in the Soviet Union and caused stagnation, for which he held wrong decisions in economic policy due to mis-assessments of further growth prospects, lack of economic integration and unrealistic growth patterns in central planning accountable. KOTZ and WEIR emphasise that, despite the growth of reserves in hard currency, internal failures trumped in the longer-term and made long-term stagnation inevitable. The economic policy adjustments in China before 1978 have not yet been embedded in a wider context in the socialist economic debate.

The aspects of US–China rapprochement and its political framing have been critically examined by EVELYN GOH[171], while the innovative examination of informal diplomacy by CHRISTIAN TALLEY[172] has shed new light on the role of non-state actors and contacts,

162 KORT MICHAEL, The Soviet Colossus, History and Aftermath, seventh edition, Armonk and London 2010.

163 ALLEN ROBERT C., Farm to Factory, A Reinterpretation of the Soviet Industrial Revolution, Princeton and Oxford 2003.

164 BEREND IVAN T., Central and Eastern Europe, 1944–1993, Detour from the periphery to the periphery, New York 1996.

165 SUTELA PEKKA, Economic Thought and Economic Reform in the Soviet Union, Cambridge 1991.

166 CHAVANCE BERNARD, HAUSS CHARLES, SELDEN MARK, The Transformation of Communist Systems, New York 2019.

167 LAVIGNE MARIE, The Economics of Transition: From Socialist Economy to Market Economy, second edition, London 1999.

168 EICHENGREEN BARRY, The European Economy since 1945, Coordinated Capitalism and beyond, Princeton and Oxford 2007.

169 HARRISON MARK, Trends in Soviet labor productivity, 1928–85: War, postwar recovery, and slowdown, in: European Review of Economic History, Vol. 2, No. 2, August 1998, pp. 171–200.

170 KOTZ DAVID, WEIR FRED (both of the following), Revolution from Above: The Demise of the Soviet System, London 1997; Russia's Path: From Gorbachev to Putin, The Demise of the Soviet System and the New Russia, London 2007.

171 GOH EVELYN, Constructing the U.S. Rapprochement with China 1961–1974, New York 2005.

172 TALLEY CHRISTIAN, Forgotten Vanguard: Informal Diplomacy and the Rise of United States-China Trade, Notre Dame 2018.

apart from official protocol. Research on the *long 1970s* is still relatively eclectic. Some aspects, including transnational ones, have been specifically analysed with regard to developments in international "high politics". A volume edited by POUL VILLAUME et al.[173] brings together perspectives concerning movements of the civil society as well as international diplomacy. With regard to the international economy, besides the contribution by ERNEST MANDEL mentioned above, notably, the volume edited by NIALL FERGUSON[174] reflects the many facets of the decade. Furthermore, CHARLES S. MAIER, ALAN M. TAYLOR and VERNIE OLIVEIRO, among others, have highlighted how the high level of interconnection between states shaped the consequences of a *bundle of crises*, and ODD ARNE WESTAD proposed that parts of the economic policy paradigm changed ever since the early 1970s.

While the economic development and policies of the PRC have been widely covered by the existing literature, certain features reappear in many of the approaches: a strong concentration on leader figures, notably Deng Xiaoping; the idea of political factions within the CCP politburo, of which one prevailed in a struggle for political power and then determined the primary developments in economic and other policies; and a strict separation of the years before and after 1978, with a strong emphasis on the latter. However, the preceding years – often defined as overshadowed by turmoil and rather irrelevant in terms of policy decisions and the nature of the political and economic system of the China – appear to be neglected, apart from some inquiries into certain areas and sectors. The stipulated isolation of the PRC is another feature, which due to the US embargo and the comparably small exchanges with the outside world might appear plausible but also detract from the interactions and influences that existed and affected the way the Chinese leadership tried to run the country before Deng's reforms.

Looking beyond dualisms

This study is located at the intersection of several current debates that have gained attention in the scientific as well as public domains. The first is China's rise as an economic and political global power[175] closely linked to the debate on economic reforms after 1978 and the key role in global value chains (GVC) particularly of industrial production the PRC assumed thereafter. The second is the debate on the legacy of socialist economic models and their transformation or transition to more or less[176] market(s)-based economies.

173 VILLAUME POUL, Mariager Rasmus, Porsdam Helle (eds.), The "Long 1970s": Human Rights, East-West Détente and Transnational Relations, New York 2016.

174 FERGUSON NIALL, MAIER CHARLES S., MANELA EREZ, SARGENT DANIEL J. (eds.), The Shock of the Global, The 1970s in Perspective, Harvard 2011.

175 As famously coined by NICHOLAS D. KRISTOF in 1993, using the telling subtitle "This time it is real" when referring to the rise of China in the World. See: KRISTOF NICHOLAS D., The Rise of China, in: Foreign Affairs, November/December 1993, available at: https://www.foreignaffairs.com/articles/asia/1993-12-01/rise-china, accessed on 1 April 2020.

176 While the transition of the countries included into the 2004 expansion of the European Union is widely accepted to have been successful, the picture is not all that clear. The heterogenous application of direct state aid and other subsidies continue to be some of the core disputed issues. Also, trends towards state intervention continue to emerge with regard to specific areas, most recently the strive towards a "European digital economy". See, for instance, GABRISCH HUBERT, HÖLSCHER

The third is the debate on ideas that matter in economic policymaking, their changes as well as origins.[177] The fourth is the series of somewhat global economic crises during the 1970s, referred to in my introductory remarks, which decisively shaped the structures of what today is considered to be the world economy.[178]

In many studies, the presumption of China's international isolation until 1979 corresponds with the approaches taken to write its national history or describe its economic development within the national framework. Perhaps, the – disputed[179] – image of the Qing Dynasty (1636–1912) that emphasised a sense of inherent Chinese superiority over foreign countries shaped this perception. The famous answer given by Emperor Qian Long toking George III. of Britain as conveyed by Lord Macartney for trade privileges denied any need for China to trade with the industrialised nation as "[...] we [the Chinese Empire] possess all things. I set no value on objects strange or ingenious, and have no use for your country's manufactures."[180] This stance, at least from a western perspective, seemed to be further underlined by the CCP's insistence on self-reliance, notably after the Sino-Soviet split. For several years, the assessment was plausible.

Authors like Chris Ogden have established causalities between a Chinese "autarkic stance" and big push-policies such as the Great Leap Forward, while Jan Prybyla noted that the relatively low foreign trade of both China under Mao and the Soviet Union under Stalin also need to be understood as an obvious function of their low per-capita income.[181] China's unwillingness to exchange with the outside world seemed at different times to be founded on apparently opposite motives: once self-perceived abundance,

---

Jens (eds.), The Successes and Failures of Economic Transition, The European Experience, London 2006. On the other side of the spectrum, Russia can only in parts be considered an economy based on free markets – as Boris Nikolayevich Yeltsin called it in his 1999 State of the Union address, "an ugly model – a cross-breed of the two systems". Quoted in: Gaddy Clifford W., Ickes Barry W., A Simple Four – Sector Model of Russia's Virtual Economy, in: Post-Soviet Geography and Economics, Vol. 40, No. 2, 2001, p. 103.

177 For a curated list of authors, see: Palgrave McMillan, History of Economic Thought, available at: https://www.palgrave.com/gp/blogs/business-economics-finance-management/exploring-economic-history/history-of-economic-thought, last accessed on 1 April 2020. For a classic history of economic thought leading to the formulation of policies by governments, see: Pribram Karl, A History of Economic Reasoning, Baltimore 1983.

178 It was no coincidence that Klaus Schwab published his *Davos Manifesto* in 1973, which was a principal building block for the creation of the World Economic Forum (WEF) – arguably the most important single event for the structure of the current global economy. Available at: https://www.weforum.org/agenda/2019/12/davos-manifesto-1973-a-code-of-ethics-for-business-leaders/, accessed on 3 July 2022.

179 For a critique of the isolationist narrative, see e. g. Pomeranz Kenneth, The Great Divergence: China, Europe and the Making of the Modern World Economy, Princeton and Oxford 2000; and Hubbell Bram, Eurocentrism and the Myth of East Asian Isolation, Decolonizing the teaching of world history, 25 January 2016. Available at: https://www.liberatingnarratives.com/eurocentrism-and-the-myth-of-east-asian-isolation/, accessed on 1 October 2022.

180 Emperor Qian Long's Letter to King George III., 1793, available at Modern History Sourcebook, http://www.fordham.edu/halsall/mod/1793qianlong.html, accessed on 22 July 2022.

181 Ogden Chris, China and India: Asia's Emergent Great Powers, Cambridge 2017, p. 84. See: Prybyla Jan S., Market and Plan under Socialism: The Bird in the Cage, Stanford 1987, p. 95.

once real scarcity. In both cases, the sheer size of China was an important factor. Generally, trade quotas tend to be lower for large economies, which dispose of a wider range of resources and bigger domestic markets.[182] It is the structure of the trade that is decisive: importing "manufactures" as mentioned in Emperor Qian's answer might be different from importing "objects ingenious" – particularly if the political goal is not merely consumption, but advancing the economy by using such ingeniosity and adopting it.

By approaching adjustments in specific areas of Chinese economic policy (in the fourth Chapter) in tandem with the development of foreign economic relations (in the fifth Chapter), I follow an approach rooted in the study of global and international history of both socialism and economic globalisation with particular attention given to exchanges across the national border and interfaces created with the outside world. In addition, certain elements of legal history, in particular the history of international economic law, are reflected. The research questions which this book intends to answer are inspired by approaches of scholars mentioned in the literature review and others, such as ROBERT WILLIAM DAVIES, JAN ADAM, RÜDIGER FRANK and SABINE BURGHART as well as JÁNOS KORNAI[183], who have sought to establish a differentiated view on socialist economic policies in the 20th century, and the way they are to be distinguished from models perceived as capitalist.

The core of this approach is a critique of a dualist view of political alternatives available to a society to organise its economic activity. Notably, with regard to the scholarly[184] and political debate on socialist economic systems, dualisms inherited from discourses during the Cold War strongly continue to influence the common understanding of the possibilities of and alternatives to policymaking. A prime example are debates among academic economists. The arguments brought forward in the so-called "Socialist Calculation Debate" of the 1920s and 1930s by economists such as LUDWIG VON MISES on the inadequacy of rigid centralised planning, appear to still be among the prime explanations for the collapse of socialist regimes in Eastern Europe and Russia until 1992. On the other hand, the opposite position defended, e. g., by OSKAR LANGE and ABBA LERNER continues to experience regular revivals.

---

182 Nonetheless, size is not the only determinant of trade integration. Other factors help to explain differences across countries: geography, history, culture, trade policy, structure of the economy (in particular the weight of non-tradable services) and integration in global production chains, where measured trade may include a significant proportion of re-exports and intra-firm trade linked to the presence of multinational firms. See: OECD, Chapter 6: Trade openness, in: OECD Science, Technology and Industry Scoreboard 2011, Paris 2011, p. 177.

183 For example, in addition to authors mentioned in the literature review, see: DAVIES ROBERT WILLIAM, The industrialisation of Soviet Russia, Volume 1: The Socialist Offensive: The Collectivization of Soviet Agriculture, 1929–1930, Cambridge 1980 [as well as the subsequent volumes]; ADAM JAN, Economic Reforms in the Soviet Union and Eastern Europe since the 1960s, London 1989; FRANK RÜDIGER, BURGHART SABINE (eds.), Driving Forces of Socialist Transformation, North Korea and the Experience of Europe and East Asia, Vienna 2009; and KORNAI JÁNOS, The Socialist System, The Political Economy of Communism, Princeton 1992.

184 ROTHBARD MURRAY N., The End of Socialism and the Calculation Debate Revisited, in: Review of Austrian Economics, Vol. 5, No. 2, 1991, pp. 51–76; and MILONAKIS DIMITRIS, New market socialism: a case for rejuvenation or inspired alchemy?, in: Cambridge Journal of Economics, Vol. 27, No. 1, January 2003, pp. 97–121.

Therefore, one core observation on which the analyses in this book are based is the *gradual* nature of economic policies. While a perfect market economy in accordance with pure neoclassic modelling, free of any politically determined interference has, and arguably rightly so, (almost[185]) never existed, the same observation is valid for an idealised socialist economy based on perfect centralised planning and allocation based exclusively on bureaucratic decisions. In practice, the abstract ideal of a centrally controlled planned economy was just as distant from reality in socialist China, even more so than in the Soviet Union, as the neoclassical model of perfectly competitive markets reflects the reality of market economies.

With regard to China and other socialist states, economic policy has been widely, and akin to the analysis of other policy areas, framed as being the result of a political and ideological struggle between political "lines"[186], "factions"[187], "blocs"[188] or "wings"[189]. These opposing parts of the political duality, in analogy to the often purported binary structure of international "high politics" during the Cold War[190], are generally established to be either a "leftist", "radical" or "utopian line" position – such as, in the case of China, those being personified in part by Mao himself[191], Lin Biao[192] and the members of the so-called

---

185 The argument may be made that the so-called Manchester Capitalism of 19th century United Kingdom might have approached this state of affairs as one of the hitherto most "*unembedded*" form of market economy, according to KARL POLANYI.

186 In the translations of sources by the Foreign Broadcast Information Service and Joint Publications Research Service that I refer to often, the term "*lines*" is usually used when the concept is referred to in official documents and speeches.

187 Prevalent in political science and international relations theory, where the notion apparently allows for analysis along the lines of approaches used for party-politics in parliamentary democracies. For example, see: DITTMER LOWELL, WU YU-SHAN, The Modernization of Factionalism in Chinese Politics, in: World Politics, Vol. 47, No. 4, July 1995, pp. 467–494.

188 Using the term most obviously with reference to the dualist perspective on the Cold War, referring to the "Communist Bloc" (geographically) and the Chinese "*reform bloc*" in an almost comparative manner. For example, see DITTMER LOWELL, Ghost of the Strategic Triangle, The Sino-Russian Partnership, in: ZHAO SUISHENG (ed.), Chinese Foreign Policy: Pragmatism and Strategic Behaviour, New York 2004, pp. 207–223.

189 Notably, when the inner workings of the CCP are in focus. See, for instance, TALAS BARNA, Economic Reforms and Political Attempts in China 1979–1989, Budapest 1991, pp. 90 f.

190 For examples mostly within the duality-approach, see e. g. GADDIS JOHN LEWIS, The Cold War: A New History, New York 2005; LAFEBER WALTER, America, Russia, and the Cold War, 1945–2006, tenth edition, Boston 2008. Broader approaches can be found in WESTAD ODD ARNE, The Global Cold War: Third World Interventions and the Making of our Times, Cambridge 2007 and LÜTHI 2020. For a useful review essay on literature with a binary twist, see: FOLLY MARTIN H., Cold War Dichotomies, in: Journal of American Studies, Vol. 34, No. 3, 2000, pp. 503–508.

191 As discussed in the second chapter, the role of Mao has been understood in various ways, ranging from leftist through the "balancing aspect" to rightist. The Central Committee of the CCP itself denounced aspects of Mao's policies between 1956 and 1976 as "ultra-leftist". Contemporary observers like PETER KUNTZE have emphasised the importance of dialectics and Mao's position between rightist and leftist "deviations": KUNTZE PETER, China nach Mao: Rechtsputsch in der Volksrepublik, Munich and Vienna 1978, pp. 39 ff.

192 Due to his mysterious death in a plane crash in Öndörkhaan, Mongolia on 13 September 1971, it is difficult to assess how the military man Lin would have positioned himself with regard to economic adjustments later on. FREDERICK C. TEIWES and WARREN SUN have argued, that "fragmentary indi-

"Gang of Four" during the struggle for Mao's succession – or a "rightist"[193], "moderate"[194] or, if the views of the observer happen to largely concur with those of the observed, "pragmatic"[195] position. In the historiography of China, the latter notably applies to political leaders such as Liu Shaoqi[196], Li Xiannian[197] and Deng Xiaoping.

This dualism is not entirely imposed by external interpretations but based on public political *formulae* used in the PRC during this period and earlier. Mao himself ominously stated the following in 1964:

> "In Beijing, and I don't mean the Beijing party committee, there are two independent kingdoms. I will let you guess; I have said enough."[198]

Lashing out against categories of alleged – and, according to the current predominant views, quite flexibly defined and redefined – political opposition has been used in China as a political instrument for purges and campaigns against deviationists from the then

cations" imply that his personal preferences was leaning towards a more moderate industrialisation paradigm than the mass mobilisation of the Great Leap Forward, e. g., stating indirectly that he and his son Lin Liguo were "not leftists". See: Teiwes Frederick C., Sun Warren, The Tragedy of Lin Biao: Riding the Tiger During the Cultural Revolution, London 1996, p. 117.

193 A term going back at least to the Rectification- and Anti-Rightist campaigns which were conducted between 1957 and 1959, and involved far-reaching persecutions and both public and state-organised violence. See: U Eddy, Dangerous Privilege: The United Front and the Rectification Campaign of the Early Mao Years, in: The China Journal, No. 68, July 2012, pp. 32–57; and for a theoretical view on mass mobilisation in China, Tsai Wen-Hui, Mass Mobilization Campaigns in Mao's China, in: American Journal of Chinese Studies, Vol. 6, No. 1, April 1999, pp. 21–48. Regularly rehabilitated, Deng Xiaoping was publicly criticised on several occasions as a "rightist" and even became the subject of a specific campaign in 1976 (Counterattack the Right-Deviationist Reversal-of-Verdicts Trend) as the Gang of Four controlled Chinese mass media. See: Vogel Ezra F., Deng Xiaoping and the Transformation of China, Harvard 2011, pp. 163 ff.

194 Perhaps the term that comes closest to the concept of a "middle line" applied in this thesis and often used in connection with Zhou Enlai.

195 The famous quote on "black and white cats", frequently referred to as a motto for economic pragmatism and attributed to Deng Xiaoping was nevertheless criticised by Mao, as its indifference reflected "bourgeois thinking". See: Vogel 2011, p. 164. The origin of the phrase seems to be a Sichuan and Anhui proverb. See: Levine Steven I., Pantsov Alexander V., Mao: The Real Story, New York 2012, p. 484.

196 Among the driving forces behind the readjustment of the early 1960s within the CCP, Liu became one of the – if not the main – meta-target of the mass campaigns during the Cultural Revolution. For a brief account, see: Gardner John, Liu Shaoqi and the Cultural Revolution: The Rise and Fall of a Chosen Successor, in: Gardner John (ed.), Chinese Politics and the Succession to Mao, London 1982, pp. 9–39.

197 Later becoming president between 1983 and 1988, Li was vice premier during the entire period of 1954 to 1980. He was apparently an important door-opener for adjustments prior to 1978, as Teiwes and Sun (2011) demonstrated, and a part of the modernisation consensus between Hua Guofeng, Deng Xiaoping, and himself.

198 As quoted in Dikötter 2016, p. 25.

current party line.[199] As Zhou Enlai pointed out in a speech at the plenary session of the ninth Party Congress on the 14th of April 1969:

> "We should often review the history of the party, review the history of the **struggle between the two lines inside the party** [emphasis added], and in particular review the history of the struggle against the right opportunism of Chen Duxiu, the "left" and right opportunism of Wang Ming and the counter-revolutionary revisionism of Liu Shaoqi et al.. We should review the positive and negative fighting experiences of victory and defeat accumulated by the party during these forty-eight years [...]."[200]

Similar dualities have also been relied on to describe political dynamics in the Soviet Union, the Polish People's Republic, the GDR and others, as it has been used by leaders within these states for similar lines.[201] For example, while political factions were officially banned in the Communist Party of the Soviet Union as early as 1921, the struggles between "Trotskyites" and "Stalinists" are a well-documented example of the framing of inner-party line struggle as a dualism. In that example e. g. as "socialist internationalism" contra "Russian nationalist socialism".While for the analysis of political debate and the classification of arguments brought forward, such approaches can be helpful and clarifying, they say very little about the actual implementation of economic policies or, for that matter, the envisioned alternatives to the current political course. With regard to China, the schematic view of – in their most exaggerated forms – two fundamentally opposing and mutually insulated factions does not help explain a number of policies actually implemented, regardless of the contemporary political rhetoric.

In a political situation wherein the construed opposition is part of the governing institutions in one way or another, the outcome of daily policymaking may follow the ideal vision of one of the "lines" to a large extent but not fully conform to it. This holds especially true for the administration of economic activities, where objective necessities and constraints set the *limits of the possible* for any idealised course, even if all proponents of the respective set of ideas were presumed to fully believe in them. *De facto* resulting policies are the expression of ideological trends and results of compromises, eventually tilting in a certain direction[202] based on those ideas that yield more political power and,

199 Which went back to practices in the Chinese communist movement before 1949, notably the "first" rectification campaign of 1942–1944. See: TEIWES FREDERICK C., The Origins of Rectification: Inner-Party Purges and Education before liberation, in: The China Quarterly, No. 65, March 1976, pp. 15–53. If and to what extent these practices were directly inspired by or even actively encouraged by the Soviet Union is still subject to debate.

200 SCHOENHALS MICHAEL, New Texts: Speeches at the Ninth National Congress of the Chinese Communist Party, in: The Stockholm Journal of East Asian Studies, No. 2, 1990, p. 93.

201 MCALOON DAVID WILLIAM, Leon Trotsky and the struggle for power in communist Russia, 1921–1923, University of Richmond Scholarship Repository Honors Theses, 1 April 2001; and PRIESTLAND DAVID, Weltgeschichte des Kommunismus, Von der Französischen Revolution bis heute, München 2009, pp. 131–141.

202 A lively example supporting this view is the intense debate on the "correct course" within the socialist movement, notably between the Soviet Union and China. Unfortunately, with a few exceptions, they have not found their way into this thesis, but e. g. the transcriptions of broadcasts of the *Soviet International Observers Roundtable* (partly available through the FBIS) offer rich insights into the – mutual – condemnation of the respective other's policies.

in a more optimistic view, also by the advancement of knowledge regarding the functioning of the economy. DWIGHT H. PERKINS, an important voice with regard to the Chinese economy and its historical development, referred to such observations in China as the result of "uneasy juxtapositions"[203] between a Maoist-socialist ideological and a more flexible, even market-driven approach oriented towards tangible outcomes rather than political conformism. Based on the hypothesis that the middle line within the Chinese leadership, as proposed by ROBERT WEIL, was decisive notably after the failure of the Great Leap Forward, this also holds true for China during the Long 1970s.

As an inquiry into economic policy and its dissemination, this study follows an understanding of the formation of such policies which is essentially dialectical. Regardless of the apparent focus on dogmas and ideological "lines" concerning the appropriate relationship between government and economic activities in a society, political decisions are a dialectical business – if such dialectics are not suppressed by authority. Therefore, the approach of this study seeks to omit dualism by focusing on the common denominators and *de facto* constraints. I suggest that *uneasy juxtapositions* were not the exception but much rather reflected the regular state of affairs in domestic and foreign economic policies. Even critical Soviet observers, claiming that China had entered a process of "de-Maoization" in 1977, noted that:

> "These journalists and even diploma-carrying Western sinologists as a rule do not make such an analysis [on disagreement in the CCP leadership]. And that is not all. They silently bypass the fact acknowledged by [Mao Zedong] himself that there were authoritative figures within the CCP who used to speak out against him. Consequently, the main thing is hushed up – the irreconcilable contradiction between Maoist dogmas and the objective requirements of China's development along the path of socialism [...]".[204]

In short, dialectical middle ground shaped the search for appropriate policies, backed by a certain tolerance for adjustments that yielded tangible results for the achievement of economic modernisation as the underlying common objective. Subsequently, economic policy in China has resembled a gigantic process of trial and error, within which changing approaches to economic development are adopted and dropped as well as constantly justified and legitimised within quite flexible ideological boundaries of Maoist socialism and its remnants. NASSIM TALEB has suggested that the strength to innovate is not merely dependent on the features of a political system, but by the opportunities the system and its leadership afford for decentralised experimentation ("maximum tinkering"). Building on this notion, SEBASTIAN HEILMANN has argued that the PRC has in fact pro-

203 PERKINS 2015, p. 200.

204 Foreign Broadcast Information Service, Galin Analyzed Chinese Domestic Political Situation, M. Galin article: "*What is happening in China*", Moscow Novoye Vremya in Russian, 22 04 1977 LD, accessed through Readex.

vided a setting conducive to such tinkering particularly after 1978.[205] This environment was not created overnight.

Experimentation and compromise for an overarching objective

With a view to concrete political decisions, one particular distinction is helpful. Decision-shaping refers to the process leading to the content of a political decision before it is decided, such as the preparation of bills for parliament or options discussed in the central committee in a one-party state. Decision-making on the other hand is the subsequent political decision that is made and communicated based on political power. It is *per se* rarely aligned with all opinions and influences that manifested themselves before.

While the decision-shaping and decision-making processes in a one-party state[206] obviously do not involve a degree of political compromise comparable to pluralistic democracies – at least, if a capable political opposition exists therein[207] – political economy is nevertheless the result of compromise and bargaining as well as the real constraints that define feasibility. Even if the duality of the "two line struggle" within the Chinese leadership had been clear cut – it was not, as authors like TEIWES and SUN and others have clearly pointed out – the resulting decisions would nevertheless have been a sort of dialectic synthesis, a middle ground between the visions based on factors such as the interpretation of ideological *limits of the possible*. I adapt the latter term from FERNAND BRAUDEL, who applied it to economic *Sachzwang*, restricting life before and up to industrialisation. There is no reason to believe that socialist societies were fundamentally different in that regard, regardless of their emphasis on the potential of human will and action as opposed to utilitarian necessity.[208]

Thus, ideology did play an important part. If it is defined as a system of beliefs and structured doctrines, covering most important aspects of human life, the term implies that the doctrine is completely accepted by the leaders of the ruling regime. This kind of interpretation would see ideology as a narrow system of coherent ideas and well-structured content – a dogma. A less absolute position is considering ideology as a more flexible system where practical matters are not bound to the dogma itself but are merely jus-

---

205 HEILMANN SEBASTIAN, Red Swan, How Unorthodox Policy Making Facilitated China's Rise, Hong Kong 2018, p. 28; and TALEB NASSIM NICHOLAS, The Black Swan: The Impact of the Highly Improbable, New York 2007, p. xxi.

206 Which, as it does today, existed in parallel and embedded in the state apparatus responsible for the implementation of policies by the organs of the Chinese socialist state. For an overview on the planning of production and allocation, see: BERGER ROLAND, Economic Planning in China, in: MAXWELL NEVILLE, China's Road to Development, second edition, Oxford 1979, pp 169–204.

207 For a contemporary analysis of democratic constituencies, factoring in the additional problems of powerful committees, see: SARTORI GIOVANNI, Will Democracy Kill Democracy? Decision-Making by Majorities and by Committees, in: Government and Opposition, Vol. 10, No. 2, 1 April 1975, pp. 131–158. Nevertheless, the technocratic rule, as in the handling of most decision-making by government bureaucrats, also found its proponents. See: MEIER KENNETH J., Bureaucracy and Democracy: The Case for More Bureaucracy and Less Democracy, in: Public Administration Review, Vol. 57, No. 3, May/June 1997, pp. 193–199.

208 BRAUDEL FERNAND, Civilization and Capitalism: The Limits of the Possible: The Structures of Everyday, New York 1981.

tified with it.[209] For instance, Maoism can be seen as having both properties, as it both re-interprets the Marxist premises and creates new ones. It uses the Marxist premises loosely yet introduces an ideological interpretation in order to reconcile them with the Chinese context.

Considering political compromises as the basis for an analytical approach requires an understanding of this interpretation, which has become known as "Mao Zedong Thought" – the agglomerate of writings and sayings attributed to Mao. Still during the 1970s, it was the ideological frame of reference for policies, including economic policy. Mao admitted in the aftermath of the catastrophic Great Leap Forward as not having a deep understanding of economics nor being particularly interested in it.[210] However, at the same time, he showed interest in Hegelian dialectic[211] thought and – with some strict "red lines"[212] – in finding a workable way of making China first, a military, and second, an economic force to reckon with. Also, the Chinese political system under Mao Zedong was particular insofar as it allowed for a remarkable degree of public dissent, both inside the apparatus as well as outside – at least in direct comparison to the Soviet Union under Stalin. Political alternatives were thoroughly and often violently criticised and were thus constantly visible in the public domain, albeit mostly in a somewhat distorted form.

True, such dissent was approached reluctantly. Mao backed down from any far-fetching attempts to invigorate public debate in earnest after the Hundred Flowers campaign produced uncomfortable results leading to a backlash, first in the form of a campaign against "rightism". In an editorial in Renmin Ribao on the 8th of June 1957 titled "What is this about", the CCP signaled publicly that criticism of the party had gone too far and that retaliation was coming, claiming that the Hundred Flowers campaign had been abused to attack socialism by some from the political right. A central directive issued on the 26th of June of the same year set forth the outline of the campaign, which initially focused on literary critics such as Ding Ling and Feng Xuefeng. Subsequent expansion of the campaign affected both general critics of the CCP as well as opponents of the policies of agricultural collectivisation.[213]

Still, the idea of integrating different political ideas into a new, whole "unity of opposites" was never entirely dismissed. In particular, concerning economic policy, a limited

---

209 KAUPPINEN MARKO, Canon vs. Charisma, "Maoism" as an Ideological Construction, Jyväskylä Studies in Education, Psychology and Social Research, No. 296, Jyväskylä 2006.

210 As quoted by WEMHEUER 2009, p. 139.

211 As emphasised by PETER KUNTZE in his description of the CCP-internal critique of the cult of personality around Mao, which stylised him as a genius of all sorts – which, as he describes, was perceived by Mao as rather awkward. See: KUNTZE 1978, p. 68 ff. RICHARD LEVY made a similar argument, concluding that "Mao's adherence to "dialectics" and "contradictions" is more than mere lip-service to "sacred" theories [...] Mao must certainly be seen as one of the foremost developers and practitioners of Marx's dialectical materialism". See: LEVY RICHARD, His views on the Soviet Union's Political Economy, New Light on Mao Chapter 2, in: The China Quarterly, Vol. 61, Special issue, pp. 116 f.

212 See the second Chapter.

213 POTTER PITMAN B., From Leninist Discipline to Socialist Legalism, Peng Zhen on Law and Political Authority in the PRC, Stanford 2003, p. 77.

tolerance with regard to deviations – the often-demoted and rehabilitated Deng Xiaoping being a case-in-point – is reflected in his writings and speeches, as seen from this example from 1965:

> "Our comrades are [also] of a dual nature; that is, they are at once correct and fallible. Don't you have a dual nature? I myself have a dual nature. [...] One must work in many fields and come into contact with people from all walks of life. The leftists cannot be in contact with leftists alone; they must also be in contact with rightists. We must not be afraid of this or that."[214]
>
> "I think there is only one basic law, and that is the law of contradiction. Quality and quantity, affirmation and negation, phenomenon and essence, content and form, necessity and freedom, possibility and reality, etc. are all **unities of opposites** [emphasis added][215]."[216]

Similarly, in a speech before the CCP Central committee in 1965:

> "Comrades who have made mistakes must always be given a chance. Mistakes must be rectified. Don't think that people who have made mistakes should not be allowed to correct their mistakes. Our policy is to learn from past mistakes to avoid future ones and cure the disease to save the patient. See them first and then help them. We want unity-criticism-unity."[217]

As the parallelism between keeping the revolutionary mass movements ongoing and simultaneously pursuing industrialisation and improving production was a core concept underlying Chinese economy policy, compromise was partly inherent to his rule. In the writings of Mao, and guidelines issued by the party and state apparatus, figurative formulae were frequently used to describe the idea of balance.

---

214 Joint Publications Research Service, Talk at Hangchow Conference (21 December 1965), p. 5, accessed through Readex. Also available as a translation from Long Live Mao Tse-tung Thought, a Red Guard Publication, at: https://www.marxistphilosophy.org/HngZhou65.pdf. Accessed on 15 October 2022.

215 As Mao Zedong had stated in a speech at the eight Central Committee of the CCP in 1956: "Everything in the world is a unity of opposites. The unity of opposites means the unity of things which are qualitatively different and opposed to each other. Water, for instance, is a combination of the elements of hydrogen and oxygen. There can be no water if either element is missing. I hear that there are now over 1 million named chemical compounds and an unknown number of unnamed ones. Chemical compounds are the unity of opposites of qualitatively different things. This is also true with things in society. The central and the local governments are the unity of opposites; this department and that department are also the unity of opposites." Joint Publications Research Service, Speech at the Second Plenary Session of the eighth Central Committee of the Communist Party of China, 15 November 1956, Peking Mao Tse-Tung Hsuan-Chi in Mandarin, 1977, accessed through Readex. Also available at https://www.marxists.org/reference/archive/mao/selected-works/volume-5/mswv5_56.htm. Accessed on 1 October 2022.

216 Talk at Hangchow Conference (21 December 1965) p. 6.

217 As expressed by Mao in a speech before the CCP Central Committee. Joint Publications Research Service, Translations on Communist China No. 90, Selections from Chairman Mao, Speech at the 11th Plenary Session of 8th CCP Central Committee, 1966, JPRS Document No. 49826, p. 7, accessed through Readex.

A famous example is being "red and expert". While the notion served as an ideological device in the context of the Three Red Banners and the Great Leap Forward, it also proved to be useful with regard to the rehabilitation of hierarchy and specialised labor later on. Based on Mao's speech on "The Correct Handling of Contradictions among the People" at the 11th enlarged meeting of the Supreme State Conference on the 27th of February 1957, in which he emphasised the importance of political study alongside practical work, Mao Zedong had a program on the management of labour published on 31 January 1958, the "Draft of the 60 Articles on Work Methods". Therein, article 4 described the relationship between being "red" and "expert" as well as between "politics" and "professional work". Mao indicated on several occasions that the notion referred to a balance, by stating that

> "On the one hand we oppose armchair politicians. On the other hand, we oppose realists who have lost their orientation. Ideological work and political work safeguard economic and technological accomplishments. Their purpose is to serve economic foundation."[218]

Another example was the formula of "Walking on Two Legs". It was used in Chinese political discourse to signify a number of different things, generally the bridging of "dialectical pairs", notably the simultaneous development of industry and agriculture, heavy and light industry, large and medium-to-small enterprises, modern and indigenous methods, and national and local enterprises. Generally, doing one thing such as developing heavy industry, without neglecting another, such as the development of light industry and agriculture. The same can be said of the pairs "foundation" and "leading factor" (as in the slogan "agriculture is the foundation and industry the leading factor") and "key link" ("taking grain as the key link") applied to express the attempt to achieve a degree of balance in economic development. Also, the expression has been used with regard to the relationship between practical work and education science, respectively.[219]

Concerning the role of economic modernisation, the slogan "Use the Best Things Foreign", and the call to firmly grasp revolution and class struggle while and even with a view to increasing production are particulary prominent examples. The formula was popularised in an editorial of Renmin Ribao on the 8th of August 1958 titled "Using both Indigenous and Foreign Methods is the Shortcut to Accelerate Industrial Development". While during the Great Leap Forward, the use of indigenous methods – most famously for the smelting of iron in so-called backyard furnaces – was promoted, the use of foreign methods was still seen in conformity with Mao Zedong Thought, as it had a basis in Mao's writings, from particularly around 1956. Different from later developments, this use did refer to the continuation of production in the existing foreign factories and plants under the premise that the Chinese and the foreign should be combined in order to become an organic whole, avoiding an indiscriminate use of "things foreign".[220]

---

218 Quoted from: Li 1995, p. 545.

219 Qiang Zha, "Walking on Two Legs", a Policy Analysis of China's Move to Mass Higher Education, in: State and Market in Higher Education Reforms, Comparative and International Education Book Series Vol. 13, 2012, pp. 167–180.

220 Leung Laifong (ed.), The Writings of Mao Zedong, 1949–1976, Volume II: January 1956-December 1957, Armonk 1992, p. 103 and Li 1995, pp. 458 f.

But, besides ideology, what was the bracket that held the trial and error together and gave it direction? At the core of this study is the observation that the objective of *catching up* with economically advanced countries – in particular the former colonial powers – by achieving *rapid* industrialisation was the principal unifying element of economic policy in China throughout periods of oscillation, adjustment and re-adjustment. While the methods applied and suggested changed several times, the core of the socialist industrialisation paradigm remained the same; the years between 1970 and 1978 are no exception. The second underlying hypothesis of this book is that the leadership of the PRC, upon being confronted with a state of stagnation and rising economical contradictions[221] in the industrialisation paradigm developed since 1949 and adjusted after the Great Leap, found itself challenged with regard to its legitimacy and self-declared objectives and, subsequently, looked for alternative approaches.

Adjustments of China's economic policy and concepts of socialism: Questions

In that process, the Chinese economic system since the early 1960s had moved in a direction akin to what HELMUT LEIPOLD called a "socialist concept of second order" (zweite sozialistische Ordnungskonzeption)[222]: the attempt to establish and maintain a system of largely decentralised planning with communal or state-centred property of the means of production as well as remaining mechanisms of political-economic control. The three distinguishing features for a further differentiation of economic policies he proposed are a viable starting-point to structure and perhaps compare changes in the Chinese adjustments to such occurrences in other socialist countries: First, the approach and methods used for economic planning; second, the political organisation and regulation of property, notably the relationship between public and private; and third, the political-economic influence of the state on people's economic actions beyond the plan itself.

One nuance concerns the phases of economic policy development in China between 1970 and 1978: It is well established[223] that the Cultural Revolution beginning in 1966 was partly the expression of power struggles within the CCP leadership and, generally speaking, within the Chinese socialist state. From the point of view of economic policy implementation, I suggest that the bottom line of economic policy had already departed from

221 See fourth and fifth Chapter.

222 LEIPOLD (ed.) 1975, p. 7. Different terms have been used to describe such approaches to economic policy, such as *Market Socialism*, *Market Syndicalism*, *Synthesis of Plan and Market*, *Third Way*, *New Economic Mechanism*, etc.

223 See e. g. DELURY JOHN, ORVILLE SCHELL, Wealth and Power, China's Long March to the Twenty-First Century, New York 2013, pp. 246 ff.. For the role of Mao's personal ambition, see DIKÖTTER, 2016; for a broad perspective on aspects within social groups such as the Red Guards or Shanghai factory workers, see WU YICHING, The Cultural Revolution at the Margins, Chinese Socialism in Crisis, Harvard 2014. FELIX WEMHEUER added perspectives to the roles of conflicts and social change in the system of class status, the rebellion of (discriminated) temporary and (privileged) permanent industrial workers, the position of cadres and workers in the newly-established revolutionary order and the particularities of the Cultural Revolution in the (much less affected) countryside. See WEMHEUER 2019, pp.193 ff.

the pre-Cultural Revolution paradigm. The relationship between the political-economical ideology of Maoism and the *limits of the possible* it defined for adjustments plays a role for the justification and legitimation of policy changes.

In addition to the overview on key developments concerning the central government, my analysis of specific internal adjustments of economic policy provides evidence for my reasoning on a number of key aspects. Furthermore, I suggest that the hinge years of 1974 and 1975[224] mark an important turn, which is mostly linked to developments in Chinese foreign economic policy. It was then that the Chinese strategy of partial opening to international trade, combined with gradual reforms of the economic model, encountered a number of internal and external constraints. At the same time, the potential for a more fundamental change in its course manifested itself, causing the internal consensus for gradual reforms to shift and leading up to more incisive adjustments after 1978. In 1970 already, China was moving towards a trading system as a part of its planned economy, oriented towards Western Europe and Japan and gradually opening towards the United States. This is worth emphasising as the 1980s policies of "opening China to the world" are frequently associated with international trade – which certainly is an important part of how the approach to economic policy changed after 1978, but not in any way a defining characteristic of "openness".

Accordingly, with regard to the classification of the Chinese economy during the 1970s, and for the purposes of this analysis, I suggest adding a fourth element to LEIPOLD's classification: economic relations with the *rest of the world*, both socialist and non-socialist, the political approach to trade and foreign investment and thus the degree of openness of the economy. How did the Chinese economy relate to the international economy during the 1970s, what legal and physical interfaces were created with whom, and how did the involvement in the international capitalist markets relate to the Chinese economic policies? The *limits of the possible* are embedded in and increasingly influenced by a wider international context and not exclusively subject to a decision of certain actors within the (national) leadership of the PRC. Particular attention is given to the development of infrastructures for international trade, such as pipelines and ports, which are nodes of exchange with the outside world. They also include the creation of legal and normative infrastructures to provide legal certainty for international transactions – trade is the business of contracts where rules matter.

Furthermore, an important distinction between socialist economies needs to be taken into account. The Eastern European socialist states LEIPOLD's classification is based on – as is the case with many contributions on economic policy and history of socialist states – were quite industrialised when adjustments were considered by their political leaders. The focus of the reforms was the *improvement* of the socialist administration and planning for an existing industry, as well as the distribution of the produce – for instance, in the form of material incentives. In the case of China, which in 1949

224 As initially proposed by the author in: LIONNET PHILIPPE, Anpassungen der Wirtschaftspolitik in der Volksrepublik China: die Scharnierjahre 1974/1975, in: WEMHEUER FELIX (ed.), Jahrbuch für historische Kommunismusforschung, Belin 2020, pp. 155–172.

was among the poorest countries in the world nominally[225], the basic orientation of the economic policy was fundamentally different. The mission, so to speak, of Chinese socialism was industrialisation itself and the pursuit of that goal; for instance, in Marx's terms, the creation of both the "material basis" and the "superstructure" necessary for industrial production.

On this basis, the research questions guiding this study are: First, which, if any, experiments and compromises in economic policy that enabled incremental or qualitative adjustments, based on the ideological limits of the possible defined by Mao Zedong Thought, were debated publicly before the end of 1978? Second, did such compromises interrelate with the expansion of international economic exchanges? Third, what external constraints influenced the course taken in economic policy making, in particular, with regard to the meta-objective of catching up with industrialised countries? With regard to the areas of economic policy relevant for the identification of experiments, I identify three areas of economic activity which I use to structure my analysis.

The first cluster concerns productive relations: How are people organised in the productive processes necessary for industrial development? In the case of China, the normative tension between the necessity to train and keep technical expertise on the one hand, and political egalitarianism on the other is an important factor, just as the rewards and administrative work to keep up labour discipline, the organisation of property and ownership as well as the distribution of responsibility for production outcomes. Also, measures intended to address the "growth conflict" between consumption and investment fall under this area, i. e. the extent to which the free exchange of goods and services at a price set by supply and demand or social convention, without direct state interference, are allowed or tolerated.

The second is about technical and technological progress and the use of resources: How are innovations and resources necessary for industrial development acquired and mobilised? This encompasses specific policies of promoting "workplace innovation" as well as the adoption of foreign technology, the idea of increasing labour division alongside the plan through "socialist cooperation", measures aimed at increasing efficiency as well as suppressing consumption through austerity and specific strategies for agricultural mechanisation.

The third addresses the perhaps most important aspect of the development paradigm, funding and distribution: How is the process of industrialisation with its need for both capital and labour financed? In that regard, I explore adjustments in policies around the acquisition of (agricultural) surplus through price-setting and the handling of private plots and subsidiary production.

---

225 Again, if the ususal metrics are applied, such as GDP per capita. While there is evidence that food grain and other consumables were in short supply, there were important improvements after 1949 that are expressed in the rising birth rates and life expectancies – which both raised the lasting pressure on the Chinese economy and its political organisation. China's life expectancy from birth rose from 35–40 years in 1949 to over 65.5 years in 1980 and is among the most rapid sustained increases in documented global history – and the increases did not happen between 1978 and 1980. See: Singer Babiarz Kimberly, Eggleston Karen, Miller Grant, Zhang Qiong, An Exploration of China's Mortality Decline under Mao: a Provincial Analysis, 1950–80, in: Population Studies, Vol. 69, No. 1, 2015, pp. 39–56.

In the years following 1970, almost none of the adjustments I refer to in these areas were entirely new. Some were tested or even implemented on a large scale since the period of readjustment in the early 1960s and re-emerged once the Cultural Revolution had passed the peak of turmoil. More important than the genuine innovation between these phases, in my view, is their relationship to foreign economic exchanges. Trade and, to the extent it was accepted, foreign debt were ways to address constraints that could not be fully overcome by incremental adjustments such as those in the second and third areas just described. In particular, international trade and investment offered a way to ease the pressure on grain acquisition, which necessary to feed the urban population and the industrial workers running the factories.

As an example, the capital goods industries – particularly the branches producing machine tools, which are used for the construction of more sophisticated machinery, literally *machines to make machines* – were main drivers of technical progress and thus industrialisation, while depending heavily on foreign technology. The central role of the capital goods industry in this process of development and diffusion of technical progress is due to several factors. First, new products generally require new machinery and changes in production processes. The implementation of innovations depends on the availability of the proper tools. Second, manufacturing is a major factor of technical progress, as the replacement of obsolete machinery is a major reason for investment and directly affects productivity. Third, such investments cause considerable technological feedback across sectors, as developments at one stage of production stimulate or even require further adaptations along the chain of production.[226] The quantity of, procedures by which and partners with whom such transactions were handled during the 1970s are indicative of a change in focus towards the adoption of foreign advanced technology.

Moreover, I present findings on what needs trade was envisaged to satisfy, notably with regard to consumables other than food. Further, and most importantly, I address the constraints and contradictions the socialist development paradigm encountered when engaging in international economic exchanges, and how those constraints influenced the trend of the "middle line".

The challenges of researching Chinese economic policy

In-depth analyses of the decision-shaping processes within the Chinese institutions' economic policies, as it is provided by authors like FREDERICK C. TEIWES and WARREN SUN, FELIX WEMHEUER, FRANK DIKÖTTER and LORENZ LÜTHI, among others, are not the objective of the analysis presented here. Such studies require the extensive use of both central and local government documents and other primary sources in Chinese language, which is beyond the scope of this book. Focusing on what was publicly communicated as the direction and vision of economic policy within shifting limits of the possible, I relied on ways to reconstruct how adjustments were envisaged and supposed to be implemented. Therefore, this book is largely based on the study of contemporary

226 STEWART FRANCES, Technology and Underdevelopment, second edition, London and Basingstoke 1982.

publications, both foreign and Chinese, stemming from various academic disciplines such as history, political science, geography, legal studies and even geology.

The sources I rely on consist of a wide array of published materials, originating both from China itself as well as other neighbouring countries. For the access to transcripts of provincial and urban Chinese radio broadcasts, newspaper articles (national newspapers like People's Daily (*Renmin Ribao*), Guangming Daily (*Guangming Ribao*) and the theoretical journal Red Flag (*Hongqi*)) as well as a number of articles and scientific papers[227] (published in Taiwan, Hong Kong and Japan) and a number of documents issued by the central and provincial governments, I relied on the extensive resources provided by the US Central Intelligence Agency's (CIA) Foreign Broadcast Information Service (FBIS).

The FBIS was established in 1941 as the Foreign Broadcast Monitoring Service. It is a US government agency which translates the text of daily radio and television broadcasts, newspapers and periodicals, government statements, books, and other sources of unrestricted information – such as databases and grey literature – from non-English language sources around the world. Reports with translations were issued for eight world regions daily and covered such topics as military affairs, politics, the environment, societal issues, economics, and science and technology. The FBIS also encompasses the Joint Publications Research Service (JPRS), which focuses on the translation of foreign language print media. Over the course of my research, I accessed both collections through the proprietary digital collection provided by *Readex*.

Being referred to as the "Two Newspapers and One Magazine" throughout the 1960s and the 1970s, the publications alongside the equally widespread People's Liberation Army Daily (*Jiefangjun Bao*) were the primary outlets of the General Political Department of the PLA. The media played a central role in informing the public of the latest policies and guidelines of the CCP. Renmin Ribao was – and still is – the official newspaper of the Central Committee of the CCP, while Hongqi published primarily theoretical pieces on the ideological line through the interpretation of political writings and their application to more or less concrete examples, quite often with regard to production and labour. This media system was set up under Chen Boda, Mao's secretary and main interpreter of Mao Zedong Thought, to deliver political education and, to a certain extent, teach language and literacy. Often, the three publications published the same editorials. During the Cultural Revolution, the three were at the core of the transmission of Mao Zedong Thought as a doctrine, later becoming important outlets to constantly prepare and legitimise changes in policies towards the public.[228]

As the analysis of public communication on economic policy for over eight years included extensive comparative reading, the fact that the sources in FBIS and JPRS were translated and cross-referenced, according to a unified standard, by experts working in

---

227 In particular Ta Kung Pao (Dagong Bao, formerly L'Impartial), the oldest still active Chinese language newspaper, published in Hong Kong, and the critical Taiwan journal Studies on Chinese communism (chung-kung yen-chiu).

228 Leung Cynthia B., Wang Yiping, Influences of the Cultural Revolution on Chinese Literacy Instruction, in: Leung Cynthia B., Ruan Jiening (eds.), Perspectives on Teaching and Learning Chinese Literacy in China, New York and London 2012, p. 52, and historical contributions to the independent China Media Project at the Journalism and Media Studies Centre at Hong Kong University available at: https://chinamediaproject.org/~/views-analysis/, last accessed on 5 May 2020.

the same institution, was a distinct advantage. Terms are used consistently to the utmost extent, which allows for the recognition of reused references and excerpts from Mao Zedong Thought and other political writings. The reports drawn from Readex are quoted with their date- and timestamps where available, otherwise – in the case of articles translated and summarised by the JPRS – with the bibliographical information as quoted in the report. By using this database, I could rely on extensive published materials from the central, provincial and county levels as well as foreign sources which, due to their consistent standards of translation, gave me highly comparable data covering the research period. It must be added that published sources from China tend to be notoriously unreliable witnesses. As my focus lies on the direction intended to be signalled to the audience, rather than the exact events, I have considered newspapers as indicators of *intention* rather than containing faithful reporting.

To gain an understanding of the changes in production and the economic paradigms that were intended, and also how potential contradictions to earlier models were addressed, in the initial phase of my research, campaign and propaganda material were at the core of my work. Over the course of several journeys to the Chinese mainland as well as Hong Kong between 2014 and 2019, I visited several collections and found new specimens. As I learned later, a lot of Chinese propaganda material is available in high quality and systematically archived outside China as well. In particular, the extensive collection of STEFAN LANDSBERGER, available at the International Institute of Social History (IISH), Amsterdam, as well as increasingly online, provided a rich and unexpectedly useful range of resources for this study. Changes in the tonality, symbolism and messages that the posters conveyed throughout the 1970–1978 period helped me obtain a better feeling for the relevant policy areas and aspects where adjustments could be found. Of course, visual propaganda is in no way a depiction of what actually happened in the factories, workshops and production units. But with regard to the direction in which the Chinese economy was supposed to move, particularly the shift from the heroic motives of the Cultural Revolution to much more down-to-earth scenes – such as farmer's markets and work performed in small shops – the differences are striking and immediately reflect policy decisions. Unfortunately, I could not use the material to its full extent in this book, but six examples were too noteworthy to be left out of this book.

With regard to the developments in Chinese foreign economic policy, especially the US, diplomatic cables accessible in electronic form at the Public Library of US Diplomacy (PlusD) as well as letters and reports of Swiss diplomats at the Diplomatic Documents of Switzerland-collection (dodis) proved to be of crucial value. They provided me not only with the assessments of Beijing- and Hong Kong-based US-experts on how trade in grain and oil as well as other commodities developed but also interna with regard to the readiness of Chinese officials of the Ministry of Foreign Trade to discuss, and eventually accept foreign loans as well as their attitudes towards technology imports. Also, reports prepared by the US embassy on initiatives by the US business community to increase economic activity in China, and the various reactions of their Chinese counterparts were insightful.

Nevertheless, the use of diplomatic documents comes with a number of issues that require a few important reservations. While diplomats are professional information gatherers and usually competent reporters, their position as representatives of their respective home countries directly influences the information that is transmitted back to the centre. If the general policy of the home country is the expansion of exports, then trade opportunities are emphasised in reports. Also, the impressions of diplomats that manifest in the same reports are often biased due to the personal attitude of the reporter towards the country and the spin that the superiors – usually the heads of mission or its economic section – want to lend to an event. On the other hand, with regard to adjustments in a given or perceived course of economic policy, this bias can also be helpful. On several occasions, US and European diplomats have expressed their surprise at their Chinese counterparts' unexpected insistence to increase international economic exchanges or willingness to test the *limits of the possible,* in particular, with regard to foreign debt.

Further, I relied on declassified documents available at the CIA under the 2004 Freedom of Information Act, such as analyses of Chinese foreign trade policy and developments on international markets. Referring to internal and published documents of the organs of the European communities, the quite unique Archive of European Integration (AEI) at the University of Pittsburgh, PA – where I have had the honour to conduct research on several occasions – was an important source. A permalink is provided for where sources drawn from PlusD, dodis, the CIA and the AEI are available online. Also, since the importance of rules, notably with regard to foreign economic relations, is an important part of this book, I have relied on both legal scholarship of the 1970s on the beginnings of Chinese foreign economic law as well as edited legal sources.

Additionally, I have used the accounts of several foreigners who visited China within my research-period. In particular, the critical report by the Swedish journalist Olof Lagercrantz was insightful, as he intended to disprove the popular notion at the time that China had somehow managed to establish a more humane and moderate form of agrarian socialism compared to the Soviet and, thus, questioned all he was presented in China. In fact, the more recent memoir by former IBM executive Allan Joseph was particularly interesting, as he described the keen interest of Chinese officials to procure the *basic innovations* of information technology as well as the pragmatism they showed when dealing with foreigners in that regard.

While this analysis relies on quantitative data to demonstrate trends and changes in the Chinese economy, it is largely based on a qualitative analysis of the published sources. Accordingly, quantitative data are mostly used to indicate trends and economic development and verify generalised statements on the state of the Chinese economy. A decisive factor for the research of the economic situation in 1970s China was the limited reliability of available macroeconomic data.[229] The available figures for the period before 1978 are mostly based on assessments by foreigners or statements made by Chinese officials and only scarcely involve publications by Chinese provinces or cities. The breakdown of the statistical system during the Great Leap Forward was still felt in the 1970s. For the 1950s, in addition to estimates in various publications, there was only one official statistical handbook called the *Ten Great Years,* published in 1959. Throughout the 1960s, statistical data was not published. In the early 1970s, some aggregated data was provided by Zhou Enlai to the American journalist Edgar Snow for the year 1970.

229 Hidasi 1979, Clark 1976.

As statistics are crucial for the running of a centrally planned economy, the scarcity of data – which is assumed to have been internal as well as public – during the 1970s indicates the weakness of the central planning system in the relatively decentralised economy of the time.[230] Domestic data sets were often incomplete or partly reconstructed afterwards.[231] China released indicators for the 1952–1978 period in the year 1998 based on the UN-SNA (System of National Accounts); these are unreliable due to several peculiarities of Chinese economic calculation which may have led to miscalculations and severe overestimation of figures[232] – especially when compared to western economies.

Therefore, figures also have to be derived from other sources, such as economic reports in newspapers, journals and other publications, in and outside of the PRC in order to recreate and verify the macroeconomic picture via cross-checking and calibrating. The development of foreign trade may be traced with more reliable data, as figures of the respective trade partners and international organisations may serve as benchmarks. When it comes to developments in migration, population growth, economic growth, gross fixed capital formation etc., the available official statistics are generally regarded as politically biased or difficult to compare with other countries', as they are based on different methods. The proposed approach, which concentrates on paradigmatic shifts and qualitative changes in economic policy, intends to clarify the picture of economic development in China during the considered period. Such changes, some of them perhaps rather of intention than action, might not be identifiable by studying key figures concentrating e. g. on economic output and thus provide additional insights.

Theoretical considerations

As mentioned above, discussing socialism in 1970s China requires a particularly important distinction. In contrast to the economic policy paradigms applied, for instance, in the industrialised socialist states of Eastern Europe after the Second World War, socialism in China was not primarily about the political administration of the economy or even the (re)distribution of the commodities it produced. From an economic point of view, socialism in China was primarily a method of social organisation to achieve industrialisation in the first place. At its core, this required the development of social relations and behaviours that were conducive to production processes shaped by extensively developed division of labour and the large-scale use of technology. In addition – and this is decisive for the analysis of economic policies during the 1970s – it meant *catching up* with the technology on which the industrialised nations of the West had built their position

230 US Government Printing Office, China: A Reassessment of the Economy, A Compendium of Papers submitted to the Joint Economic Committee, Congress of the United States, 94th Congress, first Session, 10 July 1975, Washington D.C. 1975, pp. 54 ff.

231 Official Chinese data has been released in the 1980s in the form of statistical yearbooks, covering the 1970s in retrospect. I will refer to these figures when I make statistical references, where available, comparing with data aggregated by the statistical service of the World Bank and estimates made by scholars on the plausibility. In any case, I do not assume contemporary Chinese data to provide more than an impression of the general direction, when assessed critically.

232 Klatt 1979.

in the world, particularly the basic innovations that had enabled societies to achieve high standards of living, economic productivity and, quite importantly, military strength.

It was for this reason that the steel furnace became an ubiquitous symbol of economic progress in 1950s and 1960s China. The notion of catching up with it was, if anything, the basis for compromises allowing for experimentation in economic policymaking in socialist China. Such flexibilities based on a dialectical understanding of politics were formulated within the limits of the possible set by the eclectic ideological framework of Mao Zedong Thought and its roots *inter alia* in Marxism–Leninism but covered quite a broad range of measures.

In industrialised countries, which had been the point of reference for modernisation strategies in both the Soviet Union and China – for what economic progress was conveyed and perceived to be – the secular trend of technological development had progressed since the early days of the PRC. In 1949, the founding year of the socialist state, the industrialised West was about to enter a decade of unprecedented growth driven in particular by the petrochemical industries. From a Chinese perspective, catching up in the same year meant something else than during the years of "leaning to one side" – the Soviet Union – and the first five-year plan in the mid-1950s. It is important to note that it also meant something else almost three decades later.

Accordingly, over the course of the 1970s, Chinese economic policies changed not only due to ideological considerations but also because the steel mills and furnaces pictured in the visual propaganda accompanying the Great Leap were not the singular reference points for what economic progress meant in practice. Such structural changes are in many cases not visible in numbers alone. If, as ERIK HÄNDELER suggests, the steel industry has a diminished turnover of e. g. 30 billion USD in a given year but at the same time, 30 billion more are turned over in medical services, the GDP does not account for the structural and social changes behind this shift.[233] It would not even be perceptible. Whereas a few years ago, the purchase of a simple home computer – and I am afraid to be old enough to remember that quite well – was a serious investment for a household, this book was written on one of several high-performance devices that would have been easily available for the task. The S-shaped diffusion of basic innovations – first slow, then accelerated growth, leading to the ebbing of the wave as the rollout has been completed and possible gains in productivity etc. materialised – can be perceived i. e. in the daily life of people. It also shapes changing government policy priorities.

The analysis of economic fluctuations beyond the nine-year business cycle, as WALT WHITMAN ROSTOW suggested, continues to be confusing due the difficulty to distinguish three distinct phenomena and their interrelation. First, the forces set in motion by a leading sector in growth, such as the oil or automotive industries, stemming from the introduction and diffusion of new technologies or basic innovations and, at some point, the deceleration of this process. Second, the forces set in motion by changes in the profitability of producing basic commodities, such as foodstuffs and raw materials, depending on available market prices – from a local price to different spot-prices in important marketplaces and the average world market prices, depending on whether such markets are accessible in a given situation – and the effects on investment in these sectors as well as

233 KONDRATIEFF/HÄNDELER (ed.) 2016, p. 33.

follow-up effects in income distribution, terms of trade, market distortions caused by subsidies, and capital movements;. Third, the forces set in motion by international and domestic migration as well as changes in the rate of family formation, housing demand and the size of the labour force. As international economic exchanges unfolded in the late 18th century, these three phenomena have since then operated more or less concurrently.

There is no reason to believe that these factors do not manifest themselves at all in socialist economies. The existence of fluctuations in planned economies has been denied by socialist economists with reference to a "law of proportional development" based on a two-department model of capital goods production on the one hand and consumer goods production on the other.[234] There is a number of reasons why such an "inherent proportionality" of planned economies is not a given. JOSEF GOLDMANN and J. G. OLIVEIRA have sought to derive the existence of cycles by studying the causalities behind changes in certain outputs in planned economies. Oliveira emphasised discrepancies between time preferences between planners and individuals, the former wishing to postpone consumption to a greater extent than the latter, with a continual departure from consumer preferences provoking the threat of social disturbance. This effect, forcing planners to fluctuate between higher investment and higher consumption in order to ease this pressure, amounts to a cyclical dynamic. GOLDMANN focused on insufficient knowledge of planners about economic consequences, leading to disproportions caused by "voluntarist tendencies towards maximising the rate of growth of output", leaving economic slowdown as the only stabilising option as the system itself is capable only indirectly and with some time-lag to react to market signals, resulting in a cyclical movement of action and rather abrupt reaction.[235] In both approaches, growth (the "boom") is a result of a subjective factor, the optimism and orientation towards growth above other factors of planners, while the downturn (the "bust") stems from objective factors such as contradictory price signals and the need to correct disproportions.

The role of overinvestment is a recurring explanation for economic difficulties in planned economies. Sequences of investment-related political decisions and administrative measures are an obvious approach to explain fluctuations in a planned system. As, for example at the beginning of a five-year planning cycle, investment flows in areas dictated by the new plan, growth might slow down before increasing again. Overinvestment may occur for several reasons, one being attempts of officials to "hook onto the plan" by understating the cost of projects in order to have them approved. This phenomenon leads to excess demand in the investment sector in later stages of the plan, requiring compensation by a decline in either the growth of consumption or production (incuding for export) if investment commitments are honoured.[236] In this phase, the implementation of projects tends to be hastened in order to reduce the

---

234 BAJT ALEXANDER, Investment Cycles in European Socialist Economies, A Review Article, in: Journal of Economic Literature, Vol. 9, No. 1, March 1971, p. 54.

235 J. G. OLIVEIRA, Cyclical Growth Under Collectivism, Kyklos 1960; and GOLDMANN JOSEF, Fluctuations and Trend in the Rate of Economic Growth in Some Socialist Countries, in: Economics of Planning, Vol. IV, 1964; and the commentary given in ICKES BARRY W., Cyclical Fluctuations in Centrally Planned Economies: A Critique of the Literature, in: Soviet Studies, Vol. 38, No. 1, January 1986, pp. 38–39.

236 ICKES 1986, p. 46.

stock of unfinished projects. As there can be phases of more intensive demand in large-scale construction projets, planners may face additional crunches once committed to a large number of projects.[237] In an economy trying to industrialise and facing resource-constraints, the approval process is faced with an additional challenge, as most projects viewed in isolation will appear socially beneficial to some degree, if macroeconomic opportunity costs are not strictly accounted for. This, again, requires clear priorities and sufficient information, which is difficult to ensure – just as it is in public procurement procedures in market economies.

GOLDMANN, looking at the Soviet Union, explained the period of rapid growth starting around 1958 with

> "...many investment projects, initiated in the early fifties, particularly in the 'basic' industries were successfully completed and put into full operation...playing a decisive part in overcoming or substantially alleviating the economic disproportions that had brought about the fall in the rate of growth in 1953 and 1954."[238]

Barriers such as unsustainable foreign trade deficits, agriculture and raw material production, capacity and organisational constraints lead, after particularly high rates of growth, to unavoidable cuts. "breathing periods" allow for overcoming such disproportions and preparing a new investment drive. As an example, the limited labour force in Czechoslovakia constrained the forced development of heavy industry as explained by KAREL KOUBA in 1965.[239] Resource and other constraints eventually lead to a deceleration of ambitious growth. BAJT emphasised, that social factors are not to be neglected, as assuming "infinite social patience" is not realistic.[240]

An explanation of economic fluctuations caused by reproduction or reinvestment has been brought forward by Soviet economist Alexander Notkin, supported by Oskar Lange. During certain periods, large parts of equipment (fixed capital) is replaced by newer capital goods, causing high investment activity. Between such periods, the need for reinvestment is small, giving the impression of stagnation at least with regard to investment activity. Other than in market economies, where the renewal of fixed capital by enterprises constantly competing with each other is distributed rather evenly over time, renewal in socialist economies may be caused voluntarily, for example, by forced industrialisation in certain sectors.[241] This "administrative" character of the investment cycle has been criticised notably by Yugoslav economists, who linked the "wavelike interchanges of expansion" to technological progress as the basic dynamic factor of development.[242] From that perspective, it is the political will of developing countries to catch up, that is, apply most rapidly what has been achieved in new production techniques that transmits cycles of

237 BAUER TAMÁS, Investment Cycles in Planned Economies, in: Acta Oeconomica, Vol. 21, No. 3, 1978, p. 250–252.

238 GOLDMANN 1964, pp. 92–93.

239 BAJT 1971, p. 60.

240 BAJT 1971, p. 61.

241 BAJT 1971, p. 55.

242 ČOBELJÍC N., STOJANOVIĆ R., The theory of investment cycles in a socialist economy, in: Eastern European Economics, Vol. 7, No. 1–2, 1968 und 1969; quoted from Bajt 1971, p. 56.

technological progresss in their economy. ALEXANDER BAJT has noted that for this approach to be valid, decisions by central policy-makers need to be taken into account. Also, the effect in his view would be limited to closed economies.[243]

The core ideas behind Chinese national economic planning have been described in the so-called *Feldman-Mahalanobis* model – the key assumption being that the basic choice for planners was whether investment should flow to consumer goods or producer goods, assuming that the capital–output ratio is fixed (a given amount of investment produces the same increase in output annually) and foreign trade is smaller vis a vis the size of the economy and total investment. This approach does suggest a closed economy, implying that producer goods such as machinery and electricity have to be manufactured within the economy for economic growth to occur).[244] According to this model, investment in producer goods is the only way for a country like 1970s China to achieve stable growth, limited only by people's basic needs for consumer goods.

Concerning foreign trade, the availability of alternatives for the procurement of commodities alone even in an otherwise closed economy is a factor to be taken into account. State-controlled prices and planned allocation may act as forms of subsidies, particularly if the economy is not entirely closed and allows open access to lower-priced imports as well as technology. The higher the difference between a given good as a cheaper import and the fixed price within an economy, the higher the burden on the buyer. If the international price is higher than the fixed price, the subsidy is paid by the producers who could sell at a higher price abroad, which requires a system of procurement and the restriction of exports. In both cases, the availability of more profitable alternatives puts pressure on policies in either direction.[245]

If the political structure allows for the correction of mistakes, planning may take such experiences in account and react accordingly. Polish economist Ryszard Chelínski, looking back at the stages of economic development in his home country, described such challenges and adjustments:

> "Very ambitious investment programs give rise to an expansion of the investment production that, in the beginning, consists primarily of construction work. Non-farm employment increases by taking workers from the overpopulated agricultural sector at high rates. Soon difficulties begin to turn up; agricultural production stagnates, insufficiently balanced plans targets and delays in realisation of investment programs closely connected with foreign trade sifficulties create further disproportion. Their elimination requires several years during which investment activity decreases. It consists almost exclusively of completion of investment objects, their re-equipment and readaptation and of complementary investment. [...] During the second phase the investment expansion was more modest, and so was the expansion of employment [...] and a better agricultural policy prevented stagnation of agricultural production."[246]

243 Ibid.

244 Created by Soviet economist Grigory Alexandrovich Feldman in 1928 and Indian statistician Prasanta Chandra Mahalanobis in 1953, used theoretical rationale for import-substitution strategies.

245 ROSTOW WALT WITHMAN, Kondratieff, Schumpeter, and Kuznets: Trend Periods Revisited, in: The Journal of Economic History, Vol. 35, No. 4, December 1975, pp. 719–753.

246 Bajt 1971.

Enterprise behaviour has also been identified as a factor, as incentives for over-fulfilment in the later stages of a planning period lead to under-fulfilment in the early years in order to gain flexibility for over-fulfilment in the later.[247] Barry Ickes has noted that inventory behaviour of enterprises reflects the uncertainty of the planning system, with inventories serving as insurance against supply shocks – not against demand shocks, as it could be the case in market economies. Expectations of future supply conditions play an important role: if supply conditions are expected to improve, then enterprises will reverse their behavious and increase production for delivery.[248] For these factors to play out, enterprises must have direct responsibility for the fulfilment of the plan which was disputed in the PRC.

Looking at China, fluctuations of the economy since 1949 have occurred for a plethora of reasons. They were also caused by and reacted to by changes to economic policies. As I discuss in the following chapters, factors such as overinvestment and difficult trade offs between consumption and investment have been important, just as the ability of the political system to continuously adapt and allow for experimentation.

247 Dahlstedt Roy, Cyclical Fluctuations in Centrally Planned Economies, Helsinki 1981, p. 161.

248 Ickes 1986, p. 44.

On socialist economic policy

Throughout this book, I refer to economic policy and its implementation frequently, fully aware that this is a very broad concept requiring some specifications. As a starting point, the Encyclopedia Britannica's definition of the same as "measures by which a government attempts to influence the economy" serves us well.[1] Nevertheless, the economy[2] is itself a tremendously wide term, comprising many facets of human activities and their products. If we invoke the Cambridge Dictionary definition for another most general view, e. g., "the system of trade and industry by which the wealth of a country is made and used", we obtain a few additional clarifications.[3] The qualification "within a country" we also find, implies further aspects such as"world economy", "international economy" or "global economy", necessary to account for exchanges that cross the borders of countries, the notion of which again includes the concept of modern Westphalian nation states.[4]

The "system", of course, is again shaped by the economic policies applied within one of these states to account for the important legal side of policy implementation. In a way,

1 KAY JOHN ANDERSON, MORRIS CHARLES NICHOLAS, POOLE KENYON EDWARDS, LINDBECK ASSSAR, DUE JOHN F., Encyclopedia Britannica, Government economic policy, available at https://www.britannica.com/topic/government-economic-policy , last accessed on 1 April 2020.

2 What is referred here is "economy" in its current meaning. The etymological origin of the term and its analysis also hold many important insights, but discussing them here is beyond the scope of this book. For a perspective on the ancient Greek term oikos and how it informs modern economic thinking, see: CAMERON GREGORY, Oikos and Economy: The Greek Legacy in Economic Thought, in: PhaenEx, Vol. 3, No. 1, Spring/Summer 2008, pp. 112–133.

3 Cambridge Dictionary, Economy, available at https://dictionary.cambridge.org/dictionary/english/economy, last accessed on 1 April 2020.

4 Supposedly arising from the Treaties of Westphalia in 1648, which ended the Thirty Years War, in which statehood and geographical borders are perfectly overlapping, meaning that the state within these borders had sovereignty over its territory and domestic affairs and the exclusion of all interference of external powers. For an overview, see, e. g., FARR JASON, Point: The Westphalia Legacy and the Modern Nation-State, in: International Social Science Review, Vol. 80, No. 3/4, 2005, pp. 156–159. Critical scholars like STEPHEN D. KRASNER have noted that the concept is in itself misleading, as it describes rather a legal fiction than reality, and is based on a misreading of historical fact. See: KRASNER STEPHEN D., Compromising Westphalia, in: International Security, Vol. 20, No. 3, Winter 1995/1996, pp. 115–151.

the notion of economic policy is inherently circular. The economy, as a system, is both the object and a defining factor of economic policy; how an economy is organised is a deeply political thing. Accordingly, this chapter seeks to shed light on the implications that a socialist form of government has on the economy and the political influence that is taken to influence it.

The analysis presented in this book relies on the definition of the specific Chinese economy as *socialist*. At the core of this specific system of economic organisation, as a general starting point, we find aspects such as the ownership and regulation of the production, distribution and exchange of goods and – presumably – services by the respective society. That such definitions as well are generally rather rough is, in my view, an important notion. As the American scholar JOHN MARTIN stated as early as 1911, the precise distinction between different variations is somewhat in the eye of the beholder:

> "Definitions of socialism are almost as numerous as the combatants for and against socialism."[5]

How a given society and its economic activities are organised is of great importance for the implications of this definition. In an anarchist vision of a socialist economy[6], the organisation of economic activity is greatly different from what might be termed "bureaucratic socialism" relying mainly on the state and its administrative apparatus as an underlying institutional framework[7]. In state socialism, the term "society" may, to a large extent, be substituted by the nation state and its political representation, the government. In an idealised model of state socialism, economic policy would thus be the bundle of measures and the underlying decisions by which such a national government attempts to influence the economy, which it regulates and – quite literally – owns.

This influence would be most direct in a command economy, amounting to immediate control comparable to military leadership structures. The main distinction vis-à-vis a capitalist economy is certainly that there, ownership and regulation are in the hands of non-state actors like the archetypical capitalists. Its probably most prominent critic, Karl Marx, defined capitalism as a mode of production characterized by the form in which whoever controls the means of production extracts unpaid surplus labor from the direct producers. This implies a separation of the direct producers, the working class, from the productive assets, which are controlled by the so-called "bourgeoisie" as their private property protected by the state. Ownership of the means of production enables this class to regulate the industrial labor process, so that individual workers are driven to seek em-

---

5 MARTIN JOHN, An Attempt to Define Socialism, in: The American Economic Review, Vol. 1, No. 2, April 1911, p. 347.

6 Which again approaches the arguably extreme form of libertarian capitalism, which endorses the absence of state ownership and regulation. Nevertheless, there are conceptions of anarcho-syndicalism, advocating for a society organized *"from below"*, by direct voluntary participation, going back on socialist activists and theorists like Mikhail Bakunin and Peter Kropotkin among others.

7 Basically, a socialist economy within a nation state that owns and regulates (to a large degree). On terminology, see e. g. ROBERTS ANDREW, The State of Socialism: A Note on Terminology, in: Slavic Review, Vol. 63, No. 2, Summer 2004, pp. 349–366.

ployment by the needs of their own reproduction.[8] Such quite basic definitions and models have been an important basis for political dualisms particularly during the Cold War, applied to classify countries as well as diverging political positions within societies. Going back further to the French Revolution, while being constantly reframed, the "Great Dichotomy" of the political left–right spectrum is perhaps the most obvious manifestation.[9]

Any reader familiar with the basic tenets of economic policies in various societies will rightly object that such absolute dualisms come with challenges. In some cases, they are utterly unrealistic. In actual societies, no matter their declared ideological direction, the *de facto* organisation of economic activity – irrespective of what may be perceived as the dominant political rhetoric – follows a somewhat nuanced approach. In the industrialised and basically capitalist economies of European states this encompasses i. e. some form of welfare state, meaning a social safety net as well as other public services financed by taxation and subsidised or even free at the point of delivery. Mixed economies can go quite far on that scale, including by interventions in mergers and acquisitions of enterprises, setting of fiscal or normative (dis-)incentives for certain forms of consumption and investment or its prevention along some public policy objectives and corrections of market failures.[10]

Governments regulate and also own important parts of the economy that are relevant for the production, distribution and exchange of goods and services, alongside others owned and regulated[11] by non-state actors. Despite decades of political debate on the relationship between the two forms of ownership and regulation, this basic tenet remains true and has not fundamentally changed in industrialised economies.[12] Most if not all modern economies are *mixed* to a certain degree. It may be a truism, although much less obvious, that the same tends to be true for economies, particularly industrialised ones, in

8 JESSOP ROBERT, Mode of Production, in: EATWELL JOHN, MILGATE MURRAY, NEWMAN PETER, Marxian Economics, London 1990, p. 289 f.

9 For a detailed discussion of the spectrum and its changing meanings, see: ROSAS JOÃO CARDOSO and FERREIRA ANA RITA (eds.), Left and Right: The Great Dichotomy Revisited, Newcastle upon Tyne, 2013.

10 For a liberal critique and approach at theorizing the concept of mixed economy, see IKEDA SANFORD, Dynamics of the Mixed Economy: Toward a Theory of Interventionism, London 1997, notably p. 32 ff.; and for phenomena within post-1978 China, see NEE VICTOR, Organizational Dynamics of Market Transition: Hybrid Forms, Property Rights, and Mixed Economy in China, in: Administrative Science Quarterly, Vol. 37, No. 1, March 1992, pp. 1–27.

11 Literally, as the emergence of *self-regulatory organizations* e. g. in the banking and securities industry demonstrates, which appear to fill gaps in public regulatory frameworks as they exist in the "*digital economy*", but also directly serve public policy objectives e. g. in the combatting of money-laundering.

12 Often described as a basic tenet of *neoliberal* economic policy, the extent of privatization appears to have gone beyond former basic public services in developing countries. For a case-study on the phenomenon in the (post-) Thatcherite era in the UK, see: JUPE ROBERT, FUNNELL WARWICK, Neoliberalism, consultants and the privatization of public policy formulation: The case of Britain's rail industry, in: Critical Perspectives on Accounting, Vol. 29, June 2015, pp. 65–85. On developing countries, see: United Nations General Assembly, Third Committee, 73rd Session, 25th and 26th Meetings, 19 October 2018, UN Document No. GA/SHC/4239, Available at: https://www.un.org/press/en/2018/gashc4239.doc.htm, last accessed on 1 April 2020.

which the normative basis for economic policy is socialist. Even if a basic differentiation between economies in two categories, particularly in the political context of the Cold War, might be useful and true in a general sense, things are complicated and gradual. For the analysis of economic policy in a given society at a certain time, general definitions may be helpful as a starting point but also bear the risk of misleading and oversimplifying.

With a view to discussing economic policies in socialist China outside a dualist perspective, the spectrum needs to be clarified. For that purpose, this Chapter introduces important aspects of socialist economic policy in a historical perspective, its origins and their influence on the PRC. It also follows the question what specific purpose and objective Chinese socialism had , followed by some remarks on the aspects of Mao Zedong Thought as an ideological frame of reference.

How to organise a socialist economy? The Soviet prototype

The principal archetype and most influential example for the perception of and discourse on what defines a socialist economy is undoubtedly the Soviet Union. Although its political economy was and still is widely perceived as a sort of blueprint for socialist economic policy in numerous countries falling within this category, there has always been a remarkable degree of variety among those economies.[13] Economic policy during Soviet "War Communism" was quite different from the Hungarian so-called "Goulash Communism" or what we find in late Yugoslavia under Josip Broz Tito.[14] While the Eastern European states and China – for various historical reasons and not entirely voluntarily – took experiences stemming from the consolidation of the Soviet revolutionary state at different stages as starting points for their domestic economic policy bundles, differences of a social, cultural, historical and even religious nature as well as with regard to economic and other preconditions led to divergencies that were accentuated over the years.

Likewise, for the genesis of the Chinese socialist economy, the Soviet experience and the lessons drawn from it are crucial. Many basic tenets were directly adopted after and during the implementation of the first five-year plan, which became the core of economic policy at least for the central government in Beijing after 1953. Similar to other states, in which political power was in the hands of the people adhering to socialist ideas on economic organisation, the CCP came to choose the Soviet-style planned economy – with its emphasis on the development of heavy industry. The approach aimed at advancing the economic basis of a largely agrarian society at a sufficiently fast pace in order to ensure the legitimacy of the policies and thus the political rule of the party.

Almost since its inception, the idea of centralised "rational" planning of economic activity was proposed as superior to the alleged anarchy of free markets with their inherent

---

13 Even though it appears that the perception of socialist economy within a *dualist* view is not even necessarily based on the de facto policies applied in the Soviet Union, at a specific point of its history, but at least, to a similar extent, on a generic image of the way its society and economy were organised.

14 Leipold (ed.) 1975 and Wemheuer (ed.) 2020.

instability and fluctuation, as they visibly resulted in periodic crises of over-production[15] that caused unemployment and poverty as well as threatened to destroy scarce capital.[16] Despite the notion of factual objectivity that references to "scientific" methods of economic organisation imply, the meaning of such qualifications depends on political positions. As OTA SIK, Czech economist and driving force behind the New Economic Model, developed in Czechoslovakia during the 1960s and a Third Way between socialism and capitalism stated, it tended to be synonymous with bureaucratic administration:

> "[...] we can state flatly that no move toward more scientific planning methods would help – or would actually be scientific – if market relations are not used to solve conflicts of interest and to create a genuine interest in optimum development of production, not only in the central bodies, but also in the enterprises. Everyone who has at heart the fate of socialist economics and is interested in its triumph in the historic competition with capitalism must, therefore, see that the main danger to it lies not in the system of management based on economics and in the utilization of all socialist economic incentives, but in the distorted, administrative, formal, bureaucratic system. Fighting against this and battling the new, genuinely economic, for of socialist planned management is the main task of Marxist economic theory and practice."[17]

The broad range of possible interpretations that "Marxist economic theory and practice" offered for the justification of almost any given bundle of policies becomes apparent in these lines.

The concrete influence of ideas – meta-narratives like material dialectics or the effectiveness of free markets – on political decisions is in itself a debatable subject. The analysis in this book accepts the assumption that Marxist theory, the concepts derived from it as well as their interpretation had a tangible role in the formulation and execution of economic policy in the PRC and were more than just a thin lining covering what might alternatively be considered the mere cynical politics of power. The latter notion also bears truth, as it does for any ideology applied in the real world, but it is not sufficient to explain the existence and design of socialist economies.

To what degree this notion applies, is subject to debate: Early scholars on Chinese socialism like BENJAMIN SCHWARTZ concluded that Mao's "theoretical contributions" were merely part of a continuous process of disintegration of Marxist thought for Leninism. Others, like RICHARD M. PFEFFER have dismissed this view, noting Mao's theoretical rigor and development. Nevertheless, dismissing the existence of any normative basis for decision-shaping and decision-making on economic policy within the CCP and the Chinese state would be misleading, particularly as such an approach would fail to explain

---

15 As the most obvious and well-known example. Regarding the relationship between the theory of a tendency to a falling rate of profit, underconsumption and overproduction, SIMON CLARKE critically examined the different strands of Marxist theory such as the *"neo-Ricardians"*, the *"labour-process theorists"* which in his view underestimated underconsumption (caused by expectations) as a factor. See: CLARKE SIMON, The Marxist Theory of Overaccumulation and Crisis, in: Science & Society, Vol. 54, No. 4, Winter 1990/1991, pp. 442–467.

16 WEMHEUER 2019, p. 93.

17 SIK OTA, Plan and Market Under Socialism, New York 2018, p. 390.

the genuine effort put into theoretical work both inside the party and within the public space.[18]

I see this assumption holding true for the Soviet Union as well, since the Bolshevik party had been developed along the lines of Marxist thought and the Soviet political economy. The state apparatus behind it was equally based on the specific interpretation of Marxist theory in the forms of Marxism-Leninism and Stalinism. This does not imply that doctrine never changed or was never disputed. As NEIL HARDING states, if the relationship of Leninism to Marxism is in itself a contested matter, the relationship of Leninism to Stalinism might be even more so. In particular, approaches based on the notion of totalitarianism assert that the theoretical, psychological and institutional bases of the Stalinist aspiration for "total control" over society and individuals rely themselves on Leninism and its core tenet of "professional revolutionaries" holding power in a one-party state. On the other hand, there is a persistent line of interpretation offered by a fairly broad spectrum of criticism from the political left that Stalinism was, in its essential respects, the illegitimate offspring of Leninism. The two doctrines are, in this interpretation, distinct in purpose, style and method. Also, evidence can be brought forward to support the view that Lenin himself was aware of the dangers of Stalin's ideas and tried to rouse the party to avoid them.[19]

Similarly, it is obvious that political movements and governments that can be classified or, perhaps even more so, declare themselves to be Marxist or communist in some manifestation are not ideologically homogenous. The interpretations are manifold. MICHAEL HEINRICH argues that the historical reception of Marxism as a category has always encompassed several strands of interpretation, which partly have been diametral opposites.[20] The *modernist* strand may be described generally as an ideology of technocratic economic development of expertise, central planning and, above all, an almost military sense of collective discipline in many areas of life. The *radical* variety is first and foremost an egalitarian movement of mass mobilisation, seeking progress through intrinsic motivation, enthusiasm for a political cause and far-reaching concepts of democratic control over power relations.[21]

---

18 PFEFFER RICHARD M., Mao and Marx in the Marxist-Leninist Tradition: A Critique of "The China Field" and a Contribution to a Preliminary Reappraisal, in: Modern China, Vol. 2, No. 4, October 1976, pp. 421–460. As MAURICE MEISNER argued, even the immediate post-1978 economic reforms envisioned a socialist vision for China, and the CCP put great effort into finding theoretical Marxist rationales for their course. See: MEISNER MAURICE, Mao's China and After, third edition, New York 1999, pp. 451 f.

19 HARDING NEIL, Leninism and Stalinism, in: HARDING NEIL (ed.), Leninism, London 1996, pp. 243–263, and, with regard to perspectives rooted in totalitarianism: DANIELS ROBERT VINCENT, The Stalin Revolution: Foundations of Soviet Totalitarianism, Lexington 1972; DEUTSCHER ISAAC, Stalin: A Political Biography, Harmondsworth 1966; GILL GRAEME J., Stalinism, London 1990; MEDVEDEV ROY, On Stalin and Stalinism, Oxford 1979.

20 HEINRICH MICHAEL, Kritik der politischen Ökonomie, fifth edition, Stuttgart 2007. The conflicts within the international Socialist movement are one basic feature that will continue to shape its historiography. See: MCDERMOTT KEVIN, AGNEW JEREMY, The Comintern, A History of International Communism from Lenin to Stalin, Houndmills and London 1996.

21 For instance, PRIESTLAND 2009, p. 20, who traces the thought of Marx back to the aftermath of the French Revolution, when the ideas of François Noël Babeuf, Henri de Saint-Simon and Charles

While this rough split again might be helpful in understanding and categorising writings, thinkers and political and economic systems having their roots – to some extent – in Marxist thought, it again bears the risk of being overly simplistic in its duality. Karl Marx himself as a writer noted that policy making is rarely coherent and pure but rather characterised by contradictions on the one hand and attempts to solve them by adjusting normative beliefs to constraints and practice (and *vice versa*) on the other. Despite the determinist tendency of Marx's writings based on a Hegelian understanding of history, diverse socialist ideas on the economy largely share the idea that conditions can be changed willingly in order to achieve normative goals.[22] Like arguably any human being over the course of his or her life, Marx was not overly consistent in his views. An important debate on his work concerns the distinction between the "young" – arguably more utopian – and the "old" Marx – rather a proponent of economic rationality and strict discipline in revolutionary organisations. The young Marx, conceptualised by Georg Lukács and Karl Korsch in 1923 has caused considerable controversy on the interpretation of Marx's legacy, notably as he offers perspectives for alternatives to state socialism and an ideological basis for the social democratic and *Eurocommunist* movements, thereby implying that the socialist movement can generally coexist with the bourgeois liberal state.[23]

For the CCP, it was primarily its Soviet heritage that finally shaped both its approach to statehood as well as to economic policies. Even if the utopianism[24] in Marxist (as well as e. g. Maoist) thought has undoubtedly been used to legitimise and solidify established political rule particularly when and where it fell short of providing any vaguely promised utopia, this legitimation had to be at least somewhat consistently based on terms and concepts of a Marxist origin. As it is well-established, held e. g. by Robert Marcuse, the specific strand of Soviet Marxism (or, more commonly, *Marxism-Leninism*) as an example was the attempt to unify the inherited corpus of Marx's theoretical work with a historical situation that quite obviously stood against one of its key premises: the historical necessity of a linear transition from feudalism through bourgeois capitalism to socialism.[25]

Fourier laid the groundwork for the proletarian communist, technocratic and utopian strands of socialism, respectively.

22 Combining this will to influence the underlying paradigms in a society with the certainty of the historical materialist narrative that change was inevitable and brought chances for revolutionary action, also accordingly giving rise to a historiography. See: Hobsbawm Eric, How to Change the World: Reflections on Marx and Marxism, New Haven 2011, and in particular the review by Theodore Koditschek: Koditschek Theodore, How to Change History, in: History and Theory, Vol. 52, October 2013, pp. 433–450.

23 For an overview on the debate, see: Leogrande William M., An Investigation into the "Young Marx" Controversy, in: Science & Society, Vol. 41, No. 2, Summer 1977, pp. 129–151.

24 While Marx himself used the term *utopian socialism* as a critique of theoretical competitors, the basic tenet of the abolishment of state and society as well as his vision of maximizing individual economic freedom and equality through the technological optimization of industrial production are in themselves utopian. See: Lovell David, Marx's Utopian legacy, in: The European Legacy, Vol. 9, No. 5, 2004, pp. 629–640.

25 Marcuse Herbert, Die Gesellschaftslehre des sowjetischen Marxismus, second edition, Neuwied und Berlin 1969, p. 33. It has been argued that Marx, in his lesser known writings like *A letter to Vera Zasulich* written in 1881, did in fact argue that a transition to a socialist society was possible

The constitutional ideology of the Soviet Union absorbed Lenin's views on the organization of the communist Party as a group of revolutionary "professionals" as well his theory of imperialism as the "highest state of capitalist development". The key importance of this inclusion was arguably that it allowed for a connection between revolutionary movements in developing countries with those in the industrialized centers, including peasants in the industrial-worker-centred thought of Marx. There were always other options, as the Leninism variation was strongly criticized by both leftist revolutionaries as well as liberal democrats and anticommunist exponents on the right. Notably, Rosa Luxemburg differed from Lenin in both his interpretation of imperialism and his views on the definition and status of the revolutionary party, seeing it as a pre-form of individual dictatorship. A similar critique was brought forward by the anarchists Pyotr Alexeyevich Kropotkin and Mikhail Alexandrovich Bakunin, emphasizing the centralizing and authoritarian tendencies inherent in Leninism.[26] The path the Soviet Union took was not due to any necessity inherent to socialist thought, but the consequence of political choices within a spectrum of ideas.

One premise that was adopted from the start by the socialist parties in both the Soviet Union and China in their political programmes was qualifying the notion of "communism" – still figuring prominently in their names – as a rather distant goal to be achieved some day, instead of a description of the actual day-to-day policies they sought to enforce. This again implied the necessity of a post-revolutionary transition to the promised utopian society by socialism and an allegedly temporary dictatorship of the proletariat incorporated by the state. Socialism itself, as it was implemented in various forms in many societies, was not intended to *be* an egalitarian utopia, not even in its most ambitious forms. Its political and normative function was first and foremost of an economic nature. It was an instrument to establish preconditions for the continuous elimination of private ownership of the means of production and, in theory and never achieved, the permanent dissolution of class distinctions through the abolishment of property, paid labour and the monetary system.

> In that case, after having fulfilled its functions, the socialist state would no longer be needed and would thus "wither away". As stated by Friedrich Engels: "When at last [the State] becomes the real representative of the whole of society, it renders itself unnecessary. As soon as there is no longer any social class to be held in subjection, as soon as class rule, and the individual struggle for existence based upon the present anarchy in production, with the collisions and excesses arising from this struggle, are removed, nothing more remains to be held in subjection — nothing necessitating a special coercive force, a state. The first act by which the state really comes forward as the representative of the whole of society — the taking possession of the means of production in the name of society — is also its last independent act as a state. State interference in social relations becomes, in one domain after another, superfluous, and then dies

even for economically disadvantaged societies such as Russia at the end of the 19th century. See: KA-KUI TSE, Agricultural Collectivization and Socialist Construction: The Soviet Union and China, in: Dialectical Anthropology, Vol. 2, No. 3, August 1977, p. 200.

26 MORGAN JOHN W., Marxism-Leninism: The ideology of 20th Century communism, in: International Encyclopedia of the Social and Behavioral Sciences, second edition, Vol. 14, 2015, pp. 656–662.

> down of itself. The government of persons is replaced by the administration of things, and by the conduct of processes of production. **The state is not 'abolished'. It withers away.** [emphasis added] This gives the measure of the value of the phrase 'a free people's state', both as to its justifiable use for a long time from an agitational point of view, and as to its ultimate scientific insufficiency; and also of the so-called anarchists' demand that the state be abolished overnight." [Lenin underlined the argument:] "The supersession of the bourgeois state by the proletarian state is impossible without a violent revolution. The abolition of the proletarian state, i. e., of the state in general, is impossible except through the process of 'withering away'".[27]

Even with regard to this basic tenet, ambiguity is found in many writings on which modern socialism is based. The Communist Manifesto of 1848 did not define the state, referring to modern state power only as a form of committee which supervises the common affairs of the whole bourgeoisie class. The Manifesto did nevertheless make a clear distinction between the state and the *bourgeois* state. RICHARD ADAMIAK and others have argued that the assumption of a "withering away" of the state was limited to the bourgeois and early socialist class-political state – but not the "new", communist non-political state as soon as it was created.[28] In existing socialism as well, this transition never happened and was regularly and with some creativity reframed by its governments. Sometimes, socialist governments were quite frank: In his comments to the program, and statute of the GDR Socialist Unity Party of Germany, Erich Honecker underlined that "[state] power is foremost" and that "law is a significant means to exercise power".[29]

With regard to the functioning of the economic system and the labour relations within this, many features of the bourgeois capitalist economy would continue to apply for as long as economic and social reality did not allow for their abolishment. For example, industrial and managerial expertise that was often in the hands of pre-revolutionary elites was simply necessary for keeping factories running even after the seizing of power by the self-declared representatives of the working class. Therefore, socialist states needed to find a way to assure the cooperation of people to whom they were, ideologically speaking, directly opposed and of which such cooperation could often not be expected. This issue was not necessarily – but certainly also – solved by means of coercion: During the phase of New Democracy (1949–1953) in the PRC, a basic system of capital compensation for the owners of industrial capital was established that guaranteed an annual dividend on the assets seized as long as production continued. The system endured for decades. Therefore, it is important to note that if socialist countries were criticised for their inherent inequalities, despite their egalitarian mission, this assessment, while *de facto* true, was largely due to intended or unintended

---

27 ENGELS FRIEDRICH, Herr Eugen Dühring's Umwälzung der Wissenschaft, third edition, Moscow 1969, p. 332–333, and LENIN VLADIMIR, The State and Revolution, Class Society and the State, Collected Works, Volume 25, Moscow 1964, p. 386.

28 ADAMIAK RICHARD, The "Withering Away" of the State: A Reconsideration, in: The Journal of Politics, Vol. 32, No. 1, February 1970, pp. 3–18.

29 SCHNEIDER EBERHARD, SED – Programm und Statut von 1976: Text, Kommentar, Didaktische Hilfen, Opladen 1977, p. 43.

misrepresentations of the ideological basis that did allow for certain inequalities to persist.[30]

In fact, the industrial structures of socialist states took the capitalist industrial economies as starting points for their own. Modern industrialisation as a theoretical condition for socialist revolution in Marx's writings had not occurred yet. At least not to any extent comparable to the industrial centres of the world such as the United Kingdom or Germany.[31] The Leninist answer to this ideological problem was delegating the development of industrial capitalism to the state in order to take the necessary historical step *within* a socialist economy and make use of whatever methods were available. As Lenin declared shortly after the rise to power of the Communist Party in 1918,

> "Reality shows us, that state capitalism would be a step forward for us. If we were able to realise state capitalism in Russia in a short time, it would be a victory [...] I said that state capitalism would be a salvation for us; if we had it in Russia, the transition to full socialism would be easy; then we could grasp it with our hands, because state capitalism is something centralised, calculated, controlled and socialised, **and that is exactly what we are lacking** [emphasis added]."[32]

A similar argument was made by the Soviet economist Yevgeni Alexeyevich Preobrazhensky over the course of the Soviet "Great Industrialisation Debate" of the 1920s, emphasising the weakness of the socialist sector and the necessity of learning and adopting capitalist methods and relations of production in the state sector. This pivotal debate in the aftermath of the October Revolution concerned the financing of industrialisation. While, as I argue, the need for industrialisation in China was not in itself disputed, the choice of appropriate sources of financing and technology was controversial.

The political answers given in the Soviet Union were decisive for the latter course, including arguably of world history. The debate, as argued by Raaj K. Sah and Joseph E. Stiglitz, is of historical importance despite the polemics involved, because it anticipated some of the difficult but central trade-offs that confront many less developed countries still today. Preobrazhensky argued on the basis of a closed economy model, in which rural and urban prices for consumables would be assumed as being the same throughout the country, and that there would be binding constraints on trade – such as the fact that

30 In China, this was notably true with regard to the economic status of industrial factory workers. See: Wemheuer 2019, p. 89.

31 The features of the Chinese economy before 1949 and its merits, at least up to the civil war in 1937, are controversial. The view that the economic basis was rather underdeveloped has been criticised since the early 1980s, notably by Thomas G. Rawski. He argued that substantial if not rapid growth, even in agriculture, was achieved and that cultural patterns such as a rich (internal) trade tradition were benefitting factors for latter development (see Rawski 2015, notably pp. 4 ff.). As continuities matter on this end of the history of the Chinese socialist state, some of the features of China's economy in the 1930s (such as family farms and entrepreneurship, urban consumerism) are certainly important. Nevertheless, in my view, the relatively rapid industrialisation after 1953 can, to the largest extent, be ascribed to the introduction of socialist strategies. However, major differences in emphasis remain among scholars.

32 Lenin in a polemic against "*left communists*" at the assembly of the all-Russian central executive committee in April 1918, quoted from Marcuse 1969, p. 59.

many potential partners would prefer to end the Soviet state than support it indirectly via trade.[33] The existing quasi-military War Communism – a product of the highly adverse circumstances after the October Revolution[34] – was obviously not a viable long-term alternative. A preliminary version of the Soviet planned economy, it was implemented during the turmoil of the Russian civil war of 1918–1921. Essentially, the policy-bundle aimed at the total abolition of private trade, strict control of labour, the nationalisation of all large-scale industries and, at its height in 1920, the replacement of the currency-based system of regulated prices with comprehensive state rationing.

The New Economic Policy (NEP) followed as both a compromise and an experiment. It was an attempt adjust the economic policy bundles in order to correct the most serious shortcomings of the bureaucratic economic system. Its relative success set a precedent for alternative models of socialist industrialisation that allowed for flexibilities. With the NEP, key industries ("the commanding heights"), particularly those relevant for defense, remained under the control of the state, while agriculture and a large part of trade were left to the hands of private households and individuals. Also, public discourse was far more open, particularly compared to the backlash under Stalin. For a moment, the continuation of the NEP as a more liveable path to socialist industrialisation appeared possible.[35] It set an example for a pattern of free production and marketisation of essential products by individuals and households rather than allocation by centralised planning.

Nevertheless, the function of the NEP became clear at the latest with its abolition: a remedy or "breathing period" applied in a situation, in which the lack of dynamism of the latter led to shortages that threatened political power. While the Soviet NEP ended with a serious backlash towards centralisation that hit those who had profited from the markets (in particular, the so-called "*Nepmen*") hardest, it has become a point of reference in discussions on socialist economic policy due to its immediate success in improving the livelihood of the population, despite the still limited material endowment.[36]

---

33 Erlich Alexander, The Soviet Industrialisation Debate 1924–1928, Cambridge 1960; and Allen 2003, pp. 47 ff. See: Sah Raaj K., Stiglitz Joseph E., Peasants versus City-Dwellers: Taxation and the Burden of Economic Development, Oxford 2002.

34 Figes Orlando, A People's Tragedy: The Russian Revolution 1891–1924, London 2014, in particular pp. 685 ff. for a perspective emphasising the course of the Soviet leadership being dictated by reactions to military pressure and politics of power. For a critical view taking into account the importance of political ideas and ideology, see Roberts Paul Craig, "War Communism": A Re-examination, in: Slavic Review, Vol. 29, No. 2, June 1970, pp. 238–261.

35 Allen 2003, pp. 51 ff.

36 See e. g., Farber Samuel, Before Stalinism, the Rise and Fall of Soviet Democracy, New York 1990, and the recent review by Marot John, The New Economic Policy was the Alternative to Stalinism, Jacobin Magazine, 12 August 2019, available at: https://jacobinmag.com/2019/12/new-economic-policy-stalinism-nep-bolsheviks-october-revolution, last accessed on 5 May 2020.

Towards the Soviet Industrial Revolution

After 1924, the opting for a rapid[37] transition from a situation of relative economic underdevelopment to the level of advanced industrialised economies led to the installation of an immense industrial apparatus. It was embedded within a complex system of state regulations, based on immediately planned allocation of inputs and outputs. This command economy gave rise to severe conflict, causing constant tension and state-led violence within the relatively rigid political system of the Soviet Union[38]: this included the temporary co-existence of different forms of property and ownership of the means of production, differentiating physical and cognitive labour, and new societal hierarchies between party officials, bureaucrats, intellectuals, industrial workers and peasants. Moreover, as the economy needed to collect resources at a large scale to feed its production and avoid bottlenecks[39] while simultaneously financing its growth, wealth needed to be constantly accumulated by the state that controlled all relevant investment decisions. Economic growth itself was not a dominant motive. As Vladimir Kontorovich and others have argued, national security considerations played a more important role than debates among economists and, in the end, tilted the consensus away from the more moderate NEP-policies towards a paradigm focused on heavy industry.

Outside support including foreign trade[40] as well as the acquisition of colonies[41] as possible channels for obtaining these means were practically unavailable to the early Soviet Union. These resources needed to be drawn from *within* the state's borders but, at the same time, from outside the emerging industrial sector in order to sustain high rates of investment. The primary sources of capital available were the labour of the peasantry and

---

37 Speed being a core element of the command economy as well as of socialist economic policy in non-industrialised countries for various reasons. For China, I discuss the issue in details in the fourth Chapter.

38 Kort 2010, p. 192.

39 Kontorovich Vladimir, The Military Origins of Soviet Industrialization, in: Comparative Economic Studies, April 2015, pp. 1–24.

40 Nevertheless, after the introduction of the state monopoly on foreign trade in December 1917, and a blockade imposed by Western powers until 1921, trade relations were sought and formalised with a number of countries in the west – notably with the United Kingdom and Germany in the early 1920s. See: Zolotarev Vladimir Ivanovich, Main Stages of Development of USSR Foreign Trade 1917–1967, in: Soviet and Eastern European Foreign Trade, Vol. 4, No. 2, Summer 1968, pp. 5f.; and Gueullette Agota, Soviet Concepts of Foreign Trade 1917–1945, in: Soviet and Eastern European Foreign Trade, Vol. 27, No. 3, Fall 1991, pp. 6 ff.

41 Which arguably would have been rejected at least within the pre-Stalinist CPSU, it has been argued that the Soviet Union did practice colonialism – or even imperialism, as the CCP saw it – later on, notably in the Eastern Europe, the Baltics and Central Asia. See: Librach Jan, The Rise of the Soviet Empire: A Study of Soviet Foreign Policy, New York 1964, and Zubok Vladislav M., A Failed Empire: The Soviet Union in the Cold War from Stalin to Gorbachev, Chapel Hill 1964. Also, as Jeremy Friedman argued, the ideological conflict between China and the Soviet Union with regard to their policies vis-à-vis developing countries caused a competition on influence, while lacking the extractive nature of 19th century European colonialism. See: Friedman Jeremy, Shadow Cold War: The Sino-Soviet Competition for the Third World, Chapel Hill 2015, notably pp. 115 ff.

the fertility of the soil, brought to use by, as Preobrazhensky termed it, "primitive socialist accumulation" under centralised control.[42] If the idea that the Soviet revolution had to combine several phases of economic development in one process is taken as starting point, this approach could even be reconciled with Marx's writings, at least the first volume of *Das Kapital:*

> "In the history of primitive accumulation, all revolutions are epoch-making that act as levers for the capitalist class in course of formation; but, above all, those moments when great masses of men are suddenly and forcibly torn from their means of subsistence, and hurled as free and 'unattached' proletarians on the labor market. The expropriation of the agricultural producer, of the peasant, from the soil, is the basis of the whole process."[43]

Accordingly, in the Soviet Union and later in the PRC, the control of rural-urban migration and collectivisation were important pillars of accumulation-policies.[44] Collectivisation of farms was intended to improve agricultural productivity and thus produce grain reserves sufficiently large to feed the growing urban industrial labour force. The anticipated surplus was to be extracted and supposed to finance industrialisation. This basic paradigm was supported by different strands of Soviet theorists, including, on many points, by opposing forces such as Nikolai Ivanovich Bukharin and Leon Trotsky, albeit with essential differences concerning the importance of the standard of living and the significance of foreign trade. For instance, Trotsky urged repeatedly that the focus on heavy industry needed to be tempered by awareness of "the consumer's point of view" and an openness to foreign trade, stating that a worker's state needed to "become subject to the laws governing the world market".[45]

It was the so-called Great Break[46] in Soviet economic development – or, as ROBERT ALLEN suggested, the beginning of the Soviet Industrial Revolution. It started with the first five-year plan, which laid emphasis on the collectivisation of agriculture as a means to improve the capital-base of industrialisation, and also the immediate control the state (and thus the party apparatus) was able to exercise over it. Assessments of the collectivisation period range, quite similar to the Chinese experience, from an emphasis on the

---

42 Advanced during the debates on industrialisation during the 1920s, the main tenet of primitive socialist accumulation was the concentration of capital goods (means of production) in heavy industries in order to create a basis for economic growth. This also implied that investment in agriculture was rather suppressed in favor of industrial investment. See: BURDEKIN RICHARD C.K., Preobrazhensky's Theory of Primitive Socialist Accumulation, in: Journal of Contemporary Asia, Vol. 19, No. 3, 1989, pp. 297–307, and ALLEN 2003, pp. 173–174.

43 MARX KARL, Das Kapital, Kritik der politischen Ökonomie, Cologne 2009, p. 661.

44 For the Soviet case, see: FITZPATRICK SHEILA, The Great Departure, Rural-Urban Migration in the Soviet Union, 1929–1933, in: WILLIAM G., ROSENBERG, SIEGELBAUM LEWIS H. (eds.), Social Dimensions of Soviet Industrialization, Bloomington and Indianapolis 1993, pp. 15–40.

45 On the debate, see: DAY RICHARD B., REVIEW: On "Primitive" and Other Forms of Socialist Accumulation: A Review of Preobrazhensky, Bukharin and Trotsky, in: Labor/Le Travail, Vol 10, Autumn 1982, pp. 165–174.

46 Based on an article published by Stalin on the 7th of November 1929 in the Pravda ("The Year of the Great Break" for the twelfth anniversary of the October Revolution).

violence experienced by peasants and groups more or less arbitrarily defined along political criteria, such as wealthier peasants (the so-called "*Kulaks*"), to the recognition of some economic progress. It is undisputed that collectivisation in the Soviet Union was a violent process.

Clarified by the first five-year plan and its implementation, it became apparent that socialism in the Soviet Union – as a first phase of economic and social development towards communism – was not intended to free individuals from the hardship of labour, any form of competitive pressure, or even the alienation that highly developed division of labour tended to induce according to Marx himself. In that regard, it is worth noting that even Lenin saw production methods akin to Frederick W. Taylor's "scientific management" as both deeply exploitative as well as a useful mechanism for increasing productivity and efficiency for the socialist cause. The essential question in his view was not *whether* such managerial practices were morally justified or in the interest of the workers, but *who* – which class – would make better use of such methods and command the added values they produced.[47]

Increasing labour productivity was not only a part of the socialist economic system, it was at its centre. Only through achieving and surpassing the capitalist economies' industrial achievements – of which both Marx and Engels were perfectly aware, even showing open admiration – could the socialist state finally fulfil its historical mission. Already the first phrase of *Das Kapital*, Volume one states: "The wealth of societies in which a capitalistic mode of production prevails, appears as a 'gigantic collection of commodities' and the singular commodity appears as the elementary form of wealth." In the *Grundrisse*, Marx underscored the "boundless creative force" of capitalism over and over. It has even been argued that the *Grundrisse* advocated a vision of "creative destruction" for the transition to socialism at an advanced stage of development.[48]

The possibilities of free individual development and the satisfaction of personal needs were, *per se*, dominated by the imperative of industrial development. Only if and when the wealth produced by a socialist society would be sufficiently abundant, it could be redistributed without taking a given individual's contribution to the productive processes into account. The principle "from each according to his abilities, to each according to his work" would thus be transitioned to the principle of "from each according to his abilities, to each according to his needs".[49] While the former principle was at the core

47 SOCHOR ZENOVIA A., Soviet Taylorism Revisited, Soviet Studies, Vol. 33, No. 2, April 1981, notably pp. 247–248.

48 ELLIOTT JOHN E., Marx's "Grundrisse": Vision of Capitalism's Creative Destruction, in: Journal of Post Keynesian Economics, Vol. 1, No. 2, Winter 1978–1979, pp. 148–169.

49 Usually identified with Marx's 1875 Critique of the Gotha Program: "In a higher phase of communist society, after the enslaving subordination of the individual to the division of labor, and therewith also the antithesis between mental and physical labor, has vanished; after labor has become not only a means of life but life's prime want; after the productive forces have also increased with the all-around development of the individual, and all the springs of co-operative wealth flow more abundantly—only then can the narrow horizon of bourgeois right be crossed in its entirety and society inscribe on its banners: From each according to his ability, to each according to his needs!" Marx Karl, Critique of the Gotha Program as abridged in Die Neue Zeit, Vol. 1, No. 18, 1890/1891, available at: https://www.marxists.org/archive/marx/works/1875/gotha/ch01.htm, accessed on 5 May 2020. The formula has been used in reference by other socialists during the 19th century

of both the Soviet and the Chinese socialist economic policy – and was enshrined in the constitutions of both states through several revisions[50] – the latter, to the present day, has remained a distant vision for some.

So, for any analysis of socialist economic policy it is crucial to bear in mind that the division of labour in production and thus the acceptance of social phenomena criticised by Marx would remain part of the socialist economic order. Even more so, agricultural collectivisation included attempts to expand such labour relations to the agricultural sector in both the Soviet Union and the PRC. The alienation of the individual from his work would thus be a reality even under the "dictatorship of the proletariat" – until the transition to communism would, one day, dissolve this necessity as well. Only then would the individual be allowed, in Marx' words, to "hunt in the morning, fish in the afternoon, herd cattle in the evening and criticise after dinner at will, without ever needing to become hunter, fisher or critic".[51]

Rich Nation, Strong Military - the origins of socialism in China

The founding of the PRC in 1949 and the subsequent rule of the CCP went back to two main sets of ideas. To a larger or lesser extent[52], those ideas have been the declared basis of the Chinese socialist state as well as his underlying political ideology until the present day. The first is the objective of building a socialist society capable of reaching a communist utopia by means of revolutionary struggle. The second includes ideas related to Chinese nationalism. While the Chinese Civil war is often framed as a conflict between nationalists and communists especially after the break-up of the second United Front, both sides could trace their political origins to the – arguably more important[53] – Chinese Xinhai Revolution of 1911. It had ended the reign of China's last imperial dynasty, the Qing. Still today, the first president of the post-Qing government, Sun Yat-sen, appears to be one of the few historic figures held in equally high respect in both Taiwan and (mainland) China as well as Hong Kong.

The emerging Chinese nationalism at the turn of the 19th to the 20th century had the incisive experience of weakness towards the intrusion and dominance by foreign modern industrial powers at its core. The First Opium War (1839–1842) fought between China and Britain, followed by the Second Opium War (1856–60) were manifestations of the

---

such as Louis Blanc and August Becker, the latter describing it as the foundational principle of communism.

50 As in article 12 of the 1936 Constitution of the Soviet Union, in hindsight, described by Leon Trotsky as an "inwardly contradictory, not to say nonsensical, formula". TROTSKY LEON, EASTMAN MAX (ed.), The Revolution Betrayed, Mineola 2004, pp. 194 f.

51 MARX KARL, ENGELS FRIEDRICH, ADORATSKIJ VLADIMIR VIKTOROVIC, Die Deutsche Ideologie, Vienna and Berlin 1932, p. 33.

52 Like all revolutionary movements in China, at least since the late 19th century, Chinese Communism was *"a child of nationalism"*. See: CHANG C.M., Communism and Nationalism in China, in: Foreign Affairs, Vol. 28, No. 4, July 1950, p. 554.

53 For a classic account oft he relationship between the Chinese revolutions, see: BIANCO LUCIEN, Les origines de la révolution chinoise 1915–1949, Paris 2007.

Chinese inability to assert its own borders, values and rules against violent intruders. In China, the latter conflict is also known as the Arrow War or the Anglo-French War, as it was fought by Britain and France against China. In each case, the foreign powers prevailed due to their superior military technology, imposed commercial privileges and enforced territorial concessions. These defeats marked the beginning of an era of limited sovereignty that weakened the rule of the Qing dynasty. Thus, they contributed to the rise of Republican China in the early 20th century.

In the second half of this book, international trade and economic diplomacy are at the center of the analysis. I argue that both were important aspects of the shifting compromise on economic policy in China during the 1970s. In that regard, it is important to note that the historical experiences of most Chinese were far from positive. Rather, they came to be directly associated with foreign coercion. In particular, international commercial exchanges bore and continue to bear the stigma of relating to the forced importation of narcotics. Opium, a major cash crop of British India, was shipped to China by the East India Company to offset the silver flowing to China that paid for luxuries like tea, silk and porcelain that were in high demand on European markets. The opium trade grew exponentially, reversing the balance of trade to the detriment of China while causing an increase in corruption of government officials and obvious risks to public health.[54]

The Opium Wars broke out, when Qing Emperor Daoguang attempted to exercise Chinese sovereignty to suppress this forcefully legalised drug trafficking. In a swift answer, British battleships destroyed Chinese naval defences. After three years of fighting, the war ended with the Nanjing Treaty of 1842. The agreement transferred possession of Hong Kong Island to Britain and opened up both the Chinese market to trade under "fair and reasonable" tariffs as well as Chinese society for Christian missionaries. Chinese ports were kept open by an international coalition uniting the British Empire, the United States, France as well as Russia.[55]

This commercial opening of China was anchored by legal means, backed by modern armed forces – the so-called "unequal treaties" of which the Treaty of Nanjing was among the first. Their definition and exact number of are subject to fierce debate. It appears to be general consensus that a total of at least fourteen countries concluded such treaties "with" China, and that there was a maximum of 48 ports opened for international shipping under a binding international legal instrument. In addition, three ports (Santuao, Yueyang and Qinhuangdao) were opened by Chinese decree in 1898. Not necessarily coastal, these so-called "treaty ports" were points of entry for foreign trade. In historiographical terms, they have been characterised in many ways – e. g. as sites of paramount importance for Chinese development, as centres of controversy and as points of encounter between China and the world.[56]

Surely, the opening was not reciprocal. Arguably, this would not have been of much value in the absence of a Chinese fleet required to actually exercise such rights for exam-

---

54 Hsiao Gene T., The Foreign Trade of China: Policy, Law and Practice, Berkeley, Los Angeles and London 1977, p. 3.

55 Parties to the Treaty of Tianjin of 1858, ending the first phase of the second Opium War.

56 See e. g., Bickers Robert, Jackson Isabella (eds.), Treaty Ports in Modern China, Law, Land and Power, London 2016.

ple in English ports. While, as CHRISTOPHER WAKE has argued, China was technically, perfectly capable of constructing a fleet, it had not used this capability to a notable extent for centuries: A common narrative follows the journeys of the Chinese fleet under Admiral Zheng He in the early 15th century under the Ming emperors, after which the fleet was destroyed by order of the Emperor and no new attempts at establishing a Chinese naval power – or merchant fleet – were undertaken. It appears that Zheng He has recently been rediscovered by the Chinese government under Xi Jinping as a historic precedent for Chinese trade.[57]

The foreign interventions also changed the foundations of how China's relations with the rest of the world were organised. While China was far from being secluded from the outside at the beginning of the Opium Wars[58], the imperial tribute-system that had regulated China's foreign trade was replaced by a system of international treaties based on Westphalian[59] concepts of international law. "Westphalian system", "Westphalian model", "Westphalian paradigm" or "Westphalian regime" among others are terms referring to a fundamental transformation of international relations in 17th century Europe, as a consequence of the Peace of Westphalia of 1648. This transformation largely replaced the idea of a "Christian commonwealth" governed by universal institutions with an international order consisting mainly or exclusively of sovereign states. It has been critically reflected as a continuing process which did not end multi-layered authority and jurisdiction in Europe, but rather redistributed it to the benefit of those states. The fundamental concept of sovereign nation-states having international legal personality is the basis their legitimacy to, for instance, conclude treaties on which today's international institutions and sets of rules are based on.

The system of such international treaties China found itself in was built over a period of almost sixty years and, in the end, encompassed about 300 international treaties and supplemental agreements with foreign states. It was deepened and widened in three rounds, each of which was preceded by one of the major military defeats of China mentioned before – after the First and the Second Opium War, the Sino-Japanese War of 1894 and the Boxer Rebellion of 1899–1901. One important objective of the treaty system was the establishment of certainty[60] for the access of foreign economies to Chinese resources and markets. Another was to secure the protection and status of foreigners on Chinese

57 WAKE CHRISTOPHER, The Myth of Zheng He's Great Treasure Ships, in: International Journal of Maritime History, Vol. 16, No. 1, June 2004, pp. 59–75.

58 LOVELL JULIA, The Opium War, Drugs, Dreams and the making of China, Oxford 2011. For an account on colonial life after the opium war, see BICKER ROBERT, The Scramble for China, Foreign Devils in the Qing Empire 1832–1914, London 2011.

59 SCHMIDT SEBASTIAN, To Order the Minds of Scholars: The Discourse of the Peace of Westphalia in International Relations Literature, in: International Studies Quarterly, Vol. 55, No. 3, September 2011, pp. 601–623; and BEAULAC STEPHANE, The Westphalian Model in Defining International Law: Challenging the Myth, in: Australian Journal of Legal History, No. 8, 2004, pp. 181–213.

60 In legal scholarship, it has been argued that the early experiences with western international law incentivised and shaped a particular Chinese view on the topic, rather focused on sovereignty and non-intervention. See, BURNAY MATTHIEU, Chinese Perspectives on the International Rule of Law, Cheltenham and Northampton 2018, chapter 6. Certainly, positions taken by modern China on international matters such as "cyber sovereignty" in internet governance support these views.

soil. Both objectives implied the restriction of what, in the Westphalian system, would be understood as national sovereignty of China. This was most obvious in the treaty ports where the Chinese imperial government was simply denied jurisdiction. The foreign parties to the treaties secured the legalisation of the opium trade, the control of tariffs applied to imports and even exercised extraterritorial jurisdiction, coupled with the establishment of foreign courts and armed garrisons. Later, a recommendation signed by twelve treaty powers on the 16th of September 1926 called for the establishment of an "independent" court in China, as well as the implementation of domestic laws instrumental to commerce: five such basic codes were promulgated between 1929 and 1935.[61]

By introducing the concept of most favored nation, Chinese ports and markets kept open to an equal extent to all imperial powers based on the declared objective of "free trade". At the time, the term essentially referred to the unilateral abolishment of protectionist policies such as the infamous Corn Laws by Britain after 1849. It was first enshrined in the bilateral trade agreement in the current sense, the British-French Cobden-Chevalier Treaty of the 23th of January 1860. Related policies have been associated with the work of classic anglophone economists, notably Adam Smith and David Ricardo and are understood as a crucial component of British imperialism, facilitating an economically more efficient or "informal" variety of imperial rule. While this argument has been criticised notably by MARTIN LYNN as exaggerating the impact of economic ties, a close entanglement between policies of free trade and British imperialism is not disputed.[62] The concept of most favoured nation, which formed the basis for both the British system of free trade and the later multilateral trade system as well as the bilateral legal regulation of trade relations[63], would return to China decades later, albeit under very different circumstances.

The "Century of Humiliation", as parts of Chinese historiography refer to the years from 1839 to 1949[64], could take its course particularly because no military means that

---

61 HSIAO 1977, p. 5.

62 GALLAGHER JOHN, ROBINSON RONALD, The Imperialism of Free Trade, in: The Economic History Review, Vol. 6, No. 1, 1953, pp. 1–15; and LYNN MARTIN, British Policy, Trade, and Informal Empire in the Mid-Nineteenth Century, in: PORTER ANDREW (ed.), The Oxford History of the British Empire Volume III, The 19th century, Oxford 1999, pp. 101–121.

63 The principle of most favored nation, which is the application of a non-discrimination obligation in international relations (no discrimination between states in the application of measures affecting trade such as tariffs), is both the basis of trade liberalization under the General Agreement on Tariffs and Trade of 1947 and the Agreements consolidated under the WTO founded in 1995. It is also until the present day included in Preferential Trade Agreements (PTA) as well as investment agreements. A (legal) history of MFN-treatment is yet to be written. On its genesis within the GATT, see: RUBIN SEYMOUR J., Most-Favored-Nation Treatment and the Multilateral Trade Negotiations: A Quiet Revolution, in: Maryland Journal of International Law, Vol. 6, No. 2, 1981, pp. 221–241.

64 And still refers to. Since the socialist revolution ended the Century of Humiliation, the Chinese state has become quite apt at working with and within the international system. As ALISON KAUFMAN argues, China's elites continue to harbor a degree of dissatisfaction with the current international system, and they continue to reference China's legacy of past "humiliation" as a justification for their suspicion about the intentions of other powers. See: KAUFMAN ALISON, The "Century of Humiliation", then and now: Changing Chinese Perceptions of the International Order, APSA Toronto Meeting Paper 2009.

could match the ship-based artillery and modern infantry of the industrialised European powers were available to China. Similar to the experience of Japan at the eve of the Meiji Restauration, it became apparent to many that the way to free China from foreign oppression was catching up through *rapid* modernisation. Speaking of slogans, this insight paved the way for the triumph of "rich nation, strong military" in Japan – including its implications for the organisation of the economy and the society at large – over the rather antithetical "revere the emperor, expel the barbarians" advocated by conservative forces. Accordingly, such ideas of modernisation had, since their beginning, a strong military twist to them that would prevail throughout the socialist era.

Modern industry was the only means that allowed for the construction of the very same rifles and cannons on which the powerful foreign naval powers relied to enforce their interests. An obvious approach was reproducing the basic innovations that had allowed the West to become powerful enough to dominate the remnants of the very Chinese empire that had understood itself as the center of the world. Like in Japan, the slogan "rich nation, strong military" (*fu guo, qiang bing*)[65] came to summarise the common goal of a broad movement, unifying a wide array of political strands in its pursuit.

Alternative paths towards a common goal

How exactly the shared objective of economic modernisation could and should be achieved was highly disputed within China. Concepts on offer ranged from liberal[66] to neo-Confucian[67] and beyond.[68] Some demonstrated the immense cultural and economic pressures to which the Chinese society was subjected. Slogans like "The survival of the fittest", directly adopted from Charles Darwin's writings, expressed a necessity to adapt to changed circumstances – or perish.[69]

The May Fourth Movement, which laid much of the groundwork for Chinese national liberation, saw the most viable path in the replacement of Confucianism by a new cul-

65 The same slogan that was used during the Japanese Meiji-restauration period by the Iwakura Mission. Ezra F. Vogel argued that it originated from the Chinese Warring States period. See: Vogel Ezra F., China and Japan: Facing History, London 2019, p. 106.

66 Yeh Wen-hsin, Middle County Radicalism: The May Fourth Movement in Hangzhou, in: The China Quarterly, Vol. 140, December 1994, pp. 903–925.

67 Which was fiercely attacked by the anarchist strand of the New Cultural Movement, which saw Confucianism, plausibly, as a basis of authority in China, both of the state and within families. The abolishment of Confucian thought was directly related to the idea of economic revolution (*jingji geming*), which was intended to provide individuals with the economic security necessary to guarantee their autonomy from the family. See: Dirlik Arif, The New Culture Movement Revisited: Anarchism and the Idea of Social Revolution in New Culture Thinking, in: Modern China, Vol. 11, No. 3, July 1985, p. 276.

68 Garver John W., China's Quest, The History of the Foreign Relations of the People's Republic of China, New York 2016, p. 6.

69 According to Jarkko Haapanen, evolutionary theory gained significant popularity in China after 1890. See: Haapanen Jarkko, Adaptation to World Trends, A Rereading of the May Fourth Movement Radicalization, in: Jyväskylä Studies in Education, Psychology and Social Research, No. 463, 2013, p. 13.

ture.[70] But where could a model for new patterns of social organisation and individual behaviour be found? The successful 1917 Bolshevik October Revolution in Russia made Marxism–Leninism a viable path for China in the eyes of a distinct group of Chinese nationalists. They eagerly embraced the basic tenet of achieving forced modernisation lead by a strictly organised movement in order to *save the nation*.

Who exactly was part of this nation depended on political stances. As SHAMEER MODONGAL noted, the later Chinese civil war can be understood as the struggle between two different approaches to nationalism – the CCP promoting a more inclusive form, while the Guomindang arguing for a Han-dominated nation, organised in accordance with ethnic criteria. FELIX WEMHEUER confirms that, comparable to its approaches to gender, the ideology of the CCP saw ethnicity as secondary to class. Building on an orthodox version of Marxism-Leninism, Mao emphasised several times that the national question was, at its root, a class issue. From this point of view, the Han chauvinism and local nationalism of the "old society" and the Guomindang were both instruments of the ruling class to divide the labouring masses.[71]

For the Chinese nationalists inspired by the Russian example, the socialist revolution was less a means to achieve an abstract utopia after a long process of resolving dialectic contradictions. Rather, it offered an instrumentarium for the organisation of a political movement[72] and the economic modernisation of the country. Since its beginning, foreign influence on the Chinese communist movement was not limited to the ideas it based itself. The CCP, which was founded in July 1921 in Shanghai, was closely linked to its Soviet counterpart, even considered to be a Chinese–Soviet joint venture.[73] This international support was not ubiquitous: In the absence of a bourgeois revolution in China, the Comintern chose a rather careful approach in their support of the Chinese communists: In 1923, it decided to not only support the CCP, but also the Guomindang. When the shaky alliance of the United Front broke in 1927 and the CCP was driven out of the cities and forced to conduct protracted guerrilla warfare in the countryside, the movement had to reinvent itself as a rural guerrilla organisation, relying on the support of the population in order to survive. As we know, this approach was successful. In October 1949, Mao declared that the "Chinese people had stood up" under the leadership of the CCP.

---

70 As CHU-YUAN CHENG argued, Sun Yat-sen himself saw his nationalism as a "heritage bequeathed [to him] by [his] ancestors, which need not be imported from outside". Taking pride in the heritage of classical antiquity, he advocated a restoration of traditional moral values and rejected most of the New Cultural Movement – notably those that called for westernisation. See: CHENG CHU-YUAN, China's Economic Development, 1950–2014, Fundamental Changes and Long-Term Prospects, London 2014, p. 29.

71 MODONGAL SHAMEER, Development of nationalism in China, in: Cogent Social Sciences, Vol. 2, No. 1, 2016, available at: http://dx.doi.org/10.1080/23311886.2016.1235749, last accessed on 1 April 2020; and WEMHEUER 2019, p. 35 f.

72 The argument that the superior organisation and unity of the Communist movement were major contributions to both the political and the military victories against the divided and at times chaotic Kuomintang, has been brought forward by several authors. See, CHAURASIA RADHEY SHYAM, History of Modern China, New Delhi 2004, p. 166.

73 PRIESTLAND 2009, p. 304.

After having seized political power, shaped by decades of warfare in the vast Chinese countryside, the party was confronted with the dilemma faced by all socialist states. While socialist theory legitimised revolutionary action and informed the cornerstones of a political program, it had very little to say about *how* a socialist economy was to be organised and run in practice. There was even less to be found about industrialising a country in the first place.[74] More so, similar to the Russian communist movement, theoretical justification was needed as to why the bourgeois revolution, as a prerequisite of socialist revolution, did not necessarily need to occur and fulfil its historical role in China. Nevertheless, as several authors have shown[75], a number of structural factors benefitted the establishment of socialist rule in China.

The Warlord Period, which ended with the CCP's rise to power, had given western observers the impression that the country was both fragmented (by local warlords which ruled pieces of territory while engaging in constant struggle against each other) and divided between areas under occupation by the Japanese and the combatants of the civil war. This impression, as PERKINS argued, was misleading and the exception rather than the rule in Chinese history. From the founding of the Ming Dynasty in 1368 until the early 20th century, China – despite its size and population – had been a relatively unified country. Notable exceptions are the Manchu invasion and internal conflict ending the Ming dynasty in 1644, as well as the Taiping Rebellion between 1851 and 1864, bringing about splits into administrative units. For long periods, China's imperial system was uniquely capable of ruling such a vast territory, a fact consistently noted by foreign visitors.[76]

This administrative rule required a highly decentralised administration, capable of woking in accordance with orders even if the capital and the emperor were far away.[77] In

---

74 For an original approach on the difficult origins of approaches on economic policymaking, see: BOCKMAN JOHANNA, Markets in the Name of Socialism: The Left-Wing Origins of Neoliberalism, Stanford 2012.

75 For instance, PERKINS 2015, with regard to the role of *Confucian Moral Law*, see: ZHU HONGWEN, PETERS MICHAEL A., Social governance, education and socialist rule of law in China, Educational Philosophy and Theory, Vol. 51 No. 7, 2019, pp. 670–673. For the potential positive effects of "the shock provided to the traditional economy and inducing a change desired by a portion of the domestic entrepreneurial class", as well as the introduction of modern technology and production methods, see: DERNBERGER ROBERT F., The Role of the Foreigner in China's Economic Development, in: PERKINS DWIGHT H. (ed.), China's Modern Economy in Historical Perspective, Stanford 1975, pp. 40, 42 f.; and the contribution by KANG CHAO on the effects of foreign competition on the traditional textile industry in the same volume, pp. 167–202.

76 For an innovative approach comparing the efficiency of the Chinese imperial administration, for instance, in the Han empire with the Roman Empire see: DINGXIN ZHAO, The Han Bureaucracy: Its Origin, Nature and Development; and EICH PETER, The Common Denominator: Late Roman Imperial Bureaucracy from a Comparative Perspective, in: SCHEIDEL WALTER (ed.), State Power in Ancient China and Rome, New York 2015, pp. 56–89, and 90–149.

77 Administered by a *rule of mandates*, meaning the issuing of relatively open guidelines by the central government instead of detailed orders, implemented by discipline and a system of sanctions for non-compliant subordinates. MAYLING BIRNEY applied the concept to the analysis of the current Chinese structures of power and corruption. Chinese administrative law still appears to bear factors reminiscent of imperial rule, instead of the Rule of Law. See: BIRNEY MAYLING, Decentralization and Veiled Corruption Under China's "Rule of Mandates", in: World Development, Draft Paper March 2013, available at: http://dx.doi.org/10.2139/ssrn.2279059, last accessed on 1 May 2020.

practice, this meant that imperial mandates had to be executed by local elites and magistrates in a largely independent manner and adapted to local conditions *without* constant exchanges with the central government. On the other hand, it meant that officials needed to be trained, appointed and controlled in a way that ensured sufficient loyalty, reliability and also the swift removal of non-conforming representatives. These requirements were met by a combination of shared values based on Confucian classics, a famously rigorous examination system and a standing army led by generals who were independent of the administration, capable of backing any imperial decision with robust means, if needed.

The remarkable consequence of the examination system introduced by the Han Empire was making the meritocratic principle central to the administration of the state, privileging (a concept of) individual merit over birth, combined with immense prestige for the members of the administrative hierarchy. While the ideal was never fully realised: candidates with commoner status rather than licentiate status or higher comprised 33 percent of cohorts under the Song, 49.5 percent under the Ming, and 37.6 percent under the Qing dynasties.[78] In addition, the majority of the Han Chinese[79] shared a common culture and written language, which allowed for a common identity and facilitated the rise of Chinese nationalism in the early 20th century. These preconditions did in no way guarantee stability, unity or economic development in and by themselves, as the period preceding 1949 demonstrated. Nevertheless, they provided a foundation on which any future national government could build.

In 1949, the first objective of the Chinese communist movement – national liberation – had been largely attained. The second, economic development, would become subject to decades of debate, experimentation, failures and remarkable success. After the nationalist revolution of 1911 and the socialist revolution of 1949, the objective of the socialist state centred on catching up with two other revolutions that industrialised countries had experienced. First, the Agricultural, second, the Industrial Revolution. Both implied introducing basic innovations that had laid the foundation for the economic success of industrialised nations to China. At a much faster pace.

Those industrialised societies stood at the beginning of a decade of unprecedented growth, forming the peak of a macroeconomic cycle driven notably by the petrochemical industries. The fourth long-wave technological revolution just had entered its upswing in the 1950s, establishing new patterns of sophisticated division of labour and thus unprecedented productivity.[80], A *raison d'être* of the PRC was the building of a foundation

---

78 McMullen David L., The Chinese Examination System in Dynastic China: Did it select the brightest and best?, in: Sunway Academic Journal, Vol. 8, 2011, pp. 1–11; and, for an overview, Lee Thomas H.C., Review: Imagining the Chinese Examination System: Historical Nature and Modern Usefulness, in: China Review International, Vol. 13, No. 1, Spring 2006, pp. 1–12.

79 Not referring to the Han Dynasty (ca. 206 b.C.-220 AD). In today's China, 56 ethnic groups are distinguished by the census bureaucracy, including "*Han*" which refers to the majority of Chinese people. As the proportion of Han Chinese has declined over the years, the sizes of the minority Chinese are increasing. In 2010, minority Chinese reached 113.79 million people, a little less than the national population of Mexico in 2012. See: Zhou Yun, Question of ethnic group formulation in the Chinese census, in: China Population and Development Studies, No. 3, 2019, pp. 67–83.

80 Metzler Mark, Capital as Will and Imagination: Schumpeter's Guide to the Postwar Japanese Miracle, Ithaca and London 2013, pp. 160 f.

for catching up some day. The objective continued to be economic modernisation. How to achieve it?

Oscillations of Chinese economic policy before 1970

Cycles of experimentation with economic policies can be observed in all societies at any time, regardless of the political, philosophical or theoretical beliefs their governments might adhere to.[81] The three decades of economic policy in China after 1949 have been described with a number of generic terms such as "big push industrialisation" or "policy instability"[82]. Indeed, changes of direction, experiments and their reversal marked the *de facto* course of economic policy in socialist China. While the emphasis on political control of production was distinctive enough for a number of authors to describe a distinctive Maoist model of economic organisation or transformation[83], there was never a monolithic approach or model. At all times, both some economic planning as well as flexibility remained a part of the actually implemented policies, rhetoric set aside.

The Development Centre of the OECD makes a distinction between a "Maoist Phase" of policy and performance lasting until 1978 and the Reform Period afterwards, defining three objectives as cornerstones: Changing the socio-political order, accelerating economic growth and improving China's geopolitical standing and restore its national dignity.[84] The socialist governments of the USSR and in Eastern Europa have equally gone through a number of reform cycles, which aimed at improving their systems of economic planning and management as well as the performance of their economies. In doing so, they strived for opening new sources of legitimacy.

One important reason for these oscillations was the CCP's lack of experience with running a large and complex economy. Another was a number of objective constraints painfully experienced particularly during the Great Leap Forward. Nevertheless, with regard to the outcomes of such changing bundles of economic policies, the different periods of policy oscillation yielded very different results, from quite successful to catastrophic. As CHENG CHU-YUAN proposed, these phases may be distinguished as (1) the "Stalinist Model" of the first five-year plan (1953–1957), (2) the "Maoist Model" of the Great Leap Forward (1958–1960), (3) the "Khrushchev-Type Revisionism" of a period of readjustment (1961–1965), (4) another period following the "Maoist Model" during the Cultural

81 For a classic study on cyclical phenomena of economic policy making in democracies, see: ROGOFF KENNETH, SIBERT ANNE, Elections and Macroeconomic Policy Cycles, in: The Review of Economic Studies, Vol. 55, No. 1, January 1988, pp. 1–16.

82 NAUGHTON BARRY, The Chinese economy: transitions and growth, Cambridge Mass. and London 2007, pp. 55 ff.

83 See e. g. HOFFMANN CHARLES, The Maoist Economic Model, in: Journal of Economic Issues, Vol. 5, No. 3, September 1971, pp. 12–27; PAINE SUZANNE, Balanced development: Maoist conception and Chinese practice, in: World Development, Vol. 4, No. 4, April 1976, pp. 277–304; and GURLEY JOHN G., China's Economy and the Maoist Strategy, New York and London 1976.

84 OECD, Chinese Economic Performance in the Long Run: The Maoist Transformation and its Impact, Available at https://www.oecd.org/dev/chineseeconomicperformanceinthelongrunthemaoisttransformationanditsimpact.htm, accessed on 10 May 2020.

Revolution (1966–1970), (5) a combination of (3) and (4) (1971–1975), (6) the "ultra-leftist model" shaped by the influence of the Gang of Four (1975–1976), and finally (7) a revival of revisionism in a second readjustment from 1977 to the present.[85]

This book mainly focuses on the period between (5) and (7) and proposes a further focus on overlap and nuance. The general differentiation is certainly valid from the perspective of macroeconomic development and has been adopted by a number of authors. For instance, BARRY NAUGHTON'S analysis of investment rates indicates that the main phases of economic development are marked by a number of "leaps" – phases of above-average growth of aggregate investment accompanied by political mobilisation and a degree of institutional transformation – followed by phases of retrenchment and consolidation.

Accordingly, investment cycles in China tended to correspond with policy cycles. Based on this observation, NAUGHTON has proposed the phases of (1) economic recovery (1949–1952), (2) the "Twin Peaks of the First Five-Year Plan" (1953 and 1956), (3) a first phase of retrenchment during the Hundred Flowers campaign (1956–1957), (4) the Great Leap Forward (1958–1960), (5) a second phase of retrenchment marked by "Crisis and Readjustment" (1961–1963), (6) a new expansion "hijacked by radicalism during the build-up of the Third Front" (1964–1966), (7) a third phase of retrenchment during the Cultural Revolution (1967–1969), followed by (8) a "new leap" in 1970, (9) retrenchment marked by "consolidation and drift" between 1972–1976, and finally (10) the "leap outward" and the end of Maoism in 1978, with the third plenum in December of the same year as a "final turning point".[86]

While different stages can be identified depending on the focus of a given perspective, the structure of the Chinese economy is a determining factor. Again: The society that the CCP took political control of in 1949 was largely based on agriculture, of which a major part did not go far beyond subsistence.[87] The military defeat against Japan in 1895 had opened Shanghai to foreign investment, leading to the establishment of a basic modern textile industry and industrial firms. The city saw industrial growth until the beginning of the civil war. According to estimates by DWIGHT H. PERKINS and THOMAS G. RAWSKI, this growth amounted to just over two percent per annum – which is very modest particularly given the state of underinvestment.[88] A relatively modern industrial basis existed mostly in the vicinity of the very ports that had been forcefully opened to foreign trade as well as investment. Therefore, it was mostly limited to the coastal area in the east and south of the vast country and some Japanese-built heavy industry in Manchuria, specifically in the former puppet-state of *Manchukuo*.[89]

---

85 CHENG 2014, pp. 118 f.

86 NAUGHTON 2007.

87 A state of affairs that did not change rapidly and arguably still has not fully changed. See: REYNOLDS, LLOYD G., China as a Less Developed Economy, in: The American Economic Review, Vol. 65, No. 3, June 1975, pp. 418–428.

88 PERKINS 2015, p. 13.

89 As DWIGHT PERKINS argued, from the point of view of economic development, the decisive military defeat of China by Japan in 1895 had the positive outcome of allowing – for the first time – foreign direct investment in industry and commerce. See PERKINS DWIGHT H., China's Prereform Economy in World Perspective, in: WOMACK BRANTLY (ed.) 2010, p. 118. For an overview on pre-1949 industrial

After seizing political power, the CCP was faced with a situation for which no political operating manual existed.[90] Subsequently, in a gigantic trial-and-error process[91], approaches to national economic development were adopted and dropped within the quite flexible[92] ideological boundaries of Maoist socialism. Even after bringing the rampant inflation under centralised control through the introduction of a new currency and the founding of the (People's) Bank of China, the political structures the CCP established initially remained quite different from the Soviet model.

An important yardstick for the future was the concept of New Democracy introduced by Mao in 1940. Originally, it was intended as a political vehicle to bridge differences between the CCP and the rest of the second United Front – notably the Guomindang but arguably also the majority of the Chinese people. It was based on a gradual process of persuasion, political education and coercion and was meant to be a transitional model until a socialist system could be introduced.[93] The years between 1949 and 1956, when New Democracy was embraced by the CCP, have frequently been described as a sort of "honeymoon period" between the party and the population. This is a rather optimistic view. While the approach provided remarkable stability, both within the political leadership and economically, it also saw political purges: the Campaign to Suppress Counterrevolutionaries between 1951 and 1953[94] and the Three-Anti Campaign.[95]

Such excesses were fuelled by both the fact that the CCP was essentially a military organisation and that the newly established socialist state saw itself faced with both internal and external threats and tensions. While armed uprisings in south-western China against the new rulers persisted, the threat of the exiled Guomindang attempting a re-conquest of the mainland appeared to be quite plausible during this phase. Furthermore, the Chinese involvement in the Korean War had led to a high death toll, enormous military expenses and effectively closed the door to stable diplomatic and economic ties

---

development, see Chen Nai-Ruenn, Industrial Development in Mainland China, in: Asian Affairs, Vol. 2, No. 5, 1975, p. 287.

90 The historiography of the socialist takeover in Russia is still subject to ongoing debate, notably with regard to the question about whether the October Revolution deserves to be called a revolution, or whether it was merely a coup by a distinct group which, in a way, hijacked the social movements that manifested themselves, for instance, in the uprisings of the February Revolution in the same year. For a valuable discussion of this issue, see: Bogdan Nina, October of 1917 Revisited – Revolution or Coup d'état? in: Footnotes: A Journal of History, Vol. 1, 2017. Available at https://journals.uair.arizona.edu/index.php/UAHISTJRNL/article/view/20152, last accessed on 1 May 2020.

91 After 1978, the approach of "gradual trial and error" was continued, albeit within different ideological boundaries, as I discuss later. Over the course of the 1980s, the figurative image of "touching stones to cross a river" became frequently used. See: Chen John-ren, China's Way of Economic Transition, in: Transition Studies Review, Vol. 21, September 2005, pp. 315–333.

92 The prolific writings of Mao were already reinterpreted extensively and creatively during his lifetime, even more after his death. For a helpful compilation on the development of political terms in the PRC, see: Li 1995.

93 Dittmer Lowell, On China's Rise, in: Brantly (ed.) 2010, p. 42.

94 See: Dikötter Frank, The Tragedy of Liberation: A History of the Chinese Revolution 1945–1957, London 2013, pp. 84 ff.

95 Wemheuer 2019, p. 69.

with the West. Besides its internal tensions, the PRC had become an active actor in the conflict between the two superpowers.

Despite these instances of political violence, there was a number of tangible achievements. Besides national reunification, remarkable social changes such as the move away from legal gender inequality in the form of new marriage laws were progressive. Nevertheless, regardless its name, Maoist New Democracy bore little resemblance to liberal democratic systems. Crucial institutions necessary for seriously ensuring political pluralism and the separation of powers were not established; there was neither a system of general, secret and equal elections nor a legal system assuring the rule of law for citizens let alone the political opposition. Formal rules on state power were limited to the Common Program of the Consultative Conference of the People's Government of China of 1949, rather a political pamphlet than a constitutional document. The People's Congress as an all-China representative body established by the constitution of 1954 had legislative functions – as did the executive branch, namely the CCP Central Committee and the State Council – but was not elected by popular vote.[96]

What was meant by "democracy" is still today reflected in the Chinese national flag: The large star represents the leadership of the CCP, while the four small stars grouped beside it stand for the allied classes: the working class, the petty bourgeoisie, the national bourgeoisie and the peasantry. They reflect a broad class alliance and patriotic united front, albeit under the leadership of the CCP. Together, they were intended to serve the common interest of removing power from the old, failed elites in order to give it back to the Chinese people. The concept of class alliance was neither new nor specifically Chinese. It had been applied by the Soviet Union to unite a wide spectrum of political movements against fascism. Also, after the end of the Second World War, the states of Eastern Europe under Soviet control were founded as "people's democracies" with a narrative similar to the Chinese after 1949. They were set in opposition against the "feudal remnants" of the pre-revolutionary order, establishing this political narrative in a Marxist sequence of historical determinism. The intent was the completion of the bourgeois revolution necessary as a precondition for socialism. For instance, a decisive element in the GDR as well as in China during this first phase was land reform.

The years of New Democracy in China were shaped by comparably inclusive policies and politics[97], demonstrating that the concept was taken seriously and treated as more than mere lip-service. This became particularly apparent in industry, where the management skills and technical know-how of factory owners and their foremen were needed to ensure the continuation of production. Private industrial enterprises, which were allowed to co-exist with the steadily expanding state-owned and joint state–private sectors[98], continued to be run on a profit-oriented basis and distributed their products under what were basically market conditions. As an expression of the class alliance, the

96 Wemheuer 2019, p. 51.

97 At least certainly more so than the *dictatorship of the proletariat* later on. See: Priestland 2014 p. 364 and Wemheuer 2019, p. 52.

98 While being gradually integrated into the expanding state sector, notably after 1953. In 1956, socialist state enterprises accounted for 67.5% of the total industrial assets, while joint state-private enterprises accounted for 32.5%. See: Li 2006, p. 124.

capital of private owners that was thus procured by the state was compensated for by an annual dividend of five percent. State control was ensured through production quotas and sale/purchase-contracts, while the former owners remained in charge of the factory's management, receiving both wages and a dividend at five percent on their capital shares. The transition to state ownership was supposed to happen on a voluntary basis, while pressure existed[99] The distinction between patriotic "national capitalists", who could be cooperated with to achieve the common cause, and "bureaucratic capitalists" was a subtle political tool that allowed striking a compromise for the sake of industrial modernisation and production.

It is disputed whether the concept of New Democracy was ever intended to last longer than required to establish the necessary stability, In June 1950, Mao himself reassured Chinese businesspeople at a meeting of the Chinese People's Political Consultative Conference that the mixed economy under the system of New Democracy would last two or three decades, while conditions conductive to a socialist transition would gradually develop.[100] At the same time, New Democracy was understood by the CCP, and explicitly so by Mao, as part of a global movement to achieve a socialist world revolution. Both things were about to change, as the party kept pushing towards a different direction of economic development.

"Leaning to one side" – introducing the Soviet model in the PRC

After the period of New Democracy, the Chinese leadership opted for an industrialisation paradigm that was largely based on the outcomes of the Soviet industrialisation debate and its harsh adjustments. The fifth Soviet five-year plan ending in 1955 was shaped by Stalin's ambition that the Soviet Union would be the leading industrial power by 1960 – an expression of economic competition with the USA and the reconstruction effort after the devastation caused by the Second World War. It can be argued that Soviet planning was tilted even more towards heavy industry than before, even if the plan itself narrowed the gap of allocated capital between construction and consumer goods. Heavy industry, the basis of further technological advancement and – to a changing degree – the development of light industries around the country were at the centre of economic policies.

The choice of the CCP can be explained with a number of practical arguments. However, until then, the Soviet model was the only model of a planned economy, even more so of a large country, that had been implemented in practice and showed empirically impressive results. As Jiri Kosta and Jan Meyer have argued[101], a number of important preconditions in China were very similar to those in the Soviet Union: the leadership in both countries perceived the need for an accelerated build-up of an industrial base, notably for defence purposes, the existing economic structure was still relatively simple and underdeveloped from an industrial point of view, and the size of both countries posed

---

99 Kosta/Meyer p. 39 f. and Ecklund George, Protracted Expropriation of Private Business in Communist China, in: Pacific Affairs, No. 3, 1963, p. 242.

100 Mühlhahn Klaus, Making China Modern: From the Great Qing to Xi Jinping, London 2019, p. 418.

101 Kosta Jiri, Meyer Jan, Volksrepublik China, Ökonomisches System und wirtschaftliche Entwicklung, Frankfurt am Main and Cologne 1976.

similar difficulties with regard to investment transport and the allocation of the labour force.[102] Furthermore, the Marxist–Leninist conceptions of centralised economic planning and the direct influence of Soviet advisors – both before and after 1949 – influenced the choice of the economic model. KONG HANBING noted that the Stalinist model became the very definition of socialism in China, the embodiment of Marxism and true socialism. Intellectuals and cadres were mobilised to study the "Short Course on the History of Soviet Communism", published in the Soviet Union.[103]

Also, the long history of Soviet involvement in Chinese affairs showed the need to be on good terms with a potentially, and later, actually, threatening neighbour.[104] This "leaning-to-one-side"[105], towards the Soviet model, was further reinforced by the beginning of the Cold War, which excluded support from Western nations to the CCP – a Communist party that was already close to the Soviet Union and had fought against the USA and its allies in Korea. Less than three weeks after China entered the Korean War in late 1950, the US imposed an embargo on both trade and financial transactions, freezing assets of Chinese nationals and the State under US jurisdiction. While these measures were only directly implemented in the US, the chilling effect was considerable. Between 1950 and 1955, the proportion of trade with Western countries (including Japan) plunged, from about 36 to under eight percent of the total volume.[106] While initially, the sanctions stood in the logic of external goals (ending inter-state warfare) as suggested by NICHOLAS MULDER[107], internal goals in accordance with the logic of Cold War political conflict contributed to their persistence for decades. The door to reasonable alternatives to the Soviet Union seemed closed for China.

Also, with regard to the difficult international context, the Soviet model of a command economy had the clear advantage of relatively direct political control. For a newly established and, in many ways, inexperienced government with military roots trying to consolidate political rule in a vast country marked by decades of war, this aspect was attractive. The focus on central planning of heavy industry in particular related to the production of steel and the implements necessary for its use, which is the basis for the production of weapons and military equipment.[108] Furthermore, while continuities existed

---

102 Ibid. p. 51.

103 KONG HANBING, The Transplantation and Entrenchment of the Soviet Economic Model in China, in: BERNSTEIN THOMAS P., LI HUA-YU, China Learns from the Soviet Union, 1949-present, Plymouth 2010, p. 161, and the introduction by THOMAS P. BERNSTEIN in the same volume, pp. 1 ff.

104 NATHAN/SCOBELL 2014, pp. 70 ff.

105 A policy that not only expressed the choice of a model of economic development but also the decision to adhere to the socialist world as it existed at the time – which also exposed China to the complications and conflicts within this emerging international system. See: LI DANHUI, SHEN ZHIHUA, After Leaning to One Side: China and Its Allies in the Cold War, Stanford 2011.

106 AIGUO L., China and the Global Economy Since 1840, London 2000, p. 78.

107 MULDER NICHOLAS, The Economic Weapon, The Rise of Sanctions as a Tool of Modern War, New haven and London 2022, p. 294.

108 Military defense and economic development in Sino-Soviet relations were interlinked since the beginning. During Mao's visit to Moscow in 1950 to achieve a mutual defense treaty, first, Soviet loans amounting to 300 million USD were discussed and agreed upon. See: NATHAN ANDREW JAMES, SCOBELL ANDREW, China's Search for Security, New York and Chichester 2014, p. 71.

and the institutional as well as ideational legacy of the Guomindang with regard to Chinese nation-building remained remarkable, the choice of the foreign model also allowed the emancipation of the CCP from the rest of the Chinese nationalist movement.[109]

With direct technical and administrative support by the Soviet Union, the Chinese adopted their first five-year plan in 1953. It was directly based on the Soviet system of centralised bureaucratic planning and allocation, addressing the need for industrial development by including large imports of capital goods from Russia. Ownership of all major industrial factories as well as infrastructures (transportation, finance and communication) was transferred to the state. Agricultural collectives took over the ownership of the land and managed the agricultural production using industrial methods. Compulsory procurement of grain and a government monopoly on key agricultural goods were established, forcing farmers to meet procurement quotas at low fixed prices.[110] Planning authorities issued orders assigning quantitative production targets to firms while allocating inputs. Prices were set in a way to channel resources towards industrial development, generally speaking, by undervaluing agricultural products while keeping prices for industrial products high[111], and make industrial production more profitable. A hierarchical system of managerial career paths controlled by the CCP assured political control of the production processes.[112] The core of the first five-year plan, about half of all investment in heavy industry, consisted of 156 large-scale construction projects of Soviet design, many of which involved the movement of equipment for entire factories to China.[113]

The centralised elements and complex nature of the system required large numbers of people able to draw up plans for the allocation of inputs and products. On the other hand, despite this first bundle of adjustments based on the vision of a command economy, China continued to be a largely mixed economy that allowed flexibilities in several areas until at least 1956. The collectivisation of agricultural production and the transformation of industrial enterprises under direct state control marked an important transition, so to speak, from decentralised markets to more centralised allocation. Tobias ten Brink described the shift in German terms with a transition from *Betriebswirtschaft* (the economic management of enterprises) principles to a system oriented towards *Volkswirtschaft* (the economic management of a national economy).[114]

While the Soviet Union did send advisors, the relatively successful macroeconomic outcomes of 1957 despite all shortcomings speak for the capability of the CCP to establish a fairly functional bureaucratic apparatus in a relatively short time. While there might have been conducive factors like the high morale and integrity of officials, the relatively high availability of educated and literate workers or the millennia of Chinese experienced

109 Strauss Julia, Morality, Coercion and State Building by Campaign in the Early PRC: Regime Consolidation and After, 1949–1956, in: The China Quarterly, No. 188, December 2006, pp. 893 ff.

110 Chen/Galenson 1969, pp. 162 ff.

111 Ibid.

112 Naughton 2007, pp. 59 f.

113 Chen Nai-Ruenn, Galenson Walter, The Chinese Economy under Maoism, The Early Years, 1949–1969, New Brunswick and London 1969, p. 42.

114 Ten Brink Tobias, Chinas Kapitalismus, Entstehung, Verlauf Paradoxien, Frankfurt am Main 2013, p. 94.

in running large bureaucracies, such correlations remain speculative.[115] As PERKINS has argued, it was in many ways remarkable that China was able to make a system of central planning following the Soviet model work at all. Anyway, in his words, China "could make a centrally planned command economy work, but not very well".[116]

During the period of the Chinese first five-year plan, almost forty-five percent of industrial investment went towards industry in general, ninety percent of which went to heavy industry. On the other hand, the primary sector of agriculture was allocated only about seven percent of the resources in the plan, despite being the basic source of income for over ninety percent of the population.[117] These funds were guided by proven technical know-how: Soviet experts did have a pivotal role in the implementation of large-scale projects in the defence, steel, energy, machinery and chemical industries. According to Soviet data, some 11'000 people were assigned to the construction of Chinese industries between 1950 and 1960, which is confirmed by more recent studies – for instance, on statistics in the early PRC by ARUNABH GHOSH. While those figures are lower than the higher end quoted in the literature: the Soviet contribution, particularly with regard to technical know-how and capacity-building in industry, was certainly extensive.[118]

Industrial wages rapidly increased and were subsequently stabilised, albeit with remarkable regional differences. While the planned wage-increases for the period 1952–1957 ranged from 27.1 percent in industry, nineteen percent in construction, and 20.4 percent in transport and communication compared to, for example, 65.7 percent for state employees and 33.5 percent in agriculture and forestry; wages in construction increased by more than seventy-five percent in Inner Mongolia.[119] Control over financial flows and credit was exercised through a state banking monopoly, allocating financial resources along the lines of the plan. Planning itself was based on material balance planning, meaning that the indices used were physical quantities.

The concept of socialist industrialisation in China relied on a far-reaching process of socialisation, meaning changes in ownership through the takeover of industrial enterprises by the state and collectivisation of arable land. During the first five-year plan, when this transformation was still ongoing, state ownership remained largely limited to urban industry, which existed in parallel to private enterprises. Further, centralised state planning was *de facto* limited to this industrial state-owned sector, which coexisted with other forms of ownership in industry during this period. A fact that also lent itself as an argument for emphasised heavy industry development. Large factories and mines allowed for the control of significant productive potential "under one roof". In China, it is remarkable that *mixed* enterprises remained relevant after the first five-year plan, while wholly private enterprises were abolished after 1955.[120]

---

115 PERKINS 2015, p. 15.

116 PERKINS 2015, p. 35.

117 SHARMA SHALENDRA D., China and India in the Age of Globalization, Cambridge 2009, p. 44.

118 CHENG CHU-YÜAN, Scientific and Engineering Manpower in Communist China, 1949–1963, Washington D.C. 1965, pp. 190 ff., and GHOSH ARUNABH, Making it Count: Statistics and Statecraft in the Early People's Republic of China, Princeton and Woodstock 2020, p. 77.

119 HOWE CHRISTOPHER, Wage Patterns and Wage Policy in Modern China, 1919–1972, New York 1973, pp. 47 f.

120 WEMHEUER 2019.

The state-owned enterprises were managed by experts who had little freedom to direct operations of their enterprise beyond the plan. Initially, this aspect was beneficial to economic growth. THOMAS G. RAWSKI argued that the socialist economic organisation of large industrial plants stimulated industrial output by sweeping away restraints formerly imposed by markets. As an example, iron-works in northern China idled during the 1930s because of the scarcity of capital and low prices as well as buying power, but quickly returned to production in the 1950s. On the other hand, output was in many instances maximised with disregard to actual demand, as even substandard products could be sold to the commercial organs of the state in any quantities – in addition to the availability of state-backed loans.[121] While it was basically impossible to go bankrupt as a state-owned enterprise, profits could not be retained and regular workers could not be fired for economic reasons. This was an important aspect of the "iron rice bowl" (*tiefanwan*). Living standards did not necessarily improve, but the value of these auxiliary benefits for individual workers is not to be underestimated. An important flexibility akin to the Soviet NEP concerned single households, which could use their disposable income to purchase from a – quite limited – supply of non-essential consumer goods.[122]

Despite all similarities with the Soviet system, it has been noted that even during the first five-year plan, the Chinese industrial planning system was far less centralised or tightly controlled than the Soviet system. Since the beginning of economic planning, small firms had been more important and the range of industrial products actually allocated by central planners was much lower. BARRY NAUGHTON and others have estimated that Chinese planners allocated an all-time maximum of 600 different products, while the same figure surpassed 60'000 in the Soviet Union during the 1970s.[123] In addition, the lower quality of communication and transportation systems as well as the low reliability of data contributed to the lower density of planning and its implementation in China. Centralised planning was primarily directed at heavy industry, which lend itself to centralised planning as it requires concentrated use of large amounts of capital in relatively isolated projects – such as the construction of a mine, an iron foundry or a power plant. Light industry, consisting of the whole rest of organised productive activity that has tangible goods as an output, was rather the result of indirect efforts, affecting the overall political and legal conditions of an economy as well as disposable income of potential buyers. Therefore, especially in the early stages of a political program aiming at the construction of the essential industrial production chains, the "neglect" of light industry was somewhat inherent. The collectivisation of agriculture as well a thight grip on heavy industry allowed for a degree of control over both the population and production processes, but only as long as reliable cadres were in charge of the production units.[124]

121 RAWSKI THOMAS G., The Growth of Producer Industries, 1900–1971, in: PERKINS DWIGHT H. (ed.), China's Modern Economy in Historical Perspective, Stanford 1975, p. 226.

122 CHEN LEIN-LEIN, DEVEREUX JOHN, The Iron Rice Bowl: Chinese Living Standards 1952–1978, in: Comparative Economic Studies, No. 3, Vol. 2 2017, pp. 261–310.

123 NAUGHTON 2007, p. 62 and a comparable estimate: TIDRICK GENE, China: Socialism and Reform, 1950–1990, in: GRILLI ENZO, SALVATORE DOMINICK (eds.), Handbook of Comparative Economic Policies, Vol. 4, 1994, p. 499.

124 PERKINS 2015, p. 25.

On the other hand, both the limits of the Chinese planning system and the importance of small enterprises for light industrial production meant that the mid-level, typically officials in the provinces, were crucial for the execution of policies issued by the central government. While the establishment of the central planning apparatus was far from complete in 1953, it evolved quickly into a highly organised system with layered structures and relatively clear division of labour by 1957. The State Planning Commission was responsible for overall long-term planning, while the State Economic Commission handled annual and shorter-term planning as well as the coordination of sectoral industrial ministries and key enterprises. The Ministry of Finance provided funding in accordance with the plans. Based on the principle of "the Party manages cadres", a complex "nomenklatura" system of personnel management was established. In practice, each layer of the central ministries and commissions was replicated, down to the level of individual industrial plants.[125] The importance given to social and ideological control of production, especially at the beginning of the first five-year plan, was also a consequence of limited bureaucratic control.

The development concept, which was passed to the State Council as a basis for the future development of the plan, accordingly made reference to the positive economic performance of the Soviet Union, advocating for a continuation of planned and "well-proportioned" development in China in accordance with Soviet thetoric. This implied not ignoring the "enthusiasm of the masses", but curbing "adventurist tendencies".[126] *No experiments* was the basic demand of the high political cadres responsible for economic policy. After a detailed report on the first five-year plan and its widely acknowledged success was presented by Vice Premier Li Fuchun, Premier Zhou Enlai announced the second five-year plan at the eighth party congress of the CCP on the 16th of September 1956. The plan was an extension of the first with respect to its structure and priorities, continuing the pursuit of the Soviet development pattern.

Nevertheless, the relatively successful paradigm was radically altered in 1958. It was replaced by a concept of labour-intensive development enabled by mass mobilisation along with a radical process of forced decentralisation, thus moving away from the Soviet model.[127] This shift was particularly hasardous, as the production of edible grain had always been a serious constraint for China. It continued and continues to shape the relationship between cities and the countryside, the factory and the farm. Also in socialist China.

Walled industrial cities and self-reliant peasants

Since 1949, a major objective in relation to agricultural policy was the increase of farm output and especially the marketable share or surplus. At the same time, state investment

125 LI CHEN, China's Centralized Industrial Order: Industrial reform and the rise of centrally controlled big business, New York 2015, pp. 24 f.

126 KRAUS WILLY, The Policy of the Three Red Banners. The Second Five-Year Plan, 1958–1962, and the Consolidation Phase, 1963–1965, in: Economic Development and Social Change in the People's Republic of China, New York 1982, p. 107.

127 WEMHEUER 2019, p. 122.

in agriculture was kept as low as possible. This extractive approach was as challenging as it was persistent. Still in the late 1990s, about seventy-five percent of farmland was used for grain production involving millions of farms with small holdings, using about two-thirds of grain output for subsistence consumption.

Given the extremely low ratio between arable land and the population, alimentary subsistence of China by itself can be seen as an achievement, let alone the reliable production of a surplus.[128] The marketable share of grain proved to be crucial from the beginning, because the major part of the (initially minor) exports of the PRC consisted of agricultural products, and second, urbanisation developed rapidly in parallel to industrial construction which required food for the urban population, in particular the industrial workers. Both scope and tempo of agricultural collectivisation were topics of political conflict between more radical ideas of fast collectivisation and a more gradual, careful approach. The major difference with the Soviet procurement policies, which followed the same objective, was that the CCP was dealing with a much weaker level of agricultural production.[129]

To understand the underlying paradigms of Chinese industrialisation, taking its constraints into account is crucial. They were imposed by population growth combined with a relative scarcity of food and high-yielding arable land. Additionally, the optimistic mobilisation advocated for by Maoist principles is foundational for basic policy choices, essentially centred on three apodictical assumptions: China had no "population problem" such as overpopulation, people were the primary asset of the country and certainly not a liability, and the relatively rapid population growth during the early 1950s was not an issue but proof of the superiority of socialist rule.[130] Further, the belief in the development of productive forces was key to addressing the disadvantageous relation between said growth and agricultural production, as set forth in a release by Xinhua on the 16th of September 1949, which was later included in the Collected Works of Mao Zedong:

> "It is a very good thing that China has a large population. Even if China's population multiplies many times, she is fully capable of finding a solution which is production [...] Revolution plus production can solve the problem of feeding the population [...] Of all things in the world, people are the most precious. Under the leadership of the Communist Party, as long as there are people, every kind of miracle can be performed [...] We believe that revolution can change everything and that before long there will arise a new China with a big population and a great wealth of products, where life will be abundant and culture will flourish. All pessimistic views are utterly groundless.".[131]

---

128 DAVIS JOHN, WANG LIMING, China's Grain Economy, The Challenge of Feeding more than a Billion, Oxon and New York 2018, notably chapter 2.

129 PERKINS 2015, p. 57 and ECKSTEIN ALEXANDER, Economic Development Prospects and Problems in China, in: Annals of the American Academy of Political and Social Science, Vol. 402, China in the World Today, July 1972, p. 109.

130 WANG GABE T., China's Population: Problems, Thoughts and Policies, New York 1999, in particular chapter 3.

131 As quoted in: ORLEANS LEO A., China's Science and Technology: Continuity and Innovation, in: US Government Printing Office, People's Republic of China: An Economic Assessment, A Compendium

Regardless this confident assessment, the initial conditions of both countries (Soviet Union in 1928 and China in 1952) differed in important ways. The urban population in China at the time of the first five-year plan was significantly lower than it had been in the Russian Empire, as was the estimated per capita production of grain and available arable land. Under the Soviet's first five-year plan (1928–1932), which also coincided with the first large-scale collectivisation drive, state procurement of grain absorbed about twenty-five percent of total production. The corresponding Chinese figure stood at about twenty-seven percent, despite the fact that average per capita grain output in China was more than forty percent lower than in the Soviet Union. This also explains why resales back to the countryside were much more important in China. As a result, the net procurement ratio (after redistribution) was significantly lower than the gross procurement ratio (before redistribution), even during and immediately after good harvests.[132]

The lower yield of edible grain was a particularly important constraint, as it limited the available surplus from agricultural production. Additionally, China produced far less of all major industrial commodities, such as steel, coal and cement – which is no surprise, as the relative share of the population working in industry was about six times higher in the early Soviet Union.[133]. The consequences were varied and depended directly on the socioeconomic status of Chinese people before the introduction of the first five-year plan. For the industrial workers who became an immediate part of the effort to modernise the country, this basic paradigm, by and large, was an opportunity to participate in modern, largely urban industrial production run by state-owned enterprises that used relatively modern imported technology and production methods as well as receiving benefits in various forms. As Felix Wemheuer has shown, industrial workers in Maoist China enjoyed a higher level of prestige as well as material advantages than any other class officially recognised by the Chinese central government.[134] From this perspective, the founding of the PRC brought, first and foremost, material safety, including reliable employment and the access to basic welfare for millions.

Until 1957, when internal migration in China was still relatively unregulated, this status could, in principle, be achieved by most citizens of the PRC. The result was an increase in the number of people having industrial worker status from eight to twenty-four million and the urban population from 57.5 to 99.4 million between 1949 and 1957.[135] This experience of upwards social mobility was a reality for those who managed to join the ranks of industrial workers during this period. The system provided them with entitlements to public services and urban housing – along with a reasonable expectation that these privileges could be enjoyed until the end of their lives and passed to their children.

---

of Papers submitted to the Joint Economic Committee of the Congress of the United States, 18 May 1972, Washington D.C. 1972, p. 223.

132 Ash Robert, Squeezing the Peasants: Grain Extraction, Food Consumption and Rural Living Standards in Mao's China, in: The China Quarterly, No. 188, December 2005, pp. 971 f.

133 Kosta/Meyer, p. 33 and Singh Ajit, Die politische Ökonomie der sozialistischen Entwicklung in China seit 1949, in: Hennicke Peter (ed.), Probleme des Sozialismus und der Übergangsgesellschaften, Frankfurt am Main 1973, p. 403.

134 Wemheuer 2019, p. 87.

135 Wemheuer 2019, p. 92.

The acceleration in urbanisation related to the expansion of the industrial workforce brought both the expansion of established cities and the creation of new from much smaller settlements. In 1949, there were 136 officially designated cities, a number which rose to 160 in 1952 and 176 in 1957. During the first Chinese five-year plan, cities such as Wuhan, Luoyang, Lanzhou, Taiyuan, Datong, Shijiazhuang, Xian, Chengdu, Zhuzhou, and Baotou formed the new backbone of China's industrialisation, linked to large-scale construction projects implemented there.[136] In order to limit the access to public services and control the influx of internal migrants, the household registration system (*hukou*) was first implemented in cities in 1951 and extended to rural areas in 1955. While the Chinese constitution of 1954 guaranteed citizens the right to free choice of residence, restrictive legislation in January 1958 (notably, the "Decree on Regulations on Household Registration of the People's Republic of China" of the 9th of January 1958) granted state agencies powers to control citizens' mobility through permits and certificates of enrolment or recruitment and thus enshrined the *hukou* nationwide.[137] Since then, it has served both as an instrument of monitoring as well as strict regulation of internal migration in China

For the overwhelming majority of Chinese people who were not able to follow this transition and continued working the land in the countryside, the social as well as economic consequences of the systemic changes were quite different. In its most abstract form, their role within the economy was limited to the use of their often strenuous manual labour for the production of surplus grain to feed those workers and provide raw materials as inputs for industrial production – and eventually exportation.[138] The profits from those exports were designated to procure industrial machinery and equipment as well as oil imported from the Soviet Union. Both were difficult for the PRC to obtain from other sources due to trade restrictions and the shortage of foreign exchange. While the bilateral balance of trade amounted to 178, 133, 126, 200, 163, 94 million rubles in favor of the Soviet Union in the years 1950 to 1955, respectively, Chinese exports surpassed Soviet imports by 28, 174, 223, 131, 28 and 166 million rubles in the years 1956 to 1961, respectively. These figures were considerably higher than what had been provided for by the annual trade protocols, which – at least formally – continued to be binding even after the Sino-Soviet Split.

This did not mean that the rural population was not affected by the national plan or changes of economic policy – quite the opposite was true. After the land reforms of 1947 to1951, over the course of which over forty-three percent of the land was divided among the peasants and traditional rural elites were disbanded – as well as religious sects and criminal gangs.[139] The next stage of restructuring in agricultural production was collectivisation or cooperatisation. Both terms have been used interchangeably and as distinctive parts of collectivisation policies. Cooperatisation (*hezuohua*) was initially

136 He Yimin, Zhou Mingchang, The 156 Projects and New China's Industrial and Urban Development, in: Zhang Xingxing (ed.), Selected Essays on the History of Contemporary China, Leiden and Boston 2015, pp. 64, 69.

137 Chan Kam Wing and Zhang Li, The Hukou System and Rural-Urban Migration in China: Processes and Changes, in: The China Quarterly, No. 160, December 1990, pp. 819 f.

138 Hoeffding Oleg, Sino-Soviet Economic Relations, 1959–1962, in: The Annals of the American Academy of Political and Social Science, Vol. 349, September 1963, p. 97.

139 Wemheuer Felix, Famine Politics in Maoist China and the Soviet Union, New Haven 2014, p. 39.

used as a programmatic term for collectivisation used to establish a distinction from the collective farms in the Soviet Union.[140] Cooperatisation took place in three steps: First, households would form mutual aid groups that would work together during the harvest but would not share any property among themselves. Linking back to existing traditions of family-based mutual aid in agriculture, which is not overly specific to China, institutionalising self-help from above. Similar approaches were encouraged in industry later on through the formula of "socialist cooperation".[141] Second, primary, elementary or lower stage cooperatives were formed by larger numbers of households and produced as a collective. The distribution of whatever was produced still was based on the amount of labour and capital (land, implements, cattle, etc.) that each household contributed individually. Third, the cooperatives were strengthened. Capital was transferred to collective ownership and grain was to be redeemed by each individual on the basis of work points. They were allocated according to overall and individual performance in a given period of time.

There was gradualism in these forms of ownership. According to CHRIS BRAMALL, the higher stage cooperatives established after late 1955 were collectives proper, where land was no longer privately owned and income was distributed solely on the basis of work points.[142] This payment in kind corresponded with the realities of rural lives, as very few consumer goods were available at the time of the first five-year plan that could have been purchased with any *monetary* compensation. Thus, within these cooperatives, the growing and harvesting of crop was, to a large extent, handled through organised division of labour. The improvement of the degree of division of labour within the agricultural production process made it an effective way to promote agricultural specialisation.[143] Farmers in this system were to become "agricultural workers" – employees of economic units receiving wages rather than independent owners of land and capital producers for their households. They were remunerated on the basis of time, effort, skill and also, to a changing degree, political attitude. There again, a distinction needs to be made between members of collective farms and employees of state farms, which were rare. The latter enjoyed numerous benefits comparable to those industrial workers received.

At least since 1957, the basic system of remuneration in Chinese agriculture was based on the work point system. Each task was assigned a certain number of points, and the output of a production unit was subsequently divided between members proportionally to the number of points they had acquired. Therefore, the question which work unit

---

140 WEMHEUER 2019, p. 100. The important distinction concerned the *People's Communes* established during the *Great Leap Forward*, which went further with regard to the position of the individual in the collective.

141 SIDEL R., Self-help and mutual aid in the People's Republic of China, in: KATZ ALFRED H., BENDER EUGENE I. (eds.), The Strength in Us: Self-Help Groups in the Modern World, New York 1976, pp. 216–228.

142 BRAMALL CHRIS, Chinese Economic Development, London and New York 2009, p. 116, FN 26.

143 XU J., Specialization and Agriculture Industry Organization Evolution, Social Sciences Academic Press, Beijing 2008; and for an economic model confirming the presumption, YANG DAN, LIU ZIMIN, Study on the Chinese Farmer Cooperative Economy Organizations and Agricultural Specialization, in: Agricultural Economy, No. 58, Vol 3, 2012, pp. 135–146.

served as the basic unit of accounting had an important effect on an individual's livelihood, as it made the distribution of income more or less socially abstract and flexible. The income of the collective was determined according to the number and value of the work points at the end of the year, after having deducted taxes and contributions to designated funds – usually one for investment and one for worker's welfare such as retirement benefits. This self-management was also significant, as the socialist welfare state had never been fully expanded to the countryside. Most of the rural population were excluded from the "iron rice bowl" that guaranteed industrial employment including a minimum of public services. In the term, the emphasis is on the word "iron", symbolising workplace security. Workers eating from the iron bowl owned their jobs and the associated benefits for life, resulting in the de-commodification of their labour as the main privilege, as employment was to the largest extent assigned by the state.[144]

Self-reliance *within* China mostly applied to the rural population, accounting for more than eighty percent of the Chinese people until after 1980.[145] By and large, it signified that they were economically on their own – while bearing most of the burden of industrial investment. Accordingly, the agricultural economy was, despite the rhetoric of the Cultural Revolution, riddled with thriving black markets, the hiding of seeds and crops, the underreporting of yields, lending the countryside the persistent image of being home to "capitalist tendencies".[146] Nevertheless, private ownership and use of small plots of land around the farms by rural households was generally permitted to supplement the basic needs of the families. Limited in size to five to seven percent of land, these small plots were an important source of individual income and nutrition. Estimates of the income generated by these plots before 1979 fall within a wide range, varying from a low of ten percent to more than thirty percent, with most estimates clustering between fifteen to twenty-one percent.[147]

Although the participation in collective agriculture was formally speaking voluntary, almost the whole rural population had been organised into collectives by late 1956.[148] Taking this step meant that households no longer had the right to withdraw their land from the cooperative and found themselves locked in an entirely new structure of agricultural work. More recent contributions have underlined the significance of rural uprisings in the course of collectivisation, in particular in Western Sichuan in 1954, where a crackdown including the confiscation of farm animals and the destruction of religious buildings led to a series of protests, spreading to Tibet in 1958.[149]

---

144 Wemheuer 2019, p. 17.

145 Today, the share stands at between 30 and 40 percent. See: World Bank Development Indicators.

146 During the later reform era, the same tendencies became a cornerstone of domestic reform in economic policy, as the peasants were understood as needing liberation in order to fully develop their inherent capitalist tendencies, and thus transform themselves into entrepreneurial farmers. For an overview on the debate during the Reform Era, see: Day Alexander F., The Peasant in Postsocialist China, History, Politics and Capitalism, New York 2013, pp. 18 ff.

147 Mead Robert W., China's agricultural reforms: The importance of private plots, in: China Economic Review, No. 11, 2000, p. 55.

148 Wemheuer 2019, p. 100.

149 Elleman Bruce A., Paine S. C. M., Modern China: Continuity and Change, 1644 to the Present, second edition, Lanham, Boulder, New York and London 2019, p. 458. It has been argued that the

This relatively rapid restructuring in parallel to the growing urbanisation was an answer to the fundamental economic challenge described above: The growing number of people living in cities not producing sufficient food for their own subsistence needed to eat, and their traditional suppliers – the market-going richer peasants able to produce a surplus – had been weakened, if not eradicated by land reform and political campaigns. As those who had lost land had seen serious shortages earlier in their lives, their willingness to hand over any surplus to the state without receiving any even basic social security was limited. After serious supply crises in major cities, notably in 1953, the central government reacted by imposing a state monopoly on grain – the "Unified Purchasing and Unified Supply System" – the objectives of which were described by the China News Service in 1974 as follows:

> "The unified purchasing and unified supply policy is a socialist grain distribution system. **It is a socialist, organized and unified grain market to replace the free grain market** [emphasis added]. The state directly purchases from productive units according to a definite quota, and directly sells to consumer units according to a rational price. This fundamentally eliminates speculative activities about grain that jeopardize the welfare of the people and puts grain distribution under national planning. The grains supplied to residents of cities, townships, industrial and mining areas are graded and sufficient in quantity to guarantee meeting their needs. The amount of grain needed by each resident is determined by the area where he lives, his age and his labor intensity. All residents are assured that they have enough grain to eat. For example, the amount of grain for each steel, railway, mining and petroleum worker, who has a high labor intensity, is 30 kilograms per month. This planned supply system which meets the need of every person according to his actual consumption level is different in nature from the grain rationing system of old China and that of capitalist countries."[150]

The system, combined with urban food rationing, was extended to most essential agricultural products until 1957.[151] It sought to ensure the access of the urban population to relatively cheap food and some other basic consumables, albeit in fixed quantities. As proposed by Ralph W. Huenemann, the primary reason for the introduction of the urban rationing system was to combat the inflationary pressures that developed during the 1950s due to progress in industrial production and rising incomes on the one hand and slower agricultural growth on the other.

It is remarkable that at least in this regard, Chinese economic policy was relatively successful. Inflation was effectively restrained, whereas the tension created by the fixing of artificially low prices caused an additional burden on the state budget. According to Kent G. Deng, the urban benchmark daily food intake was 2009 kilocalories per adult

---

process of collectivisation in China was comparably peaceful, in particular by Nolan Peter, Collectivization in China: Some comparisons also arise with the USSR in: The Journal of Peasant Studies, Vol. 3, No. 2, 1976, pp. 192–220.

150 Foreign Broadcast Information Service, Grain Distribution Said more than Adequate for Population, Peking Chung-Kuo Hsin-Wen in Mandarin, 08 11 1974, p. 1, accessed through Readex.

151 Hsu 1984

between 1955 and 1979, which is below the current World Bank's famine relief benchmark of 2185 kilocalories. He argues that the standard of 2600 kilocalories daily, applied under Deng Xiaoping in the 1980s with reference to a "reasonably comfortable life" (*xiaokang*) was, *de facto*, an adoption of the benchmark applied earlier under the Republic of China. For people working on farms, the setting of "rational prices" and was this meant in practice was obviously decisive. Purchase prices were notoriously low until the gradual abolishment of the system in the mid-1980s[152], putting a heavy strain on rural households with relatively little compensation, although the situation changed gradually with an improved supply of consumer goods. The setting of prices and quotas gave the state the possibility to extract whatever surplus needed, at politically defined prices, for the redistribution to urban households or export.[153]

The system also underlined the extractive nature of the development paradigm: Under the valid assumption that grain prices would have risen under market conditions at several points during the history of the PRC, the system had the characteristics of a broad subsidy for the urban population – the cost of which was once again shouldered by rural households.[154] This systemic inequity had the potential to further escalate the growth conflict in China and threaten the legitimation and therefore political power yielded by the CCP. Collectivisation of agricultural production was, in this context, an important instrument to ensure a higher degree of control of rural production and consumption. This way, production was easier to control and integrate in a planned economy than it could have been achieved with individual farms working on their own account and selling their surplus in markets.

While this approach to the financing of industrial modernisation was modified several times in both radical – the Great Leap Forward – and rather incremental ways, it still defined the fundament of the Chinese economy in 1970. It was an important aspect of the Cultural Revolution, in particular in the form of a push for the founding of "People's Communes" and the increase of repression in the procurement as well as the emerging of narratives blaming certain groups – dubbed as "rich peasants" or "landlords" – for resisting the system of procurement and hiding parts of their production.

Mobilising the masses, two disasters and readjustment

Public criticism of China's allegiance to the Soviet model began shortly after Nikita Sergeyevich Khrushchev's speech on de-Stalinisation held on the 14th of February 1956. In April of the same year, the CCP began echoing its basic tenets – the critique of a bureaucracy estranged from the people they were supposed to govern. In his speech on the "Ten Major Relationships", Mao criticised the exaggerated emphasis on heavy industry to the neglect of agriculture and light industry. He admitted grave mistakes committed in the treatment of peasants who had been "squeezed very hard", curbing their enthusiasm for production. The speech was lauded by the chairman of the standing

152 Gao et al. 1996, pp. 45 f.

153 Wemheuer 2019, pp. 104 f, notably figure 3.4 on p. 105.

154 Wang Liming, Davis John, China's Grain Economy: The Challenge of Feeding More Than a Billion, New York 2000.

committee of the National People's Congress and first vice-chairman of the CCP, Liu Shaoqi, at the eighth Party Congress held in Beijing from the 5th to the 23rd of May 1958.

While the inherent hardships of the basic paradigm were acknowledged, the policy solutions decided to address the issue of curbed enthusiasm and moderate growth were in no way intended to give the "squeezed peasants" a breathing period. Quite the opposite, the general spirit of the congress demanded that"all factors must be mobilised, all usable forces mobilised, in the struggle to make our country a modernized, rich and powerful socialist country as rapidly as possible".[155] The strategy of "Three Red Banners" or "Three Red Flags", decided at the second session of the Congress,[156] marked the shift to a more radical approach: the forced and complete collectivisation of agriculture through the People's Communes-movement, catching up industry-wise through the Great Leap Forward and a general speeding-up of socialist construction in what FRANZ SCHURMANN described as the "most momentous instance of ideology in action in the brief history of Chinese Communism".[157]

The particularity of this second phase lies in the strong reliance on mass mobilisation to increase production instead of technocratic planning. Its focus on the most symbolic commodity of industrialisation and its military applications, steel, demonstrated the will to compete with the industrial powers of the West.[158] The propagandistic guidelines that accompanied the strategy emphasised the element of *speed* as a main variable, rallying the CCP and the Chinese people to accomplish what was defined as their historical mission: catching up with and eventually overtaking the aggressors of the Opium Wars, particularly Britain, in the field of production within the following fifteen years or even a shorter period. The slogan "Go all out, aim high, and achieve greater, faster, better and more economical results in building socialism" defined this political line. The level of ambition of the Great Leap Forward was epitomised in the slogan "one day equal to twenty years".[159]

---

155 LOVBRAEK ASBJORN, The Chinese Model of Development, in: Journal of Peace Research, Vol. 13, No. 3, 1976, p. 216.

156 The prominent role and, with regard to general directives, individual responsibility of Mao in the process of policy formulation leading to the *Great Leap Forward* have been thoroughly established; see DIKÖTTER 2010. While Mao did take formal political responsibility in the aftermath of the famine in 1962, and thousands of local cadres were chosen for exemplary punishment, FELIX WEMHEUER has shown that the CCP was finally unable to convince parts of society, and even the party, to accept the official interpretation, as it did not sufficiently take the stark rural-urban divide in China into account. See: WEMHEUER FELIX, Great Leap Famine in the People's Republic of China, in: The China Quarterly, No. 201, March 2010, pp. 176–194. Also, recent scholarship has emphasised the role of other senior members of the political apparatus of the CCP. See e. g. CHUNG YEN-LIN, The Unknown Standard-Bearer of the Three Red Banners: Peng Zhen's Roles in the Great Leap Forward, in: The China Journal, No. 74, July 2015, pp. 129–143.

157 As quoted in SCHELL/DELURY 2013, p. 237.

158 Famously, reference was explicitly made to the goal of "*catching up with Britain in 15 years*" with regard to steel production – a basic innovation of the Industrial Revolution.

159 LI 1995, pp. 374 f.

A disaster in both human and economic terms[160], the undeniable dimension of the policy failure, caused by the utter ignorance of any economic rationality, paved the way for a resurgence of bureaucratic planning. Allowing for the breathing period that had been denied under the "Three Red Banners", favoured stability over huge production-numbers and acknowledged the utmost importance of agriculture for the subsistence of the Chinese people.[161] But disaster never strikes singly. Another challenge arose.

In 1959, with the perilous Great Leap in full swing, China was faced with the withdrawal of its most important foreign investor and source of technology and capital goods, the Soviet Union. Thus, the PRC found itself between the Socialist and Capitalist international systems. As LORENZ LÜTHI has shown, while it is likely that the operation of industrial plants was affected by the sudden withdrawal of technicians, the overall negative effect of the split itself on the economy was moderate. This is certainly also related to the fact that the economy was already in deep crisis by mid-1960. It is indeed difficult to believe that the whole Chinese economy could be dependent on 1'400 foreign experts to such a degree that their disappearance would have caused serious additional shocks. Also, short-term assignments for Soviet experts remained possible until the unilateral suspension of supply contracts in October 1960 by China – motivated also by the fact that raw materials to be delivered to the USSR in exchange for material and services could fetch higher prices on international markets.[162]

On the brighter side, by 1960, the political situation had gone beyond the worst purges and the stabilisation and improvement of production was slowly but steadily revived. After the forced demission of Mao as chairman of the CCP, the top leadership was divided between Liu Shaoqi and Deng Xiaoping, who made the day-to-day decisions in concert.[163] Most remarkably, after 1960, long-term planning in the PRC had lost its position as a main instrument for economic development. This was most pronounced in agriculture, where decentralisation of competences in economic planning was an important method to improve the sufficiency of food. The role of individual households was emphasised and the smaller production groups were strengthened in comparison to the production brigades and People's Communes. The principle "three freedoms and one fixed quota" (*san zi yi bao*) was a key measure. It meant that plots could be allotted for private use to a larger extent than before, goods produced on these plots could be sold on markets and enterprises were "free" to assume responsibility for their own profits and losses. The fixed quota meant that outputs were fixed for individual households in return for the granted freedoms. Production groups were charged with setting up their own production plans and distributing the surplus resulting from their work among their members.[164]

This readjustment marks an important distinction between the Chinese system and socialist economies in, for example, Eastern Europe or the Soviet Union itself. Although

---

160 DIKÖTTER FRANK, Mao's Great Famine, The History of China's Most Devastating Catastrophe, 1958–1962, London and New York 2010.

161 The paradigm of Two Decentralizations, Three Centralizations and One Responsibility. See PERKINS, 2015.

162 LÜTHI LORENZ, The Sino-Soviet Split, Cold War in the Communist World, Woodstock 2008, pp. 178 f.

163 CHENG 2014, p. 120.

164 KOSTA/MEYER 1976, p. 185, and LI 1995, p. 389.

five-year plans continued to be established albeit in a much more generic form, more short-term annual planning became more important for the actual organisation of the economy under the fourth edition. One important objective reason was the recognition of a general lack of reliable statistical data. Among other factors, it made even modest advantages of centralised control difficult to use. This constraint also had spill over-effects. As an example, the risky tendency to focus production on grain and cotton to the detriment of other crops might have been reduced, had it been possible to centralise planning of all production all the way up to Beijing, but this would have required adequate as well as timely data as a basis for informed decisions.[165] While the Chinese planning system had at no point been as centralised as the Soviet, it was further relaxed.[166] Nevertheless, the basic paradigm did not change: the industrial cities remained walled, and the peasants were expected to largely "rely on themselves".

In other aspects, the Chinese readjustment was not unique. The policies resembled post-Stalinist adjustments under Khrushchev in the Soviet Union, and were positively discussed in Soviet media. When further adjustments in Chinese economic policy materialised, Zhou Enlai was even commended as the antithetical embodiment of reason as opposed to the "adventurism" of Mao. This views were also broadcast to China through Soviet stations like radio "Peace and Progress", offering politically tinged interpretations of Chinese history. For example, a program broadcast in January 1976, commented on the Great Leap and its aftermath:

> "Amidst the acute crises caused by the Great Leap Forward, some people among the Peking leadership called for adoption of a pragmatic economic policy [...] a momentary victory of the current of thinking antagonistic to Mao Zedong's idealism. The readjustment policy provided the solution to agricultural reconstruction and development and the production of consumer goods and improved, on this basis, the supply of commodities [...] In industry the planning of production and profits were stressed, and the labor material incentive system was restored. In this respect, Premier of the PRC State Council Zhou Enlai made the greatest contribution. He had [a] profound understanding of what the people's most important interests are. With his sober mind and outstanding fortitude and perseverance, he carried out his activities under adverse conditions within the party and country, which Mao Zedong intentionally created in order to maintain his power."[167]

While local authorities emerged, bearing major responsibility for the restoration of balance in the economy and raising the level of production, the reforms were in no way a

---

165 PERKINS 2015, pp. 87 f.

166 It has been argued that in the years before Mao's death, large parts of the countryside had abandoned the planned economy as a whole – this undermining being an unintended outcome of the *Cultural Revolution*. See: DIKÖTTER 2016, p. xvii.

167 Foreign Broadcast Information Service, Chou lauded for countering Mao's Adventurism, Moscow Radio Peace and Progress in Mandarin to China, 1430 GMT 22 01 1976 TK, accessed through Readex. It may be of anecdotal interest that Marxist-Leninist parties in opposition, like the Communist Party of Switzerland, lauded the criticism against Deng Xiaoping as a "*bourgeois element*", as reported by Xinhua. Foreign Broadcast Information Service, Swiss M-L Organ Lauds PRC's anti-Teng Line, Peking NCNA in English, 1313 GMT, 06 08 1976 OW, accessed through Readex.

"restoration of capitalism". Rather, they reflected attempts to achieve economic recovery and some moderate development still within a socialist framework. Also, while bearing some resemblance with regard to the targeted opening of marginal markets, they were not comparable to deeper reform ambitions in Eastern Europe in the 1960s.[168]

The flexibility introduced in China contrasted starkly with the big push approach of the Great Leap. The policies respected important constraints, notably with regard to the dichotomy between urban industries and the countryside and acknowledged the limitations to productive capabilities of the agricultural sector. Accordingly, agriculture was given priority in terms of investment allocation, followed by light industry and heavy industry. Nevertheless, as Li Choh-Ming quoted Chinese officials commenting the third five-year plan (1963–1967): during its introduction, the longer-term objective was to create better and more stable conditions for the subsequent development of the core heavy industries, not to shift the emphasis away from those and thus change the underlying paradigm.[169] Rather, the resulting pattern had distinctive features of a transitional solution, a breathing period slowing down industrial growth for the sake of stability while in no way abandoning the goal of achieving industrialisation as a long-term goal.[170] The small workshops and backyard-furnaces erected during the Great Leap were mostly closed, restoring the central planning and command system with regard to the production of steel and other industrial products in the industrial state-owned sector, although modifying it to allow much of the planning to take place at the provincial level in practice.[171]

The commune system in agriculture was not abandoned but revised with respect to the levels of ownership, calculation and responsibility. The basic accounting unit that had the authority to determine the income of its members was changed from the People's Communes with their 4'000 to 5'000 families to the much smaller production teams that encompassed about twenty to thirty households. This measure resolved some of the most pressing disproportions with regard to labour incentives in agriculture, as incomes could be adjusted closer to the individual contribution again. As a side-effect, this approach also introduced an amount of competition between households as well as production teams, as the funds that could be used for consumption and welfare depended on the production figures each unit was able to achieve.[172] This was a large step away from communal agriculture back to the collective models of earlier days.

In the same instance, markets for side-line products other than the crops subject to the unified procurement system were tolerated again, and the private family-owned

168 Dernberger Robert F., Radical Ideology and Economic Development in China: The Cultural Revolution and its Impact on the Economy, in: Asian Survey, Vol. 12, No. 12, The Cultural Revolution and its Aftermath, December 1972, p. 1054. Also, there is yet no known evidence that any political exponents actually attempted to abandon socialism at this point in favor of a radically different system.

169 Li Choh Ming, China's Industrial Development, 1958–1963, in: The China Quarterly, No. 17, January-March 1964, pp. 34 f.

170 Cheng 2014, pp. 120 f.

171 Perkins 2015, p. 16.

172 Ibid, pp. 15 ff.

small plots that had proven to be indispensable stabilisers for the low-productivity agricultural sector sensitive to crises were allowed again. Steve Washenko, a US agricultural officer in Hong Kong reported that as a result of the pressures on local cadres, aberrations in policy implementation at the local level had occurred, giving rise to a more flexible handling of non-grain side-line production of crops, as long as the planning targets were reached.[173] Arguably, the Chinese system of food rationing started to turn towards a mixed system of rationing combined with the availability of marketed food and other consumer goods which, according to the model proposed by X.M. Gao, Eric J. Wailes and Gail L. Cramer, in comparison with a purely market-oriented system, was a more equitable and efficient solution.[174]

With regard to productive relations, steps were taken to restore labour discipline and stability by restoring the prerogatives of management as well as re-introducing material incentives as an intentional mechanism to make human motivation a factor that could be reliably controlled. The core regulations of the period were the Revised Work Regulation for Rural People's Communes, the so-called Sixty Articles for Agriculture as well as the Seventy Articles of Industrial Policy. The Sixty Articles defined three levels of organisation: commune, brigade and production team, specifying their rights and obligations. The regulation underlined that private plots could be used by members of the communes, and that products from such plots were *not* included in the calculation of the collective output and protected from being requisitioned by the state.[175] While not as a horizontal right, private property was introduced and evem protected in a very targeted manner.

Generally, the new units worked on their own account – the commune could not request more than three percent of the production team's labour force, and the brigade no more than five percent. If the commune needed to access the public fund of the brigades, such withdrawals required approval by the county's people's committee. The brigade set an output quota as well as a number of work points and an amount for other expenses for the production teams. If the quota was exceeded, the surplus was at the disposal of the production team and its members. The quotas were set at a moderate level, so that a surplus could be realistically achieved on a regular basis. Besides setting clear material incentives for households and individuals, this system also meant that rural cadres lost a lot of their influence and power, as they could not use their positions to simply deny some commune members access to the canteen or arbitrarily decide on work-points.[176]

---

173 Washenko Steve, Better Harvests in People's Republic of China, Strengthen Push for Economic Development, in: US Department of Agriculture, Foreign Agriculture, October 11, Washington D.C. 1971.

174 Huenemann Ralph W., Urban Rationing in Communist China, in: The China Quarterly, No. 26, April-June 1966, pp. 44 ff., Deng Kent G., China's Political Economy in Modern Times: Changes and Economic Consequences 1800–2000, New York 2012, p. 137, Gao X.M., Wailes Eric J., Cramer Gail L., Partial Rationing and Chinese Urban Household Food Demand Analysis, in: Journal of Comparative Economics, No. 22, 1996, pp. 43–62.

175 Ibid.

176 Tang Zaifu, Land and Property Taxation and Fiscal Reform and Land Market Control, in: Ni Pengfei, Zou Linhua, Gao Guangchun, Jiang Xuemei (eds.), Housing Reform and China's Real Estate Industry, Singapore 2020, p. 120.

Decentralisation was not reversed altogether. Particularly in agriculture as well as the production of light industrial and consumer goods, it continued. The process was reflected in the priorities accorded to those sectors, emphasising agriculture and light industries which were both not under direct control of the central government. In tandem with much more moderate production targets, this approach implied that the cities and the countryside, the farm and the factory, the oilfield and the pig-farm could be modernised and people's standard of life improved simultaneously.[177] At least in intention, this was another gradual difference from the Soviet Union's forced industrialisation, with its persistent focus on centralised investment in heavy industry and meticulous quantitative planning of allocation.

Despite this moderation of pace, the paradigmatic distinction between industrial and agricultural work discussed above persisted. It even became epitomised by two symbolic sites, the socialist model units of the "Dazhai production brigade" and the "Daqing oilfield" including the state-owned enterprises that were a part of the large industrial complex built for its exploitation. Both models served the purposes of propaganda as examples demonstrating what the Chinese people were able to achieve "self-reliantly" – which still meant *without* investment funds provided by the central government internally and without foreign aid and capital externally. They also became instruments for the transmission of "best practices" in economic management and organisation in accordance with political doctrine.

Besides their propaganda value as tangible visions of what the socialist way could achieve economically, and how socialist life was supposed to be, both Daqing and Dazhai were manifestations of the principle of self-reliance within China, providing narratives of economic growth achieved by a secluded unit that took care of its own while serving the socialist state.[178] The narrative behind the production brigade of Dazhai was a rather romantic dramatisation of the principle. After seeing their village being destroyed by a flood, so it was purported in the Chinese media, the agricultural workers of Dazhai had proudly refused aid offered by the state in the form of grain, funds or equipment. Instead, on their own initiative, they embraced the socialist revolutionary spirit and transformed their production unit into an agricultural powerhouse. The slogan, "in agriculture, learn from Dazhai" (*nong ye xue Dazhai*) was launched on the 26th of December 1964, Mao's birthday.[179]

Allegedly, the Minister of Agriculture, Liao Luyan, was sent to Dazhai in the spring of 1964 to find out about the achievements of the about eighty households belonging to the brigade. The report he delivered on the 25th of May of the same year was the basis for a conference of the CCP Central Committee to discuss enduring difficulties in agricultural

177 In principle, investment in the industries would be limited to the surplus generated in agriculture within the reasonable quotas set for production teams.

178 Or, as a critical Soviet article put it in 1975: "In industry and agriculture the Maoist leadership continues to pursue a policy aimed at dividing the country's population into closed production units like the [Daqing] oil fields and the large Dazhai production team, which must meet its own needs and provide the state with an opportunity for extorting the necessary funds for implementing the country's militarization." Foreign Broadcast Information Service, Fedoseyev Article on Peking's Economic Policy, Moscow Trud in Russian, 21 03 1975, p. 3, LD, accessed through Readex.

179 Li 1995, pp. 297 f.

production. The Dazhai campaign was interrupted by the Cultural Revolution, but had a public relaunch with an editorial in Renmin Ribao on the 23th of September 1970. The editorial stated that "the course of Dazhai is the course of building socialism under the guidance of Mao Zedong Thought", anchoring the model in the ideological basis of the PRC. The first conference on "learning from Dazhai in agriculture" was held after the fourth People's Congress between the 15th of September and the 19th of October 1975.[180]

Continuing to rely on political guiding principles and slogans of the Great Leap, the model that Dazhai offered was clear: agricultural modernisation was required to happen with as little state investment as possible. The conferences for the discussion of the implementation of these models, for example, the national and provincial Conferences on "Learning from Dazhai in Agriculture" and "Learning from Daqing in Industry" became focal points for discussions on economic policies throughout the country. Surely, these model brigades became almost religious ideals, framed as examples of Mao Zedong Thought "in action", frequently cited in speeches and articles. On the other hand, they were not actual blueprints forced upon brigades, and therefore not widely implemented *tel quel*. FROLIC quoted a worker from the South, "It may work for [Dazhai], but it is premature for us. In our commune we need material incentives. We lack [Dazhai's] spirit and political consciousness".[181]

In absence of a confirmed central plan for the longer term, the method of transmitting idealised models for economic development (earlier the "Yunnan base" had served a similar function) was a viable tool to set standards and clarify the expectations of the socialist state. Daqing survived as a formula long after the beginning of Reform and Opening as a model for state owned enterprises, in particular, in the raw materials sector. It was continuously modified to suit the contemporary economic paradigm. In 1990, General Secretary of the CCP Jiang Zemin summarised the Daqing by including the now dominant element of patriotism in the formula:

> "The patriotic spirit of winning honor for the nation, the spirit of being pioneering, independent and self-reliant, the spirit of seeking truth from facts, bearing a scientific attitude, being honest in the cause and strict in the work, and as the spirit of being devoted to the nation in general."[182]

The campaigns to promote the establishment of Daqing- and Dazhai-type enterprises and communes all over the country were combined with the publication of the best practices and guidelines such as the eight-point charter for agriculture.[183]

---

180 Ibid.

181 FROLIC, 1978, Fn. 8. DAVID ZWEIG suggested that the post-1978 reform policies had the model brigades as an important anchor point for debates on economic policy, as the "radicals" of the Gang of Four used the Dazhai-brigade as a revolutionary model for Chinese agriculture, mobilising the leader of the brigade Chen Yonggui to campaign for the abolishment of ownership and accounting at the level of work teams. See: ZWEIG DAVID, Agrarian Radicalism in China, 1968–1981, Cambridge 1989.

182 HAN ZHEN, ZHANG WEIWEN, Contemporary Value Systems in China, Beijing 2018, p. 101.

183 WASHENKO 1971, p. 4.

Towards more turmoil

The bundle of measures during readjustment has been referred to as the New Economic Policy, in reference to the eponymous period in the 1920s Soviet Union.[184] It resulted in a steady recovery of both industrial and agricultural production as well as the adjacent sectors of research and education. It also laid the foundation for remarkable technical and technological achievements notably in sectors related to the defense industries. While still being a poorer country in comparison, the PRC had made a number of technological and industrial achievements, demonstrating that a system of central planning could have its merits when it came to large and targeted projects, often of military application. They included the launch of a nuclear bomb in October 1964 and the first Chinese satellite in April 1970.

Certainly, those were relatively confined projects, demonstrating the impressive performance of the top tier Chinese industries that actually *were* under centralised control. It is interesting to note that similar to other areas – while investment was diverted from other areas perhaps more useful for the livelihood of the Chinese people – the approach of the Chinese leadership to nuclear armament was relatively modest. While already in 1956 Mao had stated that "In today's world, in order to prevent being bullied by others, we must possess these things [nuclear weapons]", the principles raised for the procurement were "to have [at all] (*you dian*), to have a few (*shao dian*)" and "of good quality (*hao dian*)". This view on nuclear weapons as a necessary deterrent against the other nuclear powers continued under Deng Xiaoping, who, due to his role in the military, may have influenced them in the first place.[185]

Nonetheless, the result of the breathing period was not a new lasting consensus within the CCP. In 1962, the Socialist Education Campaign was launched on Mao's initiative to address the concern that the newly found stabilisation of the economy, together with its emphasis on calculus and economics before politics, could cause the country to unalterably turn towards bureaucratic rule. The movement was the largest and perhaps most controversial political campaign involving rural areas throughout the 1960s, mirroring internal struggles within the CCP as a reaction to attacks against the Three Red Banners at a large party meeting in January 1962, after which Mao succeeded in putting class struggle to the forefront of intra-party controversies. While in the beginning, the declared objective of the movement was tackling administrative problems in the economy through the "four clean-ups" (clean up work points, account books, warehouses and assets), these were later overshadowed by more politically defined "four clean-ups" (clean up politics, the economy, ideology and organisation). The programme was refined in the so-called "10-Point-Decision" (a more radical and a revised version in the course of 1963), and the so-called "23-Point-Decision" adopted by the CCP Central Committee in January 1965, enshrining class struggle and the "political" "four clean-ups" as guidelines for the movement.

---

184 SCHURMANN FRANZ, China's "New Economic Policy" – Transition of Beginning, in: The China Quarterly, Vol. 17, March 1964, pp. 65–91.

185 SHIXIU BAO, Deterrence Revisited: Outer Space, in: China Security, Winter 2007, p. 6.

David S. Goodman has noted that the implementation on the provincial level was far from strict and, in some cases – as in Guizhou and Sichuan – practically non-existent. First, because the provincial leadership had partly lost political control over "their" provinces during the Great Leap; second, because there was disagreement regarding the direction of the movement.[186] Furthermore, following the models of Daqing and Dazhai was mostly lip-service. With regard to the economy, the Socialist Education Campaign was more perfunctory than real.[187] In that view, the Cultural Revolution was a rather radical reaction to the fact that production followed guidelines merely to the extent that they proved practicable.

The ensuing ideological conflict within China – which at the top level was frequently framed as a power struggle between Mao Zedong and his designated successor, Lin Biao, on one side and the duo Liu Shaoqi and Deng Xiaoping on the other – burst out in public on several occasions, leading ultimately to radicalisation within the CCP and the beginning of the Cultural Revolution. The complexity of motives behind the initiation of the Cultural Revolution is subject to an extensive literature. Ronald Coase and Ning Wang suggested that Mao's instinctive hostility toward centralisation could not tolerate a return to central planning for a long time – hence, the elimination of government bureaucracy as a central objective of the movement. Mao Zedong failed to recognise that an attack on the apparatus responsible for the organisation of large-scale economic activity would lead to a vicious circle of centralisation, rigid military rule and decentralisation for many years.[188]

Over the course of the campaign, two things became apparent: First, the Chinese leadership had seriously underestimated the extent of disruption and brutality the mass movement had caused.[189] In addition, the position of the CCP as the centre of political power was increasingly being challenged, as the criticism of "capitalist roaders" directly affected a growing number officials. Second, the revolutionary movement strongly interfered with the economy, which had not been intended even by Mao. The maxim that it was "absolutely imperative that production not be impeded" by the movement was underlined in an editorial in Renmin Ribao, issued in November 1966:

> "The national economy is an integral totality [...] if any particular unit is affected, the system may be affected. [...] Therefore, the Cultural Revolution in the factories and communes must be conducted in spare time only [...] In short, we must carry out the Cultural Revolution while at the same time making our production better, better, and even better!"[190]

186 Goodman David S., Centre and Province in the People's Republic of China: Sichuan and Guizhou, 1955–1965, London, New York and La Rochelle 1986, pp. 183 ff. Internal disputes on the focus and extent of the movement, in particular between Liu Xiaoqi and Mao Zedong, are important factors leading to inner-party radicalisation, expressed in the beginning of the *Cultural Revolution* on 16 May 1966. See: Li 1995, pp. 401 f.

187 Dernberger 1972, p.1055.

188 Coase Ronald, Wang Ning, How China became Capitalist, Houndmills 1988, p. 19.

189 Particularly with Mao Zedong sending contradictory signals. See: Wu 2014, pp. 66 f., and Tang Tsou, The Cultural Revolution and Post-Mao Reforms, A Historical Perspective, Chicago and London 1986, pp. 82 ff.,

190 As quoted by Wu 2014, p. 98.

The basic arguments on economic policy that can be identified with regard to the Cultural Revolution were known from decades of debate on the "correct" course, and they corresponded largely with the "red lines" of Mao Zedong Thought on the economy discussed which I address briefly below. The first demand was that "politics had to take command" – which meant that economic arguments based on experience or theory that took the development of productive forces as a starting point were unacceptable when used to counter political arguments along the "correct" line of thought. Moreover, economic constraints could not be given excessive regard, as they hindered the unfolding of the potential of the masses.[191] The reason was that, if having "production in command" was accepted, the socialist transformation process towards communism would be put off, perhaps indefinitely, as it was perceived to have happened in the "reactionary" Soviet Union.

The second demand was a general struggle against bureaucracy, in particular against its hierarchically organised form, within the units of production, the state administration and, arguably to a lesser degree, the party. At least the latter was limited for members who had the position and influence to protect themselves from serious political criticism. That the critique of bureaucracy was framed as a conflict between Maoism and a Soviet-style bureaucratic form of statehood and administration did not prevent Mao to call in the PLA, as soon as party rule was seriously threatened. As a response to emerging "anarchic currents" within the movement, Mao claimed that the Cultural Revolution should be properly understood as a revolution under the "dictatorship of the proletariat", which referred to the CCP as the Leninist vanguard party as well as the organs of the Chinese socialist state.[192]

Cutting through hierarchical bureaucracy was based on the underlying ideological argument that it would free the masses and give their abilities full play to break China from poverty and underdevelopment. The necessity of technical expertise and innovation – even through the import of foreign technology – was not denied. Finally, and perhaps most consequentially, class struggle was to be reinvigorated, as it had lost its momentum during the moderate years of economic readjustment. This concerned the demands for the elimination of income differentials and creation of an equilibrium in living standards both between and within different sectors as well as the replacement of the material incentives introduced during the preceding period of readjustment. Furthermore, the elimination of the main flexibilities introduced by private plots and rural markets as well as profit as a driver for the allocation of resources were to be abolished.[193]

The breathing period seemed to be over, as China entered the 1970s with turmoil and struggle seemingly reigning supreme. Rather arcane political slogans and controlled debates on ideological purity seemed once again to trump pragmatism and government action that was actually beneficial for the lives of the Chinese people and the overarching objective of modernisation. But what did those slogans have to say about the economy,

---

191 Leading, at least temporarily, to a shift in priorities from economic to ideological criteria in public political discourse. See: DITTMER 2010, pp. 46 f.

192 WU 2014, pp.192 f., and KING WHYTE MARTIN, Bureaucracy and Modernization in China: The Maoist Critique, in: American Sociological Review, Vol. 38, No. 2, April 1973, pp. 149–163.

193 DERNBERGER 1972, p. 1057.

if anything at all? Before turning to the events of this decade, the relationship between economic policy and the ideological framework of Mao Zedong Thought within which the former was formulated deserves consideration.

A political economy of Mao Zedong Thought?

In the course of a visit of a Singaporean delegation in the PRC in May 1976, less than four months before Mao's death, the delegation was brought to Dazhai to visit the model brigade. Prime Minister Lee Kuan Yew, who headed the delegation, was not impressed:

> "In the Daqing oilfields the model workers did not extract the maximum from the ground because of poor technology, and their yields were going down. Revolutionary fervour could not make up for expertise whether in agriculture nor in mining. The belief in the Mao era, "Better Red than Expert" was a fallacy, a fraud practised on the people. [...] the relentless assault of the huge slogans [...] was a surrealistic experience. To have [them] blaring forth from loudspeakers in railway stations and public parks and on the radio numbed the senses. We found little of such fervour in the people [...]. It was a Chinese kind of Potemkin village. [...]
>
> Towards the end of the tour, some fraternisation took place between their officials and members of my party who could speak Mandarin. They bantered as they helped each other to the dishes at dinner, saying ironically 'zi li geng sheng', one of the slogans Mao promoted: 'self-reliance, self-help', meaning, I will help myself to the food, there is no need for you to serve me. [...] Behind the disciplined exterior of the communist cadre was a human being who appreciated good food and good wines [...]"[194]

Although Lee's attitude towards the PRC and its political leadership certainly was critical, his demonstratively underwhelmed impressions are comprehensible. Many of the slogans used excessively and in particular with regard to production were certainly bland, without joy and often repetitive to an almost sacral extent. At times, the socialist slang seemed to be closer to the field of organised religion than of politics. Also, as Lee reports, it is only human to assume that many Chinese coped with the blaring propaganda through healthy irony, particularly after the harsh realities of the Great Leap and the Cultural Revolution had discredited at least the more radical approaches. However, to understand the implications of economic policies and the history of ideas behind during a period in which Mao still exercised political control and was used as an ideological point of reference, his political thought and particularly its public manifestations and interpretations must be taken into account. While the much quoted radical taglines "better red and expert" and "revolutionary fervour over expertise" certainly are parts of Mao Zedong Thought, it also included aspects that not only allowed, but even legitimised experiments and compromises.

The *public persona* of Mao Zedong and his role as a charismatic leader is influenced by numerous legends that were developed and spread actively by his arduous supporters and the CCP as well as by his critics and political enemies. The biographical accounts on

194 LEE 2000, p. 652.

Mao are still the subject of strong controversies in and outside of China. He has been described, among other things, as the "Emperor of the Blue Ants"[195], military strategist[196], nationalist leader of peasants[197], the "Chinese Lenin"[198], Philosopher King[199], greatest Marxist-Leninist of the present age[200], a new Emperor with his Harem[201], anti-authoritarian revolutionary or even, of course, the "Chinese Hitler"[202]. Unlike almost any other politician in modern times, Mao has stirred and provoked controversies and projections, some of which might say more about the current *Zeitgeist* in the west than the actual person he was.[203] With regard to an analysis of economic policies under his rule and after, his role and influence as a largely self-declared political theorist merits a closer look.

When discussing the implications of the Maoist interpretation of Marxism for economic policies, and the political limits of the possible it sets within its normative framework, two introductory remarks need to be made. First, an analytical perspective on his writings does not seek to "rehabilitate" the political person Mao nor the intended as well as the overtly or implicitly accepted consequences and toll on human life[204] and well-being of his deeds, under his direct and indirect leadership or in his responsibility.[205] These

195 As in PALOCZI-HORVATH GEORGE, Mao Tse-Tung, Emperor of the Blue Ants, London 1962.

196 DESHINGKAR GIRI, Mao Zedong's Military Thought: A Perspective, in: China Report, No. 31, Vol. 1, February 1995.

197 BENDIX REINHARD, Reflections on Charismatic Leadership, in: Asian Survey, No. 6, Vol. 7, June 1967, p. 341–352; and NÄTH MARIE L., Chinas Weg in die Weltpolitik, Berlin and New York 1976, pp. 50 f.

198 The US Time Magazine mentioned Mao in 1935 for the first time as *"the Chinese Lenin"*, reporting that he had "no fixed headquarters or abode but moves with his Chinese Soviet Government in nomadic fashion from province to province [...] ill that he has to be carried on a stretcher". Quoted from: HAYFORD CHARLES W., Mao's Journeys to the West, in: CHEEK TIMOTHY (ed.), A Critical Introduction to Mao, New York 2010, p. 316.

199 A picture of Mao Zedong that appears to be favored by the CCP after his death. In the West, the account of Edgar Snow has in particular been critically attributed with the spread of this image. See: PANTSOV, ALEXANDER V., LEVINE STEVEN I., Mao: The Real Story, New York 2012, p. 2.

200 As specified in a communiqué adopted at the eight CCP Central Committee. See: Mao Zedong, Important documents on the Great Proletarian Cultural Revolution in China, Beijing 1970, pp. 154 and 173. This assessment appears to have been officially reversed in China soon after. See: SCHRAM STUART R., Mao Zedong a Hundred Years On: The Legacy of a Ruler, in: The China Quarterly, No. 137, March 1994, p. 136.

201 Most famously purported by his personal physician Li Zhisui in his memoir. LI ZHISUI, The Private Life of Chairman Mao, New York 1996.

202 A description which appears to be exclusive to the West, notably the US.

203 As suggested by WEMHEUER 2010, p.9.

204 Comparisons between the number of victims of several leading figures of the 20th century appears to remain of public interest. Mao Zedong has more recently been referred to as "the greatest mass murderer in world history" (The Independent, 17 September 2010), with the Great Leap Forward as the "biggest mass murder in history" (Washington Post, 3 August 2016). It holds true that political violence was used in China, and that many millions starved to death under Mao Zedong.

205 Concerning the famine of 1962, Mao Zedong formally acknowledged his personal responsibility for the failure of the Great Leap Forward in the name of the Chinese central government – which led to the punishment of numerous cadres. Until today, the debate regarding responsibility of the catastrophe remains difficult; the official interpretation of the CCP is disputed within China

consequences are the subject of justified debate and a great number of studies[206]. The rule of the CCP and the shaping of the Chinese society towards a socialist system included violent means and does certainly not in any way conform to today's conceptions of fundamental values including human rights or any principles of good governance – which are in themselves important cultural achievements. Second, it would be misleading to frame Mao as any kind of economic theorist or even a politician who had any kind of consistent agenda on national economic policy. The approach of identifying political compromises and experiments that sought to achieve economic modernisation presentedin this book does not intend to identify a set of choices forming a doctrine of what might be plausibly called "Maoist economics".[207] The relation between Mao Zedong Thought and the economic policies implemented or envisaged appear to have been rather opposing at times, with a "best of-compilation" of general sayings and slogans attributed to Mao being quite freely reinterpreted to make them fit what actually happened on the farms and in the factories or what was intended to happen there in the future.

Accordingly, until at least the end of 1978, the concepts used by Mao to formulate the general direction of economic policies were used to justify and legitimise various policies which, despite some substantive changes, relied on his generalised remarks made at different points in time on how a socialist economy was supposed to work in China. For the analysis of economic policies during "Late Maoism", as presented in this book, basic differences between the Soviet "blueprint" and the Maoist approach are of particular interest. To encapsulate some of the main programmatic differences, I reference some of the core materials Mao's wherein views on the great lines of political economy are reflected.

After the spectacular Long March, which had decisively strengthened his position within the Chinese communist movement[208], Mao developed the basic principles of his

---

itself. See: WEMHEUER FELIX, Dealing with Responsibility for the Great Leap Famine in the People's Republic of China, in: The China Quarterly, No. 201, March 2010, pp. 176–194.

206 The earliest monograph providing a general history of the famine is arguably BECKER 1996. The account by Mao's former secretary (LI 1999) focused on central policies and changing strategies of the Chairman. More recent contributions like YANG 2008 and DIKÖTTER 2010 provide a more in-depth perspective based on files from provincial archives. The volumes edited by MANNING and WEMHEUER 2011 as well as DING and SONG 2009 include articles written by Western and Chinese scholars on the topic and present an overview of the state of research. For critical reviews see: Ó GRÁDA CORMAC, Great Leap into Famine: A Review Essay, in: Population and Development Review, Vol. 37, No. 1, 2011, pp. 191–202; WEMHEUER FELIX, Sites of Horror: Mao's Great Famine, in: The China Journal No. 66, 2011, pp. 155–162; GARNAUT ANTHONY, Hard Facts and Half-Truths: The New Archival History of China's Great Famine, in: China Information, Vol. 27, No. 2, 2013, pp. 223–246.

207 Attempts in this direction were undertaken in the 1960s and 1970s; see in particular: HOFFMANN CHARLES, The Maoist Economic Model, in: Journal of Economic Issues, Vol. 5, No. 3, September 1971, pp. 12–27; GRAY JACK, The Economics of Maoism, in: Bulletin of the Atomic Scientists, Vol. 25, No. 2, 1969, pp. 42–51; and PATNAIK UTSA, The Economic Ideas of Mao Zedong on Agricultural Transformation and its Relation to Capital Formation and Industrialization, in: China Report, Vol. 31, No. 1, 1995, pp. 87–100.

208 The narrative of the *Long March* as a heroic feat proving the leadership skills of Mao Zedong has been criticised, notably by CHANG and HALLIDAY, who argued that the myth around the episode has diverged so far from reality that its validity is questionable as a whole. Notably,

political philosophy, later canonised as Mao Zedong Thought. ANTHONY JAMES GREGOR has suggested that the idea of formulating a political program and doctrine was directly inspired by Stalin's writings. In order to survive as an economically retrograde country, this meant that some of the expectations, prescriptions and proscriptions central to Marxism were abandoned right away. The ideological term Mao Zedong Thought (*mao zedong si xiang*) was first introduced as a concept by Wang Jiaxiang, vice-chairman of the Central Military Commission, in Yunnan province's Jiefang Ribao on the 8th of July 1943, which stated in a reverent manner:

> "The correct course of Chinese national liberation, whether it is in the past, present, or future, is the course that follows Comrade Mao Zedong's thought. This is the course that has been pointed out by Comrade Mao Zedong in his writings and through his practical work. Mao Zedong Thought is China's Marxism and Leninism, China's Bolshevism, and China's Communism. Mao Zedong Thought and the correct course of the Chinese Communist Party's national liberation have emerged, developed, and matured through struggles against domestic and foreign enemies and through struggles against the incorrect ideologies within the communist party".

At its seventh National Congress held in Shaanxi province from April to June 1945, the CCP officially adopted Mao Zedong Thought as the party's guiding ideology.[209]

One important conflict between Hua Guofeng and Deng Xiaoping after the death of Mao revolved notably around the relationship between Mao Zedong Thought and Marxism-Leninism, particularly the aspects of the latter that were or could be read in favor of an economic paradigm applying material incentives, centralised planning and the use of all advanced technology that could be acquired. In 1981, the Resolution on Certain Questions in the History of our Party since the Founding of the PRC, published by the CCP Central Committee, re-examined the role of Mao Zedong Thought, affirming that "Mao Zedong was a great Marxist and a great proletarian revolutionary, strategist, and theorist [...] His contributions to the Chinese revolution far outweigh his mistakes. His merits are primary and his errors secondary." While six aspects – the new-democratic revolution, the socialist revolution, socialist construction, the building of a revolutionary army and military strategy, on policy and tactics, on ideological, political and cultural work, and on party building – were affirmed as positive, notably the Three Red Banners, "leftist errors" (meaning "excessive targets, the issuing of arbitrary directions, boastfulness and the stirring up of a communist wind"), the widening and absolutisation of class struggle, the treatment of cadres during the Socialist Education Movement and primarily the Cultural Revolution were criticised as errors. Most importantly, after 1981, Mao Zedong Thought was treated as a concept of the past.[210]

Arguably, the foundations of Mao Zedong Thought were created in the fortress city of Yunnan, were he worked on the theoretical justification for his line, aware of the fact that

---

they emphasised the importance of Soviet influence on the strategic decisions of the CCP. CHANG JUNG, HALLIDAY JON, Mao, The Unknown Story, New York 2005, pp. 119–167.

209 GREGOR ANTHONY JAMES, Marxism and the Making of China, New York 2014, pp. 141–165. See: LI 1995, p. 265.

210 LI 1995, pp. 265 ff.

it deviated from the dogmas pursued in particular by Moscow at the time. PRIESTLAND has suggested that the difficulties of adapting the complex Marxist-Leninist terminology and concepts to the Chinese language alone had led to their intermixing with traditional Chinese mythology, notably the utopian vision of a "future golden age"[211]. Furthermore, his early interest in and remarks on dialectics and the conflict between opposites have been perceived as resembling the Daoist theory on ever co-existing opposites, which is a viable approach to explain his – for once – comparably consistent insistence on the dialectic nature of politics and power.[212] Nevertheless, Mao's "sinified".[213] Marxist ideology was not specifically Chinese but came down to an initially radical and egalitarian as well as inherently militaristic variety of communism well-suited for the ideological needs of a guerrilla army in dire need of the support of the local population.[214]

Despite his relatively frequent references to Karl Marx in his writings, the foundation of Mao Zedong Thought had distinct Leninist traits for practical reasons, notably including the idea that the capitalist stage of socio-political development could be omitted or at least sped up politically, while emphasising the role of peasants as a revolutionary base – which was an obvious theorisation of the actual circumstances which the Chinese communist movement faced. Different from the Saint-Simonian, Leninist or late-Marx emphasis on technologically enabled progress, Taylorism-based industrialisation and rational economic organisation, the focus of Maoist political thought was, since its inception, focused on the potential of organised human will and ideological motivation, resulting in the concept of the "mass line". Faith in the mass' creativity and enthusiasm as an important factor for the achievement of social change as well as economic development was a core tenet of Mao's writings as well as the rhetoric of the CCP at least well into the 1980s.

Even during the period of New Democracy, the participatory aspects of the Chinese state were at best *granted* by a centralised political leadership – which, in the form of the CCP was highly centralised. Despite several processes of decentralisation in other areas of the state, including in the economic sphere, it has remained so. GRAHAM YOUNG among others has argued that Mao Zedong nevertheless shared the skepticism concerning the efficacy and possibility of mass activity as a political tool central to Leninist thought, as the masses could only be guided, not controlled. Mao Zedong's writings as

---

211 PRIESTLAND 2014, pp. 317 f.

212 See e. g. KOLLER JOHN M., Philosophical Aspects of Maoist Thought, in: Studies in Soviet Thought, Vol. 14, No. 1/2, March-June 1974, pp. 47–59.

213 The term was established in a report to the sixth plenum of the CCP Central Committee in 1938, where Mao Zedong asserted: "A Communist is a Marxist internationalist, but Marxism must take on a national form before it can be applied. There is no such thing as abstract Marxism, but only concrete Marxism. What we call concrete Marxism is Marxism that has taken on a national form, that is, Marxism applied to the concrete struggle in the concrete conditions prevailing in China and not Marxism abstractly used". Quoted from CHENG 2014, p. 40.

214 In her global history approach on Maoism, JULIA LOVELL emphasised its flexibility as an important aspect of its appeal as a transnational ideology. Mao Zedong's insistence on the primacy of practice and his call to adapt Soviet approaches to reality in China made his concepts and himself a "living advertisement" for the flexible molding of communist ideas to a national context, inspiring communist nationalisms around the world. LOVELL JULIA, Maoism: A Global History, London 2019.

well as his political activities consequently underline to the need for strong party leadership as the "highest form" of organisation of the proletariat, providing the revolutionary direction through the union of Marxist-Leninist "universal truths" with the concrete practice of the Chinese revolution.[215]

The first written example of a somewhat consolidated collection of Mao Zedong's thoughts on the national economy can be found in notes and commentaries made on the Soviet textbook Political Economy in 1960.[216] Other than Marx, and much more so than Lenin, Mao saw peasants as a strong revolutionary force. Nevertheless, he never disputed the main dictum shared by both that finally the world, and thus political power, would be inherited by industrial workers.[217] The problem to be solved by economic policies was to enable China to produce a class of industrial workers in the first place.

There was no Chinese version of the Soviet "great industrialisation debate" as a distinct period of discourse on economic paradigms within the CCP but, instead, continuous debates and struggles over strategies for the achievement of socialist construction were present.[218] Even at the height of the Cultural Revolution, the importance given by Mao to industrial production could be perceived by the public. As, for example, the amount of aluminium used for the production of Mao badges grew to excessive heights, Mao famously intervened in 1969 stating "give me back my aeroplanes".[219]

As in other communist movements – socialist movements with the declared intention to achieve a state of communism one day as mentioned above – the transformation of people's attitudes with regard to their roles in society was a main tenet of Mao Zedong Thought. This stood in absolute contradiction particularly to what might be called the "liberal" or "neoclassic" conception, famously simplified as the "homo oeconomicus"[220]; according to which individual self-interest, if left to itself and unfolding in market relations that are unfettered by external influence such as unnecessary state intervention, finally serves the common good by contributing to the maximisation of welfare. Within the frame of reference of Mao Zedong Thought, human beings could be led by the state to make selfless contributions for said common good through the power of ideas, as long as they were properly taught and discussed. Mao's professional background as a teacher might have influenced these views.

This particular concept of human motivation, notably with regard to complex production processes, found its political encapsulation in the issue of material incentives to influence a person's motivation, explaining some of the intensity of ideological conflict around the question in the PRC. The strength of this ideological opposition may also partly be explained by the insight that such incentives do yield empirically recognisable

---

215 Young Graham, On the Mass Line, in: Modern China, Vol. 6, No. 2, April 1980, p. 226.

216 Published in the west, e. g., as Martin Helmut (ed.), Mao Tse-tung, Das machen wir anders als Moskau!, Kritik an der sowjetischen Politökonomie, Hamburg 1975.

217 Priestland 2014, pp. 318 f.

218 Tse 1977, p. 208.

219 Which also illustrates the importance granted by Mao Zedong to military armament as a motive to develop and maintain industrial capacities. Quote from: Dikötter 2016, p. 100.

220 For an innovative critique, see: Urbina Dante A., Ruiz-Villaverde Alberto, A Critical Review of Homo Economicus from Five Approaches, in: American Journal of Economics and Sociology, Vol. 78, No. 1, 2019, pp. 63–93.

results, at least for a certain time, and therefore can be seen as seductive instruments. The constraints imposed on an individual's selfishness that might lead to actions detrimental to society – which is supposed to happen in the liberal conception through factual pressure and constraints resulting from competition – would also be set by ideas. In a similar vein, once workers had understood their role in the underlying undertaking of building socialism and later a communist society, individual motivation to contribute to production would become primarily based on their will to do so, and not on individual advantages and incentives.

In China, as Mao Zedong noted in 1958, conditions for an economic paradigm based on ideas were particularly favourable, as the Chinese people were both "poor and blank"[221] after the historical divide with the end of centuries-long imperial rule. In a critique written in the early years of the Great Leap (1958–1960), Mao formulated three main aspects of Soviet policies which, in his view, had been erroneous.

First, in his view, the masses of workers and peasants in the Soviet Union had not been given sufficient opportunities to participate in economic policy making. The idea of collectivisation through expropriation carried out by the government was dismissed too hastily as a "rightist deviation", combined with an all too tight control of the peasantry. Second, Mao criticised the idea of industrialisation as a necessary precondition for collectivisation as wrong, insisting on the importance of "moving forward from collectives to ownership by the whole people". Insisting already in a speech "On the question of agricultural cooperatization" in July 1955 that "only on the basis of co-operatized large-scale management will agriculture be able to make use of the supply from heavy industry of tractors and other farm machines, chemical fertilizers, modern transportation equipment, kerosene, electricity etc.". Mao argued that the demand created by a growing industry and the income created by "large-scale agriculture" would raise this rate of accumulation as well as allow for the increased availability of consumer goods produced by the industry – in particular, by light industries that would eventually be built. Also, Mao Zedong expressed his awareness of the fact that the Chinese primary sector, as it

221 "China's 600 million people have two remarkable peculiarities: they are, first of all, poor, and secondly blank. That may seem like a bad thing, but it is really a good thing. Poor people want change, want to do things, want revolution. A clean sheet of paper has no blotches, and so the newest and most beautiful words can be written on it, the newest and most beautiful pictures can be painted on it". In particular, when keeping in mind the ideas expressed by Italian Communist, Antonio Gramsci, this remark bears a relevant insight for the discussion of the success of Chinese Communism. Indeed, both institutions and *organic* exponents advocating ideas were subject to serious turmoil, with the abolishment of "old ideas" being demanded by several intellectual and social movements in early 20th century China. An "entrenched" social order comparable to those found in industrialised countries of Western Europe certainly did not prevail. Also, there is a certain irony in the fact that similar ideas, today referred to as *blank slate*-theories – with regard to individuals – have been formative for liberal images of man and continue to be divisive. For a critique, see: PINKER STEVEN, The Blank Slate: The Modern Denial of Human Nature, New York 2016; JOHN MARSH has even established the connection with Mao's concept, see: MARSH JOHN, Liberal Delusion: The Roots of Our Current Moral Crisis, Bury St. Edmunds 2012, pp. 109 f.

stood in 1955, would not be able to produce sufficient raw materials for the ambitious development of industry the CCP envisaged.[222]

His dismissal was combined with a general critique of "unbalanced" development in the Soviet Union, emphasising the importance of "walking on two legs" – developing heavy industry, agriculture and light industry in parallel – while not dismissing the general aim of building a heavy industrial base.[223] Third, Mao Zedong criticised the status assigned to the so-called "middle peasants" under Stalin as well as underestimating the dangers that the acceptance even of limited private property and subsidiary occupations posed to the integrity of the socialist system, as they stood in the way of changing the ideological consciousness as a necessary condition for advancing the revolutionary process. Mao accused Stalin of erring in his analysis of rural social classes and the closely related issues of equality and incentives. He dismissed Stalin's assertion that following collectivisation, middle peasants became the principal figures in rural villages as unsatisfactory.

Accepting this, in the view of Mao, was bound to make poorer peasants feel as if they had been "put in the shade", meaning that they did not participate in the revolutionary achievements. Also, this approach opened, in his view, the way for the same middle peasants to assume leadership that not only challenged party rule but also induced rural capitalism. In short, in Mao's view, Stalin did not sufficiently consider the importance of the worker-peasant alliance.[224]

On the other hand, writings like the 1956 essay on the "Ten Great Relations" or "Ten Major Relationships" (*lun shida guanxi*) provided some anchor-points for the handling of contradictions by compromises such as decentralisation, self-reliant foreign trade, light industrial development and more. In his speech given to an enlarged meeting of the Political Bureau of the Central Committee, Mao explained that the ten dialectical relationships needed to be "handled properly" in order to make China a powerful socialist country: (1) between heavy industry, light industry, and agriculture – developing the first through the two other sectors, (2) between industry in the coastal regions and industry in the interior – making use of the industrial bases in the coastal regions to support industry in the interior, (3) between economic and defense construction, (4) among the state, the units of production and the producers –consideration to the three sides, granting more independence and benefits to production units, increasing the incomes of workers and peasants on the basis of their increases in production, (5) between central and local authorities – to delegate more power to the local authorities and let them do more, on the premise that the unified leadership of the central authorities would be strengthened, (6) between the Han nationality and the minority nationalities – to emphasise opposition to Han chauvinism, and sincerely and actively help the minority nationalities develop

222 KUEH Y. Y., Mao and Agriculture in China's Industrialization: Three Antitheses in a 50-Year Perspective, in: The China Quarterly, No. 187, September 2006, p. 704.

223 Criticising Soviet economic policies under Stalin as "walking on one leg" in a speech on the Soviet publication "On the economic problems of socialism in the USSR" in November 1958, which he also related to the insistence of "having cadres, but not the masses", and "promoting heavy industry, but not light industries". See: MARTIN (ed.) 1975, p. 96.

224 ROZMAN 1987, p. 146.

their economy and culture, (7) between party and non-party – long-term co-existence and "mutual supervision", (8) between revolution and counter-revolution, (9) between right and wrong, (10) between China and other countries – to admit that every nation has its strong points, to learn from the strong points of all nations and countries, but learn with an analytical and critical eye, not blindly, not by copying everything indiscriminately and transplanting mechanically, to be applied in learning from the Soviet Union as well as other socialist countries.[225]

The fact that these seemingly contradictory "dialectical pairs" that encompassed the emphasis put on the sectors of the economy including defense, regions, the questions of centralisation and appropriate remuneration, minority policies and even international relations and "learning from others" (albeit still limited to socialist countries) were related without clarifying the "proper" relationship for each element made them a very flexible and thus ideologically powerful tool for the legitimation of a wide array of policies, while offering an anchor in Mao Zedong Thought. Notably, after his death (see fourth and fifth chapter), the essay with its dialectical character offered a wide interpretative margin that would be recognised and readily used as a tool of ideological legitimacy by the new Chinese leadership. As FREDERICK C. TEIWES and WARREN SUN note, it is telling that the 1956 essay was released on the day of Hua Guofeng's address to the second national conference on learning from Dazhai in December 1976, where he made his balanced approach to economic policy more concrete. Also, the treatise was highly regarded by Deng Xiaoping, urging Mao in 1975 to authorise the publication of a revised version.[226]

The comparison with industrialised countries – more so in the West than the immediate neighbourhood of China – influenced decisions on economic policy also for Mao. Their technical and technological success had enabled the industrialised countries to humiliate China by asserting their superior military and economic capacities, which was most emphasised as a political *Leitmotiv* during the Great Leap. The orientation on catching up and eventually surpassing advanced economies, such as in particular Britain, by relying on mass mobilisation was based on the fatal assumption that labour – if the people were sufficiently motivated – could substitute capital, causing one of the most catastrophic national economic crises in history (see above). Nevertheless, Mao Zedong Thought as a source of ideological guidelines including for economic production was not abandoned but recombined and reinterpreted. Notably, the profound egalitarianism that shaped both the consistently narrow income distribution as well as the standing of social groups, particularly women, was not abandoned.

What may be referred to as "red lines" (meaning: limits of the possible) of Mao Zedong Thought became quite clear during the readjustment between 1961 and 1964. As material incentives such as piece-work payment, extended bonuses and the partial liberalisation of agricultural production and rural markets, even on a small scale, emerged as successful methods for the stabilisation of production and the availability of basic consumables, the idea of immaterial motivation as the main driving force behind the socialist state was directly challenged. As a reaction, Mao emphasised the importance of constant class strug-

225 Quoted from Selected Works of Mao Zedong, Vol. V, pp. 274–306 in: LI 1995, pp. 406 f.

226 TEIWES/SUN 2011, p. 5.

gle as a "key link" and a revolutionary end in itself[227], not as a means to merely achieve a prosperous society.

This constant class struggle, even in the sphere of the economy, was to be conducted in order to perpetuate the revolution, making it permanent instead of treating it as a past event that had established the socialist state. Again, the question of material incentives was at the core of socialist industrialisation in China as it had been at the core of Maoist critique of the Soviet political economy.[228] Albeit within relatively narrow limits, wage differentials were accepted, and the emphasis with regard to the economic achievements of the Chinese socialist revolution was primarily placed on the changes in the structure of ownership in terms of land reform and collectivisation as well as the consolidation of a state-owned industrial sector.

Noting that the Soviet model asked for the timely transition of collective property to unified property of the people, Mao insisted on a step in-between:

> "The transition from collective property to socialist people's property means the transfer of the agricultural means of production in their entirety to the property of the state, to change peasants to workers, whom the state takes over in their entirety and to whom wages are paid. Today, the average per capita-income of peasants in the whole country stands at 85 yuan a year. If it reaches 150 yuan in the future and can be, to the larger extent, paid by the [people's] communes, communal property can be made a reality [...] In this way, making one step further and transition to state property will be easy."[229]

With regard to these aspects, Mao's publicly expressed views were relatively pragmatic, as quoted by Guangming Ribao in 1975:

> "Chairman Mao pointed out: 'China is a socialist country. Before liberation, she was much the same as capitalism. Even now she practices an eight-grade wage system, distribution to each according to his work and exchange by means of money, which are

227 A policy that permitted trade fairs was, according to Dorothy J. Solinger, published in mid-1959 and foreshadowed the later fairs that resembled *"free"* markets in the following years. At the eight Central Committee's 10th plenum of September 1962, concern about the risk of emerging corruption and income-polarisation was publicly expressed. Besides this meeting, three publications contributed to the radicalisation of attitudes towards rural markets. First, the "first ten points" by Mao Zedong published in May 1963, which attacked the resurgence of "speculation" and profiteering, finding's by Liu Shaoqi's wife published in 1964 concerning corruption in the Taoyuan brigade and the revised "second ten points" attributed to Liu himself, which reinforced the message of the first. Solinger Dorothy J., Chinese Business under Socialism: The Politics of Domestic Commerce, 1949–1980, Berkeley, Los Angeles and London 1984, p. 262.

228 Mentioning and underlining the issue repeatedly, also as a general critique of the Soviet approach on writing a textbook on Political Economy: "With regard to the distribution of products, this has to be written again. The style [of the textbook] needs to be changed and the hard struggle, the expansion of reproduction and the perspective of a communist future needs to be emphasised; the individual material interest ought not to be accentuated and the people shall not be led to the path of individualism instead of socialism with "wife, villa, car, piano, tv-set". 'A journey of a thousand miles begins with one step ahead', but if we only consider this one step and not the future and the perspective, what interest and enthusiasm will you bring to the journey." Martin (ed.) 1975, p. 83, translation by the author.

229 Ibid., p. 74.

> scarcely different from those in the old society. What is different is that the system of ownership has changed."[230]

Mao Zedong Thought did not contain an absolute rejection of additional material incentives. Paraphrasing the notion in Political Economy that a socialist society consists of a group of people that honestly fulfilled their duties and another that did not, he noted that material incentives could not be the only means to convince these unwilling individuals to do their share. While insisting on political education as the principal method to improve production, Mao added with a pragmatic undertone that material incentives "do not have to be changed every year". As the workers did not "necessarily need material incentives every day, every month or every year", they could be reduced during a "difficult phase" as "people will work anyway, and they will work very well". Even if "one recognised that material incentives are an important principle", so the nuance, "they are not the only principle; there is always the need for another principle, the spiritual motivation in the area of political thought".[231] Until technology allowed the Chinese much stronger productive forces, according to Mao, "distribution according to work, production of commodities, the law of value etc." had to be tackled in accordance with the actual circumstances in the PRC.[232] Even in this highly controversial field, the basic idea of balance in Mao Zedong Thought was omnipresent.

Also with regard to hierarchies in production and the value of expertise and education, some quite nuanced published views can be found. What is well-established is Mao's critical stance towards higher education, notably non-technical academic subjects. As he explained shortly before the beginning of the Cultural Revolution in 1966, he saw himself as deeply "suspicious of this university education", stating that it took "a total of sixteen, seventeen or twenty years for one to reach the university from primary school" while, during all that time, never having "a chance to look at the five kinds of cereals, to look at how the workers do their work, how peasants till their fields, and how traders do business. In the meantime, one's health is also ruined."[233]

The general critical stance in Mao Zedong Thought towards non-party hierarchies, be they based on technical or academic expertise or material differences, became an ideological pillar of the Cultural Revolution. Despite these critical views and their negative consequences, publications of Mao Zedong's writings in 1970 made a clear distinction between what kinds of university education were in need of ideological improvement. As he stated at a talk at a 1965 conference in Hangzhou:

> "A student of Nanking University came from a peasant family. He was majoring in history. [...] He confessed: "I have gone to school for a number of years, but in my mind, there was not even a trace of labor. [...] The department of literature must be reformed.

230 Foreign Broadcast Information Service, Kwangming Daily: Inequality Still Prevails in The PRC Under Socialism, Peking Kwangming Daily in Mandarin, 18 02 1975, accessed through Readex.

231 Quoted from Martin (ed.) 1875, pp. 56 f., translation by the author.

232 Ibid., p. 32, translation by the author.

233 Joint Publications Research Service, Translations on Communist China No. 90, Selections from Chairman Mao, Talk at Hangchow Conference (21 December 1965), JPRS Document No. 4982, 12 02 1970, p. 2, accessed through Readex.

> If it is not reformed, can it produce philosophers? Can it produce writers? Can it produce historians? Today, philosophers are incapable of writing anything philosophical; writers are incapable of producing novels, and the department of history is incapable of carrying out historical studies. What they all write concerns nothing but emperors, kings, generals and prime ministers. [...] The department of literature must be reformed, and its students must be asked to go to the lower levels to work in industry, agriculture, and commerce. [...] Members of the faculty should also go along, working and teaching at the same time. Can they not teach philosophy, literature, or history at the lower level? Must they teach in tall, modern buildings?
> As for the department of technology and the department of physics, things are different. They have their workshops and laboratories where they can test and put what they have learned to practice."[234]

While this distinction between perhaps more practice-oriented fields of study and the humanities may evoke associations with quite similar arguments made in numerous countries today, one aspect of Mao's views on education becomes clear: technical and technological progress was instrumental to the fulfilment of the CCP's historical mission. Nevertheless, Mao kept his egalitarian stance as he stated repeatedly that "scientific inventions" does not necessarily come from "highly educated" people, advocating for professional engineering and practical education. Many professors, he underlined in his critique of the Soviet "Political Economy", receiving perks and benefits for excelling individuals, had not "invent[ed] anything". But, in contrast to these idle academics, "simple workers make inventions".[235]

The critique of academic and technical education was less aimed at the fact that it allowed for the development of expertise and thus social differentiation within and beyond the production process, but that this expertise was too distant from the realities of workers and peasants in the production processes. This critique also extended to white-collar management functions, where the risk of social rifts was even higher:

> "Management also involves socialist education. If management personnel do not go into the shops and sections to take part in the three togethers and to learn one or more manual skills from the teachers, then they are liable to spend their whole lives in sharp struggle against the working class. In the end, they will inevitably be overthrown by the working class as members of the bourgeoisie. If they do not master a skill and remain a dilettante for long, they cannot properly perform management functions. Confusing and dazzling others will not do."[236]

The Three Togethers (*san tong*) referred to eating together, living together and work together, going back to the directive on sending cadres down to participate in manual labour, issued on the 28th of February 1958 by the CCP. The directive stated that three of the ten million cadres within the party had never participated in the revolutionary war,

234 Ibid, p. 3.

235 Quoted from Martin (ed.) 1972, p. 88, translation by the author.

236 Joint Publications Research Service, Translations on Communist China No. 90, Selections from Chairman Mao, Comment on Comrade Ch'en Cheng-jen's Stay in a Primary Unit (29 January 1965), 12 02 1970, p. 23, accessed through Readex.

mass struggles or manual labour. Accordingly, these three million, along with intellectuals, were to be "sent down" to factories and farms to live the three togethers together with workers and peasants. Similarly, the policy was implemented within the PLA. The three togethers were, since the opening of the oilfields, included as a central part of the spirit of Daqing best practices.[237]

Even so, it appears that Mao was aware that a certain degree of specialisation and expertise was simply needed to run a modern economy effectively, albeit with a constant emphasis on the contradiction with revolutionary goals: in his view, experts and cadres tended to separate themselves from the masses, the historical driving force towards communism. It is a peculiarity of Mao Zedong Thought that similar tensions tended to be understood and interpreted consistently as dialectic pairs, which meant that the two opposites – for example equality and expertise – could in fact coexist in socialist China even for an extended period of time, but needed to be constantly criticised in order to keep the balance on the "correct" side.

In a political comment issued on the 29th of January 1965, Mao highlighted that while he recognised this tension with regard to technical expertise, it needed to be understood as a "unity of opposites". According to WANG RUOSHUI, Mao adopted Lenin's proposition that such unities of opposites are merely transitory, while the struggle between opposites is absolute. This thinking extended also to the sphere of international relations: in 1964, Mao launched a campaign to criticise the "two combined into one", propagating his approach of "one divided into two" in order to establish a dialectical legitimation for the Sino-Soviet split. This was a turning point in Mao Zedong Thought, for it implied abandoning the formula "unity of opposites" and is seen as a retreat towards Stalin's more reactionary views that emphasised opposition over harmony.[238]

With regard to expertise and hierarchies, what Mao perceived as the real threat to the class struggle and thus the socialist rule in China were not differences in technical expertise but the separation between "useful" expertise and "pure", bureaucratic managerial work. While he recognised the utility of technical and practical education[239] and the acquiring of useful skills for production, managers and government bureaucrats were a liability that was at most to be tolerated:

> "The bureaucratic class is a class in sharp opposition to the working class and poor and lower-middle peasants. How can these people who have become or are in the process

---

237 LI 1995, pp. 377 f.

238 WANG RUOSHUI, The maid of Chinese politics, Mao Zedong and his philosophy of struggle, in: Journal of Contemporary China, Vol. 4, No. 10, pp. 66–80. The term "unity of opposites" nevertheless continued to be referred to in speeches by high cadres, even after Mao Zedong's death, being too practical a formula to legitimise changes over the course to be abandoned.

239 Expressing his belief in technical education, while criticising institutions of formal "higher education" as elitist, linked back to the experience of the Chinese Civil War, as in Mao Zedong's critique of the 1960 Soviet Political Economy: "We do not deny the difference between engineers and workers, and we do want engineers, but on this point [equality and the position of the non-privileged] there are problems indeed. In history, people with a lower state of culture have defeated people with a higher state. During our civil war, our leaders at all levels were inferior to the officer clique of the Guomindang, who all had gone through domestic and foreign military academies. But we defeated them." Quoted from MARTIN (ed.) 1975, p. 88.

> of becoming bourgeois elements sucking the blood of the workers be properly recognized? These people are the objective of the struggle, the objectives of the revolution. The socialist education movement cannot rely on them. We can only rely on those cadres who feel no enmity toward the workers and who are revolutionary in spirit."[240]

On the other hand, this specific scepticism of clerical and bureaucratic work did not mean that Mao stood in fundamental opposition to labour discipline and hierarchical structures at the workplace. Quite the contrary: similar to Lenin's fascination with Taylor's "scientific management" and in an expression of the scientific-technological utopianism that socialism was based on, Mao held that "because" after the transition to communism "production will be automatised to a high degree", "higher precision will be demanded" both with regard to "the labor and the behaviour of people". In this communist utopia, labour discipline would need to be "even stricter than now".[241]

While the use of the most advanced technology was the objective, Mao admitted in 1960 that the use of "backwards" technology was unavoidable "for a certain time". As in the past, underdeveloped capitalist countries had caught up with developed ones "because of the use of advanced technology in production", and the Soviet Union had achieved the same thing. Mao Zedong emphasised that China "will proceed like that and [can] achieve just as much".[242]

240 Comment on Comrade Ch'en Cheng-jen's Stay in a Primary Unit (29 January 1965), 12 02 1970.

241 Comment on chapter 57 of the Soviet Political Economy titled "On the transition to Communism", quoted from MARTIN (ed.) 1975, p. 72, translation by the author.

242 Comment on chapter 48 on the coordinated promotion of local and modern methods and the coordinated promotion of large, medium and small enterprises, Ibid., p. 64. Translation by the author.

Phases of Chinese Economic Policy Formulation, 1970–1978

Due to their prominent position in Chinese and foreign media, the period of Chinese history in focus of this study is widely perceived through the lens of political struggle and the social upheaval over the course of the Cultural Revolution. Despite undisputed spillovers into economic activity[1], the period of "late Maoism", according to CHRIS BRAMALL from 1964 to 1976, was relatively stable in economic terms. With regard to the industrial basis it created and the stabilisation of production it was quite succesful.[2] While this assessment is rather obvious when compared to the collapse of the Great Leap, the 1970s brought a number of remarkable developments.

Whereas the subsequent chapters focus on specific adjustments with regard to the organisation of economic activity, material as well as technical and technological advancements, this short chapter provides an overview of the macroeconomic situation and important political events between 1970 and 1978. Also, I introduce the phases that structured my research, referencing to the findings supporting their distinction. Following a second phase of readjustment from 1970 to 1973 – that involved, in many ways, a continuation of policies initiated in the early 1960s – adjustments both in domestic and foreign economic policies occurred that, in my view, supported qualitative changes. Therefore, the years of 1974 and 1975 can be identified as *hinge years*, where experimentation informed decision-making in economic policy in particular concerning international trade and an increasing openness to foreign debt. Both areas, albeit couched in rather restrained – one might say, "politically correct" – language first, lent themselves as possible solutions for both the challenges of technological progress and the persistent growth conflict that constrained the funding of modernisation.

---

1 In particular, a certain deterioration of urban living conditions, as argued recently by GENE CHANG, SHENKE YANG and KATHRYN CHANG, and disruption caused in the Shanghai industries. See: CHANG GENE, YANG SHENKE, CHANG KATHRYN, The Immiserizing Growth During the Period of China's Cultural Revolution, in: The Chinese Economy, Vol. 51, No. 5, pp. 387–196.

2 BRAMALL CHRIS, A Late Maoist Industrial Revolution? Economic Growth in Jiangsu Province (1966–1978), in: The China Quarterly, Vol. 240, December 2019, pp. 1039–1065.

On the other hand, experimentation with "native" solutions to provide for economic growth, both quantitative and qualitative, continued to be an important part of the applied policy bundles. The year 1975 saw the reintroduction of core concepts of the Chinese development model that were continued into the 1980s, notably the "Four Modernisations" formula (*si ge xian dai hua*). It encapsulated the intention to push modernisation in four leading sectors, namely agriculture, industry, national defense as well as science and technology under a socialist premise. The Modernisations were first presented on the 23th of September 1954 at the first National People's Congress by Zhou Enlai, being partly reiterated by Mao Zedong at the 11th session of the Supreme State Conference on the 27th of February, in his speech on the "Correct Handling of Contradictions among the People". The concept was briefly revived during the readjustment of the early 1960s, being mentioned e. g. at the Shanghai Science and Technology Work Conference on the 29th of January 1963, and the third National People's Congress on the 21st of December 1964 along with a two-step long-term development plan.

After a long hiatus, both the two-step plan and the Modernisations were relaunched in 1975.[3] In the same year, the revision of both the constitution of the Chinese state and the CCP – still under the auspices of Mao – enshrined several aspects of economic flexibility, such as the acceptance of agricultural markets in the revised founding document of the PRC. The continuity of economic policies that had been initiated before the Cultural Revolution in 1966 was re-established by setting modernisation in a long-term context, reaching forward to the next millennium.

The years 1976 to 1978 have been subject to more vigorous scholarly debate recently, notably with regards to the significance of the often ignored interim government under Hua Guofeng and its potential for the creation and implementation of a distinct path for China's modernisation, different from the post-1978 course of Reform and Opening. In many respects, flexibility in terms of economic policy quickly became more pronounced after the death of Mao Zedong on the 9th of September 1976 and the arrest of the "Gang of Four" one month later. The latter event certainly disciplined the radical left within the CCP and ended its long-held influence on the core outlets of Chinese mass media.[4] While experiments touching the core of Maoist political economy – notably, adjustments of the levels of ownership and responsibility as well as the fiercely debated material incentives in production – were rather continued than initiated during these years, the manner in which such adjustments were publicly communicated and legitimised by targeted interpretations of selected pieces of Mao Zedong Thought changed greatly.

While the latter remained the formal ideological frame that the CCP as well as enterprises, workers, newspapers and bureaucrats consequently referred to in their descriptions of and prescriptions on economic activity, specific writings from the canon of Marxism-Leninism were reintroduced to put more weight on aspects of Mao's work that supported an emphasis of production over ideological purity as well as efficiency over the necessity of political expression. I argue that this readiness to compromise within the system of reference of Chinese socialism was particularly evident in foreign economic policy, as the integration of China in the international trade system and markets as a

---

3 Li 1995, p. 422.

4 Teiwes/Sun 2007, pp. 569 ff.

tool for increasing growth and speeding up the Modernisations were pursued with less and less reluctance, especially with regard to ideological limits of the possible.

China is a large country; its society and bureaucratic administration have always been at least as complex and many-layered as they are today. This chapter cannot and does not intended to cover all aspects and events during these fast-paced years. The intention is to provide context for the reader, limited to aspects I find necessary and without any claim to be comprehensive.

1970-1973: The second readjustment and stabilisation

With regard to economic policy, the Cultural Revolution did not imply a break with the General Line of the CCP, which assumed the dominance of politics and ideology and saw the revolutionary initiative of the masses as a precondition for the achievement of economic objectives.[5] The principle of production *and* revolution was reflected in point fourteen of the "sixteen points program" of the movement, as well as its reinvigoration with revolutionary zeal as a means of "achieving more, faster, better and more economical results", one of the slogans going back to the Great Leap.

To reduce the Cultural Revolution to a struggle between technocrats and ideologists would be misleading as, while revolutionary thought was emphasised in Mao's writings notably during the 1960s as a reaction to the readjustment, the movement as it was framed by the CCP had never established economic growth and revolutionary zeal as opposites. It has been established[6] that the course of the Cultural Revolution and the stance of both the state and the CCP changed rapidly, when the movement seriously began to affect the efficiency and output of production as well as questioning the dominance of the party. Even with the Red Guards and the PLA ready to follow his instructions, the dilemma of having to justify the revolutionary movement with all its consequences while having to legitimise attacks on Party institutions was difficult to navigate for Mao.[7]

The basic economic policies had remained remarkably consistent since the first five-year plan of 1953. The general paradigm of industrial development, financed through agricultural extraction in form of the unified grain procurement system, continued. At the same time, the burden of production directly imposed on rural households and collectives was reduced during the 1960s and 1970s, being increased again after 1979 to about twenty-five percent in 1982.[8] According to Robert Hsu, the procurement ratio (percent-

5 Kosta/Meyer pp. 224 f. The general line for socialist transformation, formulated by Mao Zedong between October 1952 and September 1953 has been found to be directly influenced by Stalin's writings, most importantly the "Short Course". See: Li Hua-Yu, Mao and the Economic Stalinization of China, 1948–1953, Oxford 2006, pp. 95–120. Julia Strauss has described Mao's adoption of Stalin's program as plagiarism, being "a sign of both respect and submission by a junior partner in global communism". See: Strauss Julia (ed.), The History of the People's Republic of China, 1949–1976, Cambridge 2007, p. 28.

6 Meisner 1999, pp. 333 f.

7 Tang 1986, pp. 82 f.

8 Hsu Robert, Grain Procurement and Distribution in China's Rural Areas: Post-Mao Policies and Problems, in: Asian Survey, Vol. 24, No. 12, December 1984, p. 1231.

age of grain output procured by the state) reached its peak in 1960 at 35.6 percent, being lowered consistently until it reached twenty percent in 1977. In the same year, the net procurement ratio, the percentage of grain procurement after resales from the states to farms, hit an all-time low at 13.3 percent compared to 21.5 percent in 1960.[9] From 1967 through 1970. and from 1973 through 1976, state quotas and prices for grain were practically frozen. Some steps were taken in the years between to address disproportionalities such as overly mismatched prices, taking into account actual supply and demand. From 1971 to 1972, quota prices for sugar crops were raised twelve percent and oilseeds by twenty-five percent. Grain prices remained unchanged, but incentives in the form of a thirty percent price bonus for above-quota deliveries of grain and oilseeds were instituted in 1971, unifying and replacing existing, regionally diverse bonus programs. This was an effective raise of above-quota grain prices between four and fourteen percent. Also, the duration during which fixed quotas remained valid was expanded from three to five years, making the system more reliable for agricultural producers.[10]

At the same time, rural areas and households relying on government resales of grain for their own alimentation suffered from social stigma during the Cultural Revolution. This was particularly pronounced in cases, where the reason for this dependency was a specialisation of sideline production of crops other than grain that they had developed in the course of the 1960s readjustment. Such peasants were accused of eating "guilty-conscience grain" or as "wearing the hat of eating return-sale grain". Such social consequences were most likely related to the emphasis given by the central government to general austerity for the sake of industrial development, calling for self-sufficiency in grain even in areas where the soil was ill-suited for its production.[11]

No significant and qualitative changes occurred with regard to sectoral emphasis; the development of heavy industry remained the objective of planning and production. While the more balanced approach since the early 1960s – meaning the recognition of agriculture as the basis and light industry as an important contributing factor – has been recognised by many observers also in practice, it also contributed to the formation of myths of a slower and genuinely Chinese model of socialist development that was perceived as being more equitable and humane than the socialism practised the Soviet Union and its satellites. The Cultural Revolution contributed to this perception. MICHAEL FROLIC argued that in a "noble effort" to moderate excesses of the "Stalinist model", a distinct Chinese economic model *could* have emerged during the Cultural Revolution, genuinely emphasising slower and equitable development over big-push-approaches, while noting that the emphasis on social development would only be short-lived.[12]

Given the weakness of the bureaucratic system and the consistent attacks on new ideas especially in the domain of economic policy, the safest course for planners and cadres was to just continue doing what they were doing – and perhaps try to do a little

9 Ibid.

10 See the statistics aggregated in: SICULAR TERRY, Grain Pricing: A Key Link in Chinese Economic Policy, in: Modern China, Vol. 14, No. 4, October 1988, pp. 464 f.

11 HSU 1984, p. 1237.

12 FROLIC 1978, p. 387.

more of it.[13] On the other hand, this also meant that some distinctive features of the Chinese system of economic planning and administration during the early 1960s readjustment prevailed. Particularly the decentralisation of both planning and administration remained untouched and was even deepened. This was not necessarily only the result of political decisions: It has been noted that although various ministries and commissions of the State Council were in the midst of rebuilding their internal structures, the economic planning departments were still in a desolate situation in 1971, making it implausible that calculations necessary for effective "general balancing"[14] could be carried out in any effective way. Therefore, the output of the planning commission was reduced to a number of control targets, such as for the production of steel, coal, grain and cotton.[15] FREDERICK TEIWES and WARREN SUN hold that despite some efforts to rebalance the economy, Mao's strategic as well as more eclectic ideological concerns complicated the process.[16]

Compared to the detailed twelve-part structure of the first five-year-plan of 1953[17], the fourth five-year-plan (1972–1976) was a rather open and general bundle of directives. With a view to the decentralised structure it was supposed to work in, the was perhaps reflecting in economic policy what MAYLING BIRNEY, in her analysis of the contemporary Chinese legal order, called "rule by mandates", suggesting that political and legal directives by the central government are comparable rather to rather open mandates given by an emperor to regional governors than to acts of law.[18]. There had been no formal adoption of the announced third five-year plan immediately after the period of readjustment; it was supposed to cover the period between 1966 and 1970.[19] The already small number of control targets relating for the overall output of key commodities such as steel, coal, grain and cotton was not put on a workable basis with a detailed allocation plan necessary for its actual implementation. The tentative plan was strongly influenced by the highly confidential Third Front programme and focused on the development of agriculture while addressing issues concerning basic needs such as food and clothing, the strengthening of national defense, while endeavouring to make breakthroughs in technology and in order to support both, the development of infrastructure.[20]

---

13 As described in PERKINS 2010, p. 147.

14 HUDSON CHRISTOPHER (ed.), The China Handbook, Oxon 1997, p. 98.

15 Joint Publication Research Service, Chinese Communist Capital Construction Studied and Analyzed, Article by Ch'ien Yuan-heng: "Study and analysis of Chinese communist capital construction work", Taipei Chung-kung Yen-chiu, Vol. 7, No. 5, Original in Mandarin, 05 1973, p. 70, accessed through Readex.

16 TEIWES/SUN 2008, p. 51.

17 Which has been published outside China by the Foreign Languages Press in the form of a 231-page book. Foreign Languages Press, First Five-year Plan for Development of the National Economy of the People's Republic of China in 1953–1957, Beijing 1953.

18 BIRNEY 2014, pp. 55–67.

19 ECKSTEIN ALEXANDER, China's Economic Revolution, Binghamton 1977, p. 111.

20 Renmin Ribao, Welcoming 1966 – The First Year of China's Third Five-Year Plan – New Year's Day Message – as published in Peking Review, No. 1, 1st of January 1966, pp. 5–9, available at: https://www.marxists.org/subject/china/peking-review/1966/PR1966-1a.htm, last accessed on 20 April 2021.

Overall, the state of centralised planning in the early 1970s was marked by debates on political principles rather than its practical execution at least outside the Third Front. Still, in 1971, technical planning continued to be criticised on political grounds, as an article by the writing group of the State Construction Commission published in August 1971 titled, "Relentlessly Pursue the Struggle of the Two Lines; Intently Inaugurate the Planning Revolution" demonstrated.[21] The article referenced the fourth five-year-plan with a mixture of optimism and political fervour: "Our socialist revolution and socialist construction have entered a significant period of development." The very centrepiece of planning under the first five-year plan, i. e. the focus on the financing of large-scale investment by allowing for the use of modern – thus, necessarily foreign – technology in industrial production, had come under fierce attack. Economic planning, despite the limited influence the Cultural Revolution had on actual production output, was yet another battleground for class struggle. Accordingly, the article warned:

> "If we lose our alertness and do not question these feudalist-capitalist-revisionist ideas about planning, they will spread everywhere. Only by relentlessly grasping the class struggle and the struggle of the two lines and by taking the offensive against these feudalist-capitalist-revisionist ideas about planning, can the work of planning proceed in the correct political direction. Planning is a kind of mental attitude, which belongs in the upper strata of structural forms. If we do our planning in accordance with the feudalist-capitalist-revisionist ideas about planning, we will serve to fulfill the requirements for class exploitation and work in favor of the restoration of capitalism. [...] **the work of planning has class characteristics and is certainly not simply technological activity** [emphasis added]."[22]

The accentuation of the differences between the city and the village, one of the "Three Great Differences" (Between the city and the countryside, mental and manual labour, industry and agriculture), was a concern that reflected the consequences of the deep separation between industrial cities and rural China. What the description of planning as a mental attitude rather than a technical rational task indicated was the lack of orientation within the bureaucracy. Even the department most concerned with the coordination and organisation of economic activity and most reliant on data and predictability was not sure about how to proceed with their duties; questions remained unanswered:

> However, some persons [...] simply stress the questions of technology and economics even to the point of using technological standards to substitute for political standards. [...] The planning revolution in substance is a struggle for leadership authority between the proletariat and the capitalist. [...] The various levels of leaders in the capital construction departments must have a good grasp of the planning revolution, conscientiously inspect planning projects, and see that the Party's directives and policies are

21 Foreign Broadcast Information Service, Experts Downgraded, Worker's Role Stressed In Planning, Article by Writing Group of State Construction Commission: *"Relentlessly pursue the struggle of the two lines; intently inaugurate the planning revolution"*, Peking Jen-min Jih-Pao, Original in Mandarin, 19 04 1971, p. 2, accessed through Readex.

22 Ibid.

> thoroughly carried out in the planning. [...] Shall we depend on the "monopoly of management" of the State Planning Commission and go the expert line; or shall we under the Party's unified leadership firmly espouse the "three unities" of on-the-spot planning, and engage in a mass movement? This is an important problem of the struggle of the two lines in the planning battlefront."[23]

The primacy of politics referred to is put in the context of technological advancements, the importance of which has in no way been denied. Rather, it is claimed that relying on, for instance, expensive imports of "turnkey" foreign plants – encapsulated in the phrase "gigantism-foreignism-perfectionism" – was inferior to an approach that relied on political principle over economic "rationality". The fourth five-year plan, valid for the years 1971 to 1975, was indeed peculiar, as it held that industrial development as well as its mechanisation were to be emphasised in sectors auxiliary to agriculture as, thereby continuing the general direction of stabilising agricultural production to avoid shortages of food[24], flanked by the development of heavy and chemical industries directly linked to agricultural production.

In principle, this was a continuation of the course pursued until 1966. Shortages of light industrial products for daily use, which had been a long-standing problem most notably in the countryside, were addressed as a priority. After policies intended to support agriculture during the drought of 1972[25] were not deemed to be overly successful, due to a shortage of spare parts and technical knowledge, the reissued call to "go a step further in managing light industry well" was intended to fit the production of light industrial goods for daily use within the production plans of industry.[26]

In particular, ongoing military preparations – including the decentralised storing of large amounts of grain as a part of the Third Front that could thus not be procured for other purposes[27] – once again brought unrealistically extensive targets in the relevant sectors, especially for the demand that steel output be doubled between 1971 and 1975. The resulting misallocation was, in hindsight, dubbed the "Three Excesses": too many

---

23 Ibid.

24 Which were not new concepts, but continuations of the third five-year plan intended for the years 1966–1970 and according to Alexander Eckstein was largely made obsolete as a planning instrument by the *Cultural Revolution*. See: Eckstein Alexander, China's Economic Revolution, Cambridge 1977, p. 111.

25 In particular, the drought in North China in 1972 was an all-time high in terms of meteorological measurements of the entire period from 1921 to 1984, ranking as among the five worst droughts ever to occur in the past 500 years. Whilee it was confined to certain regions, the 1972 drought depressed the national grain output greatly. See: Kueh Y. Y., Agricultural Instability in China, 1931–1990: Weather, Technology, and Institutions, Oxford 1995, p. 285.

26 As described in: Joint Publication Research Service, Chinese Communist Industry In 1972, Article by Ch'ien Yüan-heng; Taipei Chung-kung Yen-chiu, Vol. 7, Original in Mandarin, 10 02 1973, pp. 15–26, accessed through Readex.

27 Summarised with the slogan dig tunnels deep, store grain everywhere, and never seek hegemony (*shen wa dong, guang zhi liang, bu cheng ba*); the necessity of war preparations was emphasised in the 1970s, together with the demand to not to get involved in the struggle between the superpowers.

workers, an excessive wage bill coupled with excessive sales of grain from farms to industrial cities.[28] The national planning conference between December 1971 and February 1972 was still clearly influenced by political criticism, albeit allowing for further readjustment under the auspices of Zhou Enlai.[29] Initiative was taken elsewhere.

Indices for industrial outputs during the Cultural Revolution (1966 = 100). National Bureau of Statistics of China, China Statistical Yearbook, Beijing 1982, pp. 225–231, compiled in PERKINS *2015, p. 141. Graph by the author.*

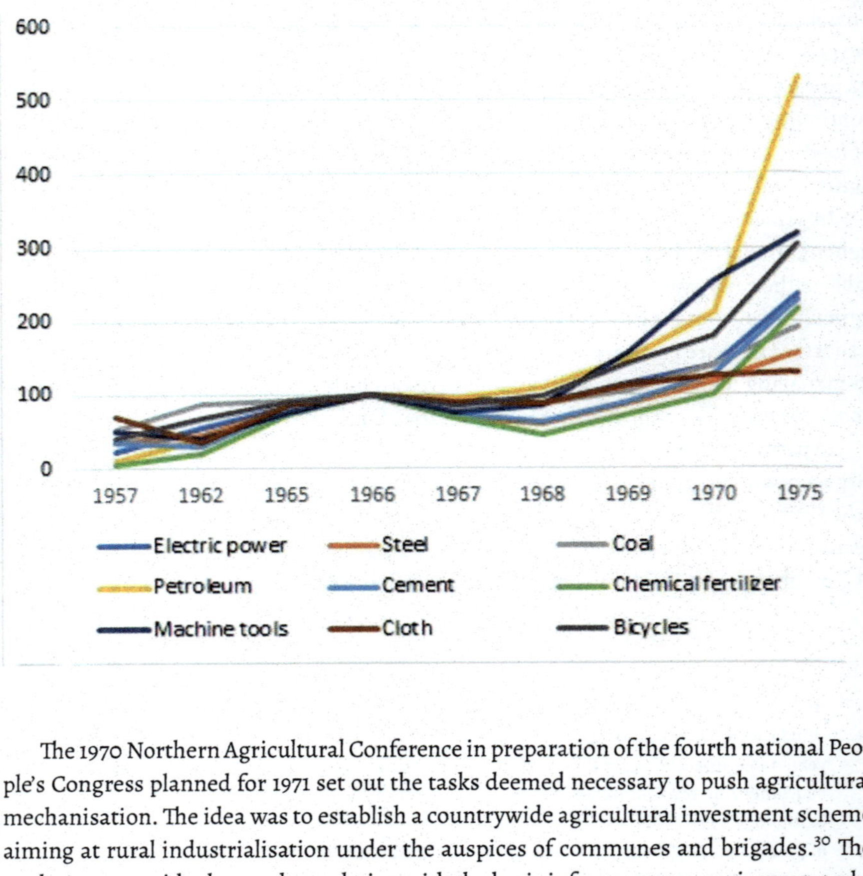

The 1970 Northern Agricultural Conference in preparation of the fourth national People's Congress planned for 1971 set out the tasks deemed necessary to push agricultural mechanisation. The idea was to establish a countrywide agricultural investment scheme aiming at rural industrialisation under the auspices of communes and brigades.[30] The goal was to provide the rural population with the basic infrastructure, equipment, tech-

28 TEIWES/SUN 2008, p. 51.

29 Ibid. p. 53.

30 Thereby laying the foundation for the later township and village enterprises (TVE) of the period of Reform and Opening. See: PUTTERMAN LOUIS, Continuity and Change in China's Rural Development: Collective and Reform Eras in Perspective, New York and Oxford 1993, p. 13.

nology and training in order to produce steady increases in agricultural output[31], and thus seriously implement the concept of "walking on two legs" and decentralised production of necessities. Nevertheless, the ongoing political struggle and the September incident leading to the death of Lin Biao delayed the Congress by four years. Towards the end of 1971, policy initiatives were being taken to set new guidelines for future development. Gathering momentum during 1972, most of them were basically designed to correct and reverse the adverse effects of the Cultural Revolution. In fact, such effects existed in the industry as well. As a glance at aggregate production figures, published by Chinese authorities in the the early 1980s shows, these effects were negative but temporary.

In macroeconomic terms, as indicated by the aggregated data, this impact was limited both in time *and* scale. First, the direct effect on a national level only became apparent in the three years of 1967 to 1969.[32] Second, particularly the heavy industrial and railroad transportation sectors were affected.[33] With regard to the quantitative level of production, the disruption merely manifested itself as a dent, which was mostly compensated by 1969.[34] This held true for Shanghai, the centre of the Cultural Revolution, where the effects could be mitigated even faster.[35] By the 1970s, both the primary and secondary sectors had surpassed the peak levels of 1966 and 1967, and their growth had realigned with the long-term trend line. These observations are particularly striking when compared to the disruptions of the Chinese economy caused by the Great Leap, when outputs fell by twenty-six percent (grain) and thirty-eight percent (cotton) compared to the peak levels achieved before.[36] The output of most industrial products kept growing through 1972 and 1973, while capital construction remained stable. PERKINS suggested that regardless of the political disruption, the overall growth rate of the Chinese economy during the third five-year plan (1966–1970) may have been as high as six percent *per annum* in average.[37] Thus, he concluded:

---

31 EISENMANN JOSHUA, Red China's Green Revolution: Technological Innovation, Institutional Change, and Economic Development under the Commune, New York, Chichester and West Sussex 2018, in particular chapter 3.

32 As PERKINS stated for the national level, and available statistics indicate. On the other hand, BAI LIANG argued that the regional differences were remarkable, depending on "revolutionary intensity". Where disruptions were more marked, effects were large in magnitude and, in some cases, began to decline decades later. Notably, social norms important to economic conduct, such as trust-based informal lending, appear to have been adversely affected, while the timing of later policy reforms was not. See: BAI LIANG, Economic Legacies of the Cultural Revolution, Berkeley 2014.

33 PERKINS 2015, p. 140.

34 At least in the walled industrial cities, meaning the production of electricity and machine tools, less so steel. Importantly, the increasingly export-oriented oil-sector was hardly affected (Chapter V).

35 PERKINS 2015, p. 142.

36 Ibid., p. 143.

37 Ibid.

> "In short, the Great Leap was a very expensive disaster. The Cultural Revolution at its peak (1967–1968) was a severe but essentially temporary interruption of a magnitude experienced by most countries at one time or another."[38]

Chris Bramall on the other hand emphasised that under a broad definition of rural industries – including industries owned by sub-provincial units such as town governments in the counties – growth accelerated markedly in the Chinese countryside during the 1960s and 1970s, making rural industrial production significant by the time of Mao's death.[39]

Although the Chinese economy still faced a plethora of challenges, it was far from being at the brink of collapse. It followed a relatively coherent strategy leading to consistent, albeit slow, growth.[40] Major capital construction projects which had been initiated before the Cultural Revolution, and interrupted for years, were completed as production caught up. It was noted that many of these projects even had their origins in the years of the Great Leap but had been postponed until the relative stability of the late 1960s, to be interrupted again by politics.[41] As Hidasi noted in 1970, quantitative indices at the time could not properly reflect the qualitative development of the Chinese industry. Despite its low efficiency and the rather small series produced, it was already capable of turning out a whole host of products, machines, equipment, instruments in a range only possible within the productive capabilities of countries with an advanced level of overall economic development and industrialisation.[42] With regard to industrial output in the centres of production, the impact was limited to a short period of stagnating growth within a general positive trend since 1962.

Nevertheless, changes in the administration of the economy did occur, in particular, within the bureaucratic apparatus of the state. As Elis Joffe argued, whatever may have been the objectives of the principal participants in the Cultural Revolution, there can be little doubt that they did not include the most striking and significant short-term outcome: the rise of the PLA to an even more decisive position in the power structure of China. Compelled by Mao himself to intervene, when the disruptive effects reached dangerous dimensions for both the economy and the position of the CCP, the PLA ascended to the commanding heights of political power in the provinces and acquired a substantial voice in the policymaking organs in Peking.

---

38 Ibid., p. 144.

39 Bramall 2007, p. 49.

40 Ibid., p. 138 f. A view shared by Wu 2015, p. 205.

41 Joint Publication Research Service, Communist China's Industry in 1969, Excerpts from an article by Ch'ien Yuan-heng, Taipei Chung-kung Yen-chiu, Vol. 4, No. 1, Original in Mandarin, 01 1970, pp. 18–28, accessed through Readex.

42 Hidasi G., China's Economy in the early 1970s, in: Acta Oeconomica, Vol. 9, No. 1, 1972, p.86.

Gross industrial output in Shanghai, million yuan. Statistical yearbook of Shanghai, 1983; as compiled by WU 2014, p. 100. Graph by the author.

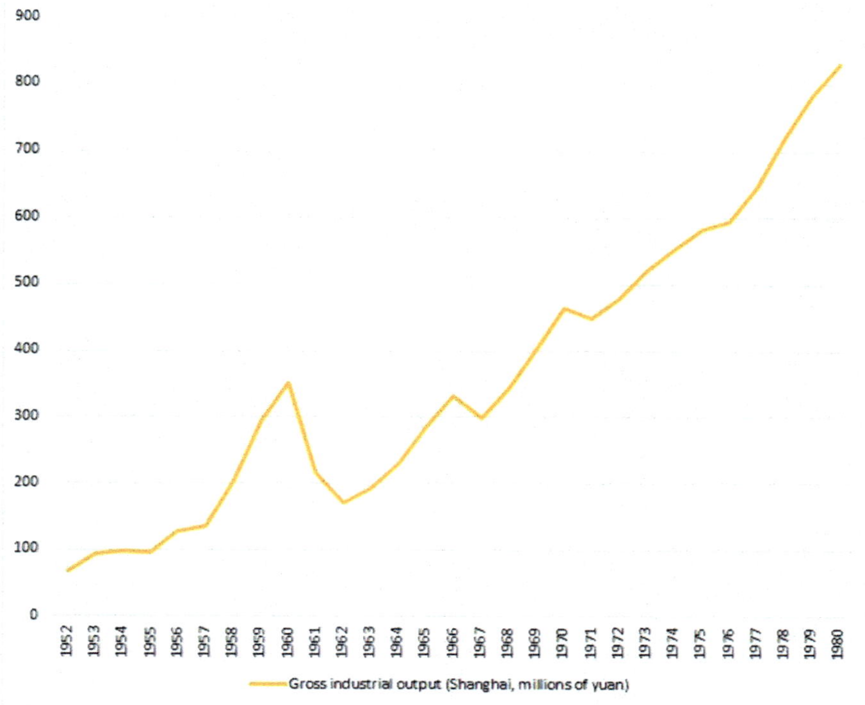

When the Ninth Congress of the CCP finally met in April 1969 to write the epilogue to the Cultural Revolution, the PLA held most of the key positions of power in China.[43] After it had taken over control in 1967 by putting military representatives in charge of the ministries and commissions, the reconstruction of the state bureaucracy after the death of Lin Biao in the so-called "September incident" of 1971[44] was an enormous challenge both for the internal workings of the parallel structure of the CCP and its legitimising narrative. Within the bureaucracy of the state, changes were largely driven by the new

43 JOFFE ELLIS, The Chinese Army after the Cultural Revolution: The Effects of Intervention, in: The China Quarterly, Vol. 55, September 1977, pp. 450–477.

44 Until the present day, different interpretations of the events explaining Lin Biao's sudden escape by plane and subsequent crash in Mongolia persist. First, the narrative put forward by the CCP itself, which states that Lin Biao attempted to take over the leadership of the Party and China by a military coup, even planning to assassinate Mao Zedong, and that he defected to the USSR after his plans were exposed. An alternate view, presented by Yao Ming-le, puts the emphasis on Lin Biao's son, Lin Liguo. His daughter Lin Liheng, and Lin Liguos' former fiancée, Zhang Ning, on the other hand, presented a narrative claiming that Lin Biao was kidnapped by his own son, who himself was manipulated by a third party. See: UHALLEY STEPHEN, QIU JIN, The Lin Biao Incident: More Than Twenty Years Later, in: Pacific Affairs, Vol. 66, No. 3, Autumn 1993, pp. 386–398.

dominant position of the PLA, reaching far into the political and economic realms. Even before the Cultural Revolution, the participation of the PLA in industrial production and construction was nothing new. For example, the military production-construction corps that was put to work in the military regions, such as Xinjiang, Shenyang, Lanzhou, Tibet, Canton and even Beijing, over the course of the Third Front-strategy were officially characterised as "a creative development" of Mao Zedong Thought on the People's War and People's Army under new historical conditions. Divisions of the Corps were specialised in engineering and agriculture, for instance, and they were in charge of large production units: A division like the Agricultural First Division controlled twenty-five farms producing cotton, rice and hemp.[45]

Before the Cultural Revolution, the State Council as the administrative centre of the PRC was among the most gigantic government organisations in the world. There were as many as fifteen vice premiers, and cadres with the ranks of minister and vice minister totalled more than 290 persons, altogether controlling forty ministries. The State Council had also established nine commissions, seven staff offices and twenty-four special agencies, such as the Civil Aviation General Administration and the People's Bank. During the Cultural Revolution, more than half[46] of the vice premiers were removed from office. Until 1971, a total of fifty-seven military representatives were instated as replacements. Some of them had been appointed ministers, such as Bai Xiangguo (Minister of Foreign Trade from July 1970 to October 1973), Yang [Cheh] (Minister of Communications), Sha Feng (Minister of Agriculture and Forestry from June 1970 to January 1978), Chen Shaokuan (Minister of Metallurgical Industry from June 1970 to 1977[47]) and Li Shuiqing (Minister of Machine Building Industry from March 1971 to July 1975).[48]

Under the responsibility of the PLA, the State Council also underwent an extensive process of condensing, simplification and curtailing of administrative units, foreshadowing the streamlining of the Chinese administration enshrined in the 1975 revision of the constitution. Ministries with overlapping or directly related fields were integrated. The reorganisation was conducted under the PLA's organisation principle of "Better troops and simpler administration", which also brought possibilities for medium cadres to rise through the ranks – often involving people who had already experienced social mobility through the PLA, like Bai Xiangguo.

---

45 Joint Publications Research Service, Communist China's 'Production-Construction Corps' studied, Article by Chang Yun-t'ien, "The Establishment and Expansion of Communist China's 'Production-Construction Corps': A Study of its Conditions and Functions", Taipei Chung-kung Yen-chiu, Original in Mandarin, 03 1970, pp. 31–40, accessed through Readex.

46 E. g. Deng Xiaoping, He Long, Tan Zhenlin, Bo Yibo, Wu Lanfu, Lu Tingi, Lo Juiqing and Tao Zhu. See: DIAO RICHARD K., The Impact of the Cultural Revolution on China's Economic Elite, in: The China Quarterly, Vol. 42, June 1970, pp. 65–87.

47 Chen Shaokuan became the second-ranking member of a new industry small group after the May Conference, when he was sidelined with others by Deng Xiaoping. However, he was identified as a minister as late as 1977, despite being prominent in attacking Deng Xiaoping in 1976. See: TEIWES/SUN 2008, p. 266, FN 57.

48 For a useful directory of Chinese state personnel between the early 1960s and mid-1980s, see: LAMB MALCOLM L., Directory of Officials and Organizations in China, Volume 1, third edition, New York 2003.

The strategy originated during the CCP's war effort against Japan and was applied to the "People's Anti-Japanese Self-defense Corps" – a militia which kept its members in their usual occupation in agriculture or industry. The guideline "Better troops and simpler administration" also applied in conjunction with the rectification campaign of 1942 to 1944, with special emphasis on "anti-bureaucratisation" aiming at a reconciliation between both the people and the army as well as officers and regular troops.[49] This also meant that officials familiar with the operational and technical levels of administration rose to positions of strategic significance. For example, the newly appointed vice minister of foreign trade, Chen Jie used to be the deputy director of the political department of the former Ministry of Commerce. His colleague and the vice minister of economic relations with foreign countries Chen Muhua rose from being a deputy director of a bureau of the former Commission for Economic Relations with Foreign Countries[50].

The newly established Ministry for Economic Relations with Foreign Countries[51] was the condensation of these organisations, directed by the former chairman of the commission, Fang Yi. The preceding Committee of Foreign Economic Relations was established in June 1964, mostly with the aim of improving the administration of foreign aid and abolishing the former Administration of Economic Relations with Foreign Countries, which had been more trade-oriented. The Committee was also responsible for foreign aid, but its organisation was based on regions and domains – very similar to Western Foreign Affairs administrations. The Ministry had six bureaus that were in charge of socialist countries, African countries, planning and financing, foreign trainees and so forth.[52] Although the staff of the new ministry was smaller in number than that of its predecessors, the change resulted in a more concentrated and literally militarily organised leadership that demonstrated and supported the ongoing pivot towards the outside world.

On the other hand, efforts to reduce the fourteen departments and other units of the Ministry of Foreign Affairs were faced with difficulties as the recent membership to the United Nations meant an additional increase in diplomatic activity.[53] Another key ministry that was streamlined was the newly founded Ministry of Light Industry, which incorporated the former first and second Ministry of Light Industry and the Ministry of

---

49 Sing Lam Lai, The International Environment and China's Twin Models of Development, Bern 2007, pp. 11 f.

50 Watanabe Shino, Implementation System: Tools and Institutions, in: Ohashi Hideo, Shimomura Yasutami (eds.), A Study of China's Foreign Aid, an Asian Perspective, New York 2013, p. 73.

51 Partly referred to abroad as the Ministry of Foreign Economic Liaison.

52 Further qualitative changes occurred later in March 1982, when in accordance with a resolution passed at the 22nd Session of the Standing Committee of the fifth National People's Congress, the Ministry of Foreign Trade was merged with the Ministry of Foreign Economic Relations, the State Import and Export Regulation Commission, and the State Foreign Investment Regulation Commission, and became the Ministry of Foreign Economic Relations and Trade, thus formally including foreign direct investment as a part of foreign economic policy. The Ministry of Foreign Trade was officially dissolved on March 8, 1982. See: Ministry of Commerce of The People's Republic Of China, The History, available at: http://english.mofcom.gov.cn/column/history.shtml, last accessed on 1 May 2020.

53 Kim Samuel S., China, the United Nations and World Order, Princeton 1979.

Textile Industry.[54] A similar consolidation occurred with the new Ministry of Machine Building, the Ministry of Agriculture and Forestry and the Ministry of Communications. Additionally, the newly established Ministry of Fuel and Chemical industry incorporated the three separate ministries for the coal, petroleum and chemical industries. These promotions not only motivated ambitious cadres but also demonstrated the will to strengthen the technical sophistication of higher administration.[55] However, many high cadres who had been attacked during the Cultural Revolution, and even by the Central Cultural Revolution Group[56], were allowed to retain their party membership and to return to important positions even before the movement had significantly slowed down.[57] Meanwhile, the fourth National People's Congress, planned for 1972 kept being postponed due to the reconstruction of the legislative branch after that of the acting bureaucracy, which thus received additional leeway within their areas of competence.

The purges and campaigns directed against "rightist deviationists" during the Cultural Revolution, personified in the forcefully convicted and politically as well as physically ruined Liu Shaoqi[58], caused uncertainty among industrial cadres and workers alike on what the line of the Party and the central government with regard to technical expertise and remuneration actually was. During the Cultural Revolution, guidelines for political action published in outlets such as Hongqi were very general, notably with regard to the treatment of cadres. When the central government called for the integration of so-called revolutionary cadres in the late 1960s, no indication was given on which cadres should be liberated and which should remain the target of the struggle. Also, the temporary breakdown of provincial and local party organisations gave considerable latitude and made the implementation of policies even more difficult. Often, it was unclear who the legitimate representatives of power at the lower levels actually were.[59] This uncertainty changed significantly in the autumn of 1970 when a great number of technical cadres were reinstated to their offices. It is important to note that cadre rehabilitation –

---

54 Whitaker Donald P, Shinn Rinn-Sup et al., Area Handbook for the People's Republic of China, Washington D.C. 1972, p. 243.

55 Joint Publication Research Service, Problems of the Chinese communist State Council Reviewed, Article by Chin Ch'ien-li: "Longstanding, Big and Difficult Problems of the Chinese Communist State Council", Hong Kong Hsing-tao Juh-pao, Original in Mandarin, 21 01 1972, p. 4, accessed through Readex.

56 The Central Cultural Revolution Group (*zhongyang wenge xiaozu*) was formed in May 1966 as a replacement organisation to the Central Committee Secretariat and the so-called "five-man-group" and initially answered directly to the politburo. It consisted mostly of the members of the Gang of Four and Mao Zedong, but also included more moderate members like Zhou Enlai. The Group at the height of the Cultural Revolution *de facto* replaced the Standing Committee of the politburo as the highest organ of the party state.

57 Wemheuer 2019, p. 227.

58 While Liu Shaoqi undoubtedly suffered a lot over the course of his purge, he was not executed – as it would have probably been the case under a leader like Stalin. He died in confinement, having been instrumentalised as a figurative enemy of the people, to an extent that made his rehabilitation unfeasible. For a critical biographical account including an extensive analysis of the connotations linked to the public persona of Liu Shaoqi, see: Dittmer Lowell, Liu Shaoqi and the Chinese Cultural Revolution, second revised edition, New York 1998, notably pp. 54 ff.

59 Wemheuer 2019, p. 225.

allowing "disgraced cadres" at all levels to return to their functions and (as in the case of Deng Xiaoping and others) even active politics, after the "rectification" of their mistakes – was a uniquely Chinese practice, which differed from the Soviet experience. HONG YUNG LEE argued that there is philosophical justification for cadre rehabilitation in the traditional Chinese belief that although people are fallible, they are also malleable through proper education. Mao repeated his belief in the possibility of rehabilitation frequently.[60]

On the other hand, approaches to economic theory and teaching in the early 1970s, like universities in general, were still heavily influenced by the Cultural Revolution. The political economy department of Nankai University reported in the summer 1972 that it had dispatched "educational revolution teams" to factories, villages, department stores and economic control units to gather materials for writing and compiling new teaching materials for courses on political economy. Specifically, observations intended for a course entitled "The Characteristics of Capitalist Exploitation in Old China" demonstrated the contents of revolutionary education:

> "...we went to Tientsin Woolen Textile Mill No. 3 – formerly the East Asia Woolen Textile Mill – to study its history. Through a study of the voluminous archives of the mill and holding talks with its senior workers and cadres, we were able to analyse and figure out its exploitation and capital accumulation processes prior to the liberation [...] During the period 1934 to 1937, that mill had an average rate of surplus value of 466 percent, and by the period 1938 to 1941, this rate increased to 929 percent. [...] In 6 years, it made a total profit of 320'000 yuan through exploitation. During this period the workers had to work 11 hours a day. After work, some of them had to pull rickshaws at night for additional income. Even so, the workers were still unable to earn enough to make both ends meet. [...] By incorporating these data into the teaching materials, it is much easier for the teachers and students to understand the basic theory of political economy. [...] We found that prior to the liberation, the workers had to work 357 days a year, 16 to 20 hours a day – 2.59 times longer than the working hours of the workers here today."[61]

On the other hand, the importance of the class struggle as a decisive factor in production was underlined:

> "In the past, the quality of products had been taken as a technical matter unrelated to political economy. But in this study, we realized that the low quality of products was caused by the counterrevolutionary revisionist line advanced by swindlers like Liu [Shaoqi] to undermine enterprise control. For this reason, the quality of products is a line problem, and it reflects on whether the enterprise is operated successfully or not."[62]

60 LEE HONG YUNG, The Politics of Cadre Rehabilitation since the Cultural Revolution, in: Asian Survey, Vol. 18, No. 9, September 1978, pp. 935 f.

61 Joint Publication Research Service, Article Explains how New Teaching Materials are Written, excerpts from an article by the political economy department of Nankai University: "Write and compile new teaching material, using society as the factory", Peking Kuang-ming Jih-pao, Original in Mandarin, 12 08 1972, p. 2 f, accessed through Readex.

62 Ibid.

The mixture of concepts from the readjustment of the early 1960s, even the "development of agriculture and light industry led by heavy industry", as well as the emphasis on iron and steel production, had persisted since the days of the Great Leap. They were combined with an insistence on the importance of relying on the masses – a core demand of the Cultural Revolution as well as the Great Leap– to improve both management and efficiency of production. Further, in the absence of effective planning, the reliance on model brigades such as Daqing as frameworks for economic development continued to be purported in party newspapers, radio programs and visual propaganda.

This propaganda poster (Fig. 1) was designed by Qi Dehan[63] and published in the Jiangxi province in April 1972, purporting the slogan industry studies Daqing (*gongye xue Daqing*) and displaying one of the "Chinese Stakhanovs". Over the course of the history of the PRC, there have been several figures stylised as "model workers" with quasi-Stakhanovite competitions inspired by the Soviet model, held even before the first five-year plan, with increased publicity during the mid-1950s via slogans such as "salute the model workers". National conferences were arranged in Beijing, reuniting such "model-workers" from all around China. They were usually small group leaders whose groups became identified through the leader's name.

A well-known example was Ma Hengchang in emerging in 1950/1951, who was a machinery worker in Liaoning province. His achievements were spread through the publication of books and articles, making him an integral part of the Chinese approach to non-material incentives. The Soviet Stakhanovite movement was widely perceived in China through the core elements of CCP campaigns and publications paralleling the Soviet handbooks and manuals.[64]

---

63 Qi Deyan, born 1932, is from the Gao'an, Jiangxi Province. After his graduation from the Lu Xun Art Academy in 1955, he worked as an editor for the Jiangxi Illustrated (*jiangxi huabao*) and taught at the Jiangxi College for Literature and Art. He is now a Professor of Fine Arts and Environmental Design at the Chongqing University in Chongqing City, Sichuan Province, China.

64 Kaple Deborah A., Dream of a Red Factory: The Legacy of High Stalinism in China, New York and Oxford 1994, p. 98.

Fig. 1: Gongye xue Daqing, Jiangxi Renmin Chubanshe, 76.5x53 cm, Stephan Landsberger Collection at the Institute for International Social History (IISH), Call number BG E13/915.

Wang Jinxi, depicted[65] here as a floating portrait in red, was popularly known by his nickname "Iron Man"[66] due to his zealous and persistent work efforts. He watches over two industrial workers handling a glowing furnace and a mining drill, backed by the three-in-one leadership of the PLA, the CCP and the workers represented by (from left to right) a soldier, a party cadre and a female worker looking over their shoulders to the left, from where a red glow emanates. The slogan left of Wang Jinxi calls to the "vanguard of the working class" to study his example.

The idealised image of Daqing, the visual narrative of which was modified later on, was particularly important with regard to two points of the course Chinese economic policy followed in the early 1970s. First, the modern industry it represented had been erected and was being maintained without foreign, particularly Soviet, support and managed by the three-in-one leadership. Thus, it was intended to demonstrate, what Chinese workers under the socialist state and the rule of the CCP were capable of on their own.

Second, Daqing, while the complex contained other industries as well, was not just any industrial plant. Daqing was an oilfield. It contributed decisively to Chinese self-sufficiency in crude oil as well as the production of a surplus. It was as much a part of industrial self-reliance as of the expansion of foreign trade, which became a defining element of economic policy in the following period.

1974–1975: Hinge years, constitutional reform and trade

As the PRC approached its 25th anniversary, its status within the Marxist timeline of development was redefined. Abroad, the aspects with regard to international economic relations were emphasized. In their inaugural speech after the "restoration" of the PRC as sole representative as China in the United Nations[67] before the 26th session of the United Nations General Assembly, the Chinese declaration declared:

---

65 Lincoln Cushing and Ann Tompkins distinguished eight principal types of visual propaganda that emerged in socialist China, being easily reproducible hand-printed woodcuts that were particularly prevalent during the Cultural Revolution, complex woodcut illustrations, graphically driven imagery resembling modern comics, classical watercolor landscape painting style, the rather romantic Huxian peasant paintings emphasising the diversity of the PRC with its minorities, watercolor paintings with graphic outlines, and large posters composed of several segments. The last category of oil paintings was arguably the most demanding artistically, and thus usually made by professional artists. The examples I refer to throughout this book fall under this category. See: Cushing Lincoln, Tompkins Ann, Chinese Posters, Art from the Great Proletarian Cultural Revolution, San Francisco 2007, p. 12.

66 It is remarkable that other than older Chinese Stakhanovites, Wang Jinxi has endured. Over the course of the expansion of Chinese foreign investment in the oil sector as well as the transfer of experts abroad to drilling projects, the figure has even "gone global". Hu Fuqing, a rig manager on the Halfaya oil field in Iraq was quoted by the official Chinese Global Times: "If our old team leader Wang Jinxi could endure the extreme cold in Daqing in the old days, we can also cope with the extreme heat in Iraq". See: Li Qiao, China's oil drilling champions take 'Iron Man' spirit to foreign fields, in: Global Times, 13 October 2019, Available at: https://www.globaltimes.cn/content/1166688.shtml, last accessed on 1 May 2020.

67 Draft Resolution 2758 (XXVI) brought forward by Albania. See: United Nations General Assembly, Twenty-Sixth Session, Plenary Meeting of 25 October 1971 at 3 p. m., Agenda Item 93, Restoration

> "Since the founding of the People's Republic of China, we, the Chinese people, defying the tight imperialist blockades and withstanding the terrific pressure from without, have built our country into a socialist state with initial prosperity by maintaining independence and keeping the initiative in our own hands and through self-reliance".[68]

By 1974, it was claimed by Xinhua, the Chinese people had turned the "poor and backward old China" into a "socialist country with initial prosperity" – the formula describing the perception of the economy by the Chinese leadership that acknowledged basic progress in the process of catching up.[69] While the observations of a Yugoslav journalist in October 1974, who saw the emergence of a "New Great Leap Forward"[70], was fortunately exaggerated in both the negative and the intended positive sense; the consolidation of the early 1970s had led to the stabilisation of industrial and agricultural production, resulting in what may be described as moderate growth. Data remains difficult to interpret and appears erratic. The World Bank estimates that the rate of GDP growth in China stood at 2.31 percent in 1974, rising to 8.72 percent in 1975 and falling to a negative -1.57 percent in 1976 assuming an exclusively positive trajectory afterwards. On the other hand, the figures provided for the years 1969 and 1970 are 16.94 and 19.3 percent respectively, which is far higher than the post-1978 peaks of 15.14 percent in 1984 and 14.2 percent in 2007, respectively.[71]

In an official publication of the Chinese Foreign Languages Press in 1974[72], the foundational principles and policies for the development of socialist economy were still directly linked back to Mao's General Line. For the years following 1953, dubbed in the same publication as the "transition period", the economic course of China was presented as having been rather reluctant: "To bring about, step by step and over a fairly long period, the socialist industrialization of China and the socialist transformation of agriculture; handicrafts and capitalist industry and commerce by the state". The new stage of economic development entered by the Great Leap was, in contrast, referenced as having

---

of the lawful rights of the people's Republic of China in the United nations, Document A/PV.1976. Available at: https://digitallibrary.un.org/record/735611?ln=en, last accessed on 15 June 2021.

68 Speech by Chiao Kuan-hua, Chairman of Delegation of People's Republic of China, Peking Review, No. 47, 19 November 1971, p. 6, available at: https://www.marxists.org/subject/china/peking-review/1971/PR1971-47.pdf, last accessed on 1 May 2020; and Kim 1979, p. 277.

69 Foreign Broadcast Information Service, China's socialist economy proves successful in 25 years, Peking NCNA in English, 0701 GMT, 24 09 1974 B, accessed through Readex. Until the present day, the formula is used by the CCP with reference to the successes of the Maoist era, serving as a platform for the "modernization drive" of reform and opening. See e. g. Speech given by President Jiang Zemin at the Sanders Theatre, Harvard University, on 1 November 1997, in: China: President Jiang Zemin Handbook, Strategic Information and Materials, Washington D.C. 2015, pp. 95 ff.

70 Foreign Broadcast Information Service, Correspondent Sees New 'Leap Forward' In PRC, Mihailo Saranovic report from Peking 'A new year for comparisons', Belgrade Borba in Serbo-Croatian, 15 10 1974.

71 The World bank, World Bank national accounts dara and OECD National Accounts data files, GDP growth (annual %) – China. Available at: https://data.worldbank.org/indicator/NY.GDP.MKTP.KD.ZG?locations=CN, last accessed on 1. June 2021.

72 Foreign Languages Press, A Glance at China's Economy, Beijing 1974.

brought the additions of "going all out, aiming high and achieving greater, faster, better and more economical results in building socialism", bridging the moderate build-up towards socialism to a fast-tracked approach to development that had so catastrophically failed in delivering prosperity. With regard to later years, the historiography presented to foreigners was even more diffuse, adding a number of points to the "general policy of developing the national economy", namely the slogan "take agriculture as the foundation, the industry as the leading factor" as well as the strategic "be prepared against war, be prepared against natural disasters, and do everything for the people, dig tunnels deep, store grain everywhere, and never seek hegemony" –referring to the Third Front.[73]

Although these principles were presented as orienting the national economic development, the existence of conflicts was not denied and Liu Xiaoqi and Lin Biao continued to be accused of sabotage. While the production figures were praised as having surpassed those of the thirteen years prior to the Cultural Revolution in eight years (1966–1973), the same, it was claimed, held true for the machine industry, with steel and energy outputs having doubled since 1965.[74] While this optimistic perspective presented to the reader was not unusual for Chinese pamphlets – as it would not have been for any other socialist state for that matter – the brochure emphasised a distinctive point: "The petroleum industry" it underlined, "has developed especially fast, its output being several hundred times what it was in the early post-liberation period. New China has not only become self-sufficient in petroleum but in recent years has some crude oil for export."[75]

The reasons why I suggest referring to the years 1974 and 1975 as hinge years bridging two quite different paradigms of economic modernisation are further elaborated upon in the fifth Chapter; the main reasons are found in the relations between socialist China and an increasing number of trade partners as well as international markets.[76] The core development can be seen in the economic opening of the PRC towards a new group of partner countries, including Japan and Western Europe, and the relatively rapid and large expansion of foreign trade as a consequence.

The developments in 1974 were more of a qualitative than merely quantitative nature. In 2007, China became the world's largest exporter, while its imports accounted for more than thirty-one percent of its GDP, surpassing by far the import-quotas of India (twenty-five percent), the United States (seventeen percent) and Japan (sixteen percent). British Plenipotentiary, Sir Henry Pottinger's hopes expressed after Britain's victory over China in the First Opium War (1842) became a reality, but much later: "[China's potential for

73 For a classic study on the effects of Third Front policies in rural China, see: NAUGHTON BARRY, The Third Front: Defense Industrialization in the Chinese interior, in: The China Quarterly, No. 115, September 1988, pp. 351–386.

74 CHENG 1974, p. 24.

75 A Glance at China's Economy, pp. 3 f., reiterates the necessity of catching up despite progress later on: "Although China's industry has made remarkable progress, it is still far behind of the industrially developed countries. The Chinese people, however, are determined to build their country into an industrially advanced socialist state in the not too distant future". Ibid., p. 31.

76 Meaning what is also referred to as the global economy, which is more than merely the whole of human economic activity: A system of industrial division of labour in industry, enabled through international trade and finance, including foreign investment. The result of the process of economic globalisation.

trade is so vast that] all the mills of Lancashire could not make stocking stuff sufficient for one of its provinces".[77]

These qualitative changes were noticed by foreign observers. For example, the Swiss delegate for trade agreements, ambassador Raymond Probst travelled to the PRC in September 1973 after having visited the political centrepiece of the Western trade system, the GATT ministerial conference in Tokio. He was the first high Swiss official responsible for trade matters to visit the socialist state. He reported that this visit was explicitly not aimed at a specific negotiation, but the establishment of contacts and a "deep exchange" on economic matters at a time, when bilateral economic relations with the PRC in his words "obviously entered a more active phase". This activity was not one-sided: while several Swiss economic delegations had announced visits for the near future and several industrial exhibitions in both China and Switzerland were being prepared, a Chinese delegation toured France, the United Kingdom and Switzerland at the same time as ambassador Probst wrote his report on his first week in the PRC.[78]

At first glance, taking inflation and the rise in real national income into account, the Chinese foreign trade ratio had merely recovered to the level of 1953–1957, the first five-year plan.[79] I argue that the figures alone are not sufficient to explain what this phase of trade expansion meant for the structure of the Chinese economy and the orientation, which saw important flexibility. *What* was traded, with *whom* transactions took place and *which* legal, financial and infrastructural framework the PRC was ready to commit to in order to pursue its economic opening towards the rest of the world is essential. Based on expansive diplomacy, the trading system built by the Chinese bureaucracy relied on agreements, oil and grain, ports and pipelines and the readiness to tweak political principles in favour of economic development.

One manifestation of this qualitative shift became epitomised by depictions of the model brigade Daqing in visual propaganda. One example is the specimen below, dated September 1975 (Fig. 2). Designed for the Dalian Red Flag Shipbuilding Factory, the slogan "study the spirit of Daqing, persevere in the great principles of acting independently and with the initiative in one's own hand and self-reliance" underlined that China should continue to catch up in terms of industrial construction on its own. At the same time, comparable with the depiction of Wang Jinxi shown above, the background in the composition of the picture reflects the orientation the oil industry and its product to take. On the left side, a ship leaves the wharf on its first route or is decorated in celebration of another occasion, while in the background the large cranes of a modern port stand densely arranged. To the right of the two workers forming the centrepiece of the picture, other workers pursue the construction of these infrastructures crucial for trade, while the masses to the left celebrate with red banners.

77 Keller Wolfgang, Li Ben, Shiue Carol H., China's foreign trade: Perspectives from the past 150 years, in: The World Economy, No. 36, Vol. 6, 2011, p. 854.

78 China – Reise Botschafter R. Probst, 16. Bis 23. September 1973, Ref. China 821 AV17. Available at dodis: dodis.ch/37716. Last accessed on 12 August 2022.

79 Perkins 2015, p. 151.

Fig. 2: Xuexi daqing jingshen, jianchi duli zizhu, zili gengshengde weida fangzhen, Renmin meishu chubanshe, 77x106 cm, Stephan Landsberger Collection at the Institute for International Social History (IISH), Call number BG E13/620.

Internally, the period of readjustment and stabilisation of the preceding years came to an end during 1974. At the party congress held in late August 1974, the CCP announced that the long-postponed fourth National People's Congress would be held shortly. In December, the rehabilitated Deng Xiaoping told Japanese journalists that preparations on "details" still needed to be completed but that the Congress would be held.[80] Priorities had shifted from the campaigns against Confucius and Lin Biao, of which the rehabilitation of Deng was a strong signal. Deng entered a position of enormous power, second only to that of Mao himself. He was undoubtedly constrained by him and the need to pay lip-service to the principles promulgated by the Cultural Revolution. However, at the highest level of the state, he was primarily responsible for policies adopted during 1975. Deng was recalled to Beijing in February 1973 to begin working in foreign affairs, seeing his role gradually expanded until being called by Mao Zedong to replace Wang Hongwen who was deemed insufficiently competent to run day-to-day affairs of the Chinese government. Deng Xiaoping became vice-chairman of the CCP as well as vice-premier close to Zhou Enlai and vice-head of the Military Commission. At the time, Zhou, who was sympathetic to economic readjustment, already suffered from his ill health.[81]

Within China, with regard to the general line of economic policy, the beginning of 1975 marked an important turning point – at least concerning the declared course of the CCP. While Deng played an important role comparable only to his status after 1960, when he and Liu Shaoqi were in charge of economic readjustment with the support of Zhou

80 Foreign Broadcast Information Service, 4th NPC May Be Held Soon, Tokyo Kyodo in English, 0014 GMT, 06 12 1974 T, accessed through Readex.

81 NAUGHTON BARRY, Deng Xiaoping, The Economist, in: The China Quarterly, No. 135, Special Issue: Deng Xiaoping: An Assessment, September 1993, pp. 497 f.

Enlai[82], it is important to note that the paradigm of the Four Modernisations – which has often been linked directly and exclusively to Deng Xiaoping's policies after 1978[83] – was developed and declared during the lifetime of Mao. Publicly, Zhou Enlai was credited with initiating the idea in a report to the fourth National People's Congress in January 1975 and the subsequent inclusion of the concept in both the state and party constitutions in the same year.[84]

GAO WENQIAN has argued that Zhou had been unwilling to be directly involved in tensions arising between Liu Shaoqi and Mao on economic policies while trying to act as a moderating force employing his Confucian strategy to find a "middle way" – while being explicitly sympathetic for policies which gave farmers more influence on basic decisions in agricultural production. In this account, his devotion to the solution of the enduring food crisis and the prevention of future crises made him a natural ally of advocates for economic stabilization and improvement, while trying to avoid the impression that adjustment meant the correction of mistakes committed by Mao – replacing the term "rectification" (*zhengfeng*) used for the policies of the third five-year plan with the milder "adjustment" (*tiaozheng*) and "filling out" (*chongshi*).[85]

The Modernisations were officially relaunched at the fourth National People's Congress in January 1975, calling for the modernisation of agriculture, industry, national defence and science and technology in order to transform China into a "powerful, modern socialist country". However, it had been part of longer-term economic planning since the mid-1950s and was advocated by Zhou Enlai until the end of his life. Already at the first National People's Congress on the 23rd of September 1954, the formula was presented by Zhou Enlai. Mao Zedong referred to it at the 11th session of the Supreme State Conference as the "need to turn China into a socialist country with modernised industries, agriculture, science and culture", adding national defense later. The longer-turn two-step plan to realise the Modernisations were introduced at the third National People's Congress on the 21st of December 1964, not to be revived officially until 1975.[86] If there ever was such a thing as a general consensus on economic development in China, it was around the commitment to the Modernisations – a guideline broad enough to

82 CHENG 2014, p. 120.

83 Tellingly, the introduction to the site on a well-known online encyclopedia explaining the term begins with: "The Four Modernizations were goals first set forth by Deng Xiaoping to strengthen the fields of agriculture, industry, defense, science, and technology in China. The Four Modernizations were adopted as a means of rejuvenating China's economy in 1977, following the death of Mao Zedong, and later were among the defining features of Deng Xiaoping's tenure as head of the party.". Wikipedia in English, Four Modernizations, https://en.wikipedia.org/wiki/Four_Modernizations, last accessed on 15 May 2020. The author has not yet succeeded in changing the entry.

84 HSÜ IMMANUEL C. Y., China without Mao: The Search for a New Order, Oxford 1990; HUA SHIPING, Chinese Legal Culture and Constitutional Order, New York 2019; and SOO FRANCIS, China and Modernization: Past and Present, A Discussion, in: Studies in Soviet Thought, Vol. 38, No. 1, Modernization in China, July 1989, p. 19.

85 GAO WENQIAN, Zhou Enlai, The Last Perfect Revolutionary, New York 2007, pp. 93 ff.

86 LI 1995, pp. 422 f. Nevertheless, the way Zhou Enlai and other leading cadres referred to the stage of completion – the beginning of phase two being in 1975 – the assumption that the long-term development plan was never interrupted was underlined.

be acceptable, notwithstanding differing ideas with regard to its implementation. The Report on the Work of the Government delivered by Zhou at the first session of the fourth National People's Congress was a synthesis of concepts for economic development that had been developed over the course of the history of the PRC.

First, the Cultural Revolution and the Movement to Criticise Lin Biao and Confucius were declared to have been a success through heightening the awareness of class struggle of the Chinese people "of all nationalities", forging "closer links to the masses", and consequently "successors to the cause of the proletarian revolution" were "maturing in large numbers".[87] The Movement was appropriately named Mao's Last Campaign by A. James Gregor and Maria Xia Chang. Merle Goldman has stated that the campaign was a deliberate retreat from the radical politics of the Cultural Revolution, an effort of retrenchment. The central themes of the campaign were centralisation, ideological unity and an emphasis on economic production. The ideological core was the perpetuation of class struggle, not to be overshadowed by bureaucratic rule and economics.[88]

The legacy of the movement, that is the political message, was addressed rather briefly: After lauding several social achievements such as the "over a million" so-called "barefoot doctors"[89] and the progress of re-education of cadres, the introduction directly passed on to the subject of economic development. The ideological success had strengthened "the all-round dictatorship of the proletariat over the bourgeoisie in the realm of the superstructure, and this further helps consolidate and develop the socialist economic base".

After a short overview of production figures and the assurance that the third five-year plan was of course over-fulfilled and the fourth was working out fine, harvests were good and agricultural output was rising, surpassing the growth of the population and thus

87 Foreign Broadcast Information Service, Chou En-Lai Report On Government, Beijing NCNA in English, 1200 GMT, 20 01 1975 OW, accessed through Readex; also in: Wang Joseph En-pao (ed.), Selected Legal Documents of the People's Republic of China, Arlington 1976, p. 108.

88 Gregor James A., Chang Maria Xia, Anti-Confucianism: Mao's Last Campaign, in: Asian Survey, Vol. 19, No. 11, November 1979, pp. 1073–1092; and Goldman Merle, China's Anti-Confucian Campaign, in: The China Quarterly, No. 63, September 1975, pp. 435–462. On the significance of Confucius in the Cultural Revolution and beyond, see: Sommer Deborah A., Images for Iconoclasts: Images of Confucius in the Cultural Revolution, in: Jones David (ed.), East-West Connections: Review of Asian Studies, Vol. 7, No. 1, 2007, pp. 1–23.

89 Often, and arguably for good reason, referred to as a principal success of the Chinese socialist state with regard to the improvement of the standard of living as well as life expectancy – it was acknowledged by the *World Health Organisation* (WHO) as a successful example of how shortages of medical services in developing countries can be solved. See: Zhang Daqing, China's barefoot doctor: past, present, and future, in: The Lancet, Vol. 372, No. 9653, November 2008, pp. 1865–1867. The term barefoot doctors (*chijiao yisheng*) debuted in a 1968 *Hongqi* article when the Cultural Revolution's most chaotic phase was abating, making the concept a household term overnight. Although, according to Chunjuan Nancy Wei, China had already in 1958 started to train barefoot doctors as, in essence, half-farming-half-medical (*bannongbanyi*) workers – they were not institutionalised nor trained *en masse*, until the Cultural Revolution commenced. In connection with the Rural Cooperative Medical Scheme operating between 1968 and 1981, a basic national primary health care system was achieved. See: Wei Chunjuan Nancy, Barefoot Doctors: The Legacy of Chairman Mao's Healthcare, in: Wei Chunjuan Nancy, Brock Darryl E., (eds.), Mr. Science and Chairman Mao's Cultural Revolution, Plymouth 2013, pp. 251–280.

"ensuring the people their basic needs in food and clothing", industrial output was on the rise, and China had proven capable of shooting satellites to space and testing hydrogen bombs, the economic situation in China was summarised in comparison to the rest of the world:

> "In contrast to the economic turmoil and inflation in the capitalist world, we have maintained a balance between our national revenue and expenditure and contracted no external or internal debts. Prices have remained stable, the people's livelihood has steadily improved and socialist construction has flourished. Reactionaries at home and abroad asserted that the Great Proletarian Cultural Revolution would certainly disrupt the development of our national economy, but facts have now given them a strong rebuttal".[90]

The reference to the crises perceived in the West and the emphasis on the financial solidity of socialist China was completed with a reference to the new international standing of the PRC:

> "We have smashed imperialist and social-imperialist encirclement, blockade, aggression and subversion, and have strengthened our unity with the people of all countries and especially the Third World countries. China's seat in the United Nations, of which she had diplomatic relations with us has increased to nearly 100, and more than 150 countries and regions have economic and trade relations and cultural exchanges with us. Our struggle has won widespread sympathy and support from the people of all countries. We have friends all over the world."[91]

To use the favourable situation thus described to the advantage of China, the consolidation of the country was a major task. The method presented to the deputies of the National People's Congress was applied dialectically, distinguishing between antagonistic and non-antagonistic contradictions to legitimise what was basically a call for stability over political differences. The basis of the argument was taken from the speech, "On contradiction", held by Mao in August 1937. "Antagonistic contradictions" (*duikang xing*) and "non-antagonistic contradictions" (*fei duikang xing*) were distinguished as follows:

> "In a class society, antagonistic contradictions refer to contradictions established on the basis of the fundamental opposition of class interests, whereas non-antagonistic contradictions are contradictions that emerge on the basis of a fundamental clash of interests between mutually antagonistic classes or cliques. When it has developed to a certain stage, a contradiction of this type is bound to manifest itself in terms of external conflict and antagonism, and can be resolved only through the form of antagonistic struggle [...] Generally speaking, non-antagonistic contradictions are contradictions produced on the foundation of the basic unanimity of interests of the people. They do not need to be resolved through the form of external conflict. Therefore, antagonism is only one form, but not the entirety, of the struggle of contradictions."[92]

---

90 Quoted from Wang 1976, p. 110.

91 Quoted from Ibid., p. 111.

92 Quoted from Leung (ed.) 1992, p. 342.

This relatively moderate course was to be combined with continued class struggle but by dealing "steady, accurate and hard blows" at the "handful of class enemies"[93], with the emphasis on accuracy and the small number of people actually requiring an opposing struggle.

The emphasis on unity over ideological struggle for the sake of economic development was also expressed with reference to Mao's sayings that supported the call, such as to "practice Marxism and not Revisionism, unite and don't split, be open and above board, and don't intrigue and conspire".[94] The unification of the country, the unity of the people and the unity of the various nationalities were to be the basic guarantees for the triumph of the socialist cause:

> "Socialist revolution is the powerful engine for developing the social productive forces. We must adhere to the principle of Grasping Revolution, Promoting Production and Other Work and Preparedness Against War, and with revolution in command, work hard to increase production and speed up socialist construction so that our socialist system will have a more solid material foundation"[95]

It was remarkable that about one-third of Zhou's speech was dedicated to international relations. Particular emphasis was put on the necessity of alliances "with all the forces in the world that can be allied with to combat colonialism, imperialism and above all superpower hegemonism".[96] Struggles of traditional allies such as North Korea as well as Vietnam, Cambodia, Laos, Palestine and the Arab countries were explicitly supported, as was the struggle of countries of the Second World (more on this later) against "superpower control, threats and bullying, in particular, the "efforts of West European countries to get united in this struggle".

Also, the willingness of the Chinese government to work together with both Japan and the United States was underlined in the report.[97] On the other hand, although the ideological debate "should not obstruct the maintenance of normal state relations", the Soviet Union was declared to have "betrayed Marxism-Leninism", and this debate would go on "for a long time" – signalling the decision that, for the moment, the internal as well

---

93 "We should unite over 95% of the cadres and the masses and unite with all the forces that can be united with in a joint effort to build our great socialist motherland." Quoted from WANG 1976, p. 114. This basic tenet of focusing ideological struggle against the "handful", indicating basic unity, was reiterated through the following years, as opposed to the broad destabilising criticism of the Cultural Revolution.

94 Which would become an important formula under Hua Guofeng, on which he would rely during potential and real crises such as the Tangshan Earthquake, in order to call out against opposition against party rule. See: PALMER JAMES, The Death of Mao: The Tangshan Earthquake and the Birth of the New China, London 2012; for a highly readable account.

95 Quoted from WANG 1976, p. 115.

96 KEITH RONALD C., Diplomacy of Zhou Enlai, New York 1989, pp. 210 ff.

97 "There exist fundamental differences between China and the United States. Owing to the joint efforts of both sides the relations between the two countries have improved to some extent in the last 3 years, and contacts between the two peoples have developed. The relations between the two countries will continue to improve so long as the principles of the Sino-American Shanghai Communiqué are carried out in earnest".

as international orientation of the PRC was not at all dependent on Moscow alone.[98] On the other hand, China had to "uphold proletarian internationalism, and get rid of great power chauvinism resolutely, thoroughly, wholly and completely." Also, in advocacy of non-alignment: "We will never seek hegemony; we will never be a superpower; we will always stand with the oppressed people and oppressed nations throughout the world".[99]

Internally, based on a compromise between revolution and the pragmatic development of productive forces, the Chinese national economy was to be built up in two stages – the first of which had already begun with the third five year plan in 1965. With this link back to the readjustment period of the early 1960, at least in the economic sphere, the Cultural Revolution was thus *de facto* declared over.[100] The objective of the first stage, the last third of which China entered in 1975, was "to build an independent and relatively comprehensive industrial and economic system in fifteen years"[101]; that is, before 1980. This reiterated the objective of assuring economic independence in order to have political independence – which signifies that China could remain independent of the superpowers and keep its non-aligned position as well as largely self-reliant.

The avowed goal of the subsequent second stage was to accomplish the Modernisations and turn China into a "relatively modern" state before the end of the century, "so that [the] national economy will be advancing in the front ranks of the World". This reflected the awareness that industrialised economies of the west were very far ahead and that the task of Chinese economic policy was the creation of a base – the implementation of the basic innovations that had allowed for the economic development in these advanced countries – in order to be able to compete thereafter. The principle of self-reliance was expressed with a nuanced quote from Mao's writings:

> "Rely mainly on our own efforts while making external assistance subsidiary, break down blind faith, go in for industry, agriculture and technical and cultural revolutions independently, do away with slavishness, bury dogmatism, **learn from the good experience of other countries conscientiously and be sure to study their bad experience too** [emphasis added], so as to draw lessons from it".[102]

Already on the 10th of April 1974, in a speech as the head of the Chinese delegation to the United Nations, Deng had defined the cornerstones of a more open approach to self-

98 The shift analysed in detail from the perspective of international relations in: Ross Robert S. (ed.), China, the United States and the Soviet Union: Tripolarity and Policy Making in the Cold War, London 1993.

99 Referring to the policy of preparedness for war. See: Wang 1976, p. 124.

100 Alessandro Russo argued that the ideological conflict within the highest leadership persisted in 1975, but was kept away from the public and contained within the political apparatus. See: Russo Alessandro, How Did the Cultural Revolution End? The Last Dispute between Mao Zedong and Deng Xiaoping, 1975, in: Modern China, Vol. 39, No. 3, May 2013, pp. 239–279.

101 Pointed out in the Report on the Work of the Government by Zhou Enlai for the third National People's Congress in December 1964, assuming that the Chinese economy, having recovered from the immediate negative consequences of the *Great Leap Forward*, was ready for a long-term development-drive beginning in 1966.

102 Quoted from Wang 1976, p. 117.

reliance towards the rest of the world, acknowledging the importance of economic cooperation and even the international division of labour, as long as it was complementary:

> "By self-reliance we mean that a country should mainly rely on the strength and wisdom of its own people, control its own economic lifelines, make full use of its own resources, strive hard to increase food production and develop its national economy step by step in a planned way. The policy of independence and self-reliance in no way means that it should be divorced from the actual conditions of a country; instead, it requires that distinction must be made between different circumstances, and that each country should work out its own way of practicing self-reliance in the light of its own conditions.
> At the present stage, a developing country that wants to develop its national economy must first of all keep its natural resources in its own hands and gradually shake off the control of foreign capital [...] Self-reliance in no way means 'self-seclusion' and rejection of foreign aid. We have always considered it beneficial and necessary for the development of the national economy that countries should carry on economic and technical exchanges on the basis of respect for state sovereignty, equality and mutual benefit, and the exchange of needed goods to make up for each other's deficiencies."[103]

While the *conscientious* adaptation of advanced technology and other experiences from abroad was thus encouraged, interdependence as an alternative to self-reliance remained excluded, at least in principle. The speech ended with a repetition of the core demand of internal consolidation to achieve the common cause:

> "We should continue to work hard, carry forward our achievements and overcome our shortcomings, be modest and prudent, guard against arrogance and rashness, and continue our triumphant advance. Under the guidance of Chairman Mao's revolutionary line, let us Unite to Win Still Greater Victories!"[104]

Zhou, who had been entrusted by Mao to revive the economy with the support of the PLA in 1972, was the proverbial moderate and continues to be interpreted as such. His views on economic policy, as his biography and writings and remarks indicate, was perhaps pragmatic in a similar way as Deng Xiaoping, but arguably more genuinely rooted in socialist principles. It has been established that many of the most important aspects of economic stabilisation after the worst turmoil in the late 1960s happened under his responsibility, as did the rehabilitation of cadres including Deng Xiaoping.[105]

Struck by terminal cancer, his immediate legacy with regard to economic policy was the programme for the development of the national economy, which was approved by

---

103 Foreign Languages Press, Speech by chairman of the delegation of the People's Republic of China, Teng Hsiao-ping , at the special session of the U.N. General Assembly, 10 April, 1974, Beijing 1974. Also available as a publication by Foreign Languages Press: Speech by chairman of the delegation of the People's Republic of China, Teng Hsiao-ping, at the special session of the U.N. General Assembly, April 10, 1974 (*Teng Hsiao-p`ing t`uan chang tsai Lien-ho-kuo ta hui ti liu chieh t`e pieh hui i shang ti fa yen*), Beijing 1974.

104 Quoted from Wang 1976, pp. 124 f.

105 Shambaugh David, Deng Xiaoping: The Politician, in: The China Quarterly, No. 135, Special Issue: Deng Xiaoping: An Assessment, September 1993, p. 466, and Vogel 2011, pp. 91 ff.

Mao. His importance as a source of legitimacy in the search for compromises was illustrated by the first Tiananmen-demonstrations after his death, while also demonstrating his role as a moral point of reference. The critical factor was the sense among large sections of the urban public that Zhou Enlai had not been adequately honored after his passing, and that some vaguely perceived struggle was continuing over his reputation. The tension originated in the period immediately following the premier's death, when official constraints on public mourning were introduced such as the prohibition of wearing black armbands, the handing out of commemorative photos and memorial activities. The decision of the CCP to prohibit any further displays of public mourning after the official ceremony on the 15th of January added to popular discontent.[106]

The "uneasy juxtaposition" with regard to economic policy was reflected in the short-lived revision of the Chinese constitution that was an important part of the fourth National People's Congress. A number of significant changes had been made.[107] In particular, the 1975 revised constitution eliminated the 1970 draft's repeated references to "the great leader Chairman Mao Zedong" and dropped any mention of the late Lin Biao, whom the earlier draft had identified as "Chairman Mao's close comrade-in-arms and successor". It also replaced Mao Zedong Thought with "Marxism-Leninism-Mao Zedong Thought" as the nation's ideological guideline while emphasising the leadership of the CCP over the state, and, most importantly, inserting the crucial and unique provision that the chairman of the Party Central Committee "commands the country's armed force".[108]

In itself, the constitution was a carefully balanced compromise that reflected what the limits of the possible with regard to general aspects of economic policy were – also for Mao, who approved the adoption. In comparison with the Soviet-inspired 1954 constitution, the document was much more streamlined, reducing the number of provisions from 106 to thirty – mostly with regard to the detailed provisions of the administrative structure of the state – thereby reflecting the much more decentralised approach wherein the CCP was the main vertically integrated power in the state. While the document reaffirmed the importance of Mao Zedong Thought together with Marxism–Leninism, it strengthened the position of the CCP in comparison to the Chinese government. The emphasis on the right of citizens to "speak out freely, air views fully, hold great debates and write big-character posters" as well as the freedom to strike had been added as an important concession to the Cultural Revolution. In the official "Report on the Revision of the Constitution", Zhang Chunqiao held that the revolutionary masses, "tempered in the Great Proletarian Cultural Revolution" would use these freedoms wisely in order to

106 Teiwes Frederick C., Sun Warren, The First Tiananmen Incident Revisited: Elite Politics and Crisis Management at the End of the Maoist Era, in: Pacific Affairs, Vol. 77, No. 2, Summer 2004, pp. 212 f.

107 Egli 2011.

108 Cohen Jerome Alan, China's Changing Constitution, in: The China Quarterly, No. 76, December 1978, p. 802. Being an expression of the compromise achieved at the fourth National People's Congress and still bearing the influence of Mao Zedong – including the flexibilities introduced in the economy – it was replaced in 1978. For an innovative analysis of qualitative changes in Chinese Constitutions during the 1970s, see: Egli 2011.

> "[...] create a political situation in which there are both centralism and democracy, both discipline and freedom, both unity of will and personal ease of mind and liveliness, and so help consolidate the leadership of the Communist Party of China over the state and consolidate the dictatorship of the proletariat".[109]

Finally, in Article nine, the principles of "he who does not work" and "from each according" were enshrined as the "socialist principles" of Chinese economic policy.[110]

The signs of a new dynamic were also noted by foreign observers. Already in early 1975, The US Liaison Office (USLO) in Hong Kong reported "various signs" indicating the Chinese leadership was "serious" after having lost sight of the goal of building a powerful and modern Socialist China often during the "past two decades". While the US-diplomats still recognised persisting structural challenges, their comparison of the current period with the PLA-dominated phase around 1967 led to an overall positive prognosis, as the political as well as governmental frameworks necessary for carrying out economic development were back in place. The report concluded that "China's political house is now in much better shape structurally".[111] After some months of observation, in late October 1975, USLO confirmed that China had "embarked on a massive development drive" following a sluggish start, resulting from inherent structural imbalances and "holdover problems from 1974". The industrial growth rate of 17.3 percent for the first eight months of the year, which the Office had obtained from Chinese sources, was estimated to be realistic, as a consequence of a resurge in production after the low growth rates of the previous year.[112] Potential obstacles for a continuation of this initial growth trajectory were recognised mostly in imbalances in key sectors such as coal, iron and steel and transport, potentially causing bottlenecks, and the particularly "rapid-growing petroleum industry". "Factionalism and labour unrest" on the other hand were described to be minor obstacles. While "remaining a problem", factionalism in the view of the USLO had *resulted* "in numerous, though probably localised factory closures or slowdowns in productions", which in severe cases were resolved by "the use of PLA troops to restore production and calm a violent factional confrontation".[113]

These instances of unrest were not primarily reported to be connected to political factionalism but rather the economic conditions:

> "Factionalism and labor unrest in China's factories are also more seriously reflective of an overall malaise that has affected responsiveness and enthusiasm across the board in China. Buffeted by long periods of political campaigning, cadres and managers have

---

109 ZHANG CHUNQIAO, Report on the Revision of the Constitution, 13 January 1975, in: Documents of the First Session of the Fourth National People's Congress of the People's Republic of China, paragraph 3, available at: https://www.marxists.org/reference/archive/zhang/1975/01/13.htm, last accessed 1 May 2020. Also in WANG 1976, pp. 91–104.

110 HOOK BRIAN, WILSON DICK AND YAHUDA MICHAEL (eds.), Quarterly Chronicle and Documentation, in: The China Quarterly, No. 62, June 1975, p. 391.

111 US Department of State, Electronic Telegram, Political Basis for Economic Development, 13 March 1975, 04:15, *Public Library of US Diplomacy* (PlusD), ID:1975HONGK02580_b.

112 Ibid.

113 US Department of State, Electronic Telegram, PRC Industrial Advance – Encouraging Despite Trouble Spots, 24 October 1975, 07:12, PlusD, ID: 1975HONGK12676_b.

often appeared hesitant to enforce center instructions on a labor force **facing greater work demands without corresponding material rewards and already somewhat disgruntled over apparent lack of response to wage issues**. [emphasis added]"[114]

The Japan-China Economic Association, having taken into account available data after one year, concluded that the new approach of Chinese economic policy of maintaining a balance between industrial and agricultural development was able to attain economic growth "within a fixed framework", calling the Modernisations "a reasonable objective well in line with the efforts of the Chinese in the past" – this while noting the persistent lack of advanced industrial equipment as an important obstacle.[115] Economically, the emphasis on the development of productive capacities as well as the flexibilities enshrined in the revised constitution – for agriculture in particular – were somewhat anticyclical as economic problems began to accumulate in late 1974.

The downturn of economic growth was attributed by the Chinese state to the spillover of "factional feuding" and the prevailing conflict and uncertainty concerning Mao's succession among other factors. While disruptive tactics were applied that certainly affected production, the Gang of Four also was a useful scapegoat to legitimise changes in the course of economic policies that followed. In addition, the losses suffered as a result of the Tangshan earthquake on the 28th of July 1976 were catastrophic – with the CCP estimating publicly in June 1977 that it had caused more human casualties than any earthquake in four centuries, with the lower end of estimates standing at around 244'000 lifes lost.[116]

Despite these challenges, over the course of 1975, what was publicly available information on political discourse over economic policy was marked by several shifts in tonality as well as an emphasis on a description of progress in the economy that was less built on ideological canon and output figures and more on qualitative growth. As foreign trade increased and gained media attention, publications directed at a foreign audience, such as the briefs published by national news agencies, underwent a particularly recognisable shift that was flanked by specific publications through the Foreign Languages Press praising the advancement of production by presenting concrete examples. Also, references to the "economic crisis in the capitalist world" were made frequently. For instance, in September 1975, a NCNA correspondent put particular weight on the balanced Chinese economy, which developed "big, medium and small" enterprises simultaneously, raising the rate of self-sufficiency in the supply of industrial products, the "broad and stable domestic market" that was "absorbing more and more industrial products", the narrowing of the price scissor between agricultural and industrial products through "rigid price

114 Ibid.

115 Joint Publications Research Service, Developmental Phases of China's Iron and Steel Industry analysed, chapter 2 on *"China's Iron and Steel Industry"* from the book *"The Developmental Phases of China's Industry and their Characteristics"*, Tokyo Chugoku Sangyo No Hatten Dankai To Sono Tokushitsu ni Tsuite, Original in Japanese, 03 1976, accessed through Readex.

116 Malcolm Andrew H., Chinese Disclose that 1976 Quake was Deadliest in Four Centuries, New York Times of 2 June 1977, p. 1, available at: https://www.nytimes.com/1977/06/02/archives/chinese-disclose-that-1976-quake-was-deadliest-in-four-centuries.html, last accessed on 10 May 2020.

control", praising the raising prices for "sideline products" and the successful differentiation of prices in foreign and domestic trade.[117]

While it remained clear that the debate on how and in what order of priorities these goals would be worked towards, a smallest common denominator as well as a timeline to temper political disagreement by referring to the need for *rapid* economic development were created that could potentially lift China from the stagnation of the post-Cultural Revolution years. The question of how was left open, but a general frame of reference other than Mao Zedong Thought was created for the experimentation that followed.

1976–1978: The Four Modernisations and a dialectical tilt

The initial impulse for the economic policy adjustments provided by Zhou Enlai was used at the highest level of political leadership, notably by Deng Xiaoping to establish a concrete program in three core documents. First, the "General Programme of Work for the Party and Country" and second, "Some problems in accelerating Industrial Development" containing a twenty point guideline for enterprise management and the "Outline Report on the Work on the Academy of Sciences".[118] While still focused on policy adjustment within China, and carefully based on Mao's writings as well as – and, in particular – the Marxist-Leninist canon, the documents laid out a consolidation and continuation of the early 1960s approaches that were directly associated with the fallen Liu Shaoqi, including several direct criticisms of radical political ideology, which saw itself as above the requirements for efficient production and modernisation.

Nevertheless, the measures proposed by Deng Xiaoping struck at the heart of conflict on appropriate economic policy in a socialist state: the full restoration and further development of managerial authority as well as the introduction of immediate material incentives for workers to increase their productivity. The criticism that followed is often reduced to the attacks associated with the Gang of Four, which popularised several indirect accusing references to Deng Xiaoping such as the "unrepentant man on the capitalist road" who worked relentlessly to subvert Mao Zedong Thought.[119] Besides these personal attacks, more subtle criticisms were formulated publicly alongside wide approval for the program. While the demonstration of some 100'000 people in Tiananmen Square in Beijing on the fifth of April 1976 was used as an occasion by the CCP politburo – on recom-

---

117 Foreign Broadcast Information Service, NCNA Correspondent on Healthy State of Economy, Peking NCNA in English, 1207 GMT, 25 09 1975 OW, accessed through Readex.

118 Published in the west, e. g., in Krott Martin (ed.), Programm für Chinas Zukunft, Deng Xiaopings Dokumente zur Lage der Nation auf dem Höhepunkt des Machtkampfes 1975, Übersetzung und Kommentar, Hamburg 1978.

119 As an article in Renmin Ribao and Hongqi on 2 March 1976 stated: "The unrepentant man on the capitalist road; who was at the origin of the rightist wind of reversal of verdicts, is the man who opposed collectivization and communization, who wanted redistribution of the land, who said 'a cat may be white or black; if it catches mice it's a good cat'; later he opposed the great cultural revolution, repressed the movement of the masses and wanted reversal of verdicts and restoration." As quoted in: Eisenmann Joshua, Red China's Green Revolution, New York 2018, p. 61.

mendation by Mao Zedong – to remove Deng Xiaoping from all official positions, the motives of the demonstrators were not primarily found in the support of his economic policies.

Talking to a US diplomat in March 1976, local deputy director of Xinhua Li Zhusheng presented the ongoing debate as a "rational activity" and a "normal process" in the Chinese political system, focusing on the universities as they were the major focal points of the debate, suggesting that opposing views were prominently displayed in the Chinese media and a "new Cultural Revolution" was not coming. Rather, the real issues in Li's view centered around the fifth five-year plan and on "who leads economic development in general". It was noted that Li's "unconcerned approach and bland exposition" was in stark contrast to the apparent anxiety of his younger interpreter. USLO reported that "Both gentlemen may have been displaying generational attitudes common in China these days".[120]

Nevertheless, the ideas introduced by the readjustment program were out and had demarcated the limits of the possible. The impressions of Journalist René Flipo working for the Hong Kong Branch of the Agence France-Presse (AFP) are noteworthy. While after Deng Xiaoping had been ousted, he presumed that the programme "hardly had the time to filter though the lower echelons [of production] before its rejection was recommended by the party" and was received by factories as late as December 1975. His exchange with cadres hinted that the fact of the dismissal changed nothing, particularly for enterprises which did not need nor use foreign trade in their production. A director of a machine tool factory in Yunnan, when asked about Deng Xiaoping and the practical consequences of his dismissal, drily responded that he had "not read the posters".[121]

While public criticism quite openly attacked Deng Xiaoping and his economic program[122], especially with regard to material incentives and the tendency of recentralisation through the proposed "direct and exclusive control of enterprises by the ministry concerned", the Modernisations as such were much less in its focus. This was an expression of the persistent tension between centralisation and decentralisation, control and bureaucratism, also referred to as the predicament "lifeless by centralisation, chaos by decentralisation" (*yi tong jiu si, yi fang jiu luan*) were ongoing topics in Chinese economic policy.[123] The Cultural Revolution combined with criticism of Deng Xiaoping's more ambitious proposals was not primarily framed as a means to keep the class struggle contin-

120 US Department of State, Electronic Telegram, Hong Kong NCNA Representative Gives Unexcited View of PRC Campaign, 8 March 1976, 09:46, PlusD, ID: 1976HONGK02649_b.

121 Foreign Broadcast Information Service, Teng Ouster should not affect 5-year plan, Hong Kong AFP in English, 1450 GMT, 22 04 1976 OW, accessed through Readex.

122 At the most extreme, the three parts of Deng Xiaoping's proposals – the General Program for the Work of the Party and the Country, Concerning an Number of Problems in Scientific and Technical Work and Some Problems Concerning the Acceleration of Industrial Development – were named poisonous weeds and put in direct opposition to Mao Zedong Thought,. For an example, see: Joint Publications Research Service, Liang Hsiao scores Teng's 'Poisonous Weeds', Article by Liang Hsiao, "Grasp the Question of the Line and Deepen the Criticism of Teng Hsiao-ping", Peking Kwangming Daily, Original in Mandarin, 26 08 1976, HK/P, accessed through Readex.

123 Qu Jingdong, Fu Chunhui, Wen Xiang, Organizational Transition and Systematic Governance, Labor Relations in Enterprises, Singapore 2018, p. 47.

uing but "a mighty driving force behind development of socialist productivity" in China, needing to be consolidated and developed to help the people "to push our country's industry forward continuously [...] along the socialist road".[124] The Modernisations and the Cultural Revolution were not primarily seen as opposites, although criticism persisted. According to the basic assumption in Chinese high politics, set forth by FREDERICK C. TEIWES and WARREN SUN, that as long as he lived, Mao Zedong was basically in command. As LAWRENCE C. REARDON has critically argued, factual limitations of his power as well as his "frequent political disengagement" need to also be considered, particularly with regard to the more detailed questions of economic policy. Nevertheless, the general lines of policies in the PRC can be assumed at least to not have been running diametrically against Mao's views.[125]

Deng Xiaoping's program of 1975 on economic readjustment was an important guideline that demonstrated how far officially endorsed policies could go – and this meant Mao Zedong's approval. It was not the only initiative aiming at adjustments. Notably, the North China Conference in agriculture and the National Conference on learning from Dazhai were important anchor points for compromises and experiments in agriculture. Albeit not throughout China, but certainly in provinces where the flexibility introduced by the 1975 constitution and the fourth National People's Congress worked out well. An article by the theory group of the Shensi provincial revolutionary committee planning committee in June 1976 – while reflecting the criticism of Deng Xiaoping at the end – included explicit references to both conferences before noting the progress made in both industrial and agricultural production, stating that: "Thanks to the development of industrial and agricultural production, financial revenue has increased, commercial business and the markets are prosperous, prices are stable and the people's living standards are rising gradually" – without referring to class struggle.[126]

The conferences also marked the entry of Hua Guofeng as a proponent of readjustment. The relatively young and publicly rather unknown Hua, formerly in charge of the national police, was appointed as the first vice chairman of the CCP and prime minister of China on the sixth of April 1976, following Deng Xiaoping's demission and the Tiananmen protests. The appointment was remarkable in two ways: First, Hua was an unlikely candidate whose record did not indicated his rise before. Second, his position was a new invention, the creation of a powerful position in government that only Mao Zedong him-

124 Joint Publications Research Service, Red Flag: Cultural Revolution Boosts Industry, Excerpts of article by Hsiang-Chi-wei: "The Great Proletarian Cultural Revolution and Industrial Development", Red Flag, No. 6 1976, Peking Domestic Service in Mandarin, 0330 GMT, 02 06 1976 OW, accessed through Readex; and: Foreign Broadcast Information Service, Red Flag on Cultural Revolution, Industry, Peking NCNA in English, 0703 GMT, 08 06 1976 OW, accessed through Readex.

125 REARDON LAWRENCE C., The Reluctant Dragon: Crisis Cycles in Chinese Foreign Economic Policy, Washington D.C. 2002, p. 36.

126 Joint Publications Research Service, Shensi Article Discusses Economic Development, Excerpts from article by the theory group of the Planning Committee of Shensi Provincial Revolutionary Committee: "*The Great Cultural Revolution Promotes the Great Development of the National Economy in our Province*", Sian Shensi Provincial Service in Mandarin, 1300 GMT, 10 06 1976 FE, accessed through Readex.

self had ever held. The situation was described by Soviet observers as an "unusual state of expectation".

In the Soviet talkshow International Observers Roundtable, where China was normally only mentioned in connection with political criticism, Vadim Nekrasov described the situation in an unusually sober tone:

> "Inside China, a situation has now come about which is unusual for recent years. At present, the antagonistic radical and moderate groups – as they are called in the West – have gone silent; they are in a state of expectation. Foreign observers think everyone is waiting for Mao's death, or at least his complete withdrawal from political activity [...] the impatience with which many Chinese await the death of their great helmsman borders on the indecent. [...] But once again, I wish to stress now that even in these circumstances, when a certain truce has arisen in relations between the most diehard extremists and moderates in China, Peking's policy of hostility to peace and socialism has in no way changed."[127]

In this state, the Tangshan earthquake, as it has been described by several authors[128], could well have been seen as a traditional sign foreshadowing the change in leadership in China. Mao Zedong died on the ninth of September 1976 in Beijing; therefore, relief-work after the Tangshan earthquakes was as challenging economically as it was politically.

On the one hand, the catastrophic earthquake was framed as yet another demonstration that human beings were not passively subject to outside forces but could shape nature. In a report on the autumn harvest around Beijing, Xinhua published an appeal to the "revolutionary spirit of 'the stronger the quake, the harder we work'", interpreting the quake in the context of class struggle: "[...] cadres and commune members used Chairman Mao's instructions as the weapon to deepen their criticism of [Deng Xiaoping's] revisionist line and the reactionary theory that everything was decided by heaven. This strengthened their confidence that man will conquer nature and greatly promoted the county's [...] anti-quake struggle and other work."[129]

As Teiwes and Sun have shown[130], it is telling that a reissue of Mao Zedong's 1956 essay, "On the Ten Great Relations" was released the day after Hua Guofeng addressed the second national conference on "learning from Dazhai" in December 1976. He had referred to the essay as forming the basis for an economic policy that would allow China to become a powerful socialist country by following a carefully balanced approach of a course of the dialectical middle – a political compromise, upholding both the improvement of production and the socialist character of Chinese society. The struggle that followed is well-documented and does not differ in its quality from similar struggles for succession after the end of impersonated rule.[131]

---

127 Foreign Broadcast Information Service, Weekly International Observers Roundtable, Moscow International Service in Russian, 0730 GMT, 25 07 1976 LD, accessed through Readex.

128 In particular Palmer 2012; and Wemheuer 2009, p. 132.

129 Foreign Broadcast Information Service, Crop Management stepped up in Peking suburbs, Peking NCNA in English, 0726 GMT, 20 08 1976 OW, accessed through Readex.

130 Teiwes/Sun 2011.

131 Tang Tsou, Mao Tse-tung Thought, the last Struggle for Succession, and the Post-Mao Era, in: The China Quarterly, No. 71, September 1977, pp. 498–527.

Enter the Gang of Four (*si ren bang*), referring to a circle aroun Mao's second wife Jiang Qing, with Zhang Chunqiao, Yao Wenyuan, Wang Hongwen and also Mao's nephew Mao Yuanxin. All of them were not necessarily representatives of a particular policy, but certainly among the main beneficiaries of the Cultural Revolution. Allegedly, the term was coined when the four were reprimanded by Mao at a meeting of the Politburo on the 17th of July 1974, where they criticised, in particular, his wife Jiang for her ambitions, stating that "she does not represent me, she represents herself [...] you people must be careful. Don't act as if you were a gang of four". The term rose to be a public formula for the expression of dissatisfaction with the political exponents of the more radical materialisations of the Cultural Revolution, particularly during the course of the protests in Tiananmen quare in 1976. It was being adopted by the CCP as a general rhetorical device to directly blame economic shortcomings.[132]

The Gang continued their attacks in the media of which they yielded significant control. Particularly, Deng Xiaoping's proposals for economic adjustment and foreign trade were targeted fiercly as deepening an already increasing dependency on foreign ideas and technology. Their position was remarkably weakened after their political protection from Mao ceased, which resulted in their arrest, ordered by Hua Guofeng on 6 October 1976. This consolidated Hua's position as a successor to Mao Zedong for the moment. On Sunday, the 24th of October, Hua was inaugurated in a lush ceremony that was still overshadowed by the conflict that had preceeded it. Swiss ambassador to the PRC Heinz Langenbacher, who was present on the square, described the ritual:

> "At three o'clock in the afternoon, before a square where the 'masses' and soldiers had been carefully placed since nine in the morning, the new president of the party was presented to the crowd. Appearing in a military uniform, his face transfigured by a radiant smile, Hua entered majestically, followed by what was left of the politbureau. One had the impression that, rather than a new chairman, it was the new emperor who was presented [...] his appearance on the ritual stage of the Tienanmen doors, the numerous portraits of Hua, carried next to those of Mao, the insistence shown by Wu Teh, the mayor of Beijing, to show that Hua had been "designated" by Mao, all was prepared so that the crowd would understand well that Hua really was Mao's successor.
>
> But to see, next to Hua, the [content] faces of the numerous military men who found themselves there, to see Wu Teh deliver his speech with the same smooth tone of a village leader he had used in this very same place last April, when he served the very same persons who were now accused of 'crimes reaching up to heaven' one had the impression that this satisfaction [...] was hiding an abyss of mental reservations and unexpressed or unexpressable thoughts that threatened to transform this respectable square in a true pandora's box."[133]

---

132 Li Kwok-sing (ed.), A Glossary of Political Terms of the People's Republic of China, Hong Kong 1995, pp. 430 f.

133 Ambassade de Suisse en Chine, Boulversement politique en Chine : revolution de palais ou coup d'Etat, Pékin, le 26 octobre 1976, Ref. RP No. 59 – DR/we. Available at dodis: dodis.ch/49033. Last accessed on 12 August 2022. Translation by the author.

How to bring about great order?

After their arrest, the members of the Gang were made responsible for "leftist deviations" before and during the Cultural Revolution, and thus served as an ideological contra point for tilting the "middle line" away from mass mobilisation towards more pragmatic policies.[134] Hua went further by directly attributing losses of "100 billion yuan of industrial output, twenty-eight million tons of steel and forty billion yuan of state revenue" to "sabotage and interference by the Gang of Four".[135] Jiefang Daily celebrated the "great historical victory" of overcoming the Gang:

> "Under the wise leadership of the party Central Committee headed by chairman [Hua Guofeng], we are fully confident in the victory of our party's revolutionary future, and we will surely carry out Chairman Mao's behest. We are confident that a political situation in which there are both centralism and democracy, discipline and freedom, unity of will and personal ease of mind, as well as liveliness, which Chairman Mao advocated for many years' past will finally emerge. The grand goal personally mapped out by Chairman Mao to modernize agriculture, industry, national defence, science and technology in an all-round way within this century and to build China into a strong socialist nation will surely be attained. The communist ideal for which Chairman Mao struggled all his life will surely be realized. Our objective will be and can be achieved. Let us advance from victory to victory under the wise leadership of the party Central Committee headed by Chairman [Hua Guofeng]."[136]

Although public criticism against Deng Xiaoping and aspects of his program of 1975 continued in various forms, openness to adjustments in economic policymaking reached an all-time high, going beyond the readjustment period of the early 1960s. Attributing economic difficulties – caused by various reasons, including production and infrastructure bottlenecks, the Tangshan earthquakes and persistent, albeit few, instances of worker's opposition to the new course – to the Gang and their acts of "sabotage" quickly became a mainstay in Chinese official media and a convenient way to explain any persisting issues in production.

Having established its legitimacy, the new leadership under Hua nevertheless deepened earlier adjustments in economic policy and developed new approaches, which were perceived by the USLO as "almost like [in] a western economics text [book]". This meant rational rules and regulations, improved economic accounting, lower production cost through improved efficiency, and increased accumulation of funds through allowing limited profits to be independently reinvested in enterprises, technical innovation and emu-

---

134 As Teiwes and Sun have argued, Deng Xiaoping and Hua Guofeng were in basic agreement on this. See: Teiwes Frederick C., Sun Warren, China's New Economic Policy under Hua Guofeng: Party Consensus and Party Myths, in: The China Journal, No. 66, July 2011, p. 2.

135 Prybyla Jan S., Industrial Development in China: 1967–76 and 1976–78, in: Challenge, Vol. 21, September/October 1978, p. 8.

136 Foreign Broadcast Information Service, Liberation Daily Acclaims Victory over Clique, Shanghai City Service in Mandarin, 0700 GMT, 26 10 1976 OW, accessed through Readex.

lation of foreign technology and raising productivity in general.[137] After the experiences of the hinge years, improvements of the Chinese economic system were sought in a number of nationwide and provincial conferences on the development of specific policies. In an article in Renmin Ribao on the 14th of November 1976, commentator Jen Ping summarised the prevalent official view on the relationship between economy and ideology:

> "By stressing the commanding role of revolution, we do not mean that production is unimportant, still less do we mean it is indispensable. Marxists regard man's activity in production as the most fundamental practical activity, and material production as the basis for the subsistence and development of mankind."[138]

As the USLO commented a few days later, it would appear that while "revolution may continue to lead production in post-Mao China", the new leadership left "no doubts as to where the motive force comes from.", which was the rapid advancement of industrialisation in China, both in quantity and quality. In March 1977, vice prime minister Wang Zhen, an old veteran of the CCP and former comrade-in-arms of Mao told Swiss ambassador Heinz Langenbacher who was about to leave for Bern as his assignment ended that China's future was "brighter and clearer than ever". This optimism would also have positive effects on bilateral relations and open new possibilities for trade, science and research as well as personal contacts.[139]

This "new optimism" allowed for much more straightforward language in Chinese media. An article by the mass criticism group of the State Planning Commission, published in December 1976, in Hongqi, answered the rhetorical question of "should we built our state into one with modern agriculture, industry, national defence and science and technology?", demonstrating the ideological re-discovery of Mao Zedong as an economic moderniser. It quoted remarks made in 1949, appropriate for that purpose, as well as Lenin's remarks on heavy machinery as the material foundation for consolidation of the dictatorship of the proletariat – arguing with the "simple logic" that "man must eat, drink and have clothing and shelter":[140]

---

137 As quoted in US Department of State, Electronic Telegram, People's Daily calls for new focus on production, 15 November 1976, 08:12, PlusD, ID: 1976HONGK13321_b.

138 Foreign Broadcast Information Service, 'Gang of Four' sabotage of production outlined, Peking NCNA in English, 1739 GMT, 14 11 1976 OW, accessed through Readex.

139 Ambassade de Suisse en Chine, China: Abschiedsbesuch beim Vize-Premierminister, Peking, den 28. März 1977, Ref. P.B.15.21.Cha. Available at dodis: dodis.ch/49021. Last accessed on 12 August 2022.

140 "After the victory of the democratic revolution we must step-by-step change China from an agricultural state into an industrial state, and build China into a great socialist nation" and "The only material foundation of socialism is the heavy machinery industry which can transform agriculture at the same time. Only with such a big industry can the proletariat consolidate its [...] dictatorship." Joint Publications Research Service, 'Gang' Undermined Modernization, Text of article by the State Planning Commission mass criticism group: "The 'Gang of Four' are the Chief Culprits in Undermining Socialist Modernization in the Four Fields", Red Flag No. 12, 1976, Nanchang Kiangsi Provincial Service in Mandarin, 1100 GMT, 12 12 1976 OW, accessed through Readex.

> "The 'gang of four' babbled: 'When revolution is carried out well, it is all right if production goes down.' We would like to ask: If factories produce no goods and farms grow no grain, what kind of socialist enterprises are they? If all enterprises cease to produce, how will people solve the problems of clothing, food and shelter? If you [the Gang of Four] had your way, not only would the revolution have been forfeited, even society would have been doomed."[141]

The article also referred to the "black cat, white cat" (*bai mao hei mao lun*) proverb, widely associated with Deng Xiaoping[142], and why it was attributed to the Gang. The folksy proverb was contrary to a common narrative not invented by Deng Xiaoping. In full, it went: "Black cat or white cat, as long as it catches mice, it's a good cat". Later on, the phrase was frequently referred to as "cat theory", "white cat theory" or "black cat theory". In the context of economic policy, the saying is particularly associated with the increased flexibility for the use of private plots since the early 1960s.

Liu Shaoqi, who defended the policy and demanded its extension, was supported by Deng and Chen Yun at a meeting of the Central Committee. Allegedly, Deng quoted a farmer from Anhui province who had used the proverb in order to advocate for results rather than political purity. After the beginning of the Cultural Revolution, the phrase was quoted frequently by Chinese mass media to criticise "capitalist roaders"; for instance, in an article published in Renmin Ribao on 3 December 1967 titled "Only socialism can save China – Repudiate the Reactionary Fallacy of 'Black Cat, White Cat'".[143] Criticism of Deng Xiaoping – while it persisted – was not any more at a level of intensity comparable to earlier struggles, which was obvious by the end of 1976, as an excerpt of a speech by Bai Jubing at the Shantung conference on "learning from Dazhai" on the third of December demonstrates:

> "[...] how do we appraise our work in 1975? We were faced with this issue at the beginning of the movement to criticise [Deng Xiaoping] and repulse the right deviationist wind to reverse verdicts. Under the pretext of criticising [Deng Xiaoping], the 'gang of four' totally denied our achievements in 1975, and smeared the party committees at all levels for 'implementing what [Deng Xiaoping] was peddling' and 'trying to restore capitalism' [...] The provincial party committee [of Shantung] held: the erroneous revisionist line peddled by [Deng Xiaoping] had some effects in our work in 1975. However, in practice, we continued to implement Chairman Mao's revolutionary line and acted upon the directives issued by Chairman Mao and the party Central Committee. Our general orientation was correct and our achievements were basically fine."[144]

---

141 Ibid.

142 Li 1995, pp. 12 f.

143 "They reversed right and wrong and called black white in an attempt to confuse people's minds, to disrupt the party organization, to disorganize the revolutionary ranks and to throw the normal socialist production order into confusion so that they could benefit from confusion". "The 'Gang of Four' are the Chief Culprits in Undermining Socialist Modernization in the Four Fields", Red Flag No. 12, 1976, GMT, 12 12 1976 OW.

144 Foreign Broadcast Information Service, Pai Ju-Ping Stresses Learning from Tachai, Tainan Shantung Provincial Service in Mandarin, 1100 GMT, 04 12 1976 OW, accessed through Readex.

The official attacks on purged members of the politburo – except to some extent Deng, who was infrequently named – increasingly focused on the disruptions that had allegedly slowed down production and the realisation of the Modernisations. The attacks reflected the shift of emphasis, notably with regard to the contradiction between revolution and production that were at the core of attacks against Liu Shaoqi during the Cultural Revolution. USLO estimated that this process could "affect the Chinese perception of sectoral development priorities", and eventually "result in a model of economic development more closely resembling the Soviet Union's".[145]

The realignment of priorities indicated that stabilisation in agriculture was apparently perceived within the Chinese leadership as sufficiently successful and on a promising growth path in order to re-focus on the traditional priority advocated consistently under Mao: the building of modern industrial facilities. The establishment of an ideological distinction between Mao and Mao Zedong Thought became a primary objective of propaganda, notably in 1977. The Thought continued to be positively referred to for the new course in economic policy, with the Gang and their "fallacies" as the counterpart and thus a source of "negative legitimation". The publication of volume five of Mao Zedong's selected works underlined the use of those aspects of Mao Zedong Thought, which could be used to support the "correct line" for Chinese economic policy as advocated by the Central Committee under Hua Guofeng.[146] As the Soviet journalist Alexander Bovin commented in May 1977:

> "Today it can merely be said that attempts are being made to prevent any kind of 'ideologues' from incompetent interference in production, to introduce some kind of diversity in cultural life and to normalize the situation in higher education establishments and schools."

Unity and the reestablishment of order became the main policy tenets under Hua, together with aspects of cultural opening. The quite obvious question "How to bring about great order?" was rhetorically asked by Renmin Ribao in April 1977 and answered in terms of the following eight main aspects. Criticism of the Gang acted as a politically useful embodiment of all that ran counter to the adjustment policies and the unity of the CCP under centralised command.

This stability was supported by constant assurances of swift and smooth successions within party ranks by "combining the old, the middle-aged and the young" in leadership work, the unified implementation of management guidelines that was encapsulated in modified Daqing- and Dazhai-models and transmitted through conferences and reports and an emphasis on the improvement of standards of living. To a certain degree, this bundle reminded observers of the "Hundred Flowers-campaign" of 1956 and 1957, which had claimed to loosen political control of culture and research to a certain degree,

145 US Department of State, Electronic Telegram, "Revolution" taking a lower Profile in Peking's Production/Modernization Priorities, 20 December 1976, 00:51, PlusD, ID: 1976HONGK14650_b.

146 Joint Publications Research Service, Bovin: Domestic Changes in PRC, No Change in Anti-Sovietism, Article by Aleksandr Bovin: "What has Changed?", Moscow Literaturnaya Gazeta, Original in Russian, 25 05 1977 LD, accessed through Readex.

strengthening the state including the PLA. Another declared objective was bringing economic planning back on track while ensuring "unity in thinking, policy, plan, command and action" and including cadres, intellectuals and the diverse nationalities of the PRC in the process.[147]

Also, the focus on the production of grain to be purchased and distributed by the unified grain procurement system was relativised by the central government, as the importance of agricultural side-line-production and markets as well as the decentralised rural industries and crops needed as industrial inputs were stressed. Before the summer harvest of 1977, the Ministry of Agriculture and Forestry held a national meeting where the strengthening of field management was a primary topic. It was held that:

> "While grasping grain production, various localities must also increase production of industrial crops. It is necessary to pay attention to the production of cotton and oil and sugar-bearing crops. It is essential to conduct overall planning and make all-round arrangements. We must combat the trend of grasping production of grain crops while ignoring industrial crops."[148]

These statements coincided with an expansion in the imports of agricultural products in mid-1977, which had been low after the experience of rising deficit in 1974 and 1975. The strengthening of regional economic independence as a *Leitmotiv* of national planning was underlined in May 1977, when Deputy Prime Minister Yu Qiuli announced the reinstitution of the regional administration system based on "large regions" in China – northwest, northeast, central-south, east and southwest – which had existed twice before as political divisions, between 1949 and 1954 and again between 1961 and 1966. The system took over from the division of military regions, which were based on a 10 to 11 region system.[149]

Deng Xiaoping was rehabilitated[150] again at the third plenum of the 10th CCP party congress in July 1977, allowing him to take up his former offices. The Third Plenum of the CCP Central Committee was held in Beijing from the 16th to the 21st of July 1977. As the official communiqué reported, the Plenum adopted a resolution confirming Hua Guofeng in the posts of both chairman of the CCP Central Committee and of the CCP Central Committee Military Commission, as well as a resolution restoring Deng Xiaoping to the posts

147 Foreign Broadcast Information Service, People's Daily On How To Bring About Great Order, Text of People's Daily 10 April editorial: "Carry out an All-Round Way the Strategic Policy Decision on Grasping the Key Link in Running the Country Well", Peking NCNA Domestic Service in Mandarin, 1700 GMT, 10 04 1977 OW, accessed through Readex.

148 Foreign Broadcast information Service, Agriculture, Forestry Ministry Meets on Summer Farming, Peking NCNA Domestic Service in Mandarin, 1246 GMT, 12 06 1977 OW, accessed through Readex.

149 Foreign Broadcast Information Service, London Times on Teng, Administrative Regions, London The Times in English, 24 05 1977, LD, accessed through Readex.

150 An "unofficial report" from Canton was quoted by the London Times already in May 1977, which stated that Deng himself had set forth three conditions for his rehabilitation: a thorough investigation into the riots in Tiananmen square in April 1976, him being reinstated to posts at least as senior as those he held before, and legitimising of his rehabilitation by a National Congress – according to the report, the politburo had accepted the proposal. Ibid.

of vice chairman of the CCP Central Committee, vice chairman of the CCP Central Committee Military Commission, vice premier of the State Council and chief of the General Staff. As the Russian Literaturnaya gazeta commented: "This figure's [Deng Xiaoping's] wheel of fortune has come full circle and he has become, if not the second, then certainly the third figure in the party and the state."[151]

Expanding limits of the possible

While the Four Modernisations were taken up again by the socialist state and made the object of numerous approaches to render them tangible, it is not yet entirely clear how the interim reign of Hua Guofeng and the drive of Deng Xiaoping towards modernisation were distinct or interrelated. In particular, while the urban political elites in Beijing went along with the rejection of the Mao regime's inherent instability after his death, they all shared – Deng Xiaoping included – a strong attachment to the collectivist system.

While these elites were divided over *how* to go about improving the lot of the poorest peasants, it was above all Hua Guofeng, who with his long experience in farming policy in Hunan and at the prefectural (*xiangtan*) and provincial levels, displayed pragmatism and tolerance: In particular, he accepted moves towards family farming and dialogue with provincial cadres about their actual needs. Thus, by authorising practices carried on earlier regionally, and with a low profile, it was primarily under Hua Guofeng that the limited liberalisation of the agricultural market continued, eventually helping to free enough capital for investing in industry and unleashing the Chinese economy. The continuities with earlier policies are striking. The interplay with other policy areas shows that the readiness to move further in economic policymaking towards a technology- and trade-driven vision was already well-established under Hua Guofeng.[152]

The two primary goals of restoring order and pushing for economic modernisation were shared by both, albeit to differing extents. As political constraints lost importance during 1977, economic constraints shifted to come under the focus of policy adjustments. Economic policy bound to the fulfilment of the meta-program of the Modernisations required increases in production and a pace dictated by the politically set timetable.

Different strategies were now within the limits of the possible, elements of which continued to be combined; primarily, the expanded purchase of foreign advanced means of production and technology to improve the basis of industrial production, approaches to increase the motivation of the workforce by raising standards of living and eventually wages, and improvements in planning and management of the economy. Additionally, after long periods of stagnation and hardship, the promise of an improved livelihood[153] yielding tangible results as a basis for a sense of national unity and purpose for the socialist industrialisation of China was overdue.

---

151 Foreign Broadcast Information Service, PRC urged to regain Socialist Fold while 'not too late', Second and final part of Fedor Burlatskiy's article: "The heavy Burden of the Inheritance", Moscow Literaturnaya Gazeta in Russian, 03 08 1977 LD, accessed through Readex.

152 Teiwes/Sun 2016.

153 While the benefits of the system of unified purchase and supply of grain continued to be praised in media outlets controlled by the CCP.

In preparation of the national day celebrations on the first of October 1977, rare statistical data on industrial output was released; it confirmed that, after the slump of 1976, industrial growth began hitting the ten percent mark again. A Xinhua report published on the 28th of September 1977, quoted by the USLO, stated that the overall industrial output had grown by ten percent during the first eight months of the year, compared to the preceding year, accompanied by the same increase in crude oil production, twelve percent in light industrial products, 27 percent in chemical fertilisers, 36 percent in tractors, and over 39 percent in hand-tractor production, with industrial output being reported to have risen to about forty percent in some provinces. While these statistics have to be considered with a grain of salt, they reflected the sectoral priorities of the leadership and signaled that agricultural mechanisation was being taken seriously.[154]

Nevertheless, the 11th CCP party congress in September 1977, while reiterating basic guidelines for management and the sectoral orientation of the national economy, gave few public answers with regard to their practical implementation – although having people figuring this out at the local levels appears to have been an integral part of economic policy. What became clearer was first, the undisputed orientation towards the rest of the world, and the acceptance of economic interdependence within the ideal of overall balanced trade, and second that Mao Zedong Thought at least in the sphere of economic policy had lost most of its authority and increasingly had to yield to classic texts and quotations by socialist writers like Vladimir Lenin, Friedrich Engels and Karl Marx himself, who lent themselves better to the legitimation of the new course. This also helped in omitting the ideological problem of reconciling the negative legitimation through criticism of the Gang of Four as convenient scapegoats for any economic shortcomings while keeping references to Mao Zedong as guiding principles.[155]

Life in the streets also seemed to change. When an USLO officer visited Wuhan, Changsha and Guangzhou between the 4th and 10th of September 1977, he noted that the three cities were "devoid of politically significant posters" while "bustling with economic activity", the general mood being one of "complete normalcy".[156] As it seemed, both objectives of stability and economic development had become a part of the street scenery in China. Accordingly, commemorating the first anniversary of the death of Mao Zedong, an article ascribed to the State Planning Commission was published on the 11th of September 1977 that connected the legacy of the former chairman directly with economic progress and the subsequent steps necessary to continue the path. "The Chinese people, once slaves bound in a hell on earth, have long since become dauntless masters of their own destiny. True indeed are Chairman Mao's verses: 'I find new scenes

154 US Department of State, Electronic Telegram, China's Industrial Growth Returns to Normal, 30 September 1977, 00:00, PlusD, ID: 1977HONGK11900_c.

155 Which was fully recognised by foreign observers, particularly with regard to the public trial in 1981, which besides its function as an instrument of ideological clarification with regard to the new course also served as a platform for the legitimation of the CCP in the longer run, despite the shortcomings in the economy. See: Xiung James C. (ed.), Symposium: The trial of the "Gang of Four" and its implications in China, Occasional Papers in Asian Studies, Vol. 40, No. 3, 1981.

156 US Department of State, Electronic Telegram, Observations in Chengchow, Wuhan, Changsha and Kwangchow, 13 September 1977, 00:00, PlusD, ID: 1977PEKING02047_c.

replacing the old'; 'The world has changed'".[157] The three parts of the long article underlined first the application of "the dialectical materialist law of the unity of opposites" by Mao Zedong, adding that through "scientific experiment", the quality of oil produced in China had reached "international standards" and eight further points underlining the correctness of the current management guidelines, and that "increasing or decreasing production is an important criterion to judge whether a revolution is successful or not".

At the first session of the fifth National People's Congress on the 26th of February 1978, Hua Guofeng presented his "Report on the Work of the Government". After underlining the importance of respecting the law of value and the profit motive within Chine, he called for an intensification of state trade within China to "provide the markets with adequate supplies [...] increase the variety of goods on the market, and improve the quality of service to customers" while tightening price and market controls to deal "resolute blows" to speculation. He also stated that there "should be a big increase in foreign trade". China needed to "build a number of bases for supplying industrial and mineral products and agricultural and side-line products for export". Further, all localities and departments were to follow developments in technology "at home and abroad" in order to "not get stuck in a groove and rest content with old practices."[158] In that vein, the blueprint for a ten-year modernisation plan was approved by Hua. It accounted for massive investments in extensive large-scale projects in the industry necessary to accomplish the Four Modernisations.[159] In his report, it was made quite clear where the focus would be:

> "We must greatly raise the scientific and cultural level of the entire Chinese nation so that our working people will master modern technique in production and scientific knowledge. At the same time, we must build a vast army of working-class intellectuals. We must catch up quickly, [Hua Guofeng] says, with the swift changes taking place in modern science and technology and rapidly eliminate our backwardness in these fields [...]"[160]

Once again, China's modernisation was about "quickly, swift and rapidly" catching up. But now, it was not the "iron man" in the factory and on the oil rig alone but "working-class intellectuals" who would ensure that the socialist state could modernise by making use of advanced science and technology.

157 Foreign Broadcast Information Service, State Planning Commission article on Socialist Construction, full text of an article written by the State Planning Commission to commemorate the first anniversary of the death of the great leader and teacher Chairman Mao: "Great Guiding Principle for Socialist Construction", Peking NCNA in English, 0102 GMT, 12 09 1977 OW, accessed through Readex.

158 Foreign Broadcast Information Service, Hua Kuo-feng 26 February Report, Unite and Strive to Build a Modern, Powerful Socialist Country, Peking NCNA in English, 1451 GMT, 06 03 1978 OW, accessed through Readex.

159 CHENG, CHU-YUAN, China's Economic Development 1950–2015, London 2014, pp. 123 ff. How foreign trade and perhaps investment were accounted for in this program is subject of an ongoing project of the author.

160 Foreign Broadcast Information Service, Hua's Work Report, Peking NCNA in English, 1207 GMT, 26 02 1978 OW, accessed through Readex.

Economic policy adjustments in China (1970–1978)

This Chapter is structured around the areas of interest stated in the introduction to this book: the policies on management and hierarchical labour division in production, the strategies to achieve improvements in efficiency and technological progress, and the question of how the meta-objective of industrialisation was to be financed, particularly with regard to the balance between investment and the Chinese people's livelihood.

Above, I have summarised the main developments at the highest political level of central government, where the issues around economic policy have been at the core of many debates. In this Chapter, based on sources including a selection of literature published in the PRC and outside on adjustments, the focus is on qualitative changes and experiments that reflected the limits of what was feasible and could be publicly expressed on the national and provincial levels. Being fully aware that the analysis cannot even by far be comprehensive and take into account all potentially relevant developments, my findings serve as a basis for a contextualisation of related experiments and qualitative changes in the economic relations between the PRC and the rest of the world.

How to organise economic activity?

This first question concerns one of the primary conflicts, if not *the* primary conflict, around the social organisation of production that was particularly pronounced during the Cultural Revolution. How could the egalitarian promise of socialism, which had been an important argument in its favour when compared to the imperial system, be reconciled with the requirements of industrial production and economic planning? While the issue has been thoroughly discussed in scholarship with regard to China, the emphasis in the approach presented here is slightly different.

On the one hand, I discuss the importance of rules and regulations as well as hierarchical relations at the workplace, which were an important feature of economic readjustment after the Cultural Revolution – in particular, over the course of the rehabilitation of cadres and the further stabilisation of production. On the other hand, as discussed further below, the indirect effect of increasing orientation towards foreign trade and advanced technology needs to be taken into account. While the CCP set out after 1949 to catch up with advanced nations based on the Soviet model, and thus to replicate the basic industrial innovations first of the Industrial Revolution and subsequently the ongoing "second long wave", the Chinese economy was increasingly confronted with constraints in economic management. For example, how could a sufficiently high, consistent and uniform standard of industrial production be reliably maintained in order to be able to compete in foreign markets?

Moreover, as the persistent point of orientation for industrial development – the advanced technology of industrialised nations to be introduced and used in China – moved away from the steel mills, coalmines, petrochemical factories to much more complex technology in the fields of electronics and machinery, how could the Chinese economy ensure the necessary expertise and specialisation of its workers? While the basic idea of having workers, experts and cadres participating in management and production on an equal footing might have worked to a certain extent on farms and in factories, where labour was largely physical and the necessary know-how could be transmitted relatively easily. Running a plant producing e. g. integrated circuits at a sufficient level of quality and output – particularly for exportation – was a different thing altogether.

Additionally, while China had proven its ability to realise large-scale projects that were technologically very advanced – notably catching up with some advanced basic innovations in cutting-edge fields like space exploration and nuclear technology – the progress of technology was not confined to such projects that could be handled by a centralised agency. Beyond grain and steel, technological progress affected the labour- and capital-intensive industrial production of all kinds of goods.

Management and hierarchy: Expertise versus egalitarianism

> "Only one, two or three percent of the cadres who really belong to the fourth category (rightists). [(premier said: Much more now)]. Do not be afraid if there is more. In the future they can be rehabilitated. Some of them who cannot continue to work in their own localities may be transferred to others."[1]

The need for experiments and compromise as well as a certain generosity when it came to the assessment of workers' political stances had been obvious with regard to the running of the economy, notably modern industry, since the end of the first five-year-plan. This was particularly the case when it came to the role and status of technical and managerial expertise, without whom production could not run efficiently.

On the one hand, industrial production required technical know-how, which not every worker could command, in order to maintain reasonable efficiency. While Lenin and other socialists were firmly committed to approaches rooted in "scientific management" along the lines of Frederick Taylor – with an emphasis on highly specialised labor and

1 Joint Publications Information Service, Translations on Communist China No. 90, Selections from Chairman Mao, Speech at Central Committee Political Work Report Meeting, 24 October 1966, JPRS Document No. 49826, p. 12, 12 02 1970, accessed through Readex. Also available as a translation of Long Live Mao Tse-tung Thought, a Red Guard Publication at: https://www.marxists.org/reference/archive/mao/selected-works/volume-9/mswv9_68.htm. Accessed on 10 October 2022.

distinct division of labour– in Maoist China, the fear of feeding an apolitical technocracy appears to have been too strong to outright embrace specialisation until the mid- to late-1975s.[2] On the other hand, the egalitarian premise of Maoism and the notion of the united working class stood in contrast to the hierarchies of both management and distribution of labour inherently created.[3] Further, different industrial branches were inherently "unequal" with regard to the value-added they were able to create as well as the relative value their products had for both the state and consumers. It was something different to work in a factory producing tanks or bicycles than, for example, cheap tin cans.

Therefore, a combination of technical expertise and political education was an important part of the organisation of enterprises and workers therein, with shifts in emphasis between the two pillars during the general oscillation in Chinese economic policies. This criticism of specialisation and abstraction of labour and rigid hierarchy also extended to the level of planning, notably concerning the purpose of state-owned enterprises. In the "Instructions to Metallurgical Organisations" issued in June 1965, Mao advocated the idea of creating and maintaining "multi-purpose enterprises" instead of specialised sectors. The concept indicated that large enterprises, such as the Wuhan Steel Factory, could be transformed to engage in the production of other products such as machines, chemicals and even engage in agriculture, commerce, education and military affairs if instructed to do so.[4] Slogans issued during the Great Leap, such as "The lowly are the most intelligent, the elite are the most ignorant", endured and were recited by newspapers and authorities throughout the early 1970s. In practice, the guidelines enshrined in the "Constitution of the Anshan Iron and Steel Company"[5] stipulated the two

2 Kirby William C., Technocratic Organization and Technological Development in China: The Nationalist Experience and Legacy, 1928–1953, in: Simon Denis Fred, Goldman Merle (eds.), Science and Technology in Post-Mao China, Harvard 1989, p. 43. On the other hand, despite changes in rhetoric and several actual purges, specialised workers as well as cadres in changing forms always existed in Chinese industries after 1949.

3 Which, as Richard Curt Kraus rightly emphasised, was a promise of material egalitarianism much more than of political egalitarianism, at least during the postulated period of the dictature of the proletariat. Nevertheless, the idea of the mass line was taken seriously by the Chinese leadership. See: Kraus Richard Curt, The Limits of Maoist Egalitarianism, in: Asian Survey, Vol. 16, No. 11, November 1976, p. 1086.

4 Joint Publications Research Service, Translations on Communist China No. 90, Selections from Chairman Mao, Instructions to metallurgical Organizations, Original in Mandarin, JPRS Document 49826, 12 02 1970, accessed through Readex.

5 Also referred to as the Charter of the Anshan Steel Company (an gang xian fa). The main points of the management guidelines originally issued as the Report by the Anshan Municipal Committee on the Implementation of Technological Reform and Revolution on the Industrial Front were: "Carry out technological reform and revolution, mobilise mass movements, give prominence to politics, implement the manager responsibility system under party leadership, and practice 'two participations, one change, and three combinations' [the participation of cadres in labour, worker's participation in management, the change of all 'unreasonable' rules and regulations within the enterprise, the combined leadership by cadres, technicians and workers]". See Li 1995, p. 2. While the charter emphasised party control and the exchange between workers and cadres as well as efficiency of administration, efficiency via references to the law of value were not part of the Anshan Constitution.

complementary directives of cadre participation in productive labour and worker participation in management – albeit the existence of a distribution of labour between the functions as such was not disputed. While people were encouraged as well as forced to move between the two functions to a certain degree, neither management functions nor industrial workers were abolished as distinct groups. The internal class division of the Chinese society, with regard to types of employment, class status and ethnical origin, did not change fundamentally throughout the late Maoist era.[6]

The necessity of functional management for the improvement of production was – despite Mao's critical views – officially declared an important aspect of the economy's organisation even in the early 1970s. With regard to the industrial management of specific enterprises, the Anshan constitution reflected principles of "close cooperation among workers, cadres and technicians" in order to "go full steam ahead with technical innovations and technical revolution".[7] While specialisation in general was not touched, keeping politics in command, notably through the assurance of the leadership of the CCP in industrial and rural production, appears to be the core of the Anshan Constitution implemented through the "Three-In-One" combination[8] of decentralised leadership that ensured a high degree of political control by the CCP and the PLA. Within the PLA, which was still *de facto* running important parts of the country's infrastructure in the early 1970s, political education for cadres was underlined while their status and importance as such was undisputed.[9]

As an example, the writing group of the PLA railway corps referred to earlier writings of Mao, quoting the expression "Cadres are a decisive factor, once the political line is determined" and underlining that "the leading bodies at various levels are leaders in giving prominence to proletarian politics". The criteria for the selection of cadres on the other hand continued to be influenced by the emphasis on political consciousness of the Cultural Revolution, as reflected in a directive on the implementation of the Dazhai-model issued in late 1970 in Hunan province shows:

> "We must carry out criticism and education to help those people who are ideologically still at the stage of the democratic revolution and who cannot pass through the gate of socialism in order to help them to continue the revolution. **We should select and promote to leadership posts only those people who have done a good job in the living, study and application of Mao** [Zedong] **Thought and who have resolutely followed**

---

6 What Felix Wemheuer has referred to as the intersectional hierarchies of Maoist China, consisting of the general urban-rural divide as well as formal and informal hierarchies based on rank, class, ethnicity and gender. Wemheuer 2019, pp. 21 ff., notably figure 1.2, p. 26.

7 Foreign Broadcast Information Service, Anshan Municipal Committee Article, Peking NCNA Domestic Service in Mandarin, 2303 GMT, 23 03 1970 B, accessed through Readex.

8 Generally referring to the setup of administrative organs at all levels that consisted of a representant of the revolutionary mass organizations, the PLA and the cadres. See: Foreign Languages Press, "On the Revolutionary 'Three-in-One' Combination", Editorial of Hongqi, No. 5, 1967, in: On the Revolutionary "Three-In-One" Combination [brochure published by the Foreign Languages press], Beijing 1968, p.1.

9 Foreign Broadcast Information Service, PLA railway-men describe successes in using Mao thought, Peking NCNA Domestic Service in Mandarin, 2136 GMT, 31 10 1970 B, accessed through Readex.

> **the socialist road** [emphasis added]. By so doing, leadership power at all levels will be tightly grasped by people who are loyal to Chairman Mao and build the leading group into a battle headquarters which will resolutely execute Chairman Mao's revolutionary line and be closely united and vigorous."[10]

Over the course of the rehabilitation of cadres at all levels in the early 1970s, technical staff were gradually brought back to their positions and assigned work according to their prior specialisations, if they had been removed in the first place. As RICHARD CIAO and DONALD ZAGORIA have noted, the purge of experts was pronounced in the field of economic policy: In Beijing, by 1969, only one-fourth of high cadres had retained their positions. Of the highest-ranking seventy-five leaders on economic affairs in the CCP Central Committee, seventy were ousted.[11] Also, cadres of basic-level plants, mines and enterprises who had been sent to perform manual labour were reinstated, but the importance of political education continued to be emphasised.

Similarly, the compulsory "May 7 Cadre Schools" continued to operate until 1976, albeit to a rapidly diminishing extent. On the 9th of November 1978, Renmin Ribao reported that the authorities of Beijing and Shanghai had decided that technical and scientific workers were exempt from cadre schools that focused on manual labour.[12] Compared to the numbers of urban residents[13] and students sent to the countryside with far more uncertain prospects and uncertainty about whether they would ever be able to return home, relatively few party officials had been sent to the May 7 Schools at all.[14] By the end of 1972, the rehabilitation on all levels was practically completed.[15]

---

10 Foreign Broadcast Information Service, Hunan Directive On Furthering Tachai Campaign Issued, Changsha Hunan Provincial Service, Original in Mandarin, 1100 GMT, 19 11 1970 V, accessed through Readex,

11 CIAO RICHARD, ZAGORIA DONALD, The Nature of Mainland Chinese Economic Structure, Leadership and Policy (1949–1969), in U.S. Arms Controls and Disarmament Agency, February 1972, pp. 181–182.

12 FEN SING-NAN, The May 7 Cadre Schools in the People's Republic of China: 1968–1976, in: Administration & Society, Vol. 18, No. 1, May 1986, p. 40.

13 Meaning non-party members. While the CCP after 1949 was an enormous political organisation that grew rapidly, it did not encompass the whole of the Chinese population. According to ANDREW WALDER, there were about 1.2 million party members at the time of the Japanese surrender in August 1945, rising to over 4.5 million until October 1949 and quadrupling in size by 1965. It is noteworthy that the political capital and personal advantages that party membership brought were significantly higher for members who had joined before the victory over Kuomintang, based on a distinction between the revolutionary members and later accessions (similarly so in the PLA). Accession procedures were complicated and selective, notably with regard to class background and the need to find a designated sponsor ready to vouch for one's integrity. Therefore, individuals were most likely to join when they were young – with highest probabilities around the ages of 22 and 23, dropping rapidly afterwards to being practically impossible after the age of 35. See: WALDER ANDREW, The Evolving Party System, in: BRODSGAARD KJELD ERIK (ed.), Critical Readings on the Chinese Communist Party, Leiden and Boston 2017, pp. 61 f. and 67 f.

14 DIKÖTTER 2016, p. 2014 f.

15 Ibid., p. 258.

The "remold first, employ later" policy towards technicians was abandoned and replaced by the dictum of "having to trust and rely on the overwhelming majority of the cadres" in combination with a rather pragmatic policy of "remolding in the course of employment".[16] Both had the distinct advantage that political instruction – while still conducted and encouraged by the state– did not affect production as much as it had. Nevertheless, the ordeals experienced by cadres and technical experts during the Cultural Revolution had shaped their attitudes towards prudence and a certain passivity. This chilling effect of extensive political campaigning found its expression in the popular proverb of the so-called "three do-nots". "Do not do what the party committee has not explicitly ordered, the masses have not unanimously decided, or for what there is no precedence", a pun on the "three points" brought forward by Mao between the "September Incident" and the 10th Party Congress: "We must practice Marxism and not revisionism; unite and don't split; be open and aboveboard and don't intrigue and conspire."[17]

The careful attitude and ideological confusion of both workers and cadres during this period was reflected later on in modern Chinese literature. In JIANG ZILONG's most famous novel first published in 1979, an ambitious and energetic manager named Qiao assumes office in a Heavy Electrical Machinery Plant. The enterprise has never fulfilled its quota and finds itself in dire straits, as expectations by the state are rising. Manager Qiao's mission is to "put things right" and by doing so, of course, protect the reputation and members of the Electrical Equipment Bureau responsible for the plants performance. Jiang describes the ideological insecurity and political divisions in a scene, in which deputy manager Shi summarises the difficult situation and negative attitudes of the workforce. Both are unknown to Qiao, who does "not really talk to workers":

> "The workers in this plant were rather confused ideologically. The idol many had worshipped had gone [Mao]. They had even lost their national pride and faith in socialism. For many years they had been cheated, manipulated and criticized. They'd become demoralized. Moreover, in this plant there were three groups of cadres: those who had been cadres before the 'cultural revolution'; or during it; or after the downfall of the gang [of four] when Ju Shen became the manager. The old people were still hurt, while the young felt resentful. Shi worried that one day they would flare up and clash head-on. There was not only chaos awaiting him and Qiao, but also bitter political rivalries. They were up against a very difficult situation."[18]

Despite this very difficult situation, the breathing period was only short. The need for the strengthening of enterprise management and both the quality and quantity of output led to new government demands directed at enterprises to do well in their management, work in planning, production, technology, on materials and financial matters, and reintroduce or improve reasonable regulations and systems.[19]

---

16 Chinese Communist Industry in 1972, Taipei Chung-Kung Yen-Chiu, 10 02 1973.

17 Ibid. and AHN BYUNG-JOON, The Cultural Revolution and China's Search for Political Order, in: The China Quarterly, No. 58, April-June 1974, p. 277.

18 JIANG ZILONG, All the Colours of the Rainbow, Beijing 1983, pp. 149–150.

19 Chinese Communist Industry in 1972, Taipei Chung-kung Yen-chiu, 10 02 1973.

The state also gave some attention to the livelihood of workers. Industrial wage adjustments were made in both 1971 and 1972 in the order of up to a ten percent[20] increase, primarily intended to compensate for measures during the Cultural Revolution. The need for compensation was obvious. For workers having permanent positions and other benefits of the "iron rice bowl", the abolishment of bonuses due to heavy criticism had put considerable pressure on their real wages. Furthermore, wage cuts and fines were re-introduced as means of imposing labour discipline. While there is no evidence of substantial hardship among industrial workers during the 1970s, life had become more difficult in particular for younger workers in lower ranks who had obligations towards their families.[21] Cadres fared best when they were affiliated with the CCP and at a relatively lower levels. Some of them continued to be chosen as examples for their efforts to push productivity through technical innovations at the workplace (see next sub-chapter).

In the early 1970s, a combination of technical expertise that rehabilitation allowed for and the moderation of hierarchies was the prevalent model of labour management purported in Chinese media. An egalitarian twist prevailed, as emphasis was put on the inclusion of workers in all processes related to production. As an example, Xinhua reported in December 1973 on how workers in the Wuhan Iron and Steel Works had difficulty in meeting their production targets and thus received the order from the leading cadres to use advanced equipment for oxygen separation. Luckily, the cadres acted "class consciously" and consulted with the workers before taking action. By this reliance on the "wisdom of the masses", a more efficient solution was found than what the cadres had initially envisaged.

Later on, A "worker-turned chief engineer", Li Feng, was reported to have stayed with the workers for days on end, checking up on the records and technical data of the furnace and investigating potentials for improvement – leading to "an output of this furnace [...] now almost twice as much as it was at the beginning of 1973". "In the battle for iron and steel", the article concluded, "leading cadres at all levels went down to the grassroots, joining the workers in productive labor, making detailed investigations, giving guidance on the spot, and thus ironing out many hitches in production work".[22] While the role and function of cadres in industrial production *was* recognised in these accounts, the ideal of their work and position was still very much based on strictly egalitarian ideals. Notably, after the 10th Party Congress, the order that was passed down put remarkable emphasis on the stability of production over the rectification of potentially deviant cadres and experts, as illustrated in a speech of a leading cadre of the Shantung provincial CCP committee from January 1974:

> "Tempered in the Great Proletarian Cultural Revolution, the broad masses of rural cadres in our province have greatly raised their consciousness of class struggle and the struggle between the two lines. Basic-level cadres, in particular, have fought on

---

20 Joint Publications Research Service, Current Chinese Communist Trends, Article by Lin Pin, "*Current Economic Trends of the Chinese Communists*", Taipei Chung-kung Yen-chiu, Vol. 7, No. 5, Original in Mandarin, 05 1973, p. 35, accessed through Readex.

21 Wemheuer 2019, pp. 241 f.

22 Foreign Broadcast Information Service, Wuhan Iron-Steel Complex, Peking NCNA in English, 1248 GMT, 30 12 1973 B, accessed through Readex.

> the frontline of the three great revolutionary movements the year round. Braving strong winds and heavy rain, they have worked vigorously for the party and have taken the lead in taking part in labor. **The overwhelming majority of them are good, or comparatively good** [emphasis added]".[23]

While cadres continually required to prove their right attitude towards revolutionary principles, their function and even additional value as workers had become a priority; especially, lower-level cadres were treated with increasing acceptance. This was also made clear in agricultural production, with regard to the guidelines that the model brigade of Dazhai had set. At the provincial conference on "learning from Dazhai", cadres were put in a positive light, as long as they participated in manual labour:

> "The cadres [...] have carried out their work well. To maintain close ties with the masses, one must be physically close to the masses. Otherwise how can you maintain close ties with them? While the masses are working in the fields, you are sauntering in the yard. You may write good reports with all the details well covered, but they may not be true. Only by sharing weal and woe with the masses, will the masses be happy. Sometimes, discussions have been carried out verbally, but no action has been taken. We must do more and talk less. We should not talk more and do less."[24]

The call for less theoretical debate and more productive work was coupled with a call for stability in leadership at all levels, even before the fourth National People's Congress in 1975. This attempt did face political headwinds. While the rehabilitation of cadres was carried out without particular interferences, criticism of "bourgeois rights"[25] re-emerged, once again focused on inequality with regard to wages and hierarchy. This reassessment of the roles of the cadres also had a very practical connection to the reactivation of stalled and initiation of new capital construction projects – as complex construction was, probably rightly so, it was perceived to work better with a hierarchical working structure in place. The Guangxi Regional Revolutionary Committee summarised this objective in a matter-of-factly tone after holding a conference on agricultural capital construction:

> "We must establish and put on a sound basis a command system for agricultural capital construction. The prefectures, municipalities, counties and communes must set up commands with a deputy secretary or vice-chairman in charge. Key projects should also set up strong commands. All projects should be led by **someone** [emphasis added].

23 Foreign Broadcast Information Service, Pai Ju-ping Speech, Tsinan Provincial Service in Mandarin, 1100 GMT, 11 01 1974 B, accessed through Readex.

24 Foreign Broadcast Information Service, Chen Yung-Kuei's Report at Heilungkiang Conference on Tachai, Harbin Heilungkiang Provincial Service in Mandarin, 2130 GMT, 24 02 1974 B, accessed through Readex.

25 Based on Karl Marx's *Critique of the Gotha Program*. He argued that people in socialist society would be paid on the basis of the amount of goods they produced. Since, some people produced more than others, equal right of reward necessarily was to result in unequal payment, turning the formally "equal right" to an "unequal bourgeois right". The critique was first raised by Zhang Chunqiao, who criticised in 1958 that the eight-point wage system was a manifestation of bourgeois rights. See: Zweig 1989, p. 24.

> The chief leadership of the commands must be assigned to comrades who have a high sense of responsibility for the proletarian cause and tremendous enthusiasm for work. They should also be relatively stable, and grasp the work to the very end. The leading cadres at all levels should all go down deep and take the lead to work in a big way and, under the centralised leadership of the party, blend the forces of all trades to support agricultural capital construction."[26]

When criticism of the implementation of the Modernisations and the course associated with Deng Xiaoping emerged in early 1976, hierarchy and leadership were particular points of conflict addressed with references to the Anshan and Magnitogorsk Constitutions. In comparison to the emphasis on the collective and the masses, the "system of one-man-leadership" affiliated with the Magnitogorsk Constitution contrasted with the leadership of the CCP "in everything".[27] Also, the focus of critique with regard to the use of technical expertise and its status in production was much more narrow compared to the Cultural Revolution, when it was claimed that "95 percent of the cadres and masses"[28] would need to join to battle against the few capitalist roaders, as a critique in Hongqi against "revisionist fallacies" in industry and communications in May 1976 stated:

> "Didn't [Deng Xiaoping] advertise that he wanted to elevate to leading posts bourgeois intellectuals whose interests were identical and who had knowledge? This shows that je wanted to rely on a small number of bourgeois 'specialists' and 'authorities. Didn't [Deng Xiaoping] prostrate himself before foreigners and regard as sacrosanct foreign specialists and equipment? Didn't he try his utmost to preach the slavish comprador philosophy and the doctrine of trailing behind at a snail's pace? This shows that he wanted to rely on foreign capitalists."[29]

In agriculture, management guidelines issued at the provincial level were important tools to transmit the priorities of the central government to individual collectives, such as the "Four Summer Tasks" in Anhui province in 1975, which, in addition to a reflection of the political canon, emphasised the importance of bringing in the summer harvest quickly and efficiently, practicing field and crop management including the

---

26 Foreign Broadcast Information Service, Kwangsi Holds Rural Conference on Agriculture, Nanning Kwangsi Regional Service in Mandarin, 1100 GMT, 08 09 1975 FE, accessed through Readex.

27 As in: Foreign Broadcast Information Service, People's Daily upholds Anshan Constitution, Article by Kung Yeh-ping, "Uphold the Constitution of the Anshan Iron and Steel Company, Criticize the Theory of Productive Forces", Peking Domestic Service in Mandarin, 2230 GMT, 18 02 1976 OW, accessed through Readex.

28 "[We must] unite with more than 95% of the cadres and masses, adhere firmly to the general orientation of struggle, and carry through to the end the great struggle to rebuff the right deviationist wind to reverse previous verdicts." Foreign Broadcast Information Service, People's Daily Scores Capitalist Key Link, Text of People's Daily 29 February Article by Liang Hsiao and Jen Ming: "Criticize 'Taking the Three Directives as the Key Link'", Peking Domestic Service in Mandarin, 2230 GMT, 28 02 1976 OW, accessed through Readex.

29 Foreign Broadcast Information Service, Revisionism in Industry, Communications scored, Excerpts of an article by Chung Shih, "Criticize the Revisionist Absurd Fallacies on the Industrial and Communications Front", Red Flag No. 5, Peking Domestic Service in Mandarin, 0800 GMT, 09 05 1976 OW, accessed through Readex.

waging of a "people's war" against pests, ensured efficient bookkeeping, settlement of payments and distribution in advance and mobilisation of all available resources during the harvest months. Provincial revolutionary committees used quite modern means like phone conferences to coordinate efforts, while the content was often more political than practical.[30]

In parallel with the rehabilitation of cadres, improvements in productivity were sought by increasing discipline at the workplace and adjusting management. While the Cultural Revolution had not officially ended until 1976, such initiatives were taken on at the enterprise level to improve efficiency and administrative procedures while retaining the requirements of a revolutionary struggle at least formally. According to a dispatch from Canton, quoted in a Taiwanese report on the state of the Chinese industry in December 1970,

> "...in order to improve the work style of the organizational cadres, the Canton Branch Bureau of Railroads has adopted four concrete measures: First, uphold one third of the cadres going to the "May seventh" cadre school to do labor, one third of the cadres settling at the basic levels in the countryside to do labor, to do investigative study, and to direct work, and one third of the cadres to uphold daily organizational work. At a set date they will all rotate. Second, uphold set dates for labor. The cadres who are upholding daily organizational work will assemble in squads every Tuesday according to the production tasks and each unit's production situation to participate in labor and to store the fulfilment of production tasks. Third, take meetings, documents and reports concise.
> **Do not call meetings which either can or cannot be called. Do not break up meetings which can be consolidated. Do not call a big meeting if a small meeting can be called. Do not call meetings at a higher level that can be called at a lower level. Make documents which you have no choice but to write and meetings which you have no choice but to call, short and to the point. Raise the quality of documents and meetings. Save time.** [emphasis added] Fourth, reduce gradations. When taking the lead in the arrangement of work, get to the bottom by one pole, implement fully to a man and avoid letting things pile up."[31]

The conflict between different management paradigms was stylised by official media such as Renmin Ribao as a choice between enterprises following official guidelines such as the "Anshan Constitution" or falling for bureaucratic or bourgeois alternatives. In short, the latter were considered to be led by managers and experts[32], profit-oriented and offering material incentives for workers and cadres in accordance with the Soviet

30 Foreign Broadcast Information Service, Telephone Conference, Hofei Anhwei Provincial Service in Mandarin, 1100 GMT, 07 06 1975 OW, accessed through Readex.

31 Joint Publication Research Service, Article by Chiang Huai, "Situation Regarding Communist China's Transportation and Communications", Taipei, Fei-Ch'ing Yueh-pao, Original in Mandarin, JPRS Report No. 89, 01 01 1970, pp. 79–82, accessed through Readex.

32 Criticised as "one-man-leadership". See: Foreign Broadcast Information Service, People's Daily Upholds Anshan Constitution, Peking Domestic Service in Mandarin, 2230 GMT, 18 02 1976 OW, accessed through Readex.

model of the "Constitution of the Magnitogorsk Steel Combinate",[33] while the former used mass movements, cadre participation in productive labour and worker participation in management as well as workplace innovations to improve production.[34] Arguably, also in this case, neither of these enterprises existed in their pure form. Decisions on management and remunerations were rather taken at the level of individual enterprises, so elements of both "constitutions" were part of the reality at the workplace.[35] At the national level, the question encapsulated the tension between the need to keep wages relatively low to generate surplus for investments and the basic egalitarian promise of Maoist socialism on the one hand and ideological demands on the other.

How could workers be motivated to be more productive beyond the time-consuming – and certainly not always overly attractive – political "incentives" manifesting themselves in the form of lengthy study sessions and debates that had shown their potentially devastating effects on cadres to implement and enforce instructions by their superiors on the other? As Lev Delyusin, head of the China Department of the Institute of Oriental Studies in of the Soviet Academy of Sciences, put it during the weekly International Observers Roundtable: "It is impossible to make workers work harder, raise labor productivity and care about turning out high-quality goods solely by having them read various leaflets and speeches by Mao [Zedong]."[36] Cadres and managers, on the other hand, were described as hesitant to enforce instructions facing greater work demands without corresponding material rewards.[37]

An important aspect of the "Anshan constitution" – read and discussed in conjunction with the systems of cadre participation in productive labour and worker participation in management as well as the requirement of close cooperation between workers, cadres and technicians – was the "reform of irrational rules and regulations". This implied a larger degree of worker participation in defining regulations at the workplace. The Anshan municipal committee underlined the importance of "rational rules" in early 1970, albeit with numerous political caveats:

> "The reform of irrational rules and regulations is a revolution. In the course of this reform, it is necessary to arouse the masses fully, consult them and ask for their opinions,

---

33 While it served as a contrast to the *Anshan Constitution* as a rule-book-oriented system run by a managerial bureaucracy, the references to the Magnitogorsk Steel Works appear to have been rather a signifier for the whole of Soviet methods of labour management than a reference to a real document. See also: Corrigan Philip, Ramsay Harvie, Sayer Derek, Socialist Construction and Marxist Theory: Bolshevism and its Critique, London and Basingstoke 1978, p. 132.

34 Foreign Broadcast Information Service, Article by Yeh Yen, The Constitution Of Anshan Steel Plant Will Shine Forever, People's Daily in Mandarin, 23 02 1974, accessed through Readex.

35 Whereby the decision to introduce material incentives was frequently criticised and protested against, as reports on big-character posters were being put up by workers declaring " „We are masters, not hired hands of an enterprise" showed. Foreign Broadcast Information Service, Fukien workers' poster lashes out at material incentives, Foochow Fukien Provincial Service in Mandarin, 1100 GMT, 25 02 1974, accessed through Readex.

36 Foreign Broadcast Information Service, International Observers Roundtable, Moscow International Service in Russian, 0730 GMT, 28 September 1975, accessed through Readex.

37 US Department of State, Electronic Telegram, PRC Industrial Advance, 24 October 1975, 07:12, PlusD, ID: 1975HONGK12676_b.

> and carefully examine the existing rules and regulations. We must make a demarcation line between the rational regulations and rules and those that 'govern, restrict, oppress, and punish'. We must uphold everything that gives prominence to proletarian politics and do away with everything that does not, uphold everything that is in the interests of our effort to increase production and practice economy and do away with everything that does not. [...] we should uphold everything which conforms to Mao [Zedong] thought and do away with everything which does not. At the same time, new rules and regulations should be established and improved in the light of the needs of the revolution and production."[38]

During the course of this criticism of intra-enterprise regulations, the political side – proletarian politics and Mao Zedong Thought – were taken as guiding principles but so was the increase of production as well as its efficiency.

"Strengthening management" and re-introducing "rational rules and regulations"

With regard to labour discipline, the tone after the Cultural Revolution shifted clearly in 1975 when the readjustment programs advocated by Deng Xiaoping gained momentum. Under the rubric of "strengthening management"[39], central directives were issued to ensure implementation of mandates over the fear of cadres that they might be ideologically disputed and that compliance may lead to political repercussions. At least ten such directives referring to the economy (notably in the coal, railway and steel sectors) emphasised the need to obey instructions and carry out orders in 1975.[40] Ensuring the implementation of instructions issued in particular by the central government, and thereby the new concentration of production goals, also bore the objective of reassuring cadres and workers that the consensus on economic policy had really shifted, and that the emphasis of ideology over production of the Cultural Revolution did not correspond with the official state line any more.

Concerning the ideological legitimation of this adjustment, with principles advocated by exponents of the CCP during the Cultural Revolution, increasing references were being made to classic writings of Marxism-Leninism. In February 1975, Hongqi published an article referencing "A Great Unprecedented Action" by Lenin.[41] The piece emphasised the sequence of the revolutionary process and its economic implications. Notably, it was explained that although part of the bourgeois rights to private ownership of the means of production had been abolished after 1949, the "right of the bourgeoisie under which different people are given the same amount of goods by doing different amounts of work" was not. Therefore, it would still be necessary to apply the principle of "to each according to his work", for it had "a role to play in the historical period of

---

38 Foreign Broadcast Information Service, Anshan Municipal Committee Article, Peking NCNA Domestic Service in Mandarin, 2303 GMT, 23 03 1970 B, accessed through Readex.

39 For a critical discussion of the role of management in the early and mid-1970's People's Republic, see: PÉAN PIERRE, Après Mao les managers, Paris 1977.

40 PERKINS 2015, p. 147.

41 Foreign Broadcast Information Service, Red Flag: Study Lenin's Work On Proletarian Dictatorship, Peking NCNA Domestic Service in Mandarin, 07:43 GMT, 09 02 1975 OW, accessed through Readex.

socialism". As it was not a communist principle, it would nevertheless – eventually – be abolished. An article published in Hongqi as well as in Renmin Ribao in February 1975 warned against sectarianism and "splittism" within the CCP and made reference to selected theoretical works such as Marx's Critique of the Gotha Program, Lenin's The State and Revolution and Mao's On the Correct Handling of Contradictions among the People. Strengthening labour discipline was notably widespread through provincial conferences on the implementation of the Dazhai and Daqing-models.

During a seven-day conference on the topic in the Jiangxi province, in April 1975, the reporting radio service praised the "warm atmosphere of soaring enthusiasm to aim high and achieve great objectives". The messages conveyed were nevertheless rather sober. The first secretary of the provincial CCP committee spoke at the closing ceremony, highlighting how industrial production was to be approached. Under the precondition of putting politics in command, as the Cultural Revolution had demanded, attention was to be paid to planning and management. Absolutes such as "it is safe to grasp production" – the "economism"[42] of Liu Shaoqi – as well as "it is dangerous to grasp politics" were deemed fallacies. The terms referred broadly to any practices perceived as putting production and economic considerations before ideology and, in particular, class struggle.

According to Xing Li, the term primarily referred to practices in the countryside such as the liberalisation of private plots and markets as well as the introduction of the profit motive as a planning device and the definition of output quotas on the basis of individual households, which were conceptualised by Mao Zedong as being capitalistic in nature. The correct principle, he declared, should be "a unity of politics and economics and a unity of politics and technology", achieved by the establishing and perfecting of "rational rules and regulations".[43] While cadres should continue to go down to the lower units, they should do so mostly to "show concern for their daily life". Practical problems in daily life were to be solved step by step, on the basis of both ideological education and increased production, and "a demarcation" should be drawn "between material incentives and concern for the masses' daily life" – a difference that would become important shortly after.

At a nationwide conference on coal mining, approved by the State Council at the Peking stadium on the 30th of October 1975, the sectoral implementation of "rational rules and regulations" was announced in an impressive public act. A large portrait of Mao hung high above the rostrum, while large streamers with the main slogan of the Great Leap "go all out, aim high and build socialism with greater, faster, better and more economical re-

42 Li Xing, The Chinese Cultural Revolution Revisited, in: The China Review, Vol. 1, No. 1, Fall 2001, pp. 137–165.

43 Foreign Broadcast Information Service, Chiang Wei-Ching Speaks at Kiangsi Meeting Closing Ceremony, Kiangsi Provincial Service in Mandarin, 1100 GMT, 01 05 1975, accessed through Readex.

sults"[44] combined with the new "learn from Taching, catch up with Kailuan"[45] and "build a contingent of particularly good fighters" decorated the auditorium. The minister of the coal industry stated:

> "With regard to strict enforcement of regulations and rules, correct application [of them] means correct application of the workers' experience gained through their long practice. It assists in raising the contingent's [of miners] fighting capacity and enables it to wage effective struggle against nature. It is crucially important to be strict in enforcing rules and regulations."[46]

After the demotion of Deng Xiaoping in April 1976, the criticism of the regulations introduced or partly introduced before and during the programme was officially endorsed by the state and formulated by various local entities, such as party committees in factories, within the framework of the Anshan/Magnitogorsk-comparison. The critique, while referring to the importance of class struggle and the dialectical struggle with regard to the interpretation of the Three Principles, appears to have been relatively nuanced, at least in its public showcasing. In the case of the iron and steel plant in Shandong, the critique was almost exclusively directed at the acceptance of foreign technology, stating that "during the critical moment of our industrial development, the Khrushchev renegade clique tore up the contracts, withdrew its experts and shipped back or destroyed technical data in order to throttle and impede our development and to put the Chinese people in a hopeless position".[47] The actual management of the daily work in the factory was not mentioned in the critique.

Similarly, one of the critiques of Deng Xiaoping's "Question on Speeding Up Industrial Development" – that had the establishment of rational rules and regulations at its core – published in Beijing in June 1976 was more specifically directed at the top–down nature of the guideline rather than an absolute dismissal of rational rules and regulations on ideological grounds. While attacking Deng Xiaoping as running counter to "Chairman Mao's consistent teachings", the stance taken was not against regulations per se: "It is not true that socialist enterprises do not need rules and regulations. The question is what kind of rules and regulations have their class nature. Proletarian rules and regulations for enterprise management should be a summarisation of the experiences of the masses of workers in actual struggle." The rules and regulations that were demanded instead were to be political in character, as "conductive to consolidating the leading role of

---

44 A general line that was used as early as 1958/1959 during the massive campaign to make iron and steel. For example, Report on Adjusting the Major Targets of China's 1959 National Plan and Further Developing the Campaign for Increasing Production and Practicing Economy, delivered by Premier Zhou Enlai to a plenary meeting of the Standing Committee of the Second NPC, August 26, 1959. Available in: Bowie Robert R., Fairbank John King, Communist China 1955–1959: Policy Documents with Analysis, Cambridge 1971, pp. 540–549.

45 Another example of socialist enterprise, the main source of coking coal in Northern China around the city of Tangshan.

46 Foreign Broadcast Information Service, Reportage On Coal Mining Conference, Peking NCNA Domestic Service in Mandarin, 1428 GMT, 30 10 1975, accessed through Readex.

47 Foreign Broadcast Information Service, Shantung Workers Oppose Teng's 'Regulations', Tsinan Shantung Provincial Service in Mandarin, 1100 GMT, 24 06 1976 OW, accessed through Readex.

the working class, to bringing into play the socialist enthusiasm of the masses of workers, to developing the socialist economy, and to carrying out the task of consolidating the dictatorship of the proletariat in every grass-roots unit."[48] The divisive issue, as pointed out by author LU TA, consisted primarily of three areas:

> "The 'rules' [as proposed by Deng Xiaoping] also use material incentives as an important means to exercise this kind of dictatorship [of the bourgeoisie over the masses of workers], using money and material gains to corrupt the souls of the workers, stifle their revolutionary spirit and undermine their unity, thus turning the relationship among men into a capitalist relationship between employer and hired hands [...] based on money. [...] [Also] the 'rules one-sidedly stress centralised unified leadership, try in every way to strangulate local initiative, and attempt to control enterprises. [...] The 'rules' dished up on his instruction advocate reliance on a small number of bourgeois 'experts' and 'authorities'"[49]

Notably, with regard to those cadres who were seen as having ascended in the hierarchy during the Cultural Revolution, sharp appeals to egalitarianism made way for more pragmatic views by 1976. The public image of good cadres reflected the compromise between the necessity of sufficient ideological credibility and productive capability.

For instance, a worker like Liu Liangshan, a thirty-nine years old miner working in Hunan province, allegedly from a poor peasant family, was made secretary of the party committee and chairman of the revolutionary committee of the Yangmeishan coal mine.[50] His career had begun as a cutter in the mine, where he joined the criticism of Liu Shaoqi and his counterrevolutionary revisionist line during the Cultural Revolution. "Though now a leader", Xinhua reported, "he regularly goes down into the pit to work alongside the miners and keeps close ties with the masses". At the mine, half of the members of the party standing committee were reported to be "ordinary miners", while one-third of the party committee were miners "who carry on with productive labour, many heading work sections and teams". The miners were quoted as saying: "We have really become masters of this socialist mine". That workers who had distinguished themselves in the Cultural Revolution had been promoted to "leading posts in factories and mines in new China" was touted as "one of the important new things that has emerged in the Great Cultural Revolution". The report on Liu Lien-sheng concluded with a description of the efficiency gains achieved by incremental technical innovations and the perseverance of the workers.

The hierarchical state unveiled (again)

After the arrest of the Gang in October 1976, hierarchical relationships quickly re-emerged openly as a centrepiece of economic organisation, with the CCP as a vanguard of the development. After the second national conference on "learning from Dazhai", where further clarifications had been delivered by Hua Guofeng, the line passed down to the

48 Ibid.

49 Ibid.

50 Foreign Broadcast Information Service, Hunan Miners Given Leadership Positions, Peking NCNA in English, 0715 GMT, 18 06 1976 OW, accessed through Readex.

provinces was clear, foreshadowing a movement of "Consolidation and Rectification" announced for 1977:

> "We must organise party members to scathingly criticise the crimes of the Gang of Four to place themselves above the party [...] and others; and strictly observe the discipline of the party, namely: The individual is subordinate to the organisation; the minority is subordinate to the majority; the lower level is subordinate to the higher level; and the entire membership is subordinate to the Central Committee."[51]

The ideal of the workers being "both red and expert" expressed in Mao Zedong Thought was a useful formula to legitimise improving technical standards, when factory-run technical schools and spare-time technical training institutions – which had previously suspended operations – were re-opened. It went hand in hand with the guideline for enterprises to ensure that workers were given merely an "adequate" amount of time for political studies.[52] Also, with regard to the long-term development plan, the participation of workers in industrial enterprises was reinvigorated under the competitive goal of surpassing the advanced world levels by 1980, with as little state investment as possible. From the Lanzhou oil refinery in Gansu province, it was reported that more than sixty planning committees following the Three-In-One combination – which were, in this context, important enterprises composed of cadres, workers and technicians – were formed.[53] The emphasis, at least in the relatively advanced oil industry, began to shift towards technical innovation. Accordingly, at the Lanzhou plant, the resulting measures demanded that old technology be abolished, manual operation be replaced with mechanisation and automation, single-item manufacturing replaced with standardised manufacturing and packing, efficiency of equipment be improved, and new technology be developed to replace the old.[54]

The tilt within the dialectical flexibility of the "red and expert"-formula was confirmed in Renmin Ribao on the 14th of November 1976 by a commentator who used a criticism of the Gang of Four as the basis for the formulation of the new priorities. The group's opposition to production, he wrote, was "anti-Marxist". While the commentary emphasised that revolution had to be prioritised over the development of productive forces, it argued for a balance between "redness" and "expertise", stating clearly that "we

---

51 Foreign Broadcast Information Service, Wang Huai-hsiang 10 Feb Speech, Speech given by Comrade Wang Huai-hsiang, first secretary of the Kirin Provincial CCP Committee, on 10 February at the provincewide conference on learning from Tachai in agriculture: "Hold High the Great Banner of Chairman Mao and Strive Hard to Carry Out the Strategic Policy Decision of Chairman Hua and the Party Central Committee to Grasp the Key Link in Running the Country" [Title read by announcer]. Changchun Kirin Provincial Service in Mandarin, 1100 GMT, 14 02 1977 OW, accessed through Readex.

52 Ibid.

53 Which were also tasked with training technicians from among the workers and were largely credited with achievements made by workplace innovations (discussed below). See: Jencks Harlan W., Politics and Professionalism in the Chinese Army, 1945–1981, New York 1982.

54 Foreign Broadcast Information Service, Long-Term Planning, Peking Domestic Service in Mandarin, 0800 GMT, 23 07 1975 OW, accessed through Readex.

[the Chinese people] want both".[55] In the very same commentary, nevertheless, both the insistence on the "Three Directives" as well as the "black cat, white cat"-quote associated with Deng Xiaoping were stated to be "extremely wrong", albeit the critique, as USLO estimated, remained quite far below earlier apodictic statements on a "conflict of two lines".

Specifically, in the key industries of coal and steel, the priorities for the implementation of the Daqing model were modified and the turn towards a management style based on hierarchy became clearer, as reported after the conclusion of the national conference on learning from Daqing in January 1977. Ideologically basing their conclusions on the Ten Relationships, the 3000 conference representatives adopted a report calling for the continuation of the selection of "particularly good fighters"[56] among the workers and making careful distinctions "in defining Marxism, socialism and capitalism, materialism, dialectics, idealism and metaphysics" in order to further clarify the relationship between production and revolution. The military connotation was quite fitting, as many of the new cadres at the highest level of governence had military experience. Minister Yu Qiuli's experience with the mobilisation of troops to fight the Japanese proved to be useful, and he replicated the habit of setting up command posts near the "front lines" in order to oversee operations. In a 1994 publication on Daqing by the military press, oil prospecting in Daqing was accordingly referred to as "the start of an important smokeless great battle" (*yige meiyou xiaoyan paohuode zhongdazhan yijijiang kaishile*).[57]

Emphasising the development of smaller coal mines as a goal, the guidelines reflected the rule- and hierarchy-based courses of economic management: "Consolidate and strengthen enterprise management, socialist cooperation in networks to direct production, consolidate labour organisation, institute and improve on-post responsibility of individual workers and cadres, standardisation of technical operation procedures, instating evaluation systems for work performance and accounting systems based on work teams, saving materials where possible and show concern for the well-being of staff and workers".[58] Clarifications on the adjustments of economic policies concerning the management of enterprise – although still referencing the Anshan Constitution and Daqing – had reached the operative level. The Gang was accused of both the harmful negation of rational rules and regulations and sabotage of enterprise management along the lines presented at the conference in several publications by provincial planning committees, linking the establishment of such regulations back to 1973 and 1975.[59]

55 As quoted in US Department of State, Electronic Telegram, People's Daily Calls for New Focus on Production, 15 November 1976, 08:12, PlusD, ID: 1976HONGK13321_b.

56 Lim Tai Wei, Oil in China: From Self-reliance to Internationalization, Singapore 2010, pp. 51 f.

57 Foreign Broadcast Information Service, Further Report On Conclusion Of Coal Industry Conference, Peking NCNA Domestic Service in Mandarin, 1713 GMT, 25 01 1977 OW, accessed through Readex.

58 Ibid.

59 Foreign Broadcast Information Service, Hunan Officials Attack 'Gang' for Local Crimes, Speech by Sun Kuo-chih, member of the standing committee of the Hunan provincial CCP committee and chairman of the provincial planning committee at the Hunan provincial conference on learning from Daqing in industry: "Indignantly Expose and Criticize the Towering Crimes of the 'Gang of Four' in Sabotaging Socialist Revolution and Construction and Conspiring to Usurp the Party

Similar instructions were repeated in several provincial conferences on learning from Daqing and Dazhai, calling for the expansion of "progressive units" – meaning enterprises and agricultural production units that adhered to the new guidelines throughout the country – albeit with differing undertones.[60] Similarly, the slogan "fewer and better troops and simpler administration"[61] became a shorthand for the course transmitted through the same conferences and published reports on their outcomes – it encompassed the solution of, as it was reported after the Hunan conference on Dazhai in February 1977, "problems of line, drive, style of work and unity and transform the situation of softness, laziness and looseness in the leadership groups of some units". Rectification of cadres, as it was understood under the adjusted economic policy paradigm, was oriented towards production and efficiency, provided that "outstanding elements" were "promoted to the leadership groups at all levels".[62]

The end of the Cultural Revolution brings new idols

The mobilisation "of all positive factors" in 1977, while reminiscent of the Great Leap was clearly linked to the end of the Cultural Revolution and distinguished from political voluntarism. Those who had "erred in their political thinking" in some way or another were declared "basically liberated", with the exception of "a few who have comparatively serious problems". Within the Daqing model-guidelines, summing up experiences became an expression of the closing of the chapter of political struggle within enterprises, which was combined with the continued selection of "model workers" and "pacesetters".[63]

That the Cultural Revolution had ended was an important message particularly to the younger workers spread through the consequent emphasis on rules, labour discipline and the degree of conformity within enterprises that both demanded. The new ideals,

---

and State Power", Changsha Hunan Provincial Service in Mandarin, 2230 GMT, 14 01 1977 FE, accessed through Readex.

60 For instance, the first secretary of the Kwantung provincial CCP committee emphasising on the "persistence in the socialist road and the communist orientation" while presenting the findings of the provincial conferences in January 1977. Foreign Broadcast Information Service, Kwantung First Secretary Addresses Taching Conference, Canton Kwantung Provincial Service in Mandarin, 1100 GMT, 28 01 1977 FE, accessed through Readex.

61 According to John Halliday and Jung Chang, the slogan originated from the Yunnan years of the CCP, being proposed by the local parliament to cut costs for the communist military administration and army. In order to appease the demands, Mao Zedong accepted, albeit being uninterested in reducing the number of troops. Chang/Halliday 2007, p. 336.

62 Foreign Broadcast Information Service, Hunan Conference on Learning from Tachai Continues, Report by Mao Chih-yung, secretary of the Hunan provincial CCP Committee, at the provincial conference on learning from Tachai: "Resolutely Respond to the Great Call of Chairman Hua and the Party Central Committee, Raise Still Higher the Red Banner of Tachai and Speed Up the Pace of Building Tachai-type Counties Everywhere", Changsha Hunan Provincial Service in Mandarin, 0330 GMT, 08 02 1977 FE, accessed through Readex.

63 As brought forward in a speech by the secretary of the Daqing oilfield CCP committee in April 1977. Foreign Broadcast Information Service, Text Of Sung Chen-Ming Speech At Taching Conference, Peking NCNA Domestic Service in Mandarin, 0103 GMT, 24 04 1977 OW, accessed through Readex.

adopting but modifying the archetypical "iron men" of earlier stages of industrial development. One example was a young worker called Meng Shao Tai, a twenty-three years old descendant of a worker's family. While being an excellent student in his earlier youth, he began reading old books as a teenager and decided "not to be afraid of pain caused by daggers through the ribs but to wander everywhere like Chin Chiung" (a famous Tang dynasty general). At one time or another, it was said, he made friends with martial artists, engaged in numerous fights and thereby injured people. Coming to Daqing in 1972, he worked only seventy out of 300 work days, being told by some of his comrades that he was incorrigible in his ways. Nevertheless, the local party branch did not leave him in this dire state, mobilising the workers and the party members to help him. Having heard the stories of forty-six comrades over the course of half a year, he learned about "their past sufferings and their criticism of [Lin Biao]".

Finally, he changed, turning his back on the "highwayman-type heroism and the bourgeois world outlook" and decided to emulate "the iron man instead of Chin Chiung". After more than three years "of hard tempering", Meng was said to have become a party member and an activist in "grasping revolution and promoting production", through which he inspired "many backward workers" to change their ways as well. Similarly, a young worker called "young lord Chia" with "long unruly hair and untrimmed whiskers" wearing "oversized and baggy jackets and trousers" was brought forward as an example of misled youth, who also had changed under the assistance and education of the party branch, even helping change another young worker by the name of Hung.[64] The core message of these anecdotes for the advanced and export-oriented Chinese industry was clear: the liberating experience that many young people had encountered during the Cultural Revolution was over; instead of such "reactionary freedoms", industrial production demanded conformity and devotion.

In a similar vein, the first secretary of the Chekiang provincial CCP committee, Ti Ying referred to the new elements of the Daqing-model as the beginning of "a new leap forward of the national economy", proven by examples of economic progress all over the province:

> "We should follow the example of the No. 1205 drilling team, let one man do three men's work and do three days' work in one day.[65] The greater the difficulties, the more we must do. The farther we lag behind, the quicker we must catch up. The less we have to start with, the harder we should work."[66]

With a reference to the coming "ten crucial years" between 1976 and 1985 for the fulfilment of the PRC's long-term development plan, Ti's speech demonstrated that without additional support, history threatened to repeat itself. The rhetoric was used variously at the

---

64 Ibid.

65 Which, in direct comparison, reflected the much more modest yet ambitious dimension of the alleged new leap. During the Great Leap Forward, slogans like "one day equal to twenty years" were purported.

66 Foreign Broadcast Information Service, Tieh Ying Speech, Hangchow Chekiang Provincial Service in Mandarin, 1100 GMT, 29 05 1977 OW, accessed through Readex.

provincial level, marking the increased pressure on production figures in the implementation of the long-term plan.[67] To speed up the pace of development, innovations were also required in planning and management. For example, the provincial revolutionary committee of Shantung explored "a quick method of seeking the best technical solution and an overall planning method" together with mathematicians of the Chinese Academy of Sciences; however, they did not report any tangible results.[68] The greatest emphasis was on speed: At the national conference on "learning from Daqing", Hua Guofeng pointed out that "as of now [1977], we have only twenty-three years left before the end of the century. To greatly increase the speed of development of our national economy is a task which brooks no delay".[69] Another formula used in 1977 was "initial success in one year, great success in three years" in industry. As the Canton provincial CCP committee held at a provincial petroleum and chemical industries conference stated: "The speed of economic development is not simply a question of economics but it is also political".

After the second rehabilitation of Deng Xiaoping, the "Twenty Points Program" advocated by him in 1975 was reactivated and yet again became a viable reference for labour discipline in public discourse.[70] Also, they were strictly presented as a consequence of the fourth National People's Congress and a continuation of Mao Zedong Thought in production. As an article attributed to the mass criticism group of the State Planning Commission in Renmin Ribao presented the narrative on the 16th of July 1977:

> "The '20 points' were drafted in July 1975 under the sponsorship of leading comrades of the State Council. Then, what was the background under which this document was drafted? First, in 1974 Chairman Mao issued important directives on studying the theory of the dictatorship of the proletariat, on stability and unity and on pushing the national economy forward. The second plenum of the 10th CCP Central Committee and

67 For instance, in an article by the Hunan provincial planning committee in June 1977. Foreign Broadcast Information Service, Hunan Article calls for Promotion of National Economy, article by the Hunan provincial Planning Committee: "Redouble Our Efforts, Realise a New Leap Forward in the National Economy", Changsha Hunan Provincial Service in mandarin, 2330 GMT, 14 06 1977 HK, accessed through Readex. Hua Guofeng used the terminology in a toast at a reception in Beijing on 30 September 1977, on the occasion of the 28th anniversary of the People's Republic, saying that "A new leap forward in China's national economy is taking shape". Joint Publications Research Service, The Toast by Hua Kuo-Feng, Chairman of the CCP Central Committee and Premier of the State Council, at the Reception Marking the 28th National Day, Peking Red Flag No. 10, Original in Mandarin, 08 10 1977, accessed through Readex.

68 Foreign Broadcast Information Service, Shantung Meeting Promotes Use Of Quick Planning Methods, Tsinan Shantung provincial Service in Mandarin, 1130 GMT, 20 06 1977 OW, accessed through Readex.

69 Foreign Broadcast Information Service, Kwangtung conducts Petrochemical Industries Conference, Canton Kwangtung Provincial Service in Mandarin, 0500 GMT, 02 12 1977 HK, accessed through Readex.

70 Foreign Broadcast Information Service, People's Daily Condemns Gang's Criticism of 'Regulations', Text of 16 July People's Daily article by the mass criticism group of the State Planning Commission: "A Counterrevolutionary Farce of Usurping Party and State Power – Commenting on the 'Gang of Four's' Criticism of 'The 20 Points'", Peking NCNA Domestic Service in Mandarin, 0717 GMT, 16 07 1977 OW, accessed through Readex.

> the fourth NPC were held in January 1975. In accordance with Chairman Mao's instructions, Premier [Zhou Enlai] set forth the task of persevering in continuing the revolution under the dictatorship of the proletariat, reiterated the grand two-stage plan for the development of our national economy and called on the entire party and the people throughout the country to strive to build our country into a modern, powerful socialist stage before the end of the century.
> Second, in 1974, due to the interference and sabotage by the 'gang of four', the party organizations of many localities and enterprises were paralyzed, capitalism was rampant, production was stagnant, the rate of industrial development decreased and steel output dropped drastically. [...] People demanded that is was necessary to conscientiously sum up experiences regarding these and to take effective measures to meet this demand, accelerate the development of industry and of the national economy as a whole and consolidate the dictatorship of the proletariat. 'The 20 points', in accordance with Chairman Mao's line, principles and policies, criticized some fallacies spread by the 'gang of four' and set forth concrete methods and measures for putting the industry and enterprises in order."

The most explicit expression of Deng Xiaoping's thoughts on the economy can be found in the document titled "Some Questions on Accelerating the Development of History". It called for defined five concrete goals for the achievement of an independent and relatively comprehensive industrial system in China. First, the establishment of complete domestic supply chains in the steel industry, second the accelerated exploration of coal, oil and gas as well as increased production of electricity, development of the petrochemical industry, notably fertiliser, the development of the machine tools industry, production of a varied supply of light industrial goods and the expansion of infrastructure of transport and communication.

The methods to achieve this goal were based on existing policies, but intended to push them further: concentration on the supply of raw materials, targeted and disciplined investments in few large-scale projects, reusing what can be reused and improving what can be improved, putting up quality, norms and variety as priorities, continuing austerity, promoting cooperation between enterprises and regions, using as much advanced technology as can be made available, raising the share of exports, primarily of industrial goods and raw materials, relying on the masses under the strict leadership of the CCP, the principle of subsidiarity in decentralisation, as long as it is not to the detriment of the central level, unified planning "of each accordingly", improving the livelihood of the masses, promoting the combination of "red and expert" in a much weaker form, simplifying administrative procedures – in particular, shortening and avoiding meetings where possible – and propagating dialectical materialism and "seeking truth from facts".[71]

Renmin Ribao continued to emphasise the importance of rules and regulations in production as necessary "at all times [...] even after 10'000 years from now [...]". "Anarchy is not in accord with the interests and aspirations of the people", which also meant reiterating Lenin's idea of turning the economic organisation of the state into an "inte-

---

71 Krott (ed.) 1978, pp. 85–109.

grated big machine, an economic body whose work plan is adhered to by several hundred million people".

The Ten Relationships were presented in tandem with Hua Guofeng's speech at the second national conference on "Learning From Dazhai", where he provided an important clarification of ideological priorities and thereby discussed the contradiction between socialism and capitalism as the key link for the resolution of dialectical opposites in the economy, in lieu of class struggle, as it had been advocated during the Cultural Revolution. The contradiction between revolution and production was presented as a "Unity of Opposites", while the Gang of Four was used as a scapegoat in official media, with the centrally coordinated relief work after the Tangshan earthquakes showing that its members cared only about political power and "not […] for the development of production and the safety of the people"[72], indulging in theoretical "metaphysics". As it was reported in the Guangxi autonomous region regarding a rally of the planning front:

> "Our country is a socialist state. Only by building up a strong socialist economy can the dictatorship of the proletariat have a strong material base, can 800 million people be fed and clothed, can we support still better the world revolution and create the necessary conditions for gradual transition to communism. The antiparty clique of the 'Gang of Four' disregarded this truth, understood even by children; used the tools of public opinion in their hands; deliberately violated Marxism-Leninism-Mao [Zedong] Thought; distorted the relationship of dialectical unity between politics and economics and between revolution and production, deliberately created all kinds of chaos and babbled that 'when revolution is done well, production will increase automatically'".[73].

Numerous conferences that followed at different levels clarified the new course and reassured of its reliability as their main objectives. Notably in the strategic coal and iron industries, these calls were increasingly bold, as references to Mao Zedong Thought were dropped in published reports in favour of concrete instructions. The Daqing model remained a point of reference although the principles attached to it had changed, as a report on the conclusion of the national conference of the coal industry on learning from Daqing in Renmin Ribao in early 1977 pointed out:

> "We should deepen education in the party's basic line; consolidate and strengthen enterprise management; set up a powerful network to direct production; persevere in the system of having leading cadres on shift duty; consolidate labor organization; institute and improve the system of on-post responsibility, technical operational procedures, the work evaluation system, the system to insure equipment maintenance and repair and quality inspection, production safety and the shift and team economic accounting system. We should economically use raw materials and other materials, improve economic accounting and show concern for the well-being of staff and workers."[74]

---

72 'Gang of Four' Sabotage of Production Outlined, 1739 GMT, 14 11 1976 OW.

73 Foreign Broadcast Information Service, Kwangsi Planning Front Rally criticizes 'Gang', Nanning Kwangsi Provincial Service in Mandarin, 1100 GMT, 16 11 1976 FE, accessed through Readex. The notion that "800 million people need to be fed" was a consistent part of language discipline of Chinese officials, in particular when interacting with foreign contacts.

74 Further Report on Conclusion of Coal Industry Conference, 1713 GMT, 25 01 1977 OW.

The objective of streamlining enterprise management was pursued with increasing intensity throughout 1977, with the Daqing model being used as a portmanteau for an increasingly wide range of measures, alongside the consolidation and further strengthening of party control at all levels. At the national Dazhai conference on the fourth of May 1977, Vice Premier Yu Qiuli presented guidelines, highlighting the PLA as a prime example for the organisation of enterprises as well as the party. Quoting Mao with "People must adapt their thinking to the changed conditions" – which Yu defined as "A political situation in which there are both centralism and democracy, both discipline and freedom, both unity of will and personal ease of mind and liveliness" – He established a direct link to chairman Hua Guofeng's "strategic policy decision" to lead the country towards a "great order".[75]

The main points of the programme were, first, that the necessary task of increasing production after the sabotage by the Gang of Four had been successfully fulfilled, ensured by a continuous criticism of their deeds, second, to continue the implementation of the Daqing model as "China's own road", and third, to link back to the comparisons of the first five-year plan and the Great Leap Forward, "Speed Up China's Industrial Growth, Strive to Catch Up with and Surpass Advanced World Levels".[76] The Shanghai conference on "learning from Daqing", held in the heart of the Chinese urban industry, on the seventh of August 1977, summarised the management guidelines as they had been decided at the third plenum of the 10th central committee of the CCP, which also formed the basis for future Daqing-type enterprises.

First, it involved an increase in the speed of the development of industrial production under the slogans of "replacing the donkey with a steed", and "if we have a hundred percent working drive, we will never waste one percent; even after we have exerted a hundred percent effort, we still will throw in something extra" as well as martial references to the iron-man movement: "Iron-man [Wang Jinxi] chose to live twenty years less in order to build the Daqing oilfield; [secretary Li Xianglin of the Shanghai No. 7 light industrial plant] would rather give up my life and see that the red banner of [Daqing] is flown on top of the Shanghai No. 7 light industrial plant." Moreover, highlighting progress in technical innovation (China's first alternate current synchronised generator), a marked increase in financial revenue at the Shanghai port, new achievements in culture, art, journalism, propaganda, education and public health as achievements, showed the right way to "make up for the time they [the Gang of Four] wasted". This general relaxation towards the performing arts was observed. When visiting several Chinese cities in the fall of 1977,

75 Foreign Broadcast Information Service, Vice Premier Yu Chiu-Li Speaks at Taching Conference, Peking NCNA in English, 2105 GMT, 07 05 1977 OW.

76 "At the first session of the preparatory meeting for the eighth party congress in 1956, Chairman Mao made a comparison between the conditions of our country and those of the United States, and suggested that we overtake the United States economically in fifty or sixty years. […] The factors for revolution and war are both increasing in today's world and the contention between the two hegemonic powers – the Soviet Union and the United States – is becoming ever more acute. A world war is bound to break out some day. The wild ambition of Soviet revisionism to subjugate China will not die. With the wolf and tiger pacing before us, we must not lower our guard. As far back as over half a century ago, Lenin made this pointed statement: 'Either perish, or overtake and outstrip the advanced countries economically as well'". Ibid., part four.

a US diplomat noted performances by local arts troupes, which included the presentation of several songs and traditional skits that had been banned for decades.[77]

Second, stability through party leadership, stating that "the dictatorship [of the proletariat] is aimed at protecting the people in carrying out their work in peace and building China into a socialist nation with modern industry, modern agriculture, modern science and modern culture." Third, scientists and technicians "who have made contributions to the socialist cause" needed to be "respected, commended, and given encouragement". Fourth, the guidelines stated that "it is impossible to develop socialist production in any enterprise without scientific management", which aimed at the establishment of "a capable, authoritative and strong production management system", based on "a set of rules and regulations" embodying the "new socialist relations of production and reflect[ing] the objective laws of productions", together with the strict implementation of "the system of personal responsibility" based on the "eight technical and economic targets".[78]

Enterprises that failed to fulfil state plans "due to internal reasons" were to be criticised and, "in serious cases", action was to be taken to pinpoint leadership responsibility. However, even with the necessity to rely on the masses being mentioned, the managers were taking over. With regard to work ethics, the need for efficiency and accountability was clearly reflected:

> "It is necessary to foster a new spirit on the enterprises, a spirit in which hard work is regarded as glorious and fear of hardship and fatigue shameful, a spirit of regarding arduous struggle as glorious and extravagance and waste as shameful, a spirit of regarding efforts to remain honest in thought, work, and deed as glorious and making false statements and empty talk and doing impractical things as shameful, and a spirit of regarding enthusiasm in studying hard to improve one's skills and work performance for the sake of revolution as glorious and the tendency to remain ignorant and make no progress as shameful."[79]

The overall implementation strategy presented was once again ambitious. Within four years, half of all enterprises in Shanghai were to follow the new management model, as well as one third of all administrative offices. The process was to be controlled by an audit, over the course of which, through "evaluation by the masses and confirmation by higher-level departments", the fulfilment of management and output criteria was to be evaluated "and see[n] to it that they continue[d] to develop and grow like rolling snowballs". By 1985, the percentage of enterprises adhering to the model needed to be at eighty percent.

---

77 The US Department of State, Electronic Telegram, Provincial Observations in Kunming, Chengtu, Sian, Shanghai, Canton, October 25 to November 4, 9 November 1977, 00:00, PlusD, ID: 1977PEKING02583_c.

78 People's Daily Condemns Gang's Criticism of 'Regulations', Peking NCNA Domestic Service in Mandarin, 0717 GMT, 16 07 1977 OW.

79 Foreign Broadcast Information Service, Peng Chung Report At Shanghai Learn-From-Taching Conference, Excerpts of 7 August report by Comrade Peng Chung at Shanghai conference on learning from Taching in industry: "Hold Aloft the Great Banner of Chairman Mao and Strive To Speed Up the Building of Taching-Type Enterprises", Shanghai City Service in mandarin, 0430 GMT, 08 08 1977 OW, accessed through Readex.

Beyond the "advanced national levels" for output and efficiency, "advanced world levels" were emphasised as the yardstick for economic success.

Regarding sectoral developments, the petrochemical and iron and steel industries were named first, with high-grade alloy steel named as the product to strive for besides "the comprehensive utilisation of petroleum resources" and petroleum equipment to contribute to the task of building "ten more oilfields like [Daqing]". The demand led to the forming of the so-called "petroleum group" made up of prominent members of the Central Committee and the Politburo such as Li Xiannian, Yu Qili, Kang Xien, Chen Muhua and Gu Mu in May 1977, who took it as their task to define the scope and direction of China's cooperation with foreign enterprises and governments in the development of oil reserves both on- and offshore.[80]

The machine-building industry was named next, tasked with providing advanced technical equipment for the national economy to realise the Four Modernisations, in particular, after having realised agricultural mechanisation in the whole country by 1980, "not only [by] numerically increase[ing] the output of large tractors, drainage and irrigation equipment and chemical fertiliser equipment but also [by] increase[ing] the variety and improve[ing] the quality". The light industrial and especially textile sectors were to increase output "to enrich the people's life and expand exports". The main directions for Shanghai's light and textile industries were to "develop products which require less raw materials, are of high quality, have a greater variety and are new in design" – all this to provide consumer goods for the Chinese people with as low a need for input materials as possible, while meeting international standards, which was still an obstacle for Chinese products in foreign markets. Also, the production of light industrial products including consumer goods "such as wrist watches, television sets, cameras and so forth" was to be greatly increased. It needs to be added, as KARL GERTH noted, that while, for example, the production of watches had ebbed and flowed depending on the state's larger economic goals – expanding even during the decade of the Cultural Revolution (1966–1976), only a small fraction of the country's potential purchasers owned a watch.[81] This was not necessarily the goal now: Additionally, the instructions stated that "it is necessary to vigorously develop exports of industrial products and build Shanghai into an important foreign trade base of our country".[82]

While this sectoral distribution mainly reflected the continuation of the established industrialisation pattern with more centralised and disciplined management, the research- and technology-heavy electronics sector was put to the front as well, needing to "provide the various types of electronic computers, automation instruments and large, precision analytical instruments for the modernisation of the petrochemical industry, coal mining, metallurgical industry, power stations, machine-building industry, light industry, public health [...] and defense industry". The Chinese industrial sector – along

80 CHOSSUDOVSKY MICHEL, Towards Capitalist Restoration? Chinese Socialism After Mao, New York 1986, p. 166.

81 GERTH KARL, Unending Capitalism, How Consumerism Negated China's Communist Revolution, Cambridge 2020, pp. 16–17.

82 "Hold Aloft the Great Banner of Chairman Mao and Strive to Speed Up the Building of Taching-Type Enterprises", 0430 GMT, 08 08 1977 OW, paragraph D.

with its public services – was envisaged to become much more technology than labour driven, using automation to increase efficiency. The orientation of objective facts was also reiterated as a guiding principle for work in agriculture, where an editorial in Renmin Ribao after the National Conference on Farmland Capital Construction on the 8th of August 1977 called for sincerity in economic work, which was underlined by the sober style of the article, almost void of ideological references: "We must make real, not false efforts, and we must not act rashly. We must not practice formalism of do foolish things, such as 'dig, fill up, dig again.' [...] pay attention to the proper arrangement of work and rest and protect the socialist enthusiasm of the masses."[83]

In a certain way, manager Qiao mentioned before was a figure fit for this new era. Not only an imposing personality with a strong drive to shake things up ("Modernisation doesn't mean technique alone. You'll have to offend some people."[84]), JIANG ZILONG also gave the character a strong affinity for the ingenious use of technology, dedicated to world market level quality. These traits were even more pronounced in entrepreneurial factory worker Lui Sijia, who's adventures he described in his novella "All the Colours of the Rainbow":

> "Gradually his interest in electrical engineering grew. Every day he ran to an electrical appliance store to buy cheap rejects, He learned to make a refrigerator and a gramophone by dismantling and then reassembling them. [...] His parents gave him as much money as he needed [...] since all universities and colleges were closed then, they could only hope that he would become a good electrician. [Later] He spent a good part of his wages on electrical appliances, and made his own tape-recorder, camera, sewing-machine, TV set, calculator, washing-machine and radio. Most of them were better designed and made than those on the market. He used stainless steel to make his Latinized trade-mark 'Cang Xian' [...] Therefore many people believed that all these home-made electronic devices of his were imports."[85]

The implementation of the new management models was to be supported by so-called "socialist emulation drives"[86], which were organised by various administrative entities up to the level of the national ministry, aiming at establishing and distributing best practices in management in different interrelated sectors, in order to ensure efficient management throughout production chains. As an example, in September 1977 the Ministry of Post and Telecommunications and the Ministry of Water Conservancy and Power were reported to have launched a joint "emulation drive" at a meeting in Beijing, including

83 Foreign Broadcast Information Service, People's Daily: Advance Farmland Capital Construction, Text of People's Daily 8 August editorial: "Farmland Capital Construction Should Be Pushed Forward Vigorously During the Coming Winter and Spring", Peking NCNA Domestic Service in mandarin, 1818 GMT, 07 08 1977 OW, accessed through Readex.

84 JIANG 1983, p. 177.

85 Ibid., p. 88.

86 A concept adopted from the Soviet Union. Certain factories, work units and individuals were periodically designated as being particularly advanced, serving as models for emulation by others. Besides the distribution of best practices in industry and agriculture – quite a modern concept – another function may be seen in the indirect competition in the absence of market pressure.

"some ten thousand cadres, workers and technicians of various offices, enterprises and research units" under the two ministries.[87]

The agreement set up a competition between the participating entities with regard to the speed, low cost and quality of construction achieved. The ministry pledged to bring about a "high tide" in the coming winter and spring in basic farm construction, ensuring that one *mou* (about one fifteenth of a hectare) of farmland would be available *per capita*, having "high and stable yields, irrespective of drought or heavy rain", while reducing cost, increasing production and ensuring energy safety. On the other hand, the Ministry of Post and Telecommunication pledged that before the year 1980, all telephones in over 2'000 counties throughout the country would be changed to the dialling system, including the use of telephotography for the transmission of telegrams, motorcycles for postal deliveries in villages accessible to such vehicles as well as other improvements in basic infrastructures. According to the central guidelines, both ministries pledged to turn one-third of their units into Daqing-type enterprises, which meant offices run according to the newly issued management-guidelines.[88]

As the control of production shifted towards a system of management responsibility, the competences of the central authorities were clearly defined as the formulation of principles and policies for the development of the national economy, the setting of major industrial and agricultural productions quotas, investment in capital construction and major projects, the distribution of important and scarce materials, the purchase and allocation of major commodities, the setting of the state budget and issuance of a common currency, accompanied by the centralisation of the banking system[89], fixing of the number of industrial workers admitted to the industrial cities as well as setting the overall wage-sums and prices for major industrial and agricultural products.[90] Monetary management and its improvement was aimed at increased credit discipline to improve the state's control of money, which was in circulation through a strict monopoly of the Bank of China, as well as for simplifying the procedures necessary to obtain credit as deemed justified by the bank. On the other hand, it also included a call for severe punishment, when financial discipline was violated, for instance, due and overdue loans not repaid or

87 Foreign Broadcast Information Service, Chinese Ministries to Compete In Emulation Drive, Peking NCNA in English, 0742 GMT, 06 09 1977 OW, accessed through Readex.

88 Ibid.

89 The centralisation of banking went under the slogan *tidying up banking work*, as reflected at a conference on the topic by the Fukien provincial revolutionary committee in November 1977: "To tidy up banking, it is essential to eliminate the remnant poison and influence of the 'gang of four's' counterrevolutionary revisionist line, bring about great order in banking and tidy up banking. We must strengthen the centralization and unification of banking work and completely implement the national unified basic banking system so as to really concentrate the power of issuing currency in the central authorities. The financial and economic discipline must be strict. We must strengthen banking management and properly concentrate financial and material resources to guarantee the fulfillment of the plans for the national economy and to guarantee the construction of the state's key projects." Foreign Broadcast Information Service, Fukien Holds Conference on Banking Work, Foochow Fukien Provincial Service in Mandarin, 0300 GMT, 20 11 1977 HO, accessed through Readex.

90 Foreign broadcast Information Service, State Planning Commission Article on Socialist Construction, Peking NCNA in English, 0102 GMT, 12 09 1977 OW, accessed through Readex.

funds misused.[91] At a designated conference in Shandong province, First Secretary Bai Yubing of the provincial CCP committee summarised the significance of this "new leap forward in finance" for economic planning as, "we must discard formalism, exaggeration and false reports."[92]

That management had become the new primary method of control was encapsulated in a programmatic article published in Hongqi in October 1977. Combining the "Twenty Points" with the "Anshan Constitution", the key to "rectifying" enterprises after the damage done by the Gang of Four was established as being leadership, as "organising modern large-scale production" required "centralised direction of production, adherence to scientific rules and regulations and observance of strict discipline", in order to enable an "all-round leap forward in the national economy". The greater the profits, the greater the contributions to the state, the piece clarified, "and this has absolutely nothing to do with 'profits in command'". Opposition of management rectification meant opposition to the Chinese socialist revolution.[93] In a speech to the Standing Committee of the fourth National People's Congress[94] on the 23rd of October 1977, Vice Premier Yu Qiuli reported on the development of China's national economy, relating the ongoing work on management back to the guidelines issued in early 1975, bringing the importance of the implementation of plans – where they existed – to the forefront, describing the "need to strengthen the system of authority in production and political work at all levels" by a system of "responsibility from top to bottom", in order to put an end to the situation "of no person accepting responsibility".

In particular, the fields where the central government was responsible for economic policy – notably, the expansion of "a number of bases for the power, fuel and raw material industries and a number of key projects in communications and transport" – "advanced technique, as possible, needed to be applied". Balanced development needed to be primarily based on changes in price-policy, addressing "the problems flowing from the relatively high prices for certain items in the means of production in agriculture" and the comparably low prices of agricultural and sideline products as well as "raw materials and fuel". In order to achieve all that, labour power was needed to be put to use rationally and productively, as Yu repeated. This was to be done by ensuring "more pay for more work

91 Foreign Broadcast Information Service, People's Bank urges strengthened Monetary Management, NCNA reporter's commentary: "Strengthen Monetary management, Quickly Bolster the National Economy", Peking NCNA Domestic Service in Mandarin, 1425 GMT, 05 11 1977 OW, accessed through Readex.

92 Foreign Broadcast Information Service, Pai Ju-Ping submits Report at Shantung Finance-Trade Meeting, Excerpts of report by Shantung Provincial CCP Committee First Secretary Pai Ju-Ping at the 28 December second provincial meeting of advanced representatives of the finance and trade front on learning from Taching and Tachai: "Deepen the Movement To Learn From Taching and Tachai on the Finance and Trade Front, Make Contributions To Grasping the key Link and Running the Country Well and Accelerate the Development of the National Economy", Tsinan Shantung Provincial Service in Mandarin, 1100 GMT, 30 12 1977 OW, accessed through Readex.

93 Joint Publications Research Service, Opposition to Rectification means Opposition to Revolution, Article by Lo Yuan-cheng, Chang Cho-yuan and Liu Fu-jung, Peking Red Flag No. 10, Original in Mandarin, 08 10 1977, accessed through Readex.

94 Foreign Broadcast Information Service, Yu Chiu-Li Speech, Peking NCNA in English, 1922 GMT, 24 10 1977 OW, accessed through Readex.

and less pay for less work"[95], which signalled that another, perhaps even more intense debate had reached its conclusion.

Managers and experts had taken over. This step was combined with a recentralisation of core industries, with the First Ministry of Machine Building announcing in June 1978 that "the salient problem" in the organisation and management of the machine-building industry was its diversity; factories were either too large or too small, leading to many duplications in construction and production. Even more, the ministry criticised the existing decentralised system as being "scattered and small-scale", with production processes being "backward, with low efficiency, poor quality and high cost". The heads of machine building industries of provincial and municipal levels were quoted by Xinhua to have "agreed that organisation and specialisation of production" was "the inevitable trend of modern industrial development". Also, in this sector, time was a pressing issue, and it was "necessary to act immediately and, in three to five years, complete the reorganisation of the entire machine-building industry in a planned and systematic way."

The recentralisation of key industries was decided,[96] and the race against time in economic development was also brought forward to tighten discipline outside the workplace. An editorial in Kirin Ribao on the sixth of July 1978 called for the strengthening of "social order", as "all fronts" in the province were "racing against time and speed and working hard and vigorously in order to realise the socialist four modernisations". In such a situation, the author asked, how could a "handful of criminals" be allowed to continue their deeds? Thus, a new situation "in which the cadres observe the law, the masses follow the law and socialist morality [is] carried forward" was promised.[97] Similarly, the first secretary of the municipal party committee of the port-city of Tianjin underlined that in line with the need "to rapidly increase the production of commodities for export", it was necessary to reform the organisations, regulations and "other aspects of production relations that are not suited to foreign trade development", insisting that "wherever problems exist, we must make revolution."[98] With regard to management, the expansion of foreign trade and the orientation towards exports had indeed replaced the class struggle as the principal subject of revolutionary struggle.

Motivation, ownership and responsibility

The use and necessity of material incentives to increase production and motivate the workforce was a heftily disputed approach, in particular during the Cultural Revolution. In practice, during the Maoist years, material incentive included the implementation of wage scales according to qualifications and the adjustment of salaries, such as by providing individual benefits, according to individual work performance as well as piece-rate

95 Ibid.

96 Foreign Broadcast Information Service, First Machine-Building Ministry Reorganised Industries, Peking NCNA Domestic Service in Mandarin, 0155 GMT, 17 06 1978 OW, accessed through Readex.

97 Foreign Broadcast Information Service, Kirin Daily Stresses Strengthening Social Order, Kirin Daily 6 July editorial: "It is Necessary to Strengthen Social Order Well", Changchun Kirin Provincial Service in Mandarin, 2200 GMT, 05 07 1978 SK, accessed through Readex.

98 Foreign Broadcast Information Service, Tientsin First Secretary Discusses Foreign Trade, Tientsin City Service in Mandarin, 2330 GMT, 23 08 1978 SK, accessed through Readex.

wages. While dismissing material incentives as such, provincial governments as well as individual enterprises and work brigades made references to the socialist (and after 1975, constitutional[99]) principles of "from each according to his ability" and "to each according to his work" when describing their practice of individual remuneration.

Nevertheless, such "revisionist tendencies" were brandished in editorials[100] and their use remained an often-used topic in political speech, especially during the "Criticise Lin Biao and Confucius"-campaign between 1973 and 1976[101] – but they were at no point officially abolished or prohibited. In practice, an eight-step wage policy – in accordance with the Soviet model – had officially allowed wage-differentiation since 1956. The system of the first five-year plan also allowed for wage standards specific to industries, sectors, regions and functions. Industries with higher significance to the national economy – such as notably heavy industries – were granted higher wage-increases over time. Among enterprises within the same industry, those based in high-priority development areas were granted the same. The position of a worker on the wage-scale was set according to the technical complexity, intensity and the conditions of labour, with a tendency towards higher wages for intellectually demanding work – notably, engineers and other technical personnel received higher wages than management personnel on the same level.[102]

Industrial wages, administrative-technical wages, and incomes of peasants in collectives had three main components throughout the 1970s: basic wages and salaries as well as incomes calculated on the basis of work points, premiums and bonuses as well as social and welfare benefits in cash and kind.[103] During the Cultural Revolution, notably bonuses and premiums had been the focus of critics, as they constituted additional income directly aimed at incentivising workers to over-fulfil their targets, and stood in opposition to the principle of ideological motivation. Measures in this direction stood at the centre of the charges brought against Liu Shaoqi and other "capitalist roaders"[104] associ-

---

99 As Article nine of the Constitution of the PRC adopted on 17 January 1975 by the fourth National People's Congress stated: The State applies the socialist principle: "He who does not work, neither shall he eat" and "from each according to his ability, to each according to his work".

100 As a worker of Paochi Bridge Works wrote to the editor of Shensi Daily on 2 February 1974: "Please think: During the years of war, did those old armament workers who produced rifles and guns for the front seek remuneration from the party? During their arduous struggle with the sky above and the barren land beneath their feet, did the Taching workers ask for cash rewards? No. Educated with Marxism-Leninism-Mao Tsetung Thought, they turned powerful spiritual strength into enormous material force. This was absolutely not the outcome of so-called material incentives." Foreign Broadcast Information Service, Shensi Daily Prints Worker's Letter Criticizing Material Incentives, Sian Shensi Provincial Service in Mandarin, 1100 GMT, 13 02 1974 V, accessed through Readex.

101 Initiated after the September incident, the campaign was intended to rectify the party line after the fall of one of its most prominent members and main exponents of the Cultural Revolution. The main theme of the attack against retrogression and restoration was in line with the long-standing critique of bureaucratic rule. See: Chang Parris H., The Anti-Lin Piao and Confucius Campaign: Its Meaning and Purposes, in: Asian Survey, Vol. 14, No. 10, October 1974, p. 876.

102 Zhang Jun, Wages in China: An Economic Analysis, Hong Kong 2012, pp. 5 f.

103 Prybyla, Jan S., Work Incentives in the People's Republic of China, in: Weltwirtschaftliches Archiv, Vol. 112, No. 4, 1976, p. 768.

104 The slogan "Oppose Economism", which was mostly associated with the critique of material incentives, first appeared in Renmin Ribao on 12 January 1967, followed by a poster campaign

ated with him. Some restrictions of such additional transfers were effectuated, without questioning the general wage system. Even during the readjustment of the early 1960s, bonuses and premiums were neither particularly important parts of the wage-sum nor were they ubiquitous. While a number of factories, mines and other enterprises (notably in sectors relying on hard physical labour) with easily quantifiable work quotas such as coal mining, steel and oil drilling used such additional material incentives for the improvement of production-performance as early as the mid-1960s, others did not.[105]

Within the Chinese development paradigm, the basic policy with regard to wages consisted in relative suppression of the prices of most consumer goods and services except the most basic. The availability of consumables was of course directly connected to the relevance of material incentives, at least insofar as they involved money. Additional buying power, as long as the necessities were covered, is only of value if it can be used for the purchase of goods or service, or as savings for any future procurements. The reasons were first to allow a larger portion of the available resources to be channelled to productive investments, second to elicit relatively high labour participation of households in conformity with the socialist principle, "he who does not work, neither shall he eat",[106] and third, allowing for a guaranteed low basic income, at least for industrial workers.[107] While there appears to have been practically universal consensus among the Chinese leadership that the raising of the general level of material income was among the core objectives of Chinese economic policy[108], the composition and distribution of this raise was disputed. Nonetheless, frugality was also equally emphasised. As WANG NING argued, the conflict for individual workers was rather between the beliefs in the future raising of standards of living by a collective effort, based on, at times, confusing contradictions on what the moral and political guidelines were, as opposed to the individual improvement of the livelihood of one's family to the detriment of this grand vision.

Should basic earnings be raised for everybody? Should bonus payments directly aligned with individual work performance be emphasised? Should the work-point-system under which allocation was often decided by the members of the respective unit collectively be expanded? Or should the gains serve the rising of the levels of consumption in the communes and cities for the benefit of all members – the vision of the Great Leap Forward? Moreover, should wages be adjusted according to the productivity and "usefulness" of the respective sector, which also concerns the differences between industrial cities and self-reliant agricultural units?

Even among the relatively well-off industrial workers in large cities like Shanghai, considerable differences of status existed, besides the nominal hierarchy and wages. As

---

unfolding in the streets of Beijing. See: DITTMER LOWELL, Liu Shao-Chi and the Chinese Cultural Revolution: The Politics of Mass Criticism, London 1974, p. 150.

105 HOFFMANN, CHARLES, Work Incentive Practices and Policies in the People's Republic of China, 1953–1965, New York 1967.

106 Originating from the Christian Bible, the verses"He who does not work, neither shall he eat" and "From each according to his ability, to each according to his work", (second Thessalonians 3:10 and Acts 4:35, respectively), had been adopted by Lenin around the time of the October Revolution.

107 PRYBYLA 1976, p. 769.

108 WANG NING, Rise of the Consumer in Modern China, Reading 2012, pp. 148 f.

Sun Tianxian, a Hong Kong citizen of Mainland Chinese origin, described in his report on a trip to several provinces in April 1972:

> "The workers of China's government organizations and enterprises are not only secure in their jobs without the worry of unemployment, but also generally entitled to benefits of labor protection. All workers are entitled to free medical care under various systems which vary only slightly in name, such as Labour Protection Regulations, or Labour Protection Contracts. For example, the workers of the Nanking Machine Tool Plant are given free medical care and paid with regular wages when they are sick, their wage is cut to 50–60 percent after a sick leave of six months. With the exception of heavy industry workers who may apply for early retirement, a male worker may retire at the age of 60, and a female worker [...] at the age of 55.[109]
>
> The retired workers are generally entitled to 70 percent of their wage for the rest of their lives. Generally speaking, all government organizations and factories have day care centers and nurseries for workers' children from the age of 2 months to 7 years. Women workers may take an hour off in the morning, and another half an hour in the afternoon to breast feed their babies. There are numerous other fringe benefits. For instance, the workers may have their haircut and baths in factory operated barber shops and bathrooms free, or meals at factory mess halls at reduced prices. In the workers' clubs, they may take part in social activities, or enjoy entertainment programs."[110]

While the enterprises Sun visited during his trip – organized by the London branch of the Bank of China – were certainly the most presentable ones, his description of the iron rice bowl offered to industrial workers was accurate. Some of the perks he described had a long tradition in the Chinese socialist economy. Already in the Draft Laws of the Chinese Soviet Republic in 1933, it was stated that women, when hired by the year, were entitled to two-month maternity leaves with pay, before and after childbirth.[111] The problem was that not all workers benefited from the system.

Since the rapid expansion of industrial production during the late 1950s, industrial enterprises had expanded their workforce with temporary workers, from amongst the

---

109 Standard retirement ages in China remain at this level until the present day. While the nationwide average age of retirement was still at 53 years in 2014, average life expectancy – already comparably high during the 1970s – was 75 in the same year. With regard to the demographic effects of the one-child policy, adjustments to the retirement age are underway. As the Economist claimed, advice from international organisations, in particular the World Bank and the International Labour Organisation, played an important role in this development. See: Paying for the Grey, The Economist, 5 April 2014, available at: https://www.economist.com/china/2014/04/05/paying-for-the-grey, accessed on 1 May 2020.

110 Joint Publication Information Service, Overseas Chinese describes industrial agricultural projects, Article by Sun T'ien-chien: "Second visit to my motherland from England", Hong Kong Ta-kung Pao, Original in Mandarin, 08 06 1972, pp. 1–3, accessed through Readex.

111 Schram Stuart (ed.), Zedong Mao, Mao's Road to Power: Revolutionary Writings, 1912–49, Volume IV, The Rise and Fall of the Chinese Soviet Republic 1931–1934, New York 2015, p. 949. While the mobilisation of the female workforce was facilitated in socialist China, with regard to political power and positions at the workplace, some progress towards gender equality was made in the state-sector during the Cultural Revolution, and women hardly "held up half the sky" in the People's Republic, as Mao Zedong had claimed. See Wemheuer 2019, p. 245.

urban unemployed and the countryside. In stark contrast to regular workers, these "peasant workers" were not entitled to medical benefits or retirement pensions. Also, they were confronted with administrative difficulties that persisted and even increased after the Cultural Revolution. When enrollment procedures for institutions of higher education and secondary vocational schools in Guangdong began in November 1977, an administrative employee of the enrollment committee indicated that temporary workers who had worked in units, factories, mines and other enterprises for more than six months consecutively could apply for studies within their work units. Otherwise, they had to apply at their place of residence, which might have been thousands of kilometers away.[112]

Development of productivity of industrial workers in Shanghai (yuan per person). Statistical yearbook of Shanghai 1983, pp. 80, 136, 329; China statistical yearbook 1983, pp. 455, 490, as compiled in WU 2014, p. 100. Graph by the author.

Some estimates of this semi-proletarian workforce were as high as thirty to forty percent of the total nonagricultural workforce by the mid-1960s. A decision by the Chinese Labour Department in 1959 distinguished between three basic forms of urban work: long-term regular employment, temporary work on an individual contract-basis undertaken by urban workers, and "peasant workers" recruited from the countryside for short-term assignments.[113] The practice was heavily criticised during the Cultural Revolution as a form of class exploitation, leading to millions of temporary and contract workers being granted permanent jobs.[114] This contract system gained importance in the organisation

112 Foreign Broadcast Information Service, Canton Radio Carries Dialog on College Enrollment, Canton Kwangtung Provincial Service in Mandarin, 0500 GMT, 10 11 1977, accessed through Readex.

113 HOWE CHRISTOPHER, Labour Organisation and Incentives in Industry, before and after the Cultural Revolution, in: SCHRAM STUART (ed.), Authority, Participation, and Cultural Change in China, Cambridge 1974, p. 235. See: WEMHEUER 2019, p. 171.

114 BIAN YANJIE, Work and Inequality in Urban China, New York 1994, pp. 53 f.

of industrial labour that a State Council directive in 1965 enshrined as the "discretionary power to reduce fixed labour and increase temporary labour" for enterprises.[115]

Wu Yiching argued that opposition to this flexible system became one of the major rallying points for dissatisfied workers during the Cultural Revolution.[116] Also, the use of piece-rates instead of fixed wages was one of the aspects of the economy which caused work teams to clamp down on factories, even being the initial reason for the rise of Wang Hongwen in the Shanghai Number Seventeen Cotton Textile Mill.[117] In 1971, the State Council regulated the use of temporary workers by limiting their legal hiring for state-owned enterprises for actually temporary and not "year round" regular work. Furthermore, there should be no more than two and a half million temporary workers across the country at a given time, engaged evenly in short-term and seasonal work. This change also had a strong gendered impact, as many temporary workers were female relatives of permanent workers.[118]

In the industrial sector, raises of basic wages was noted in 1972 and 1973, which corresponded with the amounts usually distributed as bonuses.[119] These raises were particularly remarkable, as the urban workforce expanded massively during these years. Between 1966 and 1976, the number of workers employed in state-owned enterprises rose from 39.3 million to 68.6 million, while the workforce in the collectively owned sector expanded from 12.6 to 18.1 million workers during the same period.[120] Meanwhile, as the available data reflected in the graph above shows, measures to improve the productivity of industrial labour had positive effects, at least in the industrial centre of Shanghai.

Thus, the systematic suppression of wages endured during the 1970 meant that a larger share of surplus was extracted from the productive work of a fast-growing number of industrial workers. While this allowed for the increase in industrial production noted by a number of scholars as well as a certain rise of standards of living, the pressure to raise wages also increased, more pronouncedly so, as the Cultural Revolution had emphasised the status of industrial workers as the masters of China. This pressure might have been eased partially by the slower increase in the cost of living – which mitigated the effects of stagnating wages perceived by workers – as shown in the following graphical comparison. Nevertheless, the rise of over thirty index points of the cost of living in the years of readjustment is remarkable, as compared to the years of the first five-year plan, while nominal wages stagnated under conditions of relatively stable prices.

115 Wu 2014, p. 102. and Hong Zhou, Jun Zhang, Towards a Society with Social Protection for All: A Concise History of Social Security Transformation in Modern China, Singapore 2017, pp. 27 f., in particular FN 41.

116 Wu 2014, pp. 101 ff.

117 Dikötter 2016, p. 65.

118 Wemheuer 2019, p. 241.

119 Prybyla 1976, p. 769.

120 Wemheuer 2019, p. 242.

Monthly wages of workers in state-owned enterprises in Shanghai compared to the cost of living (index, national average = 100). Statistical yearbook of Shanghai 1983, pp. 80, 136, 329; China statistical yearbook 1983, pp. 455, 490, as compiled in WU 2014, p. 100. Graph by the author.

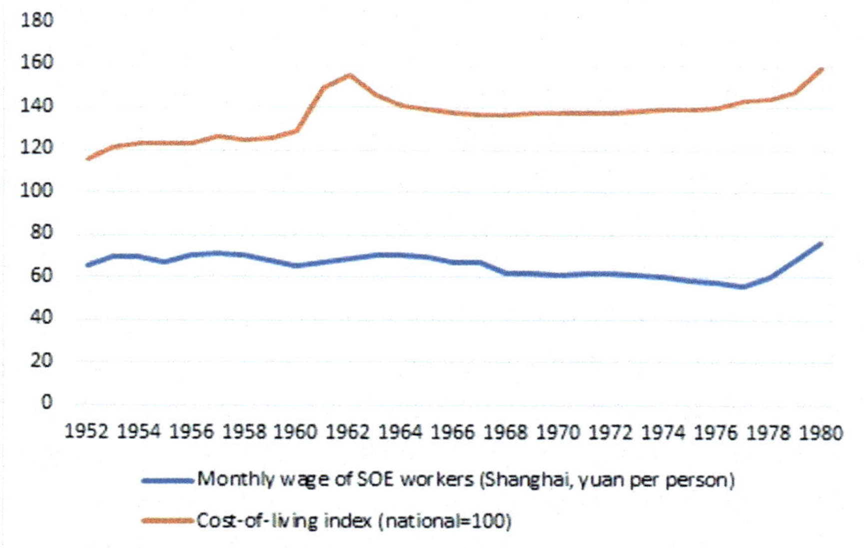

In addition to this economic pressure, which was well-perceived by the Chinese leadership[121], the conflict around material incentives was and remained essentially a conflict shaped by different views on economic *morality*. An important spill-over effect from the Cultural Revolution to industrial production was the demand for a reduction of wages for political reasons. While intellectuals and technical cadres were at the centre of political attention and wage reduction was intended and regarded as a punishment during the first stage of "Struggle–Criticise–Reform", a campaign for voluntary wage reduction expanded to industrial workers unfolded in early 1971, as a part of the fourth five-year plan.[122]

In February 1974, during the "Criticise Lin Biao and Confucius" campaign, a report by the Fuzhou Provincial radio service under the title "We are Masters, not Hired Hands, of an Enterprise" illustrated this conflict with two anecdotes, appealing to the pride of the workers.[123] Towards the end of the previous year, it was reported that workers who would fulfil the production targets well would receive a premium in kind: an extra aluminium

121 As reports on the excessive use of overtime and complaints among workers about stagnating wages were being issued since the late 1950s. See WU 2014, pp. 99 f.

122 Joint Publications Research Service, Chinese Communists Unfold All-Encompassing Campaign on Mainland for Voluntary Reduction of Wages, Hong Kong Hsing-tao Jih-pao, Original in Mandarin, 22 06 1971, p. 4, accessed through Readex.

123 Foreign Broadcast Information Service, Fukien Worker's Poster Lashes Out at Material Incentives, Foochow Fukien Provincial Service in Mandarin, 1100 GMT, 25 02 1974 B, accessed through Readex.

frying pan. Some workers expressed their stark disagreement with this idea that "the worker's enthusiasm for socialism [could] be aroused by material incentives". However, social pressure was not the way to achieve increasing production, In particular, as the standard of living stagnated even in the most advanced cities. As a cadre of a state-owned enterprise explained after the Cultural Revolution:

> "[During] the 'Cultural Revolution', we were not diligent. It should be said that before the 'Cultural Revolution', worker's attitudes were still very positive. Everyone worked hard. After the 'Cultural Revolution', there was great confusion of who was right and who was wrong. The society itself was very chaotic, which is difficult to adjust to. At that time people talked about 'fighting selfishness and criticizing revisionism'. People would rather go home to make furniture [...] than coming to work.".[124]

For instance, once, the emission claimed that there was a young worker at the cutting workshop who had been unable to fulfil her output quota, because she was not sufficiently skilled. The workers reacted by having a "heart-to-heart" conversation with her, comparing her present happiness under socialism with her past misery. This strategy, unsurprisingly, was presented as a full success. The unskilled worker raised her ideological awareness, began to see the relationship between the fulfilment of her output quota and the state plan as well as her assigned quota, and the socialist construction of China as a whole. Having recognised her part in the system, she worked hard to improve her skills and – unsurprisingly – was able to catch up with the more skilled workers.

This anecdote, representative of a plethora of comparable stories published until 1976, demonstrates a fundamental contradiction that had accompanied socialist industrialisation in China as well as in other countries. On the other hand, the differentiation between workers who felt the need to be incentivised by socialist enthusiasm and workers was framed in Renmin Ribao as a question of pride and awareness of the status of workers in the PRC. Such awareness was also a generational issue. In an article printed in July 1975, the secretary of the party branch of the consolidation workshop of the Peking Art and Craft factory, perhaps unintentionally, outlined this issue in his self-critique:

> "Do persons work merely for money? One of the senior workers in my workshop answered that question very well. He said: 'In the old society, we had to endure severe hardships that lasted through the first half of our lives. Happiness came only after the socialist system was imposed. I shall work for socialism as long as I live [...]'. A young worker in my workshop used to be apathetic at work because he held the attitude, 'I'll work only as much as I am paid'. [...] we assisted him in making comparisons between the two social systems and between the two types of dictatorships by the two classes, thus enabling him to raise his ideological consciousness. As a result he has markedly changed his work attitude".[125]

---

124 As quoted in WANG 2012, p. 148.

125 Joint Publications Research Service, People's Daily discusses 'Material Incentives', Article by Liu Yung-sen, "What kind of Question is that about 'Tangible Means of Control'?", People's Daily, Original in Mandarin, 19 07 1975, p. 3 WA, accessed through Readex. The comparison between the old society and between visible differences in the standard of living in a city like Beijing of course did not have the same convincing power.

The Soviet Union, having long since accepted bonuses and other material incentives as well as a more differentiated system of remuneration in its economic system, criticised the insistence on revolutionary zeal in China as a leftist deviation. In a commentary on radio Peace and Progress, Russian anchor Vladimir Barov stated that "keeping workers poor", as it was practiced as economic policy in China, was not only contrary to Marxism–Leninism but even a consequence of the persisting influence of "reactionary" Confucianism that had led to China being "covered by a network of concentration camps" and ruled by a bureaucratic dictatorship.[126]

In the cities, the supply of consumer goods was augmented significantly during the early 1970s. Despite the still quite limited range of available products in Beijing markets, and the effect of suppressed consumption, the level of sufficiency was estimated in 1973 to have risen from fourty-eight percent in 1965 to seventy-one percent in 1972. For goods "suitable for the countryside" (like bicycles, sewing machines, clocks, knitting wool, synthetic detergents, flashlights and batteries), increases of more than ten percent per annum were reported in 1974 as well as substantial widening of the product categories offered to the rural population.[127] As foreign trade increased, the responsible ministry of foreign trade began to signal Chinese demand for more than just grain and machinery to foreign partners. As the Swiss delegate for trade agreements Raymond Probst, reported after his visit in China in September of 1973, chemical dyes to be used by the textile industry were specifically flagged by his Chinese counterparts as prospective imports from Switzerland. According to Probst, they were not only intended for exports, but quite remarkably for "taking into account" the growing demands of Chinese women for more diversity in clothing. Probst noted that this was the first reference to consumer demand he had ever heard in the PRC.[128]

Decentralised production and distribution under the paradigm of self-reliance meant that the availability of consumer goods available for purchase differed from region to region. While even rather poor regions like Guangxi reported increases in their own production of consumer goods, availability was by far superior in the industrialised cities. Reporting on efforts in the development of the light industry in Guangxi, in March 1975, Xinhua proudly emphasised the use of local materials and self-reliance with regard to consumer goods.

> "Almost entirely dependent on other provinces for consumer goods a quarter century ago, today the region produces 60 percent of its light industrial needs. This includes wrist watches, bicycles and sewing machines. It is one of the main sugar producers in China. The gross value of light industry has more than tripled since 1965. One-third of the regional income every year is provided by light industry".[129]

126 Foreign Broadcast Information Service, Mao's Economic Theory based on Confucius, Moscow Radio Peace & Progress in English to Asia, 0800 GMT 19 03 1974 L, accessed through Readex.

127 Foreign Broadcast Information Service, PRC Bases Light Industry on Agricultural Developments, Peking NCNA in English, 0704 GMT, 27 12 1974 B, accessed through Readex.

128 China-Reise Botschafter R. Probst, 16. bis 23. September 1973, p. 6.

129 Foreign Broadcast Information Service, Industrial Output in Kwangsi Develops Rapidly, Peking NCNA, Original in English, 1210 GMT, 24 03 1975 OW, accessed through Readex.

While the suppression of wages to achieve surplus remained a crucial part of the Chinese attempt to industrialise, an increasing emphasis on the variety of available products to households demonstrated that the Chinese industrial development had entered a stage where political legitimation required more than just righteous paroles. Reporting about the increase of consumer goods in Peking, Xinhua quoted a member of the municipal commercial department saying: "The market is like a mirror, but it reflects not only the material aspects of life, but the political and cultural life as well".[130] The variety also encompassed luxury goods such as watches and radio sets, where production of the former grew by an estimated factor of eight between 1965 and 1975, and by an estimated factor of nine for the latter.[131]

In fact, differences in payment were relevant for more than just individual recognition and immediately created differences in the livelihood of people, which was emphasised by critical voices. By the transformation of private property via the means of production to public property in the socialist system, the argument was that "bourgeois rights" had ceased to exist only with regard to this change in property and mostly ownership.[132] This position, which Mao had taken in his writings, became a core argument in public discourse on material incentives. In socialist China, still far from reaching a communist society, abolishing capitalist traditions and vestiges inherited from the "old society", such as the differences between workers and peasants, between rural and urban areas as well as manual and mental labour, could not yet be done, just as it was the case with "bourgeois rights" reflecting these differences.

In Mao Zedong Thought, what is referred to as the "Three Major Differences", notably the contradictory relations between urban and rural, worker and peasant, and mental and manual labour, were to be solved politically.[133] Therefore, the distribution of consumer goods was central to this criticism. Although the socialist state adopted policies that implemented the principles of "he who does not" and "from each according", which at least guaranteed fairness to the degree that the applied yardstick was the same for everybody, the persistence of real inequality, resulting in differences in material wellbeing was being criticised.[134] The critique of "bourgeois rights" was mainly a demand for

130 Foreign Broadcast Information Service, Peking Increases Consumer Goods, NCNA Domestic Service, Original in Mandarin, 0754 GMT, 26 09 1975, accessed through Readex.

131 PRYBYLA 1978.

132 As Mao Zedong stated in his criticism of the Soviet Political Economy in 1960: "In the book, it is said [...] that the property produced by the Kolkhoz also includes personal property and individual side-line production. If, with regards to this side-line production the question of its transfer to collective property is not asked, the peasants will always remain just peasants. It is necessary, to solidify a certain socialist system in a certain period of time, but this solidification has to be limited, one cannot continue forever with it. Otherwise, the conscience reflected in this system will be entrenched and it will be impossible for people to adapt their thinking to new changes. [...] If, in a country like ours, a rectification campaign is not executed every one to two years, the contradictions among the people will never be solved." Quoted from MARTIN (ed.) 1975, p. 45, translation by the author.

133 As an example of public criticism of *Bourgeois Rights*, see: Joint Publications Research Service, Kwangming Daily: Inequality Still Prevails In PRC Under Socialism, Peking Kwangming Daily, Original in Mandarin, 18 02 1975, WA, accessed through Readex.

134 Ibid.

the equality of outcome, not merely the equality of treatment. In this regard, the role of money was criticised as well, as "educating people with the ruble" had been one of the methods used to "restore the capitalist system" in the Soviet Union.[135]

Nevertheless, it was not the abolishment of money as a means of exchange that was demanded, but strict monetary control by the state and strict accounting to ensure exchanges of "equal value".[136] However, the necessity of a certain moderate material inequality between households and production units as such – as a consequence of the eight-point wage scale, for instance – was remarkably undisputed; the political conflict on material incentives was about sequence, timing and general direction. Allowing the reintroduction and expansion of material incentives was perceived by its critics as a step away from the revolutionary path towards communism. In contrast to how it was stated by the Soviet media, in particular the News Agency TASS, that claimed in July 1976 that the core of the campaign criticising Deng Xiaoping was an "attack on the people's living standards", using the restriction of bourgeois rights as a "pretext to liquidate the eight-category system of wages and to jettison the principle of distribution according to work as well as any kind of material incentives and to do away with the crafts by which the peasants earn extra money, as well as many other things."[137]

From this point of view, all policy choices that concerned remuneration in any form meant walking on a thin line. The solutions proposed to this dilemma were not only found on the axis between material calculus and ideological re-education but also included demands for recentralisation of planning in commodity production and distribution. Material incentives, it was argued, would undermine centralised planning as different incentives through the profit motive would lead to an imbalance between supply and demand, inevitably to be filled by people harbouring capitalist ideas who would step in and engage in "graft, theft and speculation".[138] The "uneasy juxtaposition" with regard to material incentives was expressed by carefully curated statements when engaging foreigners visiting China, the number of which increased throughout the 1970s. At the Dagang oilfield near Tianjin, while a delegation from New Zealand was told that the workers did not care how they lived but were only interested in producing more oil for the state, a Brazilian delegation visiting shortly afterwards was told that workers received paid vacations at the fashionable beach resort of Beidaihe.[139]

In February 1976, political opposition towards the implementation of the Four Modernisations, notably under the responsibility of Deng Xiaoping, was voiced in a series of articles appearing in Renmin Ribao – notably on the 17th of February – which criticised

135 Foreign Broadcast Information Service, Red Flag Analyzes Use of Money as Means of Exchange, Shanghai City Service in Mandarin, 0700 GMT, 15 06 1975 OW, accessed through Readex.

136 Ibid.

137 Foreign Broadcast Information Service, 'Critical' Reassessment of Maoist Leadership under way, TASS headline: *"Concerning Political Scene Inside China"*, Moscow TASS in English, 1441 GMT, 23 07 1976 LD, accessed through Readex.

138 Foreign Broadcast Information Service, Red Flag Article Discusses Need to Restrict Bourgeois Rights, 18 02 1975, accessed through Readex.

139 US Department of State, Electronic Telegram, China's Takang Oil Field, 3 July 1975, 01:06, PlusD, ID: 1975STATE156840_b.

the "eclecticism", focus on "pure production" and the general "revisionist program" of "unrepentant capitalist roaders within the party". The critique, which was directly aimed at Deng Xiaoping and other rehabilitated cadres, particularly claimed that the interpretation of Mao's Three Points to study theory in order to combat and prevent revisionism overemphasised economic modernisation and ignored the class struggle. As the argument was intricately presented in Renmin Ribao on the 29th of February 1976:

> "Taking the three directives as the key link is an attempt to deny the existence of classes and class struggle in socialist society in order to negate the key link of class struggle and tamper with the party's basic line. The unrepentant capitalist roaders within the party babble that the three directives are interrelated and inseparable and that they form a complete entity from which no part can be removed. They sound plausible, as if they have considered everything. In fact, they are playing an eclectic trick. They deliberately include in the key link things that hinge on it, such as stability and unity and developing the national economy. Their purpose is to confuse and replace the key link with things that merely hinge on it. Through their manipulation, the contradiction between stability and instability and between unity and disunity, the contradiction between the backwardness of scientific research and the realisation of the four modernizations, and so forth all become principal contradictions. This is how they use the method of confusing the principal contradiction with the minor ones to negate the principal contradictions in socialist society, i. e., the contradiction between the proletariat and the bourgeoisie."[140]

In fact, parallels to the Soviet "revisionists" like Trotsky, Bukharin, Khrushchev and Brezhnev were drawn in the same article, followed by a critique of Karl Kautsky, the German social-democrat and "Lassalle-elements" who had been criticised by Marx as preferring opportunism over revolution. They were also blamed for other perceived shortcomings of Soviet policy, notably with regard to agriculture. Renmin Ribao stated repeatedly that agriculture in the Soviet Union had been "in a mess since Khrushchev and Breshnev usurped party and state power and staged an all-round restoration of capitalism in the country [...] with the per capita output of grain even lower than that of 1913 in the time of tsarist Russia."[141]

With regard to the pressure that stemmed from the mismatch between growing productivity and stagnating nominal wages, USLO noted on the 20th of February 1976 that the readjustments had nevertheless proven to be very popular, as "grievances over the inflexibility of the present system" were perceived as "genuine" and especially a revision

140 Joint Publications Research Service, People's Daily scores Capitalist Key Link, article by Liang Hsiao and Jen Ming: "Criticize 'Taking the Three Directives as the Key Link'", Renmin Ribao of 29 February, Peking Domestic Service in Mandarin, 2230 GMT, 28 02 1976 OW, accessed through Readex.

141 Foreign Broadcast Information Service, People's Daily derides Brezhnev over Crop Failure, Peking NCNA in English, 1702 GMT, 27 04 1976 OW, accessed through Readex. Another issue brought up regularly with regard to the Soviet Union and its economy was foreign debt, and notably the readiness to accept long-term loans. See, for instance, Foreign Broadcast Information Service, NCNA Reports Mounting Soviet Debt to West, Peking NCNA in English, 1839 GMT, 16 10 1976 OW, accessed through Readex.

of the eight-grade wage scale to allow for a raises – which was one of the focal points of the critical articles – "would appear to be a highly popular program". At least for the better-off urban population, this was certainly the case. It was further reported that a local employee of an embassy in Beijing, when being shown a poster with criticism aimed at Deng Xiaoping and asked to comment, simply answered, "It was an excellent year for the economy".[142]

Hua Guofeng, on the other hand, who had brought forward the Three Point Directive in his speech on "learning from Dazhai" in October 1975, at this time equally identified with the direction of Chinese economic policy. Much of academic scholarship on the 1975 Dazhai conference suggests that there were clear differences of opinion between multiple factions within the party leadership. The members of the Gang of Four represented a "hard radical" faction which was openly hostile to the use of markets and private plots, demanding a rapid transition towards work brigades. The "soft radicals" represented by Hua Guofeng, Chen Xilian and Ji Dengkui were more inclined towards modernisation, championed the cause of agricultural mechanisation and were opposed to curtailing the private sector completely. The role of Deng Xiaoping is less clear, as he appears to have asked for "rectification" and "honest work" without formulating concrete demands.[143] Nevertheless, the critique, once again, did not deny that building China as a "powerful modern socialist state" was the overarching objective– but that the questions were, first, "what kind of modernisation" was needed and, second,"how to achieve it".[144] The opposition to adjustments was nevertheless of a much smaller scale than what was experienced during the Cultural Revolution, particularly supported by the fact that already on the first of November 1975, a directive issued by the PLA General Political Department explicitly supported the Three Directives.[145]

The arrest and fall of the Gang of Four on the 6th of October 1976 ended the phase of reluctance with regard to what could be published on material incentives, decisively extending the limits of the possible for their implementation. Critique of the arrested exponents and their now "ultrarightist ways" was widely used in the form of articles, lectures and political reports to justify and underline the new normal. In a series of talks under the general title "The Twelve 'Whys' have Exposed the Ultrarightist Essence of the Gang of Four", which were based on the highly dialectical Ten Relationships by Mao, held in early 1977, in Beijing – and distributed among other channels by radio and material incentives – were a core topic. The underlying thread was the repeated and overly emphasised need for centralised, unified and strengthened leadership under the auspices of the CCP. For example, the ninth lecture stated: "The whole national economy is unified, and socialist production is carried out under the centralized administration of the state.

142 US Department of State, Criticism of PRC moderate Economic Policies, Electronic Telegram, 20 February 1976, 09:25, PlusD, ID: 1976PEKING00296_b, paragraph 5.

143 Weatherley Robert, Mao's Forgotten Successor: The Political Career of Hua Guofeng, Houndmills 2010, p. 125, Zweig 1989, pp. 34–35.

144 Renmin Ribao of 29 February, 28 02 1976 OW.

145 The USLO commented that this was not particularly curious as the organisation was headed by "moderates" – even if these appeared not to have been attacked politically. US Department of State, Electronic Telegram, The PLA and Criticism of the 'Three Point Directive', 27 February 1976, 00:31, PlusD, ID: 1976PEKING00327_b.

Therefore, the central authorities command economic powers and exercise centralised leadership over the whole national economy so that 'the whole economy is one chess-board'". On the other hand, the lecture series opposed other initiatives brought forward by more ambitious cadres, like Deng Xiaoping's direct and exclusive control of enterprise by the ministry concerned, with the argument that the "flood of statistical information" caused by this approach could not be handled to ensure proper allocation.[146]

With regard to material incentives, the proclamations were particularly clear, stating that while there was merit in a plain lifestyle, and Mao Zedong had advocated it, the Gang of Four had exaggerated by ignoring "the plain fact that people must first of all eat, drink, live and be clothed".[147]

More than wages: Addressing the livelihood

The lectures stated that the consolidation of the dictatorship of the proletariat and the creation of material conditions for the gradual transition to communism would not be possible without "a powerful material foundation", giving the people "visible material benefits"[148]. The lectures were remarkable because they strictly followed a format of dialogue, taking a statement from Mao Zedong Thought or associated with the late Mao, followed by an authoritative interpretation that embodied the new flexibilities. The following is a pertinent example from the seventh lecture:

> "Chairman Mao said: We should admit that some people are apt to pay attention to the immediate, partial and individual interest but fail to fully understand the long-term national and collective interest. This therefore makes it necessary to constantly, vividly and practically educate the masses politically. Forsaking the practice of putting politics in command, forgetting hard struggle and only seeking individual material benefits will invariably lead us astray and make us individualists who think only about personal gains and losses. In advocating hard struggle, we do not mean the harder the life of the workers, the better off they become. Nor do we negate the individual material benefits of the workers. Still less do we oppose improvement of the life of the workers on the basis of the development of production [...] We support being concerned with the well-being of the masses but are opposed to material incentives. Being concerned with the wellbeing of the masses is a proletarian policy and material incentives are a bourgeois policy. The two are fundamentally different."[149]

In the party press, the call for the improvement of the living standard was echoed by the slogan "pay full attention to problems concerning the livelihood of the masses". This general call was combined with new flexibilities for enterprises to keep any profits that arose from increases in efficiency they achieved themselves, as long as this happened within

146 Foreign Broadcast Information Service, Part Nine of Peking Lecture Series on 'Ten Relationships', Peking Domestic Service in Mandarin, 2200 GMT, 08 02 1977 OW, accessed through Readex.

147 Ibid. The element of "live" being new, probably referring to the importance of consumer goods.

148 Foreign Broadcast Information Service, Seventh Peking Lecture On Mao's 'Ten Major Relationships', Peking Domestic Service in Mandarin, 2200 GMT, 06 02 1977 OW, accessed through Readex.

149 Ibid.

the assigned tasks by the relevant plans and the careful and reliable maintenance and use of state resources.[150]

The question of material incentives was complex, insofar as across-the-board wage increases combined with the consequent policy of monetary stability[151] was concerned, which would simply have increased the supply of money in circulation without immediately increasing the number of products and services available for sale. If incentives by money were to be effective in the longer run, distinctions between different groups with regard to the increases in buying power caused by any such adjustments would be necessary. The raising of general standards of living was less prone to creating social tensions, or doing so much slower. In contrast to the industrial sector, as FELIX WEMHEUER noted, rural China under Mao was never more than semi-socialist. The economic failure of the Great Leap had also been the failure of policies that aimed at eliminating private property and led to the growth of social structures in rural villages. This acknowledgement had forced the CCP, and particularly Mao, to tolerate mixed structures of ownership and allow for a certain extent of private use of land since 1961.[152]

These basic compromises had not been seriously disputed even during the Cultural Revolution, and the rural households remained a crucial social as well as economic unit. In his confession to the CCP central work committee work conference on the 23rd of October 1966, Liu Shaoqi had to announce the backtracking from initiatives taken in this direction:

> "At one of the conferences of the Central Committee in February that year, comrade Teng Tzu-hui spoke on the advantages of the "responsible farm". I did not dispute it, and it acquired its legal status. Subsequently, I advocated at a number of cadre conferences fixed output for each household. Another comrade on the Central Committee suggested the division of farms by households. [...] These were all views directly contrary to the general line of socialist revolution and socialist construction expressed after an erroneous appraisal of the domestic and international situation. I had heard

---

150 "When the factory is investing a fixed amount, if there is any surplus in the investment resulting from enhancement of labor productivity or other factors, the factory may be allowed to take certain profits from such a surplus in accordance with established provisions". Ibid.

151 The extraordinary rapidity of the achievement of price stability by most measures in the early People's Republic was attributable to a variety of actions taken. Appropriate fiscal and monetary policies aiming to eliminate the budget deficits of the past and bring increases in the money supply, in line with increases in output, were at the core. Such efforts were facilitated immediately by the establishment of a unified and centralised system of public finance, through the creation of a similarly structured system of state-operated banks, by the issue of a non-convertible currency and the nationalisation of foreign trade, by the institution of (Soviet style) accounting and payments systems, in the expanding socialist sector, and by other regulations designed to reduce the uncontrolled flow of funds. See: SCHRAN PETER, China's price stability: Its meaning and distributive consequences, in: Journal of Comparative Economics, Vol. 1, No. 4, December 1977, p. 368 ff.

152 WEMHEUER 2019, p. 18.

of the proposal on the division of farms by households, but it was a big mistake that I did not refute it at the time."[153]

Nevertheless, as the presentation of the 1970 to 1974 agricultural development plan in Yunnan province shows, some flexibility with regard to the organisational structure was given back when political pressure decreased:

> "...the organisation of the people's commune may have two levels, i. e., the commune and the production team; it may also have three levels, i. e., the commune, the production brigade, and the production team. The size of the various levels in the people's commune may be determined by the commune members democratically. The size of the various levels should be determined for the benefit of production, for the benefit of management, for the benefit of solidarity, and for the convenience of the masses to oversee the affairs. [...] Currently, the rural people's communes in our province have mostly three levels and some of them have two levels. All of them are legal."[154]

While production teams that usually encompassed about thirty households – the size of a small rural village – were still a fairly large unit, this was a clear move away from the forced organisation in the largest possible production units up to the People's Communes, and a continuation of the readjustment policies of the early 1960s. Attempts at the provincial level to adopt different models of responsibility and work organisation, in an effort to increase production were reported throughout the early 1970s. They included smaller production units than the production team, ranging from the individual household to teams of ten persons.[155]

In the agricultural sector, compared to the industrial, the question of remuneration and incentives was fundamentally different. In December 1971, the Central Committee of the CCP issued a Directive on the Problem of Distribution in the Rural People's Communes (Chung-fa 1971 No. 82), endorsed by Mao Zedong, with the note to "issue accordingly".[156]

The main issues, expressed in six problems to be solved, concerned the proper calculation of rural work compensation as well as distribution of products. A document reproduced by the Taiwanese *Journal on Studies on Chinese Communism* contained the views of a district committee concerning the implementation of Directive 82, mentioned the

153 Joint Publications Research Service, Liu Shao-ch'i's Confession at Chinese Communist Party Central Committee Work Conference (23 October 1966), Taipei Chung-kung Yen-chiu, Original in Mandarin, 01 1970, pp. 122–127.

154 Referencing the Revised Draft Regulations for Rural People's Communes 1969. Joint Publications Research Service, Provincial Revolutionary Head Reveals Agricultural Woes, Article: "T'an Fu-jen's Speech at the Province-Wide Agricultural Work Conference", Taipei Chung-kung Yen-chiu, Original in Mandarin, No. 9, 09 1970, pp. 128, accessed through Readex.

155 As reported by the USLO in: US Department of State, Electronic Telegram, People's Republic of China Economic Review 1, 31 May 1974, 07:18, PlusD, ID: 1974HONGK06138_b.

156 Joint Publications Research Service, Views expressed concerning implementation of directive, Article, Views of the Chinese Communist X X X District Committee concerning the implementation of the CCP Central Committee Directive on the problem of distribution in the Rural People's Communes, Taipei Chung-kung Yen-chiu No. 8, Original in Mandarin, 08 1972, pp. 101–110, accessed through Readex.

appearance of "equalitarianism" as the "chief hindrance to the perfection of work in calculating rural work compensation and distribution". It was necessary, the declaration stated, "to clear up the relations between politics and economy, between line and policy, between communist ideological education, and the relations between having food grain as the key link and having diversified economy, and to clearly define the boundaries between 'to each according to his work' and 'letting work points take command', between reasonable encouragement through rewards and 'material stimulation', between common prosperity and equalitarianism, between the legitimate home subsidiary production of commune members and capitalist spontaneous tendency." Guidance was requested for the navigation of thorny issues, while the declaration assured that "only in this way can self-consciousness towards the implementation of Chairman Mao's revolutionary line and policies be increased, equalitarianism be conquered, the socialist positiveness of the broad masses of cadres and commune members be stimulated still more fully."[157]

This implicit and careful turn towards increased immediate responsibility of families for their own wellbeing and duty owed to the collective, was clearly complemented by the order to "maintain a system of responsibility in feed and care management of livestock". For the task of feed and care of livestock, which concerned a particularly valuable asset of the commune, it was declared necessary – "under the upholding of the principle of putting proletarian politics in command" – to select experienced commune members to take over the duties and implement the method of "making each person responsible for their own work." The regular review of the performance, measured in the "fatness of livestock at fixed periods" would lead to "reasonable compensation according to different grades, and [...] methods for appropriate encouragement and rewards." As for those "who achieve outstanding results in the protection feed and care [...], they may be given appropriate reward and encouragement". Still, it was insisted that "praise and encouragement" be the "main factors".

This did not mean that other factors were not intended to provide incentives, as the partial shift in style in visual propaganda indicates, exemplified by the following example (Fig. 3).

157 Ibid.

Fig. 3: Fengshou changshang pi xinzhuang, hanghai renmin chubanshe, 53x77 cm, Stephan Landsberger Collection at the Institute for International Social History (IISH), Call number BG E13/49.

What the poster published in the early 1970s in Shanghai titled "spreading out new clothes on a bumper harvest market" shows, is that at least the ideal purported with regard to rural markets went beyond necessities or strict utility. The textiles offered to the people vary in pattern and colour, which is also reflected in the clothes worn by the women in the foreground. In parallel, the full bags of grain underneath the scale to the right show both the success of agriculture as well as the importance of being frugal and practicing economy and accounting (also represented by the woman to the left in blue, keeping the books). In the background of the scene, a tractor establishes the connection between the bumper harvest and agricultural mechanisation, while the poles with an electric lamp and a loudspeaker attached represent electrification and the inclusion of the countryside in economic progress.

The different strands of adjustments that were experimented with in the provinces were increasingly picked up at the national level. In October 1975, a still relatively unknown member of the CCP politburo, Hua Guofeng, just having been named vice premier of the State Council, presented his report on the nationwide conference on learning from Dazhai, which explained the main directions for an incremental improvement of the agricultural developmental paradigm. The basic tenets of stability and unity, as declared by the fourth National People's Congress, were to be implemented in agriculture as well. Dazhai, until then mostly a model with regard to self-reliance and the practical aspects of collective management, was to become a model for the mechanisation of agriculture and its "all-round development" – albeit still relying on grain as the "key link".[158] Regarding the management of the counties, which were the primary geographical units

158 Foreign Broadcast Information Service, Reportage, Commentaries On Tachai Conference, Hua Kuo-feng report, Peking NCNA in English, 1204 GMT, 20 10 1975 OW, accessed through Readex.

of the Dazhai campaign, the strengthening of the CCP party committees as the "at once leading and executive organs" was at the centre of the programme, as well as setting the production team as the lowest accounting unit, as a countrywide standard.

All-round development, Hua Guofeng's report explained, was to be achieved in all areas including "side occupations", in order to generate "considerable increases in output, big contributions to the state and steady improvement in the living standards". Side occupations included a wide range of activities from the cultivation of private plots and gardens to work in construction, industries, transport as well as the production of handicrafts – which were, to a certain extent, exported – and personal services. Also, partly reproducing older patterns of rural division of labour, with men working the fields and women engaging in production at home.[159] Despite references to the People's Commune-movement of the Great Leap, clear emphasis was on mechanisation until 1980, according to the long-term development plan, based on scientific research and the construction of small industrial enterprises producing farm machinery, fertiliser and insecticides for and suited to local needs and more:

> "Party committees in all parts of the country must adopt a positive attitude and take effective measures to make the commune- and brigade-run enterprises grow up [sic!] still faster and better. In developing the commune- and brigade-run enterprises, it is necessary to keep to the socialist orientation and see to it that they devote their main attention to serving agriculture and the people's livelihood. **Where conditions permit, these enterprises should also work for the big industries and for export.** [emphasis added]"[160]

Cadres, "should" participate in collective labour "regularly".[161] With regard to further transition of ownership in agriculture, the report was very far from advocating any big pushes:

> "...with the spread and deepening of the movement to build up Tachai-type counties, with the expansion of large-scale, socialist agriculture and especially with the growth of the economy at the commune and brigade levels, this system of ownership will make a transition step by step to the system of ownership that takes the production brigade or even the commune as the basic accounting unit **when the conditions are ripe. In the still more distant future** [emphasis added], the people's commune will undergo the transition from the system of collective ownership by the whole people to the communist system of ownership by the whole people.".[162]

The development plan was remarkably modest, stating that by 1980, a mere one-third of the counties in China were expected to become Dazhai-type counties. Tendencies towards capitalism, whose existence, particularly in the countryside, was openly acknowledged in the report, were to be solved by means of persuasion and education as opposed

159 Fei Xiaotong, Rural Development in China: Prospect and Retrospect, Chicago and London 1989, pp. 222 f.

160 Hua Kuo-feng report, 1204 GMT, 20 10 1975 OW.

161 Ibid.

162 Ibid.

to coercion and violence, according to "Contradictions among the People".[163] Shortly after, a page-one editorial in Renmin Ribao lauded the direction of the report and the development blueprint it set forth, emphasising the importance of "basing [ourselves] on current realities, make long-term planning and work hard and effectively". Delegates, having left Beijing for their posts after the conference, would certainly have to devote eighty percent of their strength as well as eighty percent of local financial resources for the purpose of farm mechanisation in the future. In formulating their plans, the article claimed that the delegates had "adopted the scientific approach of obtaining truth from facts".[164]

After the arrest of the Gang, the stagnating buying power of workers and peasants was among the imperfections of the socialist economy that was blamed on their actions. With a view for the following year of 1977, the importance of improving the livelihood of people was actively underlined, and in some provinces prioritised further. At the end of December of 1976, during a telephone conference of the Kiangsi provincial party committee, the general line of agriculture as the foundation of the national economy was confirmed, emphasising that it was "necessary to make proper arrangements for light-industrial production", in particular "of light industrial products for the new year and spring festival markets". In this view, shortages of consumer goods were slated to become a thing of the past.[165] Similarly, a report regarding the Shantung province conference on learning from Dazhai on 3 December 1976 set forth the immediate goals for the province's contribution to the development of the national economy, naming "three hard battles": the improvement of (i) agricultural production conditions, (ii) markets for light industry and (iii) iron, steel and coal production.[166] In particular, agricultural mechanisation proved to be a rallying point for a compromise within the Chinese leadership.

In early 1977, increasing the production and availability of consumer goods had become a priority of economic policy as well as an integral part of the economic development paradigm. In February of the same year, even Hongqi, the more doctrinal outlet of CCP media, came out in support of higher living standards as well as a "more varied and colorful cultural life", as the speeding of economic growth was also to be applied in these fields.[167] Printing several quotes by Mao in support of raising living standards as

---

163 At the provincial level, the implementation of this guideline went further, notably by imposing financial sanctions instead of ideological re-education. In a report in late 1975, Chang Chianglin, second secretary of the Tsinghai Provincial CCP Committee at the provincial conference on learning from Dazhai, stated: "It is necessary to guard against the class enemies who always try to create turmoil and blur the demarcation line between the two different types of contradictions. Those who are corrupt, and who embezzle and speculate should be dealt with according to the party's policy, and economic sanctions should be taken against them." See: Foreign Broadcast Information Service, Chang Chiang-lin Reports at Tsinghai Meeting, Sining Tsinghai Provincial Service in Mandarin, 1500 GMT, 27 12 1975 OW, accessed through Readex.

164 Foreign Broadcast Information Service, People's Daily Stresses Tachai Importance, Peking NCNA Domestic Service in Mandarin, 1726 GMT, 25 10 1975 OW, accessed through Readex.

165 Foreign Broadcast Information Service, Kiangsi Holds Meeting On Industrial Tasks, Nanchang Kiangsi Provincial Service in Mandarin, 1100 GMT, 29 12 1976 HK, accessed through Readex.

166 Pai Ju-Ping stresses Learning from Tachai, 1100 GMT, 04 12 1976 OW.

167 Foreign Broadcast Information Service, AFP: Red Flag Calls for More Consumer Goods, Hong Kong AFP in English, 1113 GMT, 24 02 1977 OW, accessed through Readex.

socialist construction proceeded, while accusing the Gang of Four for their "luxurious and decadent" lives, the review stated that Hua Guofeng had personally given instructions for an "improvement in the market" and a "diversification" of the economy; albeit, no details were published. "Legal family occupations carried out on the side" were confirmed to be non-capitalistic and legal, even confirming that such activities were positive as they could contribute to a diversification of products in the market, especially since such products could be sold to the state – which would provide funds for the further development of light industry.[168]

This defence of private economic activity in Hongqi was qualitatively new, as was its stance that the raising of the standard of living could only be "a gradual process and no 'leap forward' should be expected." Rather, private economic activity was a means to develop China into a "powerful socialist country".[169] Similarly, the improvement of standards of living also lead to the thorny issue of material incentives being discussed, albeit not officially recognised. A German newspaper reported in late April 1977 that foreign students at Chinese universities, having close contact with their fellows, affirmed that the topic ranked high in all discussions on the economy. Further, it was alleged that jokes making the rounds among the citizens of Beijing mocked the distinction between politics and material well-being such as:

> "After his rehabilitation in 1973, [Deng Xiaoping] [...] is said to have visited Mao, bringing along his, [Deng's] grandson. The great chairman took the little boy on his lap and played with him. All went well, only to Mao's displeasure the little boy would always address him as 'great chairman' and would not call him 'uncle', as Mao wanted him to do. [Deng] then intervened and suggested giving the boy an apple from the bowl on the table, but only on the condition that he would call Mao "uncle" from then on. Mao followed [Deng's] advice. The boy hungrily bit into the apple and immediately called Mao 'uncle'. Then [Deng] pointed out: 'There you see, Great Chairman, the great effectiveness of material incentives'".[170]

Nevertheless, no official changes in wage-policy were announced. In September 1977, during visits of US officials to several Chinese cities, spokespersons for local iron and steel, machine tool and paper factories did not admit that any changes in wage policy had occurred but independently stated that a decision by the central government was

168 Ibid.

169 This reflected the line presented at various conferences on learning from Dazhai, like in Kirin province in early February 1977: "It is necessary to promote diversified economy while simultaneously developing grain production. We must vigorously develop agriculture, forestry, animal husbandry, sideline production and fishery so as to increase accumulated funds for collectives, produce more raw materials for industries, supply more merchandise for market and export, improve the people's living standards in the cities and the countryside and strengthen the worker-peasant alliance". Foreign Broadcast Information Service, Juan Po-sheng Report at Kirin Tachai Conference, Changchun Kirin Provincial Service in Mandarin, 1100 GMT, 12 02 1977 OW, accessed through Readex.

170 Joint Publications Research Service, Material Incentives New Peking Slogan, Article by Harry Hamm, Original in German, Frankfurt Frankfurter Allgemeine No. 98, 28 04 1977, accessed through Readex.

expected in the near future.[171] The chairman of the Canton Paper Factory revolutionary committee was quoted as saying that the new policy would probably involve across-the-board wage increases, targeted at lower-paid workers rather than material incentives in the form of bonuses for individual over-fulfilment of work quotas. While the need for transmitting the gains in production – announced during the year as a confirmation that the current course was right – was recognised, the form still was not; the latter remained dependent on a high-level decision.

In the countryside, indirect material incentives had become a reality through the workings of rural markets. Renmin Ribao demonstrated the fact publicly with a commentary on the ongoing harvest of "secondary autumn crops", as valuable input materials for light industrial production. To "do a good job in harvesting secondary autumn crops", the paper explained, "it is very important to arrange the labor force rationally". To this end, the rural commercial departments were called to "properly implement state procurement, price and incentive policies" and "bring into full play" the role of the commercial department's rural stores that were responsible for buying the side-line products from the peasants who were willing to harvest and sell.[172]

Just about two weeks before, the paper had published an editorial calling for the rational use of the agricultural labour force, in particular by the known methods of mobilisation and more efficient management via reduced and shortened meetings. In addition, through a reference to Karl Marx[173], the article underlined the importance of agricultural surplus for freeing workers to do labour in industry as an "objective law which cannot be violated under any circumstance". Production teams as responsible units had to be consulted if workers were being employed for other productive activities, to ensure that a sufficient amount of people were working on actual agriculture.

Also, in order to do "management work" well, the "socialist principle" of from each according to his ability, to each according to his work was to be implemented alongside a new principle – "more pay for more work" and "he who does not work, neither shall he eat". Simple, easily applicable labour remuneration methods, which were both fair and

---

171 US Department of State, Electronic Telegram, Observations in Chengchow, Wuhan, Changsha and Kwangchow, 13 September 1977, 00:00, PlusD, ID: 1977PEKING02047_c, paragraph 3. In a meeting with a delegation of the National Committee on US-China Relations Board, the Chinese People's Institute of Foreign Affairs president Hao Te-ching told his guests when announcing the fifth National People's Congress in the first quarter of 1978 together with the national conference on science and technology that wages had "already been raised", without indicating any details. US Department of State, Electronic Telegram, October 19 Hao Te-Ching Meeting with National Committee Delegation, 20 October 1977, 00:00, PlusD, ID: 1977PEKING02414_c.

172 Foreign Broadcast Information Service, people's Daily on production of Secondary Autumn Crops, Excerpts of People's Daily 15 September Commentator's article: „Pay attention to production of Secondary Autumn Crops", Peking Domestic Service in Mandarin, 0800 GMT, 15 09 1977 OW, accessed through Readex.

173 Who strongly argued in favor of the use of modern technology in agriculture in order to improve productivity. See: Perelman Michael, Natural Resources and Agriculture under Capitalism: Marx's Economic Model, in: American Journal of Agricultural Economics, Vol. 57, No. 4, November 1975, pp. 701–704.

rational were to be established.[174] While the agricultural basis of the economy was to be prevented from neglect, akin to the experience of the Great Leap, workers in agriculture were to be subject to individual incomes directly based on their work – on a more streamlined basis than the discussion-heavy attribution of work points.

A delegation of the Shanghai planning bureau met with the National Committee for Sino-US Relations, on the first of November 1977, giving the US delegations some details about the implementation of the current planning guidelines. Profit, it was confirmed, would be used as a "measure of managerial efficiency" as well as a proxy with regard to the "level of science and technology" being a means for capital accumulation. This gave planning additional importance, as one of the Chinese officials underlined, it was "sometimes necessary to produce goods that don't generate a high profit", citing cigarette manufacturing as a high-profit industry and adding that "if it was not for state planning, there would be a fight".[175] While wage increases were to be a part of general policy, priority was given to avoiding inflation by adapting increases in overall aggregate wages to the approximate supply of consumer goods that could be bought. Most of these raises were said to be in the lower brackets, except for those who had not received "a wage increase for many years and those who make a high contribution to production", thus confirming that bonuses were back on the agenda. The planners explicitly referred to a "new leap forward" taking place in Shanghai. As a major industrial city, the planners revealed that they had practically no flexibility under the state plans, as they set the "plans and the production quotas and we must obey", which was also said to be true for overall wage policy and internal and foreign trade.

The importance of learning technology from abroad was reaffirmed to be at the core of the new economic policy. Shanghai continued to contribute most of its comparative advantage to the rest of China, and the movement of parts of its textile industries to the countryside in order to remove the necessity of transporting raw materials from the source to the city was confirmed; Shanghai, in turn, was to concentrate on advanced industries, such as the high-precision electronic and chemical industries, especially fertiliser, where large increases in production were described by the delegation, "just like in the United States". Confirming another main turn in economic policy orientation, the planners emphasised that increasing labour productivity was a major target that all production plans focused on, with science and technology as major facets.[176]

At the end of their presentation, the Shanghai planners reiterated the eight areas set by the state for emphasis in industrial products: Quality, variety, quantity, low production cost, higher profits and the accumulation of working capital, labour productivity and care in the handling of materials. In addition, a seven-point system had been drawn

174 Foreign Broadcast Information Service, people's Daily on Rational Use of Agricultural Labor Force, Text of People's Daily 3 September editorial: "Strengthen the Frontline of Agricultural Production", Peking NCNA Domestic Service in Mandarin, 1816 GMT, 02 09 1977 OW, accessed through Readex.

175 US Department of State, Electronic Telegram, National Committee Delegation Meeting with Shanghai Economic Planners, 10 November 1977, 00:00, PlusD, ID: 1977PEKING02601_c.

176 Ibid.

up with regard to managerial responsibility in the industry, which was basically the Anshan Charter with the addition of individual and managerial responsibilities: clear division of responsibility for each post, attendance of workers, quality control, standardisation of operational techniques, maintenance and protection of equipment and protection, work safety and effective cost accounting.[177]

A popularised version of these revised guidelines was published in Chinese media in November 1977, as well addressing "fallacies" of the Gang of Four to explain qualitative changes in policy with regard to appropriate remuneration for work. Two articles in Renmin Ribao on the 22nd of November 1977 rather drily explained the new realities. The first by Zhao Luguan, titled "Refute the Fallacies of the Gang of Four on the Forms of Payment for Labour", dealt with the subject of why even the most radical form of material incentive – piece-rate wages – was now possible in socialist China:

> "The timerate wage system is a widely applicable form of remuneration. The piecework system, though applicable to a narrower scope, is nevertheless suited to certain trades under certain conditions. Use of necessary material rewards in given circumstances and within certain limits can make up for the weaknesses for the basic forms of payment for labor and help the implementation of the principle of distribution according to work."[178]

The second, "On Profits under Socialism" by economist Xu Tixin, defined the difference between "normal" profits under socialism and "putting profits in command" by applying four criteria:

> "[First] The purpose of socialist production is to meet the growing needs of the state and the people, whereas capitalism and revisionism regard profits as the purpose of production; [second] A socialist enterprise produces in accordance with state planning. Its primary consideration is to follow the plan while price consideration is secondary. It still has to abide by the state plan in circumstances in which it gets little profits or has to operate at a loss temporarily because some products are underpriced by the state out of consideration for the overall interests; [Third] Every Socialist enterprise must proceed from overall interests in its operation and management, cooperate well with other enterprises in accordance with state planning and must not go the anarchist way to pursue its narrow interests; [Fourth] A socialist enterprise must first of all guarantee the quality of its products and, with this precondition, strive to increase production, practice economy, lower costs and make more profits."[179]

An article in the Hongqi by economist Xue Muqiao formulated a new answer to an old question more concisely, on the 7th of November 1977:

177 Ibid., paragraph 8.

178 Foreign Broadcast Information Service, People's Daily condemns Gang's Labour Payment Theories, Peking NCNA in English, 0806 GMT, 23 11 1977 OW, accessed through Readex.

179 Ibid.

> "The proletariat must use the commodity and monetary systems and the wage system to promote the socialist economy, and therefore, must protect bourgeois rights."[180]

When wage increases were officially announced three days later, it was also made clear that those workers doing scientific research or technical work were to be given priority in recommendations for wage increases. Xinhua emphasised the importance of the evaluation by co-workers, while stating the sectoral priorities very clearly:

> "This year's wage increase will be affected in line with the principle of 'from each according to his ability, to each according to his work'. Co-workers evaluate the political consciousness, attitude towards work, contributions and technique of a person before they recommend whether his or her wage should be increased and this must be approved by the party committee. Those who make greater contributions to socialist revolution and construction, wither in production or in work, and those doing scientific research or technical work are given priority in recommendations for wage increases."[181]

Also, scientists and technicians "who really know the work but are now in improper or unrelated jobs" were to be moved to "proper posts", so that they could fully use their talents.[182] In hindsight, Xue wrote that "between 1955 and 1977", not enough attention had been given to the standard of living, barely allowing for its stability. This failure, he noted:

> "Does not mean that socialism is not a superior system. It means only, that we breached the objective laws of economic development in some points and thus prevented [it] to unfold its full superiority."[183]

---

180 Joint Publications Research Service, Red Flag criticizes Gang's view of Bourgeois Rights, Article by Hsueh Mu-chiao: "Criticize the 'Gang of Four's' Reactionary Fallacies on the Question of Bourgeois Rights", Peking Red Flag No. 11, Original in Mandarin, 07 11 1977, pp. 35–42, accessed through Readex.

181 Foreign Broadcast Information Service, Worker's Wages Increased 1 Oct, Peking NCNA in English, 1225 GMT, 10 11 1977 OW, accessed through Readex.

182 As in: Foreign Broadcast Information Service, Tseng Shao-Chan Report at Liaoning People's Congress, Summary of Liaoning Provincial Revolutionary Committee work report, presented by Tseng Shao-shan, Chairman of the Liaoning Provincial Revolutionary Committee at the fifth Liaoning Provincial People's Congress on 23 December 1977, Shenyang Liaoning Provincial Service in Mandarin, 1100 GMT, 30 12 1977 SK, accessed through Readex.

183 XUE MUQIAO, Sozialismus in China, Erfolge, Fehlschläge, Reformperspektiven, Hamburg 1982, pp. 174 f. As a commentator summarised in Hongqi, in early 1978: "We must understand and master objective laws governing economic development and constantly improve our standards of organizing and managing the economy [...] We must uphold the principles of 'to each according to his work', 'he who works more gets more' and 'he who works less gets less' and combine spiritual encouragement. We should use price laws to serve socialism." Foreign Broadcast Information Service, Excerpts of Commentator's article: "Strive to Rapidly Develop the National Economy", Red Flag, No. 1, 1978, Peking Domestic Service in Mandarin, 1200 GMT, 06 01 1978 OW, accessed through Readex.

At the fifth National People's Congress in February 1978, Hua Guofeng clarified how his objective was to be pursued concerning material incentives: "Moral encouragement" was to go "hand in hand" with material rewards, albeit "with emphasis on the former".[184]

While a qualitative shift with regard to wages had taken place, much more incisive changes were looming. What even a limited liberalisation of markets would mean in practice later on was also narrated by JIANG ZILONG, who had worked in a heavy machinery plant since 1958 and put his experiences in the late 1970s and early 1980s into literary form. While the events he describes take place after 1981, they demonstrate the dynamic inherent to this measure:

> "The [No. 5 Iron and Steel Plant] built in the seventies was virtually surrounded by a free market – a result of the boom in the countryside. At the foot of its front wall, there were baskets, carts and stalls displaying millet, lentils, turnips, Chinese cabbage and all manner of merchandise. The pedlars' shouts woke up this city of iron and steel and drowned the roaring of the furnaces. The workers in the plants living quarters no longer relied on alarm clocks because the hucksters' shouts always got them up in time for the morning shift. [...] So long as you had money you could buy whatever you fancied. Inside the plant production had slumped, while the peasants outside were doing a roaring trade [sic!].
> They had surrounded the state-run iron and steel plant, and could make as much in one day selling jelly-fish as a worker's weekly pay. However, the workers were glad to give their cash to those pedlars, even though their wares were expensive. It was better than having nothing to buy with their money. Though the plant's output was low, the workers were not short of money, for their purchasing power had gradually risen. Economic laws, like a humorous, clever magician, have played this trick on us in recent years so that we are forced to acknowledge their existence."[185]

How to make production more efficient?

A necessary condition for the rapid and large-scale industrial development was the availability of advanced technology and the means to distribute it to the factories as well as acquainting workers and cadres with its use. After having mostly been cut off from their main source of modern industrial technology, the Soviet Union, trade partners in Europe as well as Japan became the main sources for the import of technology, on an initially small scale, in the 1960s. With regard to volume. On the other hand, the import strategy was focused on large-scale imports of foreign plants that were set up as a whole – so called "turnkey"-plants. Perhaps the formative experience of the first five-year plan,

---

184 As published later in Renmin Ribao together with explanations, referring to the principle "of each according" as a means to "arouse the enthusiasm of the masses and promote the development of socialist productive forces". Foreign Broadcast Information Service, People's Daily on Moral Encouragement, Material Rewards, Text of People's Daily 9 April editorial: "Implement a Policy of Combining Moral Encouragement with Material Rewards", Peking NCNA Domestic Service in Mandarin, 1132 GMT, 09 04 1978 OW, accessed through Readex.

185 JIANG 1983, pp. 21–22.

when Soviet support was largely clustered around such large-scale production explains this as a continuity. On the other hand, as the level of industrial development in China signified that the main point of orientation was catching up with basic innovations that were required for the production of basic industrial commodities – e. g. steel – this strategy was also conditioned by the technological level.[186]

The import of technology, which had been part of Chinese economic policy since 1949, raised the fundamental issue of finance, notably the acquisition of sufficient amounts of foreign exchange (see next chapter). Another approach was the promotion of *incremental* technological innovation in China itself, relying on traditional technical know-how, the education of engineers as well as research and development in universities and attempts to encourage innovation by workers in the workplace. While systematic research and development suffered from the spill over of the Cultural Revolution on institutions, "workplace innovation" as a heritage from the Great Leap continued to be promoted as a way for Chinese industrialisation.

It is important to underline that despite the disturbance the movement caused at institutions of education and research, there was little or no denial of the importance of both for the Chinese society. Rather the criticism – albeit in a radical form – aimed at abolishing distinctions in status and limits on the access in particular to institutions of higher education. It appears that, despite some progress with regard to the opening of the historically closed Chinese approach to education, a major issue was the lack of a tangible alternative by which the egalitarian motive could be combined with the necessities for quality-assurance and reliability that the increasing technological level and even more so the ambitions for further development.

Besides the difficulties of the Chinese economy and the limited potential of bottom-up innovations, some technological successes achieved by the Chinese economy were clearly visible and even recognised by foreigners in early 1970. For instance, as the journalist Jan Deleyne wrote in a report on the Chinese economy in 1972, explaining the difficulties of assessing the state of affairs with the persistent lack of data and the cryptic and untransparent documentation, combined with the complexity of a largely decentralised system:

> "So, there remains the information that can be collected in China itself, because here, you get to know the Chinese economy better that through global estimates, which are based to a large extent on assumptions. Is it not just as informative to learn that Chinese engineers produce steel since 1965 using oxygen and are able to heat air up in their furnaces to 1250 degrees, or that they can produce electronic microscopes, hydraulic presses of 12000 tons and diesel locomotives? Is this not much more informative than knowing about the gross national product or the extent of the iron industry or the mechanical industry, numbers which can only be established in the most daring of ways?"[187]

---

186 With regard to the import of technology to China during the 1960s, see: Scranton Philip, Enterprise, Organization and Technology in China: A Socialist Experiment, 1950–1971, Cham 2019.

187 Deleyne Jan, Die Chinesische Wirtschaftsrevolution, Eine Analyse der sozialistischen Volkswirtschaft Pekings, Reinbek bei Hamburg 1972, pp. 12 f, translation by the author.

Furthermore, journalists from Taiwan reported the manufacturing of complex machinery from scratch by Chinese engineers, such as a 125'000 kilowatt dual internal water-cooled turbo-generator unit, as well as progress in the automation of textile manufacturing and the development of semiconductors used in telecommunication. Further, incremental improvements such as new processes, techniques and methods in the use of existing production capacities, e. g., of cars and locomotives, were acknowledged.[188] Nevertheless, these achievements had two significant limitations. First, they were mostly concerned with the implementation and incremental improvement of existing technology, which corresponded to a large extent with what had been built up during the first five-year plan and its aftermath, with some imported plants added in the 1960s. In the words of economist GERHARD MENSCH, by adjustments and the encouragement of technological innovation within China, improvement in innovations and not new basic innovations was the aim.

This did not mean that no progress beyond these incremental improvements was achieved. The difficulty faced by the Chinese economy was rather that the productive capacities were not sufficient to bring to large-scale serial production of what could be technologically achieved. As the editor-in-chief of the Swedish daily Dagens Nyheter, Olof Lagercrantz, wrote after having visited the PRC in 1970:

> "I took an in-depth look at the industrial exhibition in Shanghai, which took place in a huge Stalinist palace. [...] The exhibition impressed me a lot. An electric generator could be found, so strong that it could provide the necessary energy to the city of ten million, Shanghai. There were data machines, trucks, cars, an iron-ore truck of 332 tons with a loading capacity of 42 tons. There were electronic microscopes, television sets with a 31-centimeter display that cost 400 yuan in the shop, cameras, musical instruments, tractors, drills [...] all tools needed by a dentist, several chemical products."[189]

But when Lagercrantz continued to ask his guide critical questions, this first impression changed quickly.

> "At a loom that [...] produced 12 meters of cotton fabric an hour instead of five meters like the machines I had seen before, I asked how large the series were, in which this new loom was produced. The answer was that this was a unique specimen and still in the stadium of experiment. The same held true for a range of the exhibited machines – a book binding machine, a printing press, a translation device. What I saw, was partly a museum of the industry of the future: In the socialist society with its long-term planning, you do not show what there is at the moment, but what there once will be."[190]

The conditions necessary to produce a small series based on advanced technology had been created successfully, at least in some sectors. What was needed was the capability of standardised and reliable mass-production, while keeping the industry running as it was, as efficiently as possible.

---

188 Communist China's Industry in 1969, Taipei Chung-kung Yen-chiu, 01 1970, pp. 24 ff.

189 LAGERCRANTZ OLOF, China Report, Bericht einer Reise, Frankfurt am Main 1971, pp. 93 f.

190 Ibid., p. 94.

Beyond grain and steel: introducing modern technology

Based on the very limited existing modern industrial capacities and the few imports that could be afforded from trade partners in the West, ways to advance technological progress and improvements in efficiency were sought in order to yield results despite the serious constraints in material endowment. Particularly in the chemical sector, where Chinese achievements in organic chemistry were recognised internationally[191], international contacts were slowly re-established during 1971. While this opening was tangible and included e. g. visits by several large Swiss pharmaceutical companies (Ciba-Geigy, Sandoz, Hoffmann-La Roche) in the PRC, such contacts were still limited by the fact that many experts still found themselves assigned to tasks in "production" for political reasons.[192]

This balancing act produced approaches seeking to create technological progress within the range of the possible. In July 1970, the Ministry of Light Industry hosted a forum on "Grasping Revolution and Promoting Production", where it presented a strategy based on the concentration of investment in small- and medium-sized industries and employing indigenous methods in combination with the foreign technology available. The phrase "combination of indigenous and foreign methods" (*tu yang jie he*) was the fitting slogan for this strategy, aiming at doing the maximum with what was there.[193]

Still in late 1974, the official retrospective on 25 years of economic development in the PRC put self-reliance at the centre, omitting both Soviet imports of the first five-year plan and, later, imports from Japan and Europe:

> "China relies mainly on herself for machinery. Not all existing equipment is up to date. However, with wisdom and creativeness, the working class is able to make new machinery up to modern standards out of ordinary equipment. The performance of some old machines has been greatly raised after being technically transformed. After two decades of hard work, the machine-building industry is able to supply the various branches of the national economy with complete sets of equipment."[194]

"Workplace innovation" as a manifestation of the capabilities of the working class continued to be reported by news outlets in the provinces, ranging from incremental improvements in the production process and over-innovative use of materials and machinery, to the successful construction of specific projects. As an example, the Taizhou shipyard in Yangzhou special district reported that workers, by applying native methods, had started using cement instead of timber to repair wooden ships, and thus saved time and material.[195] The emphasis on native technological innovation was not new. It had been

---

191 Aktennotiz, Wissenschaftliche Zusammenarbeit / Projekt einer Mission schweizerischer Wissenschafter in die Volksrepublik China, 21. Juli 1972, Ref. O.320.China – SO/ca. Available at dodis: dodis.ch/35906. Last accessed on 12 August 2022.

192 Ambassade de Suisse en Chine, Lettre à la division du commerce, 15 août 1972, Réf: 550.1. – CJ/dx. Available at dodis: dodis.ch/35905. Last accessed on 12 August 2022.

193 Li 1995, p. 459.

194 China's socialist economy proves successful in 25 years, 0701 GMT, 24 09 1974 B.

195 Joint Publication Research Service, Communist China's transportation and communications, Taipei Fei-ch'ing Yueh-pao, Original in Mandarin, 01 09 1970, p. 10, accessed through Readex.

a part of the Chinese economic development paradigm since before the Great Leap, and throughout the readjustment of the 1960s.[196] According to RENSSELAER W. LEE, the concept of "creative labor" was encouraged by the Chinese communist movement, prior to the founding of the PRC, as a means of rehabilitating the economy and fostering the development of production.[197]

Besides their potential and, to a certain extent, real practical value for industrial production, workplace innovation had the characteristics of a political campaign. It was a revolutionary counter-example with regard to the policies of the early to mid-1960s, where imports of advanced technology from abroad as well as specialised management of enterprises were important yardsticks of economic policy. A report on the construction of a rolling mill in the Liaoning plant exemplifies this political character:

> "In the movement to criticize Lin Piao and rectify the style of work, the workers of the medium section rolling mill repudiated the doctrine advocated by [Liu Shaoqi] and [Lin Biao] of trailing behind at a snail's pace and the philosophy of servility to things foreign. This raised their consciousness of the struggle between the two lines, which in turn stimulated their socialist enthusiasm and creativeness. The 40 year old rolling mill had outdated equipment and backward technological processes. It used to depend on manual labor to turn the steel over in the process of rolling.
> Some 'experts tried to make a mechanical tilter before the cultural Revolution but failed. During the Cultural Revolution veteran worker Chang Fulai, a Communist Party Member, carefully observed the entire process of rolling and studied how to design a tilter that would meet its needs. He finally made a small and highly efficient light rail tilter with the assistance of other workers. Simpler in structure and consuming less power than imported models, it won the praise of some rolling-machine experts."[198]

The report reflects the critique of the reliance on foreign technology stemming from the Cultural Revolution in particular, as well as the trust in the ability of the masses to create innovations that were superior to those conceived by "experts". The phrase "servility to things foreign" was used particularly for the criticism of technology imports, if they were emphasised over the "native" capabilities of China to achieve technological progress. Being aware that importing whole plants meant adopting what had been in use for a long time in the industrialised countries, the criticism was based on the idea that by including the workers in the process, technological innovations that were better suited for the conditions in China could be achieved.

Also, the aim of replacing hard and potentially dangerous manual labour is reflected, which was both an issue of efficiency and – later on, more explicitly – the wellbeing of

---

196 Also translated as *first use, second criticise, third improve, and fourth make it your own*, attributed to Zhou Enlai as the *four points with respect to the import of technology*. See: KEITH RONALD C., Deng Xiaoping and China's Foreign Policy, New York 2018, p. 215.

197 LEE RENSSELAER W. III, Ideology and Technical Innovation in Chinese Industry, 1949–1971, in: Asian Survey, Vol. 12, No. 8, August 1972, pp. 648 f.

198 Foreign Broadcast Information Service, Production increases at Liaoning's Anshan Steel Center reported, Peking NCNA in English, 0728 GMT, 16 04 1974 B, accessed through Readex.

the workers. The concept of workplace innovation not only extend to incremental improvements but was also purported as a method to achieve qualitative innovations. As an example, projects in a boiler plant in Tianjin were celebrated by Xinhua in March 1970 as representing an exemplary implementation of the Anshan Constitution as well as demonstrating the productive and innovative potential of political zeal, surpassing the potential of notoriously reluctant hierarchical management:

> "In March of last year, the plant was given the task of trial producing a new type of coal-saving boiler. The time limit was within two months. Some leading cadres were not so sure whether it could be done. The party committee and the revolutionary committee started a Mao [Zedong] thought study course with nonstop cadres and veteran workers attending, and organised the masses to discuss the task. Through this study and discussion, the masses realized that the trial production of the new boiler was necessary in carrying out Chairman Mao's great strategic principle 'be prepared against war, be prepared against natural disasters, and do everything for the people' and that it was a revolution to transform China's industrial boilers. They became more confident and courageously took up the task. The workers of the whole plant soon swung into action. They applied Mao [Zedong] thought to analyze and solve difficulties. As a result, it took them only 18 days to trial-produce the new type boiler in the spirit of achieving greater, faster, better and more economical results in building socialism".[199]

While tangible outcomes stemming from these immediate workplace innovation projects were confirmed by foreign visitors and observers, the quality and usefulness has been assessed with general scepticism. As LAGERCRANTZ wrote:

> "[Mao Zedong] claims that he who is the lowest in society is also the most gifted. This hypothesis appears to me disputable, but used in practice it might contribute to lifting the mood at the workplace. Wherever I went [in China], there was a competition for showing me in what way the talent of the workers was used. The examples that were shown appeared nevertheless dubious to me. [...] I asked to see the inventions made by the workers. In a new machine hall, carrying concrete pillars were shown to me. Now they are hollow inside. This is a saving. I was also shown windows, which can be turned by a hinge in the middle – also an invention of workers. In a textile factory, the workers have invented a movable chair that slides from machine to machine. In a sewing machine factory in Canton, there is a drilling machine that drills 31 holes at the same time. In this factory, there is also an engineer sitting with his drawing board outside at the floor of the workshop, so that the workers may participate in the construction work."[200]

Similar observations were made by a delegation of eleven members of the Swiss parliament, who visited a Chinese car factory in 1971. Addressing the foreign guests, the vice president of the enterprises' revolutionary committee claimed:

---

199 Foreign Broadcast Information Service, Tientsin plant takes on new look by following Mao, Peking NCNA International Service in English, 1310 GMT, 24 03 1970 B, accessed through Readex.
200 LAGERCRANTZ 1972, pp. 94 f.

> "We are capable of giving up a bad way of working and preserve the good. [...] before, the initiative of the workers did not count. If a worker had a suggestion for an improvement, it had to be authorized by the cadres first. Often, the suggestion was ignored or the cadres used it as their own. Today, cadres, technicians, engineers and workers work together", naming 600 suggestions that had been registered since the beginning of the Cultural Revolution and 400 work improved work benches produced in cooperation."[201]

Another variety of workplace innovation was the reconstruction and declared improvement of foreign technologies and large-scale installations, such as the Sanmen Yellow River Gorge Reservoir[202], inherited from pre-revolution times. These examples show how slogans from the mobilisation of the Great Leap kept being referenced and combined with the campaigns of the Cultural Revolution, to frame tales of progress induced by ideological motivation and collective work in the industrial and economic spheres. Nevertheless, as the varying degree of detail of such accounts illustrates, not all projects in the context of workplace innovation were useless or non-existent. While certainly exaggeration and over-reporting existed and served as a means for workers to demonstrate political righteousness, Chinese industrial development was not non-existent and neither were workers idle. However, with regard to contemporary, Western as well as Soviet standards, the technological capacities of basic industries – such as the production of machine tools crucial for the expansion of productive as well as military capabilities – clearly lagged behind.

In 1978, looking back at the preceding years, a report submitted to the Joint Economic Committee of the US Congress reported that machine tool technology in China suffered from a "double lag", first running several years behind the international state-of-the-art with "mostly imitative" research accomplishments, and second from long transition periods between trial to serial production, if ever. As a result, it was estimated that the technological level in China found itself as much as twenty years behind comparable production in the West. As an example, the most common machine tool produced in China, still in 1978 was the C620 Lathe, a copy of a Soviet design that had been in production since 1959, being suitable for a wide range of needs.[203]

Technological development was an important expression of international self-reliance and co-existed with the pursuit of the expansion of technology imports, as it had earlier. After the fourth National People's Congress, the concept was nevertheless widely formulated in a much more nuanced way. The problem of raw materials for the development of the steel industry, as an example, was in autumn 1975 still presented as not to be solved by "plunder or imports" but by developing the Chinese mining industry by its own efforts.[204] Thus, domestic steel production would be placed on a solid base "which

---

201 Cortesi Mario, Meyer Frank A., Notizen aus China, Zürich 1972, p.26.

202 Foreign Broadcast Information Service, Reservoir poorly designed by foreigners is rebuilt, Peking NCNA Domestic Service in Mandarin, 0207 GMT, 19 12 1974 B, accessed through Readex.

203 US Government Printing Office, Chinese Economy Post-Mao, A Compendium of Papers submitted to the Joint Economic Committee Congress of the United States, Volume 1: Policy and Performance, 95th Congress, 2nd Session, November 9 1978, Washington 1978, p. 300.

204 Foreign Broadcast Information Service, Mines Support Steel Production, Peking NCNA in English, 0700 GMT, 15 09 1975 OW, accessed through Readex.

is independent of foreign control and the effects of economic crisis in the capitalist world". Self-reliance in that regard was less about self-sufficiency but about stability and control.

Despite attempts at improving technological innovation, the rather derivative than innovative character of research in China as well as a far-going lack of coordination after the Cultural Revolution limited what could be achieved. Further, the vertical integration of plants meant that they produced many or most of their own parts, and thus – with the exception of socialist cooperation-policies discussed below – were largely unable to use efficiency-gains from specialisation of their production capacities. Despite these difficulties, progress was noted particularly in the important machine-tool industry. One part of this progress depended on the expansion of imports (see the following Chapter). On the other hand, reports of an exhibition of machine tools of Chinese origin for export in Hong Kong in 1977 featured a wide range of machines that were certainly not Soviet-type C620s, including gear-shaping machines, cylindrical grinders, optical profile grinders, lathes and gear-grinding machines.[205]

Besides being a direct derivative from self-reliance and an expression of egalitarianism, "workplace innovation" offered narratives supportive of a spirit of cooperation under socialism. At the industrial workplace, this cooperation was less emphasised with regard to the "three-in-one"-leadership of the party, the PLA, and the workers, but more in terms of the different levels of expertise. With the shift from the logic of sending cadres to hierarchically lower positions towards the participation of workers in processes of planning and management, a similar shift occurred with regard to technical innovation. Over the course of 1975, workplace innovation, as reported in Chinese media, became less about the celebration of an alleged ingenuity of the anonymous masses but, rather, about precise reports on specific innovations that had been realised under the undisputed leadership of cadres, with the expertise of technicians *and* the participation of workers. Typically similar to this report from Shanghai, April 1976:

> "The cadres of the Shanghai Syringe Plant 2, through great technical improvements by the worker masses firmly carried out the 'combination of three' of workers, cadres and technicians and through self-reliance and getting things done by native methods, in one quarter completed 9 important innovations."[206]

Following the re-emergence of the Four Modernisations, workplace innovation was also openly put in the context of the lack of state investment, albeit explained as due to necessity rather than political priorities. For example, a September 1975 report from the Dagushan iron ore mine, part of the Anshan Iron and Steel Company – the alleged birthplace of Mao Zedong's management guidelines – stated:

> "Deep holes had been dug in the opencast deposits, making improvement difficult. Without asking the state to allocate funds and equipment to the mine, the workers

205 US Government Printing Office, Policy and Performance, November 9 1978, p. 301.

206 Joint Publications Research Service, Shanghai Instrument and Telecommunications Industry Doing Well, Article: "Shanghai Instrument and Telecommunications Industry System Revolution, Production Situation Generally Good", Hong Kong Chung-kuo Hsin-wen, Original in Mandarin, 26 04 1976, accessed through Readex.

> tackled and overcame the problems on their own. Workers, cadres and technicians joined in with the miners to improve the low-efficiency hammer drilling machine and made a new kind of saw-toothed rotary driller which increased efficiency three times over. With the help of other units, workers in charge of shoveling and loading transformed power shovels into long handled ones to double the efficiency. Workers throughout the mine were encouraged by the success of the innovations in the two major processes. They set about devising technical innovations to make up for the deficiency in ore dressing and blasting. The mine now has become a main source of ore in the Anshan Iron and Steel Company."[207]

Nevertheless, the striving for technical innovation through the participation of workers and cooperation as well as the exchange of experiences between factories of different regions, not only concerned industrial development for the advancement of industrial necessities – as it had been notably during the hardship years of the Great Leap – but also consumer goods like textiles, both for domestic and export markets. Although the examples provided to foreign observers as well as the numbers of innovations had to be seen for what they were – projections of a state of affairs as *envisaged* rather than achieved in practice – were present, the wish for inclusive cooperative processes at the workplace was genuine. This was also expressed in visual propaganda in the aftermath of the Cultural Revolution's peak, when more realistic and remarkably detailed and well-composed scenes from the workplace as envisioned partly replaced the heroic imagery of young people wearing the famous olive-green uniforms. The following example (Fig. 4) is striking with regard to its instructive character, appearing more like a management recommendation than political propaganda.

The truck repair shop depicted in the propaganda poster, published in the Jiangsu province in July 1973, shows how workers come together on the shop floor to debate how production can be improved. The title, "the factory is small, the aspirations high, striving to make great contributions" speaks of the ambition to be pursued by smaller-scale industries. The banner in the background calls for "self-reliance and frugality", while the gas cylinder in the foreground with its print indicates that the viewer is looking at a repair shop concerned with maintaining and improving existing technology as its purpose.

---

207 Mines Support Steel Production, 0700 GMT, 15 09 1975 OW.

Fig. 4: Chang xiao zhiqi gao, zhengzuo da gongxian, 54x77 cm, Stephan Landsberger Collection at the Institute for International Social History (IISH), Call number BG E12/738.

The role of research and education in the production effort

A particular variety of "workplace innovation" that emerged from the Cultural Revolution and its criticism of formalised education was the combination of institutions of technical education and production, for example, via small factories run by colleges on their premises. As was the combination of other public institutions and production. As an Egyptian report on the visit of a delegation to China in spring 1976 stated:

> "Another strange thing is the clinic of the small hospital of the air base. It produces medicine. The jobless wives of officers work there. It is a simple factory for medical production. I asked what they did with the medicine. He said that they would try to see what kind of medicines the town near them lacked. They are near Peking. They would find out if Peking lacked medicine or antibiotics of any kind. Then they would make these medicines and take them to the market to barter them for what they lacked."[208]

On the one hand, this meant using simple and Indigenous methods for light industrial production; on the other hand, the know-how still present in educational institutions was put to use, which was in line with demands for the transformation of the education system of the Cultural Revolution.

---

208 Foreign Broadcast Information Service, Mubarak speaks about his Visit to PRC, Cairo MENA in Arabic 1500 GMT, 30 04 1976 JN, accessed through Readex. The visit took place in a trade-context too, as on 6 June 1976, the yearly trade protocol – fixing trade exchanges at 60 million pounds sterling – was concluded right afterwards. Foreign Broadcast Information Service, 1976 Trade Protocol with PRC signed, Cairo Domestic Service in Arabic, 1500 GMT, 06 06 1976 ID, accessed through Readex.

As a means to advance production by assuring that theory and practice were not separated, "open door education" was a lasting legacy of the Cultural Revolution – the abolishment of admissions criteria for institutions of higher education save non-academic ones, such as class-background. College applicants were no longer required to take academic examinations in order to be admitted to college, and school grades were not taken into consideration. Grades and exams were replaced by a system of recommendations, whereby workers or peasants at each workplace recommended individuals for higher education.[209]

Following the reemphasis on production after 1975, the value of open doors for production by overcoming the separation of theory and practice was increasingly referred to as a justification, a decisive factor to explain the persistence of workplace innovation. As the Educational Revolution Group of Shanghai Normal University wrote in January 1976:

> "Open-door education has opened a wide world for universities to serve the economic base of socialism. [...] Since the great Cultural Revolution, the teachers and students of the Department [of mathematics] have already completed nearly 200 projects which moreover play a direct role in production. Some of the teachers and students designed and calculated the laying of gas and water pipes of Shanghai, rejecting the old, troublesome mathematical operations of the Soviet revisionists. [...] Still others trial made instruments to enable the shipbuilding industry to rise on its own feet. All this shows the revolutionary aspect of worker-peasant-soldier students in the fight to bring about the four modernizations."[210]

Moreover, the direct integration of education and production was that these forms of small-scale production and technical innovation did not directly rely on state-investment, and therefore corresponded with the concept of internal self-reliance. The Chinese press, notably Hongqi, reported extensively on successes of the use of such new-found synergies, such as the following example:

> "[...] we made full use of available equipment and other facilities, used simple and indigenous methods and relied on ourselves to set up a number of small and medium-sized factories which can promote various specialties, including a precision machine tool plant, an experimental multi-purpose electronics factory and a motor vehicle plant which accept some state assignments of scientific research and production. The experimental multi-purpose electronics factory, for instance, was built on the basis of a laboratory by making use of the old equipment and making some new pieces. **It has stimulated automatic control, radio technology, electronic computer technology and other specialties and turns out a wide range of electronic products** [emphasis added]."[211]

209 SCHOENENHALS MARTIN, The paradox of Power in a People's Republic of China Middle School, New York 1993, p. 47.

210 Joint Publications Research Service, Open Door Education Praised, article by Educational Revolution Group of Shanghai Normal University: *"Open-Door Education id Good"*, Shanghai Hsueh-His P'I-P'An, Original in Mandarin, No. 1, 1976, accessed through Readex.

211 Foreign Broadcast Information Service, Red Flag on transforming science-engineering schools, Peking NCNA International Service in English, 1831 GMT, 21 07 1970 B, accessed through Readex.

Both the need for technological advancement, with the particular example of electronics, as well as division of labour through specialisations were fully acknowledged, but the proposed method was based on local experimental innovation – rather tinkering than academic research. Which, notably, with regard to college-run factories and "open door education" did in no way prevent the creation of exchanges and networks. As the Dalian Institute of Chemistry and Physics of the Chinese Academy of Sciences reported in an article in Hongqi, in February 1976:

> "In 1975, our institute established ties with more than 300 units in 27 provinces, autonomous regions and municipalities throughout our country. We have sent more than 500 persons to and invited more than 200 persons from these units. Our research projects encompass industry, agriculture, national defense, foreign aid, outer space and underwater. Our institute has formed a three-in-one combination group of workers, cadres and scientific and technical personnel, and has integrated scientific research, production and application into a single process."[212]

As the factories were intended to be initiatives by educational institutions, they were remarkably free in choosing their lines of products as well as establishing their own planning and management; this was highlighted by the same article in the Hongqi:

> "The products it [the college-run factory] chooses to manufacture should be typical, varied and of advanced standards. They should be products which industry and national defense urgently need and should at the same time meet the needs of teaching of specialties; there should be a certain degree of serial-production, and in the meantime, energetic efforts should be made to conduct research and trial production and constantly introduce new techniques."[213]

The actual academic teaching was to become a function of these production processes through the students and teachers taking part in them, thereby combining education and productive labour.

> "Scientific experiment is an important task that universities of science and engineering must shoulder. While running factories, we have accelerated the reform and construction of the laboratories. Linking the university-run factories and laboratories with society, we have turned the university into an important base for training the students' ability in scientific experiment, energetically conducting scientific research, scaling pinnacles of technology, creating new technological processes and manufacturing new products, probing new theories and **catching up with and surpassing advanced world standards**.[emphasis added]"[214]

In the industrial cities, developments in complex industries such as electronics were reported with diverse applications suited to local needs, covering production needs such as grain scales, medical needs such as breathing equipment, and consumer goods like ratio

212 Foreign Broadcast Information Service, Red Flag Views Open-Door Scientific Research, Peking Domestic Service in Mandarin, 2345 GMT, 05 02 1976 OW, accessed through Readex.

213 Ibid.

214 Ibid.

and television receivers. Xinhua even claimed in July 1975 that "integrated-circuit computers capable of 1'000'000 operations per second" were produced in Beijing, together with colour television sets as well as integrated circuits of different scales.[215]

With regard to the organisation of such complex production chains, the same report claimed that the electronics industry had developed "step-by-step, from nothing to something, from small to large". The example of the East Wind Television Plant was presented as a quasi-entrepreneurial success story, albeit based on neighbourly cooperation rather than individual initiative – the enterprise, it was claimed, was organised by several copy shops, waxed wrapping paper plants and other small shops. Capable of producing both colour and black-and-white television sets, the enterprise had not only "graduated" to a state-owned enterprise of the Beijing municipality, with a set production level according to the local plan, but also provided the 19-inch television sets available in the Peking Hotel. New products in the Beijing electronics industry were, according to the report, "all new products designed through the cooperation of plants, technical universities, and scientific research units", test-produced through common efforts.[216]

The need for technological development to progress beyond the production of consumer goods in the longer term was recognised by the Chinese Academy of Sciences at several occasions, notably in a defence of Deng Xiaoping's outline report called "Scientific Research should Advance Ahead of Production and Construction", advocating for the increasing importance of advanced technology in modern production processes. As the country's electrification – reference to Lenin's famous definition of communism[217] – had created the base for further advances, there was a need to focus on the production process itself. "The development of electronic computers", the article noted, had "technically paved the way for an all-round automation of the process of production". As the controllers of these processes, "electronic computers are being developed into important means of production".[218] Another strand was the development of devices for oil exploration, which were presented as joint efforts by several units: examples reported by Xinhua in May 1977 included a catalytic and cracking unit designed and produced by the Yumen and Lanzhou oil refineries, the comprehensive research laboratory of the Petrochemical Industry Institute "after three years of experiments and preparations" and, among other things, a underwater geological prospector devised by the Yangtze River Basin Planning Board.[219]

With the introduction of the Four Modernisations in the constitution of the CCP[220] at the 11th Party Congress, the institutionalisation and professionalisation of research

215 Joint Publications Research Service, Peking's Electronics industry Develops Abundantly, Hong Kong Chung-kuo Hsin-wen, Original in Mandarin, 25 07 1975, accessed through Readex.

216 Ibid.

217 Communism being the Soviet government plus the electrification of the whole country. See: Lenin Vladimir, Our Foreign and Domestic Position and Party Tasks, in: Collected Works, fourth edition, Moscow 1965, pp. 408–426.

218 Foreign Broadcast Information Service, Academy of Sciences Article Defends 'Outline Report', Peking Domestic Service in Mandarin, 0200 GMT, 18 05 1977 OW, accessed through Readex.

219 Foreign Broadcast Information Service, New Technology Developed in Learning from Taching, Peking NCNA in English, 0714 GMT, 31 May 1977 OW, accessed through Readex.

220 Hsu 1990, p. 93.

and technical development in universities and specialised institutions became an integral part of economic policy in China. As in other policy areas, criticism of the Gang of Four became a legitimising rhetorical device for the rehabilitation of intellectuals who had been particularly affected by the Cultural Revolution. This also implied that the scope of ambition for technological progress as a whole went beyond incremental improvements of facilities through "workplace innovation" – the organised tinkering by workers – towards the systematic adaptation of foreign technology at a large scale, and the emphasis on Chinese efforts to develop advanced technology. This was particularly marked by advanced industries such as electronics and the emerging information technology.[221]

The need to catch up with the industrialised West in qualitatively new fields of technology, in particular information technology, was perceived in the Soviet Union and other socialist countries since the mid-1960s. While in the USA, a series of publicly financed projects in the defense industries had led to the development of a powerful industrial complex that confronted production and society with ever-shorter innovation cycles, the production of a small series of highly specialised appliances was predominant within the socialist world system. After 1968, the Soviet Union attempted to establish international cooperation, in particular within the Comecon, with mixed results at best. While the establishment of a unified system of cooperation in the sector could be achieved, institutional difficulties as well as prevailing mistrust between the partners hindered the development of mutually compatible solutions. In the West, the dominance of a few corporations in the sector that began to be established in the 1970s appears to have supported the development of *de facto* global standards – in particular those established by IBM for business and home computing – albeit arguably to the detriment of market competition.

In August 1977, the deputy director of the national Semiconductor Research Institute of the Chinese Academy of Sciences commented at the 11th Party Congress:

> "[...] the evil Gang of Four rabidly sabotaged our scientific and technical work. They slandered intellectuals [...] and openly clamored that the peasants could still move forward and [Daqing] could still be there even without scientific research work. Whoever attempted to do scientific research work would be charges by them with being divorced from the masses, labour and reality and 'taking the road to become specialists without a socialist conscience'. As a result, scientific workers could not make proper use of their energy and efforts and their enthusiasm was seriously hindered."[222]

Without making any reference to Mao Zedong Thought, Wang pointed to the "great march toward modernisation of science and technology", initiated by "Chairman Hua", underlining that "we veteran scientific workers" were to take the lead in this march. While learning from and absorbing the advanced science and technology of foreign

221 HERMANN FELIX, Technology Gap, transnationale Integrationsbemühungen und nationale Egoismen: Der Aufbruch des Rats für gegenseitige Wirtschaftshilfe in das digitale Zeitalter, in: WEMHEUER FELIX (ed.) 2020, pp.209-223.

222 Foreign Broadcast Information Service, Talk by Wang Shou-wu, deputy director of the Semiconductor Research Institute of the Chinese Academy of Sciences: "Resolutely Implement the Line of the 11th National CCP Congress and Strive to Realise the Splendid Goal of the Four Modernizations", Peking Domestic Service in Mandarin, 1200 GMT, 28 08 1977 OW, accessed through Readex.

countries, China would need to strive "to make discoveries, inventions, creations and progress" on its own, including by exercising concern "over the growth of the younger generation of scientific workers and encourage and help them in scaling scientific heights".[223]

Provincial conferences on scientific and technical work reiterated the points made, utilising the "red and expert" formula to justify the build-up of specialised research organisations, and emphasising that in future, science and technology needed to advance *ahead* of production and construction in order to create real progress in China. Also clarifying that science and engineering were tasks for experts, as reported by the provincial scientific and technical committee at a conference on scientific and technological work in Heilongjiang province in August 1977:

> "To develop science and technology, we must have faith in and rely on the masses and launch vigorous mass movements. At the same time, we must also bring into full play the backbone role of advanced elements and fully arose the enthusiasm of scientific and technical personnel."[224]

In September 1977, the CCP published a circular on the holding of a national conference on science on the 18th of the month, which emphasised the present and future role of specialised research and development even more. With the general justification that "without scientific experiment, without new technology, labour productivity cannot be raised greatly", the circular read like a catalogue of demands from the Chinese Academy of Sciences and technical cadres.

The Academy consisted of five departments, specialising in physics, mathematics and chemistry, biology, earth sciences, technical sciences, and philosophy and social sciences. It succeeded the *Academia Sinica* of the Republican Era. Being one of the two academies besides the Chinese Academy of Engineering, the Academy served the national governing body for research. After its founding in 1949, 233 members were appointed to the departments, which was raised to 254 two years later. According to TRONG R. CHAI, most of the members were attacked in various manners and degrees during the Cultural Revolution, with 42 members having been assaulted severely.[225]

The number and "level" of scientists was to be increased by an expansion of the education system at all levels, underlining the importance of colleges and universities. It was stated that "it is criminal to suppress free academic discussion in the ranks of the people", and scientists and technicians "who have made achievements or have great talent" were to be assured proper working conditions, by being "provided with necessary assistants", among other things. Titles for technical personnel were to be restored, technical proficiency systematically assessed and particular responsibilities allotted to technical posts. "Just as the workers and peasants are ensured that other things will not affect their work

223 Ibid.

224 Foreign Broadcast Information Service, Heilungkiang: Liu Kuang-Tao speaks at Science Conference, Harbin Heilungkiang Provincial Service in Mandarin, 2130 GMT, 07 08 1977 OW, accessed through Readex.

225 CHAI TRONG R., The Chinese Academy of Sciences in the Cultural Revolution: A Test of the "Red and Expert" Concept, in: The Journal of Politics, Vol. 43, No. 4, November 1981, p. 1217.

time, so scientific research workers must be given no less than five-sixths of their work hours each week for professional work."[226] The priority within the Four Modernisations shifted towards the importance of professionally conducted and highly specialised science and the advancement of technology, in a spectacular ideological counter-movement to the Cultural Revolution.

As it was presented at a provincial conference on learning from Daqing on the third of October 1977, the "important instructions of Chairman [Hua Guofeng] and Vice Chairman [Deng Xiaoping]" were transmitted in order to create the proper spirit for the preparation of the national conference on science in the coming year. Wang Feng, member of the CCP Central Committee and second secretary of the regional CCP committee and political commissar of the Sinkiang PLA-units, underlined that time was pressing for this task:

> "Comrades, our country is now at a historic juncture of carrying forward the revolutionary tradition and opening the road of advance. Our goal is magnificent; our tasks are arduous, time is pressing. [...] We must speed up the pace of construction and the movement to learn from Daqing in industry and build Daqing-type enterprises, seize every minute and second, go all out and achieve quick results."[227]

Once more, the CCP underlined *speed* as a centrepiece of China's economic policy. But this time, the emphasis on advanced technology increasingly replaced the "revolutionary spirit of the masses" as the historical force required for modernisation at a fast pace. "Until 1979", as the Changsha provincial forum on science and technology planning undelined in November 1977, China had to establish a rank-and-file of "red and expert" in science and technology in order to fulfil the objective. The national planning conference, concluded at the same time, established that the development of academic research on basic sciences was just as indispensable for China's rise as the practical work of engineers and experts.

Representatives of the sciences were cited by Xinhua as having brought forward numerous facts that refuted rather crude contradicting claims attributed to the fallen Gang of Four such as "theory was useless" and "divorced from practice". Implicitly, this also discarded Mao's scepticism about purely academic research. Practical examples given by Xinhua underlined both the importance of the oil industry and experts applying non-political thinking. For example, it was reported that "guided by the theory of geo-mechanics, pioneered by the Chinese geologist Li Siguang" China had finally "discovered several large oilfields and greatly developed our [the Chinese] oil industry".[228]

---

226 Foreign Broadcast Information Service, Text Of CCP Circular On National Science Conference, Peking NCNA in English, 1634 GMT, 22 09 1977 OW, accessed through Readex.

227 Foreign Broadcast Information Service, Saifudin Addresses Sinkiang Conference On Taching, Urumchi Sinkiang Regional Service in Mandarin, 1300 GMT, 03 10 1977 OW, accessed through Readex.

228 Foreign Broadcast Information Service, Importance Of Studying Basic Science Stressed, NCNA reporter's commentary: "Only When the Tree is Deep-Rooted Can It Become Leafy – On the Significance of Developing Basic Science In Our Country", Peking NCNA Domestic Service in Mandarin, 1315 GMT, 09 11 1977 OW, accessed through Readex.

In addition, references were made to the twelve-year plan that had been decided in 1956 for scientific and technological development and had enabled China to realise large projects in the military and related sectors – the satellite and hydrogen bomb of the 1960s.[229] Now, technology was to serve industrialisation directly and help push the Chinese economy beyond steel and grain. A national electronics industry conference on the 7th of November in Beijing was attended by representatives from electronics enterprises, scientific institutes as well as state and party cadres. The task of the conference, it was announced, was to devise policies and "specific lines" for the promotion of rapid growth and modernisation in this second guiding industry.[230]

The opening address by the new vice minister of the Fourth Ministry of Machine Building accentuated the importance of electronics for the needs of national defence as well as economic construction, while Minister Wang Zhen stressed technical innovation and strict quality assurance as the keys with which to *catch up* "and surpass" world levels. USLO reported that the conference was attended by the "leading lights" in the Chinese economic and science establishment, which included State Council vice premiers Yu Qiuli, Wang Zhen and Gu Mu as well as the vice president of the Chinese Academy of Sciences and member of the politburo, Fang Yi.

The Chinese Academy of Sciences greeted the "New Great Leap Forward in Scientific Research Work" and formulated its needs to support it, which were appropriately specific to match the new status their field had garnered in China. For example, its library group held in an article published in December 1977 that library work was an important foundation for the study of science and technology, but "before an army can march, food and fodder must be sent first" – referring to library reference materials as essential supplies. "Many facts have proved" that if library work is unable to catch up, scientific and industrial work suffers as "even the most experienced scientists would normally have to spend more than a third of their research time in going over relevant documented reference materials." If the documented reference materials were incomplete or inaccurate, it would "inevitably result in great difficulties".[231] Thus, science and technology as the main pillars of economic development required new heroes.

Geologist Li Siguang lent himself perfectly to the role as he combined the emphasis on science with trade orientation, manifested in the oil industry, as well as offered a possibility to establish a link to Daqing. Also, he represented an idol for younger people who might aim at a career in science, as most scientists after the gap-years of the Cultural

229 As in: Foreign Broadcast Information Service, People's Daily Urges Scientific, Technological Planning, People's Daily 8 November Commentator's article: "Do a good Job in Planning Scientific and Technological Development and Scale the World's Heights", Peking Domestic Service in Mandarin, 2230 GMT, 07 11 1977 OW, accessed through Readex.

230 US Department of State, Electronic Telegram, National Electronics Industry Conference Stresses Modernization; New Vice Minister Identified, 10 November 1977, 00:00, PlusD, ID: 1977HONGK13827_c.

231 Foreign Broadcast Information Service, Academy Library Greets Leap Forward In Scientific Research, Article by the library of the Chinese Academy of Sciences: "Take Practical Actions to Greet the New Great Leap Forward in Scientific Research Work", Peking Kwangming Daily in Mandarin, 28 12 1977 HK, accessed through Readex.

Revolution tended to be old men. Subsequently, he was built up as "a model of redness and expertness", as Hongqi called him in November 1977.[232]

Ignoring the theory that China was poor in oil "spread by the imperialist -paid scholars", Li showed pioneer spirit in proposing that general prospecting be carried out in the North China plain, receiving the support of Chairman Mao Zedong, Premier Zhou Enlai and other members of the central authorities. The results of his work "smashed the spiritual shackles" and demonstrated the ambition of the Chinese people. Moreover, he proved to be a versatile scientist: When the state needed coal, he did research on coal prospecting; when it needed uranium, he turned to uranium; when it needed to exploit geothermal sources, he took up the research in that field. Whatever the state required, he put his mental capacities to it. At his old age, he turned to earthquake research to prevent further catastrophic blows to the Chinese economy, as it had experienced in 1976. The article underlined that socialist construction had opened up grand prospects for the development of science, as the superior system provided plenty of room for the sciences, together with the practices of the masses of people, providing "inexhaustible sources for scientific studies". Li represented the "advanced world outlook and methodology" that was needed to "find a path through complex things, to know truths that have not yet been uncovered and to solve problems that no one has yet solved." A battle to capture science had begun, and Li Siguang was an example to be followed for it.[233]

In January 1978, Vice Minister Yuan Baohua of the State Planning Commission openly criticised "some conservative ideas about new technology", pointing out that "ideological hindrances of all forms" should be removed. Regions needed to advance as fast as they could, particularly with regard to the development of new energy sources, with "those which have reached advanced Chinese levels" striving to "catch up with or surpass advanced world levels".[234] In the same vein, the revised constitution that was presented at the fifth National People's Congress in late February 1978 did not introduce many major changes compared with the highly dialectical version of 1975. Approached with a systematic interpretation of their wording, articles thirteen and fourteen were remarkable: They put expansion of scientific research, the adoption of advanced technology and the development of education to raise the scientific level of China *before* political objectives.

> "[Article 13] The state devotes major efforts to developing science, expands scientific research, promotes technical innovation and technical revolution and adopts advanced techniques wherever possible in all departments of the national economy. In scientific and technological work we must follow the practice of combining professional contingents with the masses, and combining learning from others with our own creative efforts;

232 Joint Publications Research Service, A Banner which is both Red and Expert – Learning from Comrade Li Ssu-Kuang, Peking Red Flag No. 11, Original in Mandarin, 07 11 1977, pp. 24–28, accessed through Readex.

233 With an editorial in Hongqi in January 1978 calling out, "Our pressing obligation in speeding up the realization of the four modernizations is to [...] train a large contingent of scientists and technicians who are both Red and Expert." Red Flag Calls for Rapid Development of Economy, 1200 GMT, 06 01 1978 OW.

234 Foreign Broadcast Information Service, Yuan Pao-Hua Speech, Peking NCNA in English, 0700 GMT, 29 01 1978 OW, accessed through Readex.

> [Article 14] The state devotes major efforts to developing education in order to raise the cultural and scientific level of the whole nation. Education must serve proletarian politics and be combined with productive labor and must enable everyone who receives and education to develop morally, intellectually and physically and become a worker with both socialist consciousness and culture".[235]

Accordingly, the newly expanded system of higher education and the status accorded to it substantiated the technology-driven vision for the modernisation of China's economy. While the shifted compromise reflected in the articles included some elements stemming from the Cultural Revolution and the Great Leap, such as labour participation, the workers, as the descending order of the provisions indicated, were legally required to be *first* experts and then perhaps red to some degree. Accordingly, class struggle and the struggle for production and scientific experiment were to be grasped in equal measure in the future.[236]

A forum on the planning of economic sciences held in Beijing, in March 1978, emphasised that economic management was about to change even further. The discussions stood in stark contrast to the politically laden proclamations of the State Planning Commission eight years before, where the relevance of class struggle for economic planning had been at the forefront. Now, discussions on subjects like the "correct application of the law of value" and "price relations between domestic and international trade" were reported. Also, the forum reflected on the emphasis on technological advancement, which came to be the defining priority of the year, creating topics like the "widespread application of modern mathematics and computer techniques in planned statistical work."[237]

Xinhua reported days later how a worker in Daqing had improved her welding technique thanks to a "quick mathematical estimation method", taught to her by her former professor Hua Logeng. Allegedly interviewed shortly after, the sixty-eight years old professor, and then the vice-president of the Chinese Academy of Sciences, was quoted praising the new era the Chinese economy had entered:

> "Old China's backward industrial production had no room for applied mathematics. Since liberation, with Chairman [Mao Zedong's] and Premier [Zhou Enlai's] great con-

235 Foreign Broadcast Information Service, Text of the New Constitution, Peking NCNA in English, 0704 GMT, 07 03 1978 OW, accessed through Readex.

236 With Renmin Ribao declaring in April 1978 that: "None of the three great revolutionary movements of class struggle, the struggle for production and scientific experiment is dispensable. The three great revolutionary movements form an entity. They are integral parts of the continued revolution under the dictatorship of the proletariat. They are relatively independent, with each of them having its own characteristics and laws. It is impossible to substitute one of the movements with another, they are interconnected and they restrain and promote each other." Foreign Broadcast Information Service, Text of People's Daily 22 April editorial: "Seize the Three Great Revolutionary Movements Together", Peking NCNA Domestic Service in Chinese, 1725 GMT, 21 04 1978 OW, accessed through Readex.

237 Foreign Broadcast Information Service, Economic Sciences Planning Forum Discusses Work, Article by Lin Ching-sung, Hsueh Yung-ying and Fang Liu-pi: "Peking District Holds a Forum on the Planning of Economic Sciences", Peking Kwangming Daily in Mandarin, 20 03 1978, p. 3 HK, assessed through Readex.

cern and repeated instructions on mathematics serving production and construction, and with rapid industrial development and the widespread mass technical innovation's movement, applied mathematics has a much wider scope."[238]

The primacy of class struggle in the ideological sphere had also ended legally. The fact that experts would be needed was underlined in a series of public lectures delivered in Beijing, and covered at length by Renmin Ribao, on the modernisation of industry in May 1978:

"With the modernisation of industry, the output of our country's major industrial products is expected to approach, equal or outstrip that of the most developed capitalist countries by the end of this century. There will be automation of the main industrial processes, a major increase in rapid transport and communications services, and a considerable rise in labor productivity. We will be able to make extensive use of new materials and sources of energy and modernized our major products and processes of production. Our economic and technical norms will approach, equal or surpass advanced world levels."[239]

Using synergies beyond the plan: "Socialist cooperation"

While the ambition to lift China to the next level of economic development through technology grew, experiments aiming at the improvement of efficiency and productivity were also undertaken in other domains. In particular, principles of centralised planning were loosened in the industry, giving way to a form of inter-enterprise trade officially branded as "Socialist Cooperation". Referring to inter-enterprise cooperation apart from the plan, not to be confused with cooperatisation. According to RICHARD MCGREGOR, the networks created and the culture of informal agreements was the root of what would later be known as "China Incorporated" – in particular, with the concerted action of Chinese state-owned enterprises abroad and the persisting networks between various state-owned enterprises and their management.[240]

While aspects of technical collaboration, get-togethers between workers and engineers and the occasional neighbourly helping out with some spare parts did not mean turning away from centralised planning as such, allowing enterprises of different sizes to freely exchange products and inputs in order to meet common planning mandates did. Reports from Shanghai illustrated how:

"Interfactory relations in socialist new China are governed by the principle of altruistic cooperation to serve the national interests in direct contravention of the "Jungle Law"

238 Foreign Broadcast Information Service, Mathematician Discusses Practical Application of Work, Peking NCNA in English, 1225 GMT, 24 03 1978 OW, accessed through Readex.

239 Foreign Broadcast Information Service, People's Daily Looks At How To Modernize Industry, Fourth lecture on the general task for the new period by Chi Ti: "Modernize our Industry", Peking People's Daily in Mandarin, 23 05 1978, p. 2 HK, accessed through Readex.

240 MCGREGOR RICHARD, The Party: The Secret World of China's Communist Rulers, London 2010. Also, the legal implications of socialist cooperation after the 1980s has been given scholarly attention, as the spirit of socialist cooperation is somewhat averse to contractual law and, in particular, competition law. See: JONES DAVID M. (ed.), Basic Principles of Civil Law in China, New York 1989.

> that dominates the capitalist world [...] When the 200 workers of the Shanghai No. 2 Iron and Steel Plant learned that the Shanghai general petro-chemical works, then being constructed, urgently needed 300 studded tubes, they pitched in to help. [...] when the [Jiangnan] shipyard was building two 10'000 ton cargo ships, it found it urgently needed special plastic bends. The No. 6 pharmaceutical plant readily took it on and produced the bends in two days. [...] Thanks to socialist cooperation, factories of more than 20 branches of industry have widely adopted advanced techniques, such as use of laser beams, electronics, isotopes, microbiology and infrared rays."[241]

While Xinhua stressed the voluntary and selfless nature of socialist cooperation, the mandate of producing more economical results and the fact that single enterprises were keeping their own balance sheets[242] meant that emerging inter-enterprise markets were, at least in principle, tolerated. The efficiency of socialist cooperation in Shanghai became a new ideal in the course of 1975: "This has been achieved by pitching all the technical forces of the industry into a concerted, continuous battle for overall technological transformation", bringing returns that were claimed to be 63 times their investment.[243]

This practice included exchanges between large factories and so-called "neighbourhood factories" and workshops,[244] which had been allowed in the aftermath of the Great Leap. An article in Hongqi developed the idea of socialist cooperation further, referring to earlier experiences:

> „The lines between various trades should be eliminated and all related factories organized to carry out close cooperation and form a joint production line with chain-like coordination. [...] When [Zhangzhou] city organized several small factories to manufacture tractors, some people said that ‚it is impossible to stage an opera on top of a table.' Workers replied: ‚It is possible to stage an opera if we put several tables together to make a stage."[245]

The thought given to the division of labour though diversified supply chains of industrial production[246] in the piece is striking, just as its resemblance with aspects of small- and medium-sized enterprise (SME)-based structures in market economies. The success of local industries as an instrument to ensuring self-reliant industrial development in the countryside was claimed and underlined by official channels at staggering numbers. This expansion was explained as self-reliant production under state planning:

---

241 Foreign Broadcast Information Service, Shanghai Plants Foster Socialist Cooperation, NCNA Domestic Service in Mandarin, 0735 GMT, 30 09 1975, accessed through Readex.

242 While the central government continued to exercise control notably through the banking- and credit-system. See: Kosta/ Meyer 1976, pp. 238 f.

243 Foreign Broadcast Information Service, Shanghai Stresses Interfactory Socialist Cooperation, NCNA in English, 0736 GMT, 30 11 1975, accessed through Readex.

244 Correspondent on healthy state of economy, 1207 GMT, 25 09 1975.

245 Foreign Broadcast Information Service, Article by Chiang Hung, Run Medium and Small Industries Actively and Well, Red Flag No. 10, 1975, Peking Domestic Service in Mandarin, 2140 GMT, 12 10 1975, accessed through Readex.

246 Although limited at this point to what could be delivered in terms of material and labour, besides the plan. With the increase of flexibility concerning the legal retaining of surplus as profit, this phenomenon became even more pronounced.

> "The enterprises work in cooperation while maintaining a rational division of labor as far as conditions permit, so as to raise the production capacity and technical level of a city as a whole. This "streamlined" method, as the local people call it, embodies the spirit of socialist cooperation and increases production effectively."[247]

For the relatively highly industrialised Jiangsu province, state propaganda increases in industrial output by over 2000 percent since 1949 were attributed to such improvements.[248] The method of "streamlined" production went back to the initiatives in economic policy that were applied during the readjustment of 1962 in Canton. In late 1973, it was claimed that eight "streamlines" had been organised for the production of corduroy, khaki, cotton prints, "walking tractors", synthetic fibre, fiberglass, plastics and transistors.

The "walking tractors" were a particular application of technology in agriculture, which has been widely purported as being an example of the adaptability of engineering in the PRC. After the beginning of the first five-year plan, and large tractors as the symbols of agricultural mechanisation in the Soviet Union had been adopted, the State Planning Commission under Bo Yibo began to emphasise traditional farm implements in the mid-1950s in particular, as labour remained abundant in the countryside. As the use of heavy machinery was impeded by energy shortage, the emphasis shifted during 1964 and 1965 to the use of small, hand-guided tillers and tractors, which was carried on throughout the Cultural Revolution and its aftermath. When agricultural mechanisation seriously shifted to the focus of economic policy in 1975, the idea of using small, flexible machinery that could be repaired on spot and saved energy prevailed.[249]

Xinhua praised that since the beginning of "streamlined" production of tractors, output had risen "56-fold" and economies of scale had been realised, lowering the cost of a tractor "by fifty percent", mainly by cooperating with other factories outside the plan. The method, as the vice chairman of the Guangzhou municipal revolutionary committee claimed, enabled the city's enterprises "to tap their production potential and achieve quick results with little investment", allowing the gross industrial output of the city to increase "at a rate 24 times higher than state investment".[250] The method was also praised as a solution for technologically complex and large capital construction projects:

> "The construction of a 6-ton pure oxygen top-blown converter [...] is complicated, and no factory in the city can make all necessary parts independently. But, when related factories were mobilized to do the job collectively, they did it with satisfactory results. The work involved no less than 82 factories, big and small. Each of them, apart from fulfilling its own production plan, allotted a certain amount of manpower and equipment to help build the converter. [...] Several machine shops worked together [...] They

247 Foreign Broadcast Information Service, Kiangsu Cities Self-reliantly expand local industries, Peking NCNA in English, 0713 GMT, 30 12 1973 B, accessed through Readex.

248 Ibid.

249 Zhang Li, Urbanization, farm dependence and population change in China, in: Green Gary Paul (ed.), Handbook of Rural Development, Cheltenham and Northampton 2013, pp. 305 f.

250 Kiangsu Cities Self-reliantly expand local industries, 0713 GMT, 30 12 1973 B.

> completed the converter within 1 year, from collecting data and designing to trial operation.".[251]

When the implementation of the fifth five-year plan began in 1976, the consolidation of urban industries with an increase in capability to produce whole sets of equipment instead of specific machinery was still emphasised as an expression of self-reliance and the intention to create Chinese-built industrial plants from scratch. As it was reported in Hong Kong by Xinhua in January 1976 on the development of the Beijing machine industry:

> "The city's machine-building industry has now grown considerably in scale. There are many branches, basically forming more than 10 segments for the production of machine tools, heavy general machines, mining engineering machines, power generating equipment, automobiles, farm machines, instruments and meters, radios etc., and becoming an important equipment-producing force of North China and the whole country. The machine-building industry of Peking is now developing from being a producer of individual machines into one of whole sets of equipment [...] Most of the present key enterprises, such as the First Machine Tool Factory, Second General Machine Works, Heavy-Duty Electric Motor Factory, Internal Combustion Engine Factory, and Gas Analysis Instruments Factory, were established and developed in the Great Leap Forward [transcribed as: big leap forward].
>
> A marked change in the development of Peking's machine-building industry since the great proletarian cultural revolution has been the much higher level of assembly of whole sets of products [...] Peking's machine-building industry can now supply the metallurgical industry with whole sets of equipment for steel-rolling workshops capable of producing 2.3-meter medium plates, heavy and ultra-heavy machine tools equipment for aviation and navigation enterprises, and whole sets of equipment for refineries capable of producing 2'500'000 tons of oil a year [...]. Since the last 2 years, technical innovation activities of the city's machine-building industry have developed with vigor, technical levels have been rising continually, and many new products have appeared. For example, over 1000 new products, including a 24-meter rotary planer, a 30'000 ton hydraulic press, a 2-meter laser lead screw checking instrument, a fully automatic screw tap grinding machine, and a color newspaper printing machine."[252]

Also, besides the encouragement of "workplace innovation" by having workers participate – albeit under the leadership of technicians and cadres – cooperation in innovation through the sharing of experience was equally commended. Xinhua reported in January 1976 how the Shanghai industrial design departments, while they "modestly sought the worker's suggestions on how to improve their designs", visited "more than 10 other plants and design and construction units" where they sought the opinions of "experienced workers and technicians" on improvements, and thus "greatly" reduced labour in-

---

251 Ibid.

252 Foreign Broadcast Information Service, Fifth Five-Year Plans begin, Hong Kong Chung-Kuo Hsin Wen, Original in Mandarin, 01 01 1976, accessed through Readex.

tensity, shortened the period of construction "by one third" and saved "a large quantity of material and labor".[253]

While the emphasised spontaneous and voluntary nature of socialist cooperation – outside the plan and not affecting its execution negatively – could give the appearance of rather apolitical self-help, the idea became politicised in the movement to criticise Deng Xiaoping over the course of 1976. An important aspect in the critique was the idea of "direct and exclusive control of enterprises by the ministry concerned" and the call for re-centralisation of the control of key industries presented in Deng Xiaoping's comments on industry in 1975. The proposal was perceived by critics as undermining socialist cooperation and rational planning and impeding balanced economic development, notably in peripheral areas. Also, support for the light industry – which meant smaller enterprises controlled at a lower level of the state – was seen a threat by the concept that advocated for a more Leninist paradigm of organising at least a certain part of the national economy "like a factory".[254]

As an article put it in Hongqi in early September 1976:

> "Furthermore, the practice of [direct and exclusive control] is bound to undermine socialist cooperation, sabotage the comprehensive utilization of resources, impair the rational industrial planning, and impede the economic development in areas of national minorities. When this practice is in effect in the field of planning and other fields of work, only present and no long-range disadvantages or advantages will be taken into consideration for economic reasons; no political consideration will be taken into account. Big enterprise will be taken care of and the medium-sized and small enterprises will receive a cold shoulder".

Although somewhat more nuanced critiques were published later on in Hongqi, referring to Deng Xiaoping's program as "Comprador-Bourgeois Economic Concept", the authors emphasised the turn towards a "bureaucrat-monopoly-capitalist economy" amounting to letting China become a "colony or semi-colony of imperialism and social-imperialism [...] and a place for capital investments", being controlled by "a few persons in the central departments concerned" giving orders and imposing "vertical-line leadership". The negative example brought forward was not a capitalist economy, but the Soviet Union's.[255]

---

253 Further stating that for the construction of the "Chienpi Power Plant" – a large-scale project – engineers "after consulting the workers" introduced "12 new items of technique, equipment and materials which helped greatly improve the working conditions, raised quality and saved 3.3 hectares of farmland as well as 6 million yuan for the state". Shanghai Workers Make Industrial Designs, 0721 GMT, 01 01 1976 OW.

254 Joint Publications Research Service, Red Flag scores Teng on Enterprise Control, article by Chi Ping, "The Reactionary Nature of the Practice of 'Direct and Exclusive Control of Enterprise by the Ministry Concerned' Reemphasized by Teng Hsiao-ping", Peking Domestic Service in Mandarin, 0330 GMT, 09 09 1976 OW, accessed through Readex.

255 Foreign Broadcast Information Service, Red Flag scores Teng's Economic Concept, Excerpts of article by Kao Lu and Chang Ko: "Comment on Teng Hsiao-ping's Comprador-Bourgeois Economic Concept", published in Red Flag No. 7, Peking Domestic Service in Mandarin, 2020 GMT, 10 07 1976 OW, accessed through Readex.

Criticism was in many instances based on the "Ten Relations", notably the quote, "It is far better for the initiative to come from two sources than from only one. Let the localities undertake more work under unified central planning", advocating for avoiding a tilt in the dialectical relationship between the centre and decentral units to tilt in favour of the latter. As also explicitly stated in Mao Zedong's criticism of the Soviet *Political Economy* in 1960:

> "We want to achieve, that the whole country is unified, but each province is independent, this means relative unity and at the same time, relative independence. Each province follows the decisions of the central [government], but decides independently on its own issues. The decisions of the central on important issues are nevertheless not decided solely by it, but in consultation with each province, as for example the decisions of the Lushan conference. [...] While we do have a unified plan for the whole country, we advocate for each province doing alone what it is able to do. [...] Earlier, there was worry that, if each province would develop every kind of industry, the industrial products of a city like Shanghai would not find any demand. Now we see that this is not the case. Shanghai has shown the way for the development of high-grade, larger, finer and more precise [products], but there is still plenty to do [for Shanghai]."[256]

With the consolidation of the economic policy course favouring small-scale industries, the production of consumer goods and agricultural mechanisation and the idea of socialist production gained additional momentum as a means of giving full play to local initiative. The Jiangsu provincial CCP committee reported in February 1977 that through the flexibility of the localities – largely independent of centralised planning and leadership – it was possible to better "carry out great socialist coordination" and improve efficiency by "tapping the production potential".

The municipal party committee, the report claimed, had coordinated the production capabilities of various small enterprises as well as "various professions, trades and urban districts", producing "15'000 hand-guided tractors and 38'000 diesel engines"; although the necessary investment was claimed to be "only one third of that needed to build an independent [integrated, large-scale] plant". "Mass cooperation" was even credited with the construction of a "sophisticated ground satellite receiving station". Moreover, socialist cooperation was reported to allow for the increased production of core consumer goods such as clocks and watches, bicycles, sewing machines and other light industrial products.[257] The article demanded the expansion of the "right of independent action" of local authorities to enable them to "do more things". Also, with remarkable clarity, it stated that "our policy is to put production ahead of capital construction", adding that "this should not be considered as right conservatism or inactivity. This is following the objective law in economic development and ensuring the success of more important things".

---

256 Quoted from MARTIN 1975, p.75, translation by the author.

257 Foreign Broadcast Information Service, Red Flag: Kiangsu Article on Socialist Construction, article by Kiangsu Provincial CCP Committee: "The Only Road to Speed Up Socialist construction – Notes on Studying 'On the Ten Major Relationships'", Red Flag, No. 2, 1977, Nanking Kiangsu Provincial Service in Mandarin, 0330 GMT, 14 02 1977 OW, accessed through Readex.

After the presentation of revised management guidelines at the national conferences on learning from Daqing and Dazhai in May of 1977, socialist emulation as a practice amounting to the adaptation of "scientific management" in enterprises not yet audited and certified overshadowed socialist cooperation in emphasis. The unification of reliable management was to be achieved as a priority. Unified management was deemed to be particularly important due to the highly decentralised nature of light industry in China, which was in late 1977 justifiably celebrated as a core success of Chinese economic policy. Over 120'000 light industrial factories reported all over the country, with impressive output values; more importantly, the emphasis on the deployment of light industry in the countryside had toned down the inherent conflicting relationship between industrialised walled cities and the self-reliant countryside, while releasing the strain on transportation, as factories could be constructed close to the source of raw materials. Xinhua reported on the 25th of September 1977:

> "Over 70 percent of China's few and poorly equipped light industrial enterprises before liberation were concentrated in Shanghai, Tientsin and a few other coastal cities. New China has put emphasis on building factories in the interior while continuing to develop the coastal regions. Tibet, Inner Mongolia, [Ningxia], [Qinghai] and other areas inhabited by minority nationalities, which virtually produced no manufactured goods before, now have textile, paper-making, canning and other industries. Because light industry has been developed simultaneously in both coastal and interior areas, its rate of growth has been quite fast. There are now 120,000 light industrial factories located in different parts of the country. Gross output value of light industry in 1976 was 12 times the figure for 1949."[258]

Technology and equipment that were developed, acquired and adopted in the industrial centres, particularly along the coast, were intended to support the interior of China in the manufacturing of new products like watches, cameras, fibres, photographic film and electric appliances, thus distributing technologies and products that were new to China as a whole. Pressure on the rural–urban divide would rise significantly in later years, but this development was connected to the creation of a new kind of walled city close to the sea harbours that were erected during the gradual turn of the Chinese economy towards the outside world in the Long 1970s.

Agricultural mechanisation strategies

The idea that economic development in China would necessarily need to take agriculture as its basis, and that the improvement of the primary sector's productivity by the appliance of improved techniques – such as irrigation, crop change and the use of improved seeds – was not new. At their core, the Three Red Banners and particularly the Great Leap had a similar intention[259], albeit the implementation by a "big push" was more

258 Foreign Broadcast Information Service, More Balanced Deployment of Light Industry achieved, Peking NCNA in English, 0722 GMT, 25 09 1977 OW, accessed through Readex.

259 In December 1975, the second secretary of the Tsinghai provincial CCP committee, Zhang Qianglin reported at the provincial conference on learning from Dazhai that when the intended

than flawed. Mechanising agriculture, meaning the use of machinery to make human labour more efficient or reduce its need altogether, had been stated as a goal in various forms since the founding of the PRC. The *new* quality of the bundle of programs emerging in the early 1970s meant that mechanisation was given unprecedented priority and implemented in the whole country simultaneously.[260]

At the Yunnan province-wide agriculture work conference, held in August and September 1969, a member of the provincial revolutionary committee described the lack of profitability of farming, stating that even with more than fourty state-operated farms, the majority lost money annually, and that many units devoted to grain cultivation did not even produce enough food for their own use. Transmitting the general rationality of the small industries programme to the officials of his province, he emphasised that the problem needed to be solved "within the next year or two." State-operated farms not only needed to be self-sufficient – which meant not relying on investment and support from higher levels – but, on the contrary, to contribute actively to the national economy.[261]

An important manifestation of improvements in agriculture aiming at an increase in productivity was the programme for the development of "five small industries", which produced subsidiary inputs for agriculture and small rural industrial undertakings: cement, machinery, fertilizer, steel in small quantities and electricity. While not new, the implementation of the programme was remarkably improved after 1970.[262] The development of these "rural small-scale industries" was a distinguishing aspect of the early 1970s. To stabilise agricultural production and improve it through mechanisation on a local level, the programme was an expression of efforts to partly decentralise the industrialisation of China while maintaining the general course of centralized urban industrialisation. Both "rural" and "small scale" are to be understood in quite general terms in order to take into account the very diverse range of construction projects. As Dwight H. Perkins noted:

> "Rural small-scale industry is not necessarily even rural (some of it is located in county towns), or that small (the number of employees sometimes exceeds 500 per factory). And yet there are fundamental differences between large-scale urban plants and those that are termed rural and small scale [...] Being under a county's jurisdiction usually means that the greater portion of the factory's outputs and inputs are sold or obtained within that same county. When an enterprise finds itself supplying a much larger area, it usually is transferred up to a higher-level administrative unit".[263]

---

level of farm mechanisation was reached – 80% to 90% of the work in state-run farms was being carried out by machinery – the province could conduct agricultural production "as if we had doubled our manpower and bring about a new leap forward in agriculture and livestock breeding". Chang Chiang-lin reports at Tsinghai meeting, 1500 GMT, 27 12 1975 OW.

260 Bramall 2007, pp. 45 ff.

261 Provinicial Revolutionary Head reveals Agricultural Woes, Taipei Chung-kung Yen-chiu, original in Mandarin, No. 9, 09 1970.

262 Bramall Chris, The Industrialization of Rural China, Oxford and New York 2007, pp. 24 ff.

263 Perkins Dwight H. (ed.), Rural Small-Scale Industry in the People's Republic of China, Berkeley, Los Angeles and London 1977, p. 1.

Also, it familiarised a large number of people – cadres, workers and peasants – with the organisation and maintenance of industrial production. This allowed for an indirect subsidy to agricultural collectives, which was transferred to an adjustment in the internal terms of trade of the centralised grain procurement system. While the purchasing prices for agricultural products were lowered, the prices for agricultural inputs declined as well; thus, the extractive nature of the system did not change.[264] Further, the heavy droughts in 1972 marked a setback for improvements, which had consequences on the purchase of grain from foreign suppliers but did not interrupt the modernisation efforts. Moreover, improvements were observed with regard to the standard of living, even in the countryside.

PERKINS noted[265] that in the summer of 1975, China's rural industrial program had entered a new expansionary phase centred on farm mechanisation and driven by the immediate needs of the localities. As high transport costs and bureaucratic bottlenecks inherent in central planning stood in the way of the supply of local needs, the way around these barriers was for the locals to do it themselves, while decreasing the investment burden for the central government. The rationale behind the push was the rolling out of the available basic innovations to the countryside, in order to improve the economic basis of the country and achieve non-interdependence in food as well as provide sufficient agricultural raw materials for the growing light industry. This continuity was publicly established, as heard in a 1975 CCP cadre's speech at a conference on agriculture in Qinghai:

> "The fundamental line for the development of China's socialist agriculture is: After the completion of land reform, the first step is collectivization (i. e. to form mutual-aid teams, agricultural co-operatives and then people's communes). On this basis, the second step is to realise agricultural mechanization. Only by following this revolutionary line of Chairman Mao's has China's agriculture been making rapid strides along the road to socialism."[266]

While this ideal sequence still communicated the difficulties faced outside, as collectivisation was imperfect and relativised frequently, the second step of mechanisation was pursued regardless. The inclusion of the countryside in the process of industrial development also had a strong political background.

In a 1973 interview with an Egyptian journalist, Zhou Enlai was asked to explain the rationale behind the Cultural Revolution. How could a second revolution be needed in a country already being ruled by the working class? After explaining the doctrine of persisting class contradictions within China, and even within the CCP, Zhou embarked on a critique of the Soviet Union and particularly the legacy of Stalin:

> "Can we imagine that even 50 years after the revolution the Soviet Union still has been unable to solve the question of agriculture? They have an industry, but it is not a good industry. They have developed colossal nuclear weapons and they compete in space,

264 PERKINS 2015, pp. 175 ff.

265 PERKINS (ed.) 1977, pp. 252 ff.

266 Ibid.

> but what it the use of this if the question of agriculture is not solved and if industry fails to provide a good standard of production for the people?"[267]

Similarly, the second secretary of the Shandong provincial CCP committee spoke to a provincial meeting at learning from Dazhai, in early 1974, and linked back to efforts initiated in 1970s, calling for the promotion of agricultural mechanisation in a rational fashion. In particular, he called for a scientific approach that sought "truth from facts":

> "The fundamental way out for agriculture is mechanization. To develop agriculture in a big way, it is necessary to bring into full play the leading factor of industry. Since 1970, the party committees at all levels have paid great attention to the tasks of mechanization. Most of the five small industries in support of agriculture in the province have been developed in recent years. Not only must we have the revolutionary spirit of daring to think and act, but also the scientific attitude of seeking truth from facts. We must strive to do what we can do and should not insist on saying that we can do what actually cannot be done".[268]

Frequently attributed to Deng Xiaoping alone, the expression is much older. Seek truth from facts (*shi shi qiu shi*) originates from the Book of Han, describing a general investigative attitude needed for study and research. Being quoted by Mao Zedong at the Party Congress of 1938, it became an integral part of Mao Zedong Thought as a call for pragmatism over rigidity. After 1978, the expression was appropriated by Deng Xiaoping as a part of "socialism with Chinese characteristics" (*Zhong guo te se she hui zhu yi*), referring to taking the material conditions as a starting point for the development of policies instead of normative goals. Ross Terrill noted that Mao probably remembered the phrase from his time at the Hunan first teacher's training school, where it was inscribed on the main building.[269]

At its core, the idea of combining of collectivised agriculture with decentralised light industry went back to the years of the Great Leap and its campaigns for the rapid expansion of industrial output, under the slogan "go all out, aim high and achieve greater, faster, better and more economical results in building socialism". The role of the so-called "township and village enterprises", and their importance in the relative success of the domestic economic reform policies in the 1980s, has been studied extensively.[270]

---

267 Joint Publication Research Service, The Red East – a long discussion with Chou En-lai, Cairo Al-Ahram, Original in Arabic, 23 02 1973, p. 4, accessed through Readex. In his critique of the Soviet political economy, Mao Zedong argued in an even more utilitarian manner, but basically made a similar point: "If one wants to achieve the rapid development of heavy industry, then general activism and an overall happy mood are required; and when one wants to achieve this, then the simultaneous and coordinated development of industry and agriculture and of light and heavy industry are required." Quoted from Martin 1975, p. 52, translation by the author.

268 Foreign Broadcast Information Service, Pai Ju-ping Speech, Tsinan Provincial Service, original in Mandarin, 1100 GMT 11 01 1974 B.

269 Terrill Ross, Mao, A Biography, Stanford 1980, p. 28.

270 Balasubramanyam Vudayagi, Fu Xiaolan, Township and Village Enterprises in China, in: Journal of Development Studies, Vol. 39, No. 4, pp. 27–46; the analysis of the relationship between TVEs and state-owned enterprises in Perotti Enrico C., Sun Laixiang, Zou Liang, State-Owned

It is worth emphasising though that their establishment, mostly based on local investments, had begun earlier under different paradigms. A leading member of the town planning committee of Shashi emphasised in November 1975:

> "Ours is a developing socialist country and there is a lot of work to be done. In transforming consumer cities, it is wrong to rely on state investment to build up bis factories. It is up to us to develop small-scale industries in a planned way and expand them step by step so as to speed up industrial construction [...]"[271]

Very different from the Cultural Revolution rhetoric on the importance of revolutionary criticism as a means to improve the situation, his description of plans for agricultural development in the years 1970 to 1974 was practical:

> "Step by step, we must establish a complete industrial system for the service of the agricultural production. The local industries must concentrate their financial, material, and technical efforts to develop all types of machines, power tools, chemical fertilisers, agricultural drugs, and tools of transportation suitable for the varied conditions of all the different localities of our province for the purpose of agricultural development."[272]

That the intended local industries would also serve other purposes was made clear:

> "The direction of local industries must be in such a manner that both wartime and peacetime conditions are taken into consideration. In times of peace, local industries must serve socialist agricultural production and construction; in times of war, local industries must serve the war effort. [...] In times of war, they must be able to repair guns and cannons, and to manufacture hand grenades, mines, and bullets do as to serve the war effort."[273]

PERKINS predicted that the day would come when these enterprises can no longer be called "small-scale". Interestingly, in hindsight, this process appears to have been further developed in cities already, were factories branching out from central-state financed ones grew rapidly. This process was not only tolerated but also actively supported by the central government.

Factories equipped themselves for the production of new machinery from the prominent hand tractors to machines used for the arduous task of rice planting and harvesting, while factories producing inputs such as cement and chemical fertilisers were also expanded. "Under the party's centralised leadership", Hongqi reported in November 1975, "[a] municipality [in Jiangsu] made an overall plan for its existing enterprises, organised coordination, broke down boundaries between different trades" and "carried out rational division of labour and production". As a consequence, the required investment "was equivalent to only thirty percent of what would have been needed to build a new factory

---

versus Township and Village Enterprises in China, in: BRADA JOSEF C., WACHTEL PAUL, TAO YANG DENNIS, China's Economic Development, London 2014, pp. 33–59; and PERKINS 2015, pp. 446–448.

271 Foreign Broadcast Information Service, Hupeh city industrializes via self-reliance, Peking NCNA in English, 0706 GMT, 01 11 1975, accessed through Readex.

272 Ibid.

273 Ibid.

with the same production capacity". Moreover, the lower production costs and higher quality were praised.[274]

The programme focused on three aspects: Providing electric power supply to villages, developing small machinery plants and repair shops to supply tools, and the development of small chemical fertiliser plants. Fertiliser was particularly scarce, and Chinese efforts to improve and promote strains of agricultural crops went back to the first five-year plan, where the sixth clause in the fourth article on measures for "increasing agricultural production" stated that the use of "high quality seeds" would be actively promoted and technical assistance to farmers strengthened.[275]

As the US Department of Agriculture reported, increased use of chemical fertilisers had made a major contribution to the progress in Chinese agriculture. During the years 1964 to 1974, fertiliser production was estimated to have risen at an annual average rate of about sixteen percent – which would have been remarkable under any circumstances. While official statements on fertiliser production were patchy and partly conflicting, production in 1975 was estimated to even be twenty percent above the 1974 level.[276] The improvement of seeds had already been part of the "eight character code" authorised by Mao in 1958, which aimed at the improvement of grain production.[277]

Using superior varieties was a viable alternative, but the lack of experience with their use lead to unpredictable harvest yields and unintended degeneration. According to some estimates, China imported over 6.5 million tons of chemical fertiliser and purchased over 5.36 million tons of grain in 1970 – a trend to be continued (see next chapter) later on. To increase yields, new seeds were imported; for instance, 5'000 tons of dwarf wheat varieties were obtained from Mexico in 1972, which increased to 15'000 tons in 1973.[278]

In February 1975, at a conference of the US Committee on Scholarly Communication after a visit to China, in the late summer of 1974, concluded that Chinese agriculture had reached a high technological level for basic commodities such as rice, where "efforts by scientists, engineers and farmers have been concentrated" before the Cultural Revolution.[279] New techniques thus developed were perceived to be in widespread use, part of

274 Foreign Broadcast Information Service, Article by Tang Feng "Speed up Mechanization of Agriculture", Red Flag No. 11, 1975, Peking Domestic Service in Mandarin, 2130 GMT, 13 11 1975, accessed through Readex.

275 As stated in a speech on Article 29 of the National Programme for Agricultural Development, published in 1957, at the fourth session of the first National People's Congress, in July 1957. Ma Yinchu, A new theory of population, in: Howe Christopher, Walker Kenneth R. (ed.), The Foundations of the Chinese Planned Economy: A Documentary Survey, 1953–65, London 1989, p. 312.

276 The US Department of Agriculture, the Agricultural Situation in the People's Republic of China and Other Communist Asian Countries, Review of 1975 and Outlook for 1976, Foreign Agricultural Economic Report No. 124, Washington D.C. 1976, p. 30.

277 Joint Publication Research Service, Study and Analysis of Chinese Communist Scientific and Technical Activities in Agriculture, article by Ch'iung Wen, Taipei Fei-ch'ing Yueh-pao, Original in Mandarin, September 1972, pp. 56–63, accessed through Readex.

278 Perkins Dwight H., A Conference on Agriculture, in: The China Quarterly, No. 67, September 1976, p. 601.

279 Ibid., pp. 607 f.

which was explained as a consequence of the more efficient rural organisation standard, with the production team as the main accounting unit encouraging the efficient use of inputs and rapid introduction of new technology, once developed. A member of the Plant Studies Delegation was quoted stating,

> "I came back [from China] and told my foundation: integrated rural development is possible. I have just seen a large, successful project that involves 650 million people."[280]

Nevertheless, further development prospects were assessed more cautiously, as high agricultural productivity, notably in much of northern China, was found being dependent on finding sufficient and adequate supplies of water, which in turn required solutions to silting, therefore extensive investment and time. Another limiting factor was the availability of fertiliser, even with the sufficient production, more was required by the larger crop varieties, which also meant more research investment and time.[281]

As long as both population and incomes were growing, agricultural output would have to rise in order to sustain the economy. Also, expectations from the state rose with the income – how could necessary investments be financed, if the main source of surplus in China was to be only found in agriculture for the time to come? Despite visible and acknowledged progress, the basic dilemma of Chinese economic development was far from solved. While the initial efforts to increase agricultural mechanisation were largely based on a decentralised system of production and application, the recentralisation efforts after the fall of the Gang of Four began emphasising standardisation, with party officials at the provincial level issuing calls for the creation of standardised blueprints to enable production of successful appliances in large numbers, while keeping production small during local "trial-periods" to minimise waste.[282]

After the fourth National People's Congress, the mechanisation of agriculture emerged quickly as the smallest common denominator for economic policy in the PRC, appealing to those who had advocated for the deepening of People's communes as well as decentralisation and economic development by any means necessary. As a fairly technical issue which involved the industrial cities and sites, while focusing on improving the life of the overwhelming majority of the Chinese population living in the countryside, it was a perfect focal point to create unity with regard to a broad economic issue. Hongqi, which during the Cultural Revolution had risen as the core publication of the dogmatic strands of Maoism, embraced agricultural mechanisation and praised its advantages in the consolidation of socialism as it required the local communities' cooperation, the accumulation of capital, an increased availability of food, raw materials

---

280 Ibid.

281 Ibid., p. 608.

282 Foreign Broadcast Information Service, Chang Ping-Hua Speaks on Agricultural Mechanisation, speech by Chang Ping-hua, second secretary of the Hunan Provincial CCP Committee, at the provincial conference on learning from Tachai in agriculture on 9 February 1977, titled: 'Thoroughly Expose and Criticise the Gang of Four and Promote Agricultural Mechanization" [Title read by announcer], Changsha Hunan Provincial Service in Mandarin, 1100 GMT, 19 03 1977 OW, accessed through Readex.

and, subsequently, labour and an enlargement of the range of products that people in the countryside could access.[283]

On the other hand, the competition for investment funds and resources between agricultural mechanisation projects, small enterprises and the construction of large-scale enterprises was noted. If the concept of self-reliance was to be taken seriously – independence as far as possible from funding by the central government – the construction of large-scale enterprises would either be strictly limited or require a shift in paradigm.[284] Be it for the simple reason that the alternative would have been no industrial progress.

Vice President Hosni Mubarak of Egypt, who visited China with an official delegation in spring 1976, reported:

> "[...] I visited a town called [Oshi]. At 1400 on the following day, while walking, I asked the governor about the industries of the province, which is like one of our provinces. He said: We have the cotton and silk textile industries. We have hides. We have all the industries that will guarantee our needs because we are proceeding according to the principle of self-reliance. We [do not ask] Peking for anything at all. On the contrary, we produce, we work, and we feed ourselves. After this we give the surplus to the national interest."[285]

The light industry directly related to agricultural production, such as sugar refineries, and the necessary infrastructure for mechanisation, such as repair shops and smaller sources of raw material like coal mines, shifted slightly from the periphery to the focus of economic policy, while heavy industry remained at the centre, with production and growth figures being placed prominently in reports on industrial development. The manufacturing of farm machinery at the lowest possible level also increased the need for quality assurance to enable mechanisation to be rolled out as evenly and equitably as possible. The necessity to ensure sufficient capacities for the repair and maintenance of equipment in the state plans as well as avoidance of below-standard products being checked out of plants were emphasised. The ideal purported at conferences on learning

283 While stating that the struggle between the "two lines" would still be unavoidable, the programme itself was presented as undisputed. "Speed up Mechanisation of Agriculture", Peking Domestic Service in Mandarin, 2130 GMT, 13 11 1975 OW.

284 "In the process of socialist construction, it is absolutely necessary to build a number of large-scale enterprises in a planned and systematic manner and to strengthen our leadership over such enterprises. However, large amounts of capital investment and major equipment are needed in order to build up large-scale enterprises and the technical requirements for building such enterprises are very high. Take a province or a region, for instance, since its funds, equipment and other conditions are limited. It is impossible for it to build many large-scale enterprises. If a province or region wants to build many large-scale enterprises, it must ask the central authorities for funds and equipment." Foreign Broadcast Information Service, Red Flag Discusses Medium, Small Industries, Article by Chiang Hung: "Run Medium and Small Industries Actively and Well", Red Flag No. 10, 1975, Peking Domestic Service in Mandarin, 2140 GMT, 12 10 1975 OW, accessed through Readex.

285 Mubarak Speaks about his Visit to PRC, 1500 GMT, 30 04 1976 JN.

from Daqing, with regard to the role of industry, demanded a system of "guaranteeing free repairs, exchanges and refunds" for farm machines.[286]

While agricultural mechanisation was an important compromise in economic policy, as it addressed core contradictions of the development paradigm while fitting the Mao Zedong Thought neatly, its consequences in the longer run were prone to sharpen other contradictions. In early 1976, in a meeting with USLO in Hong Kong, senior representatives commented on the upcoming five-year plan that continued prioritising agriculture, stating that was possible to increase grain production as well as the mechanisation of farms. These improvements, while positive, would potentially cause the "transfer of ten million workers from agriculture to industry".[287]

The improvement of productivity in the agriculture and rural industries promised to solve a number of crucial problems but also threatened to create new challenges. The development of rural small-scale industries remained a policy priority throughout the 1970s, their development being among the most reported successes in official Chinese media. In November 1976, Xinhua reported that "eighty percent of the counties" had their own small cement works that were able to fulfil the local needs to a large extent, while "most of the provinces, municipalities and autonomous regions" were reported to have set up "a network of big, medium and small cement works" that were "rationally distributed" – allegedly improving the quality of the cement produced steadily, at annually dropping cost.[288]

Regarding the overall line in economic policy, the relatively pragmatic course of the leadership under Hua Guofeng had already become granular – achievements in rural small-scale industry remained linked to the Great Leap and the Cultural Revolution as main political enablers.[289] An editorial in Renmin Ribao, published in late December 1976, was published with an editor's note stating that the text had been written "five years ago, but was then suppressed by the 'gang of four'", titled "The Fundamental Way Out for Agriculture Lies in Mechanisation" and covered the national conference on the mechanisation of agriculture held in August and September 1971, "in accordance with the instruction of the party Central Committee headed by Chairman Mao".

---

286 As at a provincial conference in Anhui province in June 1976, where the importance of reliability of tools was particularly emphasised. Foreign Broadcast Information Service, Kuo Hung-chieh addresses Anhwei Meeting, Hofei Anhwei Provincial Service in Mandarin, 1100 GMT, 10 06 1976 OW, accessed through Readex.

287 US Department of State, Electronic Telegram, PRC-Controlled Organizations' Representatives Comment About Economic Aspects of Hua Kuo-Feng Appointment, 13 February 1976, 09:30, PlusD, ID: 1976HongK01688_b.

288 Foreign Broadcast Information Service, Small Cement Industry Progressing Rapidly, Peking NCNA in English, 0700 GMT, 19 11 1976 OW, accessed through Readex.

289 As Xinhua put it: "The rapid development of the small cement industry is a fruit of the Great Proletarian Cultural Revolution. The drive to build small cement works was started by workers and commune members in 1958 under the impetus of the party's general line for building socialism. But this drive was gradually running out of steam owing to interference and sabotage by [Liu Shaoqi's] counterrevolutionary revisionist line and did not pick up momentum until the start of the Cultural Revolution when [Liu Shaoqi's] line was criticised. The small works require small investment and get quick returns" Ibid.

Yao Wenyuan, officially identified as a member of the Gang of Four, was accused of having stopped the text from being published, quoted as stating that the mechanisation of Chinese agriculture until 1980, as foreseen in the 1975 long-term development plan, was impossible. However, as the prospects for the accomplishment of this task were stated to be "very good", the editorial was framed as a contribution to a "revolutionary mass movement" to speed up the process. Referencing Mao Zedong Thought and the "going all out" slogans of the Great Leap, the text praised mechanisation as a strengthening factor for the "worker-peasant alliance", demonstrating the superiority of the collective economy that allowed elimination of the vestiges of small-scale peasant economy and the concept of private ownership, "plugging the channels from which the spontaneous forces of capitalism grow."

The article also criticised Deng Xiaoping via the idea of "direct and exclusive control", while not naming him directly. Dazhai was referred to as a model to follow, but so where other brigades that had been successful in their efforts towards mechanisation, like the Liuqi commune in Hubei.[290] The model advocated for the future was strictly decentralised and based on cooperation, emphasising management over planning and paraphrasing the dialectical unity of being "red and expert" simultaneously as a main tenet of adjustment:

> "Our motherland is vast; its natural conditions vary and many types of crops are grown. Leading members at various levels should make overall planning and arrangements according to their local conditions. From bottom to top, they should work out plans for agricultural mechanization which can be effectively implemented by stages. Strong and effective management organizations should be set up from the province down to the prefecture, the county and the commune in order to do a good job in the manufacture, maintenance, supply, operation and management of farm machinery, and in scientific research and in training technicians. It is necessary to build a contingent of agricultural mechanisation workers who are both Red and Expert, efforts should be made to implement the party's policy of uniting, educating and transforming intellectuals and to bring the role of scientists and technicians into full play."[291]

Decentralised industrialisation was underway in the latter half of the 1970s, albeit with great regional differences.[292] Difficulties that were reported mostly related to shortages as well as labour organisation. In early 1978, the secretary of a provincial party committee reported how "some comrades" had not yet emancipated themselves from small-scale production and lacked "the bold vision to develop modern, socialist large-scale agriculture". In his view, many were "not farsighted enough". Further, he reported uneven development, with some prefectures being faster than others. The principal problem he stated, was the "inadequate or unsatisfactory" supply of complementary equipment and parts as well as fuel. As a solution, he proposed that scientific research and the trial production of

---

290 Foreign Broadcast Information Service, Editorial on Farm Mechanization Resurrected, Peking NCNA Domestic Service in Mandarin, 2008 GMT, 22 12 1976 OW, accessed through Readex.

291 Ibid.

292 Bramall 2019.

new products that "suit the characteristics of [our] province" needed to be pursued with more vigour.[293]

Of course shifting the investment burden down to the provincial level – which in some cases refers to entities larger than, say European countries – while defining the role of the centrally controlled industries as "technology-hubs" and sources of capital goods were also methods to loosen financial pressure and free assets for other projects. In this regard, agricultural mechanisation and the promotion of rural small-scale industries were also strategies to stabilise the periphery within China to strengthen the centres. It appears that the question of how the industrialisation of China – based on the imported basic innovations of the preceding decades as well as some native adaptations – could be financed without threatening the supply of its people's most basic necessities, found its momentary solution. At the same time, there were other measures aiming in that direction.

How to finance self-reliant development?

As established above, after the period of New Democracy, China basically followed the Soviet paradigm in economic policy with regard to the accumulation of funds for industrial development. Reluctant to accept any financial dependency from foreigners, and paying back debts to the Soviet Union after the Sino–Soviet Split well ahead, China was left with the procurement of the surplus of grain production as its primary source of funding. Sales of grain, as I discuss in the next Chapter, was crucial for acquiring foreign exchange to pay for imports of advanced machinery. Until the early 1970s, there had not been any alternatives with the exception of a small share of the textile sector. Besides this marginal flexibility that the limited trade offered, pushing for more efficiency and curbing unnecessary investments as far as possible became an integral part of Chinese economic policy.

In particular, compared to the partly uncontrolled and wasteful pig push investment initiatives of the Great Leap Forward, this was a formative feature of the way the socialist economy of China worked during and after the Cultural Revolution. While one part of this orientation towards diligence can be linked to policies aiming directly at the preparation for war – particularly with regard to the storage of grain beyond what might be necessary – using and improving the scarce technology and resources with the maximum possible outcome was a direct consequence of factual circumstances in the PRC. The principle of self-reliance as well as the insistence on decentralisation of both production and investment related to it were, among other factors, driven by this scarcity.

As the improvement of the livelihood of the people as a political objective was increasingly underlined in the early 1970s and the partial acceptance of rural markets be-

293 Foreign Broadcast Information Service, Chin Ho-Chen Speech at Agricultural Mechanization Meeting, Excerpts of speech by Chin Ho-chen, secretary of the Shantung Provincial CCP Committee, at the Third National Conference on Agricultural Mechanization: "Develop Agricultural Mechanization on the Basis of Self-Reliance", date not given, Peking NCNA Domestic Service in Mandarin, 1302 GMT, 05 01 1978 OW, accessed through Readex.

came both part of national policy and propaganda, the pictures of abundance of markets and shops that were presented might have initially seemed contradictory to the omnipresent insistence on austerity. While wages did continue to stagnate as shown before and the availability of consumables was slow to grow, the differentiation between frugality and efficiency in production and the alleged abundance in consumption was striking. Of course, the contradiction only held at first glance since providing an improved standard of living with serious constraints with regard to the available technology, everpresent risk of food shortages from bad yields, and economic policies aiming at increasing the levels of consumption in both cities and the countryside required even more efficiency than the meta-objective of industrial development.

Fig. 5

The poster (Fig. 5) published by the People's Art Publishing House in 1972 by Lu Pan and Pan Honghong titled "Another good harvest"[294] expressed the objective of being able to reliably provide for the basic needs of everybody, with famines as an experience of the

294 Picture and reference from: Wolf Michael, Chinese Propaganda Posters, Cologne 2011, pp. 174 f.

past. The scales to the right show the importance of measuring production and keeping the books tidy, in this case the notebook on the left that lies with a pen attached on the abacus. The print on the cup assures the viewer that "socialism is good", while the hand tractor in the top right corner stands for mechanisation. The print on the bag in the lower half indicates that this is successful work being conducted within the collective of a production brigade.

Austerity

The call for saving scarce resources was a part of Mao Zedong Thought, frugality being promoted as a core value of Maoist socialism. Most famously, title 20 of the "Little Red Book", Quotations from Chairman Mao Zedong, that was widely distributed even in the West during the Cultural Revolution, demanded that China be built "through diligence and frugality".[295] While the opposition against individual waste and thrift and the mobilisation of labour as far as possible were part of socialist practice, the drive to achieve higher efficiency on the macroeconomic level was particularly pronounced in the early 1970s.

Letters sent to the Chinese living in Hong Kong, in 1974, described that an "economic clearing" movement aiming at the settlement of overdrawn work-point accounts was underway in the countryside. Despite the relatively good harvests after 1972, the work-point system, allowing only for insufficient consumption, had been stretched, leading to a form of credit:

> "Although this year is a big bumper year, with good farm production and sufficient rations, compensation for labor is very low. [...] Each work-day earns 10 work-points and the highest limit is 50 cents per workday. Therefore, most people have overdrawn [their work-point credit]. Take our family for instance. Our family of eight had four working members originally, but two of them left home, earning no work-points for the year. My wife has been sick frequently. In fact, my oldest boy is the only one working.
> As a result, we overdrew several ten yuan [...] it is estimated that the total amount overdrawn by our family will exceed 200 yuan by the time the year-end account settling period comes. [...] in the past the amount overdrawn each year could be paid off gradually in one's account. But this year is different. The "economic clearing" movement is a brigade-wide drive led by cadres. All old accounts of past years will be checked and all debts, loans and overdrawn amounts must be repaid. **Those unable to do so must sell their bicycles, watches, sewing machines, valuable household items and even their piglets.** [emphasis added]"[296]

At the same time, the expansion of rural credit cooperatives was praised, which in autumn 1974 were declared would cover every rural People's Commune, claiming that "one-

295 Quoting Mao Zedong's speech On Contradictions of 27 February 1957. ZEDONG MAO, Quotations from Chairman Mao Tse-tung (The Little Red Book) & Other Works, published independently.

296 Joint Publications Research Service, Movement to clear all debts underway in Chinese Communes, Hong Kong Ming Pao, Original in Mandarin, 23 12 1974.

third of the production brigades" would offer credit service stations and that a "socialist rural monetary network" had been set up.

While the cooperatives – where members could deposit their surplus income at a fixed interest rate – had existed since earlier, an increase in funds by 2.1 times as compared to 1965 rates was reported.[297] In order to have this decentralised system of savings and loans serve the national industrialisation effort, the general policy consisted of an increase of the share of loans given to the collectives for mechanisation purposes and, more importantly, the share of deposits made in the state banks. Nevertheless, the share of loans issued to individual households was officially reported to be at twelve percent of funds in late 1974, which indicates that a significant number of households were in need of loans to – as the dictum went – "solve temporary difficulties".[298] Measures akin to austerity were already a part of the general economic policy, but were strongly emphasised in early 1975. Industrial departments inventoried enterprises and stores, took in overstocked goods and organised the collection of scrap iron and steel. Also, specific political movements aiming at decreasing the use of resources were initiated; one of these was the "three-electricity" movement, which aimed at limiting the use of non-essential electrical appliances, the number of lamps and the brightness of light bulbs used in households and enterprises and ordered the cutting of in rotation supply of electricity to plants and residential areas by declaring "plant's Sunday" days of rest, to be used for activities such as political studies.[299]

In order to motivate the masses to learn from good experiences in accordance with the socialist principle of "to each according". Generally, work points were allocated according to two systems. First, the "four-fixed"-system[300], which defined the time, quality and quantity of work necessary to receive a fixed number of points. It was a regulation on the economic relationship between the production team, its individual members and households, indicating what was to be defined by the higher level of administration: the number of work days to be contributed, the quantity of manure to be delivered for the production team, the quantities of subsidiary products to be sold by the household to the state and the rations to be provided by the team. With regard to the setting of production quotas, the four-fixed referred to the factors of production assigned to a production team – labour, land, animals and tools – which were taken as a basis for the calculation of the quota. Second, according to the category of work, which basically boiled down to a payment scale on the individual level that followed the industrial wage policy.

The problem of distribution was particularly relevant for the national economy, as the rations distributed to the members of the collective finally determined the quota that

297 The rural credit cooperatives (*nongcun xinyong hezuoshe*) were the primary credit institutions in rural China, introduced in the mid-1950s to serve the financial needs of peasants on a non-commercial basis.

298 Joint Publications Research Service, Rural Credit Cooperatives Established, Article "Monetary Network established in our country's rural areas", Hong Kong Wen Hui Pao, Original in Mandarin, 22 11 1974, accessed through Readex.

299 Portraying the theme of self-reliance in unusually stark terms. US Department of State, Electronic Telegram, PRC Publicises Austere Investment Policy, 27 March 1975, 03:16, ID: 1975HONGK03204_b.

300 Donnithorne Audrey, China's Economic System, Abingdon 1967, pp. 53, 57–58.

could be sold to the state at fixed prices. The declaration reminded that "on the problem of distribution, we must, at the same time, take care of state interests, collective interests, and the interests of the individual." It was demanded that fixed prices be maintained for periods of five years and "absolutely" prevent the purchase of "an excess of grain". The basic ration needed to be strictly determined by the commune members through discussion, thereby teaching them to utilise and conserve grain "in a planned manner". The state, after a careful criticism, deemed it necessary to rationally arrange purchasing assignments or joint marketing targets in order to ensure comparable rations for commune members in all areas.[301]

Under the subtitle strengthen labour management, make rational use of manpower, the declaration demonstrated, that the necessities of production required more than revolutionary spirit. "To facilitate the organisation of production, the strengthening of work discipline, and to guard against absenteeism and waste, the production team [...] should set up a wholesome and strict system of production responsibility." The same held for subsidiary production such as animal husbandry, forestry, fishery and other productions. Manpower needed to be "rationally utilised" so that full-time workers, part-time workers, male workers, female workers, and incidental workers could "each according to his ability fully develop their roles". On the other hand, the "non-productive use of manpower" was ordered to be "strictly controlled". "It is necessary to reduce to a minimum the number of people who are not in production work, insist that literary and art and sports activities of the communes and brigades must be held during leisure hours." After the years of encouraged criticism and debate of the Cultural Revolution, the regulation held that "it is necessary to simplify meetings, hold fewer meetings, and hold brief meetings." Measures of austerity with regard to the use of material resources went hand in hand with the efficient use of human labour through management and, well, more authoritarianism.[302]

The rise in efficiency also required the strengthening of financial management, which meant ensuring independent bookkeeping. "The accountants, trustees and tellers, each have their own responsibilities and they cannot hold two positions at the same time." While "financial democracy" in the form of discussions on "relatively large sums" in the member's congress was emphasised, the financial management teams had the authority to reject payments for expenditures which did not "conform to regulations". To improve statistical reporting, accounting items such as work points, grain, and cash were required to be reported monthly. "The phenomena of advanced withdrawals and personal loans" were to be strictly controlled. Just as in the cities and the industrial sector, policies of austerity were implemented; this also meant that the existence of richer and poorer brigades was officially accepted: "Collective welfare work conducted by the communes and brigades should be adaptable with the level of economic development" – this implied that families which had been allowed to subsist in the communes despite being less productive would face a tougher stance. On the "problem of overdrawn households", it was demanded to

301 Views of the Chinese Communist X X X District Committee concerning the implementation of the CCP Central Committee, Taipei Chung-kung Yen-chiu, No. 8, 08 1972.

302 Ibid.

> "[...] teach the commune members to become self-reliant, wage hard struggle, and keep house diligently and frugally. As for the aged, sick and disabled commune members, it is necessary that reasonable arrangements be made to place them in work which they can handle, as to distressed households which have many people but little manpower, it is necessary to have them report for work more often, as to such overdrawn households which are active in production and practice strict economy but are still meeting with difficulties, public welfare funds may be given to them as an appropriate supplemental aid by the commune members through discussion".[303]

One key to the increasing of efficiency was the improvement of unified accounting[304], the importance of which was underlined in visual propaganda. In a brochure on the significance, mission, and requirements of the financial and accounting work of production teams[305], issued in late 1972, it was reiterated that

> "[...] it is necessary as well as possible to develop production according to a plan, conduct economic accounting, enforce austerity, and reduce cost. This requires the strengthening of financial and accounting work so that it will factually reflect all economic activities during the production and distribution process, and the strict management of such activities."[306]

While the text dismissed the attempts of "swindlers like Liu Shaoqi", blaming him for having tried to distract accounting by overemphasising production, the mission stated for production teams' financial and accounting work was quite sober.

> "(1) Strict control and accounting of funds, property and material; expose corruption, theft , and speculative activities; prevent sabotage by class enemies and safeguard public property, (2) Prepare and execute financial plans; actively develop sources of revenue; organize income from production; strengthen economic accounting; make full and rational use of financial and material resources; strive to economize on expenditure; and earnestly implement the policy of "running the communes with diligence and frugality", (3) Keep the books in order; record the work points of commune members correctly; accurately calculate the results of production; earnestly implement the party's distribution policy; and do a good job in earnings distribution, (4) constantly analyse economic activities as reflected by accounting data; improve management; and guarantee the realization of production and financial plans."[307]

---

303 Ibid.

304 Besides assuring efficiency, accounting in the People's Republic was in particular a tool for facilitating economic planning and allocation of funds. On the political dimension of bookkeeping, see: Xi Lina, Cortese Corinne, Zhang Eagle, Exploring hegemonic change in China: a case of accounting evolution, in: Asian Review of Accounting, Vol. 21, No. 2, pp. 113–127.

305 Joint Publications Research Service, Brochure: The significance, mission, and requirements of the financial and accounting work of production teams, 01 01 1973, accessed through Readex.

306 Ibid.

307 Ibid.

In addition, despite the numerous references to class struggle and the frequent quotations from Mao Zedong Thought, running the economy was held to be beyond the line struggles:

> "...develop the collective economy by following the principles of 'self-reliance', 'hard struggle' and 'running communes with diligence and frugality', put the national interest, collective interest, and individual interest in proper perspective; and persist in the socialist distribution policy of 'from each according to his ability, to each according to his needs'; fully execute the party's policy and resist all interference from the right or the left in matters of food distribution, pricing and taxation."[308]

In this vein, increasing economic production through austerity directly affected workers, as additional shifts including night-shifts were introduced.[309]

Capital construction, meaning investments in means of production, remained a main pillar of Chinese economic policy – it being the basis of heavy industrialisation in particular – but it too was affected by the policies of austerity. At a national planning conference in February 1973, the State Planning Commission defined principles regarding investment in capital construction in order to save scarce resources. Projects had to be limited to those absolutely necessary for the realisation of the production and construction targets of the fourth five-year plan, and those had to be completed with "concentrated efforts" as fast as possible. Any capital construction project required approval on the basis of complete design documents.

Projects with unresolved problems with the availability of raw materials, construction techniques or the availability of infrastructure were to be postponed until further notice. In addition, "hidden potentials" of factory as well as military enterprises needed to be developed in order to minimise necessary capital construction. The same requirements were declared with regard to rural industry projects carried out by local governments.[310] In short, capital construction was to be reduced to a small number of essential construction projects, in a manner reminiscent of the readjustment policies of the early 1960s. Thus, two main priorities were set: first, the prioritisation of agriculture; second, the reduction of the scope of capital for construction projects. For the second aspect, five principles of the 1973 Capital Construction Plans were set, urging the planning bureaus

308 The significance, mission, and requirements of the financial and accounting work of production teams, 01 01 1973.

309 Leading to difficulties for workers, which the local party committees tried to mitigate. After the Shanghai rubber industry jointly introduced both measures to save energy (reporting shortages of coal) as well as extended shifts into the night for its 36 enterprises, "the party organisations of all levels of Shanghai's rubber industry actively adopted measures to solve the difficulties as much as possible. After readjusting the shifts, the party organisation of the fourth rubber products plant tried its best to avoid assigning old, weak, sick, and handicapped staff and workers to the night shift [and] also made appropriate readjustments of the nursery shifts and solved the difficulties of those women comrades with infants." The burden placed on workers kept on increasing. Joint Publications Information Service, Shanghai's Rubber Industry Overcomes Power Shortage, Peking Jen-min Jih-pao, Original in Mandarin, 11 03 1977, accessed through Readex.

310 "Study and Analysis of Chinese Communist Capital Construction Work", Taipei Chung-Kung Yen-Chiu, Vol. 7, No. 5, 05 1973.

to clarify the need for the continuation of projects. On the other hand, specific campaigns for tackling droughts were financed by the state, with an emphasis on small and medium-sized projects.[311]

Calls for austerity were directly linked to the possibilities of the central government for providing machinery and investments, which became a more noticeable problem when the balance of payments in foreign trade shifted and deficits became a serious issue (see next chapter). The reduction of imports over the course of 1975 was accompanied by an increase in spending discipline inwards, especially outside the main industrial centres, which were ideologically bolstered by appeals for increasing self-reliance. The USLO reported in March 1975 that requests from lower levels, provinces, counties, communes, brigades and state-owned enterprises, for increased amounts of equipment, war material, manpower and funds were forestalled, if not cut off, combined with an urge to look to the Shanghai model to improve management and put existing resources to better use.[312]

The already austere budgets were thus increasingly tightened, putting more pressure on labour for efficiency and raising the need for technological advances to attain the same goal. In fact, in sectors relevant for exports, innovations that improved production were noted. In the textile industry, the traditional export sector of the Chinese economy and use of modern equipment also made improved working conditions possible. As a report in Hong Kong – albeit from a pro-communist source – stated:

> "The introduction of the fine yarn automatic 'lo-sha' machine, eliminating the use of hands, is most popular with the workers. In the past, the fine yarn and cloth weaving workers had to walk around [...] 15 to 25 km a day. In recent years, some mills experimentally introduced the automatic 'tang-ch'e', making it possible to eliminate walking".[313]

In addition, experiments with alternative energy sources were underway since the late 1950s, in particular with marsh gas as an alternative to firewood, coal, kerosene or electricity for cooking, light and heating. They were continued in order to free other more expensive resources, including labour. A reportage by Xinhua in the summer of 1975 described such efforts:

> "The use of marsh gas has many advantages. In addition to cutting fuel costs, commune members can now devote the time previously used for gathering firewood and delivering coal to agricultural production. Large amounts of firewood, coal and kerosene can thus be conserved for industrial construction. Some agricultural waste products, which were usually used for fuel, can now be used for improving the fertility of the soil. Timber resources can also be conserved. As a result of effective management and use

311 Foreign Broadcast Information Service, NCNA Reports 1973 Water Conservation Achievements, Peking NCNA in English, 0707 GMT 31 12 1973 B, accessed through Readex.

312 US Department of State, Electronic telegram, PRC publicizes austere investment policy, 7 March 1975, 03:16, PlusD, ID:1975HONGK03204_b.

313 Joint Publications Research Service, Textile Industry Meets Needs of Nation's 800 Million People, Article by Ching Wen, "The Textile Industry of the New China", Hong Kong Ching-chu Tao-pao in Mandarin, 26 03 1975, accessed through Readex.

of human and animal waste, environmental sanitation can also be improved. Leadership is the key for successful exploitation of marsh gas. The great success of Szechuan [Sichuan] province in exploiting marsh gas is a very convincing example. The Szechwan [Sichuan] provincial CCP Committee regards the task of mobilising the masses to exploit marsh gas as an important step in improving the people's livelihood and promoting agricultural production. A special leading group and a special office led by a responsible comrade of the provincial party committee have been formed to take charge of this task".[314]

The further shift towards the saving of energy – notably in the form of electricity and oil – was remarkable after 1976. Under the slogan "conservation while promoting production", conserving energy emerged as a key factor of economic planning, while conservation work was promoted as a core task for party committees at all levels. Statistics on quantities of energy that had been saved in previous time periods became just as important figures as the ones reporting on industrial output. The State Planning Commission was quoted after a meeting in Canton: "According to incomplete statistics, a total of over ten million tons of coal, 700'000 to 800'000 tons of oil and four to five billion kwh [kilowatt hours] of electricity were conserved throughout the country in 1976."[315]

As an attachment to economic plans, energy conservation plans were attached that addressed efforts to curb the consumption of raw and other materials.[316] The objective was not only the increase of efficiency but also the mitigation of regional differences, e. g., to counteract the dependency of the south from resources like coal from the north, the transport of which was energy-intensive and required continuous investment in infrastructure – not to speak the energy required. and even the protection of the environment. Which was named frequently as a motive, leading to the introduction of a specific provision on the state's responsibility for the protection of the environment in the Chinese constitution of 1978. As a part of the emphasis on frugality in the economy, reusing materials and turning "harmful things into useful things" were propagated practices, albeit stemming from a rationale of improving productive processes.[317]

A part of the conservation campaign was the promotion of technical innovations – connecting to the concept of workplace innovation – to conserve natural resources. Aspects of the campaign were also presented on the international stage as part of a broader effort to protect the environment in China. As the Chinese delegate stated at a meeting on environmental problems at the third session of the Governing Council of the UN Environment Program on the 22nd of April 1975:

"In the field of protection and improvement of the environment, we have formulated the principles of comprehensive planning, rational distribution of enterprises, multi-

314 Foreign Broadcast Information Service, Marsh Gas Fuel Experiments Conducted in Rural Areas, NCNA reporter's commentary: "An innovation to solve the rural areas' fuel problem", Peking NCNA Domestic Service in Mandarin, 0246 GMT, 20 06 1975 OW, accessed through Readex.

315 Foreign Broadcast Information Service, State Planning Commission Meets in Canton, Peking NCNA Domestic Service in Mandarin, 0107 GMT, 17 01 1977 OW, accessed through Readex.

316 Ibid.

317 Strohm Holger, Umweltschutz in der VR China, Hamburg 1978, pp. 76 ff.

> purpose utilization of materials, turning bane into benefit, relying on the masses and promoting universal effort to protect the environment and benefit the people. According to these principles, we have reformed old cities and built new industrial and mining areas in a planned way, actively prevented and eliminated contamination by harmful substances from industries and widely unfolded mass movements for water conservancy projects, soil improvement and afforestation, thus improving urban and rural environments in our country."[318]

In early 1977, a national conference on the conservation of electricity and other forms of energy was organised in Canton by the State Planning Commission, officially stating in Renmin Ribao in January of the same year that the event served as exchanges of experiences between delegates from various parts of China. As the conference was part of the preparations for a national industrial conference that was planned for the first semester, it showed the priority given to energy conservation in the context of industrial development.[319] The conference reported proudly that "about 800'000 tons of oil, ten million tons of coal and 5'000 million kilowatt hours of electricity were saved by Chinese industrial and transportation workers", attributing these savings to technical innovations and increases in efficiency achieved by the workers.[320]

With the rise of importance of foreign trade and its acknowledgement by the Chinese leadership after October 1976, the aspect of energy saving – particularly with regard to oil – was increasingly put at the centre of austerity measures. After the Canton conference, the State Planning Commission lauded notably the popularisation of boiling stoves that used stone coal as fuel and contributed to the conservation of large amounts of fuel throughout the country.[321] The reports on energy savings resembled earlier celebrations of attained production goals, as a correspondent of Xinhua reported in July 1977:

> "Some people hold that in order to raise production, it is necessary to consume more power, and that without electric power, enthusiasm alone will not help. Such a view apparently overlooks man's subjective initiative and the potential for conserving and consuming electric power in a planned and rational manner. For example, in spite of the fact that a big gap exists between the power consumption target and the actual amount of power needed in Kiangsu's Nanking Municipality this year, the gross industrial output value of this municipality during the first 5 months registered an increase of 12.5 percent over the corresponding period last year, thus setting a record for that period by the city [...] it is of equal importance to increase power output for production

318 Foreign Broadcast Information Service, PRC Delegate Addresses UN Meeting on Environment Problems, Peking NCNA in English, 1529 GMT, 23 04 1975 OW, accessed through Readex.

319 According to the commentary of the Hong Kong branch of AFP. Foreign Broadcast Information Service, Conference on Energy Conservation held, Hong Kong AFP in English, 0705 GMT, 18 01 1977 OW, accessed through Readex.

320 Foreign Broadcast Information Service, Innovations allow Savings in Fuel, Electricity, Peking NCNA in English, 0707 GMT, 22 01 1977 OW, accessed through Readex.

321 Foreign Broadcast Information Service, State Planning Commission meets in Canton, Peking NCNA Domestic Service in Mandarin, 0107 GMT, 17 01 1977 OW, accessed through Readex.

and to tap potentials for consuming power in a rational way [...] it is essential to bear in mind that conservation is one of the basic principles of a socialist economy."[322]

After the adaptation of management guidelines in the summer of 1977, reporting on enterprise success shifted increasingly towards the reporting of profits, which were partly also reported, in hindsight, for the years of the Cultural Revolution to show that management had been effective. In August of the same year, the party committee of a textile industrial bureau of Shanghai reported that the industry for which the bureau was responsible had "accumulated large amounts of funds for the state" for ten successive years, "from 1966 to 1976", doubling the output value over the period and turning over reserve funds at 2.6 billion RMB to the state – this was claimed to be "equal to nine times the fixed assets of the bureau and nine times the total reserve of the fourteen years before the Great Cultural Revolution".[323] In addition, successful innovation projects during the period were reported, in order to explain the double-digit increases in profitability that had thus stemmed from the own efforts of the enterprises involved.

The "socialist emulation drives" that served the implementation of new management guidelines after May 1977, also concerned the practice of economy, the importance of surplus and the profit motive to ensure it. A report of the provincial conference on enterprise management in Guangdong in September 1977, before referring to Mao Zedong Thought, first quoted Lenin: "We should ensure that every state-owned enterprise, far from running at a loss, should be able to make a profit", before paraphrasing Mao Zedong's demand that all socialist businesses had to increase accumulation. "Hence", the report concluded, "to strive to increase accumulation and profits for the state is the glorious duty of socialist enterprises".[324]

The inevitable criticism of the Gang of Four was presented as a trinity: the Gang needed to be criticised vigorously for inciting anarchism, sabotaging management of norms and opposing economic accounting and, in turn, strictly observe rational rules and regulations, grasp the eight economic and technical indexes and fulfil the state plans and use sober accounting to increase accumulation. "When rectifying and strengthening management", all enterprises had to "proceed from reality [and] the demand to turn loss into profit". In order to create the discipline necessary, the feeling of "it is shameful to run at a loss and glorious to provide accumulation for the state" was to be promoted and pur-

322 Foreign Broadcast Information Service, East China Progress in Electric Power Conservation, NCNA correspondent's commentary: "There Are Tremendous Potentials for Conserving Electric Power, for Power Consumption in a Planned Manner and for Running Electric Power Stations by the Masses", Peking NCNA Domestic Service in Mandarin, 0332 GMT, 20 07 1977 OW, accessed through Readex.

323 Foreign Broadcast Information Service, Shih-Chia-Shuang's Textile Industry shows Large profits, Article: "Shih-chia-chuang Textile Industrial Bureau Strengthens Party Guidance, Improves Enterprise Management, and Accumulates Large Amounts of Funds for the State for 10 Successive Years", Peking Jen-Min Jih-pao in Mandarin, 27 08 1977, accessed through Readex.

324 Foreign Broadcast Information Service, Kwantung Meeting Demands Improved Enterprise management, Canton Kwantung Provincial Service in Mandarin, 0500 GMT, 19 09 1977 HK, accessed through Readex.

sued by "mass activities to innovate, improve and tap potentials [to] achieve high output, fine quality and low consumption of materials" as the "fundamental way".[325]

What rose from earlier attempts to ensure efficiency through political calls for frugality were measures to ensure reliable results. One was immediate control through management, which was part of the general tendency towards more rules-and-regulations-based production and labour discipline in the early 1970s. The second aspect, particularly in the state-owned enterprises that remained a part of the centrally managed economy, was the official introduction of the profit motive – first, as a reference number to be used in planning and bookkeeping. Building on the abstract guideline of self-reliance, which advocated the efficient use of the available resources in order to produce as much surplus as possible for the state, this appeared only as a small step that did not even require much interpretative work. Another matter was the emergence of rural markets, which had begun earlier and been the explicit target of criticism by Mao himself.

Private plots and subsidiary production

That absolute positions with regard to the collectivisation of agriculture were bent in favour of compromises during the 1970s was well illustrated by an article in Hongqi, discussing experiences in communes in the Hunan province of Yuehyang county.

> "To defeat capitalism with socialism, we must be good at helping the masses distinguish between socialism and capitalism. In working in the countryside we often come across some confusing problems. If we won't understand the nature of these problems well, we are apt to deviate from the socialist orientation. [...] some comrades hold that they can increase the masses' enthusiasm by rewarding them with material incentives. Some production brigades have even temporarily allowed commune members to plant rape and other minor autumn crops on collective land. Is this practice in accord with socialist principles?"[326]

The question of material incentives in the countryside was different per se from the discussion with regard to employees in industrial factories. As the attempts to turn peasants into agricultural workers through collectivisation and communalisation were never entirely successful – and steps away from these attempts were made both in the 1960s and again in the early 1970s by switching the basic accounting units closer to the individual households – peasants were plausibly seen as natural-born capitalists. The experience of the 1960s had shown that allowing households to farm plots for the needs of their families was an excellent stabiliser with which famines could be prevented, which led to the right being inscribed in the PRC's constitution during the lifetime of Mao.

On the other hand, as the basic industrialisation paradigm continued to rely on the production of a sufficient and reliable surplus, grain quotas needed to be filled nevertheless. The increased supply of consumer goods was one aspect that became important in the mid-1970s, as affordable goods for sale such as the bicycles, watches and radios were

325 Ibid.

326 Foreign Broadcast Information Service, Red Flag Article reviews Hunan commune's experiences, Peking domestic service in Mandarin, 2130 GMT, 14 09 1974 B, accessed through Readex.

an incentive for participation in paid agricultural labour. On the other hand, the risk that the products grown on private plots entered into competition and put more pressure on the already low grain prices was real. As XUE MUQIAO noted:

> "For a long time, the demand for grain could not be satisfied. For years, we did not raise the grain price, but forced the peasants in areas where industrial plants were grown as well as in mountainous and pasture areas to supply themselves with grain. Accordingly, the production of agricultural raw materials and products of forestry and animal husbandry diminished. Because, thereby, incomes of peasants and herders also sank, they were not in a position to invest in order to increase their yields. [...] Because the agricultural collectives were themselves responsible for profits and losses, they have a strong interest in prices. Too low prices necessarily affect their work motivation negatively. [...] In order to ensure the supply of grain and other foodstuffs at relatively low prices, the Chinese government has to spend billions of Yuan in subsidies and acquire foreign exchange in substantial amounts for the export of agricultural products like grain and cotton."[327]

The solution, it appeared, was flexibility – even before the revised constitution was presented at the fourth People's Congress. Accordingly, with regard to Hunan province, Hongqi noted:

> "Last year when (Meishu) production team of the (Taolin) production brigade was drawing up its sowing plan, some people suggested that it would be better to plant medicinal herbs instead of grain crops because herbs have a higher value. They proposed that the acreage for grain crops should be reduced so that more medicinal herbs could be planted. But the poor and lower-middle peasants rejected this proposal, saying 'When we draw up a plan or do a job, we must think of the state and socialism. If we only strive to make more money for a small collective, we are liable to depart from socialism and thereby encourage capitalism.'
> Having criticized the capitalist tendency that placed money above everything, the cadres and the masses drew up a production plan on the basis of the principle of taking grain as the key link and ensuring all-round development and the principle of subordinating the interest of the collective to that of the state. Thus the acreage for grain production as described by the plan was guaranteed. **At the same time, they also made use of mountain slopes and planted medical herbs there.** [emphasis added]"[328]

Besides the centralised grain distribution system as the prime mechanism for the alimentation of urban workers, self-sufficiency in vegetable production on the city outskirts was expanded. While Xinhua underlined in December 1974 that grain production remained the focus of agriculture, appropriate amounts of land were reported to have been devoted to vegetables to "meet urban market demands".[329] The city of Shanghai was

327 XUE 1982, pp. 150 f, translation by the author.

328 Red Flag Article reviews Hunan commune's experiences, 2130 GMT, 14 09 1974 B.

329 Foreign Broadcast Information Service, PRC cities attain self-sufficiency in vegetable production, Peking NCNA in English, 0753 GMT, 28 12 1974 B, accessed through Readex.

presented as an example, having allegedly procured "over 70 percent" of its vegetables from other areas but achieved self-sufficiency and more: "The city outskirts now grow 12'000 hectares of vegetables, averaging annual sales at over 1 million tons. In the peak year, it was 1'350'000 tons. Shanghai also cans and dehydrates vegetables for other parts of China and exports frozen vegetables".[330]

With more than eighty tons of "annual sales" per hectare, these figures are hardly credible. In any case, not all cities were as successful, so purchases from outside were still necessary, based on subsidised prices. State commercial departments placed orders with the communes and brigades and "consulted them" with regard to prices. That the unified grain purchase system was at its core an instrument of subsidy was fully recognised – even with reference to potential market prices:

> "The market price falls below state purchasing price when vegetables are in abundance, but the growers do not lose because of government subsidies that average two yuan a year per city resident. This is an indication of the non-profit nature of socialist commerce in China".[331]

Sideline production was notably criticised in poorer provinces, where the potential improvement of livelihoods by collective labour were greater. If extensive projects to affect adverse natural conditions for agriculture through large-scale irrigation and other labour- and capital-intensive projects comprised the primary approach to improving livelihoods, then under the paradigm of rural self-sufficiency, sideline production was a plausible hindrance. Also, if a part of a collective engaged in sideline production, the contribution to other, less successful units suffered. The deputy secretary of the party committee of a commune with a population of reportedly 43'000 people at the time, consisting of 9,100 households that were organised in 56 production brigades in Qixia county, Shandong province, complained in early 1975,

> "A brigade in our commune has relatively good natural conditions. In 1971, the commune demanded 24 labor teams from it. However, it only assigned seven people to the commune, most of whom were old and sick, while retaining most of its labor force to engage in sideline production. [...] Another brigade kept to the socialist orientation at first. Production developed, collective income increased and the living conditions of the commune members greatly improved. Under these circumstances, some people began to busily arrange their private homes and started to build houses for themselves. As a result, the collective production was adversely affected. The aforesaid conditions were duly corrected by the brigade party branches by suppressing the capitalist tendencies and persisting in the socialist orientation."[332]

In his report on the 1975 Constitution, Zhang Chunqiao paraphrased the acknowledgement made by Zhou Enlai in his "Report on the Work of the Government", that the task

330 Ibid.

331 Ibid.

332 Foreign Broadcast Information Service, Shantung County Struggles Against Peasant Economy Concept, Tsinan Shantung Provincial Service in Mandarin, 1100 GMT, 29 01 1975 OW, accessed through Readex.

of socialist transformation of the ownership of the means of production – the *raison d'être* of the 1954 constitution – had "in the main been completed".[333] The new constitution affirmed this success and enshrined the two different forms of ownership in China: socialist ownership by the whole people and socialist collective ownership by the working people, which referred to the People's Communes and enterprises directly owned and controlled by the state.[334]

While this was not genuinely new, the additional flexibility granted in the founding document of the PRC was: Article five allowed for the agricultural workers to engage in individual labour, "involving no exploitation of others, within the limits permitted by law and under unified arrangements by neighborhood organisations in cities and towns or by production teams in rural People's Communes". Simultaneously, these individual workers "should be guided on the road to socialist collectivisation step by step" so that they do not formally give up the long-term ideal.

Article seven added the already practiced rural accounting system with the production team as the basic level and accounting unit. Then, provided that the development and absolute predominance of the collective economy of the people's commune were ensured, People's Commune members were allowed to "farm small plots for their personal needs, engage in limited household side-line production, and in pastoral areas keep a small number of livestock for their personal needs". The report explicitly referred to flexibility as a concept of economic policy while attributing tendencies to abolish private plots to one of their firmest advocates, the fallen Liu Shaoqi:

> "These provisions integrate the principle of adherence to socialism with the necessary flexibility and are sharply demarcated from such fallacies as those advocated by Liu Shaoqi and Lin Biao on the fixing of farm output quotas for individual households with each on its own and the abolition of farm plots for personal needs."[335]

The introduction of flexibilities in individual agricultural production did not necessarily mean that the ideals of the People's Commune movement were forgotten in their entirety. With a view towards the stabilisation of the production of necessities, the aspect of timing was an argument that supported the acceptance of a certain degree of "peasant capitalism" in the Chinese countryside. In an article by the theoretical study group of the Ministry of Agriculture and Forestry in August 1975, the transformation of small production was defined as a long-term task of the dictatorship of the proletariat. Based on an interpretation of Mao Zedong Thought, the group concluded that socialist ides would not "spontaneously come into being in the minds of peasants". However, other than by ideological education, the transformation was presented as a function of development to be achieved in the long term.[336]

---

333 Report on the Revision of the Constitution, 13 January 1975, paragraph 4.

334 In article six of the Constitution of 1954, there was a reference to "State ownership, that is, ownership by the whole people; co-operative ownership by the working masses, ownership by individual working people; and capitalist ownership." See: Hook et al. (eds.) 1975, p. 389.

335 Report on the Revision of the Constitution, 13 January 1975, paragraph 4.

336 Foreign Broadcast Information Service, Mao's Agricultural Cooperation Work Hailed, Article by the theoretical study group of the Ministry of Agriculture and Forestry: "Transformation of Small Production Is a Long-Term Task of the Dictatorship of the Proletariat – Some Experience in

The handling of private plots was a prime example of the paradigmatic shift in 1975, over the course of which ideological goals were declared to be long-term objectives, while economic development was conceptualised in a clear-cut and ambitious, albeit relatively realistic, timeframe. This view was still criticised publicly with reference to the importance of keeping up the class struggle and the observation that capitalism was active in the countryside on a high level. For instance, Jiang Qing addressed it at the National Conference on Learning from Dazhai, openly contradicting the decisions of the fourth National People's Congress: "The capitalist restoration in agriculture is dangerous, for the pernicious influence of Liu Shao-ch'i's revisionism has been thoroughly eliminated. It is reported that in some production teams there still exists the revisionist policy of San Zi Yi Bao [extension of plots for private use, extension of free markets, increasing the number of small enterprises with sole responsibility for their own profits or losses, and the fixing of output quotas on the basis of individual households] [...] Only through self-reliance can we achieve triumph over difficulties."[337]

Nevertheless, private plots and sideline production had become an integral part of the development paradigm of the PRC. As the account of a reporter from Hong Kong underlined in early 1976:

> "With the advent of the busy season of collection of agricultural sideline products, rural markets in all parts of [Guangxi province] present a picture of prosperity marked by brisk activity of buying and selling. People can see everywhere that commune members [...] are arriving in steady streams in collection centers to deliver and sell to the state various industrial crops, native special produce, mountain produce, and poultry and animal products. These agricultural sideline products are coming continuously to the market for the selection and purchase of customers."

The report also emphasized the benefits rural markets in combination with light industrial development offered to the nationalities in their autonomous regions:

> "Five nationalities [...] live together in Teo commune [...]. Over 60 kinds of commodity were newly added to the special shelves for the nationalities in the commune store in 1975, including blue-black umbrellas, colored silks, lace and various silver ornaments popular with Miao women, hair clasps and pins popular with Chuang women, and belts decorated with colored butterflies, colored silk thread, scarves and leggings popular with I and I-lao women. [...] income of commune members of all nationalities has risen, and their purchasing power has gone up. In the period from January through November, 1975, total sales of industrial products of everyday use in Pai-se district [...] were up 9.8 percent compared with the corresponding period of 1974; sales of cotton cloth [...]

Studying Chairman Mao's Work 'On the Question of Agricultural Cooperation'", Peking Domestic Service in Mandarin, 1130 GMT, 30 08 1975 OW, accessed through Readex.

337 Excerpts of Chiang Ch'ing's Address at the National Conference on Learning from Tachai in Agriculture, in: Classified Chinese Communist Documents: A Selection, Taipei 1978, p. 639, available at: https://www.marxists.org/archive/jiang-qing/1975/september/15.htm, last accessed on 1 May 2020.

> were up 26 percent and those of bicycles and sewing machines were up 43.5 and 21.5 percent respectively."[338]

On the other hand, in poorer provinces such as Guizhou, serious concerns with regard to private plots and their effect on collective agriculture were publicly expressed. In a report at the provincial conference of cadres, Ma Li, first secretary of the Kweichow provincial CCP committee, underlined that the provinces had to "solve existing problems in accordance with the party's policies", which required sending "strong cadres" to production units where "capitalist trends" existed. With regard to extending private plots that went as far as "taking over the collective's land, draft animals and [...] dividing up the collective's mountain forests [...] we must, on the basis of carrying out ideological education and enhancing people's socialist awareness, insure that these things are returned to the collective in accordance with party policies".

Additionally, Ma reported that in many places in the province, "a considerable number of peasants leave to attend rural fairs, thus affecting collective production", which required persuading them "not to go to such fairs very often, but to participate more in collective productive labour". As "more than 80 percent of the funds for provincial, prefectural and county capital construction" were to be used in agricultural capital construction as well as in the "five small industries" supporting agriculture, sideline production in Guizhou province was – according to the report – to be performed by communes and production brigades rather than private households selling such products in markets.[339]

As rural industries grew and other sources for the advancement of economic modernisation – notably in the area of foreign trade by increased use of deferred payments and emphasis on technological development on a grand scale –opened up, pressure on rural households with regard to grain procurement was loosened over the course of 1977. The coordinated procurement of main agricultural products (like grain, cotton, oilseeds, pig meat and more) and sideline products was still an important mechanism in Chinese economic policy; but in the handling of rural markets, avoiding overbuying by the state became the maxim. Leaving as many products as possible to the population, so that an improvement in living standards could also be felt in the countryside was given real priority over procurement figures. A commentary in Renmin Ribao on the 20th of October 1977 celebrated the prosperity of "both rural and urban markets", and emphasised the importance in "doing a good job in the procurement of agricultural and sideline products".

What this meant was expressed in the call for paying "attention to the interests of the state, collectives and individuals". Purchase targets needed to be "rational" and carried out in a "timely" manner, accompanied by proper arrangements for the peasant's livelihood. Through higher prices, sales to the state were to be encouraged, while communes and brigades that had "kept too much grain for themselves" needed to be moved to

338 Joint Publications Research Service, Rural Market in Kwangsi, Article: "Rural Market in Kwangsi Presents Scene of Prosperity", Hong Kong Chung-kuo Hsin-wen, Original in Mandarin, 17 01 1976, accessed through Readex.

339 Foreign Broadcast Information Service, Ma Li delivers report at Kweichow Cadre Conference, Kwieyang Kweichow Provincial Service in Mandarin, 1300 GMT, 08 07 1977 HK, accessed through Readex.

sell these quantities through "good planning and strict control". Where loans were outstanding, they were to be recalled quickly to make additional funds available to support the production of agricultural and sideline products. The rule about the distribution that was established in the article stated, "the countryside should have priority over the city when an industrial product is needed by both and the city should take precedence over the countryside when non-staple food is needed by both".[340] This policy favoured accumulation through markets while trying to reduce the pressure of procurement by the state and was supported by the good yields in 1976 and 1977.[341]

The importance of the countryside as a market for industry, and light industry especially, growing and contracting in parallel with the quality of harvests, was recognised. An article published in Guangming Ribao, in November 1977, while praising Mao Zedong Thought as the "beacon shining on China's road to industrialisation", surmised the following: "The worker-peasant alliance will be impaired if the peasants cannot get industrial products in return for their grain". In November 1977, a representative of Cargill visited Beijing, where he was told that while cotton as an industrial input was still a commodity interesting for China, wheat, soybeans and other edible crops were not. USLO noted that winter wheat, as far as it could be observed, looked exceptionally good, with plants much higher than usual in many fields.[342]

Remarks on population control in China

At the UN World Population Conference, in a plenary meeting on the 21st of August 1974, the Chinese delegate Huang Xuze delivered a speech that summarised the Chinese position towards contemporary claims of overpopulation:

> "One superpower [the USA] asserts outright that there is a 'population explosion' in Asia, Africa and Latin America and that a 'catastrophe to mankind' is imminent. The other superpower [the Soviet Union], while pretending at some conferences to be against Malthusianism, makes the propaganda blast that 'rapid population growth is a mill-stone around the neck of the developing countries'. Singing a duet, the two superpowers energetically try to describe the Third World's population growth as a great evil.
>
> If this fallacy is not refuted, there will be no correct point of departure in any discussion on the world population. Of all things in the world, people are the most precious. Once the people take their destiny into their own hands, they will be able to perform miracles. Man, as worker and as creator and user of tools, is the decisive factor in the

---

340 Foreign Broadcast Information Service, People's Daily calls for Strengthening Agricultural Procurement, People's Daily 20 October frontpage Commentator's article: "It Is Necessary To Grasp Firmly and Well the Procurement of Agricultural and Sideline Products", Peking Domestic Service in Mandarin, 2230 GMT, 19 10 1977 OW, accessed through Readex.

341 US Department of State, Agricultural Highlights: Crop and Trade Situation in PRC; Code 24M Alert, 9 November 1977, 00:00, PlusD, ID: 1977PEKING02585_c.

342 Joint Publications Research Service, Mao's Teachings on Industrialization Praised, Article by Su Hsing: "The Beacon Shining on China's Road to industrialization – A Study of Volume V of the 'Selected Works of Mao Tsetung'", Peking Kwangming Daily, Original in Mandarin, 07 11 1977 HK, accessed through Readex.

> social productive forces. Man is in the first place a producer and only in the second place a consumer. Historically, the valiant, industrious and talented people of Asia, Africa and Latin America made outstanding contributions to human civilization."[343]

Reminding other delegations that "the notorious Malthus" had underestimated the ability of economies to raise yields, and thus the availability of food. Nevertheless, admitting that there was a "population problem", he explained the "primary way" for its solution was by combating "the aggression and plunder by the imperialists, colonialists and neo-colonialists, and particularly the superpowers", breaking down the unequal international economic relations, winning and safeguarding national independence, and developing the national economy and culture "independently and self-reliantly in the light of each country's specific conditions and differing circumstances as well as raising the living standards of the people." His statements aligned with the demands for a new international economic order. To establish a link to Mao Zedong Thought, he referred to the formula revolution plus production can solve the problem of feeding the people.

Besides, some tension between these statements and the reality of Chinese economic policy with regard to foreign economic relations as well as the programmatic introduction of the speech were also not entirely representative of Chinese policies on population control. At the end of his statement, Huang added more pragmatic remarks "on the formulation and implementation of population policy". Underlining the necessity of sovereignty in these questions, he stated that "some countries need to lower, and others to raise the rate of population growth to a proper extent". In China, this meant the "planned regulation of the rate of population growth". Already, in the years following the revolution of 1949, the household registration system (*hukou*) put strict controls on the movement of people within China. As pull-factors in the cities were prevalent, and demand for cheap labour existed, migrants were nevertheless tolerated to a certain extent – creating a class of workers often relegated to arduous tasks, without secure status and at the risk of being deported back to the countryside.

From Shanghai alone, until 1975, well over a million people were removed.[344] The importance of birth control was underlined by the state at all levels throughout the 1970s, albeit implemented on a voluntary basis. When ex-US-President Richard Nixon visited China in late February 1976, the Japanese news-agency Kyodo reported that a man in the crowd greeting him near the Beijing history museum held up his son to shake hands with the visitor, explaining that this was his only child. As Nixon reportedly asked whether he planned to have more, the man was quoted as replying: "Answering the call of our government, we are practicing birth planning and will at most have two".[345] Conferences on family planning were organised at the provincial level, under the auspices of the State Council's responsible family planning leadership group office. Until 1975, these fora were limited to the reiteration of the ideological foundations of family planning – which in-

343 Foreign Broadcast Information Service, PRC Delegate Scores Superpowers at UN population conference, Peking NCNA in English, 1845 GMT, 21 08 1974 B, accessed through Readex.

344 Dikötter 2016, p. 200.

345 Foreign Broadcast Information Service, Nixon 'Campaigns' among Peking Crowds, Tokyo Kyodo in English, 0613 GMT, 24 02 1976 TK, accessed through Readex.

cluded a wide array of Mao Zedong Thought[346] – accompanied by the exchange of experiences from the responsible administrative units. A principal ideological difficulty with regard to the enforcement of family planning was the postulate of relying on the masses, as the contradiction to the fundamental tenet by the introduction of compulsory birth control would have stretched the interpretative creativity of even its most arduous supporters.

In an interview with the French journal Le Monde, an anonymous high official in Beijing stated in accordance with the official language discipline that "800 million people have to be fed, and this is a very serious problem". Family planning, as it had a direct influence on this "problem", was, according to him, encouraged in China, but the task was described as being "easier in the cities than in large rural areas where Confucius' influence persists. Whenever there are already two or even three daughters in the family, the parents try to have yet another child in the hope that this time it will be a boy".[347] Accordingly, Xinhua reported positively about the development of the Chinese population throughout 1977, stating that due to the instructions on family planning, "young people are marrying later so that they can devote more energy to revolution and production [...] and young couples are taking measures to limit the size of their families".[348]

Talking to Swiss federal councillor Max Petitpierre in may 1973, Zhou emphasised the precarious situation: "China has a population too large to import sufficient grain or rice and has to rely on its own forces". In 1971, according to Zhou, the PRC had produced 250 million tons of grain, which had allowed for the creation of a small buffer stock of ten million tons. In 1972 again, the yield was around 240 million tons, which had used up the reserve. China's objective was producing 400 million tons by qualitative improvements and quantitative expansion of production, in parallel to "a policy of birth control".[349]

In 1977, Li Xiannian underlined the importance of family planning policies along with the assurance that the methods chosen were to remain moderate:

> "Yes, we have reduced the rate of population growth with our family planning policy. We have not resorted to drastic methods of birth control or to sterilizing people. That, we shall never do. Our family planning education policy has given us a growth rate of 1 percent (the lowest rate). But even that rate represents 10 million more children every

346 At a symposium organised in Hunan province in October 1975, reference was made to "bourgeois rights" and the "doing away" of private ownership by birth control, as well as the strategic principles of *being prepared against* and the strengthening of the leadership of the CCP. Foreign Broadcast Information Service, Hunan Holds Symposium on Family Planning, Changsha Hunan Provincial Service in Mandarin, 1100 GMT, 26 10 1975 FE, accessed through Readex.

347 Joint Publications Research Service, 'High Official' discusses economic situation, Alain Jacob and Jean de la Gueriviere Peking dispatch, "It Appears That the Population Has Exceeded the 800 Million Mark", Paris Le Monde, Original in French, 04 11 1976 LD, accessed through Readex.

348 Foreign Broadcast Information Service, Population Growth Rate Declines Through Birth Control, Peking NCNA in English, 0703 GMT, 27 02 1977 OW, accessed through Readex.

349 Ambassade de Suisse en Chine, Visite de M. Petitpierre à Pékin, Pékin, le 16 mai 1973, RéPf. 101.0, 712.0 – NT/hw. Available at dodis: dodis.ch/37713. Last accessed on 12 August 2022.

> year. We are told that if we go on like that, China will become a country of old people in a few years' time. We do not believe it. Conditions will have changed by then."[350]

While no official policy on the number of children allowed to couples was yet to be formulated, the tendency was evident; however, mandatory birth control was not implemented until 1980. That there was persistent unease with population control was openly communicated to foreigners. In Sichuan, officials told USLO in late 1977 that while the current population growth rate for the province was around 1.1 percent, the target was "between .6 and .8".[351]

350 Foreign Broadcast Information Service, Li Hsien-Nien Interviewed, Interview with vice-premier Li Hsien-nien in Peking on 1 June 1977 by Antonio Fernandez Arce, Lima La Prensa in Spanish, 12 06 1977, accessed through Readex.

351 Provincial Observations in Kunming, Chengtu, Sian, Shanghai, Canton, PlusD, ID: 1977PEKING02583_c, paragraph 4.

Chinese foreign economic policy in a volatile world (1970–1978)

On the international stage, the PRC continued to cultivate an image as the champion of the world's poor, non-aligned and exploited nations. The Chinese development model[1], or what it was perceived to be, became a political asset in both developing and developed countries. It served as an example of what could be done *on one's own*, without entering into a relation of dependency on either the Soviet Union or the West.[2] At the same time, the departure from self-reliance as a core paradigm of Chinese foreign affairs became increasingly clear. The fact that Chinese diplomats did not disrupt the daily business within the organisation after China's accession to the United Nations was noted, as well as the dismissal of earlier plans associated with Mao to establish a rival international body.

China's interest in finding a "new international economic order" within the existing Westphalian framework was pronounced, while Zhou Enlai stated publicly that new and increasing links with the United States was making the Chinese Leadership feel more secure with regard to Soviet military threats.[3] As John W. Garver has suggested, China pursued a second push to build a global coalition to counter Soviet efforts during the 1970s, the first having been the efforts of the 1960s to advance socialist revolution abroad. Even if the socialist state still was relatively weak in economic and military terms: China acted strategically, like a global power. Most importantly, this second push allowed for cooperation instead of confrontation with the United States and other countries.[4]

The idea of an emerging alternative to the dualist world order was appealing to many outside China, as the occupation of Czechoslovakia in 1968 had taken place recently. A generally anti-Soviet mood was at a peak, even within European leftist movements. It led, for example, to the founding of no less than three self-declared Maoist parties in the Federal Republic of Germany (FRG) between 1967 and 1973, namely the Communist Party

1 As it was presented abroad, e. g., through the publications of the Foreign Language Press (FLP), such as: Foreign Languages Press, a Glance at China's Economy, Beijing 1974.

2 Frolic 1978.

3 Terrill Ross, China and the World: Self-Reliance or Interdependence? in: Foreign Affairs, Vol. 55, No. 2, January 1977, p. 298.

4 Garver 2016, pp. 344 f.

of Germany-Marxist Leninist (KPD-ML), the Communist Party of Germany Organisation to Rebuild (KPD-AO) and the Communist League of West Germany.[5]

The proposition that a secretive and mysterious eastern culture had succeeded in finding a (technically or morally) superior way to modernise was easy to accept and created a wave of, as FROLIC suggested, "Voltaire Syndromes" – the want and will to discover that the heathens were, so to speak, more Christian than the Christians themselves. The culture of the European Enlightenment left a number of well-established marks on China, accelerated by authors with diplomatic experience – usually within the British Empire. While the narrative that China was a stagnant country, stuck in the past and paralysed by subservience to tradition proved to be powerful, the rather enthusiastic views of China in the tradition of exceptionalist discourses reappeared with the perceived and actively claimed success of the PRC.[6]

Religious themes were also applied to the world outside China and its economic situation, which after 1973 was marked by the combined effects the crises referred to in the introductory Chapter with the industrialised economies entering a phase of broad economic contraction. Policy involvement in international markets had grown to an extent that – even if there had been quite similar phenomena with regard to price hikes in commodities in the past, e. g. in the wake of the Great Depression – the answers needed to be more far-reaching than merely a further expansion of production. In particular, the creation of divides through regionally different reactions to the crisis was a consequence that defined, among other things, international relations in the late twentieth century.[7]

The particularity was the parallelism of several crises affecting many economies at once. Trying to describe the prospects for trans-Atlantic trade in the face of growing protectionism and galloping inflation in 1975, the head of the Delegation of the European Communities in Washington, Jens Otto Krag, resorted to the Bible:

> "According to the Holy Bible Egypt, once upon a time, was sent seven plagues. I think it is fair to liken the Western industrialized countries position now to Egypt's position then. We have inflation, recession, unemployment, energy crisis, floating exchange

---

5 ALEXANDER ROBERT JACKSON, Maoism in the Developed World, Westport 2001, pp. 79 ff. The attraction of Maoism, the version that was generally perceived abroad, for the European left was summarised by JOHN F. MELBY in 1972 as "In a world which has lost faith in its values and ideologies, it may well be that the greatest impact of Maoism will be its demonstrated belief in its destiny, superiority, and rightness". See: MELBY, JOHN F., Maoism as a World Force, in: The Annals of the American Academy of Political and Social Science, Vol. 402, July 1972, p. 26. On the other hand, even critical observers expressed admiration for visible successes in Chinese development, as numerous publications show. Illustrative examples are reports by western journalists such as the report on the visit of a number of Swiss parliamentarians to China in 1972, documented by the journalists MARIO CORTESI and FRANK A. MEYER. See: CORTESI/MEYER 1972, and DELEYNE 1972.

6 OLLÉ MANEL, China in the World: Historiographical Reflection, in: ELIZALDE MARÍA DOLORES, WANG JIANLANG, China's Development from a Global Perspective, Newcastle upon Tyne 2017, p. 7; and ABBATTISTA GUIDO, Europe, China and the Family of Nations: Commercial Enlightenment in the Sattelzeit (1780–1840) in the same volume, pp. 140 ff.

7 ROSTOW WALT WHITMAN, The Developing World in the Fifith Kondratieff Upswing in: The Annals of the American Academy of Political and Social Sciences, Vol. 420, July 1975, pp.113 ff.

> rates, high interest rates and high food prices. In Egypt, the plagues followed one after the other. But we have gotten all our plagues over our sinful heads at one and the same time. If we could trust that this would mean a fast ending to the plagues, it might be an advantage. But here I am a sceptic."[8]

With these introductory remarks, Krag summarised the dominant feelings at a conference on trans-Atlantic trade *"in an era of two-digit inflation"*, on the 7th of February 1975, in New York. What had happened? For the diplomat Krag, the immediate consequences perceived to affect international economic relations were arguably at the centre. In the face of the synchronised economic downturn in capitalist economies over the course of 1973, calls for avoiding the unilateral protection of what was conceived as being the immediate national and regional economic interests would irrevocably damage the established rules-based system of international trade between these countries.

In order to preserve the wealth that international trade and investment had helped to create, alternative policies were sought. In a speech at a luncheon of the Oil Industries Club in London in February 1975, vice president of the Commission of the European Communities, Christopher Soames, summarised the need for finding new ways of organising international economic relations:

> "So, the challenge which now faces both the industrialized world and the developing countries is to build a new consensus as a basis for the management of our interdependence. The industrialised countries must work to narrow the gap between us and the developing world. And for their part the developing countries must sit down with us so that we can work out together the ground rules under which the world economy should operate in the rapidly changing conditions of the 1970s and 80s. For let there be no mistake – just as in the past so also in the future the prosperity and stability of us all depends upon the existence of an effective framework of international rules and disciplines."[9]

To protect their economies from the impact in particular of inflation, the same economies were not reluctant to take measures that impeded international trade flows. The US Trade Reform Act of 1974 authorised the executive branch to reduce American trade barriers but also ease the path for new import barriers. The bill made it easier for industries to collect state assistance when import competition caused injury to their businesses. It also opened the criteria for invoking an "escape clause" stipulated therein to provide for increased tariffs or quotas when industries or organised labour could demonstrate that imports were a "substantial cause of serious injury, or the threat

8 Address by Jens Otto Krag, Head of the Delegation of the European Communities, Washington D.C., to the Conference on Trans-Atlantic Trade in an Era of Two Digit-Inflation at State University of New York at Albany. 7 February 1975, Archive of European Integration, Document No. 8315, available at: http://aei.pitt.edu/8315/, last accessed on 1 May 2020.

9 The World Economy: Towards a New Consensus, Extract from a speech by the Rt. Hon. Sir Christopher Soames, Vice-President of the Commission of the European Communities, at a Luncheon given by the oil industries club at the Connaught Rooms, London, At 01:30 p.m., Tuesday, 1 July 1975, AEI, Document No. 8493, available at: http://aei.pitt.edu/8493/1/8493.pdf, last accessed on 1 May 2020.

thereof", to the domestic industry. Substantial cause was defined as "important and not less than any other cause", which gave a wide margin of interpretation to both industries and the implementing government.[10]

Using the new legislative guidelines, the US International Trade Commission (appropriately called the Tariff Commission before), in early 1976, determined that imports of footwear and specialty steels were injuring those two industries. Increased tariffs were recommended for footwear and quotas for specialty steel. In both cases, the question of real injury was at least questionable. More important is the fact that these findings could encourage other industries to apply for similar protection, notwithstanding legitimate need. That the Trade Reform Act whetted the appetite of protectionist forces by liberalising and expanding the criteria for restricting imports can be seen from the fact that within ten months of the bill's passing, fifty-one petitions for import relief had been filed. It is remarkable that this trend occurred while the overall US trade surplus was reaching historic highs.[11]

In the European communities that had just seen an enlargement from the original six to nine member states in 1973, progress in internal trade liberalisation contrasted with measures such as import restrictions and subsidies aimed at the protection of domestic industries.[12] As the crises had deeper reasons than merely an overproduction of commodities or the impact of oil prices – in particular, the fact that already in the late 1960s, European economies had basically depleted the technological backlog consisting of the *basic innovations* inherited from the Second World War and the early post-war economy[13] – attempts to increase potential for intra-community growth and innovation took priority over trade liberalisation at a larger scale.

With these international developments in mind, I suggest that qualitative and quantitative changes in foreign economic relations deserve special attention with regard to Chinese economic policies in the 1970s. Regardless of the best efforts to keep international exchanges to a minimum in line with self-reliance, their growth and the resulting affiliation of the Chinese economy with the capitalist world economy[14] introduced ele-

---

10 While multilateral trade negotiations among the industrialised countries of the West were seen as an essential instrument for the mitigation of the faltering demand on markets, the Tokyo Round of negotiations that formally opened in 1973 could not begin in earnest under the Trade Reform Act that had passed, as the European Communities and Japan alike were not ready to negotiate before the content had become clear. See: ERB GUY F., The Trade Reform Act of 1974, in: Challenge, Vol. 18, No. 1, 1975, pp. 60–61.

11 European Community Information Service, The United States and the European Community: Their Common Interests, second edition, New York 1973, p. 20, AEI, Document No. 9617, available at: http://aei.pitt.edu/9617/1/9617.pdf, last accessed on 1 May 2020.

12 PRICE VICTORIA CURZON, Industrial Policies in the European Community, London 1981, pp. 85 ff.

13 Which may be understood in particular as a coordinated attempt to catch up with the middle-class living standard that existed in the USA and, in particular, the extensive, liberalised market that had decisively facilitated its development. See EICHENGREEN 2008, pp. 257, 261.

14 As defined by IMMANUEL WALLERSTEIN as having been stabilised with regard to its three main structural positions – core, periphery, and semi-periphery – by about 1640. See: WALLERSTEIN IMMANUEL, The Rise and Future Demise of the World Capitalist System: Concepts for Comparative Analysis, in: Comparative Studies in Society and History, Vol. 16, No. 4, September 1974, pp. 387–415. With regard to the world economy of the 1970s, the degree of synchronisation among

ments of volatility to the system of economic planning. Also, dealing with foreigners required lasting structural adjustments, most notably in infrastructure and law, which the responsible ministries quite readily provided once the political backing was given. Regardless of the US trade embargo[15] which lasted until 1972, as well as the economic consequences of the Sino-Soviet Split, the foreign trade of the People's Republic had never ceased entirely. Enacted as retaliation in the context of the Korean War, the embargo had raised the cost for trade with the West between 1950 and 1972, albeit not making it impossible. As CHEN XIN-ZHU J has shown, trade with Japan resumed in 1959, while also being restricted by the strict implementation of self-reliance in trade after 1956 as a consequence of deficits incurred in trade with the Soviet Union.

After reaching its peak in 1959, Chinese foreign trade declined again, rebounding to the level of 1959 in 1966 before stagnating until 1972. CHEN argued that the trade embargo after 1960 became "all but a joke", as China could procure most Western products through Western Europe and Japan. While also Canada and Australia were sources for imports, this absolute view does not hold entirely true. Restricted goods, in particular anything related to the defense industries, were still difficult or impossible to obtain. Also, even were transactions were possible, the cost of trade was significantly increased due to the complications caused by the embargo and the profits of necessary middlemen. Longstanding channels of exchange with the rest of the world, such as the Canton Trade Fair or Canton Fair, had served as platforms for the Chinese economy to sell produce to foreigners in order to obtain foreign exchange since the 1950s and even earlier, which in turn was used to purchase specific products abroad, largely according to the plan. Therefore, the extension of trading capacities advanced throughout the early 1970s.

On the other hand, while the domestic Chinese strategies with regard to the distribution of investment, and even income in a balanced way showed at least some moderate success and the stabilisation of production as well as the rehabilitation of technical expertise were well underway, these mostly incremental adjustments, improvements and experiments (discussed above) obviously had inherent limits. Motivating the workforce with some additional material incentives and a higher standard of living in real terms would not by itself raise the productivity of the industries or the farms. Improving existing technologies through small improvements in individual factories, even if those genuinely proved to be useful and could be spread through "socialist cooperation" and the transmission of best practices could not by themselves generate ground-breaking new basic innovations needed to enter a new industrial cycle. All that such adjustments were able to do was improve the output, perhaps also cleanliness and safety of industrial production based on existing technology. Even if a steel mill was operated by a highly motivated and well-managed crew who constantly improved their processes and even the machinery, it was still a steel mill that would never produce anything else but steel.

Austerity was implemented with tangible results, yielding gains in efficiency and even growth. This was remarkable in particular with regard to the constraints the Chi-

---

capitalist states was at an incomparably higher level, and the industries were based on a much more advanced set of technologies.

15 CHEN XIN-ZHU J., China and the US Trade Embargo, 1950–1972, Vol. 13, No. 2, October 2006, pp. 12 f. and 15.

nese economy faced. Nevertheless, saving materials and keeping wages as low as possible did not contribute to technological progress in production, but was merely suited for maximising the outcomes *without* the use of advanced means of production. Even more so, austerity measures seemed to improve the performance of factories and farms in the books, which could actually prevent investment in a situation of general scarcity. Giving some enterprises the flexibility to allocate their surpluses for investment purposes independently was an effective remedy if the management was capable, but even so, creating industry-led growth of the whole economy required access to acvanced technologies.

Considering a contra-factual line of thinking against the professional instinct of the historian, it cannot be excluded that a relatively closed system like the Chinese economy, with the basic policies described in the previous chapter, could have self-reliantly or – as I suggested in the beginning of this book – *non-interdependently* delivered new basic innovations to the Chinese people in the longer run. There is no basis for the assumption that China, particularly with knowledge about the existence of more advanced technology abroad, would *not* at some point have come up with similar, even better digital technologies, robotics or materials as the West commanded. I argue that there are two main reasons why this scenario did and could not materialise under the given conditions and why the path that materialised consisted of rather small and gradual adjustments; both reasons emerged before 1978.

The first reason is the expansion of foreign trade which had started during the lifetime of Mao Zedong, with his authorisation. Among the normative and tangible structures built to conduct this trade were expensive investments in infrastructure and the acceptance of legal concepts, both of which anchored economic exchanges in the Chinese economy through newly established rules and ports, pipelines and ships. Daqing as the symbolic heart of socialist industry in China was actually at the centre of these networks, as oil was the prime commodity that led China to seek trade offensively. Another structure or custom that was introduced specifically during the 1970s to China was the voluntary acceptance of foreign debt, only faintly covered as "deferred payments" bound to a particular supply contract. The legal form did not change the fact that the PRC accepted indebtedness to industrialised foreign countries and was ready to pay interest in exchange. Through these decisions, China also experienced the effects of fluctuations on foreign markets and even tried to use them for its advantage. As the scope for action with regard to foreign trade including debt grew, so did the number of opportunities to acquire advanced technology much faster and cheaper than by waiting for the Chinese to develop similar things autonomously. In a situation of serious material constraints and scarcity, there was no real alternative.

The second reason is related to the overarching objective of the Chinese revolutions discussed the first half of this book. The Chinese communist movement was based on the urgent demand of a generation that China needed to become a modern and powerful nation to be able to defend itself (*rich nation, strong military*). This core tenet had united the major modernisation movements within the remnants of the Chinese empire at the turn of the century and was the basis of Chinese socialism. It implied that the Chinese economy needed to *catch up* with the technologically advanced foreigners, in order to rise to their ranks and assert itself. Obviously, catching up with one who is far ahead requires moving much faster than whoever one is pursuing. Accordingly, the timelines the CCP set for the state it had created were immensely compressed to the point of farce, stating the need to look at days as if they were years. Keeping this requirement of speed inherent to the basic tenet in mind, the stabilisation that could be observed in the Chinese economy in the early 1960s and 1970s stood merely for the taking of a breath. It was the temporary acceptance of a slower pace for the sake of an improved livelihood at the current section of the race that was the *raison d'être* of the CCP.

China, as one might say with reference to one of the most arduous critics of the centralised command economy, FRIEDRICH VON HAYEK, had at least partly solved many problems of distribution and incomplete information by reducing its central planning to the commanding heights and relying on decentralisation where it was possible without risking political power. HAYEK's basic argument with regard to centralized economic planning is made in abstract form in Volume II of his Collected Works:

> "This argument [that public utilities need to be provided by government and technology makes planning even more necessary] is based on a complete misapprehension of the working of competition. Far from being appropriate only to comparatively simple conditions, it is the very complexity of the division of labor under modern conditions which makes competition the only method by which such coordination [of the "complete economic process"] can be adequately brought about. There would be no difficulty about efficient control or planning were conditions so simple that a single person or board could effectively survey all the relevant facts. It is only as the factors which have to be taken into account become so numerous that it is impossible to gain a synoptic view of them that decentralisation becomes imperative. But, once decentralization is necessary, the problem of coordination arises – a coordination which leaves the separate agencies free to adjust their activities to the facts which only they can know and yet brings about about a mutual adjustment of their respective plans. As decentralization has become necessary because nobody can consciously balance all the considerations bearing on the decisions of so many individuals, the coordination can clearly be effected not by 'conscious control' […] This is precisely what the price system does under competition and which no other system even promises to accomplish."[16]

The leadership of the PRC had moved even further away from central planning at its (hypothetical) most extreme – the "single person or board" mentioned by HAYEK, surveying all the relevant facts. But the main challenge was not merely coordination, it was modernisation: how could the challenge of technological innovation be tackled when the potential of "creative destruction" or "Schumpeter's gale"[17] that markets were supposed to

16 HAYEK FRIEDRICH AUGUST, Caldwell Bruce (ed.), The Road to Serfdom, The Definitive Edition, Chicago 2007, p. 95. China at the end of the 1970s had moved as far away from a system of centralised control of allocation towards a system of *coordination* that the argument would not fully apply.

17 Describing the "process of industrial mutation that incessantly revolutionises the economic structure from within, incessantly destroying the old one, incessantly creating a new one", which was based on a detailed reading of Karl Marx' writings, in particular the Grundrisse and the Capital. Being established as an integral part of capitalist economies, the process driven by competition and the changing demand on markets leads to the constant revolutionising of the economic

cause through competition and the business cycle could not be uncovered without sacrificing even more control and stability? In that regard, it was decisive that for Mao's successors – be it Deng Xiaoping or even Hua Guofeng – moving *slowly* was ruled out as an option early on. In the latter half of the decade, when speed emerged again as an explicit *Leitmotiv*[18] for industrial development in China, the hypothetical scenario of moderate and fully self-reliant growth was de facto ruled out.

The experiences gained with foreign economic exchanges in the earlier years were, even more than before, put to use for the primary objective of obtaining technology of the most advanced kind to allow China to move on to the next set of basic innovations that had emerged. This corresponded with the Maoist vision of communism, as much a technology-driven vision as Marx' and Lenin's (see the second Chapter). Only one red line that crystallised clearly would not be crossed – accepting ownership and participation by foreign capital in China. At least not lightly.

Self-reliance and the rest of the world

The chinese political paradigm of self-reliance had and has two sides: addressing structures within the PRC as discussed above is one. Referring to the socialist state's relations with the rest of the world the other. One origin story in the latter context has a military background. As the number of US troops began to rise in South Vietnam in 1965, chief of staff of the PLA Liu Ruiqing proposed the notion of "active defence" to frame the Chinese readiness to intervene as it had before in the Korean War. Minister of defence Lin Biao intervened and proposed an alternative strategy that sought to avoid both a confrontation with the United States and collaboration with the Soviet Union: self-reliance.[19] With regard to Chinese international relations and, in particular, foreign economic relations,

---

structure from within. See: SCHUMPETER JOSEPH A., Kapitalismus, Sozialismus und Demokratie, Stuttgart 2005, pp. 137 f.

18 In his report on the work of the government, Hua Guofeng underlined this aspect, naming the mobilisation of the whole country for agriculture, speeding up the development of the basic industries and giving full scope to the leading role of industry, doing a "good job" in commerce and developing foreign trade, the encouragement of socialist emulation and technical innovation and "technical revolution", the strengthening of unified planning and giving "full play" to the initiative of both the central and local authorities, and lastly upholding the principle of "from each according" and the improvement of the livelihood of the people as cornerstones of economic development – followed by the call to build "a vast army of working-class intellectuals". Foreign Broadcast Information Service, Hua's Work Report, Peking NCNA in English, 1207 GMT, 26 02 1978 OW, accessed through Readex. In July 1978, a draft decision of the Central Committee "concerning some problems of speeding up the development of industry" was issued to all party committees and groups for implementation on a trial basis. The main points included the system of responsibility of the plant director, the expansion of fuel, energy, raw material and transport industries, technology and reorganisation, "in accordance with the principle of specialisation and coordination". Foreign Broadcast Information Service, CCP issues Decision on Speeding up Industrial Development, Peking NCNA in English, 0743 GMT, 04 07 1978 OW, accessed through Readex.

19 DIKÖTTER 2016, p. 44.

self-reliance found its expression in the synonymous departing from national independence and development of the national economy.[20]

Even before the socialist rule, trade exchanges within China had taken place largely without the direct influence of foreigners. Once goods were unloaded at Chinese ports, their sale and transportation were almost exclusively handled by Chinese merchants.[21] Even exports from China, while transported by foreign ships from Chinese ports, were only taken care of by foreigners for this last leg. Business activities related to foreign trade handled by specialists were referred to as "compradores" *and* criticised heavily *post factum* for their collaboration with foreigners, both by Chinese nationalists and the CCP.[22]

The rise of the so-called comprador merchants was due partly to the opening of the treaty ports after 1842, a process which provided more opportunities for foreign and Chinese merchants to pursue their business. When the imposed doctrine of "free trade" replaced the monopolistic imperial trade system, western merchants found that it was not easy to establish reliable contacts with their Chinese counterparts. These difficulties were due to the language barrier, the complexity of the monetary system, the great variety of commercial customs and practices and the still influential guilds and merchant groups in China. Therefore, middlemen were quite easily able to find demand for their services.[23]

With regard to China's relationship with the rest of the world, the risk of creating a new class of compradores was frequently referred to in order to justify the course of self-reliance at the international level. Nevertheless, the fact that foreign trade had never played a major role in China after 1949 is also related to the choice of the Soviet model of economic planning in the early 1950s. As it had been the case in the Soviet Union in its beginnings, the high rates of investment and a strong emphasis on the development of heavy industry as well as the bureaucratic planned economy to run it, were also functions of the (in part involuntary) closedness of the economy. Such a path to economic development with the sacrifices it required – stemming from the constant pressure on wages and individual consumption as well as the arduous labour – would have been much less obvious if both economies could have been opened up to foreign trade and investment right away. The PRC did not have the choice to focus on the downstream end of industrial value chains in order to industrialise, like it had been done by the much smaller economies of say, Hong Kong and Taiwan.

In the years following 1970, self-reliance on the international level was as much a part of political ideology as it was a description of reality. The US trade embargo had at least discouraged trade and diplomatic relations with the rest of the west for decades after

20 Chiang Ching's Address to Diplomatic Cadres, March 1975, Classified Chinese Communist Documents: A Selection, Taipei Institute of International Relations, 1978, pp. 537–545, available in: Chinese Law & Government, Vol. 9, No. 1–2, 1976, pp. 49–61.

21 Perkins 2015, p. 10.

22 Despite the persisting shortcomings with regard to the organisation of foreign economic relations and trade between the planned economies of the Comecon/CMEA, the notion of two separate and competing world markets was adhered to by Soviet theorists in the 1970s. See: Brun Ellen, Hersh Jacques, Soviet-Third World Relations in a Capitalist World: The Political Economy of Broken Promises, New York 1990, p. 74.

23 Hao Yenping, A "New Class" in China's Treaty Ports: The Rise of the Comprador-Merchants, in: The Business History Review, Vol. 44, No. 4, Winter 1970, pp. 446–459.

the Korean War. Also, the Sino-Soviet split after 1956 had burned bridges with the PRC's principal ally and crucial trade partner. Thus, the PRC saw itself at least partly excluded from international markets. First the capitalist world market, the underlying principles of which were legally enshrined in the General Agreement on Tariffs and Trade (GATT),[24] and the socialist based on the Council for Mutual Economic Assistance (CMEA). The formula of self-reliance in the international context also served as a useful theoretical device to fit this situation in the CCP's political narrative.

The political rhetoric was quite radical: After member of the Swiss Federal Council Pierre Graber visited the PRC in summer of 1974, he described the Chinese world view, as it had been presented to him, in rather bleak terms to the conference of Swiss ambassadors in Bern in September of the same year:

> "[Thus,] Peking sees two possibilities for the future of the world: either the superpowers [US and the Soviet Union] start a world war, or the countries of the third world – which [in the Chinese view] are those who determine the course of history – take the lead and start the revolution in order to assure their freedom. Such a situation is considered "excellent" over there."[25]

Accordingly, as Graber reported, the Chinese had signalled interest and sympathy towards the Swiss conception of neutrality, particularly *armed* neutrality, as it seemed to confirm their concept of international self-reliance.[26] Despite such alleged political parallels, with regard to trade and foreign investment, the PRC followed a very different approach compared to the small, highly industrialised and open Swiss economy.

Chinese foreign trade had stagnated at a low level between 1959 and 1972. Socialist China continued to rely on the institutional interfaces with the world to conduct its limited trade operations, but also developed them further to ensure compatibility with the centralised organisation of foreign trade. Due to the strict state monopoly on international and national trade, foreign buyers and sellers were both not allowed to do business directly with Chinese buyers or sellers. About a dozen state trading companies were responsible for negotiating prices and drafting contracts, which was described as tedious and requiring a lot of patience and insistence.[27]

In the mid-1950s, foreign trade organs were also established at the provincial level and in the cities of Shanghai and Beijing. The most important of these second-tier bureaus were those in Canton and Shanghai, a consequence of the importance of their

24 The GATT is a post-Second World War treaty signed in 1947 and designed to limit national barriers impeding international trade. Both tariff and non-tariff barriers (i. e., import quotas, licensing requirements, and regulatory actions designed to limit imports) are covered by the agreement. As a result of the so-called Uruguay round of multilateral trade negotiations, the GATT was revised and integrated in the Agreement establishing the World Trade Agreement (the so-called Marrakesh Agreement), which entered into force on the first of January 1995.

25 Conference des Ambassadeurs 1974, Rapport de M. le Conseiller fédéral P. Graber, Chef du Département politique, sur son voyage en Chine, Bernerhof, mercredi 4 septembre 1974, 14.30 h, Annexe III, pp. 3–4. Available at dodis: dodis.ch/35124, last accessed 12 August 2022. Translation by the author.

26 Ibid., p. 2.

27 Deleyne 1972, 141.

ocean ports and the Canton Fair. Paralleling the consolidation of the Chinese Ministry for Trade in the same period, the structure of specialized sectoral foreign trade corporations was set up and underwent only few changes until 1970. In 1971, in the course of the reorganization of the state administration, it underwent a major reorganization, during which the number of foreign trade corporations was reduced from fourteen to seven, expanding the competences of each unit. These seven corporations were the China National Cereals, Oils and Foodstuffs Import-Export Corporation, the Chemicals Corporation, the Light Industries Corporation, the Machinery Corporation, the Metals and Minerals Corporation, the Native Produce and Animal By-Products Corporation and the National Textiles Corporation.[28]

A crucial institution for Chinese foreign trade was not a corporation or a ministry, but a combination of a showroom and a marketplace. The annual Canton Fair allowed foreign companies and governments to exchange with state trading companies and foreign trade corporations. The Fair had inherited the tradition of medieval Chinese trade fairs, going back centuries in large cities along the coast, notably Hangzhou and Canton itself.[29] Taking place for the first time in 1957, when the first five-year plan was in full swing, the Canton Fair was held without interruption twice a year between the 15th of April and the 15th of May as well as between the 15th of October and the 15th of November. More than half of all foreign trade in the 1970s was handled directly through the Fair, making it a major instrument in Chinese foreign trade activities.[30] The Fair even spawned its own branch of management literature in the West, advising businesspeople how to approach Chinese representants and lead negotiations effectively.[31]

The Fair served two purposes: first, the acquisition of foreign goods and negotiation of trade contracts with foreign companies; second, and more importantly, the sale of Chinese products which were displayed only there. As DELEYNE suggested, while some of the more complex products were only on display in small quantities, the technical progress demonstrated at the Fairs allowed for at least a qualitative assessment of the capabilities of the Chinese industry. The only line of products that he described to be consistently available to foreign buyers until 1975 in significant quantities were textiles, which were offered at competitive prices. In terms of quality and design, however, they were only regarded by buyers as adequate for customers of Chinese origin in Hong Kong and Singapore.[32] Nevertheless, growing export potential was seen and attempted to create for goods with higher value added during the 1970s, such as conserved food, frozen seafood, small agricultural machinery, simple machine tools and some number of basic electronic and electric utilities.

28 KLEIN DONALD W., The Foreign Trade Apparatus, in: Li Victor H. (ed.), Law and Politics in China's Foreign Trade, Hong Kong 1977, p. 313.

29 The Canton Fair, http://www.cantonfair.org.cn, last accessed 1 May 2020.

30 TRETIAK DANIEL, The Canton Fair: An Academic Perspective, in: The China Quarterly, No. 56, October-December 1973, pp. 740–748.

31 BRUNNER JAMES A., TAOKA GEORGE M., Marketing and Negotiating in the People's Republic of China: Perceptions of American Businessmen Who Attended the 1975 Fair, in: Journal of International Business Studies, Vol. 8, No. 2, Autumn/Winter 1977, pp. 69–82.

32 DELEYNE 1972, p. 140.

The Canton Fair also had other limited effects on the "openness" of China, for example, the expansion of telephone connections. As the importance of the so-called China trade increased, the Sino-British Trade Council proposed to the British General Post Office to expand the length of time during which the international phone lines between the Chinese mainland and Britain were open during the duration of the 33rd Canton Fair opening on 15 April 1973. The request was granted, and the timeframe doubled from four to eight hours.[33] Similarly, shortages in Chinese industry and agriculture were noticed at the Canton Fair of 1974, which particularly Japanese businessmen hoping for growing trade prospects with China found to be a major disappointment according to US reports.[34]

In early 1975, after the re-introduction of the Four Modernisations as the main paradigm for economic development, the flexibility with regard to the interpretation of self-reliance concerning the procurement of advanced technology to support industrialisation was communicated in increasingly open form in the Chinese official press. Looking back at twenty-five years of socialist construction, "adhering to the principle of self-reliance and going in for industry, independently" was referred to as a past success that had laid "a solid basis for socialist industrialisation".[35] But how would this basis be used with regard to the second stage of economic development after 1980, as the long-term strategy demanded? While "Walking on Two Legs" and the mixed system between centralisation and decentralisation as well as measures of austerity and the importance of the livelihood of the people as aspects of "internal" self-reliance remained, self-reliance with regard to the world outside China got a rather different connotation. NCNA reported in March 1975:

> "The policy of independence and self-reliance does not mean a 'closed-door' policy. It is conductive to and necessary for industrialization to develop economic and technical exchange with other countries, especially mutual help and support among developing countries on the principle of respect for state sovereignty, equality and mutual benefit and a **complementary interchange of goods** [emphasis added]."[36]

The reference to complementarity was a rather small step, but also a move away from the stricter import-substitution strategy – which was critically perceived by Soviet observers, accusing the Chinese leadership of hypocrisy. As stated in a Soviet commentary on an Albanian commentary that had accused the Soviet economic relations with the US as introducing capitalism to the Soviet Union in March 1975:

> "...in 1974 alone the United States sold to China goods worth a total of $807 million, whereas U.S. imports from China totaled $114 million. Last year China's overall trade deficit with the United States was $500 million (as heard). Furthermore, it becomes

33 Joint Publications Research Service, State of PRC Communications Sector analysed, article by Chiang Huai, Taipei Fei-ch'ing Yüeh-pao, Original in Mandarin, 10 03 1973, p. 109, accessed through Readex.

34 People's Republic of China Economic Review 1, 31 May 1974, 07:18, ID: 1974HONGK06138_b.

35 See e. g. Foreign Broadcast Information Service, Industrialization Achieved via Self-Reliance, Peking NCNA in English, 1200 GMT, 15 03 1975 OW, accessed through Readex.

36 Ibid.

> even clearer that China, compelling some countries not to take credits, increasingly takes advantage of credit in its relations with the capitalist countries, a common practice in present international economic relations. It is known that since 1972 Peking has bought equipment from the United States, Japan and other countries of Western Europe according to the payment system (based) on 5-year credits given to China at 6 percent interest. This once again confirms the hypocritical nature of what China's Maoist leadership says about the theory of relying on one's own resources. In imposing this theory on other countries so as to restrict their cooperation with other countries, primarily with the states of the socialist family, the Maoists want at the same time to receive scientific-technical successes from the developed capitalist countries, primarily as regards a further increase of China's military and economic potential."[37]

In the face of the steady Soviet expansion of foreign trade as well as the use of foreign credit, this criticism in hindsight appears outright defensive. At the 25th Congress of the Communist Party of the Soviet Union (CPSU), Premier Kosygin announced that Soviet export potential was to be expanded and widened, one direction being the organisation of industrial plants designated for export, while imports would continue to – all too similarly to China – be aimed at the introduction of modern technology to speed up Soviet industrial development. Kosygin noted that Soviet Trade and Cooperation would develop more rapidly with countries that insured the "Provision of normal, mutually-beneficial conditions for development".[38]

In international relations, self-reliance as a concept was applied as an alternative to interdependence, which also had some overlap with the tension between multilateralism aimed at integrated solutions and the increasing bilateral and unilateral measures taken by industrialised countries in the course of the persisting economic crisis. For example, the head of the Chinese delegation at UNCTAD criticised a proposal to establish an international resources bank for the financing of commodity trade as well as the US-practice of using bilateral commodity-agreements – which allowed the US to "maintain control, plunder and exploitation over developing countries". The participation of China in international fora and self-reliance were contradictory to some degree. It was nevertheless noted at the same meeting in mid-May 1976 that the Chinese delegate Zhou Huamin, Vice Minister of Foreign Trade, conceded to the earlier sweeping statements on principle; he stated that while independence and self-reliance remained crucial, due consideration had to be given to the specific situation of each developing country – in particular referring to the possibility of "gradually" getting rid of "imperialist control".[39]

In the Chinese media, while the emphasis on self-reliance in international affairs as well as trade was frequent, the language with regard to the expansion of Chinese trade shifted gradually after the fourth National People's Congress. Complementarity of trade

---

37 Foreign Broadcast Information Service, Nikolayev on Albanian Press Treatment of Peking's Trade, Moscow in Albanian to Albania, 1530 GMT, 16 03 1975 AU, accessed through Readex.

38 US Department of State, Electronic Telegram, Kosygin on the Soviet Economy, 3 March 1976, 07:23, PlusD, ID: 1976MOSCOW03250_b, paragraph 13.

39 US Department of State, Electronic Telegram, The PRC at UNCTAD – Response to the Secretary's Speech, 13 May 1976, 06:02, PlusD, ID: 1976HONGK05470_b.

was put into principle with reference to the Five Principles of Chinese foreign policy, stating equality and mutual benefit and "the supply of each other's needs" as the general direction. That self-reliance did not mean self-seclusion became the official line, coupled with criticism of measures taken by capitalist countries to "shift their economic and monetary crises" onto the developing countries. Addressing a foreign audience, NCNA summarized the official Chinese views on trade policy in September 1975, stating that:

> "China's adherence to the line of independence and self-reliance in construction in no way means 'self-seclusion'. In accordance with the principle of proletarian internationalism, China has actively developed relations of friendly cooperation and mutual assistance with socialist countries, broadening the scope of economic exchange, learning from each other and drawing on each other's merits, and together promoting the cause of construction. In addition, China has maintained trade contacts and developed economic relations with countries of different social systems on the basis of the five principles of peaceful coexistence."[40]

Selective opening and the expansion of Chinese diplomacy

Economic policies in the PRC also need to be understood in light of the international situation China was facing, more precisely with regard to its powerful potential military adversaries: Soviet armies to the north, US military forces across the East Asian littoral and an increasingly aggressive India – or so it was perceived – to the south. It was a political dictum that the greatest threat was posed by the former Soviet allies.[41] As JOHN W. GARVER argued, China pushed to improve its relations with India in particular in the late 1970s. The reasons behind this can be traced back to the mid-1970s. Several interrelated factors were involved. One was the recognition of India's clear pre-eminence in South Asia after Pakistan's defeat in the 1971 war and the successful 1974 nuclear test. While China rushed to help Pakistan rebuild after its 1971 defeat, and began to court Bangladesh more intensely after Mujibur Rahman was assassinated in 1975, it was now clear that no combination of South Asian countries could balance India. A second factor was a reappraisal of India's relations with the Soviet Union. Since the early 1960s, Beijing had seen Moscow and India as colluding to oppose China. This dogma began to give way as India gave clear signs of independence from Moscow after 1971. Perhaps, most importantly, New Delhi refused to sign a collective security treaty with Moscow despite strong Soviet pressure to do so. A third factor was the mounting concern of China's leaders about the increasingly aggressive Soviet foreign policy which they perceived emerging in the wake of the American defeat in Vietnam.[42]

---

40 Foreign Broadcast Information Service, NCNA on PRC Foreign Trade Policy, Peking NCNA in English, 0700 GMT, 07 09 1975 OW, accessed through Readex.

41 LÜTHI 2020, p. 131; see also CHENG JOSEPH Y. S., Mao Zedong's Perception of the World in 1968–1972: Rationale for the Sino-American Rapprochement, in: The Journal of American-East Asian Relations, Vol. 7, No. 2/4, Fall-Winter 1998, p. 242.

42 GARVER JOHN W., The Indian Factor in Recent Sino-Soviet Relations, in: The China Quarterly, No. 125, March 1991, p. 56.

According to LORENZ LÜTHI, it was the Soviet-led intervention of the Warsaw Pact in Czechoslovakia in the summer of 1968 that triggered a major overhaul of China's domestic and foreign policies. The PRC began to denounce the former Soviet ally as a socialist-imperialist power, thus subsuming it under the same category as the reactionary-imperialist United States. A possible Soviet invasion in China, in order to restore Soviet-style socialism as it had been done in Czechoslovakia was perceived as the most dangerous and immediate threat the PRC was facing. The restoration of state organs and the de facto end of the Cultural Revolution by spring of 1969 was another consequence of this shift in international affairs. In 1969, after renewed clashes with Soviet troops in Xinjiang, the threat of war had become very concrete for China. Despite some important technological advances, the country was far from being militarily ready or able to challenge the Soviet Red Army. Military mobilisation was decreed in August 1969, and the population prepared for the possibility of a large-scale invasion.[43] Also, the PLA had proven in the course of the Cultural Revolution and the violent stabilisation of its most intense phase in 1967 that it was an indispensable means for the CCP to safeguard its dominant position.

On the other hand, the observation that China had gained more self-confidence in foreign affairs could hardly be dismissed. In a report dated 22 February 1972, looking back at the past five years of his presence the Swiss ambassador to the PRC, Oscar Rossetti, indicated what he saw as the positive effects of the Cultural Revolution for China:

> "From the revolutionary turmoil of the past five years, an entirely new China has emerged. People and leadership, who never had learned to think and act in a Marxist way, think and act in a Maoist way today, which means in a Chinese way. Communism, like everything that was introduced to China from abroad, has been assimilated. This process of assimilation has given back the Chinese people its self-confidence, destroyed in the past century, together with a feeling of national unity and national responsibility, until now foreign to the Chinese. The economic stability achieved in a short period of time that has brought a modest but constantly improving supply situation of the country, is today – together with the sense of national responsibility – an inducement for great achievements.
> It is not mere coercion that is giving rise to this increasing commitment, but also national enthusiasm and above all, self-interest. This internal stability that is increasingly consolidated, is also the basis of the new Chinese foreign policy. China can dare to step out of its self-induced isolation, to demand its place in world politics. The events of the past years have shown that the world is ready to accept China as a major power, if not superpower, despite it not yet commanding the according economic and military power."[44]

Approaching the status of a major power – perhaps even the third superpower, even if the Chinese leadership consistently denied any ambitions in this direction – the major

43 DIKÖTTER 2016, p. 209.

44 Ambassade de Suisse en Chine, China 1967–1972, Politischer Bericht Nr. 5, Peking 22 Februar 1972, Ref: 382.1 – RO/hw. Available on Diplomatic Documents of Switzerland (dodis): www.dodis.ch/35819, last accessed 1 May 2020. Translation by the author.

factors constraining this regained status in the world were the limited economic and military power.

An active Chinese foreign and trade policy towards non-socialist countries in Western Europe, Japan and later the US, had two ideological preconditions. First, the belief had to be established and maintained that the Soviet Union – as opposed to China – was no longer a socialist country but capitalist and, even worse, deeply imperialist. Second, the division of the world in three distinct spheres, the "Three Worlds", gave normative grounds for the PRC to seek alliances with non-imperialist countries in the intermediate zone between the two superpowers. Further, it enabled a rapprochement towards the US, which was cognitively impossible as long as the Soviet Union, from a Chinese perspective, was a part of socialist internationalism.[45]

In response to the perceived adverse development on the international sphere for Chinese interests, a diplomatic offensive in the early 1970s aimed at nudging global politics in a more favourable direction, creating an alternative front against the common threat that was referred to as "Soviet expansionism". It constituted the second concerted effort by Beijing to influence the global power structure. The first had been the effort in the 1960s to advance world revolution by supporting movements abroad that were seen as instrumental for this goal. As John W. Garver argues, with pushes in Chinese foreign policy both during the 1960s and 1970s, there were strong links between China's domestic politics and the international sphere. In the first push, the key purpose was to create a wave of global anti-capitalist revolution, with the second, the key purpose was to contain the threat posed by Soviet "revisionist socialist imperialism" to the emancipated Chinese direction that emerged from the Cultural Revolution. Importantly, while the first push was premised on Chinese-US confrontation, the second enabled cooperation with the latter. It may be added that the economic dimension of the second push needs to be underlined as well, in particular as it facilitated the access to foreign exchange and increasing technology imports. Also, the first push did not cease and make way for the second, there was a parallelism of both.[46]

The "Three Worlds Theory" was explained to the World by Deng Xiaoping at the Special Session of the United Nations on raw materials and development in 1974. The speech was drafted by Qiao Guanhua, then vice-minister and later minister of Foreign Affairs. He infused a strong political vision into the text, taking into account the contemporary state of the international capitalist economy:

> "At present, the international situation is most favourable to the developing countries and the peoples of the world. More and more, the old order based on colonialism, imperialism and hegemonism is being undermined and shaken to its foundations. International relations are changing drastically. The whole world is in turbulence and unrest. The situation is one of 'great disorder under heaven', as we Chinese put it. This 'disorder' is a manifestation of the sharpening of all the basic contradictions in the contemporary world. It is accelerating the disintegration and decline of the decadent

45 Garver 2016, p. 288.

46 Ibid., p. 344.

> reactionary forces and stimulating the awakening and growth of the new emerging forces of the people."[47]

According to the theory, the "imperialistic superpowers", i. e. the Soviet Union and the United States, together constituted a First World, seeking global hegemony and colluding in that effort. The Second World, and this was the core political innovation of the concept compared to Beijing's earlier declared worldview, consisted of the other industrialised countries, namely Europe (West and East), Canada, Australia, and also the former nemesis, Japan. The Third World, which still today is being used as a denominator albeit with a different meaning[48], consisted of the developing – meaning non-industrialised – countries of Asia, Africa and Latin America. They were the "new emerging forces of the people" (also referred to as NEFOs) Qiao made reference to. China at the time declared itself to be a part of the Third World, establishing that both the Second and Third Worlds were oppressed by the two superpowers and expanded the *limits of the possible* for both foreign and foreign economic policy.

As Zhou Enlai declared at the first session of the fourth People's Congress, praising the importance of China in leading the Third World countries against the influence of both the USA and the Soviet Union:

> "The third world is the main force in combating colonialism, imperialism and hegemonism. **China is a developing socialist country belonging to the third world** [emphasis added]. We should enhance our unity with the countries and people of Asia, Africa and Latin America and resolutely support them in their struggle to win or safeguard national independence, defend their state sovereignty, protect their national resources and develop their national economy."[49]

As the countries of the Second World were determined to be equally oppressed, China could rely on this persistent contradiction within the capitalist as well as the socialist world systems to seek cooperation with aligned states. It also served as an explanatory formula for the rapprochement between China and the US, as the Soviet Union was firmly established as being the most dangerous source of war.

Furthermore, visible in the Chinese government's public expressions in international organisations as well as domestically, the theory sought to establish moral superiority of the Second World over the First and of the Third over both the others. Europe, as one of the centres of tension of the Cold War between the two superpowers, was crucial for efforts to influence international power structures in a favourable direction for China's

47 Quoted from Altehenger Jennifer, Social Imperialism and Mao's Three Worlds: Deng Xiaoping's Speech at the UN General Assembly, 1974, in: Hammersley Rachel (ed.), Revolutionary Moments: Reading Revolutionary Texts, London 2015, p. 175.

48 Referring to the *Three World Model* created by the demographer Alfred Sauvy where the first world is the capitalist Allies of the Second World War, the second the socialist countries including the People's Republic, and the third the underdeveloped countries including the members of the nonaligned movement.

49 Quoted from: Carneiro Corrêa Vieira, From Third World Theory to Belt and Road Initiative: International Aid as a Chinese Foreign Policy Tool, in: Contexto Internacional, Vol. 41, No. 3, September/December 2019, p. 533.

military security and economic interests. As Mao explained to Henry Kissinger in 1973, the Soviet Union would not be able to launch a full-scale attack on China as long as control over Europe and the Middle East was not established. The great danger, in Mao's view, was that the European countries would allow Soviet domination, not being aware of its imperialist ambitions. Therefore, it was important for China to take a firm line with the political leaders of Western European countries to make them aware of the threat. Kissinger found Mao well-informed about European politics and politicians.[50]

France was among the first countries to answer the Chinese call for the renewal of diplomatic and economic ties. On 13 July 1970, Mao and Lin Biao met a French government delegation led by André Bettencourt, at the time minister delegate in charge of planning and territorial development[51] in Paris. The delegation that accompanied the chairman was impressive: Premier of the State Council Zhou Enlai, Vice Chairman of the standing committee of the National People's Congress Fang Sheng, and Vice Premier of the State Council Li Xiannian. The meeting was in itself historical: Bettencourt was the first high-ranking Western political envoy to go to China on an official visit since the CCP came to power in 1949. Paris was pushing to increase trade relations with Peking. Once he had returned to Paris, Bettencourt expressed optimism:

> "China wishes to resume its links with the world. After an epoch of withdrawal, I think we are back in an epoch of opening".[52]

But the trade boycott of the West endured. Shortly thereafter, foreshadowing the normalisation of bilateral diplomatic relations in the following year, Zhou Enlai met the grandson of Japan's late Prince, who was accompanied by the honorary president of the China–Japan Friendship Association, Guo Moruo, and a representative of the trade office. Both heads of delegation affirmed that they were looking forward to regular meetings in the future.[53] In May 1971, Italy's Minister of Trade Mario Zagari visited Peking[54]; in fall 1971, the National China News Agency openly mentioned the objective of developing trade relations with suitable partners. After a reception at the Chinese embassy in

50 Garver 2016, p. 341.

51 A policy programme aimed at mitigating the uneven regional development that was a consequence of the highly centralised French system of administration –before and after the Second World War – the first objective of the *aménagement du territoire à la française* was to reduce the development gap between Paris and the province and, since 1973, simultaneously to regenerate the declining industrial areas as a part of the industrial policies that followed the decline in industrial growth since the end of the 1960s. Since the mid-1980s, this policy has been more sensitive both to international competition and to the growing local powers, also because of the progress in European economic integration. See: Baudelle Guy, Peyrony Jean, Striving for Equity: Polycentric Development Policies in France, in: Built Environment, Vol. 31, No. 2, 2005, p. 103.

52 Foreign Broadcast Information Service, Possibility Of Chou En-Lai Trip Raises Speculation, London Reuters in English, 1059 GMT, 27 08 1970 X, accessed through Readex.

53 Foreign Broadcast Information Service, Saionju Calls On Chou Before Returning To Japan, Tokyo Kyodo in English, 1035 GMT, 31 07 1970 T, accessed through Readex.

54 China and the European Community. European Community Background Information No. 9, 22 May 1974, p. 5, AEI, Document Nr. 56842, available at: http://aei.pitt.edu/id/eprint/56842, last accessed 1 May 2020.

Helsinki, it was reported that "...the hosts and guests repeatedly drank to the steady development of the friendly relations and trade interflows between China and Finland."[55]

Looking back at his first nine months in office in early 1973, the Swiss ambassador to the PRC Albert Natural noted that the intensity of contacts with Chinese officials had exceeded all his expectations. Contrary to his initial impressions, his time in Beijing was not "dedicated to literature, the study of China and of Maoism", but to "around 200" meetings with officials. He also noted that all Swiss requests for Chinese visa had been granted since he arrived. That Henri Honegger, a famous violoncellist from Geneva, was invited to play classical music in Beijing as the first foreign artist since 1966 was just another manifestation of the unexpectedly welcoming dynamic.[56]

The priorities of the diplomatic expansion were clarified by Zhou Enlai in August 1972, when he assured Kenzo Nakajima, the president of the Japan–China Cultural Exchange Associations, that China intended to normalise diplomatic relations with Japan and the FRG, "before it does with the United States". The Chinese–Japanese rapprochement was shortly after substantiated, when Zhou Enlai indicated in January 1973 that China was about to reveal its plan on a bilateral civil aviation agreement between the two countries, at a meeting with Yasushiro Nakasone, the minister of international trade and industry in Peking.[57] At the same occasion, he also made the first public announcement of a formalisation of the Chinese–German rapprochement, which had become visible with a visit from the former foreign minister of the FRG, Gerhard Schröder, one month earlier. An aviation agreement was signed in August 1974 after protracted negotiations, starting direct commercial air traffic between China and Japan in September of the same year. The inaugural flight on September 29 marked the second anniversary of bilateral diplomatic relations.[58] A new flexibility towards prospective trade partners in accordance with the theory of three worlds was emphasised, as Zhou and Schröder had agreed at their meeting that neither the existing FRG–Soviet nor the FRG–Polish treaties would pose any problems for the establishment of formal diplomatic ties.[59]

Aviation was a pioneering sector when it came to international instruments agreed by Beijing. The expansion of international transport also concerned air travel, while landbound international travel stagnated. In 1974, the Civil Aviation Administration of China (CAAC) operated under the slogan "Fly to faraway places, fly to the world" and made bold promises albeit with regard to a modest number of destinations:

> " [...] today, one can visit one's friends in Albania on the Adriatic Sea in 10 odd hours. The friendship bridge in the sky has turned far corners of the world into close neighbors

55 Foreign Broadcast Information Service, PRC Ambassador's Reception, Peking NCNA International Service in English, 1633 GMT, 14 09 1971 B, accessed through Readex.

56 Ambassade de Suisse en Chine, Lettre à Ernesto Thalmann, Pékin, ke 3 janvier 1973, Réf. 12.21.Cha. Available at dodis: dodis.ch/37712. Last accessed on 12 August 2022.

57 Foreign Broadcast Information Service, Tokyo Kyodo On Chou Meeting, Tokyo Kyodo in English, 0040 GMT, 19 01 1973, accessed through Readex.

58 Foreign Broadcast Information Service, Air Agreement, Tokyo Kyodo in English, 1317 GMT, 30 08 1974 B, accessed through Readex.

59 Foreign Broadcast Information Service, Chou On U.S., Bonn, Tokyo, Tokyo Kyodo in English, 0438 GMT, 21 8 1972 T, accessed through Readex.

> and further reinforced the intimate link between the Chinese people and the people of Albania, Romania, Tirana".

But already by September of the same year, connections had been expanded beyond these immediate allies. Indirect and direct international connections operated on the Beijing-Tokyo, the Beijing-Karachi-Paris and the Beijing-Teheran-Bucharest-Tirana lines, resulting in a total of seventeen international flights from Chinese airports in addition to eighty domestic routes. Ambitions were high as this was officially declared to be only a "preliminary framework" and "just a beginning".[60]

The prototype for an international agreement in the area had been concluded with France as early as 1966, followed by years of inactivity as the Cultural Revolution began.[61] While the Soviet national airline Aeroflot still was the only company allowed to fly to the capital in the early 1970s, this situation changed rapidly. Before the bilateral agreement between China and Japan was signed, aviation agreements with Albania, Romania and Yugoslavia marked a first opening. Also, talks with Switzerland on such an agreement began in June 1972 on Chinese initiative. One reason for this outreach was pragmatic and had to do with mail, an international infrastructure in which the PRC was integrated: Swissair had been transporting large quantities for the Chinese postal administration. When General Director of the Swiss Postal Service (*Post-, Telefon- und Telegrafenbetriebe*, PTT) travelled to Beijing in August 1971, he was told that China wished to use Switzerland as a transshipment point for air mail going to African states. At the same occasion, the Chinese delegation signalled interest in deepening cooperation on civil aviation.[62]

The Swiss Federal office for aviation (*Eidgenössisches Luftamt*) noted that, since the accession to the UN, China seemed to increasingly turn away from self-isolation in aviation matters – quoting the procurement of six Soviet Ilyushin-62 jetliners to be delivered to Beijing by the end of 1972 as an obvious expansion of the Chinese fleet, so far largely limited to domestic transport, with long-distance capabilites. The office also noted that the Western aviation industry was courting the PRC hoping for procurements – also, delegations of the leading European aviation companies (Alitalia, British Overseas Airways Corporation, KLM Royal Dutch and Scandinavian Airlines) had visited Beijing in the course of 1972. That these negotiations were both high on the list of Chinese priorities and forward-looking was underlined by the fact, that Li Xiannian himself – literally the second-in-command in the PRC – received the Swiss Delegation in Beijing for an hour of "casual exchange".[63]

With a view to the future of bilateral aviation, the Chinese delegation showed remarkable flexibility when it came to agreeing flight routes to China: with some exceptions for political reasons (e. g. Bangkok, Hongkong, Dacca), access to both Beijing and Shanghai was also granted from alternative points, i. e. other than through the Soviet Union,

60 Foreign Broadcast Information Service, China Civil Aviation develops international flights, Peking Kuang-Ming Jih-Pao in Mandarin, 11 12 1974, accessed through Readex.

61 Eidgenössisches Luftamt, Bericht der Vorgespräche über ein Luftverkehrsabkommen Schweiz – Volksrepublik China vom 11.–16. Juni 1972 in Peking, 4. Juli 1972, Ref. 14/China-Ae, p. 2. Available ar dodis: https://dodis.ch/35859. Last accessed on 12 August 2022.

62 Ibid.

63 Ibid.

particularly Tokio. The Chinese head of delegation assured that while access to Beijing continued to be restricted for foreign companies, an opening was just a matter of time.[64] While technical issues continued to be linked to political issues in the PRC as discussed above, this was only partially the case with regard to these treaties. On the one hand, the Chinese side strongly insisted on reciprocity and mutual benefit – by granting just as many entry points for Swiss planes in China as Switzerland would grant. On the other, worries by the Swiss embassy in Beijing that critical exhibitions on the fate of Tibetan refugees held in Bern, which had caused some (albeit mild) Chinese protest[65], might negatively influence the negotiations were unfounded:

> "[Earlier] the Tibet-refugees were named "former slave traders" and the activities of supporting circles in Switzerland anti-chinese and harmful for the developing [bilateral] relations. [This time] The Chinese interlocutor was extremely friendly and declared, that solely his worries about the good relationships caused his open intervention. [...] Although this exchange, compared to earlier occasions, took place in an extremely amiable way, it would not be surprising if it was the beginning of a new, adamant push of the Chinese on the Tibet issue."[66]

Similarly, the leaving Swiss ambassador Albert-Louis Natural noted that the visit of the Dalai Lama to Switzerland in 1973 had not caused even the slightest criticism by Chinese authorities.[67] When years later, based on the aviation agreement, Swissair was able to operate its inaugural flight to Beijing, federal councillor Willy Ritschard was received by a rising politician: Hua Guofeng, then minister of national security. Impressed by their counterpart who did not engage in political ritual or ideological orthodoxy, the Swiss delegation noted that again, there had been not the least allusions to the "little Tibetan or Taiwanese clouds" – but that Hua would certainly have a role to play "at the moment of succession".[68]

The perception of China as an alternative, offering a different path in international relations beyond mere non-alignment was expressed by the Maltese prime minister during a visit to China in April 1972:

> "Fortunately, not all the big countries of today want to engage in the old colonialist power game. China is today one of the biggest and most powerful countries and yet China has repeatedly given evidence of wanting to establish an international system

64 Ibid., p. 6, para. 326.

65 Ambasuisse, Peking, Telegramm Nr. 34, 2. 6.1972, 11h10. Available at dodis: dodis.ch/35822. Last accessed on 12 August 2022.

66 Ibid. Translation by the author.

67 Ambassade de Suisse en Chine, Rapport de fin de mission, 24 juin 1975, Réf : 004.5 – NT/PI/vi, p. 2. Available at dodis : dodis.ch/37707. Last accessed on 12 August 2022.

68 Ambassade de Suisse en Chine, Vol inaugural Swissair, les entretiens de M. Willy Ritschard, Conseiller fédéral, et de M. Thalmann, Secrétaire général, Pékin, le 14 avril 1975, Ref. p.B.15.21.Cha, pp. 9–10. Available at dodis: dodis.ch/37728. Last accessed on 12 August 2022. Translation by the author.

> in which it will be impossible for one nation to subjugate another economically, politically or ideologically."[69]

An important aspect of the newly construed Chinese foreign policy was a marked rise in technical exchange activities, most notably in 1972, which foreshadowed the later turn towards technological progress as the main means to achieve economic development. Various industrial and technical missions were dispatched from China to Japan, such as a "chemical fibres investigation group" (ten persons), a "shipbuilding technical investigation mission" (twelve persons), a "work machinery investigation commission" (twenty persons), a "metallurgical investigation commission" (fifteen persons), a "television industry investigation commission" (twelve persons), a "rubber investigation commission" (eight persons) and a "mining investigation commission". Also, in early 1973, a "textile technical delegation" was sent to Britain. On the other hand, invitations going beyond the controlled environment of the Canton Fair were issued to foreign companies directly, for example, to the Radio Corporation of America (RCA) and the International Business Machines Corporation (IBM) in the United States to negotiate on the import of electronics to China. Moreover, Norwegian companies were invited to hold a technical forum in Beijing, as was the Tokyo Can Company. The British government accepted an invitation to hold a British Industries Technical exhibition in Beijing, where more than 340 British firms exhibited their products.[70]

Invitations to other industrialised countries to present their production capabilities in China were issued as well, with moderate success. An Austrian industrial exhibition held in Peking in April 1974 was visited by Vice Premier Li Xiannian as well as the highest officials of the State Planning Commission, the Ministry of Foreign Trade (MoFT) and the China Council for the Promotion of International Trade (CCPIT).[71] A similar Swiss industrial technology exhibition (Swiss Industrial and Technological Exhibition SITEX) taking place from the 28th of August to the 10th of September of the same year was visited by Deng Xiaoping and a comparable delegation of high-ranking officials.[72] Over 200 Swiss companies were represented, the originally announced number of Chinese participants was surpassed by more than 30'000 (150'000 in total, more than 10'000 per day). The SITEX also encompassed around 150 technical symposia, where specific technologies, products and applications were presented in depth.[73] The Swiss Office for export promotion (*Office Suisse d'Expansion Commerciale*, OSEC) reported that only "technologically most advanced products" were desired as exhibits by the Chinese side. This was not

---

69 Foreign Broadcast information Service, Maltese Prime Minister's Speech, Peking NCNA International Service in English, 1819 GMT, 02 04 1972 B, accessed through Readex.

70 Current Chinese Communist Trends, Taipei Chung-kung Yen-chiu, 05 1973, p. 36.

71 Foreign Broadcast Information Service, Visits Austrian Industrial Fair, Peking NCNA in English, 1554 GMT 05 04 1974 B, accessed through Readex.

72 Foreign Broadcast Information Service, Teng Hsiao-Ping Visits Swiss Industrial Technology Exhibit, Peking NCNA in English, 1525 GMT, 1308 1974 B, accessed through Readex.

73 China – Reise 1974, Ergänzende Information von Botschafter Probst zum "volet économique" anlässlich der Botschafterkonferenz 1974 (4. September 1974), Beilage Nr. IV, p. 7. Available at dodis: dodix.ch/37654. Last accessed on 12 August 2022.

deemed an issue, particularly as quality was given preference over price by Chinese buyers.[74] During the still limited but significant Chinese foreign trade boom of 1974, trade and agricultural delegations of countries such as Brazil[75] and Sweden[76] were met by high-ranking officials as well.

While the application of the Three-Worlds Theory legitimised an opening towards certain capitalist nations, other political sensitivities remained relevant. As an example, talks between the Japanese Toyota Motor Sales Co. and the Chinese National Machinery Export and Import Cooperation on new shipments of cars to China were immediately suspended after representatives of Toyota referred to Taiwan as the "Republic of China". The Chinese market nevertheless proved to be too important for having the emerging business relations endangered by political semantics. Toyota admitted its "fault" immediately and sent a clarifying letter to Beijing, accompanied by a personal apology by Shoichiro Toyoda, vice president and part of the founding family of the major corporation. The Toyota Company promised to continue "to observe the spirit of the Tanaka-Enlai Communiqué".[77]

On the other hand, a Chinese delegation on a trade mission to Japan in fall 1973 underlined that there was no general objection to trade between Japan and the ROC, as long as no action was taken by Japanese firms that would imply the recognition of the ROC as a separate government.[78] The head of the Chinese delegation even took the stance that the "four principles" issued by Zhou Enlai as guiding posts for Chinese foreign relations had been "superseded" – at least with regard to Chinese–Japanese relations – by the Tanaka-Zhou Enlai Communiqué and that Toyota had "learned its lesson". He signalled that China always honoured its treaties. The four principles reflected past approaches: First, recognise that boundary disputes are the result of imperialism and unequal treaties. Second, do not assert claims to traditional tributary areas, nor assert older historical claims. Third, negotiate new boundaries based upon earlier boundary agreements (despite the fact that imperialist-era agreements were forced upon a weak China). Fourth, maintain China's "national stand", but avoid "big nation chauvinism."[79]

---

74 Schweizerische Zentrale für Handelsförderung, Interner Bericht über den Besuch in der Volksrepublik China vom 20. bis 31. Oktober 1972 betreffend die Durchführung einer Schweizerischen Industrie-Ausstellung in Peking 1974, verfasst von Dr. H. J. Halbheer, Stellv. Direktor und Leiter des Sitzes Zürich der OSEC. Available at dodis: dodis.ch/35904. Last accessed on 12 August 2022.

75 Foreign Broadcast Information Service, Li Hsien-Nien Meets Brazilian Exporters Delegation, Peking NCNA in English, 1646 GMT, 11 04 1974 B, accessed through Readex.

76 Foreign Broadcast Information Service, Meeting with Hua Kuo-Feng, Peking NCNA In English, 1243 GMT, 25 09 1974 B, accessed through Readex.

77 US Department of State, Electronic Telegram, PRC Halts Talks with Toyota Over Roc Issue, 7 September 1973, 02:30, PlusD, ID: 1973TOKYO11490_b.

78 US Department of State, Electronic Telegram, Chinese Economic Mission Concludes Visit to Japan, 12 October 1973, 08:30, PlusD, ID: 1973TOKYO13258_b.

79 Hyer Eric, China's Policy of Conciliation and Reduction and its Impact on Boundary Negotiations and Settlements in the Early 1960s, CWIHP Working Paper 85, December 2017, available at: https://www.wilsoncenter.org/publication/chinas-policy-conciliation-and-reduction-and-its-impact-boundary-negotiations-and, last accessed on 10 May 2020.

Miscellaneous sports and new partners

Establishing diplomatic relations and expanding trade with China was more than once attempted using international exchanges in the area of sports – beyond the famous US ping-pong teams sent to China. The visit of the national badminton team of Thailand to China between the 7th and 20th of August 1973 was accompanied by two officers of the Thai Ministry of Foreign Affairs, who used the occasion to prospect for the future development of trade relations.[80] In a press conference held shortly after the visit, Thai Prime Minister General Thanom Kittikachorn, on being asked by a journalist about the concrete consequences of the sports team visit with regard to a possible expansion of trade, emphasised the common history of trade relations and depicted future prospects optimistically:

> "We have known throughout that relations between Thailand and China have existed since ancient times because we Thais came from China and [we] originally lived in China. It is true that relations between us have existed for over 2000 years, as stated by the deputy Premier of the People's Republic of China to the Thai Badminton team that went to Peking last month [...] we are of the view that contacts between the peoples of the two countries, dating back to ancient times, should be continued."[81]

Using professional sports as a door-opener was extended to other disciplines, as Kittikachorn explained. After the return of the badminton team to Thailand, a Thai table tennis team went to take part in the tri-continental table tennis contests held in Peking. Thailand would soon have the opportunity to welcome a badminton team from China, returning the visit. Further, technicians "such as medical groups" were slated to exchange dialogue in the future.

> "Trade with the China Mainland will most probably be started in the near future [...] consideration will have to be paid to goods we will buy from China and what goods we have it needs, in order to preserve a proper balance of trade to the greatest extent possible. Under no circumstances must anybody be allowed to buy or sell anything as he pleases. All goods China offers to sell us will have to be considered by the Minister of Commerce first in order to decide whether we really need those respective goods [...] as well as whether we could buy tham [sic!] elsewhere at lower prices."[82]

Shortly after, during a regular weekly meeting, the Thai cabinet decided to make intergovernmental trade with China possible by amending the Revolutionary Party Announcement No. 53, which had until then prohibited the entry of Chinese goods into Thailand. The Decree had been introduced in 1959 in order to restrict contacts with communist states in order to protect the stability of the state, was progressively eliminated

80 US Department of State, Electronic Telegram, Comments on Recent Visit To China, 6 September 1973, 04:53, PlusD, ID: 1973BANGKO13889_b.

81 US Department of State, Electronic Telegram, Prime Minister Thanom On Trade With China, 24 September 1973, 10:46, PlusD, ID: 1973BANGKO14918_b.

82 Prime Minister Thanom on Trade with China, ID: 1973BANGKO14918_b.

and finally repealed after the overthrow of the Thai military regime in October 1973.[83] A new governmental corporation in the Thai Ministry of Commerce was established. Plans to control the new Chinese trade on a case-by-case price and quantity negotiations for purchase and sale drew criticism from businesses but was strictly implemented as the risk of an imbalance of trade was estimated to be substantial.[84]

These worries persisted, as on the 22nd of December 1975, fourteen local firms were reported by the Bangkok Post to have applied to the Thai Foreign Trade Department to allow imports of products on which import restrictions had been imposed – light industrial and agricultural goods such as textiles, fruit and herbs. Local businessmen on the other hand, it was reported, had objected strongly to the import of Chinese goods in general, claiming that these would damage the local industry which was not perceived as sufficiently competitive and result in a loss of foreign exchange. USLO commented that there was a clear conflict between these worries and a pronounced Chinese desire to influence the trade balance in the longer run in their favor – minimizing imports to China while maximizing exports.[85]

In his memoirs, the political leader of Singapore Lee Kuan Yew noted how Beijing quietly changed its stance towards the rapidly modernising and quite authoritarian city-state:

> "In those capitals where we [Singapore] were represented, our heads of mission were invited to China's national day receptions. China's priority then was to get as many governments as possible to close ranks against the Soviet Union and the check the expansion of its influence into Southeast Asia. [...] By 1971 China stopped public attacks on the Singapore government. That year, the Bank of China's branch in Singapore hoisted the Singapore flag on our national day, something it had not done before."[86]

Lee stressed that bilateral trade with China had always been in favour of the latter, the city-state being the second most important source of foreign exchange after Hong Kong. Still, economic relations were hampered by bureaucracy on both sides: all firms e. g. of Singaporean Chinese that dealt with the PRC needed to register with a government agency that controlled trade with socialist economies. Every Chinese franchise required government permission.[87] Further bilateral contacts followed, again on the basis of sports diplomacy, already in 1971 as Lee remembered. These contacts did not come without undesired expressions of Chinese soft power even in rising Singapore:

> "The first contact came through "ping pong diplomacy" in 1971. We allowed a Singapore ping-pong team to accept an invitation to play at the Afro-Asia Table Tennis Friendship

83 CAMILLERI JOSEPH, Southeast Asia in China's Foreign Policy, Institute of Southeast Asian Studies of Singapore ISEAS, Occasional Paper No. 29, April 1975, p. 30.

84 US Department of State, Electronic Telegram, Thailand Decides to Trade Directly with The People's Republic of China, 25 September 1973, 10:58, ID: 1973BANGKO15000_b.

85 US Department of State, Electronic Telegram, Thai-PRC Trade Negotiations, 8 January 1976, 05:12, PlusD, ID: 1976BANGKO00393_b.

86 LEE KUAN YEW, From Third World to First, The Singapore Story: 1965–2000, Singapore 2000, p. 637.

87 Ibid., p. 638.

> Games in Beijing. A few months later, a second delegation went for the Asian Table Tennis Union. We then accepted a Chinese offer to send their ping-pong team for a friendly visit to Singapore the following year, a few months after [US-] President Nixon had been to China. We had refused two previous offers, one of a troupe of acrobats, the other a Beijing trade mission. Raja [Rajaratnam] as foreign minister thought a third rebuff would be unnecessarily offensive. [During the matches] I was angered when a large part of the audience jeered at the home team and shouted slogans in praise of Mao. I publicly castigated these infantile left-wingers as Singapore's 'mini-Maos'."[88]

Even old alliances lost some of their meaning when it came to the development of trade relations. Since 1973, various government representatives and businesspeople from the Republic of Korea had tried unsuccessfully to establish contacts with Chinese officials in Hong Kong, as the Chinese side had not answered any queries in this direction. This changed in late 1974, despite the sensitivity contacts with the former military adversary that bore notably for China's North Korean ally. As the Hong Kong Standard reported on the 4th of November 1974, businesses in Seoul had reached agreement with a Chinese trading firm over the delivery of 1000 tons of red pepper – a response to the demand caused by a poor Korean pepper crop that year, leading to skyrocketing prices especially during the ongoing kimchi preparation season.[89]

These worries were not unfounded, albeit with a protectionist motive. The PRC was planning to stage the largest trade exhibition ever held in Bangkok, in March 1976; CCPIT announced that 300–500 tons of goods of 3'000 varieties, and about 200'000 pieces in all would be displayed in a 25'000 square meter space in a newly erected shopping centre complex called the "Bangkok Bazaar", lying between Rajdamri road and Chitlom Road, based on an agreement reached between Lu Fung-Chun, a Council representative and the managing director of the company owning the Bazaar. In contrast to the state-to-company sales at the Canton Fair in China, many of the displayed goods would be available for sale to the public – ranging from handicrafts from the provinces and light industrial goods such as tools, household goods, sports goods, readymade clothes, fruit and other foodstuffs.[90]

An important consequence of the Three Worlds Theory was that the general Chinese stance towards the project of European economic integration was modified. Visiting Dutch parliamentarians in 1973, Zhou Enlai had underlined that "America and Russia are not to be trusted", and that "Europe must build her own strength". To the French President Pompidou, Zhou also expressed his support for the accession of Britain, Denmark and Ireland in the same year, telling him that China

---

88 Ibid.

89 US Department of State, Electronic Telegram, PRC-South Korean Trade Contact in Hong Kong, 6 November 1974, 02:20, PlusD, ID: 1974HONGK12040_b.

90 US Department of State, Electronic Telegram, Thai-PRC Trade, 3 February 1976, 03:30, PLusD, ID: 1976BANGKO02204_b.

> "supports the peoples of Europe in uniting themselves to support their sovereignty and independence [...] the cause of European unity, if it is carried out well, will contribute to the improvement of the situation in Europe and the whole world."[91]

Underlining that China did not believe in *détente* between the two superpowers, Zhou Enlai told member of the Swiss Federal Council Max Petitpierre during a meeting on the fifth of May 1973 in Beijing that on the other hand, reinforcing the NATO and thus the process of European integration was absolutely in the interest of the socialist state. The only thing Zhou expressed concern about was a lack of vigilance of the Europeans vis-à-vis the soviet Union.[92] The rising interest of the Chinese MoFT also found its expression in the establishment of an autonomous division for European Affairs in 1972. This pivot was registered within the European Community as well. As all the nine member states recognised the PRC by 1974 – Ireland having been the last in 1972 – the path was open for the Community to seek its own relationship with Beijing. Recognising Japan as the Community's principal rival for industrial trade with China, it was realised that formal relations would strengthen the nine's position, as a background document by the EC information service claimed. EC Commission Vice President Christopher Soames noted in a speech before the British Overseas Banking Association in London on February 5, 1973:

> "We are glad to note China's increasing interest in the enlarged European Community and are conscious of the human and economic potential of the vast country. It is too early to see just how our future relations could develop, but there is surely scope for the tenuous links between us being strengthened to our mutual economic advantage and in ways that could also bring real political benefits".[93]

Shortly after, in May 1973, EC Commission president François Xavier-Ortoli openly declared that the Community was ready to establish relations with China, "if she wishes".[94] The doors were open for the Chinese trade expansion towards the European continent and beyond. Affirming the allegiance of China with Western Europe, an article in Renmin Ribao assessed the decline of superpowers referred to Lenin's analysis of imperialism to explain that the Soviet "revisionists" were attempting to expand their "colonial empire" in Eastern Europe to the West.[95] Even Switzerland, frequently praised for its neutrality by Chinese politicians and diplomats, was assessed on the basis of its contribution to European unity. According to Swiss ambassador to China Heinz Langenbacher in October 1975, this position had its advantages for the diplomatic profession: once defined, such

---

91 China and the European Community, AEI, Document Nr. 56842.

92 Ambassade de Suisse en Chine, Visite de M. Petitpierre à Pékin, Pékin le 16 mai 1973, Réf. 101.0, 712.0 – NT/hw, pp. 3–5. Available at dodis: dodis.ch/37713. Last accessed on 12 August 2022.

93 The World Economy: Towards a New Consensus, Tuesday, 1 July 1975, AEI, Document No. 8493, available at: http://aei.pitt.edu/8493/, last accessed on 1 May 2020.

94 China and the European Community, 22 May 1974, AEI, Background note to Document No. 56842 of 22 May 1974, available at: http://aei.pitt.edu/56842/1/BN_9.74.pdf, last accessed on 1 May 2020.

95 Foreign Broadcast Information Service, People's Daily assesses superpowers' decline, contention, Peking NCNA in English, 2115 GMT, 27 09 1974 B, accessed through Readex.

a stance was persistently adhered to by Chinese officials. He quoted one of his European colleagues in Beijing:

> "I could do any nonsense here without affecting our good bilateral relations, as long as China has set the European flag on fairweather [Schönwetter]. And currently, it flutters merrily in the east wind."[96]

In this spirit, in a speech on the "current world situation" at the political department of Tientsin city, Minister of Foreign Affairs Qiao Guanhua underlined that while the French leaders and the leadership of the PRC did not belong "to the same family", China would support their "resistance against Soviet Russia and America" while not subscribing to the current system of France, which had to be "overthrown in the future". In the same speech, however, he dismissed the idea of exporting the revolution at the current stage.[97] Apparently, the limitation of the Chinese view on international affairs to two possible outcomes – world war or world revolution – as it had been described by member of the Swiss Federal Council Pierre Graber a year earlier had become a thing of the past as new alliances had become possible.

Like anything that concerned economic policy, the opening of Chinese foreign relations was all but undisputed within China; remarkably, discussions mostly concerned the way diplomacy was to be conducted towards countries of the Second World than whether they were to be conducted at all. In her speech given to diplomatic cadres in Beijing in March 1975[98] – shortly after the fourth National People's Congress and the announcement of the Four Modernisations – Jiang Qing, Mao Zedong's wife and one of the leading figures of the Gang of Four, underlined the PRC's allegiance with developing countries and their importance for the revolutionary cause in the longer term. In passing, she did not refrain from branding US Secretary of State Henry Kissinger as an "adventurist and defeatist"[99]. Her instructions, mostly directed at the importance of diplomats retaining contact with the central government in Beijing to strengthen party leadership, were nevertheless quite pragmatic:

---

96 Ambassade de Suisse en Chine, Die Schweiz und China, Peking, den 24. Oktober 1975, Ref. PB Nr. 36 / LB / we, pp. 5–6. Available at dodis: dodis.ch/37717. Last accessed on 12 August 2022. Translation by the author.

97 And even making the point that self-reliance was a uniting concept within the unsuccessful United Front with the Kuomintang: "That so-and-so Chiang Kai-shek is still better than most. He is not superstitious. When we fought him, he proposed 'independence and self-strengthening' against our 'self-reliance'. One may say that he still has some Chinese backbone. It is a pity that it is used in the wrong place." Joint Publications Research Service, Ch'iao Kuan-Hua on World Situation and Foreign Policy, "Ch'iao Kuan-hua's Speech on the Current World Situation and Communist China's Foreign Policy", Taipei Fei-Ch'ing Yueh-Pao, Original in Mandarin, Vol. 18, No. 3, 05 10 1975, accessed through Readex.

98 Chiang Ching's Address to Diplomatic Cadres, March 1975.

99 Adding that "Both Nixon and Kissinger have admitted that the US policy of the past, i. e., the policy of strength pursued after World War II, is unfeasible today. The United States should return to the world of reality and should not dabble in interfering with the sovereignty and interests of other countries". Ibid.

> "The task of the diplomatic front line is different from that on other front lines. Because diplomatic workers have to spend a considerably longer time working abroad, our demands of them cannot be the same as those on our people at home. You cannot go to the streets in New York or Paris to put up big-character posters criticizing the foreign minister or the ambassador. Nor can you interfere in the domestic affairs of others by presenting your views to the president of a foreign country of shelling him with heavy artillery."[100]

In a similar speech to diplomatic personnel of consular rank in the same month, Jiang Qing added with reference to guidelines for the behaviour of Chinese diplomatic staff abroad that "just because an ambassador attends a banquet with capitalists, one must not consider him as being corrupted by the bourgeoisie".[101] In international economic relations, practical thinking was pursued not only by China, but also new partners formerly known for their rather critical stance towards the socialist state. The then-deputy chairman of the Singapore Economic Development Board, Tang I Fang, showed interest in joining the new China trade by accompanying Rajaratnam on a visit to the PRC, in the spring of 1975. He reported back to his ministry that while the state of Singapore had "an anti-communist government", the very same would welcome the further development of relations, especially an expansion of trade which could redress existing imbalances in favour of China and provide impetus for Singapore's industrial development program. The official reaction of the PRC was not adverse, thanking the potential new partner for this "straight talking", noting that Singapore – acknowledged by China as a member of the Third World – was to be allowed to go its own way.[102]

Accordingly, the pragmatic instructions reflected in Jiang Qing's speech were valid even more in the domain of economic and trade diplomacy. Tang noted that his delegation was treated very courteously, being taken out to restaurants in the public, proposing toasts to the President and Prime Minister of Singapore. Chinese officials were also reported to have specifically indicated that imports from factories in Singapore to China could include those from foreign-owned, including US firms. Tang offered to be of assistance by liaising with the USLO when it came to legal questions around the application of US export controls to China, in particular with regard to electronic components such as integrated circuits.[103] The visit also resulted in some concrete business: China ordered two oil-exploration rigs at 60 million USD from Singaporean companies for delivery within fourteen to eighteen months – Tang added that, in his view, the Chinese side would order more rigs soon, as the country was giving priority to the oil sector.[104]

After Hua Guofeng was named acting premier in 1976, a next wave of economic diplomacy followed, in particular from the already experienced Japanese business com-

100 Ibid.

101 Ibid. and as quoted in Taiwanese media: Joint Publications Research Service, Chiang Ch'ing's Address to Diplomatic Cadres, Taipei Fei-ch'ing Yueh-pao, Original in Chinese, 05 10 1975, accessed through Readex.

102 US Department of State, Electronic Telegram, Singapore Mission to PRC, 3 April 1975, 10:27, PlusD, ID: 1975SINGAP01324_b.

103 Ibid.

104 Ibid.

munity. It included an increasingly diverse array of industries. As Kyodo called it, a "high-powered" economic mission in March 1976 of the Kansai Economic Federation (*Kankeiren*), led by Yoshishige Ashihara, chairman of Kansai Electric Power Co., left Osaka with the goal to "Discuss ways for [the] expansion of Sino-Japanese trade". It included chairmen of general trading companies (*sogo sosha*), such as Sumitomo as well as the Toyobo Textile Co. The delegates even brought their spouses with them.[105] With regard to China trade, the goal of its expansion was not only directed at the import side – beyond oil – but strongly so.

In addition to positive prospects with regard to the future development, the increasingly dim economic prospects in Japan might have been an encouraging factor; while inflation continued to increase through 1976 as a consequence of internal and external factors, and domestic demand stagnated, Japan's total trade surplus continued to expand totalling nearly six billion USD for the first half of the year. The surplus was also due to weak domestic demand and was not perceived as beneficial, mostly to the risk of imported inflation it presented – while import promotion programmes were announced for August of the same year – which were mostly with regard to monetary instruments such as discounts on import bills denominated in Yen and subsidised loans issued by the Bank of Japan. The so-called "Yen-shift" also aimed at avoiding monetary intervention to appreciate the Yen – which might have interrupted the slow recovery underway. The Bank of Japan named markups by enterprises aided by government-supported production cuts, the rise in international commodity prices and an "unexpectedly" swift increase in demand for some manufactured products as main reasons – two of which were at least related to the international economic crisis.[106] On the other hand, Japan was criticised for its substantial increases in exports, on which monetary policies would have less of an influence as eighty percent of exports from Japan were invoiced in USD – and partly financed with USD.[107]

Lee Kwan Yew was invited for a lengthy visit of China, spending almost two weeks (10th to 23rd of May 1976) in the PRC, meeting three times officially with Hua Guofeng and even once with the already frail Mao Zedong. Expecting the Chinese side to push for liaison offices or trade representatives in a similar vein as earlier, trade-oriented contacts, the Singaporean delegation was rather stupefied by the Chinese focus on the Three Worlds Theory and the status of Taiwan and the Malayian communist party. Despite this emphasis on political issues and the "lack of sophistication and subtlety" of Hua compared to the recently deceased Zhou Enlai in the eyes of Singapore foreign minister Rajaratnam, it was finally Lee who had reservations with regard to economic aspects. They concerned namely a proposed Chinese trade mission to Singapore. Hua insisted that although important differences between the two countries existed given the different social systems, they did not matter because both sides had found "many common points

105 Foreign Broadcast Information Service, 'High-Powered' Economic Mission Leaves for PRC, Tokyo Kyodo in English, 0110 GMT, 25 03 1976 TK, accessed through Readex.

106 US Department of State, Electronic Telegram, Financial and Economic Developments – Week of July 15–21, 21 June 1976, 08:55, PlusD, ID: 1976TOKYO10975_b.

107 US Department of State, Electronic Telegram, Financial and Economic Developments – Sept 2 – Sept 8, 8 September 1976, 09:20, PlusD, ID: 1976TOKYO13483_b.

through a frank exchange of views". Lee on the other hand noted that the front page publicity in Renmin Ribao of his recent meeting with Mao would "not be received with joy in Southeast Asia" and sending a mission to Singapore should wait until "our neighbours' suspicions from this publicity had subsided." The more China would embrace Singapore as a "kinsman country", the greater the neighbours' suspicions.[108] The shadow of Mao was long and lingering.

The impact of the intense earthquakes around Tangshan on the 28th July 1976 halted the expansion of foreign relations as official visits were called off and visitors were asked to leave China for the time being. The event also overshadowed the remarkable opening of the Beidaihe beach resort to foreign tourists on the first of June 1976, with the 99 guests being guided home via Beijing in a designated PLA aircraft on the 29th of July 1976.[109] Trade diplomacy nevertheless continued.

The US National Council on United States-China Trade (NCUSCT) was formed in 1973 to promote and facilitate trade between the United States and the PRC. Although trade between the two countries had resumed in June 1971, the impetus for a trade council came from President Nixon's visit to China in February 1972. At the end of the visit, a joint communique addressing the issue of trade was issued in Shanghai, stating,

> "Both sides view bilateral trade as another area from which mutual benefit can be derived, and agreed that economic relations based on equality and mutual benefit are in the interest of the people of the two countries. They agree to facilitate the progressive development of trade between their two countries."[110]

The NCUSCT became the main facilitator for US-China trade with CCPIT as its counterpart. In a conversation between Christopher Phillips, the president of the NCUSCT, and Li Quan, vice chairman of CCPIT, in the summer of 1976, the former reiterated that he was not able to say when a canceled visit of an US agricultural chemicals delegation could be rescheduled. Nevertheless, future visits of US delegations from the mining, construction and petroleum equipment industries were discussed. According to Li, a NCUSCT delegation that planned to visit China in October would be welcome and free to visit all cities it was interested in. Another item concerned an issue that had risen in importance with the increase in formalised trade relations: a visit of the US legal affairs committee to discuss arbitration in trade matters.

On the other hand, the question of the status of Taiwan remained an obstacle, as Li-Quan insisted that a visit by a representative of Union Carbide would be "not convenient" as a subsidiary of the company had joined the US/ROC Economic Council – "If Union Carbide takes steps to have its subsidiary withdrawn, the CCPIT will consider this fact".[111] Similarly, the PRC withdrew from the Izmir Trade Fair in Turkey in the same

108 LEE 2000, pp. 641, 648–649.

109 Foreign Broadcast Information Service, Foreigners Restricted, Tokyo Kyodo in English, 0007 GMT, 30 07 1976 OW, accessed through Readex.

110 Quoted from: CHEN LUNG-CHU (ed.), The U.S.-Taiwan-China Relationship in International Law and Policy, New York 2016, p. 359.

111 US Department of State, Electronic Telegram, CCPIT-NCUSCT Relations, 3 August 1976, 08:08, PlusD, ID: 1976PEKING01490_b.

month, with the director of the fair Cumhur Guruz stating that it had learned that a Taiwanese firm planned to exhibit – after having demonstrated the same policy in connection with a Montreal trade fair before.[112]

Further, contacts pursued with other non-aligned states served as an opportunity to demonstrate Beijing's "universalist" approach to foreign policy in connection with the expansion of the trade network, as with the visit of Papua New Guinea's Prime Minister Michael Thomas Somare to China from the 11th to the 17th of October 1976. Vice Premier Li Xiannian provided China's views during a general discussion of foreign relations that was – by accident – held in parallel with the consolidation of Hua Guofeng's leadership in Beijing, with the arrest of the Gang of Four. These included the well-known denunciation of the Soviet Union, but explicitly not of the USA – except in the form of the assertion that the rivalry between the two superpowers would inevitably result in a war not desired by the PRC. Both countries decided to initiate a series of trade missions pertaining to specific items – copper, copra and lumber – as being cited by the USLO. Also, exchanges with regard to the Chinese model of agricultural management were discussed, with the possibility of the Papua New Guinea's minister for primary industry visiting later to examine its practical aspects. Somare was quoted as appreciating Chinese "efficiency" but abhorring the coercive aspects of the regime.[113]

Secretary of Foreign Affairs and Trade Tony Siaguru described the routine of Chinese diplomats in the handling of delegations, stating that the delegation had been closely cloistered and the movement limited to official scheduling. When people were encountered on the street, Siaguru noted their lack of "spontaneity", as "they have a group through Peking each week and simply change the banners".[114] Similarly, Lee Kuan Yew remembered his arrival in Beijing in May of 1976, rather irritated by the intensity of political rituals:

> "That afternoon we were flown in their [Chinese] British-built Trident to Beijing where a welcome ceremony awaited us at the airport. I inspected a guard of honour mounted by units of the [PLA], the navy and the air force after the PLA band played the Singapore and Chinese national anthems. Then some 2'000 schoolgrils in colourful costumes waved Singapore and Chinese paper flags and flowers, chanting 'Huan ying, huan ying' [welcome, welcome] and 'Re lie huan ying, Re lie huan ying' [warmly welcome, warmly welcome]. There was a large banner in Chinese which read 'Jian jue zhi chi xin jia po ren' [resolutely support the people of Singapore]. They did not express support for the government of Singapore.
> [...] We flew to Shanghai, to be greeted once more by dancing schoolgirls in gay-coloured clothes carrying paper flags and flowers. [...] The next morning they gave us a colourful send-off at the Canton railway station before we boarded the special train for Shenzhen. For the final time, hundreds of schoolgirls bounced up and down

---

112 US Department of State, Electronic Telegram, PRC withdraws from 45th Izmir International Trade Fair, August 20 – Sept. 30, 1976, 9 August 1976, 11:30, PlusD, ID: 1976IZMIR00245_b.

113 US Department of State, Electronic Telegram, Visit of PNG Prime Minister Somare to PRC OCT 11–17 and to the Philippines Oct 19–23, 3 November 1976, 05:05, PlusD, ID: 1976PORTM01206_b.

114 Ibid., paragraph C.

> carrying paper flags and flowers, chanting goodbye. I wondered how they could allow students to miss classes for such displays."[115]

The expansion of diplomatic relations that Beijing pursued consistently were not limited to industrialised countries of the west and developing countries. In August 1977, the first meeting between the highest ranks of China and Yugoslavia was announced as the result of a process of normalisation that had lasted almost seven years. Belgrade Radio Chief Editor Milutin Milenkovic noted in a commentary that the most important questions to be clarified between the two countries were the ways of changing the system of international economic relations and exchanges of natural resources, adding that China was "planning to join the ranks of the most highly developed countries of the world". With a view to "very important strategic-political reorganisations and re-examinations" of China's practice of socialist construction, Milenkovic noted the need to further examine this process.[116]

As he rightly observed, the PRC wanted to join the most advanced economies on the same level. One method to pursue this goal was the expansion of foreign trade, which had taken place in parallel and conjunction with the diplomatic offensive.

The expansion of Chinese foreign trade

As the emancipation from both foreigners in general and the concept of "free trade" that had been imposed on China by violent means in particular could be considered a founding principle of the PRC, the role of foreign trade was limited to the strictly necessary until the early 1970s. In specific areas and at various stages, it was nevertheless important. During the period of New Democracy, strategic goods for national defence were acquired by exchanging goods and currency with foreigners. The choice to lean-to-one-side and the first five-year plan brought a concentration on one main trade partner – the Soviet Union – and a first export-drive to avoid a trade deficit and dependency.[117] In 1978, a director working at the Peking Foreign Trade Institute summarised the Chinese position:

> "After the founding [of the People's Republic] we acted in accordance with the directives of Chairman Mao; we took over control of foreign trade; reformed the customs system; abrogated with immediate effect all the special rights of the imperialists in China; nationalized the customs service; freed ourselves from imperialist monopoly of foreign trade, foreign exchange, finance, navigation and transportation, insurance, commodity inspection, and arbitration; confiscated bureaucratic capital, set up state-owned foreign trade enterprises; gradually transformed private export firms; and thus put an end to old China's dependence upon imperialism in foreign trade. In the process,

115 Lee 2000, pp. 642, 652.

116 Foreign Broadcast Information Service, Belgrade Radio Previews Tito-Hua Kuo-Feng Talks, Commentary by Milutin Milenkovic, Belgrade Domestic Service in Serbo-Croatian, 1800 GMT, 29 08 1977 AU, accessed through Readex.

117 Hsiao 1977, pp. 10 f.

> we have transformed the semi-colonial foreign trade of old China into a new socialist foreign trade, controlled by the proletarian state power, completely independent, and serving the people. From then on, China's foreign trade has entered into a new period of development."[118]

While self-reliance as a programmatic term remained important as a strategic concept, both within the PRC and in its foreign relations, it did at no time amount to a course of absolute *autarky* – meaning the absence of economic and political exchanges with the rest of the world. The, as far as possible, independent accumulation of funds on all levels (the province independently from the central government, the commune independently from the province and the country independently from the rest of the world) to finance industrial development[119] did not imply anything like that.

Besides the remarkable increase of diplomatic relations discussed before, trade relations expanded as well beyond the well-known rapprochement with the USA.[120] These were, as the director of the Chinese Foreign Trade Department explained, still in 1978 conducted as *socialist* foreign trade based on political principles:

> "In her socialist economic construction China pays attention to cooperation and exchange with other countries on the basis of equality and mutual benefit. But she does not rely on others. The Chinese experience shows that the economy of a given country can be developed at a fairly fast pace provided the country relies on itself. On the contrary, reliance on foreign countries would only bind the people's hand and foot, hamper the progress of economic construction and harm political and economic independence."[121]

This course of non-interdependence resembles the foreign policy ideas promoted by Zhou Enlai as early as the early 1950s, eventually to be enshrined as the "five principles of peaceful coexistence" (*Panchsheel*), in the preamble of the Sino-Indian agreement on the status of Tibet of the 29th of April 1954.[122] In a way, the principle of peaceful coexistence that advocated non-interference in other countries' internal affairs and self-reliance in international economic affairs were two sides of the same coin, as both followed a spirit of non-alignment combined with the intent to cooperate in several areas. Nevertheless, the expansion of the economic limits of the possible as a political meta-objective allowed for new flexibilities in the domain of trade, moving away from strict non-interdependence for the sake of industrial development.

First, the organisation of foreign trade needed to be understood as an integral part of the unified planning system as well as of the general industrialisation paradigm of walled industrial cities and self-reliant peasants. While the line of decentralisation and self-reliance inside China allowed for a certain flexibility from the perspective of the central government, foreign trade was a different thing altogether. The fixed prices and prevailing *ex ante*-allocation of inputs in both the industrial and agricultural sector in the PRC

---

119 As presented in: China's socialist economy proves successful in 25 years, 0701 GMT, 24 09 1974 B.

120 On diplomatic relations, see in particular GARVER 2016 and above.

121 CHUNG 1978, p. 2.

122 LÜTHI 2020, p. 122.

framed the limits of the possible: volatility of prices as well as supply and demand on international markets were potentially destabilising factors. Foreign trade was therefore kept centralised[123] – under the direct control of the central government.

Regarded as a sector of the national economy, foreign trade was planned, based on a strategy akin to import substitution. In order to be sustainable, this approach needs to be implemented in parallel with the improvement of domestic efficiency, diminishing the need to indirectly subsidise domestic production by legally and physically blocking the access of buyers to cheaper foreign products. With the increasing availability of foreign products as well as of buying power, the relevance of the costs imposed by an import substitution strategy increased, as alternative sources abroad become increasingly real options compared to a situation where international markets are inaccessible for political, legal, physical or simply financial reasons.[124]. Accordingly, in principle, only goods complementary to domestic production were to be imported in the PRC, while a balanced current account was considered paramount.[125]

The foreign trade plans fell in two categories: the long-term programme and annual foreign trade plans. In setting up the latter, the MoFT was bound to the State Planning Commission's mandates within the plan and needed ratification by the State Council, but conducted its own process of consultations with local foreign trade departments, Party committees, enterprises and their own specialised trade corporations. While foreign trade in general was conducted through national corporations under the Ministry of Foreign Trade, with countries with which China did not maintain diplomatic relations, foreign trade was handled by the offices of CCPIT, in which the corporations were represented (comparable to trade promotion agencies existing other countries that are indirectly financed by governments including in market economies today).[126] Albeit the discourse on internal reforms of the system of economic planning was led on official papers and quite publicly, foreign economic policy itself was in the hands of small groups of experts in the MoFT who concluded treaties with foreigners annually.[127]

This undertaking was pursued with vigour: the trade volume of 1974 was more than three times the figure of 1970. Rising from about four to over fourteen billion USD between 1971 and 1976, while Chinese exports increased from about 1.6 billion to more than six billion USD over the same time span. With individual trade partners, the rise was even more pronounced. The entries concerning "Letters of Credit and Guarantee" with which the clearing of payments between the PRC and other countries was handled by the

123 In the hands of the Ministry of Foreign Trade, which the 1975 constitution placed directly under the State Council. See: Hsiao 1977, pp. 71 ff.

124 Which in economic literature refers to the increase of local production while reducing the consumption of imported goods, in so far as local production capacities allow for substitution. See e. g. Ershova Irina, Ershov Aleksei, Development of a Strategy of Import Substitution, in: Procedia Economics and Finance, No. 39, 2016, p. 621.

125 Economic Information & Agency, China's Foreign Trade and its Management, Hong Kong 1978.

126 Paxton John (ed.), The Statesman's Year-Book, Statistical and Historical Annual of the States of the World for the Year 1975–1976, London and Basingstoke 1975, p. 824.

127 As it is, in fact, in most nations. For an intriguing analysis of elite formation and function with regard to trade policy and its (legal) implementation, see: Fairbrother Malcolm, Elites, Democracy, and the Rise of Globalization, New York 2020.

Bank of China, grew from a nominal value of 700 million USD in 1971 to 4.7 billion USD in 1975.[128]

Foreign Trade Volume of the PRC, 1950–1976 (Million USD). Central Intelligence Agency, China: Foreign Trade Policy in the 1970s, National Foreign Assessment Center, Research Paper, ER 78–10455, pp. 4–6., available at: https://www.cia.gov/library/readingroom/docs/CIA-RDP80T00702A000200060012-0.pdf. Accessed on 1 May 2021. Graph by the author.

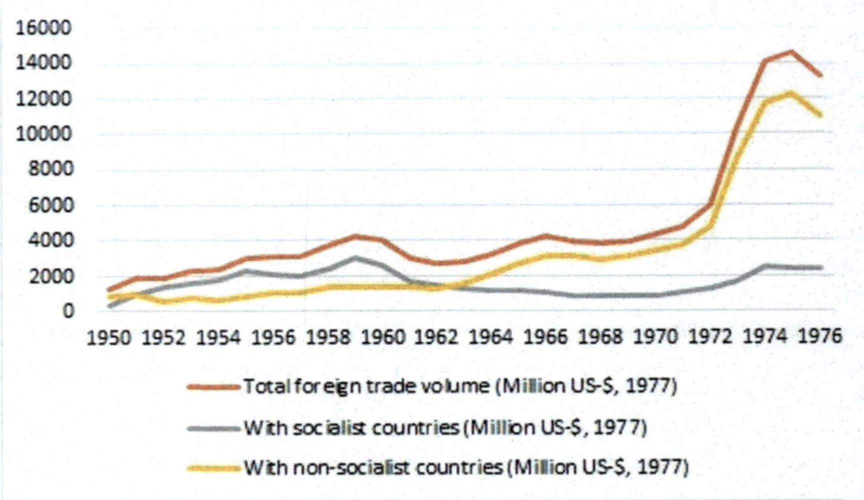

Nevertheless, despite increasing trade volumes, the avoidance of foreign debt remained the one central paradigm that limited the *marge de manoeuvre* for Chinese foreign trade and investment. The principle that the PRC was free of foreign debt and needed to remain so was frequently emphasised by the central government (first and foremost in comparison with the Soviet Union and other socialist states). In January 1974, Renmin Ribao published an optimistic outlook on financial matters which, particularly from a western European perspective of the time might, have sounded bitterly ironic:

> "The result of sticking to the budget [is] a balanced budget with a slight surplus. This has not only ensured funds for economic construction, but has also replenished the state's reserve funds. [...] In early 1965 we repaid in full ahead of schedule the loans extended to our country by the Soviet Union under Stalin. During the [...] Cultural Revolution, we redeemed in full all the national bonds issued during the early stages of national reconstruction. Our country has become a socialist state having neither external nor internal debts."[129]

128 Morrison Kent, Domestic Politics and Industrialization in China: The Foreign Trade Factor, in: Asian Survey, Vol. 18, No. 7, July 1978, pp. 691, 698.

129 Foreign Broadcast Information Service, People's Daily Article by Tsai Cheng: "Victory of Chairman Mao's Policy of ‚Building the Country by Self-Reliance and through Diligence and Thrift` – on the

This course seemed to be confirmed by macroeconomic developments in the region, where the rates of inflation spiked after 1972. It was regarded, to a large extent, as imported.[130] The optimistic outlook was even topped with a possible solution of China's need for foreign exchange that stood in contrast to self-reliance and the declared belief in the superiority of the Chinese way:

> "In the past, our country calculated the value of its foreign trade and foreign aid and other international economic exchanges on the basis of foreign currencies. However, according to the principle of equality and mutual benefit, more than 60 countries and regions have in recent years used the people's currency [the renminbi] to calculate the value of trade and settle accounts with our country. The capitalist world is now facing mounting financial and monetary difficulties. The crisis is becoming worse and it is having a very difficult time. On the other hand, the financial and monetary situation in our country is daily becoming more consolidated and stable. This has fully demonstrated the incomparable superiority of our country's socialist system."[131]

The official quarterly magazine "China's Foreign Trade" advertised the wide array of Chinese export goods: coal and cereals from Tibet, turtles and tuna from the South China Sea, ivory and jade, porcelains and lacquers, rosewood furniture, rattan, silver and gold jewellery, microscopes, medical apparatuses, electronic equipment, complete machinery plants for cotton textiles, rubber processing metal working and the like. Nevertheless, *Xinhua* reported in early 1974 that while energetic efforts had been made to increase exports, China still could not produce enough to meet foreign demand or satisfy requirements for quality, variety or pattern – an insight that matched the impression of foreign agents at the Canton Fair discussed above and motivated targeted investment in several sectors to produce more competitive goods. An important example was precisely the textile industry present at the Canton Fair. Beginning in 1975, the use of electronics in the production process was tested and implemented by certain plants in Peking to meet the demand of both the domestic and foreign markets for higher quality and quantity.[132]

In a brochure published by the Foreign Languages Press on the Chinese economy, the palette of products available to foreign buyers was praised perhaps in a rather forward-looking manner, insisting that "China's machine-tools, hardware, scientific instruments, meters, medical apparatus, bicycles, sewing-machines, cameras and other items find markets in many distant countries and regions" and promised improvement in manufactured goods, "especially light industrial items such as textiles and foodstuffs, and art and

Magnificent Achievements Scored by our country on the Financial and Monetary front", Peking Domestic Service in Mandarin, 0200 GMT, 13 01 1974, accessed through Readex.

130 For example, in Malaysia, inflation between 1972 and 1973 was up to 17.8 percent, in Singapore 22.9 percent, in Indonesia and South Vietnam well above 20 percent. See: De Silva, S.B.D., The Region: Economic Trends – Inflation, Industrialization, and Growth, in: Southeast Asian Affairs, 1975, pp. 5–14.

131 Article by Tsai Cheng, 0200 GMT, 13 01 1974.

132 Joint Publications Research Service, Textile Industry propagates electronic technology, Hong Kong Ta Kung Pao, Original in Mandarin, 10 10 1975, p. 6, accessed through Readex.

handicraft products. China now offers more patterns, colors and designs, while quality, packing and presentation have improved".[133]

That Chinese foreign trade should maintain a strict equilibrium of exchanges as a guiding principle was strictly communicated and repeatedly emphasised in publications within China as well as towards foreign trade partners. In exchanges with European diplomats and journalists, the cancellation of contracts with other partners in 1975 was openly explained with this policy to signal the Chinese insistence on balanced trade. The doubling of trade volumes between the two countries as well as the recently agreed establishment of a joint committee on trade exchanges, an upcoming Italian industrial exhibition in Tientsin and the participation of China in the Milan fair and the Florence artisan exhibit were emphasised by the Chinese trade official – which would be referred to today as location marketing.[134]

Moreover, a direct consequence of this policy was a high sensitivity for price and quality, as expressed in a declaration by Vice Minister Cai Shufan to Italian journalists in March 1975. While the growth in mutual trade exchange was seen as a positive thing, the "first motive" for which trade exchanges had not seen a greater development was because, on "some occasions", offers from Italian industries were perceived to be less competitive than those of other countries by Chinese buyers. Cai indicated that there were other opportunities approaching, particularly in the petrochemical, oil drilling and refining equipment, agricultural machines, electronics and transportation sectors. There, "better prospects [...] however, not in the immediate future" for Italo-Chinese exchange were expected, reflecting on the core economic policy lines of agricultural mechanisation and the development of the oil industry.

In the same vein, the benefits of self-reliance in the face of economic crisis were regularly praised by Chinese officials Cai denied accordingly that China was in any way affected by "the current economic crisis", indicating that it was "a phenomenon inherent in the logic of the capitalist system", recalling the lack of unemployment and price stability as well as the constant increase in agricultural and industrial production in the PRC.[135]

Cai stressed how China's principle to depend primarily on its own forces was particularly important in a moment of international economic crisis, as it "screened it from the turmoil of the world situation". At the same time, he admitted that the equilibrium of exchanges was challenged due to consequences of inflation on international prices as well as the restrictions on imports in "various countries"; this not only limited imports but also forced exports to the maximum in the attempt to "transfer on to others the burden of the crisis of the capitalist world". In western economics, what Cai made reference to here – for good reasons – is frequently and quite accurately referred to as "beggar-thy-neighbor". With regard to international trade, the term refers to an economic policy that benefits the country that implements it while harming that country's neighbours or trading partners. It usually takes the form of a quantitative of non-tariff trade barrier, imposed on the neighbours or trading partners. More recently, the practice of in-

133 CHINH 1974, p. 44.

134 Foreign Broadcast Information Service, Deputy Foreign Trade Minister on Basic PRC Directives, Rome Ansa in English, 0812 GMT, 18 03 1975 AU, accessed through Readex.

135 Deputy Foreign Trade Minister on Basic PRC Directives, 0812 GMT, 18 03 1975 AU.

tentionally devaluating the domestic currency to gain competitive advantage over them has gained some actuality. The term has been used to describe measures by governments taken in the wake of both the Great Depression of the early 1930s and the international economic crisis of the mid-1970s.[136]

Criticising joint ventures in Poland and the USSR undertaken with the Italian company Fiat[137], the vice minister repeated the readiness of China to accept "installment payments" as the "only form of facilitation", absolutely excluding the eventuality of opening up credit or allowing joint ventures as well as any kind of foreign investment. In the same manner, he excluded that China would make investments in turn, or take part in joint ventures in the Third World "for the exploitation of resources". Also in March 1975, the first secretary of the Central Committee of the Hungarian Socialist Party made very similar comments on the state of the national economy:

> "The economic and natural conditions of our fatherland are linked to the world economy by extensive relations. Our exports approach 50 percent of our national income. In the present stage of economic development, in order to raise our national income by one percent, we have to raise imports and exports in our foreign trade by some 1.5 to 2 percent. Therefore, processes and changes taking place in international economic life affect us to a large extent and we must always take them into account in our work. [...] Along with the acceleration in the inflation rate, the world market price of fuel and power sources and raw and basic materials rose by leaps and bounds. This was only slightly balanced by an increase in the price of finished goods. Consequently our foreign trade balance worsened and our national economy had to face significant losses.
>
> These changes are not temporary. In our economic work we must, now and in future, take into account the higher prices our country has to pay in world markets for the raw materials and sources of fuel and power we need. [...] despite external difficulties, we can attain continuing development in our national economy in the coming years at a rate approaching that of previous years, along with a continuing rise in the standard of living. The solution lies partly in better work and better use of our domestic economic resources and opportunities and partly in making far better use than so far of the excellent opportunities available within the economic cooperation of the socialist countries. The success of our work depends, first and foremost, on our own efforts. [...] We cannot put the blame on the international economic situation for shortcomings in our own economic work. The question is arising more forcefully: Are we making satisfactory use of our resources in our national economy?"[138]

136 Ibid. and Stiglitz Joseph E., Beggar-Thyself versus Beggar-Thy-Neighbour Policies: The Dangers of Intellectual Incoherence in Addressing the Global Financial Crisis, in: Southern Economic Journal, Vol. 66, No. 1, July 1999, pp. 1–38.

137 Deputy Foreign Trade Minister on Basic PRC Directives, 0812 GMT, 18 03 1975 AU.

138 Proposing another approach to solve the problem: "Building on the opportunities of the international division of labor and of being part of the world economy", criticising discriminatory measures taken by the US and the European Common Market. Foreign Broadcast Information Service, Kadar Speech, Speech by Janos Kadar, first secretary of the MSZMP Central Committee, at the opening session of 11th MSZMP Congress in Budapest, Budapest Domestic Service in Hungarian, 1326 GMT, 17 03 1975 LD, accessed through Readex.

With the fifth five-year plan, the importance of an intensified export drive was reinforced as a *Leitmotiv*. In February 1976, a senior representative of a Hong Kong-based bank controlled by the PRC assured the USLO that while allegiance to the principle of self-reliance would be upheld, "prospects will be very bright" for the expansion, in particular, with regard to imports to China. As a banker, he also expected a further intensification of the Chinese interest in foreign credits for "up to five years" to finance the import of capital equipment and technology. On the other hand, any form of joint ventures or other forms of capital participation would remain strictly excluded.[139]

This decisive element was handled differently by other socialist states, in particular China's main trade partners – although the political narrative allowing for joint ventures appears to have been difficult. When the Bulgarian Foreign Trade Minister visited Japan in November 1977, he asked for "industrial cooperation", which was estimated by the Japanese Foreign Office's second East Europe division director Ryoji Ondera to be a system, in which Japanese equipment, experts, materials and financing that would be provided to build plants in Bulgaria, the products of which would be either exported to Japan, or to third countries through Japanese trading companies. Ondera told USLO that Japanese companies, having little possibilities to export to Bulgaria otherwise, might be "more willing now to consider such a system than they have been in the past".[140]

The equally present senior editor of the Chinese controlled newspaper Ta Kung Pao added that the Taiwan issue would need to be solved for a meaningful expansion of trade with the US. Nevertheless, both sources confirmed and intensified the Chinese export-drive with "considerable emphasis on oil", with "very rich potential" of new oil fields near Canton.[141] Similarly, the USLO reported in August 1976 that Chinese trade officials, Li Quan of CCPIT and others, consistently took the position that reductions in Sino-US trade were only a temporary phenomenon "caused by economic factors", while the establishment of formal diplomatic relations would be a contributing factor.[142] As the Soviet press criticised at the time:

> "[...] the Maoists have in fact been trying to resolve the problem [overcoming industrial backwardness] by bringing Western technology into the country on as big a scale as possible. One of the main means towards achieving this objective became, at the beginning of the seventies, Peking's intensified propagation in foreign business circles of the most rosy-hued ideas regarding the prospects for exporting Chinese oil in exchange for Western industrial equipment. The Maoists would have liked thereby to assure the West of their credit worthiness which, back in 1974, was placed in serious doubt by China's buildup of a foreign trade debt to the West [...]."[143]

139 US Department of State, Electronic Telegram, Bulgarian Foreign Trade Minister's Visit to Japan, 22 November 1977, 00:00, PlusD, ID: 1977TOKYO18023_c, paragraph 5.

140 Ibid.

141 PRC-Controlled Organizations' Representatives comment about Economic Aspects of Hua Kuo-Feng Appointment, PlusD, ID: 1976HONGK01688_b.

142 US Department of State, Electronic Telegram, Sino-US Economic Relations, 5 August 1976, 04:23, PlusD, ID: 1976PEKING01510_b.

143 Joint Publications Research Service, PRC use of Oil as Policy Tool Scored, Article by A. Karpenko, "The Maoists' 'Oil Diplomacy'", Moscow Economicheskaya Gazeta in Russian, No. 6, 02 02 1976, accessed through Readex. It needs to be added that oil prospects in China were put in a favorable

A survey conducted by USLO among trade officials at other foreign embassies in Beijing, nevertheless indicated that the slowdown in sales to China – less so for exports – also extended to other trading partners in the West, even the FRG and Italy, who had particularly good results with regard to their exports to China in the first half of 1976. In the two middle quarters of the year, almost no major sales to the PRC had been successfully negotiated. Even with regard to the undoubtedly disruptive effects of the Tangshan earthquake, the purchases appeared exceptionally low.[144] Nevertheless, Chinese trading corporations were reported continuing their *courant normal* by organising trips abroad and meeting in Beijing, and even "forging ahead" with several foreign exhibitions like the Swedish transportation exhibition and a Japanese environmental machinery exhibition in October of the same year, the latter of which had been postponed due to the earthquake.[145] Chinese exporters also remained relatively active, e. g., with a Chinese industrial exhibition in Manila in early October –opened by CCPIT's Li Quan who allegedly had already departed for Manila in late September, quoted that he intended to do "labour" during the setting up of the exhibition.

While a "good number" of US importers were present in Beijing, the observance of rituals of grief for Mao Zedong hindered business as trading corporations refused to make afternoon appointments, stating that time was needed for political study sessions.[146] Regardless of these temporary obstacles for the continuation of trade expansion, China actively proposed to Japan in September 1976 that negotiations on iron and steel trade be opened in Beijing towards the end of the month – the request being sent by telegram from the China National Metals and Minerals Import and Export Corporation to the Japan Iron and Steel Federation on the 17th of September. Immediately, six major Japanese iron and steel firms set up a delegation for Beijing with the hope to reach an agreement in October, which was expected to raise exports of iron and steel to China by contract from about 700'000 tons in the first semester to over a million in the second.[147] Even this would have been a rather minor recovery, as exports of iron and steel had amounted to over four million tons the year before, prior to trade moving into the focus of political criticism. In Japanese media, the perception of developments in China trade was rather concerned, with the Japanese Economic Journal weekly speculating that the advocates of "self-sufficiency" were on the rise again, shattering the hopes of the Japanese industry for a sustained expansion of Japan-China trade, quoting a twelve percent drop in orders of industrial equipment in particular for energy, transport, mining and the textile industry, as "a sign of serious difficulties experienced by a number of the most important industries of Japan".[148]

light in the West as well, already before 1974 – also an expression of hope for a source of petrol independent of the OPEC price-setting power.

144 US Department of State, Electronic Telegram, Fall-off in trade activity, 22 September 1976, 08:38, PlusD, ID: 1976PEKING01894_b, paragraph 1.

145 Ibid., paragraph 2.

146 Ibid., paragraph 4.

147 Foreign Broadcast Information Service, PRC proposes Iron, Steel Negotiations this Month, Hong Kong AFP in English, 1418 GMT, 17 09 1976 OW, accessed through Readex.

148 Ibid.

Soviet TASS asserted that China's foreign trade showed a chronic deficit and was in serious difficulties. China, economic commentator Igor Vasilyev stated, had overestimated the strength of western economies on which it had staked its industrial development and which were injured by inflation and not willing to give China preferential treatment in trade. The best hopes, he concluded, were for exports of the light industrial sector and raw materials, accomplished "by belt tightening at home". The import of foreign technology, in his view, was prone to failure due to a shortage of technicians and the "general low level" of Chinese technical leading to the imported equipment laying idle. USLO noted that the Soviet trade deficit with the US in the same four-year period up to 1976 was about 3.2 billion USD – or twice as high as the Chinese.[149]

Towards the 40th Canton Fair

While the ground was actively prepared for a continuation of trade expansion for selected goods, everybody else waited for the next Canton Fair for reliable clues for the future of China trade. In the background, talks between western economies on the maintenance or adaptation of trade restrictive measures – notably import restrictions – continued within the framework of the multifibre arrangement on textiles, the main value-added export product of the PRC. In a meeting on the arrangement in Washington D.C. on the 9th and 10th of September 1976, in particular the EC stated that it was under considerable pressure by its industries to seek protectionist changes in the arrangement. Industry and Labour particularly in the UK, according to the Director of the Directorate for External Affairs Benedict Meynell, were exerting pressure to import growth rates for textiles, notably stating handloom products from India as an issue. The EC sought to reduce the levels of permissible restraints (quotas) and introduce the explicit authority of members to the agreement to reduce growth rates permitted to exporters to less than six percent. On the other hand, an interest in tariff cuts was signaled.[150]

After the arrest of the Gang of Four in early October of the same year, the proponents of foreign trade in the Chinese administration relaxed their communication concerning trade, openly referring to the slump of 1976 as a temporary event. When Minister of Foreign Trade Li Qiang met a delegation of the FRG in late October 1976, he was asked directly about the elephant in the room – the prospects for a future expansion of bilateral trade. Li admitted that foreign trade had faced some setbacks during the year, citing the Tangshan earthquake as an obvious factor together with bottlenecks notably in the railroad system. He also added that there had been "interference by some of our countrymen". As a German embassy official who was present in the room told USLO, all Chinese representatives in the room burst out laughing.[151]

149 US Department of State, Electronic Telegram, TASS ridicules PRC Economic Performance, 8 September 1976, 16:31, PlusD, ID: 1976MOSCOW14150_b, paragraphs 2 and 3. It may be noted that the Soviet Union at the time was seeking Japanese technology, capital and know-how for the further exploitation of energy resources in Siberia.

150 US Department of State, US – Japan – EC Trilateral Textile Consultations, 25 September 1976, 15:26, PlusD, ID: 1976STATE239215_b.

151 US Department of State, Electronic Telegram, Li Chiang's Remarks on Foreign Trade, 21 October 1976, 04:30, PlusD, ID: 1976PEKING02163_b.

Having visited China and Chinese trade officials in autumn 1976, President of the NCUSTC Christopher H. Phillips confirmed to US businesses that after what he had been told in these meetings, bilateral trade would increase in the future. First, obstacles to trade were mainly reported to be on the Chinese side in the diplomatic domain. In fact, persistent interest had been signalled in the purchase of wood manufactures, machinery, technology, raw materials such as cotton and even complete "turnkey" facilities.[152] "Turnkey" refers to a type of a complex construction project that is sold to any buyer as a completed site, which has usually already been in use with identical or very similar specifications somewhere else. This is quite different from build to order projects, where the contractor builds a project or parts of it in accordance with the buyer's exact specifications, or when an incomplete product or parts thereof sold with the assumption that the buyer will complete it. In China, turnkey projects usually were complete industrial facilities that were literally copied from existing foreign technology and followed foreign standards – thus symbolizing the criticism of "trailing behind at a snail's pace".

From the point of view of modernisation as a meta-objective of Chinese economic policy may appear to be justified, as the procurement of tunkey-plants amounts to the use of basic innovations that are well established elsewhere or even already dated. On the other hand, as China still lacked many of these basic innovations and their implementation in the economy through concrete technology, allowing the construction of turnkey-facilities was a way to put the productive capacities of such technologies to use relatively quickly and arguably at a lower price compared to constructing "from scratch". On the other hand, Chinese turnkey projects in particular in agriculture were already a major part of Chinese foreign aid to developing countries – and continue to be in the industrial sector today.[153]

The broad lines of Chinese trade policy, as Li Qiang clarified, would remain "unchanged from the past", aiming at the fulfilment of the objectives of the Four Modernisations and the long-term development plan leading to them.[154] Besides the well-known Taiwan issue, the absence of most favoured nation treatment was actively named as the most significant obstacle to the development of trade. An address given by President of the NCUSCT Phillips at a luncheon organised by the American Chamber of Commerce (AmCham)[155], attended by Chinese and foreign business people as well as Chinese officials, was widely covered in the press. Ta Kung Pao in Hong Kong even carried a reprint of

152 US Department of State, Electronic Telegram, NCUSCT Views on China Trade Policy, 30 October 1976, 04:18, PlusD, ID: 1976HONGK12720_b.

153 Shinn David H., Eisenmann Joshua, China and Africa: A Century of Engagement, Philadelphia 2012, p. 151. Nevertheless, as Jan Deleyne noted, China was one of the few – if not the only – countries which did not conclude any services contracts relating to the procurement of machinery, being determined to learn the use and maintenance of machinery on its own. Deleyne 1972, p. 108.

154 The report by USLO Beijing made explicit reference to the fourth National People's Congress and Zhou Enlai's presentation thereafter. NCUSCT Views on China Trade Policy, 30 October 1976, 04:18, paragraph 1.

155 Having been called the "single most influential organization in American politics, outside the Republican and Democratic Parties apparatuses" by Alyssa Katz, Amcham had been present in Beijing since 1919, with eight founding member-companies including Standard Oil. The organization disbanded when war broke out, and the chamber did not formally reform in China until

the trade newsletter published by NCUSTC on the address, on its front page.[156] The visit had been taken by the Chinese Ministry of Foreign Trade as an opportunity to reassure trade partners in the West that China trade could be counted upon in the future.

The long-awaited 40th Canton Fair in 1976 closed on the 15th of November. It confirmed these optimistic signals – at least with regard to how it was covered by Chinese media. Attendance was reported to have surpassed 25'000 participants from more than 110 countries, with both the value of exports and imports rising, the former reaching a record high. These figures were confirmed by USLO. Business transactions covered a wide range of products from chemicals, textiles, light manufactures, metals and minerals, foodstuffs, and animal products that showed further increases in variety as compared to earlier trade fairs, thus demonstrating the productive capabilities of the Chinese industry.[157] In a Hong Kong newspaper, it was reported that the share of industrial, mining and auxiliary agricultural products and processed ready-made products had risen from 50 percent in 1966 to more than 70 percent in 1976, while the volume of crude oil produced in China amounted to 6.7 times the 1965 production – the total amount of exports from China in 1976 being "equivalent to 15 times that of 1965".[158]

Criticism of increased foreign trade within China – reportedly stemming from the Gang of Four and their followers – was noted as having significantly decreased compared to the earlier Fair in spring of the same year. Ta Kung Pao quoted workers at the Canton Fair speaking out openly against the Gang of Four in turn for opposing and impeding the export of crude oil, which was at the centre of the Chinese foreign trade expansion (see next subchapter). The policy of increased oil export was presented in this criticism as having been "sanctioned by Mao [Zedong] and Zhou [Enlai]" and thus beyond criticism. USLO reported that a similar message had been carried by a Canton provincial broadcast on the 15th of November of the same year. US diplomats noted that such statements gave oil exports as an important part of foreign economic policy a "certain inviolability, which would seriously undermine any lingering opposition to using, if not boosting, China's natural resources as exports."[159]

While foreign trade had thus been confirmed as a sustained part of the Chinese economic policy bundle by both statements and action, expectations were well-managed. Meeting a French delegation visiting China in early November 1976, CCPIT chairman Wang Yaoting told the interested guests that despite all efforts, China's foreign trade would not expand "rapidly" before "1977 or 1978". He gave three reasons for this cautious prognosis: first, China needed to "repair the damage done to production" by the Gang

1981. See: KATZ ALYSSA, The Influence of the Machine: The U.S. Chamber of Commerce and the Corporate Capture of American Life, New York 2015.

156 NCUSCT Views on China Trade Policy, 30 October 1976, 04:18, paragraph 2.

157 It was nevertheless noted that while sales of cereals, oils and foodstuffs had risen to varying degrees, the supply of some products offered fell short of demand – such as rugs and feathers – perhaps indicating the focus on increased efficiency and focus in agriculture and light industry. US Department of State, Electronic Telegram, Canton Fair – Interference in Oil Trade by 'Gang of Four', 17 November 1976, 07:31, PlusD, ID: 1976HONGK13424_b.

158 Joint Publications Research Service, More Products Exported, Hong Kong Chung-kuo Hsin-wen, Original in Mandarin, 02 11 1976, accessed through Readex.

159 Ibid., paragraph 4.

of Four, second "numerous natural disasters" like the Tangshan earthquake, had negatively affected them, and third – and perhaps most importantly, concerning the import-side of trade – China's foreign exchange reserves were still *"inadequate"*. USLO remarked that similar "frank admissions" had been made by Vice Premier Li Xiannian to another foreign delegation, underlining major constraints while "still supporting what seems to be a new, strongly positive line on foreign trade".[160] Given China's still substantial and, albeit after the reaction to the experiences of 1974/1975, more moderately growing debt service obligations, the promotion and increase of high-value exports would be needed to finance the Four Modernisations, particularly given their ambitious timetable. Any imports needed for that goal would require an expansion of foreign debt to not slow down the promised economic development of the PRC.

Self-reliance as a political tenet did not disappear from propaganda and political speeches, but the openly positive assessment of foreign trade in Chinese media after late 1976 is striking. A Xinhua dispatch from Guangxi province held that "foreign trade is a component of China's national plan". China having a "vast territory and rich resources with latent capacities in foreign trade", the prospects were deemed "excellent" for the "further development of China's socialist economy and trade with foreign countries". The article further stated that "much had been learned from the strong points" of China's trading partners, which had "strengthened the Chinese people's ability to build socialism independently and self-reliantly" and expedited socialist construction.[161] Embedding such assessments in Mao Zedong Thought, selected quotes like this example of 1949 were placed:

> "The Chinese people wish to have friendly cooperation with the people of all countries and to resume and expand international trade in order to develop production and promote economic prosperity"[162]

The quote went back to a moment, in which the PRC sought international recognition actively. In March 1949, when he was anticipating the coming victory in the Chinese civil war with the Kuomintang, Mao hinted repeatedly at the possibility of a conciliatory policy towards the US. In his report to the second plenum of the seventh CCP Central Committee, he referred to the possibility of imperialist economic and cultural establishments existing in the major Chinese cities, at least until victory had been won nationwide. While the Soviets began to praise the forthcoming victory of the Chinese communists already in April, Mao underlined his conciliatory stance toward the US even more explicitly, stating that the CCP and its future regime would be prepared to establish diplomatic relations with any foreign government if it severed relations with and ceased any support to Chiang Kai-shek, stating the phrase quoted above.[163] That the quote was used at this point

160 US Department of State, Electronic Telegram, China's Trade Expansion Limitations, 5 November 1976, 09:17, PlusD, ID: 1976HONGK12958_b.

161 Ibid.

162 NAKAJIMA MINEO, Foreign relations: from the Korean War to the Bandung Line, in: MACFARQUHAR RODERICK, FAIRBANK JOHN K. (eds.), The Cambridge History of China, Volume 14: The People's Republic, Part 1: The Emergence of Revolutionary China 1949–1965, Cambridge 1987, pp. 262 f.

163 Ibid.

in time was an important signal indicating that China was again open to international cooperation – not only with the US.

The article closed by proclaiming that the Chinese people were "resolved to adhere to Chairman Mao's directives on foreign trade" and to "encourage continued development of economic and technical exchanges and trade relations with other countries".[164] While USLO assessed the outcomes of the Canton Fair of autumn 1976 more reluctantly, the statements on rich resources were seen as a sign of the Chinese leadership's readiness to expand trade in the area of oil and other raw materials – a point criticised prominently before the fall of the Gang of Four – and left the trade officials hopeful for 1977.[165] It is remarkable that the mentioned Xinhua-articles were confirmed to be "important policy statements" by the deputy secretary general of the Canton Fair, Jin Jingshan, in November 1976. They signalled China's readiness to continue the path of trade expansion including in raw materials to foreigners. Accordingly, their first publication was exclusively in English.[166]

Criticism of the Gang of Four as a propaganda tool and rhetorical device for the explanation and legitimation of adjusted priorities in economic policy was applied in particular under Hua Guofeng, with regard to foreign trade. An article associated with the theory group of the Peking Foreign Trade College[167] in Renmin Ribao in December 1976 delivered a description of this particular sabotage, which focused on the "distortion" of the concept of self-reliance into "a closed-door policy and cutting back exports" while relativising the importance of Chinese oil exports:

> "With ulterior motives, the 'gang of four' made a big fuss about exporting petroleum and importing complete sets of equipment. [...] This was an attack on our great leader Chairman Mao and our esteemed and beloved Premier [Zhou Enlai] and other leading cadres of the central organs. [They] took the correct decision to export petroleum, which is of great political and economic significance [...] [the Gang of Four] alleged that 'China exports petroleum to shift the world energy resources crisis onto the Chinese people. China exports petroleum under the country's unified all-round planning in accordance with Chairman Mao's revolutionary line in foreign affairs and the socialist foreign trade principle of equality, mutual benefit and supplying each other's needs. The amount of crude oil China exports accounts for only a very small fraction

164 As quoted in: US Department of State, Electronic Telegram, NCNA heralds expanded trade, 4 November 1976, 02:06, PlusD, ID: 1976HONGK12840_b.

165 Ibid., paragraphs 3, 4 and 5.

166 US Department of State, Electronic Telegram, NCNA statements on Foreign Trade, 5 November 1976, 04:00, PlusD, ID: 1976PEKING02284_b.

167 Based on a college-level program to train experts for foreign trade, based on which the Peking Foreign Trade Specialists' School was founded. A 1954 guide to higher education in China lists two departments in this school: The first for experts on foreign trade, the second for the study of foreign languages for practical use, namely Russian, German, English, French, Korean, Vietnamese, Japanese and Spanish. The school, it is presumed, was the basis for the establishment of the Peking College of Foreign Trade no later than 1954, headed by the then-vice of foreign trade. See: KLEIN 1977, p. 313.

of the country's total output, and an extremely tiny proportion in the world's crude oil production and consumption."[168]

With regard to the ideological legitimation of the import of foreign advanced technology and industrial equipment, the approval given by Mao in earlier years was underlined in the article, while alleged imports of "means of espionage and luxuries for [the] corrupt, decadent life [of the Gang of Four]", such as lipstick, hair dyes, artificial eyelashes, swimming suits, pornographic films and even vitamin B – "a very ordinary item produced in China" – were highlighted.[169] The public defence of foreign trade expansion by issuing harsh criticism of its critics became more detailed in the course of 1977, with Xinhua in Mandarin – thus directed at a Chinese audience – stating in January that attacks against the "wise petroleum exporting policy" as well as the import of industrial equipment, approved by Mao Zedong, had been "reactionary" and that the Gang had placed "their people in the Ministry of Foreign Trade, foreign trade departments in a number of localities" as well as in the administrative structures of the Canton Fair "to steal trade secrets and economic information like spies".[170]

That such alleged activities had affected the Chinese oil exports was brandished as having harmed China's "international credibility", having negative effects both politically and economically. Stating that the reliability of the PRC as a trading partner was an important objective and cause for political discipline stood in stark contrast to earlier insistence on self-reliance. In contrast, Xinhua underlined the drastic change of China as a country "that was poor in oil and which had to import it" to an exporter, describing the process enthusiastically as "soul-stirring happy tidings". The positive narrative underlying the oil-technology interdependence that China sought was underlined by quoting alleged Daqing workers having said "What we are exporting is not simply crude oil. We are exporting 'honour-winning oil' to win honours for Chairman Mao's revolutionary line in foreign affairs!"

Still, the red line with regard to finances was held. "Our socialist country simply does not permit foreign capital to develop our country's resources, neither does it ever enter any joint enterprise with a foreign country nor solicit foreign loans", denouncing the claim that China had become colonised anew. For the future, the diversification of exports was presented as the way forward: "We are only exporting petroleum now. We need to constantly increase the proportion of our export in industrial and mining products to gradually change the long-standing situation in which our exports are mainly agricul-

---

168 Foreign Broadcast Information Service, Sabotage of Foreign Trade, excerpts of an article by the theoretical group of the Research institute under the Peking Foreign Trade College: "Questions of International Trade", Peking NCNA in English, 1207 GMT, 10 12 1976 OW, accessed through Readex.

169 Ibid.

170 Foreign Broadcast Information Service, NCNA on 'Gang' Sabotage of Foreign Trade, Report by NCNA correspondent: "A Grave Step for Usurping Party and State Power – Exposing the Towering Crimes of the 'Gang of Four' in Rampantly Opposing Chairman Mao and the Party Central Committee and in Viciously Attacking Premier Chou in Foreign Trade", Peking NCNA Domestic Service in Mandarin, 0141 GMT, 13 01 1977 OW, accessed through Readex.

tural products, handicrafts and local specialty products." Any attempt to isolate China from the world was denounced as "historic retrogression".[171]

The Chinese trade offensive as an act of patriotism and internationalism

Accordingly, communication towards foreign trade partners shifted further in the course of 1977. First, to an increasingly less reluctant, and subsequently towards an openly celebratory tone. This mood-shift concerned in particular discussions on future trade in manufactured goods. USLO reported in late February 1977 that an official of the Light Industry State Trading Corporation had provided an "extremely forthcoming and positive assessment of the prospects for US trade in light industrial products", quoting an "unusual degree of flexibility" to be expected at the Canton Fair in discussing labelling, safety standards and exclusive representation for Chinese goods on foreign markets by trading enterprises.

More US firms than ever would be invited to the Fair. While shortages in some lines of products were admitted to be a persistent problem in China, the spring edition was declared to be a platform for the discussion of "means of assuring increased sales to the US in the future", highlighting toys as well as rubber and canvas shoes as examples. It was announced that the Crystal Company, a US toy distributor, was holding a trade seminar in March 1977 in Shanghai, where representatives of the Chinese light industry would notably focus on US product safety regulations. In addition, the official stated briefly, that China "would be buying US technology" to further improve production in the PRC.[172] In later meetings with the CCPIT, it was also noted by the USLO that Chinese officials signalled "at least some degree" of increased flexibility with regard to political obstacles to further trade expansion, notably the Taiwan question and the implementation of the Shanghai communiqué.[173]

In May of the same year, this tendency became even clearer regarding exports, as intricate structures for the facilitation of bilateral trade were tested by the PRC. Chinese trade and industry officials increased their efforts to expand exports to the US through organisations based in Hong Kong, including the establishment of a factory in the British colony. This factory was intended for the assembly of Chinese machinery to be sold afterwards by branches of a Hong Kong-based company under Chinese control in the US. Additionally, a request by a Chinese trading company based in Hong Kong regarding the registration of trademarks in the US and a similar request for the acquisition of US visas for three staff members of the China Resources Company for a trip to six US cities in order to meet with US textile importers were placed with US authorities.[174]

Furthermore, trade was also expanded with former partners: three Indian businessmen attended the spring Canton Fair, concluding contracts valued over 1.6 million USD,

171 Ibid.

172 US Department of State, Electronic Telegram, US Trade Prospects in Light Industry, 23 February 1977, 00:00, PlusD, ID: 1977PEKING00345_c.

173 US Department of State, Electronic Telegram, National Council for US-China Trade: Canton Meetings, 28 April 1977, 00:00, PlusD, ID: 1977PEKING00842_c.

174 US Department of State, Electronic Telegram, China Highlights, No. 11, 26 May 1977, 00:00, PlusD, ID: 1977HONGK06049_c, paragraph 3.

particularly on shippings of steel. This apparently positive reestablishment of commercial contacts was immediately followed by an announcement in September 1977 that the delegation at the fall edition of the Fair would encompass twenty-five members, in particular from the steel industry that hoped to sell finished steel products to China, which Chinese officials answered quickly and positively.[175] With regard to persisting border issues, the Indian embassy in Beijing indicated that Delhi wished to improve relations by trade, while leaving sensitive political issues for later consideration.[176] At the same time, Sino-Soviet trade was declining continually, which was explained by the USLO as the inability – or unwillingness – to deliver agricultural products as well as a focus on obtaining foreign exchange that the Soviet Union would not provide under the existing annual agreement.

That these positive observations were not merely coincidences or wishful thinking was confirmed in a farewell call of the Chinese Minister of Foreign Trade Li Qiang with US ambassador – formally the head of USLO – Thomas S. Gates, on the 7th of May 1977. Li described the prospects for Sino–US trade in ever more positive terms, for once providing more specific detail. In the second half of the year, imports were intended to increase remarkably, notably with regard to consumables. Emphasis within this import-expansion, however, would be on technological know-how, either in the form of complete plants of licensed technology or patents. These imports would be selected from among international offers on a competitive basis, with the three most important criteria being terms of delivery, quality and price. Li stated openly that in this international competition for the enormous and growing Chinese market, the US had an edge over others. Japan and the FRG, he added, were also seen as competitive in Beijing. He quoted the faster delivery of Boeing airplanes as compared to Tridents as an example of a particularly positive experience with US companies and the government, of which the PRC would be happy to see more in the future.

The Chinese Ministry of Foreign Affairs and its directly affiliated organisations sought to use the expansion of international trade for political purposes. When the Mid-America Committee, a group of twenty-four leading businesspeople from the US visited the Chinese people's Institute of Foreign Affairs on the 25th of October 1977, the organisation's president disturbed the visitors with a welcome far less friendly than expected. According to Hao, US businesses had only themselves to blame if they did not get a share in the growing Chinese import market, as it would go to Japanese and European exporters whose governments had normalised relations with the PRC long ago while the US "lagged behind", as not being willing to accept the Chinese Three Principles on Taiwan. The group was scheduled to meet with Minister Li Qiang on the 27th of October, where they were expecting to receive a much less antagonistic presentation on the future of China Trade, as USLO estimated.[177]

175 US Department of State, Electronic Telegram, Sino-Indian Relations, 28 September 1977, 00:00, PlusD, ID: 1977PEKING02195_c.

176 Ibid., paragraph 1.

177 US Department of State, Electronic Telegram, Mid-America Committee Meeting with Hao Te-Ching, 27 October 1977, 00:00, PlusD, ID: 1977PEKING02472_c.

This expansion of trade would play out in the open: While US technology had been obtained in the past by purchases made though third countries, China would in the future be buying directly from the US if"favourable terms" could be guaranteed. The indirect purchase of US soybeans earlier in the year was named as a first example of this change, although the USLO estimated that the prices of other basic US commodities, in particular, wheat, tended to be too high for the Chinese customers due to the transportation cost to the US West Coast for shipment. An extension of credit to China was said to be under consideration – as long as they were granted directly by the suppliers, on the basis of a designated transaction or contract. Nevertheless, Li strictly denied that the PRC would accept any foreign bank loans.[178]

That China had officially entered international trade with less politically primed reluctance was also underlined by Li's offensive demand for the lowering of US tariffs, which were rising considerably in the wake of the economic crisis and the protectionist backlash it had caused. Still, in September 1978, the US ITC reported to the White House that it had determined that high-grade ferrochromium – a complex, high-value metal alloy – was imported into the US in such quantities "as to be a substantial cause of serious injury to the domestic industry" that was "producing an article like or directly competitive with the imported article". This finding justified, at least legally, measures (trade remedies) for the limitation of imports. Whether such measures were appropriate, was and still is controversial. Reporting to the GATT secretariat in Geneva, the ITC underlined that the affected industries were in particular injured by domestic factors such as the "idling of productive facilities, the inability to operate at a reasonable level of profit, unemployment within the industry, decline in sales and a downward trend in domestic production".[179] In the wake of the economic downturn in the capitalist international market, socialist China had become a major advocate of international trade.

Similarly, Foreign Trade Secretary Vicente Paterno of the Philippines was quoted a few days later, after a visit to Beijing, as being confident that bilateral trade could reach the mark of 100 million USD soon. The necessary condition according to Paterno was that Chinese projections concerning the export of crude oil proved to be realistic. He was reported to have been particularly struck by Minister of Foreign Trade Li Qiang's vehement statements against the earlier opposition to foreign trade, which he exclusively associated with the Gang of Four. According to Paterno, the matter was personal as Li held a "real grudge". Li told him that he was particularly upset by the fact that his ministry had been dubbed the "Ministry of Betrayal", as he saw his work as guided by patriotism. Paterno echoed the statements probably made by his host that the Gang of Four had "held back the development of foreign trade, but that is now in the past".[180]

---

178 US Department of State, Electronic Telegram, Conversation with Foreign Trade Minister, 7 May 1977, 00:00, PlusD, ID: 1977PEKING00922_c.

179 General Agreement on Tariffs and Trade, Article XIX – Proposed Action by the United States, High-Carbon Ferro-Chromium, 3 October 1978, Document L/4702, available at: https://www.wto.org/gatt_docs/English/SULPDF/90950256.pdf, last accessed on 10 May 2020.

180 US Department of State, Electronic Telegram, Secretary Paterno Returns from China Visit, 18 May 1977, 00:00, PlusD, ID: 1977MANILA07574_c.

The outcomes of the third plenum of the 10th central committee were received well in trade circles, being notably mentioned by CCPIT as favourable to both the realisation of the Four Modernisations in China and – directly linked to this goal – the development of trade in both ways. Well aware of China's potential as a market for foreign enterprises, Chinese trade officials actively promoted the future prospects. Li Quan of CCPIT was quoted by USLO on several occasions as having emphasised repeatedly the almost proverbial "competitive edge" the US economy had, notably with regard to European countries, when it came to trade with China. As one way of "acquainting Chinese end-users with US-technology", he sought to include as many representatives of Chinese industries as possible in delegations going to the US, hoping in turn for the visit of many US businesspeople in China.[181] As US diplomats reported, Li mentioned "almost as an afterthought" certain political limits to trade which "of course" existed, without entering into specifics. Being asked by an USLO officer whether an expansion of trade within these given limits would nevertheless be possible, he answered without hesitation that this was indeed possible. He added that he believed these obstables would be overcome in the future, expressing his hope that this future would not be "too long".[182]

Li's hopes were justified, for between the 14th and the 28th of July 1977, a two-weeks-long national foreign trade conference on "learning from Dazhai and Daqing" was held. It was not only the largest political conference on foreign trade ever held in the PRC (with over 1400 participants from the administration in Beijing and regional organisations) but also included both the renewed management models for agriculture and industry that had been established in Chinese domestic economic policy, in their common mission to promote the economic development of China through exchange with the rest of the world. At the conference, Premier Minister Li Xiannian underlined the crucial importance of trade for the realisation of the Four Modernisations, while asserting that China would still need to remain self-reliant.[183]

The report on the conference prepared by Vice Premier Yu Qiuli predicted a "big increase" in the volume of foreign trade, while urging foreign trade workers to study international markets in order to optimise the acquisition of advanced technology and equipment as well as understand what China really needed from abroad to support its economic development. This was deemed relevant for more than the economy in the narrower sense. In an editorial published on the 24th of September 1977, the media outlet of the PLA, the Liberation Army Daily, underlined that the modernisation of the army consisted of two main aspects. First, obtaining "sophisticated weapons and equipment, including constantly improved and renovated conventional weapons, guided missiles and nuclear weapons". Second, men needed to be trained to handle these sophisticated weapons, possessing knowledge of modern military technology and the tactics for their

181 At a banquet given by the mining delegation of the national council for US-China trade in late July 1977. US Department of State, Electronic Telegram, US-PRC Trade Relations, 27 July 1977, 00:00, PlusD, ID: 1977PEKING01550_c.

182 Ibid., paragraph 5.

183 US Department of State, Electronic Telegram, PRC Foreign Trade Conference July 14–28, 2 August 1977, 00:00, PlusD, ID: 1977PEKING01597_c.

deployment.[184] Also, the report made reference to the import of required raw materials and supplies to support agricultural production as well as the light industry.

With regard to Chinese exports, the intention to align all relevant domestic production processes with foreign standards was remarkable. While the call for the production of more export-ready commodities was not new, oil and grain were to be only a part of the export structure. Agricultural sideline products were increasingly produced, thanks to flexibilities introduced in the previous years alongside light industrial goods and in particular textiles to complement these basic products. What was reflected in the earlier instructions on management given to industrial and agricultural units was emphasised even more at the conference – adjusting the variety and quality of products to the requirements of international markets as well as implementing improvements in packing.[185]

This also meant that the units producing these additional goods should follow the example of Daqing in its orientation towards foreign markets, introducing export orientation to most core sectors of the Chinese economy to increase the ratio of industrial as well as mining products in the trade mix. As it had been the case in domestic production for years, the importance of effective and precise cost accounting was emphasised in order to realise the maximum profit for the state in foreign trade. Accordingly, staff members working in foreign trade required better training, as foreign exchanges as well as standardised production on a large scale required expertise and professionalism. This broad orientation of the Chinese economy towards the industrialised part of the world also applied to the political and administrative structure of the socialist state.

Foreign trade, the report concluded, was the concern of the entire CCP – not only the responsibility of a single ministry or province, municipality and or autonomous region – and all ministries and commissions were to put foreign trade on their daily agenda.[186] This also meant that the *political* control of foreign trade was now truly centralised. Besides reaffirming what had been foreshadowed even before the fourth National People's Congress in 1975, the conference marked a comprehensive departure from the critical assessment of foreign trade in the past. The report provided written proof of this new orientation, approved at the highest level – seeking to reassure workers, cadres and officials who had been subject to severe political criticism and violence during and in the immediate aftermath of the Cultural Revolution.

Minister of Foreign Trade Li Qiang had an article published in Hongqi in October 1977 which presented the direction of foreign trade at the occasion of the 28th anniversary of the PRC, referring to trade as "not only **not** [emphasis added] betrayal, but, on the contrary, the combination of patriotism and internationalism". The article also questioned the administrative centralisation of foreign trade by mentioning that local authorities might be allowed to "do more things" in foreign trade, as long as "unified standards"

---

184 Foreign Broadcast Information Service, Liberation Army Daily on Modernization of National Defense, Excerpts of Liberation Army Daily 24 September editorial: "March Toward the Modernization of Science and Technology for National Defense", Peking NCNA Domestic Service in Mandarin, 1204 GMT, 25 09 1977 OW, accessed through Readex.

185 Ibid.

186 Ibid., paragraph 6.

were applied.[187] As it was "common sense" that imports needed to be paid by exports, Li advocated for the setting up of "bases for producing export commodities", as "practice has shown" that doing so would "facilitate meeting the requirements of the international market", promoting the sales of commodities of high quality and well-known brands and stabilising the supply of export items on a regular basis according to "fixed schedules and established norms for quality and quantity." Already in 1957, Chen Yun had proposed to establish specialised bases for the production of commodities designated for export. According to Fu Gaoyi, some of them were already set up during the late 1950s and 1960s in Guangdong, providing products in particular for Hong Kong. New bases were set up until 1972, carrying out export contracts concluded at trade fairs. In the area of Foshan, a first "unified export production base" was set up after 1973, with the explicit purpose to generate foreign exchange.[188]

Furthermore, Li underlined the importance of foreign trade for the domestic economy beyond the availability of imports, stating rather optimistically that the efficiency as well as the technical levels of Chinese production would be raised by the increased exposure to international trade and thereby support the socialist cause by promoting "the growth of the collective economy, increase the incomes of the communes, brigades and the masses, increase the accumulation of capital for the mechanisation of agriculture and promote a flourishing domestic market". These administrative adjustments could take different forms, "such as joint operations by several departments, division of work on the basis of product categories, or separate operations under a zoning system".[189] As an example, in late 1977, the separate China National Arts and Crafts Import and Export Corporation with headquarters in Beijing was founded from the former arts and crafts division of the China National Light Industrial Products Import and Export Corporation. USLO estimated that this step was due to the dissimilarity of the respective products and because markets for pieces of art in developed countries grew much faster than demand for other light industrial products. The flexibility of the Chinese administration in reacting to such trends and reorganise is in itself remarkable.[190]

Additionally, Li emphasised the importance of rules and reliability, as well as his adherence to the idea of mutual advantage, which in his words not only reflected a support of market forces but also of a basic tenet of civil and international law, *pacta sunt servanda*:

187 Foreign Broadcast Information Service, Li Chiang Discusses Foreign Trade policy, Article by Minister of Foreign Trade Li Chiang: "Distinguish between Right and Wrong in Line and Actively Develop Socialist Foreign Trade", Peking Red Flag No. 10 in Mandarin, 08 10 1977, pp. 31–38 HK, accessed through Readex.

188 As quoted in: Tao Yitao, Lu Zhiguo (eds.), China's Economic Zones, Design Implementation and Impact, Reading 2012, p. 140. For a global history approach on export processing zones and special economic zones, see: Neveling Patrick, Export Processing Zones/Special Economic Zones, in: Callan H. (ed.), The International Encyclopaedia of Anthropology, Hoboken 2018, pp. 2179–2185; and Neveling Patrick, Export Processing Zones and Global Class Formation, in: Carrier James, Kalb Don (eds.), Anthropologies of Class: Power, Practice and Inequality, Cambridge 2015, pp. 164–182.

189 Article by Minister of Foreign Trade Li Chiang: "Distinguish Between Right and Wrong in Line and Actively Develop Socialist Foreign Trade", 08 10 1977, pp. 31–38 HK.

190 US Department of State, Electronic Telegram, Establishment of New Chinese Foreign Trade Corporation, 8 December 1977, 00:00, PLusD, ID: 1977PEKING02878_c.

"We oppose the raising or holding down of prices by taking advantage of monopoly positions. We should mutually adhere to contracts, act in good faith and meet the deadline, quality and quantity set down in contracts." Beyond the subtitle "is it necessary to do business flexibly", referring to the adoption of "some flexible practices" under the "imperialist blockade, embargo, restriction and discrimination" – the article underlined that China definitely was on a path on which it needed to learn doing business:

> "In addition, we have to learn from foreign experiences, strengthen our investigation and studies on the international market and continue to make an effort to learn to do business. We must be good at using different products, times and markets in importing and exporting and flexibly use all trading methods under various complicated conditions."[191]

China had entered not only international trade but the international markets for real. In 1977, China's foreign trade with over forty major partners was estimated to have risen about eight percent, reaching about the same volume as in 1975. Exports had risen consistently, albeit mostly in crude oil, resulting in a trade surplus of more than 1.4 billion USD that increased China's foreign exchange reserves to 3 billion USD, according to the Japan External Trade Organisation.[192] In August of the same year, Kyodo reported that as both trade and production figures had been surpassed, Chinese economists had concluded that both were too low and needed to be expanded.[193]

Inside China, this shift was incorporated in the published reality of production as a wide-ranging success. In January 1978, the provincial government of Anhui reported that, thanks to the increase in exports, the local financial situation had been consolidated after the quotas for foreign trade had been fulfilled. The municipal banks, it was reported, had fulfilled their savings quotas well ahead of schedule and the funds for the support of agricultural production was twenty percent above that of 1976. "Foreign export enterprises", subordinate to the province, allegedly reduced the number of such enterprises suffering losses by twenty percent as well. It was proudly reported that profits had increased "by 2.64 million Yuan". The introduction of the profit motive in calculation and planning together with foreign trade as a new *Leitmotiv* was established.[194] The look outside was also promoted by the Academy of Sciences, when a draft plan for "promoting study of the world economy throughout China between 1978 and 1985" was discussed at a ten-day forum on scientific research planning in Changchun, on the 22nd of July 1978.[195]

Renmin Ribao published a commentary on the necessity to "emancipate the mind" in order to develop foreign trade fast in a short period of time. As sufficient sources of commodities suitable to the demand on international market were deemed necessary,

---

191 Ibid.

192 Foreign Broadcast Information Service, PRC Trade Volume Increases Steadily in 1977, Tokyo Kyodo in English, 1225 GMT, 15 03 1978 OW, accessed through Readex.

193 Foreign Broadcast Information Service, Kyodo Delegation told of PRC Plans to Revise 10-Year Plan, Tokyo Kyodo in English, 1241 GMT, 24 08 1978 OW, accessed through Readex.

194 Foreign Broadcast Information Service, Anhwei Finance and Trade, Hofei Anhwei Provincial Service in Mandarin, 1100 GMT, 11 01 1978 HK, accessed through Readex.

195 Foreign Broadcast Information Service, Forum on World Economy held in Changchun, Changchun Kirin Provincial Service in Mandarin, 2200 GMT, 22 07 1978 SK, accessed through Readex.

all forces needed to be mobilised. In order to do so, the commentary noted, it was "essential to clear away the ideological obstructions in people's minds, particularly those in the minds of leading cadres." Referring to Hua Guofeng and his "Report on the Work of the Government", one of these "ideological obstructions" was referred to by the author as "the theory of little account". Certain comrades, the article lamented, held that socialist construction in China dependent "upon self-reliance and development of foreign trade seems to be of little account". This thinking, as Li Xiannian was quoted, reflected the state of "being bound by the habits of small production." What these misguided comrades failed to understand, the author reminded, was "the fact that no country in the world can produce all that it needs."[196]

New rules for trade

The expansion of Chinese foreign trade had consequences that went beyond the mere exchange of commodities. The domain of legal rules and concepts accepted and applied by China was subject to increasing alignment as well. First, within China, after decades of relatively unregulated transactions, the legal framework for aspects concerning the exchange and transportation of goods was expanded and deepened. In early 1972, regulations for waterway cargo transportation were issued[197], which were applicable both to waterway cargo transport carried out by enterprises under the ownership of the Chinese state as well as leased foreign freighters.

The rules underlined the principles of planned management and rational economic organisation, explicitly clarifying the responsibilities for the joint drawing up of transport plans between different ministries, provinces, municipalities and autonomous regions. Besides the aspects of planning, the regulations contained detailed rules for the handling of cargo, the unification of the related paperwork (waybills), declaration requirements, freight costs and fees including payment terms, and state-designated packing standards. As the responsibilities of the crew and the receiving port were an important point of the regulation, the specialised position of cargomasters was underlined – although framed in a way that still conformed with the egalitarian spirit of the Cultural Revolution:

> "Section 17: Cargomaster
> Each port and shipping unit should strengthen cargomaster work, resolutely implement specialized cargomaster work as the leading factor, do cargomaster work with the workers committee, link up with the crew to examine the hold according to the principles of cargomaster work, sum up in a timely fashion, propagate the advanced experience of cargomaster work, establish a secure cargomaster receiving system, do

196 Foreign Broadcast Information Service, People's Daily, NCNA Commentary on Foreign Trade, People's Daily and NCNA correspondent's commentary: "It is Necessary to Vigorously Develop Foreign Trade; it is Necessary to Emancipate the Mind", Peking NCNA Domestic Service in Mandarin, 1228 GMT, 08 07 1978 OW, accessed through Readex.

197 Joint Publication Research Service, PRC regulations for waterway cargo transportation, Excerpts from a book by the Ministry of Communications, Peking Shui-lu Huo-wu Yun-shu Kuei-tse, Original in Mandarin, 02 1972, pp. 1–14, 23–27, 32, accessed through Readex.

cargomaster work precisely, receive clearly, and continually raise the quality of cargomaster work."[198]

Furthermore, as the cargo shipping sector was crucial for the division of labour both nationally and internationally, the importance of proper management and labor discipline was emphasised in the regulation:

"It is necessary to strengthen management of consolidated shipping equipment. Between the port and the shippers, and between the port authorities and the cargo shipping units, there must be strict exchange and receiving procedures for the consolidated shipping equipment, there must be timely return of the equipment, and there must be strengthening of measures to protect and repair the equipment. In case of loss or damage, compensation must be made in accord with the tariff rate."[199]

The regulation went as far as to set appropriate shipping speeds (150 nautical miles for coastal, a 100 on the Yangtze for state, 100/50 for provincial and municipal vessels per day) and pick-up dates for cargo stored at a port for the receiving party (ninety days), imposing fines if the deadline was surpassed. The same went for liability, which – as no liability insurance system existed in the PRC– was defined for cases of cargo shortage. This effort to issue clear rules on internal and coastal shipping was needed. According to a Xinhua dispatch issued from Wuhan on the 23rd of June 1973, the state-owned Yangzi Shipping Company had over-fulfilled the shipping plan and reported an increase of cargo shipping by thirteen percent compared to the previous year – achieving an all-time record.[200] Also, it was reported that although the total tonnage of ships sailing the river had increased seven times since 1949, it still fell short of the actual demand.

In parallel, the creation of legal certainty for shipping extended beyond the Chinese seas; in May 1973, a marine commerce agreement was signed with Greece – the most important European harbour in proximity to the still closed Suez Canal. The main stipulations were the mutual non-discrimination of vessels in ports, regardless of whether the cargo was destined for contracting parties or another country.[201] Further, as mentioned before, a core concept of international economic law originating in a Westphalian conception of statehood was accepted by the Chinese – despite its highly negative connotation with regard to the colonial past – most favored nation treatment was to be granted mutually. Legally, while giving China and the ships flying its flag the right to be treated in a non-discriminatory way, within the scope of the agreement, this also meant that China was not allowed to treat even its closest ally, Albania, any better than Greece in its own ports and waterways. The Chinese harbours were opened, but this time on a mutually agreed contractual basis. Additionally, other transportation agreements, e. g., concerning aviation, were signed. The aviation agreement with Greece, signed in parallel with

198 Ibid., p.24.

199 Ibid., Section 18, p. 25.

200 Joint Publications Research Service, Taiwan Reports on current status of PRC transportation, Article by Chiang Huai, Latest Chinese Communist Transportation, Taipei Fei-ch'ing Yueh-pao, Vol. 16, No. 5, Original in Mandarin, 10 07 1973, p. 105.

201 Taiwan Reports on current status of PRC transportation, Taipei Fei-ch'ing Yueh-pao, 10 07 1973, p. 104.

the maritime agreement, also stipulated non-discriminatory treatment – but, in addition, clarified that flights would pass through countries where this treatment had already been guaranteed contractually.[202]

By mid-1973, China had signed maritime transport agreements with Sweden, Canada, Britain and Greece and connected the destinations of this network by arrangements through stopovers. Remarkably, as the Chinese legal system was still almost inexistent, especially in the domain of public law,[203] regulations on the taxation of incoming foreign vessels were implemented in July 1974,[204] which stipulated an industrial-commercial unified tax and income tax to be levied on the gross transportation income derived from each voyage of a vessel of foreign nationality, carrying cargo or passengers from a port of China, set at three percent of gross income. Exemptions and reductions on the basis of reciprocity for ships flying the flag of a country having concluded a maritime transport agreement with the PRC were explicitly enshrined in Article three of the regulation. Through the negotiation of trade agreements, the Chinese MoFT, within its administrative authority, introduced further legal concepts that notably differed from the "five principles" generally emphasised in the PRC's foreign relations. Explorations of a Chinese-Japanese trade agreement aiming at extending the most favored nation treatment and, according to a joint statement issued by both governments in September 1972, creating a "rather broad, vague framework within which trade could be carried out",[205] began in August 1973. The establishment of a commission which would allow Japanese enterprises and the government to be regularly informed about Chinese planning priorities was a declared objective of the Japanese side. In addition, lists of commodities were to be traded; these would not be fixed quotas but the expression of the quantities desired to be exchanged. Systemic differences between both economies proved to be problematic. The first issue, right between established western concepts of international law and Mao's postulate of "learning from the best things foreign",[206] was

---

202 Ibid., p. 104. It was clarified, that Chinese airplanes would start from mainland China, pass through Karachi or Rawalpindi (Pakistan), Kabul or Kandahar (Afghanistan), Teheran, Baghdad, Kuwait, Damascus, Beirut, Ankara or Istanbul (Turkey) or Kairo, and then arrive at Athens or Salonika.

203 With the development of non-informal legal rules suffering a serious setback during the Cultural Revolution, as many legislative projects i. e. in the area of maritime law were halted and the existing legal structure became a major target for the Movement. See: Leng Shao-Chuang, The Role of Law in the People's Republic of China as Reflecting Mao Tse-Tung's Influence, in: Journal of Criminal Law and Criminology, Vol. 68, No. 3, September 1977, pp. 356–373.

204 Regulations for Taxation on the Transportation Income of Vessels of Foreign Nationality [expired], , Peking University Law Repository, Regulation No. CLI.2.378(EN), available at: https://en.pkulaw.cn/Search/SearchLaw.aspx [no permalink available], last accessed on 1 May 2020.

205 Joint Statement issued by the governments of Japan and the People's Republic of China at Peking, September 28 1972 in: Hsiao 1977, Appendix D, pp. 196–198.

206 Or, as Suisheng Zhao put it, looking back at the Mao years from a foreign policy perspective: "The basic goal of the Chinese revolution is to get rid of weakness, which plagued China for a hundred years, and to make China wealthy, powerful, and modernized. The way to realize this goal is to begin with the reality of China, to seek truth from facts, and to combine the basic principles of Marxism within the context of Chinese reality. To sum it up with a single phrase, it is to have a practical attitude. For things foreign, our principle is to learn whatever is good and put it into Chinese practice and never to imitate indiscriminately. To sum up, we will accept

the protection of intellectual property through the recognition of Japanese patent rights in China.[207] Such fears by certain branches – with regard to the systematic policies of adopting foreign technology in China that were justified from a commercial point of view – were demonstrated in October of the same year, when Japanese camera makers declined entry to production plants of a Chinese economic mission as they feared Chinese competition and industrial espionage.[208]

The second issue was the negotiation of a national treatment clause for the establishment of commercial presence by Japanese firms (obviously privately owned companies) in China. Sadao Uchida, the head of the North Asia division of the Japanese Ministry of Trade and Investment, described the problem effectively by stating that China did not have any private firms, and thus a formula that could legally enshrine the notion of "equal" treatment would be difficult to arrive at. An important Chinese demand foreshadowing the later technology-orientation of the Chinese development paradigm was the loosening of export controls on technology exports from Japan, particularly of computers.[209] On the Japanese side, the risk of "rapidly increasing imports" from the PRC and the need for safeguarding and emergency consultation clauses[210] showed foresight, despite the large export surplus of Japan at the time, and demonstrated that China was taken seriously as an exporter at least with regard to its potential. The agreement was negotiated quickly and signed in January 1974,[211] establishing non-preferential most favoured nation treatment – as the PRC was not a member of the GATT – for Chinese exports as well as mechanisms for consultations and arbitration. While the Chinese foreign trade companies generally insisted on integrating mediation-clauses in contracts, arbitration-mechanisms (excluding the jurisdiction of Chinese courts for disputes!) were readily accepted and even prepared with standard clauses after 1973.[212]

The conclusion of the agreement was timely, as bilateral trade in 1973 already amounted to more than 1.78 billion USD, an increase of over 85 percent over 1972.[213] It also paved the way for a political rapprochement, and the reopening of talks for a Japan–China peace and friendship treaty was announced in late 1974; nevertheless, this

---

whatever can make China modernized and can make Chinese people well of. This is what we understand as socialism. Chinese people believe that their choice is right, and history has shown that the chosen road is the right one." Suisheng Zhao, Beijing's Perception of the International System and Foreign Policy Adjustment after the Tiananmen Incident, in: Suisheng Zhao (ed.), Chinese Foreign Policy, Pragmatism and Strategic Behavior, New York 2016.

207 US Department of State, Electronic Telegram, Japan PRC Trade Negotiations, 16 August 1973, 08:41, PlusD, ID: 1973TOKYO10520_b.

208 Chinese Economic Mission Concludes Visit to Japan, PlusD, ID: 1973TOKYO13258_b.

209 Ibid.

210 US Department of State, Electronic Telegram, Japan-PRC Trade Negotiations, 10 August 1973, 07:48, PlusD, ID: 1973TOKYO10227_b.

211 US Department of State, Electronic Telegram, Amconsul Hong Kong to Secstate Washdc, 12 January 1947, 05:45, PlusD, ID: 1974HONGK00476_b.

212 Weggel, Oskar, Das Aussenhandelsrecht der Volksrepublik China, Hamburg 1976, pp. 447 ff.

213 US Department of State, Electronic Telegram, People's Republic of China Economic Review 1, 12 January 1974, 05:45, PlusD, ID: 1974HONGK00476_b.

proved to be much more difficult than expected.[214] Negotiations continued through the following year, complicated by political demands. Beijing sought to introduce larger concepts of its foreign policy with the bilateral relationship, notably by demanding the inclusion of a "hegemony clause" to declare the common struggle against the hegemony of a non-defined "third country"[215] in Asia. The Japanese side, on the other hand, despite the long-held position of equidistance from and to both Moscow and Washington and the will to bring Soviet–Japanese and Chinese–Japanese relations to the same level, was concerned that such a clause might one day be invoked by Beijing against aspects of the US–Japan relations, which were of strategic importance to Tokyo.[216]

That socialist China in parallel with its manoeuvring against Soviet influence actively sought and accepted its inclusion of the most favoured nation principle in its relations with other countries had two important implications. One was economical and primarily stemming from the rights of which Chinese exports would benefit. As Chen Hong, a sub-manager of the People's Bank of China, remarked in a conversation with a representative of the US treasury in late 1973, the use of western legal concepts and the most-favoured nation had important economic benefits for China, because it was "in competition on many products with other exporters who enjoyed it [...]. China in this situation would have to accept lower prices to make sales"[217]. Relying on the concept would thus ensure that Chinese exports to non-socialist countries were competitive on a basis of legal certainty. The second implication, primarily related to the legal *obligations* China accepted, was political. In principle, it implied that socialist China was legally bound, with regard to goods at the border, to treat its capitalist treaty partners equally, just as any socialist state. Accepting the most favoured nation as the basis for China's relations with other countries meant that, at least legally, China bound itself to new partners and was ready to do so to the potential detriment of others.

This openness towards an increase in China trade was also seen in the immediate neighbourhood, besides Japan. Shortly after the progress achieved in the Sino–Japanese trade relations, the Thai government agreed to abolish its Decree No. 53, which prohibited the import of goods from the PRC, and established a designated state trading company for China instead.

As a follow-up to the Swiss Industrial and Technological Exhibition (SITEX) of 1974 mentioned before, Minister of foreign trade Li Qiang had signalled an interest in negotiating a trade agreement with Switzerland. Already three weeks after the topic was discussed during a visit of Swiss delegate for trade agreements Raymond Probst in China,

---

214 Foreign Broadcast Information Service, Peace Treaty Talks with PRC may resume in January, Tokyo Kyodo in English, 0648 GMT, 31 12 1974, accessed through Readex.

215 According to Soviet sources, China did not try to hide that the term exclusively referred to the Soviet Union. A similar clause had been accepted in the earlier joint Japan-China statement of 1972 (Article 7). Foreign Broadcast Information Service, Commentary on Proposed Hegemony Clause in Japan-PRC Pact, Radio Moscow in Japanese to Japan, 1200 GMT, 30 04 1975 TK, accessed through Readex.

216 US Department of State, Electronic Telegram, Japan's National Interest and Foreign Policy in Northeast Asia, 4 June 1975, 08:57, PlusD, ID: 1975TOKYO07399_b.

217 US Department of State, Electronic Telegram, PRC Trade and Finance, 28 November 1973, 08:05, PlusD, ID: 1973HONGK11899_b.

a first Chinese draft was submitted. Aware of the importance of an adequate political framework for effectively conducting trade with the (in this area) highly centralised Chinese state, the Swiss side entered into negotiations, being aware that bridging the differences between the two systems as well as addressing concrete issues on patent protection and currencies would be challenging.

Similar issues had already been addressed by Swiss negotiators in earlier negotiations with eastern European countries, also the trade agreement between China and the FRG concluded in 1973 was a useful blueprint.[218] The trade agreement with Switzerland was concluded on the 20th of December 1974 and mentioned equality and mutual benefit in its preamble while establishing the most favored nation principle as its centrepiece with regard to tariffs and customs procedures. This meant that, with regard to tariffs and their application, the PRC would be treated like a Member of the GATT which Switzerland had acceded in 1966. The agreement was thus not preferential, but granted the contemporary minimal standard. Further, in an attempt to account for the state-controlled nature of still large parts of the Chinese economy, it even held that exchanges of goods and services should be conducted at "reasonable prices in conformity with market conditions".[219]

As it had been the case with Japan's trade agreement with the PRC, the clause was motivated by Swiss concerns about the possibility of Chinese dumping. The association of Swiss textile industrialists (*Verein Schweizerischer Textilindustrieller*) even demanded stricter conditionalities to be negotiated, which were rejected by the federal administration with reference to the structure of trade – particularly high-value inputs for the Swiss textile industry – and the limited risk that Chinese exports posed for the Swiss economy overall.[220] Also, the agreement documented the intention of the Chinese Ministry of Foreign Trade to establish the RMB as a convertible currency, to ease the pressure to obtain expensive foreign exchange in order to pay for imports. These provisions were nevertheless of limited substance, as they were limited to transactions conducted voluntarily in RMB.[221]

The agreement was concluded successfully, with the first Swiss–Chinese joint committee meeting in Beijing, on the 10th of October 1977, for the first time, when the bilateral annual trade volume reached about 200 million USD, consisting mostly of imports of food, chemicals, textiles and some handicrafts to Switzerland and machinery, chemicals,

---

218 China – Reise 1974, Ergänzende Information von Botschafter Probst zum "volet économique" anlässlich der Botschafterkonferenz 1974 (4. September 1974), Beilage Nr. IV, p. 7. Available at dodis: dodis.ch/37654. Accessed on 12 August 2022.

219 "Les deux Parties contractantes conviennent que les échanges de marchandises et les prestations de services s'effectueront à des prix raisonnables conformes aux conditions du marché." Swiss Confederation, Accord de commerce entre la Confédération suisse et la République populaire de Chine, Conclu le 20 décembre 1974, Recueil systématique (RS) 0.946.292.491, available at: https://www.admin.ch/opc/fr/classified-compilation/19740367/index.html. Accessed on 1 May 2020.

220 Antwort Botschafter Probst auf Brief des Vereins schweiz. Textilindustrieller vom 18.10.74, 5. November 1974. Available at dodis: dodis.ch/37711. Last accessed on 12 August 2022.

221 While limited to transactions *where both parties accept the currency*. Ibid., Article 4.

technical instruments and – in particular – watches to China.[222] It is remarkable that the about one million Swiss watches sold to China in 1974, a complex and high-priced consumer good, amounted to about one quarter of Swiss exports in the same year.[223] This reflected the careful shift towards more consumer options within the socialist state discussed in earlier chapters – albeit for a narrow group of privileged buyers.

The negotiations were handled with confidence on the Chinese side, as the technical know-how with regard to the drafting of international agreements had been firmly established. In a bilateral exchange with member of the Swiss Federal Council Pierre Graber in Beijing on the 5th of August 1974, shortly before the agreement was concluded, Li Qiang underlined the Chinese ability to negotiate internationally and defend the interests of the socialist state:

> "With regard to the redactional questions in the trade agreement in the making, there are some different views. We should not impose one's own views on the other party. In the past, when certain countries submitted the text of an agreement to us, we had to accept it tel quel. Today, it is very different: we can discuss."[224]

Throughout the early 1970s, China's legal framework for foreign trade grew more and more sophisticated, amounting to a convergence with what were legal standards in the West.[225] By the end of 1974, the PRC had signed more than sixty agreements on economic relations with forty non-socialist countries' joint committees, whose yearly meetings with alternating capitals had become a standard provision in Chinese trade agreements, leading to a further increase in regular contact between Chinese trade officials and their foreign counterparts. In the spring of 1974, such meetings were held with Mexico, Italy and Australia in Beijing and Mexico City.[226] On the multilateral level, while China did not attempt to become a member state of the GATT, the inclusion of socialist economies also reached a new level. Czechoslovakia, Cuba, Yugoslavia, Poland and Romania had already joined the agreement but under conditions that accounted for their planned economies.

Czechoslovakia was an original member of the GATT drafting group; Cuba was an original signatory – both countries joined prior to the transition to socialism. Yugoslavia,

222 US Department of State, Electronic Telegram, First Meeting of the Swiss-PRC Mixed Commission, 11 October 1977, 00:00, PlusD, ID: 1977BERN04736_c.

223 China als zukünftiger Handelspartner der Schweiz, Vortrag von Botschafter Raymond Probst, Delegierter des Bundesrates für Handelsverträge, gehalten in Basel am 25. Februar 1975 vor dem Hausverband der CIBA-GEIGY A. G., 20.2.1975, p. 14. Available at dodis : dodis.ch/37700. Last accessed on 12 August 2022.

224 Entretien du Conseiller fédéral Pierre Graber, Chef du Département politique, avec M. Li Chiang, Ministre chinois du Commerce extérieur, Grand Palais du Peuple, Minutes (PV), Beijing, 5 August 1974, dodis, document No. 37708, p. 16, available at : dodis.ch/37708, last accessed 1 May 2020. Translation by the author.

225 Despite the People's Republic not having acceded to the Vienna Convention on the Law of Treaties – legal practice with partners in the West appears to have had its inherently normative effect.

226 US Department of State, Electronic Telegram, PRC Trade Talks: Mexico, Italy, 3 May 1974, 06:26, PlusD, ID: 1974HONGK04925_b.

Poland, Romania and Hungary were admitted after negotiations and accepting individual conditions permitting for a gradual participation in the most favoured nation-based trading system, requiring the introduction of a compatible customs system and their own schedules of tariff concessions. Open questions with regard to Article XVII GATT which allows state trading as long as the responsible state-owned enterprises "act in a manner consistent with the general principles of non-discriminatory treatment" and needed to make transactions "solely in accordance with commercial considerations, including price, quality, availability, marketability, transportation". The issue was left unsolved, relying on constructive ambiguity, until the socialist governments were replaced by their successors.[227] Trade flows from and to these countries were not based on the general multilateral most favoured nation[228] and non-discrimination obligations of the agreement, regulated mostly by bound tariffs, but on negotiated trade flows that fixed the quantity of legally bound trade flows by quantitative quotas.

Nevertheless, when the legal framework of Chinese foreign trade grew and trade prospects expanded, rumors on a Chinese interest in joining the GATT emerged in early 1976, while being probably unfounded. USLO commented that Japan was highly skeptical about the possibility and agreed. Nevertheless, a number of plausible arguments speaking for an accession of China were discussed, notably that China would be able to counteract trade discrimination, better use its export potential for oil, and, as it was emphasized by the US representation in Geneva, support a "heightening shift towards readjusting the domestic economy so that the investment is not predominantly in the agricultural sector" – which would have meant that food imports would need to grow.[229]

The participation of socialist economies in the multilateral legal framework of the capitalist world market was nevertheless not excluded, *per se*. When Hungary joined the agreement on the 9th of September 1973, after years of negotiation as the sixth socialist economy, a new element of trade integration between socialist and capitalist economies was created. The rights and obligations for Hungary were defined under the assumption that its foreign trade regime would be treated as if the country were a market economy, thus enabling the country to negotiate reductions of trade barriers and receive most

227 Grzybowski Kazimierz, Soviet International Law and the World Economic Order, Durham and London 1987, pp. 55–59.

228 As stated in paragraph 1 of GATT 1947: "With respect to customs duties and charges of any kind imposed on or in connection with importation or exportation or imposed on the international transfer of payments for imports or exports, and with respect to the method of levying such duties and charges, and with respect to all rules and formalities in connection with importation and exportation, and with respect to all matters referred to in [...] any advantage, favor, privilege or immunity granted by any contracting party to any product originating in or destined for any other country shall be accorded immediately and unconditionally to the like product originating in or destined for the territories of all other contracting parties.", which in practice meant that no trade partner could – generally speaking, as there were derogations – be accorded more favorable treatment than any of the GATT member states. The General Agreement on Tariffs and Trade (GATT 1947), available at: https://www.wto.org/english/docs_e/legal_e/gatt47_01_e.htm, last accessed on 1 May 2020.

229 US Department of State, Electronic Telegram, Press Speculation about Chinese Interest in MTN, 13 April 1976, 17:18, PlusD, ID: 1976MTNGE02869_b.

favoured nation treatment from GATT member states.[230] The accession of Hungary also marked the readiness of a reforming socialist economy to deviate from the doctrine of non-equivalent exchange and of capitalist economies to willingly accommodate socialist states to credibly introduce the elements of a market economy into their system.

While some trade between China and the Soviet Union continued despite their differences, governed by annually renewed short-term trade agreements, these inter-socialist trade relations were not unaffected by developments in international markets to which both economies were increasingly interlinked. While the exchanges under the agreements were in place since 1958, based on fixed prices calculated in Swiss Francs, Soviet Deputy Trade Representative Vladimir Ivanovic Korolyov confirmed to USLO, in early June 1975, that Chinese representatives had taken the initiative to switch to world market prices instead of predetermined prices during the same year.[231] While this step sharply increased the nominal value of bilateral trade, it also made prices comparable to those being offered abroad.

As the position and importance of foreign trade in Chinese economic policy grew, the socialist state that was looking to expand its foreign trade with the West found itself confronted with increases in protectionist measures imposed by its prospective trade partners. The persisting economic crisis in 1975 affected the economies of trade partners in Europe as well as Japan, leading to more unilateral measures in these countries – such as restrictions on exports and imports through various instruments – which directly impeded Chinese trade and its potential. In exchanges with foreign governments, requests for loosening import restrictions on Chinese products were repeated consistently, as were delegates traveling to China. When presidents of Japanese regional banks visited China in autumn 1978, while the entanglement of the PRC in the international monetary disruptions was denied, the hope that Japan would relax import restrictions was a primary demand.[232] Also, the growing trade and exports from China led to business-driven demands for the expansion of import quotas of the European communities. In particular, in September 1976, a number of member states expressed their wish on behalf of their industries that import quotas for China be published earlier than usual for the year 1977 so that the firms would be aware of the import possibilities before attending the Canton Fair – "a very important event for the purpose of concluding trade agreements[233] with China". The Commission followed suit, proposed a number of adjustments for the textile sector that was especially important in Chinese trade, and even

230 Reuland James M., GATT and State-Trading Countries, in: Journal of World Trade Law, No. 3, 1975, pp.318-339.

231 US Department of State, Electronic Telegram, 1975 Sino-Soviet Trade Agreement, 4 June 1975, 01:11, PlusD, ID: 1975PEKING01057_b.

232 Joint Publications Research Service, Japanese Bankers Impressed by Tour of Mainland, Hong Kong Ta Kung Pao, Original in Mandarin, 18 10 1975, accessed through Readex.

233 Being not international trade agreements (in the narrow sense, *between states*), but agreements between European buyers – mostly privately-owned companies – and Chinese state-trading organisations.

proposed to include in the minutes of the decision the guarantee that the definitive quota arrangement for 1977 would "not be more restrictive than the one in force for 1976".[234]

In an interview with ROBERT HEUSER on the 8th of November 1977, the director of the legal affairs department of CCPIT and one of his employees confirmed that the cornerstones of a legal system able to handle international economic transactions were in place in China. They also admitted that, of the eighteen volumes in total, most of the Chinese laws and regulations were completely or partly out of date; thus, progress with regard to rules concerning trade within China was also mentioned. The basic rules were still laid down in the 1950 provisional regulations concerning the administration of foreign trade and decision for unifying the administration of state-owned trade in all of China.[235] The most essential additions were the 1963 trademark regulations, based on which no right to a patent was recognised which applied as an absolute protection against infringements through third parties – such as, e. g., a state-owned enterprise. The regulations made it clear that "all inventions" were the property of the state, and that no individual or unit could "monopolise" an invention. All production units were free to use any invention if it was of use to them. While patents could be registered, this did not mean the protection of exclusive rights but was rather an incentive for Chinese inventors as they could attach their name to an invention. The regulations defined inventions quite broadly as technical and scientific accomplishments that bring forth new knowledge, that had proven useful in practice and that were *"more advanced"* than appliances used so far.[236]

The functions of the department were described as giving legal advice to foreign trade corporations, particularly with regard to the drafting of contracts and the interpretation of clauses – and serving as an interface for the registration of trademarks, foreign trade and maritime arbitration and participation in research activities of the United Nations Commission on International Trade Law (UNCITRAL). While the concept of mutual benefit was repeatedly named as the basic principle for trade relations with China, the instruments to secure these relations were based on the standards established by westphalian international law. With regard to trademarks, the Chinese officials confirmed that those were protected in China, as they served as an indicator for the quality of a foreign product. On the other hand, patents were not protected in China, as granting and enforcing this protection would have infringed the practice of adopting and adapting foreign technology; only the contracts served as a legal basis.

Tellingly, the director clarified that for the settlement of disputes, no substantive law was stipulated, but that the place of arbitration could be either in China, a third country, or the defendant's country. In the case of a dispute on an infringement, the settlement would have to take place in China or a neutral state, stressing "the application of the three principles", as "only when we apply these principles organically can we settle the dispute

---

234 Commission of the European Communities', proposal for a council decision, provisionally extending in advance for 1977 the import quotas laid down for 1976 by Council Decision 75/788/EEC in respect of the People's Republic of China, COM (76) 496 final, 24 September 1976, AEI, Document No. 57880, available at: http://aei.pitt.edu/57880/, last accessed on 1 May 2020.

235 HEUSER ROBERT, Chinese Law of Foreign Trade: An Interview, in: The China Quarterly, No. 73, March 1973, pp. 159–165.

236 WEGGEL 1976, pp. 395 f.

fairly and seek truth from facts". Besides assuring that "due regard" would be given in such cases to mutual benefit and "international practice", he stated:

> "In short: we protect foreign patent rights, only the method of protection is different. Temporarily, we protect it in the contracts. Perhaps there will be other methods in the future. Our foreign friends can be reassured. our Party and government are against imitating as this only shows our inability. The best way to learn is to invent by yourself and not to copy from others."[237]

Connecting nodes: Infrastructures and ships

> "Such a small country as Japan has a trade fleet with a volume of four million tons. That a country of the size of ours does not have such a fleet for the transport of its own goods cannot be talked away."[238]

That the expansion of foreign trade was accounted for in China can be seen not only in the planning documents and political declarations but also when looking at investments in infrastructure and transport capacities that were made in that regard. The exportation of oil was connected to remarkable projects which, so to speak, erected huge monuments in the PRC's signifying newly established openness, railways and pipelines, pointing from the inland to the harbours.

In late 1969, the port of Tianjin – which is, to date, the largest freight port in Northern China[239] – and its facilities were expanded remarkably. In addition to three piers that were each able to accommodate four seagoing ships, construction of an additional pier was completed by the end of the year. In parallel, the shallow water areas in the port were deepened by large dredgers to accommodate larger freight ships. As the empty ground was paved with cement, in addition to the three warehouses available, cargo storage at the port was increased greatly as well.[240] This expansion was accompanied by an extension of shipping capacities bound to Japan, as two large cargo ships constructed by the Shanghai Red Flag Shipyard were added to the fleet bound for Japan which, by the end of 1969, consisted a mere thirteen vessels.[241] This push for an increase of Chinese shipping capacities had as much symbolic value as monetary. The largest single item causing a current account deficit for China in 1970 and 1971 was the cost imposed by the necessity to rent freight capacities – in a situation where foreign trade was still even more marginal.[242]

In January 1973, the number of ships running the China-Japan route regularly had tripled to a still very modest thirty-nine, being managed by five Japanese firms acting as

---

237 Ibid., pp. 163 f.

238 Additional remarks on the Soviet *Political Economy*, quoted from Martin (ed.) 1972, p. 87, translation by the author.

239 Shiphub, Shipping ports in China, available at: https://www.shiphub.co/the-biggest-ports-in-china/, last accessed on 1 May 2020.

240 "Situation Regarding Communist China's Transportation and Communications", Taipei, Fei-Ch'ing Yueh-pao, JPRS Report No. 89, 01 01 1970.

241 Ibid.

242 Deleyne 1972, p. 154.

shipping agents.[243] Running a modern fleet that spearheaded the expansion of foreign trade required technical know-how, which had been built up constantly since the early 1960s, when land-bound trade after the Sino-Soviet split was marginalised. In September 1977, a US corporate trader in metals told the US Department of State that China had become his largest supplier of tungsten, while the Soviet Union was his largest customer. Asked to buy Soviet aluminum for delivery to China, the Chinese trade administration clarified that delivery by rail over the border would not be accepted as it was "not practical". Both the emphasis on seaports as primary nodes of international trade as well as political considerations might have contributed to this refusal.[244]

The building of oceangoing vessels was a complex and technically demanding feat. Accordingly, engineering and technical expertise were needed and supported. From the Dalian shipyards, Xinhua reported in autumn 1974 that "more than a hundred shipbuilders are receiving two years' training at a worker's spare-time college run by the [Hongqi]-shipyard in northeast China", and that the shipyard had established its own technical schools. This did not mean that the participatory ambitions of the Cultural Revolution were not presented as playing an important part in this particular industry. As an example, Chang Bicai, a graduate of 1964, heading the designing team for diesel engines, was presented by Xinhua:

> "A former bench worker with little schooling, [Chang Bicai] became director of the planning office of the engine workshop in 1959 after graduating from the evening school. Later he studied in the spare time college and, by applying what he learned there to his work, helped solve many problems in production. Through participation in designing and building a 3000 hp [horsepower] low-speed marine diesel engine in the day time and studying hard in the evening, he has improved his technical knowledge remarkable [sic!]."[245]

While such distinctly optimistic reports on the successes of technological development through the education of workers were issued frequently throughout the history of the PRC, tangible successes in the shipbuilding industry were recognised even by critical observers. Despite his rather contemptuous views on the Chinese economy and particularly its political leadership, a Taiwanese observer recognised the progress made in production methods:

> "...solid tower type sectional assemblies were used in assembling the hull rather than plane tower type sectional assemblies as in the past. The new techniques of plane welding, automatic welding and carbon arc planning were utilized fully to raise work efficiency. On 29 September, a rake hydraulic type dredge of the 10,000 ton class, the "Chinsung" was launched at the Shanghai [Jiangnan] Shipyard. It is claimed that the structure of the hull is practical, its maneuverability is good, it is highly automated and it can dredge up a full boat load of mud in only 15 minutes. Its major use is in keeping the

243 State of PRC communications sector analyzed, Taipei Fei-ch'ing Yüeh-pao, 10 03 1973, p. 108.

244 US Department of State, Electronic Telegram, Sino-Soviet Trade for 1977, 1 September 1977, 00:00, PlusD, ID: 1977PEKING01946_c.

245 Foreign Broadcast information Service, Talien shipyard raises workers' technical level Peking NCNA in English, 1200 GMT, 09 09 1974 B, accessed through Readex.

seaways along the coast and harbors clear and it has important significance to the development of shipping. [...] The situation in the shipbuilding industry for 1969 shows that after the Chinese Communists, through their own efforts, solved the manufacturing techniques for the 8,824-horsepower large scale low speed supercharged ship's main diesel engine, the shipbuilding industry attained rapid development."[246]

Decisions for the expansion of these gateways to the world were taken in the immediate aftermath of the turmoil brought by the Cultural Revolution; the expansion of the shipbuilding industry was focused on the construction of naval vessels. This included passenger ships with diesel engines, such as the Dongfanghong 38, built in 1971, which was defined as a prototype for the further expansion of passenger shipping capacities, in particular on the Yangtze River. Like the pioneering freighter Dongfeng, it was used as a model for oceangoing cargo ships to be constructed in the future.[247] The "all-people shipbuilding" campaign, launched in March 1970, increased the number of technical workers in large shipyards and demanded an effort by "all types of business to give support to the shipbuilding industry".[248] In line with the principle of self-reliance – keeping in mind that the Chinese shipbuilding industry could not rely on a long tradition and that there would have been quite extensive capacities available abroad – the necessary technology for advanced shipbuilding resulted to some extent from "native" Chinese industrial and technological development. Additionally, it not only included shipbuilding but also the necessary auxiliary technology for the sector's development.

On the 21st of June 1973, the ship unit of the first shipping construction division of the Chinese Ministry of Communications announced their independently produced a 100-ton floating crane used for the construction of ports.[249] The shipbuilding industry, as the Chinese naval tradition had been interrupted centuries ago, was also a prime example of the Chinese need for foreign technology. The technical school of the Dalian shipyard, it was proudly added, also offered "a foreign language class for technicians to facilitate their study of foreign technical data and reference books".[250] The expansion of shipping also meant the opening of new routes. On 10 August 1974, the 10'000-ton ocean freighter Dongfeng, constructed solely in the PRC, arrived in Vancouver after having crossed the Pacific. It was the first time a Chinese freighter had ever entered a Canadian harbour.[251] Ties with Canada were deepened when the Hong Kong branch of the Canadian Pacific Airlines announced that the Canadian government had formally allowed it to fly to both Shanghai and Peking in exchange for granting landing rights in Vancouver and Ottawa

---

246 Communist China's Industry in 1969, Taipei Chung-kung Yen-chiu, 01 1970.

247 Dai Wusan, Communication Technology, in: Lu Yongxiang (ed.), A History of Chinese Science and Technology, Volume 3, Heidelberg, New York, Dordrecht and London 2015, pp. 486 ff.

248 Communist China's Transportation and Communications, Taipei Fei-ch'ing Yueh-pao, 01 09 1970, p. 63.

249 Taiwan reports on current status of PRC transportation, Taipei Fei-ch'ing Yueh-pao, 10 07 1973, p. 103.

250 Foreign Broadcast information Service, Talien shipyard raises workers' technical level Peking NCNA in English, 1200 GMT, 09 09 1974 B, accessed through Readex.

251 Ibid.

to Chinese airlines. Similar talks were held with the Chilean government – at the time still under president Salvador Allende, and Japan.[252]

Despite this effort to raise shipbuilding capacities, the supply did not satisfy the demand for ocean-going tonnage in China. In early 1973, it had become obvious that the continued purchase of vessels from abroad was systematic rather than merely based on some *ad hoc* decisions aiming at a temporary stabilisation or expansion of available shipping capacities in the PRC. To simplify the transactions, purchases and payments were handled by Chinese shipping companies based in Hong Kong.[253] The acquired ships ranged from newly produced – such as an order placed with the Netherlands Associated Shipbuilding Industry in Rotterdam for two 101-meter self-propelled dredgers, intended for the clearing of ports, which were delivered in late 1973 – to the takeover of used ships. Two examples show how Japan served as a gateway for these purchases: The used Norwegian freighter Fraen of 31'825 tons was bought from Norway. Forty-six Chinese crew-members travelled to Sasebo in Japan, renamed the vessel and took it to the seas to ship wheat from Canada and Australia to Chinese ports. After this assignment, the freighter joined the Chinese fleet on the Japan-route and was handled by the Japanese Yamashita New Nippon Steamship Company. Similarly, six old refrigerator ships were acquired for the transportation of meat and perishable goods. The transaction was executed in Japanese yen and, remarkably, was based on delayed payment over three years.[254]

Despite this bold move away from the programmatic avoidance of debt of any sort, procurement increased constantly. The Japanese Nihon Jiji News Agency cited an announcement from the Nishii Shipping Company, on the 20th of June 1973, that the company had signed a contract with the China National Machinery Import and Export Corporation to sell nine 1000-ton refrigerator-equipped cargo ships at approximately four billion yen, to be delivered before the end of 1974. It was communicated that China planned to have those vessels run international lines with cargoes of frozen fish and meat.[255] While the Chinese fleet was mostly built up by 1975, shipping agreements provided for cargo sharing with other fleets, which reduced the necessity for an expansion of the Chinese fleet by legal arrangement. For example as agreed with Argentina, where a cargo-sharing arrangement in 1977 provided for a fifty-fifty split of cargo volume in bilateral trade – which, in the view of an Argentinian diplomat, would result in most cargo being carried on Argentine ships, given their larger capacity.[256]

Shipbuilding in China, in particular of large oceangoing vessels, also became the target of political campaigns. Zhou Enlai, who had also advocated for the fleet's build-up through the chartering of foreign shipping capacities, was attacked for following a "slavish comprador philosophy". Chartering was used extensively in the course of the expan-

---

252 Joint Publications Research Service, Situation of Chinese Communist communications sector, Article by Chiang Huai, Taipei Fei-ch'ing Yueh pao, No. 2, Original in Mandarin, 10 04 1973, p. 105, accessed through Readex.

253 Ibid.

254 State of PRC communications sector analyzed, Taipei Fei-ch'ing Yueh-pao, 10 03 1973, p. 109.

255 Taiwan reports on current status of PRC transportation, Taipei Fei-ch'ing Yueh-pao, 10 07 1973, p. 103.

256 US Department of State, Electronic Telegram, Sino-Argentine Trade, 6 July 1977, 00:00, PlusD, ID: 1977PEKING01339_c.

sion of grain exports during the Great Leap Forward, with chartered tonnage in Northern China rising from 51'847 tons in 1958 over 184'511 tons in 1959 and 190'125 tons in 1960, with almost a quarter of cargo in the area transported by chartered ships in 1960. In 1974, two-thirds of Chinese cargo moved in chartered ships, a figure that was cut approximately in half by 1982.[257] The formula criticised an alleged preference of foreign technology over natively developed innovations. In the course of 1974, a large freighter developed and build in China called Fengqing became an important symbol for the claim that China could put modern and complex technology to use on its own – which was true – as building large ships is among the most demanding industrial undertakings. Even though imports of technology had, according to FREDERICK C. TEIWES and WARREN SUN, been explicitly authorised by Mao Zedong in 1972 and 1973, shipping became, for a short time, the focal point of controversial political rhetoric.[258] That China needed additional shipping capacities was not disputed as such; again, the *how* stood at the centre of debate.

The following propaganda poster (Fig. 6) was produced after the fourth National People's Congress – in April 1974 – depicting the Fengqing. It is anchored in the Shanghai harbour, with the characteristic architectural landmarks of the Bund waterfront visible on the right. The title, "32,000 miles that make us feel proud and elated" refers to her maiden voyage through the Pacific, Indian and Atlantic Oceans, to Asian, African and European countries. In an official publication of the Foreign languages Press for a foreign audience, published in 1975, under the title, China's First Quarter Century, the scene was described vividly:

> "The eve of new China's 25th anniversary saw the gala sailing of her 10,000 ton freighter, the Fengqing, from the mouth of the Yangtze River towards Shanghai Harbour. Amid the beating of drums and the clashing of gongs thunderous cheers of 'Long live Chairman Mao!' and 'Long live the policy of independence, initiative and self-reliance' burst forth along the banks of the [Wangpu] river. [...] This freighter, designed and made by China's own efforts and consisting entirely of domestic-made equipment, had returned from her 32,000 -nautical-mile maiden voyage [...]."[259]

The long voyage of the Fengqing was also presented as an example of Chinese industrial quality, as a case proving the "reliability of China-made ship equipment".[260] The increase in Chinese shipping capacities was registered in other countries, as was the interest of Chinese shipping in the international market for tonnage. In the course of the early 1970s, the market for ships and shipping capacity was hit by the consequences of the international economic downturn. The monthly price index applied by UNCTAD for voyage charter dry cargo freight rates, which had fallen to 66 (of 100 points) in 1972, rose to 215 in October, 222 in November, and 241 in December 1973.[261] Shipping was more expensive than

257 See: LI LIANJUN, Study of China's maritime shipping policy, Malmö 1990, p. 85; and MULLER DAVID G., China as a maritime power, New York and Oxon 1983.

258 TEIWES/SUN 2008, pp. 206 f. and 209.

259 New China's First Quarter-Century, Beijing 1975, p.119.

260 Ibid.

261 United Nations Conference on Trade and Development, Review of maritime transport 1972–1973, Report by the secretariat of UNCTAD, TD/B/C.4/117, New York 1975, available at: https://unctad.org/en/PublicationsLibrary/rmt1972-73_en.pdf, last accessed on 1 May 2020, p. 45.

ever before since the beginning of 1969. The development of time charter freight rates was similar. The cost of new builds, which had risen gradually throughout the 1960s, accelerated sharply in 1969 and 1970, with a further moderate increase in 1971.[262]

Fig. 6 Yangmei tuqide sanwan erqian li, Shanghai renmin chubanshe, 53x77 cm, Stephan Landsberger Collection at the Institute for International Social History (IISH), Call number PC-1975-002 (Private collection), picture from: https://chineseposters.net/posters/pc-1975-002.php, last accessed on 1 May 2020.

The rapid increase of these prices between 1969 and 1971 reflected both increases in production costs (principally in wages and in steel prices) and the ability of the shipbuilders to control prices, taking advantage of the high demand for tonnage in relation to the manufacturing capacity of the world shipbuilding industry.[263] During 1972, the prices for most sizes of bulk carriers and tankers dropped below 1971 levels as a result of the lower volume of new orders. However, prices rose sharply in 1973, though not in a uniform pattern, for all types of vessels, with a steeper rise for tankers.

Shortly after, the shipping markets turned to the opposite. From the mid-1970s to the mid-1980s, the shipping sector went through a crisis that was longer, deeper, and more dramatic than any other previous downturn.[264] The tonnage surplus during the last ship-

262 Ibid., p. 27.

263 The shipping industries were hit by the economic crises, primarily in two ways. First, the devaluation of the USD relative to revalued currencies, e. g., the Japanese Yen and the German Mark, improved the comparative cost position of the US shipyards, relative to other suppliers. Second, the immediate effect of the devaluation of the USD for non-American shipyards having long-term credits repayable in dollars, inflicted losses on these shipyards, in so far as their currencies had been revalued, relative to the USD.

264 Tenold Stig, The Shipping Crisis, in: Norwegian Shipping in the 20th Century, Cham 2018, pp. 195–230.

ping crisis in the 1920s was higher, but markets stabilised relatively quickly and the crisis did not have any immediate long-term effects on the sector. While the difficulties during and after the Great Depression lasted longer than those in the 1920s, it was still a much tamer downturn than the one occurring in the 1970s and 1980s. The shipping crisis was characterised by rapidly falling freight rates, increasing lay-up rates and, accordingly, diminishing profits. Freight rates in the tanker market – that was almost exclusively relevant for the transportation of oil, which was not in high demand as the supply was cut – declined instantly, with rates in the spot market for large tankers falling by more than 75 percent from October to December 1973.[265]

It became difficult for shipping companies to operate, even at the depressed level of rates, as the large oil companies had reserved the cargoes for their own ships and those they had were taken on long-term charter. The build-up of the domestic shipping industry had thus taken place immediately before the decline of prices would have made the continuation of a rental-strategy much more tempting. But, as it were, the production of Chinese ships was a sensible path in economic terms, during the peaks of shipping rates in the early 1970s, and a symbol of China being a trading nation. The number of Chinese maritime freighters handled by Japanese agents increased further, as both used and new ships were bought from European countries and Japan.[266] From mid-1972 until the end of 1973, China ordered 120 ships from Japan alone, of which more than sixty percent were for dredging and improving ports.[267]

On the 7th of June 1973, the Philippine Secretary of Commerce Troadio Quiazon announced that a Philippine trade delegation had visited Peking a month earlier and had subsequently submitted a report on the Chinese interest in sending Chinese ships to Philippine ports to undertake commercial shipping orders.[268] In particular, China had signalled that it would like to extend the China–Singapore–Malaysia shipping route to the Philippines and that the freight cost would be lower than that charged by any other company. In its report, the delegation further stated that China would be willing to designate a vessel under Chinese flag to run regularly between Canton and Manila via Hong Kong.[269] The prospects were also taken note of in Europe. A delegation of businessmen from the FRG undertook a "scouting mission" in 1973 with clear intentions, as Claus Rickmers, principal of the Rickmers Line Shipping Company emphasised:

> "…not to seek contacts, […] rather to obtain, first of all, a knowledge of China's economy, industry, trade and shipping industry by personal inspection [and] draw the attention

---

265 Ibid., p. 215, FN 30, and Fig 7.2, p. 202, and Fig. 7.3, p. 203.

266 State of PRC Communications Sector analysed, Taipei Fei-ch'ing Yüeh-pao, 10 03 1973, pp. 106–109.

267 COHEN/PARK 1975, p. 36.

268 Taiwan reports on current status of PRC transportation, Taipei Fei-ch'ing Yueh-pao, 10 07 1973, p. 105.

269 Ibid.

> of shipping organizations to the capacity of the German shipping industry as regards both liner traffic as well as tramp shipping".[270]

Nevertheless, the voyage proved to be lucrative. Shipowner Rickmers was not only able to negotiate an increase in freight rates at a "completely new tariff" (quoted in RMB) but also found his worries about long waiting times at Chinese ports readily addressed; in the future, his ships would be serviced at a modern port, where loading and unloading could be carried out simultaneously. Allegedly, Premier Zhou Enlai personally assured Rickmers that in "two or three years", the problem of waiting times would be solved.[271] Rickmers assessment of the situation was accordingly optimistic, stating that in his opinion, the Chinese traffic would "undoubtedly get lively". The composition of traded goods as at the time of his visit was, in his view, potentially about to change; it consisted of mostly iron and steel products, pipes, nonferrous metals, chemicals, locomotives, and trucks as well as some machinery, machine tools and, occasionally, complete factory equipment from the European Economic Community in exchange for oil seeds, vegetable oil, skins and furs, silk and bristles, tea, tobacco, canned goods, textiles, basic chemicals, and high-grade ores like manganese, wolfram and antimony as well as bauxite and fluorspar. In addition to the "traditional" goods, trade would increasingly shift to high-grade machinery, chemicals and metals in exchange for light industrial goods. On principle, however, Rickmers warned against expectations that the China trade will assume large proportions, due to it being "self-sufficient" and foreign trade being traditionally complementary to its domestic trade.[272]

When foreign trade had moved to the centre of economic policy in 1977, Renmin Ribao concluded that in Chinese ports, many new berths had been built in "the combined 23 years since the founding of new China." The construction of seaports as well as the engineering projects necessary for their operations, needed to be assessed with regard to whether they were developing, "in step with a new leap forward in the national economy and the daily expansion of foreign trade and foreign aid". No delay could be afforded. At the interface of a new China shaped by the re-emerged Four Modernisations, the nodes connecting the Chinese economy to the world needed to be prioritised. Seaports as large projects, "often requiring the wholehearted cooperation of tens and even hundreds of plants", were also a stress test for the implementation of planning and, where necessary, socialist cooperation. The commentary pushed, "There are only a few months left this year [...]. If we slacken our efforts even a little, our plans may become a mere flash in the pan." During the last two quarters of the year, according to the new priority of foreign trade, "great volumes of cargo will come to China to be unloaded or transshipped at a few large seaports. Time is pressing and the task is urgent."

The necessity of *speed* in Chinese economic development, while still primarily directed by political ambition and the perception of military threat, also increasingly stemmed from the need to conduct trade reliably and on an increasingly larger scale.

270 Joint Publications Research Service, Article by Hansjörg Heinrich: "China Trade Shipping: No grounds for Euphoria", Germany DVZ Deutsche Verkehrszeitung, Original in German, 28 08 1973, p. 9, accessed through Readex.

271 Ibid.

272 Ibid.

With the right spirit, as the commentary assured, the workers could certainly fulfil this task that was crucial for China's future. The outlook given promised even more work with regard to trade infrastructure: "As long as we persist in [achieving of not only greater and faster but also better and more economical results in the building of ports], many new seaports will appear one after another along our motherland's long coastline and make contributions to the task of achieving initial success this year and great success within three years [until 1980]."[273]

In a report directed at a foreign audience, Xinhua confirmed in September 1977 that ports along the Chinese seacoast had handled about twenty-five percent more cargo during the month of August compared to the same month in 1976, with cargo-handling activity at the ports of Qinhuangdao, Qingdao, Shanghai and Changjiang hitting an "all-time high". While faster processes of loading and unloading were claimed to have cut the average time of anchorage by more than three days – a problem that had been complained about by foreign seamen in earlier years – it was reported that Chairman Hua Guofeng had "learned from a letter to a newspaper that some of the ports were congested with accumulated goods", and that ships had to wait at sea for long periods of time for unloading and loading. The very same day, the report underlined, the chairman directed the departments concerned to work out ways to solve the issue. The State Planning Commission, the State Capital Construction Commission and the Ministries of Communications, Railways and Foreign Trade decided at a joint meeting to send joint work teams to the major ports – which were Dalian in Northeast China, Tianjin in North China, Huangpu in South China and Shanghai in East China – coordinated by a joint office. The report concluded that "Chairman Hua's personal attention to the work of the ports" was "a tremendous inspiration to the workers there". They "warmly responded" by starting a socialist labour emulation drive – the establishment and application of best practices – which allegedly helped eliminate the congestion of the ports within a short time.[274]

In accordance with this mandate, which was in fact a continuation of a pattern that had begun earlier in the decade, the development of shipping capacities focused primarily on efficiency and the improving of loading capacities alongside the continuous expansion of the Chinese seagoing fleet. Ships needed to be large, standardised and use advanced modes of transportation, which was primarily the capacity to handle standard freight containers. From a publication of the Ministry of Communications (and Transport):

> "We must actively build large ships, standard cargo ships and special purpose ships, and popularise such advanced modes of transportation as container transportation, loose packed transportation, gas and liquid transportation etc. Accordingly, we must build new ports, increase the number of docks and berths, and continue to improve

273 Foreign Broadcast Information Service, People's Daily Outlines Seaport Construction Tasks, People's Daily commentator's article: "Earnestly Do a Good Job in Completing the Supplementary Projects and Final Engineering Tasks in Seaport Construction", Peking People's Daily in Mandarin, 19 08 1977 SK, accessed through Readex.

274 Foreign Broadcast Information Service, Cargo Congestion at Shipping Ports Eliminated, Peking NCNA in English, 1221 GMT, 22 09 1977 OW, accessed through Readex.

> port facilities. The development of ocean transportation must be in line with the development of our country's foreign trade and aid to other countries".[275]

Chinese coastal cities re-emerged as centres of economic development, after their status had been somewhat relativised by the Third Front policies, and the emphasis was on balanced development between cities and the countryside. This was underlined by ambitious demands published in both Hongqi and Renmin Ribao in early December 1977. While Shanghai might have already been termed China's largest industrial city before liberation, "in reality, it only had some light industrial plants." Now, due to its predisposition as a harbour city, it needed to be built into "an industrial base on the advanced world level".[276]

In addition to shipping capacities, infrastructures directly related to crude oil were extended and improved within China. In October 1973, Chinese officials signalled China's readiness to extend pipelines from the Daqing oilfields to Fushan and then "a port" – one of the main Chinese large ocean ports, Yantai, being mere kilometres away – to Japanese officials.[277] With the impressive, 1152-kilometres long Daqing–Qinhuangdao pipeline, which was completed in spring 1974 after about two years of construction, the oilfields of Daqing were directly connected to a sea harbour capable of handling the crude oil destined for export.[278] Other than earlier pipeline projects which connected the industrial centres and their refineries within China with the major oilfields (Daqing, Shengli and Dagang), this pipeline literally cast China's export orientation in steel and concrete.

Furthermore, the necessary capacities for augmenting oil exports and other trade activities were built rapidly. in 1974: some forty deep water berths were constructed; subsequently, introducing a technical innovation that would shape international trade in goods arguably like no other[279], container facilities, though still limited mostly to Shanghai and Tianjin, were built in Huangpu and Xingang.[280] In late 1975, Tianjin,

---

275 Foreign Broadcast Information Service, Ministry Calls for Modernization of Communications, Article by theoretical group of the Ministry of Communications: "Implement Chairman Mao's Behest, Speed up the Modernization of Communications.", Peking People's Daily in Mandarin, 06 11 1977 HK, accessed through Readex.

276 Foreign Broadcast Information Service, Peng Chung Article on Developing Shanghai's Industry, article by Peng Chung: "Make Full Use of and Actively Develop Shanghai's Industry So as To Make Still Greater Contributions to the Realization of the Four Modernizations", Red Flag No. 12 and People's Daily of 8 December, Peking NCNA Domestic Service in Mandarin, 0226 GMT, 07 12 1977 OW, accessed through Readex.

277 Chinese Economic Mission Concludes Visit to Japan, PlusD, ID: 1973TOKYO13258_b.

278 BARTKE WOLFGANG, Oil in the People's Republic of China, Industry, Structure, Production, Exports, Hamburg 1977.

279 After a refitted oil tanker carried 58 shipping containers from Newark to Houston, in April 1956, container shipping developed steadily into a major industry that made the boom in global trade in goods and the development of highly efficient multi-modal logistics possible. See MARC LEVINSON's innovative study: LEVINSON MARC, The Box: How the Shipping Container Made the World Smaller and the World Economy Bigger, Princeton 2010.

280 Joint Publications Research Service, Article by Akio Akagi and Morihiko Sato of the Japan Broadcasting Corporation: "Tach'ing Oil Fields and China's Industrial Technology", Tokyo Shizen, Original in Japanese, 05 1974, pp. 62–74, accessed through Readex. See also: WHEELER SNOW, LOIS, China's Foreign Trade and Aid, in: Journal of World Trade Law, Vol. 11, Issue 2, 1977.

north China's major industrial city, reported the completion of its state-financed key projects and proudly pointed out that the newly constructed Tanggu harbour had added eight berths capable of accommodating ships up to 10,000 tons deadweight and commanded "cargo-handling capacity equal to the total handled in the past twenty-three years since Liberation".[281] At the port of Dalian, port facilities able to handle both tankers of a tonnage above 100'000 and a pipeline from Daqing were installed in 1974, followed by the procurement of a Japanese tanker of this tonnage in November of 1975. In the first nine months of 1976, the shipyards of Dalian finished three tankers of 24'000 tons and one of 50'000 tons.[282]

While insisting on self-reliance, China was eager to show the achievements of the socialist state in the expansion of its trade infrastructures to the world. The newly constructed port capacities were promoted abroad with dedicated publications[283] that laid out the respective technical advantages and capabilities in cargo handling, climate, hydrography and even ongoing and planned projects for their further expansion. The purchase of oil extraction and petrochemical facilities from Western European countries and Japan was considerably emphasised. While the technological know-how and the major part of facilities used in extraction and refining were inherited from the Sino–Soviet cooperation, the Ministry of Fuel and Chemical Industry, newly founded in late 1970 with the telling abolishment of the former Ministry of Coal Industry[284], looked to the West for further development capacities.

By January 1974, six countries (France, Italy, the FRG, Japan, Denmark, US) had received orders for oil production facilities worth over half a billion USD.[285] Interestingly, while some of these orders were placed already in the mid-1960s, and focused on refining equipment, later orders in 1972, 1973 and 1974 included the obtainment of deep-water drilling vessels from Japan and, in February 1974, the purchase of equipment designed to control pressure in wells during drilling from the US company Rucker & Co., which demonstrated the willingness to expand exploitation to offshore oilfields.[286]

A Soviet radio commentary broadcast in Moscow in March 1974 described the Chinese rapprochement with international markets sceptically, from a staunchly Leninist perspective.[287]

---

281 Foreign Broadcast Information Service, Tientsin Capital Construction Develops Rapidly, Peking NCNA in English, 1200 GMT, 20 11 1975 OW, accessed through Readex.

282 Péan 1977, p. 166.

283 Such as: Foreign Languages Press, The General Condition of China's Seaports, Beijing 1974.

284 Yang Chi-Jen, Energy Policy in China, New York 2017, in particular table 2.5.

285 US Department of State, Electronic Telegram, People's Republic of China Economic Review 2, 12 January 1974, 05:45, PlusD, ID: 1974HONGK00476_b.

286 See data cited in Bartke 1977, Table K, p. 43.

287 In particular his remarks on monopoly capitalism and raw materials: "The main particularity of modern capitalism is the rule of the monopolist associations of the large entrepreneurs. Such monopolies are the strongest, when all sources of raw materials are in one hand, and we have seen, how eager the international capitalist associations are striving to make [entering into] competition impossible for any adversary, how eager they are to buy up e. g. iron ore deposits or petroleum sources etc. Only colonial property offers full reassurance for the success of monopolies vis-à-vis all contingencies including that the adversary might wish to entrench himself behind a law on state monopoly. The higher developed capitalism, the stronger the shortage of raw materials can be felt,

> "The superiority of foreign trade of socialist countries is also known to the Chinese people. During China's first 5-year plan period, the socialist countries had provided China with production means totaling 12.500 million yuan [...] Now let us look at the current situation. The volume of China's foreign trade with capitalist countries accounts for 75 percent of its total, whereas that with socialist countries accounts for only 25 percent. [...] The question arises: What purpose do the capitalist countries have for trading with China? The answer: They want China's rich mineral deposits. [...] Dear Chinese listeners: You must realize that imperialists never give anything free of charge. Prices for China's mineral products are not high, but those for finished products made with Chinese raw materials and then sold to China are. The unfavorable balance in China's trade with Western capitalist countries and Japan is now greater than ever, and China is in debt. Of course, the closer its contacts with the capitalist markets, the greater China will suffer from the impact of the monetary crisis and the turbulence in the Western countries."[288]

Having turned away from the "politically correct" way to conduct trade – meaning with and among socialist economies – the Chinese had given in to imperialist demands to open their economy. Inevitably, this could, in the view of the commentator, only lead to the exploitation of China's raw materials and its economy through unjust terms of trade, forcing overpriced goods on Chinese people in order to realise a profit. Also, the establishment of economic connections to the West would inevitably subject the economy of socialist China to the unpredictable and anarchic volatility of the capitalist markets, at the time, notably visible in the ongoing generalised crisis in the capitalist world system. Certainly, the commentary duly ignored that exports of raw materials to the West were already an important part of the Soviet economy.[289]

Was this criticism justified, and did the establishment of a legal framework, infrastructural nodes and an increased exchange of goods lead to perilous effects? Did China become nothing but a source of raw materials and a market for goods? In the longer-run, this is certainly not true, as China has become one of the major importers of the former and the most important exporter of the latter. Certainly, it has not again become a colony subject to the will of foreign governments and corporations.[290] Nevertheless, in

---

the sharper the concurrence and the hunt for sources of raw materials around the world, the more the struggle for the acquisition of colonies is fought bitterly." LENIN VLADIMIR, Der Imperialismus als höchstes Stadium des Kapitalismus, München 2001, p. 92, translation by the author.

288 Foreign Broadcast Information Service, PRC Seen Heading for Total Dependency on Imperialists, Unattributed station observer's commentary: "Why China does not publish information on its economic conditions", Radio Moscow in Mandarin, 1030 GMT 27 03 1974 B, accessed through Readex.

289 In 1971, Soviet Trade with capitalist countries (except West Berlin) had risen to 21.7 of the total, rising further to 22.6 percent in 1972 and 27 percent in 1973, also consisting to a large extent of purchases of grain and industrial equipment and increasing exports of crude oil. See: US Department of State, Electronic Telegram, Comment on Preliminary Soviet Foreign Trade Figures, 24 April 1974, 08:44, PlusD, ID: 1974MOSCOW06059_b.

290 As of today, China's five most important commodity imports are mineral fuels including oil at over 116 billion USD p.a., iron ore at over 57 billion USD p.a., copper and copper ore at over 53 billion USD p.a., oil seeds at over 38 billion USD p.a. and coal at over 11 billion USD p.a.,

the short run, raw materials did indeed play a decisive role in shaping the structure of Chinese exports, as did industrial goods on the import side.

In order to understand the path to China's rise, I suggest that it is crucial to analyse first, the kinds of goods and raw materials that were traded, and second, how the structure of this trade changed over time. I suggest that two commodities are of particular relevance during the long 1970s – the main product of Daqing, crude oil, is the first. The second, important in Dazhai, is grain. Both were linked through foreign trade.

Of oil and grain

As the energy crisis drove prices up, quadrupling until late 1974, a new rift between the Three Worlds appeared: both superpowers were able to find alternative sources of energy or produce themselves, whereas the other industrialised states of the West, were most strongly affected. Within the third world, however, the crisis revealed a fourth: all non-oil producing countries, which were also the least developed. The PRC, still a developing country, was clearly not one of them.

On the occasion of the 25th anniversary of the socialist state, the fact that the PRC had been able to build modern industries that produced for foreign markets was publicly and proudly pointed to, alongside a more pronounced shift of the Chinese economic development:

> "China has built the [Daqing], [Dagang], Shengli and other oilfields, and modern oil refineries and petro-chemical complexes. She is self-sufficient in both variety and output of oil products and now exports oil and oil products from a surplus."[291]

As it was largely fuelling the industrialised economies of the West, oil was the ultimate commodity with which to obtain foreign exchange, without requiring the construction of industries that could actually produce internationally competitive goods or undermining the basic livelihood of the people by resorting to the agricultural resources that were notoriously scarce in China. The Chinese entry and participation in the world market were a novel and distinctive phenomenon of the 1970s. It was driven, first, by the necessity to supplement the domestic industrial cities with grain that the production units in the countryside were not able to provide consistently and, second, by the targeted use of investment, manpower and technology on the scarce oilfields of Northern China.

These driving factors were established before the expansion of trade had been decided. After the second National People's Congress declared in 1963 that the country was basically self-sufficient in oil, minor exports began in the late 1960s.[292] Oil had been a priority of economic planning since the first five-year plan, which had earmarked almost

---

accounting for a significant proportion of global trade in natural resources, generally consuming more than it exports. See: Commodity.com, China Commodity Imports & Exports, 8 June 2020: How China Continues to Dominate World Trade, available at: https://commodity.com/china/, last accessed on 10 June 2020.

291 China's socialist economy proves successful in 25 years, 0701 GMT, 24 09 1974 B.

292 Cohen, Jerome Alan, Park, Choon-ho, The Politics of China's Oil Weapon, in: Foreign Policy, No. 20, 1975, p. 28.

two-thirds of the national energy budget for the development of these resources.[293] The discovery of the Daqing oil field in the Heilongjiang province in 1959 gave rise to a national symbol of successful "socialist construction" and laid the base for a major asset for the financing of modernisation efforts in the 1970s. While the Chinese production figures remained on a relatively modest level when compared to major producers of oil such as the USA, the Soviet Union and Saudi Arabia, their growth during the early 1970s was remarkable and only surpassed by enthusiastic projections of future output. In 1975, the New York Times quoted estimates that were as high-flying as they were wide ranging:

> "China's oil reserves during the nineteen-fifties were put at less than 6 billion metric tons by most industry estimates, and increases in Soviet oil output were planned on the assumption of China's rising import needs. Meanwhile, industry estimates have been increased to more than 10 billion metric tons albeit with a wide range of estimates: In 1973, Shell estimated China's recoverable oil reserves at only 2.7 billion metric tons, while at the other extreme there reportedly is a United States industry estimate that puts the reserves, including offshore deposits, as high as 50 billion metric tons. **Shell's estimate would place China about 10th in the worldwide ranking of reserves; the latter estimate would make it first** [emphasis added]. Most United States experts assume China's proven reserves to be in the neighborhood of 10 billion metric tons. (As a comparison, Saudi Arabia's are set at 22.5 billion.) More accurate estimates may become available as the Chinese authorities seek outside help in the development of their oil resources."[294]

US estimates concerning the prospect of oil exports from China, which in 1973 were still very modest and did not project a remarkable potential, despite the fact that alternative sources for oil apart from the Arab members of the Organisation of Petrol Exporting Countries (OPEC) were desperately sought, were toppled by Zhou Enlai's claim at the end of the year that Chinese oil production had increased more than 150 percent compared to prior, rather conservative, Chinese and over sixty percent compared to US estimates.[295] Even if these figures were probably exaggerated, they signalled that Chinese crude oil would be available for foreign buyers in large quantities. As the consequences of the international energy crisis for industrialised countries were well-known to Zhou and the Chinese leadership[296], this isolated production figure at a time when statistics on the Chinese economy were extremely scarce abroad, the message was well-placed and well-received.

---

293 Ibid, p. 29.

294 Ronall Joachim O., China as an Oil-Exporting Nation, *The New York Times*, 5 January 1975, Section F, p. 3, available at: https://www.nytimes.com/1975/01/05/archives/china-as-an-oilexporting-nation-reserves-stir-wide-range-of.html, last accessed on 1 May 2020.

295 People's Republic of China Economic Review 1, 12 January 1974, 05:45, ID: 1974HONGK00476_b.

296 US Department of the Interior, Minerals Yearbook 1973, Volume III, Area Reports: International, Washington D.C. 1976, p. 232, available at: https://pubs.er.usgs.gov/publication/70048196, last accessed on 1 May 2020; and Lelyveld Joseph, Chinese Oil-Output Figures Are a Puzzle, The New York Times, 9 January 1974, p. 2, available at: https://www.nytimes.com/1974/01/09/archives/chinese-oiloutput-figures-are-a-puzzle-assess-french-revolution.html, last accessed on 1 May 2020.

As global demand for this commodity with almost global demand increased, the PRC seemed to have found an incomparable source of revenue. The export orientation of the capital-intense oil industry was also decisively enabled by the fact that the Chinese economy was mostly running on coal.[297] Due to its formation of coke, coal was a key resource for the production of iron and steel, which remained the key output of the heavy industry. Further, coal was used for the production of synthetic plastics, rubber and fibres as well as for the industries directly linked to the central policy of agricultural improvement, chemical fertilisers, pesticides and electricity generation. Coal was the lifeblood of Chinese industry and energy production, while the relatively small supply of oil for a long time had prevented the Chinese economy from becoming as dependent on oil as Western economies at the time had become.[298]

While many of the appliances introduced by the push for agricultural mechanisation would need refined fuel produced from crude oil, the extent of the undertaking and the timeframe set for it created a window of opportunity during which the production capacities for oil could be held high enough to create a surplus. The policies of austerity discussed above – whose focus shifted remarkably towards energy saving with growing oil export – allowed for the slight extension of this *marge de manoeuvre*. To underline that China would be able to sustain the extraction of an oil surplus as long as needed, prospects for an expansion of Chinese oil production were framed as highly positive and an important part of self-reliance. A description of the Chinese economy published in May 1973 and tellingly titled "The Fatherland's Good Mountains and Rivers" stated:

> "From a very early time China discovered and utilized petroleum. [...] However, before the liberation, reactionary leaders did not engage seriously in the survey of actual oil deposits, and more than 90 percent of the areas in the entire country was ignored without any investigation. [...] The three American and British controlled companies of Caltex, Standard Oil, and Asia Col monopolized the China market and sold 'western oil' at exorbitant prices. According to statistics, during the 42-year period between 1907 and 1948, these three companies extracted high profits totaling 30 million dollars. In order to monopolize the Chinese petroleum market, these imperialists invented 'a theory of oil-poor China'. They irresponsibly stated that there was very little likelihood of oil discovery in the southeastern section of China, and the possibility in the southwestern sector was even less."[299]

This "theory", of course, was debunked by the success of the industrial model brigade of Daqing, as well as the pioneering spirit of Chinese engineers and scientists such as

297 Which was estimated to cover about 85 percent of its energy needs, while the USA and Japan relied on oil at 44 percent and 73 percent respectively.

298 With regard to the unfolding and regression of the international oil economy see: NEU AXEL D., Die Entfaltung der internationalen Erdölwirtschaft seit 1950, in: PFISTER CHRISTIAN (ed.), Das 1950er Syndrom, Der Weg in die Konsumgesellschaft, second edition, Bern, Stuttgart and Vienna 1996, pp.179-200.

299 As quoted in: Foreign Broadcast Information Service, Article by Akio Akagi and Morihiko Sato of the Japan Broadcasting Corporation, "Tach'ing oil fields and China's industrial technology", Tokyo Shizen in Japanese, 05 1974, pp. 63, accessed through Readex.

Li Siguang whose rise to the official heroes fighting alongside Wang Jinxi – who, not by accident, was an oil worker – has been discussed in the previous chapter.

Despite the need for extensive investment, the oil sector was kept strictly isolated from foreign influence. In 1973, when the Japanese minister of international trade Nakasone signalled that there was a strong desire among the petroleum refining industry circles in Japan to help with the development of such resources on the continental shelf of China, Zhou Enlai harshly ruled out any such joint ventures.[300] In this regard, China acted remarkably different from other socialist states, like the Soviet Union or Bulgaria. Leonid Brezhnev was reported in March 1973 to have answered to a letter from the Japanese Prime Minister Kakuei Tanaka that the Soviet Union had disposed of "sufficient capabilities and foreign exchange to develop these resources independently", but nevertheless accepted to cooperate with Japan and supply resources for thirty to forty years.[301]

This reluctance vis-à-vis foreign capital participation and cooperation did not prevent oil prospects from becoming a core topic of Chinese economic diplomacy. When a 33-member economic mission headed by the Vice Minister of Foreign Trade Liu Xiwen concluded a month-long visit to Japan, in October 1973, Japanese participation for the extension of oil pipelines was discussed. Liu had represented the PRC in the negotiations of the first bilateral trade memorandum in the 1960s. Later, Liu was responsible for the implementation of agreed principles aimed at organizing Chinese shipments of oil and coal for Japanese industries on a reliable and long-term basis agreed in March 1977.[302] While the Chinese side did not promise an extension of oil exports to Japan, Liu recommended his counterparts that Japan should, for the moment, maintain reserves in RMB rather than exchange them to convertible currencies – indicating the Chinese side's wish to establish their own currency internationally.[303]

A major line of conflict with regard to the compromises in Chinese economic policy that could not the resolved until the partial shift after 1978 was the question of financing investment. How could the massive need for capital and technology of the large-scale exploitation of oil be covered by the still poor Chinese economy, particularly since stability and balanced development had arisen as sacrosanct priorities from the Great Leap Forward and the Cultural Revolution to consolidate and protect the legitimacy of the CCP? The active interest with which the emerging Chinese oil industry was approached by industrialised countries in the wake of the energy crisis made the temptation of inviting foreign capital and participation to ease the ever-present pressure. Very different from earlier years, particularly after the Sino–Soviet split, self-reliance had really become a matter of choice, not merely a figure of speech theorising the realities China faced anyway. On the other hand, as the oil price and thus the economic potential of exports rose,

---

300 Foreign Broadcast Information Service, Tokyo Kyodo on Chou Meeting, Tokyo Kyodo in English, 0040 GMT, 19 01 1973, accessed through Readex.

301 US Department of State, Electronic Telegram, Special Summary No.3, 11 March 1973, 03:12, PlusD, ID: 1973STATE044839_b.

302 LEE CHAE-JIN, China and Japan: New Economic Diplomacy, Stanford 1984, pp. 20 f.

303 Chinese Economic Mission Concludes Visit to Japan, PlusD, ID: 1973TOKYO13258_b.

an economic policy bundle that was at once self-reliant and allowed for relatively fast results became more realistic.

The market price of Chinese crude oil increased from under four USD to about thirteen USD a barrel between 1970 and 1974 (from 3.14 USD per barrel to 8.60 USD per barrel, adjusted for inflation), while still remaining competitive as compared to other producers.[304] Selling it abroad also appeared as an insurance from a possible debt trap when imports were to be further increased. Accordingly, the total output of Chinese oil grew at an estimated twenty percent per annum, surpassing domestic demand.[305] Besides the actual demand, the export share was also directly dependent on the development of Chinese refinery capacities. While they were able to keep up with total production of crude oil until 1972, the latter surpassed the former in the following year. The first exports of Chinese crude in 1973 to Japan were limited to the resulting surplus of crude oil, which grew as refining capacities continued to lag behind the production.[306] That the status of China as an oil exporting nation with direct vested interest began to interfere with the Chinese stance as the defender of the interests of developing countries, was deemed acceptable. The Chinese delegate at the 57th UN Economic and Social Council (ECOSOC) meeting on the 13th of July 1974 cited the success of the OPEC in controlling the price of their natural resources as "welcomed by all African people", directly contradicting the prior statement of the ECA Executive Secretary on serious economic difficulties the same African economies were facing with regard to the hike in oil prices.[307]

While the first exports to Japan were a modest 0.2 million tons, the Japanese industry reacted with great expectations. No less than six Japanese trading companies and twelve refineries founded the designated Council for the Importing of Chinese Crude Oil in March 1974 as imports rose, offering cooperation in the development of loading capacities in ports and the supply of tankers. The Chinese Ministry for the Fuel and Chemical Industries followed suit by reducing regulated export prices and announcing that exports of crude oil to Japan would rise to at least eight million tons in 1975. Accordingly, the first contracts for the year were signed in February, covering 5.4 million tons of crude oil to be delivered to Japan. While this was an increase of eighty percent in quantity, the price was moderately lower than in the previous year, thus undercutting the competition, e. g., Indonesian oil.[308] The contract was both denominated and settled in USD, with thirty days usance.

In parallel, a Japanese fertiliser trade mission visiting Beijing accepted a Chinese proposal to import Japanese fertiliser during the first half of 1975, based on USD-denominated prices as well as cash settlement on delivery. According to the Japan Ammonium

304 KLINGHOFFER, ARTHUR JAY, Sino-Soviet Relations and the Politics of Oil, in: Asian Survey, Vol. 16, No. 6, 1976, pp. 546 ff.

305 BARTKE 1977, p. 22.

306 Ibid, p. 31.

307 US Department of State, Electronic Telegram, 57th ECOSOC: July 9 Plenary, Agenda Items 4, 6, 7, 8, and 14 (D), 13 July 1973, 12:30, PlusD, ID: 1974GENEVA04469_b.

308 The Indonesian Vice President of the Far East Oil Trading Company was quoted by an officer of the US embassy: "Dr. Kissinger pushed on Saudi Arabia, but it [the oil] came out in China". See: US Department of State, Electronic Telegram, Japan-China Oil Trade, 19 February 1975, 08:45, PlusD, ID: 1975TOKYO02137_b.

Sulphate Industry Association, the quantity of fertiliser sold and shipped was not limited by Chinese reluctance to spend, as the 1.2 million tons in standard ammonium, to be delivered during a six-month period, was much less than the disappointed Chinese delegation had wanted to buy. Even here, the generalised economic crisis put constraints on the expansion of trade. The Japanese industry, facing continued worldwide supply shortage, was reluctant to commit greater quantities.[309] The most difficult item had been the financial settlement which, according to the association's Chairman Toshio Ariyoshi, was solved by the unexpected Chinese proposal to use "internationally recycled oil dollars" which had flowed into China.[310]

At the same time, the relatively slow growth of the Chinese agricultural sector failed to meet the demand for food and raw materials of consumers in the cities and the industrial sector.[311] The production of sufficient consumables – primarily food – had been an absolute priority of Chinese economic policy since the aftermath of the heavy famines of the late 1950s.[312] While the continuation of agricultural mechanisation remained the main policy response and was further emphasised after 1975, as discussed above, the trade relations of the PRC had included agricultural since its founding.[313] The importance of ensuring the food supply had rendered the import of grain for use in industrial cities an important means of balancing, which the unified grain procurement system could not provide for various reasons, making China's agricultural trade mainly import-oriented.[314] This was no different in the 1970s. Between 1971 and 1974, agricultural exports in grain increased from about 2.6 million tons to about 3.6 million tons[315], a number not to be reached again until the mid-1980s.

With regard to the ratio of grain export volume to the aggregate grain output, as far as it was statistically registered, the 4.9 percent reached in 1974 was an absolute peak.[316] Asked about the significance of grain imports by China in early 1971 by a journalist of the Yugoslav weekly *Vus*, Premier Zhou Enlai emphasised that the quantity of grain imported was only very small in comparison with the overall production and the available

---

309 Ibid.

310 Foreign Broadcast Information Service, Kyodo: PRC will import Japanese fertilizer; export oil, Tokyo Kyodo in English, 10:22 GMT, 13 02 1975 TK, accessed through Readex.

311 Watson, Andrew, Agricultural Reform and China's Foreign Trade, in: The Australian Journal of Chinese Affairs No. 14, August 1985, p. 42.

312 Gurley, John G., Rural Development in China 1949–75 and the Lessons to be Learned from it, in: Maxwell, Neville (ed.), China's Road to Development, second edition, Oxford 1979, pp. 5–25.

313 Either directly as raw products, or indirectly as processed goods. See: Watson 1985.

314 Since the early 1960s, Canada, Australia and Argentina became major suppliers of grain to China, while rice was firmly established as the main export commodity from the People's Republic. Most of the rice, up to 75 percent, was exported to neighboring Asian countries and regions such as Hong Kong, Malaysia, Singapore and Sri Lanka, as well as to Cuba and Indonesia. The import volume remained stable in the 1960s. Estimates on the total expenditure in foreign exchange on net grain import amounted to 13 percent from 1961 to 1965. See: Mao Yushi, Zhao Nong, Yang Xiaojing, Food Security and Farm Land Protection in China, Singapore 2013, p. 177.

315 People's Republic of China Economic Review 1, 12 January 1974, 05:45, ID: 1974HONGK00476_b.

316 With the lowest ratios during the 1960s and 1970s being under one percent. Generally, China's aggregate grain import volume from 1961 to 1978 was 2.4 times higher than the aggregate export volume. See: Mao et al. 2013, p. 176.

reserves. Nevertheless, he underlined that "wheat is cheaper than rice in the world market, so it pays to China to participate in the world trade of grain."[317] As aggregated data based on estimates by the CIA shows, imports of grain – which had been a part of Chinese trade since the readjustment after the famine of 1959–1961 – reached a peak in 1973, as grain from the US was imported for the first time in the years 1972–1974 (0.9, 4.3 and 2.8 million metric tons, respectively). Since the Great Leap Forward, imports of agricultural products had been used to maintain domestic supply in food as well as raw materials for industrial production while avoiding the administrative and transport cost of procuring grain from surplus areas and compensating for fluctuations in domestic production.[318]

Chinese imports of grain and chemical fertilizer in million USD. Central Intelligence Agency, China: Demand for Foreign Grain, National Foreign Assessment Center, Research Paper, ER 79–10073, pp. 1f. and 4, available at: https://www.cia.gov/library/readingroom/document/cia-rdp83b00551r000100060009-4, last accessed on 1 May 2020. Graph by the author.

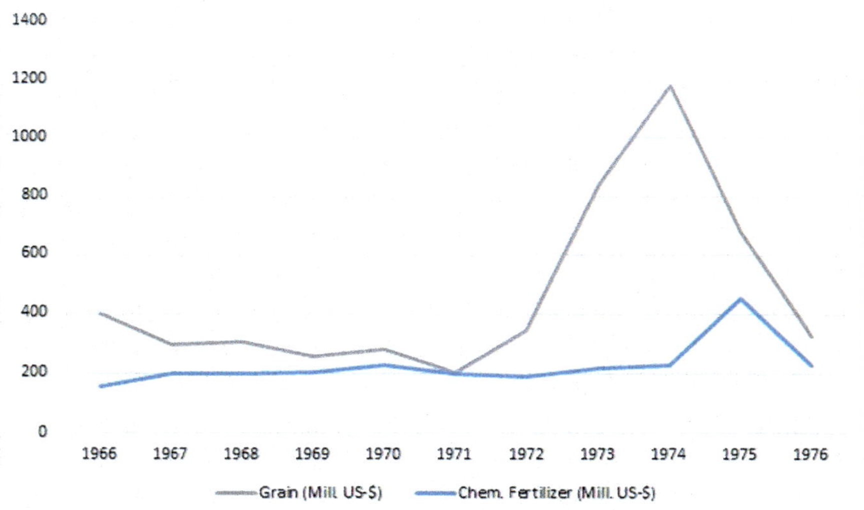

Imports of grain were supplemented by imports of fertiliser as the construction of domestic production capacities was still underway; this was a priority for the construction of rural industries discussed above. As Minister of foreign trade Li Qiang told Swiss member of the Federal Council Graber in August 1974, China was "probably" not only the most important buyer worldwide, but also cooperated directly with foreign trading companies such as the Swiss Nitrogen Chemical Fertilizer Export Cartel NITREX since

317 Foreign Broadcast Information Service, Chou discusses China's foreign trade in interview, Tanjug International Service in English, 1110 GMT, 16 03 71 T, accessed through Readex.

318 WATSON 1985, pp. 56 ff.

1962.[319] Until 1974, imports of wheat increased from about 3 million tons to about 5.4 million tons or over 1.1 billion USD. The attempt to achieve self-reliance in grain is also visible in the increase in fertiliser imports after the correction of 1974, which I address below[320], considered an input required for the improvement and stabilisation of domestic yields.

The necessity for grain and fertiliser imports as well as the emphasis on agricultural mechanisation were not merely due to the fact that the unified grain procurement system in itself did not perform well enough. As estimates on the *per capita* availability of grain show[321] the level required at the end of the first five-year plan was not achieved and certainly not surpassed during the 1970s. The relative liberalisation of side-line production, private plots and rural markets might have mitigated the real stagnation, but the situation was certainly not comfortable. In particular, the stagnation, despite improved yields, was directly connected with population growth on which improved living standards tended to have a positive effect, leading to the first policy responses concerning family planning discussed above.

While it was claimed that prices in the domestic and in foreign markets "were separated by fixing different prices for each" in 1975,[322] the very fact that foreign produce was available made this kind of artificial price-differentiation an expensive *de facto* subsidy. In other words, cheaper grain that was produced by high-yielding modern agriculture, which commanded the mechanical and chemical means China tried to create and procure, and was made available for import on international markets put additional pressure on the fixed purchase prices for grain that were the centrepiece of the Chinese economic development paradigm, as discussed in the first half of this book. Practice shows that the Chinese leadership was fully aware of this tension and tried to use it to the advantage of the country.

As Vice Minister of Foreign Trade Yao Yilin stated to US officials, in October 1975, China had bought wheat and exported rice "because of the price differential", and that "this year, there will be no wheat imports, since the price of rice is low that of wheat high, 'because of massive Soviet purchases', so it is not necessary to sell rice and buy wheat."[323] Similarly, Minister Li Qiang told Pierre Graber in August 1974:

> "We [China] have suffered consequences from the oil crisis. Concerning supply, there is no problem for China: we have sufficient quantities of petrol and its price inside China does not change. We have to reserve a certain part of production for exportation. Because of the oil crisis, we have to pay more for chemical fertiliser, up to more than a hundred percent. Grain has also become more expensive, the same goes for steel. Transport cost are also higher. The prices of small cars have not augmented, but we don't import those...We have gained by exporting petrol, but lost by importing certain products [...] Our exports are satisfactory. There has not been an increase in the price

319 Entretien du Conseiller fédéral Pierre Graber, p. 9. See also: MITCHAM CHAD J., China's Economic Relations with the West and Japan, 1949–79: grain, trade and diplomacy, Oxon 2005, p. 98.

320 Data from: Central Intelligence Agency, ER79 – 10073, p.1. Graph by the author.

321 Data from ibid., p. 4. Graph by the author.

322 Correspondent on healthy state of economy, 1207 GMT, 25 09 1975.

323 US Department of State, Electronic Telegram, US Trade with China: Yao I-Lin Statements to World Affairs Delegation, 14 October 1975, 08:18, PlusD, ID: 1975PEKING01951_b.

of textiles in 1974. But I can assure you that it is easier for us to sell petrol. One million tons equal more or less 100 million dollars."[324]

The planning of such purchases thus included an inherent element of speculation, which in turn required reliability of trade flows to work as an instrument in a still, at least partly planned economy. When the US administration pressured US companies to cancel sales of 125 million bushels of grain to the Soviet Union, due to political considerations, the Hong Kong representation of the Chinese Trading Corporation urgently requested a meeting with US grain trading firms to discuss the implications of this decision for China's trade. As he was lauded by US senator Henry M. Jackson as chairman of the permanent subcommittee on investigations of the Committee on Government Operations of the US Senate on the 1st of March 1974:

"Our President, much to his credit, took quick, decisive action. The sales, he concluded, were not in the Nation's interest. The rights and needs of the American consumer were allowed to take precedence over the requirements of the Soviets. President Ford applied the pressure necessary to force the grain companies to cancel the sales. I am pleased to note that there is at least one person in the Federal Government who saw the pitfalls in selling that much grain to the Soviets – the President himself."[325]

The Chinese side expressed their worries about a possible "hard line" of the US in trade matters, referring to the tough stance taken towards the OPEC. Even if no sympathy for the Soviet Union could be expected, the cancellation was questioned as "arbitrary" by Chinese officials, claiming that in China, top officials would "not get thus involved" in administrative action like the US President did.[326]

324 Entretien du Conseiller fédéral Pierre Graber, pp. 10–11.

325 US Government Printing Office, Sales of Grain to the Soviet Union, Hearing before the Permanent Subcommittee on Investigations of the Committee on Government Operations, United States Senate, Ninety-Third Congress, second session, 8 October 1974, Washington 1974, p. 3.

326 US Department of State, Electronic Telegram, PRC Concern of U.S Cancellation of Soviet Grain Purchase [sic!], 11 October 1974, 05:59, PlusD, ID: 1974HONGK11229_b. Similarly, Senator Jackson argued that on the US-side "Things should have never progressed that far. Contracts should never have been signed. President Ford should not have to step in at the last minute and do the work his subordinates in the bureaus are supposed to do." Sales of Grain to the Soviet Union 1974, p. 3.

Prices of important commodities (index relative to 1900 real prices = 100), for crude oil first US purchase price in USD, China Foreign Trade in percent of GDP (estimate). Graph by the Author.[327]

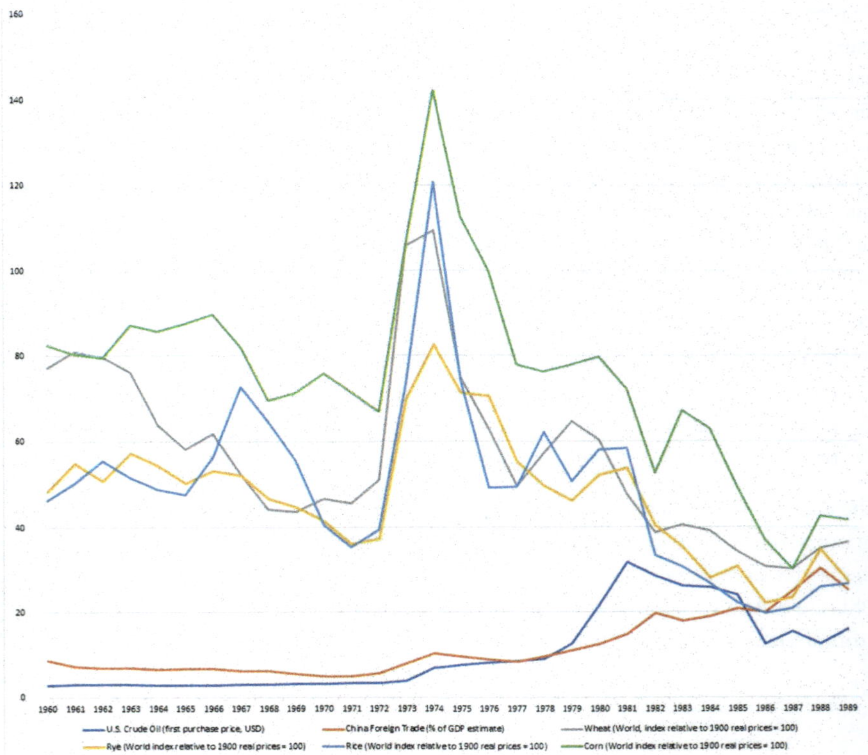

The increases in price indices for edible grains were enormous. At the same time, the price of crude oil, represented here by the first purchase price of US crude oil (right axis in USD), had entered a historical rise. The Chinese foreign trade quota until 1974 grew remarkably fast, foreshadowing the later trend. Besides the increases in imports and exports, inflation in commodity markets was an important contributing factor to this spike.

Effectively, the first signs of reluctance towards US grain shipments came from the Chinese side in late 1974. Reuters carried a news item on the 15th of December 1974 according to which China had asked the US to postpone some grain and other commodity shipments because "American exports have been accounting for almost ninety percent of

327 Data from: U.S. Energy Information Administration, Petroleum & Other Liquids, available at: https://www.eia.gov/dnav/pet/hist/LeafHandler.ashx?n=PET&s=F000000__3&f=A, last accessed on 15 May 2020; World Bank national accounts data, https://data.worldbank.org/indicator/NE.TRD.GNFS.ZS?end=1990&start=1960, last accessed on 15 May 2020; and Roser May, Ritchie Hannah, Our World in Data, Long-term price index in food commodities, 1850–2015, World, 1960 to 1989; https://ourworldindata.org/food-prices, last accessed on 15 May 2020.

the total volume of trade between the two countries". USLO was not informed of this request.[328] On the international stage, China found itself taking an increasingly defensive stance. At the 1974 World Food Conference in Rome, the head of the Chinese delegation and the Vice Minister of Agriculture and Forestry denied any connection between the international food crisis and the oil price hike:

> "Of late, one superpower [the Soviet Union] is spreading another absurdity [other than blaming population growth], asserting that the food problem is caused by the increase in oil prices, and threatening to use grain as a means against the Third World. Chiming in with this, the other superpower describes the rise in oil prices as an important factor for the increase in food prices. Everyone with a little relevant knowledge knows that food prices had increased long before the rise in oil prices last year. This argument of the superpowers is entirely untenable. Their resort to such absurdity only shows that they are not reconciled to the just action taken by the oil-producing countries of the Third World to control their own oil production and pricing and break imperialist monopoly and domination. The superpowers are trying a thousand and one ways to riposte and make reprisal. [...]
> China has also imported some food-grains from the world market, but China does not rely on imports for feeding her population. The main purpose of our imports is to change food varieties. In about 3 years from 1972 up to now, we have imported over 2 billion US dollars' worth of grain, mainly wheat. In the same period, we have exported grain, mainly rice, valued at the same total amount. [...] We have never engaged in any speculation in food. [...] We hold that international trade should be based on the principles of equality, mutual benefit and the exchange of needed goods. We support the demand of the developing countries for food imports at fair and reasonable prices. We support their reasonable demand for improved trade terms, removal of the developed countries' tariff and non-tariff barriers, expansion of sales markets and the fixing of fair prices".[329]

Thus, exports of raw materials were a decisive factor of Chinese foreign economic policy in the early 1970s and so were imports of grain to ensure the alimentation of workers in the industrial walled cities. Using differences in world market prices did allow China to use it to the advantage of its own economy, but it also meant a dependency on conditions that could not be predicted and planned.

Accordingly, possibilities to mitigate the risk stemming from this dependency were sought, including by playing the markets themselves. When the Chinese Vice Minister of Foreign Trade Cai Shufan met with US senators Charles H. Percy, Jacob Javits and Adlai Ewing Stevenson III. and Representative Pete McCloskey, on the 5th of August 1975, he emphasised that China was overall satisfied with the growth of trade and general commercial relations with the US but that a number of problems persisted: first, the US bilateral trade surplus was too large; second, Chinese exports were still unable to meet the

328 US Department of State, Electronic Telegram, UD-PRC Grain Trade, 19 December 1974, 18:29, PLusD, ID: 1974STATE277891_b.

329 Foreign Broadcast Information Service, Delegate to World Food Conference gives PRC view on crisis, Peking NCNA in English, 2030 GMT, 07 11 1974 B, accessed through Readex.

US administrative requirements and demand with regard to quality and kind on the US consumer market. Moreover, the expression of the role of and involuntary advocate of free trade that China found itself in, tariffs imposed on Chinese exports to the US were too high. Nevertheless, Cai noted that prospects for bilateral trade were and remained good if diplomatic relations could be normalised.

With regard to the key commodity, grain, Cai told the politicians that the limitation of imports to just the absolutely necessary was not merely an ideological decision, but simply a matter of fact: China, according to Cai, had to rely on its own production, because not even the US could supply Chinese needs. Therefore, he stated that his country was, at the time, not interested in importing from the US, adding that "The Soviet Union has already bought all of your [the US] grain and we will not add to your burden".[330] Concerning the second key commodity, oil, Cai expressed carefully that China could not become a "major" exporter due to its large domestic demand but was undertaking "some surveys" with a view to exploiting possible off-shore resources. Openly admitting that China still lacked the technical equipment for this undertaking, he raised the possibility of future purchases of technology and machinery from the US – reiterating that China would not accept loans or foreign direct investment, albeit describing the use of "deferred payments" as "normal commercial practice" – a peculiar instrument of trade financing based on supplier credit, discussed below.[331] With regard to purchases from the US, Cai appeared to have told only half of what the policy actually was. While there were no significant agricultural exports from the US to China in July 1975, and the overall trade volume did not go down to zero. The level of imports to China was maintained by increases in a range of non-agricultural products, including scrap metal and pulp at 3.5 million and 2.3 million tons, respectively.[332]

With regard to the import side of the new China trade, the Leninist prophecy was also not entirely wrong. Imports did consist of goods, of which the value added abroad at the time of their import was significantly higher than it was the case in the raw material-heavy export mix until 1975. Nevertheless, the declared intention of the Chinese leadership to change this state of affairs became increasingly clear. That the Four Modernisations had officially moved the oil industry and the affiliated industries downstream to the centre of Chinese economic policy, in early 1975, was also noted by China's main trading partners, in particular Japan. The Japanese Industry, seeing possibilities to loosen its notorious oil-shortage, embarked on substantive lobbying in China. They were warmly welcomed. In October 1975, a delegation of Keidanren received a formal invitation from CCPIT and announced openly that it wished to exchange views on the expansion of Sino–Japanese trade in parallel with the new five-year plan beginning the

330 US Department of State, Electronic Telegram, Highlights of Codel Percy/Javits Meeting with PRC Foreign Trade Vice Minister, 8 August 1975, 08:45, PlusD, ID: 1975PEKING01478_b., paragraphs 2, 3 and 4.

331 Ibid., paragraph 6.

332 US Department of State, Electronic Telegram, July 1975 U.S. PRC Trade Figures, 30 August 1975, 00:10, PlusD, ID: 1975STATE207273_b.

following year and specifically on an expansion of Japan's crude oil imports from China as "a measure to redress the current trade imbalance between the two nations".[333]

Trade missions sent to China focused even more on the oil industry, like a visit of the presidents of the above-mentioned six Japanese leading oil refining companies, organised by the Kansai chapter of the International Trade promotion Association of Japan (*Kokubosoku*), in June 1975. Again, the declared goal was the strengthening of "cooperation" with China in the oil sector in accordance with the long-term development plan that had re-emerged after the fourth National People's Congress.[334] Optimistic production figures published on the Chinese oil industry woke interest in several other countries, where industries experienced in exploration and exploitation existed. While Kokubosoku prepared its visit, delegations led by the Foreign Trade Minister Freer of New Zealand and the Brazilian embassy visited the Dagang oilfield, following an Australian delegation that had visited an off-shore rig of Chinese production nearby the year before. The visitors were shown only parts of the plants, but received briefings by Chinese experts on the operations.[335]

While the CCPIT confirmed the visit and signalled and interest in fulfilling the agreement, considerable gaps between the two sides were reported with regard to the oil-price to be applied in the transaction, with both sides insisting to improve the terms of trade to their favour.[336] When the Sino-Japanese long-term trade agreement was finally concluded in 1977, Japanese oil-refining firms were the first to announce and plan further visits to China, to fulfil the exchange of Chinese oil and cooking coal to Japan in exchange for Japanese coal mining equipment and industrial plants as well as technology. Before the treaty was signed in early 1978, the Chairman of the Japan-China Economic Association Inayama announced a visit to China on the 14th of February. The trade relations, as they were described in preparation of the visit, were described as an exchange of "equipment for developing oil and coal resources, petrochemical plants, harbour and other transportation machinery, steel and construction materials and other transportation machinery and industrial knowhow". Inayama stated that Japan would import fifteen million tons of Chinese crude annually by 1982, the price of which would be "roughly based" on the "prevailing international price" of around 13.20 USD a barrel at the time. About twenty Japanese business leaders were announced to be participating in the signing, sealing the contract on which the exchange of oil for technology would be based.[337]

After the agreement was signed in a ceremony, during which Li Xiannian emphasised the great prospects for trade, now that the Gang of Four was not interfering anymore. A delegation of the China State Petroleum Corporation was visiting Japan on a round-trip,

333 Foreign Broadcast Information Service, Business delegation plans PRC visit, Tokyo Kyodo in English, 1130 GMT, 06 10 1975, accessed through Readex.

334 Foreign Broadcast Information Service, Mission Hopes to Strengthen Economic Cooperation with PRC, Tokyo Kyodo in English, 1230 GMT, 04 06 1975 TK, accessed by Readex.

335 China's Takang oil Field, PlusD, ID: 1975STATE156840_b.

336 Foreign Broadcast Information Service, Firms plan to send Oil Mission to Peking in August, Tokyo Kyodo in English, 0013 GMT, 26 07 1977 OW, accessed through Readex.

337 Foreign Broadcast Information Service, Economic Treaty with PRC to be signed, Hong Kong AFP in English, 2104 GMT, 13 01 1978 OW, accessed through Readex.

including the US; the president of the corporation and head of delegation, Sun Qingwen announced that the Chinese government was planning to open 15 oilfields comparable to Daqing in scale, as it sought to increase exports as much as possible. According to a Japanese source quoted by Kyodo, China was testing the waters for an increase of the supply to thirty million tons, with the Japanese government ready to accept.[338] The Petroleum Association of Japan reacted quickly, stating that the government needed to "make sure there is enough [for] domestic demand", fearing that the Japanese industry might be forced by their path-dependent public servants to buy and process undesirably heavy amounts of oil in exaggerated quantities.[339] The long-term trade agreement was nevertheless prolonged for an five additional years when the Japanese trade minister Toshio Komoto visited Beijing in September 1978.[340]

Following the transition of highest office from the late Mao to Hua Guofeng and the consolidation of his leadership with the arrest of the Gang of Four, oil moved even more to the centre as a main enabler for the pursuit of fast economic development. Its potential to finance the economic development was even more necessary to fulfil the high expectations of the Four Modernisations and the additional emphasis on speed raised by the new leadership, especially when the general policy with regard to foreign debt and investment did not change. Nevertheless, the sector that had appeared like an almost guaranteed source of funding during the height of the international energy crisis saw itself increasingly confronted with important difficulties, such as capacity problems and even the unwillingness of large importers like the US and Japan to buy Chinese oil – perceived as more difficult to refine – at international market prices, in accordance with those charged by the OPEC cartel, as long as there were alternative sources.[341]

In Western sources discussing the prospects for Chinese oil, the argument of its difficult treatment in refineries due to the high wax-content of Chinese oil was often brought forward as an argument against the expansion of oil trade with China, or the acceptance of OPEC-level prices. According to Hu Xuetao, the paraffin content in Chinese crude oil depended – and still depends – on its origin, with some oilfields, in particular in Northern China, providing "high-wax oil" while others produced "low-wax oil".[342] The wide geographical dispersion of the Chinese oilfields has also been named by Selig S. Harrison as one of the principal reasons why the investments required to develop oil production at a high pace would have been enormous, and would probably have proven unbearable in the longer run, based on a self-reliance strategy.[343] On the other hand, in April 1977, the

338 Foreign Broadcast Information Service, PRC May Export More Oil to Japan, Tokyo Kyodo in English, 0015 GMT, 03 02 1978 OW, accessed through Readex.

339 Foreign Broadcast Information Service, Oil Industry unhappy over Japan-PRC Trade Pact, Tokyo Kyodo in English, 1243 GMT, 06 03 1978 OW, accessed through Readex.

340 Foreign Broadcast Information Service, PRC-Japan long-term Trade Agreement extended by 5 Years, Moscow TASS in English, 1038 GMT, 14 09 1978 LD, accessed through Readex.

341 China had kept its prices within the acceptable for OPEC, which would have made significant cuts of export prices politically difficult.

342 Hu Xuetao, The Physical Properties of Reservoir Fluids, in: Hu Xuetao, Hu Shuyong, Jin Fayang, Huang Su, Physics of Petroleum Reservoirs, second edition, Beijing 2017, pp. 175 f.

343 Harrison Selig S., China, Oil and Asia, Conflict Ahead?, New York 1977, p. 12 ff.

acceptance of the Chinese government of US grain imports without the cumbersome certification processes, which had complicated shipments in 1974 and 1975, was noted by US officials in Beijing. The procurement of an option for the sale of 200'000 tons of soybeans by China was noted to be concluded without the usual clause that had explicitly excluded the US from origin contracts,[344] indicating that availability and price was being given priority over politics.[345] In parallel, Chinese statements at the 8th UNCTAD special session, where the conflict between the NIEO-movement[346] and the superpowers was constantly looming in the background, were noted for their absence of criticism directed against the US.[347]

After the State Planning Commission had made it clear that China would sell "more and more petroleum, coal and other products in order to buy advanced foreign equipment"[348], results followed suit. In the first week of December 1977, negotiations for a long-term Sino-Japanese trade agreements continued. The Japanese negotiator Yoshiro Inayama agreed that Chinese petroleum exports to Japan would rise from the 1977 level of 6.8 million tons to fifteen million tons by 1982, with prices set at "world levels".[349] Most of the oil was to be produced in Daqing, but added to by supplies from Shengli and newly explored fields in northern China. This also demonstrated the readiness of Japan to accommodate the wish of the Chinese to expand the possible volume of imports by agreeing to an expansion of exports to Japan – the USLO reported that Japanese refiners and the electric power industry could not, at the time, absorb more than eleven million tons each year, so a use needed to be found for the rest.[350] However, the prospects that the Chinese hunger for technology imports represented proved to be convincing beyond simple calculus. This expansion of nodes to the outside world had awoken the interes of trade partners early on, leading to offers of support by advanced technology in the hands of their companies. Japan was an obvious partner. Press reports in 1973 claimed that the Japan Petroleum Development Corporation had actively signalled readiness to transfer technology for semi-submersible drilling ships that could be used in shallow waters, such as those of Bohai bay, which was crucial for the shipping especially of crude oil to Japan

344 Earlier purchases, while acknowledged by Chinese trade officials to be partly of US-origin, had been possible as not all purchases through traders were bound to origin.

345 US Department of State, U.S. -PRC Wheat Trade, Electronic Telegram, 5 April 1977, 00:00, PlusD, ID: 1977STATE075459_c.

346 Promulgated as a UN declaration in 1974, the NIEO was arguably among the most widely discussed reform initiatives for international governance of the 1970s. Its fundamental objective was the transformation of the international economy, in order to redirect benefits stemming from interdependence through trade and investment to developing countries, as a consequent continuation of decolonisation.

347 US Department of State, Electronic Telegram, UNCTAD: 8th Special Session of TDB on R&A: General Debate Speeches on April 26–27, 28 April 1977, 00:00, PlusD, ID: 1977GENEVA03198_c, paragraph 5.

348 Foreign Broadcast Information Service, Planning Commission Official Reports on Modernization, Peking NCNA in English, 0700 GMT, 31 12 1977 OW, accessed through Readex.

349 US Department of State, Electronic Telegram, Sino-Japan Long-Term Trade Agreement, 5 December 1977, 00:00, PlusD, ID: 1977PEKING02841_c.

350 Ibid., paragraph 6.

and beyond.[351] But using foreign technology in order to speed up China's modernisation also beyond the oil sector brought both ideological and very concrete challenges.

Imports of advanced technology

In the early 1970s as well as before, consumer goods other than food were practically absent from Chinese imports. Grain was bought to compensate shortages in agricultural production in the walled cities. Additionally, the rest of the imports had industrialisation at its core. In accordance with the notion that economic planning was primarily an instrument of development, not merely administration and distribution, imports consisted overwhelmingly of capital goods.

An important aspect of Chinese industrialisation policies were the so-called capital construction projects, which were basically industrial greenfield investments that aimed at increasing the production capacities at a large scale.[352] Between 1969 and 1972, the number of completed projects had increased from eleven to twenty-five annually, which was a modest number despite the scale of some of these projects.[353] To build and maintain complex industries and infrastructures, foreign technology had been imported at a relatively large scale from the Soviet Union during the first five-year plan and to a much smaller extent during the period of readjustment of the early 1960s; this was after the attempt to achieve industrialisation by modest means and mass mobilisation of the Great Leap Forward failed. Combined with the organised tinkering discussed in the previous chapter, that despite its partly impressive results was finally limited to what could be done with the existing means of production. When new technology was genuinely needed, resorting to their adoption through imports, as far as it was feasible, was the only means available to achieve reliable and fast-paced progress.

Besides tinkering, procuring and copying advanced foreign technology was an obvious way to drive modernisation forward, which had been demonstrated in particular by the Japanese. Western companies were aware of this risk, while seeing the enormous potential of the Chinese market. In preparation of the Swiss industrial exhibition on Beijing in Summer 1974 mentioned before, OSEC warned explicitly that both "technical seminars" as well as the Chinese insistence on only receiving the most advanced exhibits was obviously motivated by the will to emulate the technology. On the other hand, the distance between the centralized China Machinery Import Export Corporation (MACHIMPEX) and the end-users was frequently raised as a structural issue for foreign sellers,

351 Chinese Economic Mission Concludes Visit to Japan, PlusD, ID: 1973TOKYO13258_b.

352 Following a generally fluctuating pattern of regional distribution, as shown by ZHOU QINGSHENG. In the early 1970s, the central government began to shift emphasis in the distribution of investment capital from the inland to the coastal regions. See: ZHOU QINGSHENG, Capital Construction Investment and its Regional Distribution in China, in: International Journal of Urban and Regional Research, Vol. 17, No. 2, June 1993, pp. 159–177. This coincided with the general policy of moving the investment burden to decentral units, in the course of small-scale industrialisation and agricultural mechanisation.

353 Current Chinese Communist trends, Taipei Chung-kung Yen-chiu, 05 1973.

as the corporation was considered to be too far away from the actual end-users to know their needs and requirements.[354]

Foreign technology was important for the operation of infrastructure; for instance, forty electric locomotives produced by the French Alstom-MTE-group, which were ordered in 1970 as a follow-up to a 1960 procurement of material and delivered in 1973, were used on the growing number of electrified rail lines.[355] These orders also led to the exchange of technicians – in the case of the French locomotives, several Chinese visited France to accompany tests on the French east network, while, in turn, French specialists travelled to China either to assist with the launching of the locomotives or to attend fairs where the most recent achievements of the European rail industry were displayed.[356] Dagang's total labour force of over 22'000, including workers assigned to agriculture and side-line production, as well as its schools, hospital and factories producing lightbulbs, cement and acetylene from local materials were shown to the Brazilian delegation. At the time, no exports from Dagang were noted, but recently arrived Italian equipment was reported to be installed for the efficient use of the large quantities of natural gas available.[357]

In 1972, picking up the pace of the early 1960s and accelerating it carefully, at least twelve major facilities in other sectors were ordered from abroad, precisely from Japan and Western European countries. These included hydroelectric power plants produced by the French companies Alstom and Creusot-Loire, a German Steel rolling mill by DEMAG, estimated at eighty million USD, and Dutch urea plants.[358] In October 1973, the Japanese Prime Minister Kakuei Tanaka was quoted by US intelligence reports that the indirect purpose of diplomatic visits to Japan by Chinese officials was to study which types of Japanese plants China might wish to purchase in the future. Tanaka noted that the "first round" of whole plant export contracts featuring petrochemical plants and a steel mill complex was nearly complete, to be followed by a "second phase" encompassing the sale of automobile manufacturing facilities and shipyards.[359] The renewed and massively expanded imports of foreign technology were heavily attacked in the course of the campaign to "criticise Lin Biao and Confucius", as an expression of a "slavish comprador mentality" and the idea of "trailing along at a snail's pace". In an editorial in Renmin Ribao on the 22nd of March 1974, independence and frugality were stressed as the proper road to industrialisation:

> "...the policy of maintaining independence and keeping the initiative in our own hands and relying on our own efforts has become more deeply implanted in the hearts of the

---

354 Schweizerische Zentrale für Handelsförderung, Interner Bericht über den Besuch in der Volksrepublik China vom 20. bis 31. Oktober 1972 betreffend die Durchführung einer Schweizerischen Industrie-Ausstellung in Peking 1974, verfasst von Dr. H. J. Halbheer, Stellv. Direktor und Leiter des Sitzes Zürich der OSEC. Available at dodis: dodis.ch/35904. Last accessed on 12 August 2022.

355 Joint Publications Research Service, Railroads in the People's Republic of China, Paris La vie du Rail Outre-Mer, Original in French, No. 249, 01 05 1975, accessed through Readex.

356 Ibid.

357 China's Takang Oil Field, PlusD, ID: 1975STATE156840_b.

358 Current Chinese Communist Trends, Taipei Chung-kung Yen-chiu, 05 1973, Table 1.

359 Chinese Economic Mission Concludes Visit to Japan, PlusD, ID: 1973TOKYO13258_b.

> people [...] however it is necessary to see that the struggle is still continuing. The pernicious influence of the counterrevolutionary revisionist line of Lin Piao has still not been eliminated. The erroneous notion of blind faith in the 'advanced technology' of foreign countries still exists among some of the comrades. Could it be that we could not create the equipment and techniques ourselves and could only rely on foreign countries? In their eyes, they see only the foreign countries, and seek only to import things [...] if they were permitted to have their way, they would take the evil road of revisionism."[360]

Even if "blind faith" in foreign technology was criticised as revisionist, the article expressed a more nuanced view. With regard to the Four Modernisations, it referenced in its last paragraph, the question was what degree of foreign technology was permissible.

> "...we do not mean that we should not introduce foreign technology. The introduction of a bit of foreign technology is permissible. [...] we can only use them as reference and must actively catch up with them. We must make discoveries, inventions and progress. [...] we are not advocating a policy of exclusion or isolation. We always hold that on the basis of equality and mutual interests, the development of trade with various countries for the exchange of goods is beneficial to strengthening the capacity of our country for self-reliance as well as beneficial to promoting friendship among the people of various countries. Adhering to maintaining independence and keeping the initiative in our own hands and relying on our own efforts does not mean discriminating against practicing economic cooperation and mutual assistance with fraternal countries".[361]

In terms of their daily operations, officials in the responsible Chinese Ministries were neither impressed nor visibly worried about the existing doubts – as Fang Yin, deputy general manager of the responsible state trading organisation for technology import (Techimport[362]) told USLO Beijing on the 23rd of June 1975; notably, the extent of importation of complete plants in the course of the upcoming five-year plan was still under discussion. Such imports would continue to be "a small but important part" of Chinese economic policy, stating that he wished to find a way to speed up trade by facilitating the processing of export licenses with his US counterparts.[363]

While the export of industrial equipment began to increase after the brief hiccup of spiking foreign debt in 1975, the demission of Deng Xiaoping in April of 1976 brought the issue to the centre of the political debate. In practice, the import drive was extended. Ken Morse, a representative of the Rockefeller bank, spoke to Chinese trade officials in early 1976, and mentioned the possibility of importing computers to China – perhaps unaware

---

360 Foreign Broadcast Information Service, People's Daily stresses independence, frugality in building socialism, Article by Tien Chih-Sung: "Adhere to the policy of independence and self-reliance – some understanding acquired from the study of 'on the correct handling of contradictions among the people'", Peking Renmin Ribao, Original in Mandarin, 22 03 1974 V, accessed through Readex.

361 Ibid.

362 The China National Technical Import Corporation responsible for the importation of complete plants and technology.

363 US Department of State, Electronic Telegram, Call on Fang Yin of Techimport, 24 June 1975, 07:11, PlusD, ID: 1975PEKING01174_b.

of the embargo that was formally still in force. Techimport reacted promptly by actively inviting IBM in late spring 1976 by telex to Beijing for "technical talks" – which was well understood by the company management as a request for technology imports. The meeting was delayed because of Mao's death, but was finally scheduled for October 1976. The first contract with a US manufacturer was drafted and signed over the following months for the computerisation of the production in a compressor factory in North China.[364]

While, as I have argued in the previous chapters, public criticism on Deng Xiaoping's economic programme of 1975 was comparably nuanced and – with the exception of the fundamental divisions around material incentives – rather concerned about the *how* than the *whether*, the import of foreign technology proved to be a second fundamental question. The article published on the 7th of June 1976, quoted above, summarised the division apodictically:

> "In addition [to the other fallacies], [Deng Xiaoping] openly advocated pinning our hopes on the foreign bourgeoisie for the development of production, science and technology in our country. The 'rules' claim that 'to achieve the four modernizations, our country should introduce more and more advanced foreign techniques and rely on foreign countries for complete sets of modern equipment.' He slandered self-reliance as 'self-conceit' and 'a closed-door policy.' He advertised his slavish comprador philosophy and his doctrine of national betrayal as a 'most reliable big policy'. If he were allowed to have his way, would China not become a market and a raw material base for imperialism and social imperialism and an appendage of international capital?"[365]

The 16th lecture in the series on the Ten Relationships held in Beijing was directly concerned with the import of foreign capital goods and technology to support economic development in China. It opened with affirming quotes by Mao that "learning from the strong points of all nations" had always been a feature of socialist rule in China, and that self-reliance was "never to be turned into a "closed-door" policy.[366]

---

364 In the words of then-IBM executive ALLAN JOSEPH in hindsight: "Ultimately, we created personal bonds that crossed the cultural and political divide and helped to open China to the new world economy. That little computer deal exploded into the greatest industrial metamorphosis the world has seen since the Industrial Revolution! We also created one of the largest markets for IBM in a long, long time. By the end of our discussions across the negotiating table, we developed friendships lasting more than thirty years. The People's Republic of China embarked on a journey towards modernization that is still not over." JOSEPH ALLAN, Masked Intentions, Navigating a Computer Embargo on China, Bloomington 2010, p. 11.

365 Foreign Broadcast Information Service, Teng Line on Industrial Development Scored, Article by Lu Ta: "A Set of Rules for Speeding up Capitalist Restoration – Criticizing 'The Questions on Speeding Up Industrial Development' Concoted [sic!] on the Instruction of Teng Hsiao-ping", Peking Domestic Service in Mandarin, 0200 GMT, 07 06 1976 OW, accessed through Readex.

366 Foreign Broadcast Information Service, Part 16 of Peking Lecture Series on 'Ten Relationships', 16th in a series of lectures under the general title: "A Brilliant Document, a Powerful Weapon", written by the worker-theorist group of the Peking internal combustion engine general plant and the philosophy and social sciences department, and planned economy group of the Economics Institute of the Chinese Academy of Sciences on studying Chairman Mao's 'On the Ten Major Relationships', part 16 being titled: "Adhere to the Policy of Maintaining Independence, Keeping the Initiative in Our Own Hands, and Relying on our own Efforts – Criticising Those Who Worship

Taking the introduction of vinylon in the Chinese textile industry in the early 1960s as a success story for the adaptation of technology in China, the lecture made reference to Mao's formula of the Chinese people being "poor and blank". "We advocate learning from foreign countries" – it was held in the lecture, as it supported the continuous change. "Poverty is being transformed into prosperity and strength and a backward situation is being transformed into an advanced one. We believe that this transformation can be accelerated under the leadership of the party Central Committee headed by Chairman Hua [Guofeng]". Achieving this goal was stated to be dependent on the mobilisation of all "positive factors, both inside and outside the party [and] from abroad, both direct and indirect, that are conclusive to serving China. In this way, we will increase strength even more. Our socialist construction will advance at a faster rate." Accordingly, inquiries were made with foreign companies whether technology could be acquired independently of the import of actual industrial products. In a meeting of the China Resources Company and the New Yorker Phelps Dodge Cable and Wire Company in February 1977, the Chinese representative expressly stated the interest in developing domestic production capabilities, allowing for the production of sophisticated cable products and encouraging the holding of a technical seminar in China for that purpose.[367]

The sale of technology to China was not a condition imposed by the Chinese trading corporations but, at this stage, actively sought by western companies. While the only contract signed – in that regard – during February 1977 was with the Pullman-Kellog Company, negotiations with the International Business Machines Corporation and Interdata were reported as well as discussions with other US companies. The subjects were the conversion of fertiliser plants in several provinces to the use of natural gas and naphtha feedstock and computer sales, respectively. The best prospects were still reported with regard to the oil and petrochemical industries as well as mining, wherein foreign experts supervising the construction projects associated with these sales were regularly present in China.[368]

The will to develop information technology in China at a sophisticated level was confirmed by Donald Nielsen of the Passavant Corporation, based in Alabama, who visited the China Resources Company in Hong Kong on the 20th of June 1977 to discuss the sale of magnetic tape manufacturing equipment. The appointment demonstrated the professionalism of the Chinese Trade representation, as it was easily arranged on one hour's notice. According to Nielsen, the Chinese official greeting him at the office had a "very sophisticated understanding of magnetic tapes' manufacturing processes". This was a consequence of policies directed at building specific know-how in China, as observed by Joseph Allan:

Foreign Things and Fawn of Foreigners", Peking Domestic Service in Mandarin, 2200 GMT, 15 02 1977 OW, accessed through Readex.

367 Which was received positively by the company, which was also interested in exporting large quantities of copper sulfate to China. US Department of State, Electronic Telegram, US Business Visitor Trade Proposal to PRC Through China Resources Company in Hong Kong, 17 February 1977, 00:00, PlusD, ID: 1977HONGK01995_c.

368 US Department of State, Electronic Telegram, US Businessmen Visitors to PRC: February, 1 March 1977, 00:00, PlusD, ID: 1977PEKING00373_c.

> "Early in 1976, long before Techimport [...] contacted IBM, the First Ministry of Machine Building Science and Technology Bureau sent orders to the Worker Bureau in Shenyang. [...] The Worker Bureau in Shenyang, based on the requirements from the Ministry in Beijing, assigned and moved seven electrical engineers from a factory that built boats. They formed the Blower Works computer staff. I met each one of them later on. Not one of them ever was involved in manufacturing or designing a compressor of any kind. None of the computer center staff came from the compressor factory itself even through there were many engineers there."[369]

He openly acknowledged to Nielsen that the PRC had to import all magnetic tape for whatever application, be it audio recording or computer memory from abroad; therefore, the immediate interest was the import of a complete production plant capable of manufacturing said tape as well as "suitable for experiments and product development". Nielsen was asked to prepare a detailed proposal for the "smallest" feasible plant for Techimport and Machimpex in Beijing as well as the CRC. The Chinese representant also claimed that another proposal had reached his office, but, demonstrating his knowledge of Western markets, was reported as having expressed particular eagerness to receive a submission from Passavant after having heard that its customers included Sony, the German Badische Anilin & Soda Fabrik (better known as BASF), and other major tape users. Further, he appeared surprised, almost amused, when told that the plant would require only ten employees to operate at full capacity. With regard to restrictions on the export of technology to China, Nielsen underlined that the Passavant Corporation in the US, being a wholly German-owned subsidiary of the Passavant-Weke Michelbacher-Hütte, did "not care" whether it sold its products to China with an US-origin or a FRG-origin, "whichever suited PRC policy and practica". The CRC also asked for descriptions of other products of Passavant as well as services available.[370]

Restrictions on exports of sensitive technology to China were still in place as a consequence of the formally applied international trade embargo[371] and became an important point of insistence for Chinese trade officials, besides the promotion of Chinese exports, as the general course for an expansion of foreign trade had been set by mid-1977. A dinner table initiated by NCUSCT President Christopher H. Phillips in June of the same year revealed diverging interests between Chinese ministries according to their function – expectedly the CCPIT and the State Machinery Corporation representatives – pointing to good prospects in future trade, and the representative of the Ministry of Foreign Affairs, Nancy Tang, emphasized the need for political constraints.

US officials stated at the meeting that increased bilateral trade could serve as "political ammunition" in favour of a quick normalisation of diplomatic relations between the countries. Nancy Tang underlined the political nature of such questions, openly attacking the "ignorance" of those present who considered the level of trade, however high it might be, to take precedence over political realities – citing the US fear of an immediate collapse of the "corrupt" Taiwan regime under Chiang Kai-shek (*jiang jieshi*) when faced

---

369 Allan 2010, p. 6.

370 US Department of State, Electronic Telegram, US Business Visitor Trade Proposal to PRC through, 22 June 1977, 00:00, PlusD, ID: 1977HONGK07150_c.

371 Chen 2006.

with a withdrawal of US support as "further proof of the rottenness of the Chiang government and of the immortality of the US support of it", and second, the fear of offending the Soviet Union.[372]

Phillips, while agreeing that "some people in the US" might be holding these opinions, dismissed these factors and restated that, politically, the volume of "US trade and investment in other areas" provided strong political ammunition for opponents for the normalisation in Sino–US relations. Tang was quoted as replying sharply, "The more you give the Chiang regime, the more you stand to lose". The deputy director of the Chinese State Machinery Corporation, seeing his chance to push the conversation in a direction favoured by his Ministry, re-entered the discussion by restating complaints about US export restrictions, citing a concrete case where the US administration failed to license the export of a computer-controlled machine tool to China; he noted that although the machine tool could be purchased without restrictions in a version without automatic control, this variety was not nearly so attractive to buy. Similarly, Cheng cited the purchases of the Boeing aircraft, which unfortunately was followed by a purchase of the Trident aircraft due to complications caused by US restrictions.

After the 1972 visit of US president Richard Nixon, it was announced that China would purchase ten Boeing B707 – the aircraft in which Nixon arrived in Beijing. The purchase was interpreted as a political gesture of goodwill. Certainly, it was a signal that the reestablishment of trade relations was wished on the Chinese side as well as a signal that the Chinese market was deep. Shortly before, as mentioned above, China had bought five Ilyushin IL-62s from the Soviet Union, giving Chinese civil aviation the possibility to fly longer non-stop flights, e.g,. from Beijing to Guangzhou. Also, the purchase of US aircrafts gave Chinese engineers the opportunity to study advanced western technology in aviation for the first time in over twenty years, showing them the state of the art that had developed in aviation since the 1950s. Accordingly, it was attempted to reverse-engineer the B707, which of course was not in line with the terms and conditions of the transaction. In 1973, the purchase of thirty-five second-hand British Trident jets as well as direct technology-imports (the Spey engine) from Rolls-Royce were concluded, to which it was referred in this conversation.[373]

The same example that had been referred to by Chinese officials in order to assure the US of their "competitive edge" shortly before. On Phillips' remark that other countries like the United Kingdom also applied similar restrictions on the export of technology to China, Chen answered quickly that at least the United Kingdom did not discriminate in tariffs. That the implementation of restrictions on technology were handled in a case-by-case manner was confirmed by Phillips, as he pointed to the sale of Spey engines from Europe[374] which "even had a military application" and could not have taken place without

372 US Department of State, Electronic Telegram, Sino-US Trade, 28 June 1977, 00:00, PlusD, ID: 1977PEKING01301_c.

373 DOUGAN MARK, A Political Economy Analysis of China's Civil Aviation Industry, Oxon and New York 2002, in particular the second Chapter.

374 As mentioned above, at 267 million USD, as reported in US Government Printing Office, United States-China Trade Agreement, Hearings before the Subcommittee on Trade of the Committee on Ways and Means, House of Representatives, 96th Congress, First Session on Agreement on

US consent. This, according to him, had been a sign of goodwill.[375] That China worked with several suppliers and played the market was also experienced by the Swiss, who in earlier years were glad to state that the PRC preferred quality over price: arguably a valid description of Swiss exports. After having travelled with a group of Chinese journalists to Swtzerland, a revolutionary veteran heading the delegation told the Swiss embassy in Beijing that while Swiss watches had been appreciated in the past, their imports would decrease as "we have other priorities". The Swiss, he said, were "sometimes the best, but expensive. Prepare to be competitive."[376]

The import of complex technology, such as the engines, also demonstrated that practices in Chinese foreign trade were about to change: The license agreement held that China would produce the engines in the PRC but that British engineers would survey the construction of the required plant as well as the service during the first ten years; this indicates that cooperation necessarily grew closer as the complexity of the imported technology increased.[377] Another obstacle was the frozen assets in the US as an indirect consequence of the embargo, which had shortly before been the topic of a major story in the New York Times. As the experience showed that the sectoral foreign trade corporations were the more pragmatic and open partners for exchanges on trade expansion, the USLO requested a list of direct contacts in those bodies. Such a list was delivered by MoFT on the 1st of July 1977, containing both the general managers and deputies of the textile, light industrial, native and animal by-product, cereals, oil and foodstuffs, technical, machinery, metals and minerals, chemical and shipping corporations, thereby demonstrating the width of trade representations open for direct foreign contact.[378]

Within China, the rehabilitation of the "Twenty Points" also brought a decisive change in the official stance towards the importance of technology imports to China in the state media. Under the subtitle "opposing the introduction of advanced technology on the basis of independence and self-reliance", the article associated with the mass criticism group of the State Planning Commission published on the 16th of July 1977 conveyed the following:

> "The sphere of science and technology is extremely broad. Each country and each nation with its different conditions, has its own strong as well as weak points. All countries and nations should learn from the strong points of other countries and nations in order to overcome their own weak points. It is impossible and unnecessary for any country to do all things from scratch by itself."[379]

Trade Relations between the United States and the People's Republic of China, November 1, 2, and 29 1979, Washington D.C. 1980, p. 171.

375 Sino-US Trade, 28 June 1977, paragraph 10.

376 Ambassade de Suisse en Chine, Lettre à Peter Bettschart, Pékin, le 29 décembre 1977, Ref. 613.2 – DY/jg. Available at dodis : dodis.ch/49050. Last accessed on 12 August 2022. Translation by the author.

377 Weggel 1976. p. 402.

378 US Department of State, Electronic Telegram, PRC Foreign Trade Corporation Personnel, 1 July 1977, 00:00, PlusD, ID: 1977PEKING01323_c.

379 People's Daily condemns Gang's Criticism of 'Regulations', Peking NCNA Domestic Service in Mandarin, 0717 GMT, 16 07 1977 OW.

While a strong commitment to the interdependence of the Chinese economy with the world, certain limits were still underlined, as was the "approval by Chairman Mao". In all exchanges, the article explained, there were no political conditions attached, no foreign country "was allowed to meddle in the management of our enterprises" and "no profit was turned over to foreign capitalists".[380] Chinese trade policy was once more justified with international customs, stating that "they were all normal trade deals with foreign countries according to the principle of equality and mutual benefit" – and the establishment of infrastructure by "export bases and [...] production points" as "question[s] of method", for the purpose of "guaranteeing that the products meet export needs and for facilitating organization of transportation".[381]

The line presented in Renmin Ribao was subsequently taken up in a series of criticisms published by provincial foreign trade bureaus, with slightly differing emphasis, partly referring to oil trade as rather a means of foreign policy than economic development and emphasising the complementary nature of trade taking into account the livelihood of the people; production was increased in a targeted manner where goods fit for export were short in supply. Even in remote Xinjiang, the local foreign trade bureau underlined the compromise made in the domain of socialist foreign trade:

> "Marxism tells us that the law of the unity of opposites is the fundamental law governing materialist dialectics. The relationship between maintaining independence, keeping the initiative in our own hands, relying on our own efforts and developing foreign trade, introducing needed new technology and earnestly learning the good experience of foreign countries is one of the unity of opposites."[382]

The justification for the technology-focus of economic policy was transmitted in another series of talks under the general title, "Deepen the Criticism of the Gang of Four and Clarify the ten Do-s and Don't-s on the Economic Front", the ninth of these talks addressing the import of advanced technology directly. In a further step away from Mao Zedong Thought, the talk construed the import of technology as being a consequence of socialist internationalism, as technological progress was "the summing-up of the practical experience of the working people", which was circulated among countries, as for example "the compass, gunpowder, printing paper and porcelain wares", as invented by the Chinese.

380 That China would not make use of the international "credit system" was also reiterated, when trade negotiations were slowly reactivated after a visit by Roland de Kergolay, the deputy director general of the European Commission's Department of External Affairs, had visited China in 1977. Joint Publications Research Service, Trade Negotiations between PRC, Common Market viewed, Unattributed 'Current Affairs Analysis' column: "The Trade Negotiations between China and the Common Market", Hong Kong Wen Wei Po, Original in Mandarin, 11 07 1977 HK, accessed through Readex.

381 Ibid.

382 Foreign Broadcast Information Service, Sinkiang Foreign Trade Bureau Criticizes Gang, Article by mass criticism group of Sinkiang autonomous Regional Foreign Trade Bureau: "Strive To Develop Socialist Foreign Trade – Studying 'On the Ten Major Relationships' and Criticizing the Gang of Four's Crimes in Undermining Foreign Trade Work", Urumchi Sinkiang Regional Service in Mandarin, 1115 GMT, 11 07 1977 OW, accessed through Readex.

Since the working people of foreign countries could learn from Chinese innovations, why could China not "learn and import advanced science and technology from foreign countries?" – this was posed as a rhetorical question. Denying imports of technology would be equal to "strangl[ing] the scientific achievements scored by the working people of foreign countries"[383] "If we act according to the logic of the gang of four that all foreign things must be rejected, what choice do we have besides substituting ox carts for trains, oil lamps for electric lights, or even prohibiting people from eating rice and wheat flour? It is indeed absurd!"[384]

In practice, there was no doubt regarding the technological focus of Chinese foreign economic policy. Minister of Foreign Trade Li Qiang, when scheduling visits to the UK in late November and France in mid-December 1977, asked to see factories, research institutes and more, directly relating to a wide variety of advanced equipment and machinery, including steel, coal, railways and aviation. The British embassy was informed that the emphasis of the visit "across the board" was to be on advanced technology.[385] The procurement of complex technology deepened cooperation with trade partners beyond the exchange of goods, as the transaction involving the Spey engine deliveries had foreshadowed. For the construction of a major steel mill expected to be built in Hubei province, China, was reported by Kyodo in August 1978 to be actively seeking support from Japanese steel companies after having contacted the Nippon Steel Corporation earlier in the same year for technical assistance at the Baoshan refinery.[386]

When the president of the Japan National Oil Corporation Hisatsugu Tokunaga conferred with the presidents of the Japan Petroleum Producer's Association in November 1978, he told them that China had actively requested for Japanese support in developing oil deposits off Lianyun port in the Yellow Sea as well as the Gulf of Bohai and other areas. The request was a follow-up of a recent visit to China for talks on oil development. Within the arrangement, Japan would be solely responsible for planning and providing the necessary deep-sea probes for drilling work at up to 200 meters of depth.[387] Also, German engineers were involved in a project to extend coal mining in China, but by receiving Chinese mining engineers for training in Bad Godesberg, the German industry hoped to gain follow-up orders in the dimension of around one billion Marks. The first Chinese miners were scheduled to arrive in mid-1978.[388] – another long-held red line that was crossed to ensure the future flow of precious crude. In parallel, possibilities of

---

383 Foreign Broadcast Information Service, Introduction of Foreign Technology Discussed, Ninth in a series under the general title: "Deepen the Criticism of the Gang of Four and Clarify the 10 Do's and Don't's on the Economic Front" titled "Do We Need to Import Advanced Technology", Peking Domestic Service in Mandarin, 1040 GMT, 29 10 1977 OW, accessed through Readex.

384 Ibid.

385 US Department of State, Electronic Telegram, PRC Minister of Foreign Trade visit to UK and France, 14 November 1977, 00:00, PlusD, ID: 1977PEKING02645_c.

386 Foreign Broadcast Information Service, Japan Expected to Assist PRC in Construction of Major Steel Mill, Tokyo Kyodo in English, 0038 GMT, 24 08 1978 OW, accessed through Readex.

387 Foreign Broadcast Information Service, Oil Firms asked to help develop PRC Oil Resources, Tokyo Kyodo in English, 0040 GMT, 09 11 1978 OW, accessed through Readex.

388 Foreign Broadcast Information Service, Details of FRG Firms Assistance to PRC Coal Industry, Hamburg DPA in German, 1150 GMT, 06 11 1978 LD, accessed through Readex.

an expansion of scientific and technical cooperation in agriculture and agricultural trade were discussed with the US. When US Secretary of Agriculture Robert Bergland returned from a visit to Beijing, he reported that the two sides had "identified many areas for co-operation". The US, he underlined, stood ready to help and cooperate and that the growth in agricultural trade was encouraging.[389]

In September, Xinhua's commentator answered another rhetorical question: whether the introduction of foreign technology stood in contradiction with self-reliance. The answer was concise, stating that science and technology were "assets created jointly by the human race" and could not belong only to one country.[390] Advanced technology was imported in large quantities by the end of 1978, with an order of seven geological and geophysical data processing centres for use by the oil industry in December being one of the largest ever concluded. The *Compagnie General de Géophysique* expected to begin talks with Chinese officials on further purchases in the following month.[391] With a view to the extensive financing necessary to back such transactions, the French journal Le Monde commented critically on the increase of large-scale transactions between France and the PRC:

> "However, there is still a possibility that China could run into debt. The choice seems already to have been made in Peking: $5 billion in currency reserves – more than half in gold – give safe but certainly not unlimited [marge de manoeuvre]. For example, what would China do if there were a very bad harvest? The present industrialization policy would certainly suffer the consequences."[392]

The issues of foreign debt and investment

As foreign trade expanded and the political attention given to the oil sector and its potential for exports increased, the issue of foreign debt constantly lingered in the background. The use of loans would have allowed the People's Republic to expand its financial possibilities, and thus import capital goods it would otherwise not be able to afford. Despite this apparently simple logic, using foreign credit was held to be a red line not to be crossed if China was to stick to self-reliance – avoiding interdependence. Flexibilities were nevertheless gradually introduced in the early 1970s. According to Japanese Prime Minister Kakuei Tanaka, the economic mission in Tokyo in October 1973 had been aimed at China's future purchase of Japanese production plants, of which he saw the "first round" featuring petrochemical facilities and a steel mill complex as nearly complete.[393]

---

389 Foreign Broadcast Information Service, Secretary Bergland addresses 8 November Peking Banquet, Peking NCNA in English, 1753 GMT, 08 11 1978 OW, accessed through Readex.

390 Foreign Broadcast Information Service, NCNA stresses Need to introduce Foreign Technology, Peking NCNA Domestic Service in Mandarin, 1139 GMT, 16 09 1978 OW, accessed through Readex.

391 Foreign Broadcast Information Service, $69-Million Contract for Oil Prospecting Equipment with France signed, Hong Kong AFP in English, 1625 GMT, 27 12 1978 OW, accessed through Readex.

392 Foreign Broadcast Information Service, Le Monde weighs Credit Risk of Trade with PRC, Le Monde editorial: *"An Immense Appetite"*, Paris Le Monde in French, 05 12 1978 LD, accessed through Readex.

393 Chinese Economic Mission Concludes Visit to Japan, PlusD, ID: 1973TOKYO13258_b.

While Liu continued to emphasise that China did not seek any kind of finance that implied economic assistance from Japan, there were other means. Trade with capitalist countries also meant that currency and finance became factors to consider. When trading with socialist countries, exports would usually not be paid for in hard currency but in products – unless exports were a part of a Chinese aid programme. As an example, the annually renewed trade agreements between China and Czechoslovakia included fixed quantitative quotas that defined the kind and quantity of machinery and equipment to be traditionally exchanged for Chinese foodstuffs and raw materials. Imports from capitalist countries, on the other hand, could not be handled purely by this method of large-scale barter. Generally speaking, they needed to be paid in convertible currency, if the respective trade partner could not be convinced to accept RMB as a means of payment (which was rare). Chinese imports were paid for by debiting Chinese accounts in foreign banks and their branches, usually through letters of credit. Those were issued in various currencies, sent to China and collected by the Bank of China.[394]

1973 ended, and it had become clear that a new export drive was underway in China, prospects for China to become a strong exporter of labour-intensive products were recognised. At the same time, the option of acquiring capital goods more cheaply from abroad than they could be produced domestically offered a shortcut away from the slow pace of Chinese industrialisation. Remarkably, this meant an openness towards the use of another core mechanism of the capitalist world economy: foreign capital. First, imports of Japanese capital goods were financed through payment in instalments, provided by Japanese banks at an interest rate of around six percent over five years.[395]

While this policy of trade expansion and medium-term borrowing was a departure from the patterns of the 1960s, US estimates in late 1973 recognised that China had a "fairly firm grasp of its future receipts and payments" and was not likely to "suffer a significant balance of payments deficit [...] that would require import retrenchment". As the topic of balanced trade was brought up regularly when the expansion of economic relations was addressed, the Chinese leadership was well aware of the thin line it was walking.

The foreign debt of other socialist countries had increased in the past decade and was visibly affecting the stability of political rule by socialist parties. The CCP apparently wanted to avoid such political risk under all circumstances. The problem was also recognised on the side of the creditors, albeit the solution was often seen in more of the same. The President of the (West) German Industry and Trade Association, Otto Wolff von Amerongen, pointed out the increasing debt in the East to Federal politicians, stating in an interview in October 1975 that

> "The amount of debts can be such today that the debt problem can become a political problem. I am convinced that the socialist countries are good debtors due to their tradition and education; they have always paid their commercial and other debts punctually. But this does not eliminate our duty of looking after the addition of all external

394 US Department of State, Electronic Telegram, PRC Trade and Finance, 28 November 1973, 08:05, PlusD, ID: 1973HONGK11899_b.

395 Current Chinese Communist Trends, Taipei Chung-Kung Yen-Chiu, 05 1973.

> debts. Some countries are in a difficult situation in this respect. This is being plainly said in negotiations. In other words, the position of debtor can become a very strong political position some day. Better offers of East bloc states would be a solution. Their offers are too limited, they do not permit intensification of goods exchange through constant turnover increases. We need more consumer goods from them, more industrial goods, and better service if you think of such industrial goods as machines and automobiles." [On the other hand, von Amerongen recommended "sobriety" with regard to China.] "The Chinese always have been good customers of the Federal Republic and Japan. We did not have the same turnover increase with China as with other socialist countries. The Chinese have no external debs, in contrast to European Communist countries, and they are proud of it. There exists no impulse via credits, delivery credits, or long term bank credits. [...] I would call this [Chinese industrialization] a long-term plan [...] everybody going to Peking knew that they were medium-term or long-term hopes. I continue to consider China as a highly interesting market, as I did 10 years ago."[396]

Nevertheless, the use of deferred payments as a form of crypto-credit was extended. First, in quantity. Over the course of 1973, China purchased nine complete plants at an estimated price of 810 million USD on five-year-terms at six percent from Japanese, French and Italian suppliers. Second, in scope, from the purchase of whole plants to single orders – initially, in a transaction concerning the import of machinery produced by the UK Dowty Mining Equipment Company in late 1973.[397] This enabled the Chinese import companies to increase their imports of machinery, while distributing the burden of payment over a longer period of time. The increase in machinery imports was remarkable – purchases between January and September of 1973 from Japan, the FRG and the UK totalled an estimated 190 million USD, compared with 81 million for the whole of 1972. A preference towards European suppliers was noticed by US officials, as Chinese trade corporations specified at several occasions. Kodak reported a specific request that films be supplied from its British plant rather than from the United States. Also, while China signalled interest in a proposal by the Continental Can Corporation to supply canning equipment, trade corporation officials requested the UK-based Metal Box Ltd., with which the CCC had "an agreement" that they could supply the equipment.[398] Deferred payments continued to be used and were expanded through 1974, enabling China to increase imports while distributing the burden of repayment over a longer period.[399]

The use of such instruments also woke the interest of the financial sector in the West. OSEC noted already in fall of 1972 that a participation of Swiss banks in official delegations traveling to the PRC would be useful, to ensure that their prospective clients in the socialist state would be informed about available services as soon as the political winds would change:

---

396 Foreign Broadcast Information Service, Trade Official Assesses Debts of Socialist Countries, Cologne Deutschlandfunk Domestic Service in German, 1600 GMT, 28 10 1975 DW.

397 People's Republic Of China Economic Review 1, PlusD, ID: 1974HONGK00476_b.

398 US Department of State, Electronic Telegram, PRC Specifies European Sources for U.S. Equipment, 12 December 1974, 07:03, PlusD, ID: 1974HONGK13424_b.

399 People's Republic of China Economic Review 1, PlusD, ID: 1974HONGK00476_b.

> "For the banks, a participation would be useful, to create personal contacts. For the time being, they should not travel to China to offer credit. [...] they [the Chinese] are still proud to have repaid all debt to the Russians, accept no new debt and pay all imports in cash. Under the impression of the Soviet policies, which open the doors to foreign capital and "know how", also the Chinese seem to have a more positive attitude [today] towards foreign credit. [...] In any case, the banks should already today travel to the Middle Kingdom for courtesy visits. The Chinese know, what services Swiss banks can offer, so they do not need to be explained in detail. It is well possible, that the Chinese change their policies already in 1974 and resort to the services of foreign banks to finance their increasing foreign trade and investment. Here, again, Swiss banks have the advantage that the Chinese seem to be more open to accept credit by a small, neutral state, whose power they do not need to fear.The question then will rather be, whether our banks are in a position to offer the required credit".[400]

In a discussion with Hong Kong bankers, Qiao Peixin of the Bank of China confirmed three main points with regard to the financing of China's imports. First, China intended to use RMB in its foreign transactions and as an accounting unit, and extended this practice to as many countries as possible.[401] Second, China did not intend to make the RMB an international (convertible) currency, which meant that the currency could not be traded freely among foreigners. China would also not grant discounts from the official exchange rate, as this would appear as if the currency was traded internationally. The third point, underlining the semantic difference, that China would not take foreign credit, but was still interested in using deferred payments.[402] The exchange rate of the RMB fixed by the Bank of China fluctuated over days and weeks, which lead to the introduction of forward contracts (options) in USD/RMB in an agreement between the US and China on the "Financial Aspect of Trade between the US and PRC".[403] US firms could now hedge their trade contracts against arbitrary fluctuations in the RMB exchange rate.

The expansive strategy soon experienced a notable backlash. By the end of 1974, the PRC had incurred a substantial trade deficit, the estimates of which varied between 200 million to 1.3 billion USD and had a negative prognosis. As its foreign exchange reserves were insufficient to meet debt of this dimension, the limits of the possible for the continuation of trade suddenly became very narrow: reduce imports, increase revenue from exports, or borrow money. The reluctance to be further involved in global division of labour appears to have excluded an export-led strategy at the time. After the October 1974 Canton Fair, a delegation by AmCham consisting of acting president Bob Goodwin (Alcoa),

400 Schweizerische Zentrale für Handelsförderung, Interner Bericht über den Besuch in der Volksrepublik China vom 20. bis 31. Oktober 1972 betreffend die Durchführung einer Schweizerischen Industrie-Ausstellung in Peking 1974, pp. 14–15..

401 In that regard, it is interesting to note that in trade relations with Socialist economies, China consistently referred to the Swiss Franc as an accounting unit. Whether this was because of the insistence of the respective trade partner (a compromise avoiding the use of the Ruble as it was common in the COMECON) is not clear.

402 US Department of State, Electronic Telegram, Hong Kong Bankers Delegation Visit to The PRC, 10 October 1974, 07:10, PlusD, ID: 1974HONGK11158_b.

403 US Department of State, Electronic Telegram, Commerce Department Draft Of "Financial Aspect of Trade Between the U.S. And PRC", 13 November 1974, 02:50, PlusD, ID: 1974HONGK12331_b.

Bill Baker (General Electric), Lou Sabolle (Bank of America) and Herbert Minch (AmCham Executive Vice President) reported that Chinese officials were "overlooking" opportunities to indirectly expand exports to the US through Hong Kong. The proposal that was presented to the Chinese representatives consisted of large volume acquisitions of Chinese "components" and raw materials by US manufacturers in Hong Kong to be incorporated into their end products, which would thereafter be exported to the US. Although not being registered statistically as Chinese exports to the US, this integration, in a transnational value chain, AmCham proposed, could ease the pressure on China's "unfavourable trade balance".

In addition to advances of proximity, the plan would also have enabled the PRC to bypass the most favoured nation treatment[404] and technical issues, such as packing and logistics for the final products. Public estimates by AmCham indicated that these "indirect" exports could amount to 100–150 million USD per annum. As the AmCham delegation reported, representatives of CCPIT and Machimpex had signalled eagerness to start a detailed examination of the proposal, including detailed discussions on terms with Chinese officials concerning the quantities, delivery dates, specifications, "competitive prices" and kind of such intermediate products.[405]

At a press conference, Baker expressed confidence that a large import potential existed with the local electronics industry as well as textile and "other industries".[406] While USLO in Beijing approved of the proposal, as it "may generate more fair invitations and PRC contacts for local US companies. This could lead to a better understanding of US market requirements and eventually, may even generate more PRC exports." Further, increased competitiveness of Hong Kong through the use of cheap inputs from the mainland was established as a possible advantage. Still, the US State Department expressed doubts about the ability of the Chinese industry to supply the desired types of products at a sufficient quality standard and competitive price point in a timely manner. With the increased revenue, time and capital would have been required to increase the value-added of exports or production capacities of oil, and debt as such was not a viable option politically; therefore, the the suggestion was given suit. In January and February 1975, two contracts for one million tons of wheat and 200'000 bales of cotton from the USA were cancelled, with the outspoken intention to avoid a deficit.[407] Large-scale capital construction projects were strongly minimised and policy guidelines issued earlier (the five prin-

404 In December 1974, the US Department of State confirmed that the plan would enable Chinese exports to bypass the non-MFN trade barriers only, if a substantial change of the product occurred in Hong Kong giving it a Hong Kong origin according to Rules of Origin applied by US customs. See: US Department of State, Electronic Telegram, PRC Exports to US Manufacturers in Hong Kong Proposed by Amcham, 2 December 1974, 23:55, PlusD, ID: 1974STATE264606_b.

405 US Department of State, Electronic Telegram, PRC Exports to US Manufacturers in HK Proposed by Amcham, 25 October 1974, 00:45, PlusD, ID: 1974HONGK11668_b [extended report].

406 Ibid., para. 2.

407 US Department of State, Electronic Telegram, PRC Agricultural Import Policy Toward US, 18 March 1975, 07:15, PlusD, ID: 1975PEKING00474_b; and: US Department of State, Electronic Telegram, PRC Agricultural Import Policy Toward US, 14 March 1975, 03:45, PlusD, ID: 1975HONGK02621_b.

ciples of the 1973 capital construction plans[408] that resulted from the national planning conference in February) to use hidden production capacities and scrutinise the need for projects requiring massive investment were brought to attention.[409] Large-scale development projects were strictly limited to small- or medium-sized projects.[410]

Despite these measures, the estimated deficit remained at almost half a billion USD throughout 1975, while the total trade turnover rose by the same amount to about 14.5 billion by the end of the year (as mentioned above, in 1970, turnover had been at about four billion USD).[411] This was not only due to the quantitative relation between imports and exports. As the PRC had to pay its imports mostly in foreign currency, the deficit was also a function of the inflationary trend in the rest of the world. The prudence resulting from the experience was also reflected in MoFT's negotiation priorities: while the PRC–Swiss trade agreement mentioned above was a straightforward instrument aiming at trade liberalisation, a later agreement with the European communities negotiated between early 1976 and February 1978 appeared to be more balanced, at least when it came to the inclusion of Chinese demands.

The Chinese side insisted on including a clause aiming at the realisation of an equilibrium of exchanges with the possibility of taking measures if evident disequilibrium occurred. Somewhat ironically, the EC insisted on the inclusion of anti-dumping and safeguard provisions, as it feared that subsidised products of Chinese State-owned enterprises might have a distorting effect.[412]

Nevertheless, the political agenda of modernisation, including through large-scale projects, did not change substantially. In a speech in January 1975, Zhou Enlai not only stated that the PRC was still free from foreign debt, but also made clear that the decision to do what was necessary to develop the economic potential of the PRC until the end of the century had been taken. Production could be grasped as revolution could be sized simultaneously. The Four Modernisations were confirmed as essential goals.

In October 1975, Vice Minister of Trade Yao Yilin gave a general outline of China's trade policy toward the US to a delegation of the State Department. While denying that China would become a major exporter of oil and emphasising that it would develop its

---

408 A concentration on the goals of the five-year plan, a screening-mechanism for design documents, focus on water, electric power and transport, postpone what can be postponed, cut down standards and speed up construction, screening of all ongoing projects.

409 As Taiwanese reports show, the number of completed *„above-norm"*-construction projects was increasing from twenty to thirty between 1971 and 1972, but appeared rather negligible compared to the 671 projects reported in 1959. Chinese Communist Capital Construction studied and analysed, Taipei Chung-kung Yen-chiu, 05 1973, accessed through Readex.

410 Of about eighty capital construction projects announced for the year 1972, only about twenty-five were of large scale.

411 Central Intelligence Agency, People's Republic of China, International Trade Handbook, Washington D.C. October 1976.

412 Accord Commercial entre la Communauté économique européenne et la république populaire de Chine, Article 3 : „Les deux parties contractantes déploieront tous leurs efforts pour favoriser l'expansion harmonieuse de leurs échanges commerciaux réciproques et contribuer selon leurs moyens propres à la réalisation d'un équilibre de leurs échanges." Bureau de l'Intégration du DPF et du DFEP, Rapport de synthèse no 2/79, Les Relations entre la CEE et la Chine, Mars 1979, Universitätsbibliothek Basel UB Wirtschaft, SWA Magazin, SWA Vo H XI 1b CHN.

production without cooperation with foreign companies, he pointed at an upcoming expansion of Chinese trade. The PRC would rely on its own efforts, but not adopt a "closed-door policy", continuing to import advanced technology and equipment. He emphasised that trade was about to expand "to better achieve independence", as the increased effort put in socialist construction "in the next 5–10 years" would accelerate. As to the question on how China would handle its balance of payment difficulties, Yao mentioned the maintenance of balanced trade, overseas Chinese remittances and currency controls and noted that the "normal practice" of deferred and instalment payments was "not excluded" in the future.[413]

Shortly after, in November 1975, the deputy general manager of CCPIT, Xiao Fangzhou told USLO that the "just adopted"[414] fifth five-year plan would bring "great development" of the economy as well as foreign trade.[415] The "kiss of debt", as coined by STEPHEN KOTKIN[416], had grazed the socialist state, as had the immediate consequences of the global crisis. While mostly agricultural imports from the USA were reduced between 1974 and 1976 – from about 67 million USD to merely 11 million USD – imports of capital goods from the EC and Japan kept on increasing or were reduced only to a minor extent in the same period – from 165 million USD to 138 million USD (Japan) and 80.5 million USD to 109 million USD (EC).[417]

Increases in deferred payments would have raised the possibilities for increased imports of technology, with the potential estimated by USLO in November 1976 to be between one to two billion USD a year. The political situation had stabilised insofar that while the criticism towards any appearance of foreign debt had been substantial in the past, it was perceived as being much more conductive to such an expansion.[418]

Similarly, the overall outlook for future imports of whole industrial plants in particular was perceived as being positive in late 1976 by USLO, stating that "given normal harvests and a healthy world economy" as well as agricultural production keeping ahead of population growth, increases in investment in that particularly capital-intense sector

---

413 US Trade with China: Yao I-Lin Statements to World Affairs Delegation, PlusD, ID: 1975PEKING01951_b.

414 Ibid.

415 US Department of State, Electronic Telegram, PRC Five Year Plan, 12 November 1975, 07:00, PlusD, ID: 1975PEKING02160_b.

416 KOTKIN, STEPHEN, The Kiss of Debt: The East Bloc goes Borrowing, in: FERGUSON et al. 2010, pp. 80–93.

417 Organisation for Economic Cooperation and Development (OECD), Statistics of Foreign Trade, Paris 1977. The foreign trade quota (percent of GDP) is estimated by the World Bank to have risen from about 2.4 percent in 1970 to almost five percent in 1974 and subsequently stayed around 4.2 percent in 1977 and 1978. See: World Bank Statistics, Exports of goods and service (% of GDP) – China, available at: https://data.worldbank.org/indicator/NE.EXP.GNFS.ZS?end=1978&locations=CN&start=1970, last accessed on 1 May 2020. After 1977, foreign trade grew exponentially until 1982.

418 As USLO reported in November 1976: "[Deferred payments] would have a long term rather than an immediate effect on the economy. Even then, there will undoubtedly be political opposition in the party [the CCP], but these complaints should be manageable". US Department of State, Electronic Telegram, Chinese Economy as seen from Peking, 13 November 1976, 03:00, PlusD, ID: 1976PEKING02343_b, paragraph 4.

were to be expected for the following year. Given the potential for a change in the commodity composition of China's trade, as China had obtained self-sufficiency, at least in the short term, of many industrial raw materials or import substitutes and could increasingly export manufactured items in addition to agricultural products and raw materials. On the import side, USLO estimated that given the adjustments in the Chinese economy, light manufactures and, in particular, electronic devices would show the greatest growth potential besides capital goods, including whole plants scheduled to begin production during the sixth five-year plan from 1980 to 1985.[419]

In particular, due to China striving for the modernisation of oil production as well as the build-up of refining, mining, transport and communications capacities, it was expected that China would rely even more heavily on technology transfers and imports of advanced equipment, with raising import-rates "noticeable by late 1977".[420] To finance these in the present structure of the economy, China would continue to rely upon agricultural and raw materials exports. If strategies in agricultural mechanisation and birth control in particular were to prove successful, spending large amounts of scarce foreign exchange on the import of food grain as they were necessary in 1974 could be avoided. Medium-term deferred payments up to five years, as USLO estimated, would remain the only politically accepted means to expand these constraints for the moment.[421] Nevertheless, USLO concluded that:

> "The substantial increase in trade in prospect during the latter part of the decade [the 1970s] will not necessarily cause China's overall economy to become much more trade oriented than is presently the case. We doubt Chinese planners envisage turning China into a 'major' trading nation. China's trade program has a clear, if long-term, import substitution objective".[422]

That loosening these constraints was considered as early as January 1977 was indicated by contacts of FRG officials and Hong Kong-based Ta Kung Pao, where it was indicated that the question of accepting foreign credit was currently under discussion in Beijing. In parallel, USLO noted a request by Chinese officials with regard to the possibility of a deferred payment, over a seven-year period instead of the usual five years in connection with the purchase of a petrochemical plant.[423] Differences in communication between CCPIT and the Chinese MoFT were also noted, as the former kept to a strident tone in stating consistently that China would not accept foreign loans, while the Ministry merely

419 US Department of State, Electronic Telegram, PRC Trade Prospects 1977–1980, 21 December 1976, 06:30, PlusD, ID: 1976HONGK14729_b.

420 Ibid., paragraph 6.

421 Estimating a potential of one billion USD for the purchase of whole plants during 1978 and 1979. Ibid., paragraph 9.

422 Ibid., paragraph 13. Also, the USLO report stated: "Technology and the systematic expansion of exports will require significantly increased Chinese contact and cooperation with the Western World. The extent to which this will influence Chinese foreign policies is uncertain. Probably more significant of [sic!] westerners intrest [sic!] will be the accelerated economic development in China as a partial result of technology imports". Ibid., paragraph 14.

423 US Department of State, Electronic Telegram, Possible Changes in PRC Trade Financing, 20 January 1977, 00:00, PlusD, ID: 1977HONGK00824_c.

stated that China would not beg.[424] While several credit offers had been turned down in the past, limited flexibility was anticipated.

The constraints set by the concept of balanced trade were narrow. In April 1977, the embassy of the FRG was informed that the small surplus announced by the Chinese government referred specifically to the trade account, but not to the current account.[425] The trend that had become evident in the second half of 1976 was to combine sharp cuts in imports with increases in exports of goods of as high a value-added as possible; this stood in contrast with the ambitious goals of increased standards of living and technological development – at least, if these were to be realised within the political timeframe of 1980/2000, which still was the point of reference and the legitimising core of Hua Guofeng's leadership. By mid-1977, this tension was accentuated as relatively large purchases of grain and sugar from Argentina, Canada, Australia and other countries were concluded and shipped – tending to counterbalance the feeble surplus that was additionally relativised through persisting inflationary pressure on international markets.[426]

When the Peruvian journalist Antonio Fernandez Arce interviewed Vice Premier Li Xiannian in early June of 1977, he asked about rumours concerning the Chinese foreign reserves deficit and an approaching economic crisis. The second highest state official readily clarified the changes in paradigm to the foreigner:

> "China is a very large country and it has many resources. If we had a negative balance of $1 billion, $500 million or $300 million, it would not be a problem. We can recover easily. Besides, our economy is based on domestic savings and is not dependent on foreign trade. Right now, we have a positive balance and the comrades from many organizations are in a hurry to spend it in the purchase of foreign technology which we lack. Naturally, we cannot do things in a hurry, everything must be planned. We believe that we shall never make a wrong move. We have vast experience and we have learned even from the negative aspects of the Soviet economic policy; you see, today the USSR has a foreign debt amounting to $40 billion. We do not owe a cent to anybody, either at home or abroad."[427]
>
> "We are not suffering from inflation or from the phenomenon of unemployment affecting other powers and other countries. Nor do we suffer at all from an energy crisis. We have oil, coal, gas and hydroelectric power plants; in the future we shall have thermonuclear plants as well. Agriculture is and has always been our big problem. We have a population of 800 million who must eat every day; but we also have huge human resources. Naturally it would be better if we had the manpower and if the people did not have to eat. Right? [...] But the agricultural problem has been solved and we are on the road to achieve total mechanization by the end of the century."[428]

---

424 Ibid., paragraph 2.

425 US Department of State, Electronic Telegram, PRC Trade Surplus, 19 April 1977, 00:00, PlusD, ID: 1977PEKING00764_c.

426 China Highlights, PlusD, ID: 1977HONGK06049_c, paragraph 2.

427 Li Hsien-Nien interviewed, 12 06 1977, p. 26.

428 Ibid.

The article made references to ongoing oil drilling operations, quoting Li saying that "we have discovered oil deposits with reserves comparable to the most important ones in the Middle East. Just imagine what China will have by the end of this century".

As the import of machinery, which was usually based on long-term contracts, had a deferred effect on trade figures, the slight surplus of 1977 was estimated by the USLO to be realistically maintainable through 1978, particularly because the "receding of the drought danger" indicated that imports of grain and other foodstuffs would not be necessary in the following years.[429] Politically, the readiness to take the risk was established by July 1977, when Renmin Ribao published a defence of the "Twenty Points", explicitly stating that "in order to bring in some advanced foreign technology", it was necessary "to increase exports – to import whole sets of foreign equipment to be paid for with our coal and crude oil under conditions of equality and mutual benefit". He also added that these transactions might be conducted "according to methods of deferred payment or installments generally practiced in international trade". The article rhetorically asked, "what is wrong with these two points?"[430]

The national foreign trade conference of August 1977 underlined this stance, outlining the strategy to be pursued in foreign trade for the timely accomplishment of the Four Modernisations: Approximate balancing of the trade account, imports in foreign technology, consumer goods and some – mostly agricultural – raw materials as well as food, if necessary was to be gradually expanded. Deferred payments would provide some flexibility for purchases, while additional export markets for Chinese products were to be sought. Deng Xiaoping underlined in an interview with French journalists in October 1977 that China was at the time not prepared to change its policy and accept long term credit from the West to finance its imports, stating that "We accept the notion of deferred payments. But we are only going into short term debt and only on the condition that we will be able to repay it", assuring that China was open to the outside and anxious to develop its industries.[431]

Increases in exports were to be facilitated by a general orientation in both agricultural and industrial production on international standards of quality and delivery speed, as well through unified vertical management stressing discipline, while the living standard, especially in industrialised cities, was to be constantly raised – if necessary, by imports. That this strategy would be an arduous task was confirmed by several trade partners when assessing the future of their China trade.

After a visit to Beijing in September 1977, New South Wales Premier Neville Wran announced at a press conference on 10 September that he had talked to Vice Premier

429 Also estimating that in the "present period of expanding foreign trade, US should be able to use its position as the residual supplier of agricultural commodities and as the best source for many high-technology products. In some cases (soybeans, cotton) the US has already begun to do so" US Department of State, Electronic Telegram, PRC Trade Policy and Sino-US Trade, 9 June 1977, 00:00, PlusD, ID: 1977PEKING01157_c, paragraph 4.

430 Foreign Broadcast Information Service, People's Daily Condemns Gang's Criticism of 'Regulations', Peking NCNA Domestic Service in Mandarin, 0717 GMT, 16 07 1977 OW, accessed through Readex.

431 Foreign Broadcast Information Service, Teng on Terrorism, Trade, Alliance, Hong Kong AFP in English, 1330 GMT, 26 10 1977 OW, accessed through Readex.

Yu Chiu-li, Chairman of the State Planning Commission, confirming that bilateral trade with Australia would expand as the country stood "high on the [Chinese] list of friendly nations". Nevertheless, as Wran noted, the trade balance – standing at about six to one in Australia's favour – could not be easily corrected, as exports to China consisted mostly of wheat and cotton which China required. On that basis, China had renounced possible imports of uranium from Australia to serve its energy needs.[432] In general, the balance did not appear to bother the Chinese MoFT all that much as, at a later visit in September 1977, the points of setting up a permanent Chinese trade mission in Australia and Chinese imports of coal from new South Wales were the main topics discussed.[433]

The move away from the remaining red line in the general acceptance of international economic interdependence in Chinese economic policy was lobbied for by foreign exporters, who saw a tremendous potential to increase their business with the socialist state. Again, the Japanese were pioneers, followed notably by the Swiss. Both countries were also the first to be invited to send speakers to the Chinese Institute of Foreign Trade.[434] In November 1977, the Japanese Export-Import Bank sent a delegation to China, led by Vice President Daizo Hoshino at the invitation of the Bank of China, following similar missions during the hinge years of 1974 and 1975. A spokesman of the Japanese bank was quoted by Kyodo, during the preparations for the visit in October of the same year, that the visit "was designed to inspect some of the plants built with loans made by the bank in the past", which had been five-year deferred payments. It was also indicated that talks with Bank of China officials would be used to discuss the possibility of extended loans, being necessary to finance machinery and equipment that Japanese companies planned to sell in return for Chinese crude oil and coal.[435] A delegation of the Bank of China visited the Bank of Japan in May 1978. The leader of the Chinese delegation and vice president of the bank praised the friendly cooperation of the past. He was quoted by Xinhua: "together with the new upsurge in our economic construction, there will be a new development in our economic and trade relations with foreign countries", adding "as well as in banking services".[436]

Reporting on an official trade mission in the PRC in September 1978, the foreign trade division of the Swiss Department of Economic Affairs described the emerging business environment:

> "it is not to be overseen that a new spirit reigns in China. The new government seems determined to catch up economically and establish the performance principle [Leistungsprinzip]. Political dogma is not denied, but it shall no more impede economic

432 Foreign Broadcast Information Service, Continuing Trade, PRC Mission, Hong Kong AFP in English, 1046, 10 09 1977 OW, accessed through Readex.

433 Foreign Broadcast Information Service, State Planning Minister, Hong Kong AFP in English, 1812 GMT, 07 09 1977 OW, accessed through Readex.

434 Der Direktor der Eidgenössischen Handelsabteilung, Bericht über China-Mission (18. bis 29. September 1978), Bern, den 5. Oktober 1978, p. 7. Available at dodis: dodis.ch/49077. Last accessed on 12 August 2022. Translation by the author.

435 Foreign Broadcast Information Service, Bank Delegation to PRC, Tokyo Kyodo in English, 0450 GMT, 21 10 1977 OW, accessed through Readex.

436 Foreign Broadcast Information Service, Japanese Bank Governor Fetes PRC Bank Delegation, Peking NCNA in English, 1813 GMT, 24 05 1978 OW, accessed through Readex.

and scientific progress. The modernisation of factors of production is sought in cooperation with foreigners, with Japan and Europe in the focus at the moment. On our trip, we have met Japanese delegations twice)one mission for the extraction of oil and one for the import of oil) as well as a German scientific delegation of the Max Planck Institute. The conditions for an important increase of Swiss foreign trade with [the PRC] and an expansion of mutual economic relations seem particularly favourable today, because the Chinese are obviously serious about their modernisation policies and are in a hurry"[437]

After a systematic investigation of possible sources in European countries and Japan over the course of several official visits in the course of 1978, the implementation of a number of important projects was beginning in the second half of the year. Even at the highest level of the socialist state, the desire to expand the limits of the possible was expressed in an only slightly veiled manner. Vice premier Gu Mu who visited Switzerland was described as tireless by his Swiss hosts, while the rest of the delegation showed clear signs of exhaustion – but even so, Swiss companies complained that they were not part of the tight schedule that had been organised according to Chinese demands.[438]

The vice premier noted several times during his visit of enterprises such as Ciba-Geigy, Omega and Brown Boveri & Cie that if he had enough foreign exchange, he could make a number of important purchases "right here and right now". Asked for China's attitude towards foreign credit which would allow for such procurements, Gu Mu indicated that there not only was the ambitious modernisation plan not likely to be fulfilled without foreign credit, but also that a certain amount of foreign debt would be quite reasonable for a country rich in raw materials as the PRC.[439] Also, he made positive remarks on possible licensing contracts, meaning the production of products based on Swiss technology in the PRC, for power plants, pesticides and the ship engines needed to further develop infrastructures for trade. With a view to the structure of trade, the Swiss side felt obliged to emphasise the importance of the well-known Chinese principles of foreign trade, pointing out the necessity to increase Swiss imports from the PRC as well. Gu was reported to be quite satisfied by these remarks, while only mentioning coal and oil as potential Chinese exports.[440] On the other hand, the Chinese ministry for trade was eager to receive a confirmation by Switzerland, that the neutral country did not itself impose export restrictions for military goods, even if it was in some cases obliged not to re-export sensitive materials.[441]

In Bern, these signals were well noted.

Former member of the Federal Council Ernst Brugger, head of the Swiss Department of Economic Affairs from 1970 until January 1978, suggested in September 1978 that the

---

437 Bericht über China-Mission (18. bis 29. September 1978), p. 2.

438 Besuch Ku Mu, Bericht an Direktor Jolles, Bern, 18. Mai 1978. Available at dodis.ch/49051. Last accessed on 12 August 2022.

439 Handelsabteilung EVD, Besuch Ku Mu, Bern, 25. Mai 1978, Ref. vT/Ze – China 821.AVA. Available at dodis : dodis.ch/49054. Last accessed on 12 August 2022.

440 Ibid., p. 2.

441 Der Direktor der Eidgenössischen Handelsabteilung, Bericht über China-Mission (18. bis 29. September 1978), p. 6.

time was right to propose a "framework credit" or "transfer credit" of 200 million Swiss francs to the PRC. The Swiss *Volksbank* had confirmed its willingness to take the lead together with a consortium of banks. The Swiss embassy in Beijing commented that any credit with government involvement particularly on the Swiss side would be unacceptable for the PRC, while chances for an arrangement between banks could be explored. Mentioning a future visit of minister (first ministry of machine building) Zhou Zeming in November of the same year, the embassy made reference to contacts in Beijing indicating that the minister did not come to Switzerland "only for window-shopping". A credit arrangement with favourable conditions had the potential to "positively influence the minister's buying decisions".[442] The *Volksbank* visited China in the same month, presenting different models of Swiss credit to deputy director of the People's Bank of China and chairman of the board of directors of the Bank of China, Qiao Peixin. Brugger was part of the delegation. The Swiss *chargé d'affaires* in Beijing reported that while formally there had been no change in the PRC's official position on foreign credit – no debt on a government level – the dogma had been quite remarkably reinterpreted.

Vice prime minister Li Xiannian clarified the issue in a meeting with the president of *Keidanren*: "Whatever non-government entities do, is not the government's business".[443] Accordingly, at a similar meeting with the Swiss Bank Corporation (*Schweizerische Bankgesellschaft* SBG), the Chinese delegation repeatedly insisted on the question whether any credit offered would really be of a "private nature" and whether the Swiss authorities would know about such arrangements. As this issue was obviously sensitive, mentioning it at all to any Chinese official outside the Bank of China was strongly discouraged inside the Swiss federal administration.[444] According to an internal memo prepared for the director of the Federal Office for Foreign Economic Affairs, Paul Jolles, by mid-september 1978 several offers for "transfer credit" had been submitted by Swiss banks to the bank of China, ranging from about 100 million Swiss francs to about 200 million at four percent interest.[445]

Even concerning the direct involvement of foreign capital in the form of joint ventures, flexibilities were obvious albeit still experimental. While there was no model for the "appropriate modalities" of such cooperation, Chinese officials signalled their interest to receive proposals. Exchanges between Swiss diplomats and businesspeople in Hong Kong revealed that while it was important for the Chinese state not to transfer any property, production sites working with foreign know how were glad to use the commercial connections of their foreign partners. They actually preferred to pay them by passing over a part of the goods produced. Chinese enterprises even proposed to use "made in Switzerland" as a designation for such products. Also, at least in the early stages of the

442 Minister von Tscharner Chinareise Dir. Jolles: Bankgeschäfte, Peking, 12.9.1978, 13:00, Ref. 5.6.41.Cha.152.0. Available at dodis: dodis.ch/49076. Last accessed on 12 August 2022.

443 Schweizerische Botschaft in China, VR China: Besuch der Volksbank, Peking, den 11. September 1978, Ref. 101.0, 512.0 – SC/em. Available at dodis: dodis.ch/49083. Last accessed on 12 August 2022.

444 Notiz an Herrn Minister Zwahlen, China Gelder, Bern, den 14. September 1978, Ref. S.C.41.Cha.731.1. – PF/dem. Available at dodis: dodis.ch/49086. Last accessed on 12 August 2022.

445 China: Finanzprobleme, 13. September 1978, Ref. 821 AVA – vT/rf. Available at dodis: dodis.ch/49084. Last accessed on 12. August 2022.

production process, technical management was more than gladly left to foreign partners – albeit indirectly, in the form of a consultancy mandate.[446]

The Chinese intention of not only importing products but also build production sites with foreign help was received positively, as delivering to the huge Chinese market would go beyond the capacities of Swiss industries anyway – nevertheless, still in october 1978, the Chinese red lines with regard to their adaptation of international business practices were reported to be firm: no credit involving foreign governments and no foreign direct investment.[447] Besides these limits, former obstacles such as the lack of contact with the Chinese end-users, the prohibition of commercial presence in China and the protection of intellectual property were addressed in Beijing, e. g. by issuing longer-term visa to foreign businesspeople and the construction of new hotels to ensure their accommodation.

Christopher H. Phillips of NCUSCT informed the Swiss delegation during their mission in September that the first of those "partnerships" had been founded Chinese companies established in Hong Kong. Machinery and technology from the West were bought by these companies on the international market and brought to the partnership company in the PRC. The goods produced there were were brought back to Hong Kong and marketed from there.[448] Anticipating the increase of requests by Swiss companies for support under these circumstances, the need of eventually assigning more diplomatic staff to Beijing was noted in Bern – while underlining the strong international competition for market entry in socialist China.[449]

In November 1978, an article in Ta Kung Pao published in Hong Kong made reference to a practice called "compensation trade" that had "only been recently implemented in China", and presented a number of problems. If foreign equipment was brought to China, did it belong to China even if reimbursement was not completed? And what if the cost was agreed to be reimbursed "through deductions from the processing expenses and the factory price of the products?" Also, who would guarantee that the equipment would work? The article proposed a look at an agreement recently published by the UN, where three clauses stipulating the liability of foreign businessmen delivering equipment to another country and could serve as a reference for future agreements concluded by China. The text was referred explicitly to as the "Agreement on Industrial Joint Ventures".[450]

The signs of qualitative change multiplied, culminating in a decision from the top of the socialist state. Vice prime minister Wang Chen, head of the fourth ministry of machine building travelled to Europe in November 1978 to negotiate on the procurement of harrier fighter jets with the United Kingdom. On the way, he proposed to the Swiss Federal Council, he would make a stopover in Geneva and proposed a meeting. As the reason for his travel was of a military nature, a bilateral meeting was approached rather

446 Ibid. p. 9.

447 Bericht über China-Mission (18. bis 29. September 1978), p. 5.

448 Ibid. p. 10.

449 Ibid. p. 13.

450 Probably the: UNIDO Manual on the Establishment of Industrial Joint Venture Agreements in Developing Countries, UN Doc. 10/68 (1971). Foreign Broadcast Information Service, Second Installment, feature article by Tsai Wei-heng: "Ownership, Maintenance and Insurance – Second Comment on problems Concerning 'Compensation Trade'", Hong Kong Ta Kung Pao in Mandarin, 02 11 1978 p. 10 HK, accessed through Readex.

hesitantly in Bern. Also, as official Chinese missions to Switzerland had become more and more frequent, it was estimated that an official meeting could not be offered "every time". As Wang planned to visit Swiss firms outside the military sector such as Rolex and Nestlé, an official dinner with director Jolles was arranged out of courtesy.[451]

This gesture was also guided by the fact that Wang was a member of the CCP central committee and therefore the highest Chinese government representative to visit Switzerland since Hua had taken control.[452] Wang accepted the invitation to dine with Jolles in Geneva. Later, the Swiss trade diplomat noted in his report that this "improvised" meeting was obviously worthwhile:

> "First, the personality of my guest: a stone old Chinese with a finely chiselled face, who walks on a stick and had participated in the Long March. He tells us that he had been wounded and underwent field surgery eight times. Being an old man, he seems to fall asleep at the table. We assume him to be totally senile. He barely opens his eyes and only mumbles quietly to himself".[453]

The contrast between this arcane scene with the new dynamic that the seasoned trade diplomat had encountered in the PRC could not be greater. He seemed to be sharing the table with a ghost of the past, a relict of the revolutionary struggle that appeared to on the verge of disappearance in the socialist state he had helped to create. But quickly, the new path to China's rise came up:

> "Suddenly, he raises his head and speaks with a loud and emphatic voice. The interpreter translates: 'I would like to inform you that we have just decided to accept foreign investment, that is 'joint ventures', and of course also loans, and not only private, but also by states, as these are offered at more favourable conditions. I hope that Switzerland as a friendly country will join in.'"[454]

Jolles and his delegation believed to have misunderstood, as only one and a half months back, during his visit in the PRC, private investment had been explicitly excluded as incompatible with the socialist system. Also all indications of the performance and efficiency of Swiss capital markets as a source of credit had been registered with interest, but only commented with the formula, that any state involvement would be unacceptable. Was the old man really senile or was there a mistranslation? Jolles and his team inquired, what kind of investment would be possible and in what form? Suddenly, the old man seemed to be quite lively, answering quickly with a reference to the reinterpretation of Mao Zedong Thought:

> "We have misinterpreted the words of Mao. We have examined and considered the issue in the highest panning committee and came to the conclusion, that Mao was not

451 Notiz an Herrn Direktor Jolles, Volksrepublik China, Bern, den 7. November 1978, Ref. China 877.3 – Ro/ne. Available at dodis: dodis.ch/52802. Last accessed on 12 August 2022.

452 Die erstaunlichen Chinesen, Notiz des Direktors der handelsabteilung des Volkswirtschaftsdepartements P. R. Jolles, Bern, den 29. November 1978. Available at dodis: dodis.ch/49088. Last accessed on 12 August 2022. Translation by the author.

453 Ibid.

454 Ibid.

against investment and loans, as long as they were in the mutual interest. As long as this basic principle is applied, the form of foreign economic cooperation is secondary. Concerning investment, foreign companies can without any further ado build joint production sites with our Chinese state organisations und import capital, machinery and technology for that purpose. We would prefer to pay for those with our raw materials, though. We are rich in raw materials and Swiss companies would be accepted everywhere. In China, heaven and earth and all that is under it is open to the Swiss."[455]

Jolles probed further, asking Wang whether such projects had already been put into action or whether the idea was genuinely new. Again, the old man reacted emphatically:

> "The idea is new. We have taken this decision recently, but we are already negotiating with some American companies for 'joint ventures'. This might surprise you, as the United States have not yet recognised the People's Republic diplomatically. But this circumstance is not an obstable for economic cooperation with private enterprises. I hope, that the Swiss magistrates will encourage the Swiss private sector to propose such projects. Every enterprise that wants to send a delegation with proposals to Peking, is welcome there."[456]

Both the Chinese ambassador in Bern – who had not announced Wang's visit to Jolles – and the Swiss ambassador in Beijing were not informed by this groundbreaking decision. The former, present at the table, nodded sympathetically despite just having explained and confirmed the opposite Chinese policy and accepted the new line respectfully and as a given. Member of the Federal Council Arthur Honegger asked Wang about the timeframe for such project decisions, receiving the optimistic answer of "a few weeks". Despite his age, Wang showed no signs of leaving, staying at the restaurant until the Swiss delegation began to move in their chairs when the hour was approaching midnight. The spectacular dinner ended with a Chinese invitation to Honegger to visit China soon, for example for the Swiss trade fair Humatex in Shanghai.

On the 15th of December 1978, Minister of Foreign trade Li Qiang talked with businesspeople from Hong Kong. As Ta Kung Pao reported, he told his audience openly that only little time was left for China to achieve the Four Modernisations. Therefore, trade policies were flexible now, with China accepting "all the common practices known to world trade" now. Not long ago, Li said, China had two important "forbidden zones" in its dealings with other countries – the acceptance of government-to-government loans and foreign investment. "This has since changed", he assured. China had also embraced "compensation trade" now: "You help us mine coal and we shall give you coal. You help us with oil drilling, and we shall give you oil. You supply us with equipment and we shall compensate you with what it produces". Li Qing was ready to assist, if any issues persisted for foreign investors. If anybody in the audience thought, he asked, that there were still "some 'forbidden zones' left, or that we are still comparatively conservative in the respect of certain trade practices, please let us know." Also, he added, China was now prepared to enter into joint ventures, as they were "in fact practicable". He wrapped up with a

455 Ibid.
456 Ibid.

reference to the European countries that had accompanied China's opening up to foreign trade during the long 1970s:

> "In the world the production of many forms of important equipment is jointly undertaken. Countries in Europe exist side by side with each other, more or less like our provinces. The short-distance and giant 'airbus' with 300 seats was jointly developed by West Germany, France, England, [the] Netherlands and Spain, each responsible for the manufacturing of certain parts. Now Western European countries want us to produce for them automobile parts which cost less. This we can accept. They can either supply us with the necessary raw materials or semi-finished products for us to process for them. Our practices are becoming more flexible, and our 'forbidden zones' are being broken down. But nothing can change overnight. We need time for us to introduce the changes step by step."[457]

China was ready to enter interdependence.

457 Foreign Broadcast Information Service, Ta Kung Pao reports on Li Chiang's Talk with Hong Kong Businessmen, Report on Foreign Trade Minister Li Chiang's talk with Hong Kong businessmen on 15 December, Hong Kong Ta Kung Pao in English, 21 12 1978 p. 19 HK, accessed through Readex.

Conclusions

For the purposes of my research, I chose a perspective focused on the position of China within the capitalist world economy, by which I mean the non-socialist countries and the international markets in which they participated. I opted for this transnational approach based on the hypothesis that processes in the increasingly interrelated international economy affected the People's Republic, even if the beginning of its economic relations with foreign markets and inclusion in the international division of labour is frequently set *after* 1978.

The CCP had emerged from a larger movement that intended to unite and modernise China after the experiences of the late imperial and early post-imperial period. Therefore, the *Leitmotiv* of economic modernisation in order to make China a rich nation with a powerful army was an important, if not the most important normative basis of Chinese socialism and its legitimacy as a political system. Looking at aspects of Mao Zedong Thought related to the economy, it becomes clear that this objective was a consistent and far-reaching component of the ideological system of reference, within which policies in the PRC were formulated and communicated. While some aspects of the readjustment period of the early 1960s, in particular forms of private ownership, if not property, in the countryside and the establishment of formal and informal hierarchies and differences in material statuses collided with the core tenets of Mao Zedong Thought, the basic idea that China needed to industrialise and *catch up* was not ideologically disputed. The question was *how* this industrial development could be achieved, how economic activity was organised, how technological progress could be achieved and how it could be financed.

Over the course of the Cultural Revolution movement, questions of equality were major causes of violent conflict, and so was the issue of interdependence with the rest of the world. As the existing literature shows, despite some spillover from the revolutionary movement, the Chinese economy did not falter or even merely stagnate during the Cultural Revolution. While production remained relatively stable, it continued to develop along the lines established earlier. The Four Modernisations formula, which had emerged in the mid-1960s as a general concept that, if anything, stood for a *smallest common denominator* in economic policy. It was the basis for a long-term development plan running up to the end of the millennium, which vanished from public perception in 1966, only to be resurrected during the second phase of readjustment and stabilisation, between 1970 and

1973. Despite having relied on the Soviet approach to economic management during the first five-year plan from 1953 to 1957, the approach to economic planning in the PRC had moved to a much less centralised form by the mid-1960s, as a consequence of the Great Leap Forward and its devastating effects.

This paradigm of decentralisation, particularly with regard to the self-reliant farms in the countryside, was intended to reduce the central government's investment burden. It prevailed in the 1970s and continued to be developed through the serious promotion of agricultural mechanisation, which had been a declared objective of economic policy since the 1950s. Generally, this initiative sought to improve the balance between the relatively well-off industrial cities and the countryside that carried a large part of the burden as the primary source of capital accumulation. Based on the construction of industrial capacity in the provinces and counties, the set of strategies aimed at rolling out the available level of technology to the countryside would contribute to an increase in agricultural yields and, thus, somewhat loosen the pressure on peasants.

Self-reliance within China played an important role, as the investment burden for construction projects was shifted to the provincial and lower levels, with the central government providing political guidance. De facto, the Chinese economy moved further away from a planned towards a rather coordinated economy, with unified planning as a concept that relied on common standards, cooperation and "best practices" rather than centralised allocation.

The Cultural Revolution and its aftermath had made important aspects of economic policy such as wage differentials and technical expertise highly controversial, so adjustments, if any, were only approached in a gradual way. As cadres were rehabilitated in the early 1970s, backed by the PLA that had *de facto* taken over an important part of political control, their status was partly assured by calls for order and putting production before revolutionary struggle. At first, production was stabilised by management guidelines that did not as such emphasise hierarchy, but rather a general demand to work efficiently and respect the rules. With the fourth National People's Congress, the revised constitution and Deng Xiaoping's programme for the implementation of rules and regulations, production in factories grew steadily. In parallel, while concepts that had been at the core of the Cultural Revolution, such as the worker's participation in management tasks and the obligations for cadres to perform manual labour, were continued, some of these aspects were of tangible use in production. One way to improve economic performance relied on measures of austerity, which included guidelines on conducting work frugally, avoiding waste and improving processes and their management. In 1974, the importance of rules and efficiency as well as of material incentives appears to have been outright downplayed and marginalised compared to public calls for revolutionary orthodoxy; however, such policies gained traction in the following year in parallel with a tightening of austerity.

In the early 1970s, China continued to have only limited access to advanced technology, with a small number of large-scale projects being implemented using imported facilities in the 1960s and an industrial base inherited from the Soviet support during the first five-year plan (1953–1957); due to this, the improvement of production through incremental innovations and improvements of existing facilities was encouraged and even purported as a specifically Chinese way of achieving progress. The participation of institutions of technical education continued the idea of general participation in physical labour. While these narratives were at least in part attempts to theorise a *given* situation, some genuine progress was reported by foreign visitors and traders attending the Canton Fair. Nevertheless, even if it was demonstrated that the Chinese economy with its workers and engineers was *able* to develop even complex machinery, their production and implementation was limited through the constraints set by the limited access to modern capital goods and in particular technology. There was much that could be achieved with incremental changes, but it meant that the pace of economic development would continue to be relatively slow.

The principal compromise that was struck in the early 1970s was the opening of the Chinese economy to the world by an active expansion of international trade. This expansion took place through diplomatic initiatives with Japan and other countries of East and Southeast Asia as well as Western Europe. The Three Worlds Theory provided the ideological justification for seeking contact with the intermediate zone, also in order to find allies as the struggle between the two "imperialist" powers – the US and, in this revised view on international relations, the Soviet Union – was perceived to be at the brink of escalation. The opening to new partners were backed by the construction of infrastructures as prerequisites for trade, such as ports capable of handling oceangoing freighters and eventually even containers, pipelines to transport oil to said ports as well as the development of legal instruments to formalise relationships and make them more reliable.

In the course of this formalisation, Chinese officials were ready to accept legal concepts such as most favoured nation, stemming from the legal regulation of trade relations between countries of the West, in a way linking back to the unequal treaties that had once symbolised China's submission to the colonial powers. This time, arrangements were made on a basis of sovereign equality. The meta-objective of economic development on the Chinese side drove these trade relations as well, as they opened new possibilities for the purchase of advanced machinery and other capital goods. China had in the past exchanged agricultural products for foreign exchange, in particular grain collected through the state procurement system. As the availability of fertile land and advanced farming methods continued to be limited in the 1970s, exporting grain was risky.

The development of China's oil resources in particular by the model brigade of Daqing created an alternative, giving China a commodity that could be sold at a relatively high price and would almost certainly find reliable buyers. The production of crude oil was crucial for the further development of the political compromise in economic policy in two ways: first, it gave the Chinese leadership an instrument with which the technological means necessary for *catching up* with the industrialised countries could be financed – without threatening the supply of basic consumables to the Chinese people. Second, the exploration and exploitation of oil was in itself a capital-intense undertaking that eventually required technology that China could not produce, or in part even apply on its own. While the oil fields of Northern China were within the reach of the Chinese industry, the exploitation in particular of offshore-deposits would require more than the "spirit" of Daqing's heroic oil workers.

Two particular commodities were decisive for China's foreign trade in the early to mid-1970s. Besides the oil of Daqing, Dagang and other fields, China relied on foreign imports of grain in order to ensure the supply to its industrial cities while keeping the pressure of grain procurement on peasants moderate. Until 1974, this balance – combined with attempts to use the price differential between rice and wheat to China's advantage – worked relatively well. In 1974 and 1975, what I refer to as the *hinge years*, another practice accepted by China under Mao Zedong caused a backlash. Despite not accepting any direct involvement of foreign capital in industrial or other undertakings in China, and refusing to take government-to-government loans, experiments with so-called deferred payments – in fact, a form of credit granted by a supplier repayable over an agreed period of time with interest – had led to China accepting foreign debt, for the repayment of which it needed to export more. As a consequence, economic fluctuations outside China began to directly influence the Chinese economy. The price hike in both agricultural commodities and crude oil around 1974 hit China at a moment when it was still rather a buyer of grain and capital goods than an exporter of oil.

The Chinese oil industry was not yet at a stage of development in which large-scale exports of manufactured goods were feasible, nor had the necessary relations with buyers been established. Immediately, contracts on the import of both grain and machinery were cancelled by China, reducing the growth of its foreign trade for the moment. The deficit of 1974/1975 raised a number of questions – if such deficits could appear beyond any direct control, how could necessary imports of food be paid for in the future? Especially, as the temptation of debt in the form of deferred payments had led even the self-reliant PRC into a situation, where it owed hard currency to outsiders?

While the fourth National People's Congress brought the Four Modernisations back as a guiding principle for economic development, the foreign trade of China began to experience a serious slump. For a moment it looked like its expansion had merely been an experiment gone awry. Nevertheless, as the key sectors of steel, railway and coal were further disciplined, in order to fulfil the ambitious ten-year-plan, presented in 1975, the networks and harbours necessary for a further expansion of foreign trade continued to be built. The persistently high oil price at the time was not the main argument for keeping in touch with potential foreign customers, but surely a persuasive one. That China was ready to increase its oil exports to achieve the Four Modernisations was signalled by Zhou Enlai in 1974, as he communicated a piece of information that was rare at the time outside of China: statistics on oil prospects which surpassed even the most optimistic estimates.

While the revised Constitution of 1975 reflected the political *limits of the possible* as a compromise, combining elements of the Cultural Revolution such as rights concerning political expression with elements of earlier readjustment policies such as the acceptance of private plots and, to a certain extent, rural markets as stabilisers for the economy, the Four Modernisations introduced another element in Chinese economic policy. This aspect, although not new, became increasingly important in the course of the latter half of the decade. It established a rough timetable for the mid- to long-term economic development of China that was emphasised with objectives in shorter intervals, such as the achievement of agricultural mechanisation – the rollout of the technology China could provide – until 1980.

Based on this schedule, the element of *speed* (again) became a core element of economic policy. Not only would China catch up and eventually surpass the industrialised nations, it would do so particularly fast. When Mao died in 1976, this notion was anchored again in the Chinese development paradigm. Under his designated successor,

Hua Guofeng, speeding up was emphasised to an extent that was reminiscent – albeit arguably much more realistic – of the Great Leap Forward. But different from the sole reliance on mass mobilisation, this fast development was to be technology-driven, extending China's economic capabilities by relying on the most advanced means of production that could be procured.

At the same time, the point of reference for what advanced technology was had changed. It moved away from the focus on the basic innovations in heavy industry that had shaped Chinese economic policy in the 1950s and 1960s towards the next wave of innovations, in particular information technology. In parallel, an offensive in higher education placed the Academy of Sciences and the Chinese universities – only years before the primary objective of harsh political criticism – at the top of the Chinese nomenclature. Research and science would no more serve the incremental improvement of the existing technological basis as in the years prior, but was required to move *ahead* of the economy. Western companies were not reluctant to provide technology to their new customers in China, expressing their admiration for the level of technological sophistication demonstrated during their contacts.

In China's trade diplomacy, the import of technology soon rose to be *the* defining issue. Speed was the objective, technology the means. In the course of 1978, the oil industry as the flagship of the Chinese export industry, and the main source of foreign exchange, was opened to foreign participation in order to expand the supply of oil available for China to finance its technology imports. Even before the famous third plenary in December 1978, Chinese officials declared to foreign businessmen that joint ventures would be accepted in China.

It is remarkable that politics played an ambiguous role in this process, while seeming omnipresent in the public. The focus of the economic policy bundles that were publicly communicated seemed increasingly shaped by the path-dependency and problem-solving view of government officials and politicians who, in the case of the PRC, merely happened to work for a socialist state. Many of the adjustments discussed in the fourth Chapter and, in particular, the foreign economic policies under the fifth, appear primarily to be reactions to a given situation or newly emerging opportunities than acts based on political principles. The dialectic character of the political writings of Mao Zedong indicates that many decisions on policy depended on what appeared to be needed at the moment. This ideological flexibility was and could be applied without much more editing than a careful selection of quotations and pieces, notably after the fourth People's Congress. The broad middle line that was created could be redefined by the CCP as well as provincial governments quite quickly, which became quite obvious particularly after the fall of the Gang of Four. Exchanges between experts, such as the trade-officials of the CCPIT or technicians deployed by State Corporations for the procurement of foreign technology, showed that the meta-objective of modernisation was a primary unifying factor within the bureaucracy.

In a way similar to the Soviet Union, the PRC began its existence as an almost closed economy that had only limited access to resources to support its economic development. That China ended up following an approach that first followed a Soviet model was not a given but the result of specific circumstances. Similarly, attempts to solve the fundamental questions of funding and technological development by "native" means was certainly not purely the consequence of political choice – at least not for all, as the dispute around the freighter *Fengqing* exemplified. The expansion of foreign trade and foreign economic relations were also among other reasons a reaction to an external shock, namely the Sino–Soviet split. The availability of potentially large amounts of crude oil in an environment of rapidly rising world market prices opened the *limits of the possible*, primarily economically and not politically.

The notion arising under Hua Guofeng that time was running out and a schedule needed to be kept might have been helpful for the mobilisation of workers. It certainly put additional pressure on policies that did not serve such rapid development. That the "red lines" – or "forbidden zones", as Li Qiang called them – were crossed before the Third Plenary of December 1978 underlines this notion.

Literature and sources

Sources

US/USLO Cables – Public Library of US Diplomacy

US Department of State, Agricultural Highlights: Crop and Trade Situation in PRC; Code 24M Alert, 9 November 1977, 00:00, PlusD, ID: 1977PEKING02585_c.

US Department of State, Criticism of PRC moderate Economic Policies, Electronic Telegram, 20 February 1976, 09:25, PlusD, ID: 1976PEKING00296_b, paragraph 5.

US Department of State, Electronic Telegram, "Revolution" taking a lower Profile in Peking's Production/Modernization Priorities, 20 December 1976, 00:51, PlusD, ID: 1976HONGK14650_b.

US Department of State, Electronic Telegram, 1975 Sino-Soviet Trade Agreement, 4 June 1975, 01:11, PlusD, ID: 1975PEKING01057_b.

US Department of State, Electronic Telegram, 57th ECOSOC: July 9 Plenary, Agenda Items 4, 6, 7, 8, and 14 (D), 13 July 1973, 12:30, PlusD, ID: 1974GENEVA04469_b.

US Department of State, Electronic Telegram, Amconsul Hong Kong to Secstate Washdc, 12 January 1947, 05:45, PlusD, ID: 1974HONGK00476_b.

US Department of State, Electronic Telegram, Bulgarian Foreign Trade Minister's Visit to Japan, 22 November 1977, 00:00, PlusD, ID: 1977TOKYO18023_c.

US Department of State, Electronic Telegram, Call on Fang Yin of Techimport, 24 June 1975, 07:11, PlusD, ID: 1975PEKING01174_b.

US Department of State, Electronic Telegram, Canton Fair – Interference in Oil Trade by 'Gang of Four', 17 November 1976, 07:31, PlusD, ID: 1976HONGK13424_b.

US Department of State, Electronic Telegram, CCPIT-NCUSCT Relations, 3 August 1976, 08:08, PlusD, ID: 1976PEKING01490_b.

US Department of State, Electronic Telegram, China Highlights, No. 11, 26 May 1977, 00:00, PlusD, ID: 1977HONGK06049_c, paragraph 2.

US Department of State, Electronic Telegram, China's Industrial Growth Returns to Normal, 30 September 1977, 00:00, PlusD, ID: 1977HONGK11900_c.

US Department of State, Electronic Telegram, China's Takang Oil Field, 3 July 1975, 01:06, PlusD, ID: 1975STATE156840_b.

US Department of State, Electronic Telegram, China's Trade Expansion Limitations, 5 November 1976, 09:17, PlusD, ID: 1976HONGK12958_b.

US Department of State, Electronic Telegram, Chinese Economic Mission Concludes Visit to Japan, 12 October 1973, 08:30, PlusD, ID: 1973TOKYO13258_b.

US Department of State, Electronic Telegram, Chinese Economy as seen from Peking, 13 November 1976, 03:00, PlusD, ID: 1976PEKING02343_b.

US Department of State, Electronic Telegram, Comment on Preliminary Soviet Foreign Trade Figures, 24 April 1974, 08:44, PlusD, ID: 1974MOSCOW06059_b.

US Department of State, Electronic Telegram, Comments on Recent Visit to China, 6 September 1973, 04:53, PlusD, ID: 1973BANGKO13889_b.

US Department of State, Electronic Telegram, Commerce Department Draft Of *"Financial Aspect of Trade Between the U.S. And PRC"*, 13 November 1974, 02:50, PlusD, ID: 1974HONGK12331_b.

US Department of State, Electronic Telegram, Conversation with Foreign Trade Minister, 7 May 1977, 00:00, PlusD, ID: 1977PEKING00922_c.

US Department of State, Electronic Telegram, Fall-off in trade activity, 22 September 1976, 08:38, PlusD, ID: 1976PEKING01894_b.

US Department of State, Electronic Telegram, Financial and Economic Developments – Week of July 15–21, 21 June 1976, 08:55, PlusD, ID: 1976TOKYO10975_b.

US Department of State, Electronic Telegram, Financial and Economic Developments – Sept 2 – Sept 8, 8 September 1976, 09:20, PlusD, ID: 1976TOKYO13483_b.

US Department of State, Electronic Telegram, First Meeting of the Swiss-PRC Mixed Commission, 11 October 1977, 00:00, PlusD, ID: 1977BERN04736_c.

US Department of State, Electronic Telegram, Highlights of Codel Percy/Javits Meeting with PRC Foreign Trade Vice Minister, 8 August 1975, 08:45, PlusD, ID: 1975PEKING01478_b.

US Department of State, Electronic Telegram, Hong Kong Bankers Delegation Visit to the PRC, 10 October 1974, 07:10, PlusD, ID: 1974HONGK11158_b.

US Department of State, Electronic Telegram, Hong Kong NCNA Representative Gives Unexcited View of PRC Campaign, 8 March 1976, 09:46, PlusD, ID: 1976HONGK02649_b.

US Department of State, Electronic Telegram, Japan PRC Trade Negotiations, 16 August 1973, 08:41, PlusD, ID: 1973TOKYO10520_b.

US Department of State, Electronic Telegram, Japan's National Interest and Foreign Policy in Northeast Asia, 4 June 1975, 08:57, PlusD, ID: 1975TOKYO07399_b.

US Department of State, Electronic Telegram, Japan-China Oil Trade, 19 February 1975, 08:45, PlusD, ID: 1975TOKYO02137_b.

US Department of State, Electronic Telegram, Japan-PRC Trade Negotiations, 10 August 1973, 07:48, PlusD, ID: 1973TOKYO10227_b.

US Department of State, Electronic Telegram, July 1975 U.S. PRC Trade Figures, 30 August 1975, 00:10, PlusD, ID: 1975STATE207273_b.

US Department of State, Electronic Telegram, Kosygin on the Soviet Economy, 3 March 1976, 07:23, PlusD, ID: 1976MOSCOW03250_b.

US Department of State, Electronic Telegram, Li Chiang's Remarks on Foreign Trade, 21 October 1976, 04:30, PlusD, ID: 1976PEKING02163_b.

US Department of State, Electronic Telegram, Mid-America Committee Meeting with Hao Te-Ching, 27 October 1977, 00:00, PlusD, ID: 1977PEKING02472_c.

US Department of State, Electronic Telegram, National Committee Delegation Meeting with Shanghai Economic Planners, 10 November 1977, 00:00, PlusD, ID: 1977PEKING02601_c.

US Department of State, Electronic Telegram, National Council for US-China Trade: Canton Meetings, 28 April 1977, 00:00, PlusD, ID: 1977PEKING00842_c.

US Department of State, Electronic Telegram, National Electronics Industry Conference Stresses Modernization; New Vice Minister Identified, 10 November 1977, 00:00, PlusD, ID: 1977HONGK13827_c.

US Department of State, Electronic Telegram, NCNA heralds expanded trade, 4 November 1976, 02:06, PlusD, ID: 1976HONGK12840_b.

US Department of State, Electronic Telegram, NCNA statements on Foreign Trade, 5 November 1976, 04:00, PlusD, ID: 1976PEKING02284_b.

US Department of State, Electronic Telegram, NCUSCT Views on China Trade Policy, 30 October 1976, 04:18, PlusD, ID: 1976HONGK12720_b.

US Department of State, Electronic Telegram, Observations in Chengchow, Wuhan, Changsha and Kwangchow, 13 September 1977, 00:00, PlusD, ID: 1977PEKING02047_c.

US Department of State, Electronic Telegram, Observations in Chengchow, Wuhan, Changsha and Kwangchow, 13 September 1977, 00:00, PlusD, ID: 1977PEKING02047_c.

US Department of State, Electronic Telegram, October 19 Hao Te-Ching Meeting with National Committee Delegation, 20 October 1977, 00:00, PlusD, ID: 1977PEKING02414_c.

US Department of State, Electronic Telegram, People's Daily calls for new focus on production, 15 November 1976, 08:12, PlusD, ID: 1976HONGK13321_b.

US Department of State, Electronic Telegram, People's Daily calls for new focus on production, 15 November 1976, 08:12, PlusD, ID: 1976HONGK13321_b.

US Department of State, Electronic Telegram, People's Republic of China Economic Review 1, 12 January 1974, 05:45, PlusD, ID: 1974HONGK00476_b.

US Department of State, Electronic Telegram, People's Republic of China Economic Review 2, 12 January 1974, 05:45, PlusD, ID: 1974HONGK00476_b.

US Department of State, Electronic Telegram, People's Republic of China Economic Review 1, 31 May 1974, 07:18, PlusD, ID: 1974HONGK06138_b.

US Department of State, Electronic Telegram, Political Basis for Economic Development, 13 March 1975, 04:15, PlusD, ID:1975HONGK02580_b.

US Department of State, Electronic Telegram, Possible Changes in PRC Trade Financing, 20 January 1977, 00:00, PlusD, ID: 1977HONGK00824_c.

US Department of State, Electronic Telegram, PRC Agricultural Import Policy Toward US, 18 March 1975, 07:15, PlusD, ID: 1975PEKING00474_b.

US Department of State, Electronic Telegram, PRC Agricultural Import Policy Toward US, 14 March 1975, 03:45, PlusD, ID: 1975HONGK02621_b.

US Department of State, Electronic Telegram, PRC Concern of U.S Cancellation of Soviet Grain Purchase [sic!], 11 October 1974, 05:59, PlusD, ID: 1974HONGK11229_b.

US Department of State, Electronic Telegram, PRC Exports to US Manufacturers in Hong Kong Proposed by Amcham, 2 December 1974, 23:55, PlusD, ID: 1974STATE264606_b.

US Department of State, Electronic Telegram, PRC Exports to US Manufacturers in HK Proposed by Amcham, 25 October 1974, 00:45, PlusD, ID: 1974HONGK11668_b [extended report].

US Department of State, Electronic Telegram, PRC Five Year Plan, 12 November 1975, 07:00, PlusD, ID: 1975PEKING02160_b.

US Department of State, Electronic Telegram, PRC Foreign Trade Corporation Personnel, 1 July 1977, 00:00, PlusD, ID: 1977PEKING01323_c.

US Department of State, Electronic Telegram, PRC Foreign Trade Conference July 14–28, 2 August 1977, 00:00, PlusD, ID: 1977PEKING01597_c.

US Department of State, Electronic Telegram, PRC Halts Talks with Toyota Over Roc Issue, 7 September 1973, 02:30, PlusD, ID: 1973TOKYO11490_b.

US Department of State, Electronic Telegram, PRC Industrial Advance – Encouraging Despite Trouble Spots, 24 October 1975, 07:12, PlusD, ID: 1975HONGK12676_b.

US Department of State, Electronic Telegram, PRC Industrial Advance, 24 October 1975, 07:12, PlusD, ID: 1975HONGK12676_b.

US Department of State, Electronic Telegram, PRC Minister of Foreign Trade visit to UK and France, 14 November 1977, 00:00, PlusD, ID: 1977PEKING02645_c.

US Department of State, Electronic telegram, PRC publicizes austere investment policy, 7 March 1975, 03:16, PlusD, ID:1975HONGK03204_b.

US Department of State, Electronic Telegram, PRC Specifies European Sources for U.S. Equipment, 12 December 1974, 07:03, PlusD, ID: 1974HONGK13424_b.

US Department of State, Electronic Telegram, PRC Trade and Finance, 28 November 1973, 08:05, PlusD, ID: 1973HONGK11899_b.

US Department of State, Electronic Telegram, PRC Trade Policy and Sino-US Trade, 9 June 1977, 00:00, PlusD, ID: 1977PEKING01157_c, paragraph 4.

US Department of State, Electronic Telegram, PRC Trade Prospects 1977–1980, 21 December 1976, 06:30, PlusD, ID: 1976HONGK14729_b.

US Department of State, Electronic Telegram, PRC Trade Surplus, 19 April 1977, 00:00, PlusD, ID: 1977PEKING00764_c.

US Department of State, Electronic Telegram, PRC Trade Talks: Mexico, Italy, 3 May 1974, 06:26, PlusD, ID: 1974HONGK04925_b.

US Department of State, Electronic Telegram, PRC withdraws from 45th Izmir International Trade Fair, August 20 – Sept. 30, 1976, 9 August 1976, 11:30, PlusD, ID: 1976IZMIR00245_b.

US Department of State, Electronic Telegram, PRC-Controlled Organizations' Representatives Comment About Economic Aspects of Hua Kuo-Feng Appointment, 13 February 1976, 09:30, PlusD, ID: 1976HongK01688_b.

US Department of State, Electronic Telegram, PRC-South Korean Trade Contact in Hong Kong, 6 November 1974, 02:20, PlusD, ID: 1974HONGK12040_b.

US Department of State, Electronic Telegram, Press Speculation about Chinese Interest in MTN, 13 April 1976, 17:18, PlusD, ID: 1976MTNGE02869_b.

US Department of State, Electronic Telegram, Prime Minister Thanom on Trade with China, 24 September 1973, 10:46, PlusD, ID: 1973BANGKO14918_b.

US Department of State, Electronic Telegram, Provincial Observations in Kunming, Chengtu, Sian, Shanghai, Canton, October 25 to November 4, 9 November 1977, 00:00, PlusD, ID: 1977PEKING02583_c.
US Department of State, Electronic Telegram, Secretary Paterno Returns from China Visit, 18 May 1977, 00:00, PlusD, ID: 1977MANILA07574_c.
US Department of State, Electronic Telegram, Singapore Mission to PRC, 3 April 1975, 10:27, PlusD, ID: 1975SINGAP01324_b.
US Department of State, Electronic Telegram, Sino-Indian Relations, 28 September 1977, 00:00, PlusD, ID: 1977PEKING02195_c.
US Department of State, Electronic Telegram, Sino-Japan Long-Term Trade Agreement, 5 December 1977, 00:00, PlusD, ID: 1977PEKING02841_c.
US Department of State, Electronic Telegram, Sino-Soviet Trade for 1977, 1 September 1977, 00:00, PlusD, ID: 1977PEKING01946_c.
US Department of State, Electronic Telegram, Sino-US Economic Relations, 5 August 1976, 04:23, PlusD, ID: 1976PEKING01510_b.
US Department of State, Electronic Telegram, Sino-US Trade, 28 June 1977, 00:00, PlusD, ID: 1977PEKING01301_c.
US Department of State, Electronic Telegram, Special Summary No.3, 11 March 1973, 03:12, PlusD, ID: 1973STATE044839_b.
US Department of State, Electronic Telegram, TASS ridicules PRC Economic Performance, 8 September 1976, 16:31, PlusD, ID: 1976MOSCOW14150_b.
US Department of State, Electronic Telegram, Thailand Decides to Trade Directly with The People's Republic of China, 25 September 1973, 10:58, ID: 1973BANGKO15000_b.
US Department of State, Electronic Telegram, Thai-PRC Trade Negotiations, 8 January 1976, 05:12, PlusD, ID: 1976BANGKO00393_b.
US Department of State, Electronic Telegram, Thai-PRC Trade, 3 February 1976, 03:30, PlusD, ID: 1976BANGKO02204_b.
US Department of State, Electronic Telegram, The PLA and Criticism of the 'Three Point Directive', 27 February 1976, 00:31, PlusD, ID: 1976PEKING00327_b.
US Department of State, Electronic Telegram, The PRC at UNCTAD – Response to the Secretary's Speech, 13 May 1976, 06:02, PlusD, ID: 1976HONGK05470_b.
US Department of State, Electronic Telegram, UD-PRC Grain Trade, 19 December 1974, 18:29, PlusD, ID: 1974STATE277891_b.
US Department of State, Electronic Telegram, UNCTAD: 8th Special Session of TDB on R&A: General Debate Speeches on April 26–27, 28 April 1977, 00:00, PlusD, ID: 1977GENEVA03198_c.
US Department of State, Electronic Telegram, US Business Visitor Trade Proposal to PRC through, 22 June 1977, 00:00, PlusD, ID: 1977HONGK07150_c.
US Department of State, Electronic Telegram, US Business Visitor Trade Proposal to PRC Through China Resources Company in Hong Kong, 17 February 1977, 00:00, PlusD, ID: 1977HONGK01995_c.
US Department of State, Electronic Telegram, US Businessmen Visitors to PRC: February, 1 March 1977, 00:00, PlusD, ID: 1977PEKING00373_c.
US Department of State, Electronic Telegram, US Trade Prospects in Light Industry, 23 February 1977, 00:00, PlusD, ID: 1977PEKING00345_c.

US Department of State, Electronic Telegram, US Trade with China: Yao I-Lin Statements to World Affairs Delegation, 14 October 1975, 08:18, PlusD, ID: 1975PEKING01951_b.
US Department of State, Electronic Telegram, US-PRC Trade Relations, 27 July 1977, 00:00, PlusD, ID: 1977PEKING01550_c.
US Department of State, Electronic Telegram, Visit of PNG Prime Minister Somare to PRC OCT 11–17 and to the Philippines Oct 19–23, 3 November 1976, 05:05, PlusD, ID: 1976PORTM01206_b.
US Department of State, U.S. -PRC Wheat Trade, Electronic Telegram, 5 April 1977, 00:00, PlusD, ID: 1977STATE075459_c.
US Department of State, US – Japan – EC Trilateral Textile Consultations, 25 September 1976, 15:26, PlusD, ID: 1976STATE239215_b.

Readex – Foreign Broadcast Information Service (FBIS) reports

Foreign Broadcast Information Service, $69-Million Contract for Oil Prospecting Equipment with France signed, Hong Kong AFP in English, 1625 GMT, 27 12 1978 OW, accessed through Readex.
Foreign Broadcast Information Service, 'Critical' Reassessment of Maoist Leadership under way, TASS headline: "Concerning Political Scene Inside China", Moscow TASS in English, 1441 GMT, 23 07 1976 LD, accessed through Readex.
Foreign Broadcast Information Service, 'Gang of Four' sabotage of production outlined, Peking NCNA in English, 1739 GMT, 14 11 1976 OW, accessed through Readex.
Foreign Broadcast Information Service, 'Gang' Undermined Modernization, Text of article by the State Planning Commission mass criticism group: "The 'Gang of Four' Are the Chief Culprits in Undermining Socialist Modernization in the Four Fields", Red Flag No. 12, 1976, Nanchang Kiangsi Provincial Service in Mandarin, 1100 GMT, 12 12 1976 OW, accessed through Readex.
Foreign Broadcast Information Service, 'High-Powered' Economic Mission Leaves for PRC, Tokyo Kyodo in English, 0110 GMT, 25 03 1976 TK, accessed through Readex.
Foreign Broadcast Information Service, 1976 Trade Protocol with PRC signed, Cairo Domestic Service in Arabic, 1500 GMT, 06 06 1976 ID, accessed through Readex.
Foreign Broadcast Information Service, 4th NPC May Be Held Soon, Tokyo Kyodo in English, 0014 GMT, 06 12 1974 T, accessed through Readex.
Foreign Broadcast Information Service, Academy Library greets Leap Forward in Scientific Research, Article by the library of the Chinese Academy of Sciences: "Take Practical Actions to Greet the New Great Leap Forward in Scientific Research Work", Peking Kwangming Daily in Mandarin, 28 12 1977 HK, accessed through Readex.
Foreign Broadcast Information Service, Academy of Sciences Article Defends 'Outline Report', Peking Domestic Service in Mandarin, 0200 GMT, 18 05 1977 OW, accessed through Readex.
Foreign Broadcast Information Service, AFP: Red Flag Calls for More Consumer Goods, Hong Kong AFP in English, 1113 GMT, 24 02 1977 OW, accessed through Readex.

Foreign Broadcast information Service, Agriculture, Forestry Ministry Meets on Summer Farming, Peking NCNA Domestic Service in Mandarin, 1246 GMT, 12 06 1977 OW, accessed through Readex.

Foreign Broadcast Information Service, Air Agreement, Tokyo Kyodo in English, 1317 GMT, 30 08 1974 B, accessed through Readex.

Foreign Broadcast Information Service, Anhwei Finance and Trade, Hofei Anhwei Provincial Service in Mandarin, 1100 GMT, 11 01 1978 HK, accessed through Readex.

Foreign Broadcast Information Service, Anshan Municipal Committee Article, Peking NCNA Domestic Service in Mandarin, 2303 GMT, 23 03 1970 B, accessed through Readex.

Foreign Broadcast Information Service, Anshan Municipal Committee Article, Peking NCNA Domestic Service in Mandarin, 2303 GMT, 23 03 1970 B, accessed through Readex.

Foreign Broadcast Information Service, Article by Akio Akagi and Morihiko Sato of the Japan Broadcasting Corporation, "Tach'ing oil fields and China's industrial technology", Tokyo Shizen in Japanese, 05 1974, pp. 63, accessed through Readex.

Foreign Broadcast Information Service, Article by Chiang Hung, Run Medium and Small Industries actively and well, Red Flag No. 10, 1975, Peking Domestic Service in Mandarin, 2140 GMT, 12 10 1975, accessed through Readex.

Foreign Broadcast Information Service, Article by Tang Feng "Speed up Mechanization of Agriculture", Red Flag No. 11, 1975, Peking Domestic Service in Mandarin, 2130 GMT, 13 11 1975, accessed through Readex.

Foreign Broadcast Information Service, Article by Yeh Yen, The Constitution of Anshan Steel Plant will shine forever, People's Daily in Mandarin, 23 02 1974, accessed through Readex.

Foreign Broadcast Information Service, Bank Delegation to PRC, Tokyo Kyodo in English, 0450 GMT, 21 10 1977 OW, accessed through Readex.

Foreign Broadcast Information Service, Belgrade Radio Previews Tito-Hua Kuo-Feng Talks, Commentary by Milutin Milenkovic, Belgrade Domestic Service in Serbo-Croatian, 1800 GMT, 29 08 1977 AU, accessed through Readex.

Foreign Broadcast Information Service, Business delegation plans PRC visit, Tokyo Kyodo in English, 1130 GMT, 06 10 1975, accessed through Readex.

Foreign Broadcast Information Service, Cargo Congestion at Shipping Ports Eliminated, Peking NCNA in English, 1221 GMT, 22 09 1977 OW, accessed through Readex.

Foreign Broadcast Information Service, CCP issues Decision on Speeding up Industrial Development, Peking NCNA in English, 0743 GMT, 04 07 1978 OW, accessed through Readex.

Foreign Broadcast Information Service, Chang Chiang-lin reports at Tsinghai meeting, Sining Tsinghai Provincial Service in Mandarin, 1500 GMT, 27 12 1975 OW, accessed through Readex.

Foreign Broadcast Information Service, Chang Ping-Hua Speaks on Agricultural Mechanization, Speech by Chang Ping-hua, second secretary of the Hunan Provincial CCP Committee, at the provincial conference on learning from Tachai in agriculture on 9 February 1977, titled: 'Thoroughly Expose and Criticize the Gang of Four and Promote

Agricultural Mechanization" [Title read by announcer], Changsha Hunan Provincial Service in Mandarin, 1100 GMT, 19 03 1977 OW, accessed through Readex.

Foreign Broadcast Information Service, Chen Yung-Kuei's Report at Heilungkiang Conference on Tachai, Harbin Heilungkiang Provincial Service in Mandarin, 2130 GMT, 24 02 1974 B, accessed through Readex.

Foreign Broadcast Information Service, Chiang Wei-ching speaks at Kiangsi Meeting Closing Ceremony, Kiangsi Provincial Service in Mandarin, 1100 GMT, 01 05 1975, accessed through Readex.

Foreign Broadcast Information Service, Chin Ho-Chen Speech at Agricultural Mechanization Meeting, Excerpts of speech by Chin Ho-chen, secretary of the Shantung Provincial CCP Committee, at the Third National Conference on Agricultural Mechanization: "Develop Agricultural Mechanization on the Basis of Self-Reliance", date not given, Peking NCNA Domestic Service in Mandarin, 1302 GMT, 05 01 1978 OW, accessed through Readex.

Foreign Broadcast Information Service, China's socialist economy proves successful in 25 years, Peking NCNA in English, 0701 GMT, 24 09 1974 B, accessed through Readex.

Foreign Broadcast Information Service, Chinese Ministries to Compete in Emulation Drive, Peking NCNA in English, 0742 GMT, 06 09 1977 OW, accessed through Readex.

Foreign Broadcast Information Service, Chou discusses China's foreign trade in interview, Tanjug International Service in English, 1110 GMT, 16 03 71 T, accessed through Readex.

Foreign Broadcast Information Service, Chou En-Lai Report on Government, Beijing NCNA in English, 1200 GMT, 20 01 1975 OW, accessed through Readex.

Foreign Broadcast Information Service, Chou lauded for countering Mao's Adventurism, Moscow Radio Peace and Progress in Mandarin to China, 1430 GMT 22 01 1976 TK, accessed through Readex.

Foreign Broadcast Information Service, Chou on U.S., Bonn, Tokyo, Tokyo Kyodo in English, 0438 GMT, 21 8 1972 T, accessed through Readex.

Foreign Broadcast Information Service, Commentary on Proposed Hegemony Clause in Japan-PRC Pact, Radio Moscow in Japanese to Japan, 1200 GMT, 30 04 1975 TK, accessed through Readex.

Foreign Broadcast Information Service, Conference on Energy Conservation held, Hong Kong AFP in English, 0705 GMT, 18 01 1977 OW, accessed through Readex.

Foreign Broadcast Information Service, Continuing Trade, PRC Mission, Hong Kong AFP in English, 1046, 10 09 1977 OW, accessed through Readex.

Foreign Broadcast Information Service, Correspondent on healthy state of economy, Peking NCNA in English, 1207 GMT, 25 09 1975, accessed through Readex.

Foreign Broadcast Information Service, Correspondent sees new 'Leap Forward' in PRC, Mihailo Saranovic report from Peking 'A new year for comparisons', Belgrade Borba in Serbo-Croatian, 15 10 1974.

Foreign Broadcast Information Service, Crop Management stepped up in Peking suburbs, Peking NCNA in English, 0726 GMT, 20 08 1976 OW, accessed through Readex.

Foreign Broadcast Information Service, Delegate to World Food Conference gives PRC view on crisis, Peking NCNA in English, 2030 GMT, 07 11 1974 B, accessed through Readex.

Foreign Broadcast Information Service, Deputy Foreign Trade Minister on Basic PRC Directives, Rome Ansa in English, 0812 GMT, 18 03 1975 AU, accessed through Readex.

Foreign Broadcast Information Service, Details of FRG Firms Assistance to PRC Coal Industry, Hamburg DPA in German, 1150 GMT, 06 11 1978 LD, accessed through Readex.

Foreign Broadcast Information Service, East China Progress in Electric Power Conservation, NCNA correspondent's commentary: "There Are Tremendous Potentials for Conserving Electric Power, for Power Consumption in a Planned Manner and for Running Electric Power Stations by the Masses", Peking NCNA Domestic Service in Mandarin, 0332 GMT, 20 07 1977 OW, accessed through Readex.

Foreign Broadcast Information Service, Economic Sciences Planning Forum Discusses Work, Article by Lin Ching-sung, Hsueh Yung-ying and Fang Liu-pi: "Peking District Holds a Forum on the Planning of Economic Sciences", Peking Kwangming Daily in Mandarin, 20 03 1978, p. 3 HK, assessed through Readex.

Foreign Broadcast Information Service, Economic Treaty with PRC to be signed, Hong Kong AFP in English, 2104 GMT, 13 01 1978 OW, accessed through Readex.

Foreign Broadcast Information Service, Editorial on Farm Mechanization Resurrected, Peking NCNA Domestic Service in Mandarin, 2008 GMT, 22 12 1976 OW, accessed through Readex.

Foreign Broadcast Information Service, Excerpts of Commentator's article: "Strive to Rapidly Develop the National Economy", Red Flag, No. 1, 1978, Peking Domestic Service in Mandarin, 1200 GMT, 06 01 1978 OW, accessed through Readex.

Foreign Broadcast Information Service, Excerpts of speech by Premier Chou En-lai, 24 03 1968, p. 117, accessed through Readex.

Foreign Broadcast Information Service, Experts downgraded, worker's role stressed in planning, Article by Writing Group of State Construction Commission, Relentlessly pursue the struggle of the two lines; intently inaugurate the planning revolution, Peking Jen-min Jih-Pao, Original in Mandarin, 19 04 1971, p. 2, accessed through Readex.

Foreign Broadcast Information Service, Fedoseyev Article on Peking's Economic Policy, Moscow Trud in Russian, 21 03 1975, p. 3, LD, accessed through Readex.

Foreign Broadcast Information Service, Fifth Five-Year Plans begin, Hong Kong Chung-Kuo Hsin Wen, Original in Mandarin, 01 01 1976, accessed through Readex.

Foreign Broadcast Information Service, Firms plan to send Oil Mission to Peking in August, Tokyo Kyodo in English, 0013 GMT, 26 07 1977 OW, accessed through Readex.

Foreign Broadcast Information Service, First Machine-Building Ministry Reorganized Industries, Peking NCNA Domestic Service in Mandarin, 0155 GMT, 17 06 1978 OW, accessed through Readex.

Foreign Broadcast Information Service, Foreigners Restricted, Tokyo Kyodo in English, 0007 GMT, 30 07 1976 OW, accessed through Readex.

Foreign Broadcast Information Service, Forum on World Economy held in Changchun, Changchun Kirin Provincial Service in Mandarin, 2200 GMT, 22 07 1978 SK, accessed through Readex.

Foreign Broadcast Information Service, Fukien Holds Conference on Banking Work, Foochow Fukien Provincial Service in Mandarin, 0300 GMT, 20 11 1977 HO, accessed through Readex.

Foreign Broadcast Information Service, Fukien Worker's poster lashes out at material incentives, Foochow Fukien Provincial Service in Mandarin, 1100 GMT, 25 02 1974 B, accessed through Readex.

Foreign Broadcast Information Service, Fukien workers' poster lashes out at material incentives, Foochow Fukien Provincial Service in Mandarin, 1100 GMT, 25 02 1974, accessed through Readex.

Foreign Broadcast Information Service, Further Report on Conclusion of Coal Industry Conference, Peking NCNA Domestic Service in Mandarin, 1713 GMT, 25 01 1977 OW, accessed through Readex.

Foreign Broadcast Information Service, Galin Analyzed Chinese Domestic Political Situation, M. Galin article: "What is happening in China", Moscow Novoye Vremya in Russian, 22 04 1977 LD, accessed through Readex.

Foreign Broadcast information Service, Grain distribution said more than adequate for population, Peking Chung-Kuo Hsin-Wen in Mandarin, 08 11 1974, p. 1, accessed through Readex.

Foreign Broadcast Information Service, Heilungkiang: Liu Kuang-Tao speaks at Science Conference, Harbin Heilungkiang Provincial Service in Mandarin, 2130 GMT, 07 08 1977 OW, accessed through Readex.

Foreign Broadcast Information Service, Hua Kuo-feng 26 February Report, Unite and Strive to Build a Modern, Powerful Socialist Country, Peking NCNA in English, 1451 GMT, 06 03 1978 OW, accessed through Readex.

Foreign Broadcast Information Service, Hua's Work Report, Peking NCNA in English, 1207 GMT, 26 02 1978 OW, accessed through Readex.

Foreign Broadcast Information Service, Hunan Article calls for Promotion of National Economy, Article by the Hunan provincial Planning Committee: "Redouble Our Efforts, Realize a New Leap Forward in the National Economy", Changsha Hunan Provincial Service in mandarin, 2330 GMT, 14 06 1977 HK, accessed through Readex.

Foreign Broadcast Information Service, Hunan Conference on Learning from Tachai continues, Report by Mao Chih-yung, secretary of the Hunan provincial CCP Committee, at the provincial conference on learning from Tachai: "Resolutely Respond to the Great Call of Chairman Hua and the party Central Committee, Raise Still Higher the Red Banner of Tachai and Speed Up the Pace of Building Tachai-type Counties Everywhere", Changsha Hunan Provincial Service in Mandarin, 0330 GMT, 08 02 1977 FE, accessed through Readex.

Foreign Broadcast Information Service, Hunan Holds Symposium on Family Planning, Changsha Hunan Provincial Service in Mandarin, 1100 GMT, 26 10 1975 FE, accessed through Readex.

Foreign Broadcast Information Service, Hunan Miners given Leadership Positions, Peking NCNA in English, 0715 GMT, 18 06 1976 OW, accessed through Readex.

Foreign Broadcast Information Service, Hunan Officials Attack 'Gang' for Local Crimes, Speech by Sun Kuo-chih, member of the standing committee of the Hunan provincial CCP committee and chairman of the provincial planning committee at the Hunan provincial conference on learning from Daqing in industry: "Indignantly Expose and Criticize the Towering Crimes of the 'Gang of Four' in Sabotaging Socialist Revolution and Construction and Conspiring to Usurp the Party and State Power", Changsha

Hunan Provincial Service in Mandarin, 2230 GMT, 14 01 1977 FE, accessed through Readex.
Foreign Broadcast Information Service, Hupeh city industrializes via self-reliance, Peking NCNA in English, 0706 GMT, 01 11 1975, accessed through Readex.
Foreign Broadcast Information Service, Importance of studying Basic Science stressed, NCNA reporter's commentary: "Only When the Tree is Deep-Rooted Can It Become Leafy – On the Significance of Developing Basic Science In Our Country", Peking NCNA Domestic Service in Mandarin, 1315 GMT, 09 11 1977 OW, accessed through Readex.
Foreign Broadcast Information Service, Industrial Output in Kwangsi develops rapidly, Peking NCNA, Original in English, 1210 GMT, 24 03 1975 OW, accessed through Readex.
Foreign Broadcast Information Service, Industrialization Achieved via Self-Reliance, Peking NCNA in English, 1200 GMT, 15 03 1975 OW, accessed through Readex.
Foreign Broadcast Information Service, Innovations allow Savings in Fuel, Electricity, Peking NCNA in English, 0707 GMT, 22 01 1977 OW, accessed through Readex.
Foreign Broadcast Information Service, International Observers Roundtable, Moscow International Service in Russian, 0730 GMT, 28 September 1975, accessed through Readex.
Foreign Broadcast Information Service, Introduction of Foreign Technology Discussed, Ninth in a series under the general title: "Deepen the Criticism of the Gang of Four and Clarify the 10 Do's and Don't's on the Economic Front" titled "Do We Need to Import Advanced Technology", Peking Domestic Service in Mandarin, 1040 GMT, 29 10 1977 OW, accessed through Readex.
Foreign Broadcast Information Service, Japan Expected to Assist PRC in Construction of Major Steel Mill, Tokyo Kyodo in English, 0038 GMT, 24 08 1978 OW, accessed through Readex.
Foreign Broadcast Information Service, Japanese Bank Governor Fetes PRC Bank Delegation, Peking NCNA in English, 1813 GMT, 24 05 1978 OW, accessed through Readex.
Foreign Broadcast Information Service, Juan Po-sheng Report at Kirin Tachai Conference, Changchun Kirin Provincial Service in Mandarin, 1100 GMT, 12 02 1977 OW, accessed through Readex.
Foreign Broadcast Information Service, Kadar Speech, Speech by Janos Kadar, first secretary of the MSZMP Central Committee, at opening session of 11th MSZMP Congress in Budapest, Budapest Domestic Service in Hungarian, 1326 GMT, 17 03 1975 LD, accessed through Readex.
Foreign Broadcast Information Service, Kiangsi Holds Meeting on Industrial Tasks, Nanchang Kiangsi Provincial Service in Mandarin, 1100 GMT, 29 12 1976 HK, accessed through Readex.
Foreign Broadcast Information Service, Kiangsu Cities Self-reliantly expand local industries, Peking NCNA in English, 0713 GMT, 30 12 1973 B, accessed through Readex.
Foreign Broadcast Information Service, Kirin Daily Stresses Strengthening Social Order, Kirin Daily 6 July editorial: "It is Necessary to Strengthen Social Order Well", Changchun Kirin Provincial Service in Mandarin, 2200 GMT, 05 07 1978 SK, accessed through Readex.

Foreign Broadcast Information Service, Kuo Hung-chieh addresses Anhwei Meeting, Hofei Anhwei Provincial Service in Mandarin, 1100 GMT, 10 06 1976 OW, accessed through Readex.

Foreign Broadcast Information Service, Kwangming Daily: Inequality still prevails in the PRC under socialism, Peking Kwangming Daily in Mandarin, 18 02 1975, accessed through Readex.

Foreign Broadcast Information Service, Kwangsi Holds Rural Conference on Agriculture, Nanning Kwangsi Regional Service in Mandarin, 1100 GMT, 08 09 1975 FE, accessed through Readex.

Foreign Broadcast Information Service, Kwangsi Planning Front Rally criticizes 'Gang', Nanning Kwangsi Provincial Service in Mandarin, 1100 GMT, 16 11 1976 FE, accessed through Readex.

Foreign Broadcast Information Service, Kwangtung conducts Petrochemical Industries Conference, Canton Kwangtung Provincial Service in Mandarin, 0500 GMT, 02 12 1977 HK, accessed through Readex.

Foreign Broadcast Information Service, Kwantung First Secretary Addresses Taching Conference, Canton Kwantung Provincial Service in Mandarin, 1100 GMT, 28 01 1977 FE, accessed through Readex.

Foreign Broadcast Information Service, Kwantung Meeting Demands Improved Enterprise management, Canton Kwantung Provincial Service in Mandarin, 0500 GMT, 19 09 1977 HK, accessed through Readex.

Foreign Broadcast Information Service, Kyodo Delegation told of PRC Plans to Revise 10-Year Plan, Tokyo Kyodo in English, 1241 GMT, 24 08 1978 OW, accessed through Readex.

Foreign Broadcast Information Service, Kyodo: PRC will import Japanese fertilizer; export oil, Tokyo Kyodo in English, 10:22 GMT, 13 02 1975 TK, accessed through Readex.

Foreign Broadcast Information Service, Le Monde weighs Credit Risk of Trade with PRC, Le Monde editorial: "An Immense Appetite", Paris Le Monde in French, 05 12 1978 LD, accessed through Readex.

Foreign Broadcast Information Service, Li Chiang Discusses Foreign Trade policy, Article by Minister of Foreign Trade Li Chiang: "Distinguish Between Right and Wrong in Line and Actively Develop Socialist Foreign Trade", Peking Red Flag No. 10 in Mandarin, 08 10 1977, pp. 31–38 HK, accessed through Readex.

Foreign Broadcast Information Service, Li Hsien-Nien Interviewed, Interview with vice-premier Li Hsien-nien in Peking on 1 June 1977 by Antonio Fernandez Arce, Lima La Prensa in Spanish, 12 06 1977, accessed through Readex.

Foreign Broadcast Information Service, Li Hsien-Nien meets Brazilian exporters delegation, Peking NCNA in English, 1646 GMT, 11 04 1974 B, accessed through Readex.

Foreign Broadcast Information Service, Liberation Army Daily on Modernization of National Defense, Excerpts of Liberation Army Daily 24 September editorial: "March Toward the Modernization of Science and Technology for National Defense", Peking NCNA Domestic Service in Mandarin, 1204 GMT, 25 09 1977 OW, accessed through Readex.

Foreign Broadcast Information Service, Liberation Daily Acclaims Victory over Clique, Shanghai City Service in Mandarin, 0700 GMT, 26 10 1976 OW, accessed through Readex.

Foreign Broadcast Information Service, London Times on Teng, Administrative regions, London The Times in English, 24 05 1977, LD, accessed through Readex.

Foreign Broadcast Information Service, Long-Term Planning, Peking Domestic Service in Mandarin, 0800 GMT, 23 07 1975 OW, accessed through Readex.

Foreign Broadcast Information Service, Ma Li delivers report at Kweichow Cadre Conference, Kwieyang Kweichow Provincial Service in Mandarin, 1300 GMT, 08 07 1977 HK, accessed through Readex.

Foreign Broadcast information Service, Maltese Prime Minister's Speech, Peking NCNA International Service in English, 1819 GMT, 02 04 1972 B, accessed through Readex.

Foreign Broadcast Information Service, Mao's Agricultural Cooperation Work hailed, Article by the theoretical study group of the Ministry of Agriculture and Forestry: "Transformation of Small Production Is a Long-Term Task of the Dictatorship of the Proletariat – Some Experience in Studying Chairman Mao's Work 'On the Question of Agricultural Cooperation'", Peking Domestic Service in Mandarin, 1130 GMT, 30 08 1975 OW, accessed through Readex.

Foreign Broadcast Information Service, Mao's economic theory based on Confucius, Moscow Radio Peace & Progress in English to Asia, 0800 GMT 19 03 1974 L, accessed through Readex.

Foreign Broadcast Information Service, Marsh Gas Fuel Experiments Conducted in Rural Areas, NCNA reporter's commentary: "An innovation to solve the rural areas' fuel problem", Peking NCNA Domestic Service in Mandarin, 0246 GMT, 20 06 1975 OW, accessed through Readex.

Foreign Broadcast Information Service, Mathematician Discusses Practical Application of Work, Peking NCNA in English, 1225 GMT, 24 03 1978 OW, accessed through Readex.

Foreign Broadcast Information Service, Meeting with Hua Kuo-feng, Peking NCNA in English, 1243 GMT, 25 09 1974 B, accessed through Readex.

Foreign Broadcast Information Service, Mines Support Steel Production, Peking NCNA in English, 0700 GMT, 15 09 1975 OW, accessed through Readex.

Foreign Broadcast Information Service, Ministry Calls for Modernization of Communications, Article by theoretical group of the Ministry of Communications: "Implement Chairman Mao's Behest, Speed up the Modernization of Communications.", Peking People's Daily in Mandarin, 06 11 1977 HK, accessed through Readex.

Foreign Broadcast Information Service, Mission Hopes to Strengthen Economic Cooperation with PRC, Tokyo Kyodo in English, 1230 GMT, 04 06 1975 TK, accessed by Readex.

Foreign Broadcast Information Service, More Balanced Deployment of Light Industry achieved, Peking NCNA in English, 0722 GMT, 25 09 1977 OW, accessed through Readex.

Foreign Broadcast Information Service, Mubarak Speaks about his Visit to PRC, Cairo MENA in Arabic, 1500 GMT, 30 04 1976 JN, accessed through Readex.

Foreign Broadcast Information Service, NCNA Correspondent on Healthy State of Economy, Peking NCNA in English, 1207 GMT, 25 09 1975 OW, accessed through Readex.

Foreign Broadcast Information Service, NCNA on 'Gang' Sabotage of Foreign Trade, Report by NCNA correspondent: "A Grave Step for Usurping Party and State Power – Exposing the Towering Crimes of the 'Gang of Four' in Rampantly Opposing Chairman Mao and the Party Central Committee and in Viciously Attacking Premier Chou in Foreign Trade", Peking NCNA Domestic Service in Mandarin, 0141 GMT, 13 01 1977 OW, accessed through Readex.

Foreign Broadcast Information Service, NCNA on PRC Foreign Trade Policy, Peking NCNA in English, 0700 GMT, 07 09 1975 OW, accessed through Readex.

Foreign Broadcast Information Service, NCNA Reports 1973 Water Conservation Achievements, Peking NCNA in English, 0707 GMT 31 12 1973 B, accessed through Readex.

Foreign Broadcast Information Service, NCNA Reports mounting Soviet Debt to West, Peking NCNA in English, 1839 GMT, 16 10 1976 OW, accessed through Readex.

Foreign Broadcast Information Service, NCNA stresses Need to introduce Foreign Technology, Peking NCNA Domestic Service in Mandarin, 1139 GMT, 16 09 1978 OW, accessed through Readex.

Foreign Broadcast Information Service, New Technology Developed in Learning from Taching, Peking NCNA in English, 0714 GMT, 31 May 1977 OW, accessed through Readex.

Foreign Broadcast Information Service, Nikolayev on Albanian Press Treatment of Peking's Trade, Moscow in Albanian to Albania, 1530 GMT, 16 03 1975 AU, accessed through Readex.

Foreign Broadcast Information Service, Nixon 'Campaigns' among Peking Crowds, Tokyo Kyodo in English, 0613 GMT, 24 02 1976 TK, accessed through Readex.

Foreign Broadcast Information Service, Oil Firms asked to help develop PRC Oil Resources, Tokyo Kyodo in English, 0040 GMT, 09 11 1978 OW, accessed through Readex.

Foreign Broadcast Information Service, Oil Industry unhappy over Japan-PRC Trade Pact, Tokyo Kyodo in English, 1243 GMT, 06 03 1978 OW, accessed through Readex.

Foreign Broadcast Information Service, Pai Ju-ping Speech, Tsinan Provincial Service in Mandarin, 1100 GMT, 11 01 1974 B, accessed through Readex.

Foreign Broadcast Information Service, Pai Ju-Ping Stresses Learning from Tachai, Tainan Shantung Provincial Service in Mandarin, 1100 GMT, 04 12 1976 OW, accessed through Readex.

Foreign Broadcast Information Service, Pai Ju-Ping submits Report at Shantung Finance-Trade Meeting, Excerpts of report by Shantung Provincial CCP Committee First Secretary Pai Ju-Ping at the 28 December second provincial meeting of advanced representatives of the finance and trade front on learning from Taching and Tachai: "Deepen the Movement To Learn From Taching and Tachai on the Finance and Trade Front, Make Contributions To Grasping the key Link and Running the Country Well and Accelerate the Development of the National Economy", Tsinan Shantung Provincial Service in Mandarin, 1100 GMT, 30 12 1977 OW, accessed through Readex.

Foreign Broadcast Information Service, Part 16 of Peking Lecture Series on 'Ten Relationships', Sixteenth in a series of lectures under the general title: "A Brilliant Document, a Powerful Weapon", written by the worker-theorist group of the Peking internal combustion engine general plant and the philosophy and social sciences department and planned economy group of the Economics Institute of the Chinese Academy of Sciences on studying Chairman Mao's 'On the Ten Major Relationships', part 16 being entitled: "Adhere to the Policy of Maintaining Independence, Keeping the Initiative in Our Own Hands, and Relying on our own Efforts – Criticizing Those Who Worship Foreign Things and Fawn of Foreigners", Peking Domestic Service in Mandarin, 2200 GMT, 15 02 1977 OW, accessed through Readex.

Foreign Broadcast Information Service, Part Nine of Peking Lecture Series on 'Ten Relationships', Peking Domestic Service in Mandarin, 2200 GMT, 08 02 1977 OW, accessed through Readex.

Foreign Broadcast Information Service, Peace Treaty Talks with PRC may resume in January, Tokyo Kyodo in English, 0648 GMT, 31 12 1974, accessed through Readex.

Foreign Broadcast Information Service, Peking increases consumer goods, NCNA Domestic Service, Original in Mandarin, 0754 GMT, 26 09 1975, accessed through Readex.

Foreign Broadcast Information Service, Peng Chung Article on Developing Shanghai's Industry, article by Peng Chung: "Make Full Use of and Actively Develop Shanghai's Industry So as To Make Still Greater Contributions to the Realization of the Four Modernizations", Red Flag No. 12 and People's Daily of 8 December, Peking NCNA Domestic Service in Mandarin, 0226 GMT, 07 12 1977 OW, accessed through Readex.

Foreign Broadcast Information Service, Peng Chung Report at Shanghai Learn-From-Taching Conference, Excerpts of 7 August report by Comrade Peng Chung at Shanghai conference on learning from Taching in industry: "Hold Aloft the Great Banner of Chairman Mao and Strive To Speed Up the Building of Taching-Type Enterprises", Shanghai City Service in mandarin, 0430 GMT, 08 08 1977 OW, accessed through Readex.

Foreign Broadcast Information Service, People's Bank urges strengthened Monetary Management, NCNA reporter's commentary: "Strengthen Monetary management, Quickly Bolster the National Economy", Peking NCNA Domestic Service in Mandarin, 1425 GMT, 05 11 1977 OW, accessed through Readex.

Foreign Broadcast Information Service, People's Daily Article by Tsai Cheng: "Victory of Chairman Mao's Policy of ‚Building the Country by Self-Reliance and Through Diligence and Thrift' – on the Magnificent Achievements Scored by our country on the Financial and Monetary front", Peking Domestic Service in Mandarin, 0200 GMT, 13 01 1974, accessed through Readex.

Foreign Broadcast Information Service, People's Daily assesses superpowers' decline, contention, Peking NCNA in English, 2115 GMT, 27 09 1974 B, accessed through Readex.

Foreign Broadcast Information Service, People's Daily calls for Strengthening Agricultural Procurement, People's Daily 20 October frontpage Commentator's article: "It Is Necessary to Grasp Firmly and Well the Procurement of Agricultural and Sideline Products", Peking Domestic Service in Mandarin, 2230 GMT, 19 10 1977 OW, accessed through Readex.

Foreign Broadcast Information Service, People's Daily Condemns Gang's Criticism of 'Regulations', Text of 16 July People's Daily article by the mass criticism group of the State Planning Commission: "A Counterrevolutionary Farce of Usurping Party and State Power – Commenting on the 'Gang of Four's' Criticism of 'The 20 Points'", Peking NCNA Domestic Service in Mandarin, 0717 GMT, 16 07 1977 OW, accessed through Readex.

Foreign Broadcast Information Service, People's Daily condemns Gang's Labor Payment Theories, Peking NCNA in English, 0806 GMT, 23 11 1977 OW, accessed through Readex.

Foreign Broadcast Information Service, People's Daily Condemns Gang's Criticism of 'Regulations', Peking NCNA Domestic Service in Mandarin, 0717 GMT, 16 07 1977 OW, accessed through Readex.

Foreign Broadcast Information Service, People's Daily derides Brezhnev over Crop Failure, Peking NCNA in English, 1702 GMT, 27 04 1976 OW, accessed through Readex.

Foreign Broadcast Information Service, People's Daily looks at how to modernize industry, Fourth lecture on the general task for the new period by Chi Ti: "Modernize our Industry", Peking People's Daily in Mandarin, 23 05 1978, p. 2 HK, accessed through Readex.

Foreign Broadcast Information Service, People's Daily on How to Bring about Great Order, Text of People's Daily 10 April editorial: "Carry out an All-Round Way the Strategic Policy Decision on Grasping the Key Link in Running the Country Well", Peking NCNA Domestic Service in Mandarin, 1700 GMT, 10 04 1977 OW, accessed through Readex.

Foreign Broadcast Information Service, People's Daily on Moral Encouragement, Material Rewards, Text of People's Daily 9 April editorial: "Implement a Policy of Combining Moral Encouragement with Material Rewards", Peking NCNA Domestic Service in Mandarin, 1132 GMT, 09 04 1978 OW, accessed through Readex.

Foreign Broadcast Information Service, People's Daily on production of Secondary Autumn Crops, Excerpts of People's Daily 15 September Commentator's article: „Pay attention to production of Secondary Autumn Crops", Peking Domestic Service in Mandarin, 0800 GMT, 15 09 1977 OW, accessed through Readex.

Foreign Broadcast Information Service, People's Daily on Rational Use of Agricultural Labor Force, Text of People's Daily 3 September editorial: "Strengthen the Frontline of Agricultural Production", Peking NCNA Domestic Service in Mandarin, 1816 GMT, 02 09 1977 OW, accessed through Readex.

Foreign Broadcast Information Service, People's Daily Outlines Seaport Construction Tasks, People's Daily commentator's article: "Earnestly Do a Good Job in Completing the Supplementary Projects and Final Engineering Tasks in Seaport Construction", Peking People's Daily in Mandarin, 19 08 1977 SK, accessed through Readex.

Foreign Broadcast Information Service, People's Daily scores Capitalist Key Link, Article by Liang Hsiao and Jen Ming: "Criticize 'Taking the Three Directives as the Key Link'", Renmin Ribao of 29 February, Peking Domestic Service in Mandarin, 2230 GMT, 28 02 1976 OW, accessed through Readex.

Foreign Broadcast Information Service, People's Daily Scores Capitalist Key Link, Text of People's Daily 29 February Article by Liang Hsiao and Jen Ming: "Criticize 'Taking the

Three Directives as the Key Link'", Peking Domestic Service in Mandarin, 2230 GMT, 28 02 1976 OW, accessed through Readex.

Foreign Broadcast Information Service, People's Daily stresses independence, frugality in building socialism, Article by Tien Chih-Sung: "Adhere to the policy of independence and self-reliance – some understanding acquired from the study of 'on the correct handling of contradictions among the people'", Peking Renmin Ribao, Original in Mandarin, 22 03 1974 V, accessed through Readex.

Foreign Broadcast Information Service, People's Daily Stresses Tachai Importance, Peking NCNA Domestic Service in Mandarin, 1726 GMT, 25 10 1975 OW, accessed through Readex.

Foreign Broadcast Information Service, People's Daily Upholds Anshan Constitution, Peking Domestic Service in Mandarin, 2230 GMT, 18 02 1976 OW, accessed through Readex.

Foreign Broadcast Information Service, People's Daily upholds Anshan Constitution, Article by Kung Yeh-ping, "Uphold the Constitution of the Anshan Iron and Steel Company, Criticize the Theory of Productive Forces", Peking Domestic Service in Mandarin, 2230 GMT, 18 02 1976 OW, accessed through Readex.

Foreign Broadcast Information Service, People's Daily urges scientific, technological planning, People's Daily 8 November Commentator's article: "Do a good Job in Planning Scientific and Technological Development and Scale the World's Heights", Peking Domestic Service in Mandarin, 2230 GMT, 07 11 1977 OW, accessed through Readex.

Foreign Broadcast Information Service, People's Daily, NCNA Commentary on Foreign Trade, People's Daily and NCNA correspondent's commentary: "It is Necessary to Vigorously Develop Foreign Trade; it is Necessary to Emancipate the Mind", Peking NCNA Domestic Service in Mandarin, 1228 GMT, 08 07 1978 OW, accessed through Readex.

Foreign Broadcast Information Service, People's Daily: Advance Farmland Capital Construction, Text of People's Daily 8 August editorial: "Farmland Capital Construction Should Be Pushed Forward Vigorously During the Coming Winter and Spring", Peking NCNA Domestic Service in mandarin, 1818 GMT, 07 08 1977 OW, accessed through Readex.

Foreign Broadcast Information Service, PLA railway-men describe successes in using Mao thought, Peking NCNA Domestic Service in Mandarin, 2136 GMT, 31 10 1970 B, accessed through Readex.

Foreign Broadcast Information Service, Planning Commission Official Reports on Modernization, Peking NCNA in English, 0700 GMT, 31 12 1977 OW, accessed through Readex.

Foreign Broadcast Information Service, Population Growth Rate Declines Through Birth Control, Peking NCNA in English, 0703 GMT, 27 02 1977 OW, accessed through Readex.

Foreign Broadcast Information Service, Possibility of Chou En-Lai trip raises speculation, London Reuters in English, 1059 GMT, 27 08 1970 X, accessed through Readex.

Foreign Broadcast Information Service, PRC Ambassador's Reception, Peking NCNA International Service in English, 1633 GMT, 14 09 1971 B, accessed through Readex.

Foreign Broadcast Information Service, PRC bases light industry on agricultural developments, Peking NCNA in English, 0704 GMT, 27 12 1974 B, accessed through Readex.

Foreign Broadcast Information Service, PRC cities attain self-sufficiency in vegetable production, Peking NCNA in English, 0753 GMT, 28 12 1974 B, accessed through Readex.

Foreign Broadcast Information Service, PRC Delegate Addresses UN Meeting on Environment Problems, Peking NCNA in English, 1529 GMT, 23 04 1975 OW, accessed through Readex.

Foreign Broadcast Information Service, PRC Delegate Scores Superpowers at UN population conference, Peking NCNA in English, 1845 GMT, 21 08 1974 B, accessed through Readex.

Foreign Broadcast Information Service, PRC May Export More Oil to Japan, Tokyo Kyodo in English, 0015 GMT, 03 02 1978 OW, accessed through Readex.

Foreign Broadcast Information Service, PRC proposes Iron, Steel Negotiations this Month, Hong Kong AFP in English, 1418 GMT, 17 09 1976 OW, accessed through Readex.

Foreign Broadcast Information Service, PRC Seen Heading for Total Dependency on Imperialists, Unattributed station observer's commentary: "Why China does not publish information on its economic conditions", Radio Moscow in Mandarin, 1030 GMT 27 03 1974 B, accessed through Readex.

Foreign Broadcast Information Service, PRC Trade Volume Increases Steadily in 1977, Tokyo Kyodo in English, 1225 GMT, 15 03 1978 OW, accessed through Readex.

Foreign Broadcast Information Service, PRC urged to regain Socialist Fold while 'not too late', Second and final part of Fedor Burlatskiy's article: "The heavy Burden of the Inheritance", Moscow Literaturnaya Gazeta in Russian, 03 08 1977 LD, accessed through Readex.

Foreign Broadcast Information Service, PRC-Japan long-term Trade Agreement extended by 5 Years, Moscow TASS in English, 1038 GMT, 14 09 1978 LD, accessed through Readex.

Foreign Broadcast Information Service, Production increases at Liaoning's Anshan Steel Center reported, Peking NCNA in English, 0728 GMT, 16 04 1974 B, accessed through Readex.

Foreign Broadcast Information Service, Red Flag analyzes use of money as means of exchange, Shanghai City Service in Mandarin, 0700 GMT, 15 06 1975 OW, accessed through Readex.

Foreign Broadcast Information Service, Red Flag Article Discusses need to restrict bourgeois rights, 18 02 1975, accessed through Readex.

Foreign Broadcast Information Service, Red Flag Article on Mechanization of Agriculture, Article by Tang Feng, "Speed up Mechanization of Agriculture", Published in Red Flag No. 11, 1975, Peking Domestic Service in Mandarin, 2130 GMT, 13 11 1975 OW, accessed through Readex.

Foreign Broadcast Information Service, Red Flag Article reviews Hunan commune's experiences, Peking domestic service in Mandarin, 2130 GMT, 14 09 1974 B, accessed through Readex.

Foreign Broadcast Information Service, Red Flag Discusses Medium, Small Industries, Article by Chiang Hung: "Run Medium and Small Industries Actively and Well", Red Flag No. 10, 1975, Peking Domestic Service in Mandarin, 2140 GMT, 12 10 1975 OW, accessed through Readex.

Foreign Broadcast Information Service, Red Flag on Cultural Revolution, Industry, Peking NCNA in English, 0703 GMT, 08 06 1976 OW, accessed through Readex.

Foreign Broadcast Information Service, Red Flag on transforming science-engineering schools, Peking NCNA International Service in English, 1831 GMT, 21 07 1970 B, accessed through Readex.

Foreign Broadcast Information Service, Red Flag scores Teng's Economic Concept, Excerpts of article by Kao Lu and Chang Ko: "Comment on Teng Hsiao-ping's Comprador-Bourgeois Economic Concept", published in Red Flag No. 7, Peking Domestic Service in Mandarin, 2020 GMT, 10 07 1976 OW, accessed through Readex.

Foreign Broadcast Information Service, Red Flag Views Open-Door Scientific Research, Peking Domestic Service in Mandarin, 2345 GMT, 05 02 1976 OW, accessed through Readex.

Foreign Broadcast Information Service, Red Flag: Cultural Revolution Boosts Industry, Excerpts of article by Hsiang-Chi-wei: "The Great Proletarian Cultural Revolution and Industrial Development", Red Flag, No. 6 1976, Peking Domestic Service in Mandarin, 0330 GMT, 02 06 1976 OW, accessed through Readex.

Foreign Broadcast Information Service, Red Flag: Kiangsu Article on Socialist Construction, Article by Kiangsu Provincial CCP Committee: "The Only Road to Speed Up Socialist construction – Notes on Studying 'On the Ten Major Relationships'", Red Flag, No. 2, 1977, Nanking Kiangsu Provincial Service in Mandarin, 0330 GMT, 14 02 1977 OW, accessed through Readex.

Foreign Broadcast Information Service, Red Flag: Study Lenin's work on proletarian dictatorship, Peking NCNA Domestic Service in Mandarin, 07:43 GMT, 09 02 1975 OW, accessed through Readex.

Foreign Broadcast Information Service, Reportage on Coal Mining Conference, Peking NCNA Domestic Service in Mandarin, 1428 GMT, 30 10 1975, accessed through Readex.

Foreign Broadcast Information Service, Reportage, Commentaries on Tachai Conference, Hua Kuo-feng report, Peking NCNA in English, 1204 GMT, 20 10 1975 OW, accessed through Readex.

Foreign Broadcast Information Service, Reservoir poorly designed by foreigners is rebuilt, Peking NCNA Domestic Service in Mandarin, 0207 GMT, 19 12 1974 B, accessed through Readex.

Foreign Broadcast Information Service, Revisionism in Industry, Communications scored, Excerpts of an article by Chung Shih, "Criticize the Revisionist Absurd Fallacies on the Industrial and Communications Front", Red Flag No. 5, Peking Domestic Service in Mandarin, 0800 GMT, 09 05 1976 OW, accessed through Readex.

Foreign Broadcast Information Service, Sabotage of Foreign Trade, excerpts of an article by the theoretical group of the Research institute under the Peking Foreign Trade College: "Questions of International Trade", Peking NCNA in English, 1207 GMT, 10 12 1976 OW, accessed through Readex.

Foreign Broadcast Information Service, Saifudin Addresses Sinkiang Conference on Taching, Urumchi Sinkiang Regional Service in Mandarin, 1300 GMT, 03 10 1977 OW, accessed through Readex.

Foreign Broadcast Information Service, Saionju calls on Chou before returning to Japan, Tokyo Kyodo in English, 1035 GMT, 31 07 1970 T, accessed through Readex.

Foreign Broadcast Information Service, Second Installment, feature article by Tsai Wei-heng: "Ownership, Maintenance and Insurance – Second Comment on problems Concerning 'Compensation Trade'", Hong Kong Ta Kung Pao in Mandarin, 02 11 1978 p. 10 HK, accessed through Readex.

Foreign Broadcast Information Service, Secretary Bergland addresses 8 November Peking Banquet, Peking NCNA in English, 1753 GMT, 08 11 1978 OW, accessed through Readex.

Foreign Broadcast Information Service, Seventh Peking Lecture on Mao's 'Ten Major Relationships', Peking Domestic Service in Mandarin, 2200 GMT, 06 02 1977 OW, accessed through Readex.

Foreign Broadcast Information Service, Shanghai plants foster socialist cooperation, NCNA Domestic Service in Mandarin, 0735 GMT, 30 09 1975, accessed through Readex.

Foreign Broadcast Information Service, Shanghai stresses interfactory socialist cooperation, NCNA in English, 0736 GMT, 30 11 1975, accessed through Readex.

Foreign Broadcast Information Service, Shanghai Workers Make Industrial Designs, Peking NCNA in English, 0721 GMT, 01 01 1976 OW, accessed through Readex.

Foreign Broadcast Information Service, Shantung County Struggles Against Peasant Economy Concept, Tsinan Shantung Provincial Service in Mandarin, 1100 GMT, 29 01 1975 OW, accessed through Readex.

Foreign Broadcast Information Service, Shantung Meeting Promotes Use of Quick Planning Methods, Tsinan Shantung provincial Service in Mandarin, 1130 GMT, 20 06 1977 OW, accessed through Readex.

Foreign Broadcast Information Service, Shantung Workers oppose Teng's 'Regulations', Tsinan Shantung Provincial Service in Mandarin, 1100 GMT, 24 06 1976 OW, accessed through Readex.

Foreign Broadcast Information Service, Shensi Article Discusses Economic Development, Excerpts from article by the theory group of the Planning Committee of Shensi Provincial Revolutionary Committee, "The Great Cultural Revolution Promotes the Great Development of the National Economy in our Province", Sian Shensi Provincial Service in Mandarin, 1300 GMT, 10 06 1976 FE, accessed through Readex.

Foreign Broadcast Information Service, Shensi Daily Prints Worker's Letter Criticizing Material Incentives, Sian Shensi Provincial Service in Mandarin, 1100 GMT, 13 02 1974 V, accessed through Readex.

Foreign Broadcast Information Service, Shih-Chia-Shuang's Textile Industry shows Large profits, Article: "Shih-chia-chuang Textile Industrial Bureau Strengthens Party Guidance, Improves Enterprise Management, and Accumulates Large Amounts of Funds for the State for 10 Successive Years", Peking Jen-Min Jih-pao in Mandarin, 27 08 1977, accessed through Readex.

Foreign Broadcast Information Service, Sinkiang Foreign Trade Bureau Criticizes Gang, Article by mass criticism group of Sinkiang autonomous Regional Foreign Trade Bureau: "Strive To Develop Socialist Foreign Trade – Studying 'On the Ten Major Relationships' and Criticizing the Gang of Four's Crimes in Undermining Foreign Trade Work", Urumchi Sinkiang Regional Service in Mandarin, 1115 GMT, 11 07 1977 OW, accessed through Readex.

Foreign Broadcast Information Service, Small Cement Industry Progressing Rapidly, Peking NCNA in English, 0700 GMT, 19 11 1976 OW, accessed through Readex.

Foreign Broadcast Information Service, State Planning Commission Meets in Canton, Peking NCNA Domestic Service in Mandarin, 0107 GMT, 17 01 1977 OW, accessed through Readex.

Foreign Broadcast information Service, State planning Commission Article on Socialist Construction, Full text of an article written by the State Planning Commission to commemorate the first anniversary of the death of the great leader and teacher Chairman Mao: "Great Guiding Principle for Socialist Construction", Peking NCNA in English, 0102 GMT, 12 09 1977 OW, accessed through Readex.

Foreign broadcast Information Service, State Planning Commission Article on Socialist Construction, Peking NCNA in English, 0102 GMT, 12 09 1977 OW, accessed through Readex.

Foreign Broadcast Information Service, State Planning Commission meets in Canton, Peking NCNA Domestic Service in Mandarin, 0107 GMT, 17 01 1977 OW, accessed through Readex.

Foreign Broadcast Information Service, State Planning Minister, Hong Kong AFP in English, 1812 GMT, 07 09 1977 OW, accessed through Readex.

Foreign Broadcast Information Service, Swiss M-L Organ Lauds PRC's anti-Teng Line, Peking NCNA in English, 1313 GMT, 06 08 1976 OW, accessed through Readex.

Foreign Broadcast Information Service, Ta Kung Pao reports on Li Chiang's Talk with Hong Kong Businessmen, Report on Foreign Trade Minister Li Chiang's talk with Hong Kong businessmen on 15 December, Hong Kong Ta Kung Pao in English, 21 12 1978 p. 19 HK, accessed through Readex.

Foreign Broadcast information Service, Talien shipyard raises workers' technical level Peking NCNA in English, 1200 GMT, 09 09 1974 B, accessed through Readex.

Foreign Broadcast Information Service, Talk by Wang Shou-wu, deputy director of the Semiconductor Research Institute of the Chinese Academy of Sciences: "Resolutely Implement the Line of the 11th National CCP Congress and Strive To Realize the Splendid Goal of the Four Modernizations", Peking Domestic Service in Mandarin, 1200 GMT, 28 08 1977 OW, accessed through Readex.

Foreign Broadcast Information Service, Telephone Conference, Hofei Anhwei Provincial Service in Mandarin, 1100 GMT, 07 06 1975, accessed through Readex.

Foreign Broadcast Information Service, Teng Hsiao-Ping visits Swiss Industrial technology exhibit, Peking NCNA in English, 1525 GMT, 1308 1974 B, accessed through Readex.

Foreign Broadcast Information Service, Teng Line on Industrial Development scored, Article by Lu Ta: "A Set of Rules for Speeding Up Capitalist Restoration – Criticizing 'The Questions on Speeding Up Industrial Development' Concoted [sic!] on the Instruction of Teng Hsiao-ping", Peking Domestic Service in Mandarin, 0200 GMT, 07 06 1976 OW, accessed through Readex.

Foreign Broadcast Information Service, Teng on Terrorism, Trade, Alliance, Hong Kong AFP in English, 1330 GMT, 26 10 1977 OW, accessed through Readex.

Foreign Broadcast Information Service, Teng Ouster should not affect 5-year plan, Hong Kong AFP in English, 1450 GMT, 22 04 1976 OW, accessed through Readex.

Foreign Broadcast Information Service, Text of CCP Circular on National Science Conference, Peking NCNA in English, 1634 GMT, 22 09 1977 OW, accessed through Readex.

Foreign Broadcast Information Service, Text of People's Daily 22 April editorial: "Seize the Three Great Revolutionary Movements Together", Peking NCNA Domestic Service in Chinese, 1725 GMT, 21 04 1978 OW, accessed through Readex.

Foreign Broadcast Information Service, Text of Sung Chen-Ming Speech at Taching Conference, Peking NCNA Domestic Service in Mandarin, 0103 GMT, 24 04 1977 OW, accessed through Readex.

Foreign Broadcast Information Service, Text of the New Constitution, Peking NCNA in English, 0704 GMT, 07 03 1978 OW, accessed through Readex.

Foreign Broadcast Information Service, Tieh Ying Speech, Hangchow Chekiang Provincial Service in Mandarin, 1100 GMT, 29 05 1977 OW, accessed through Readex.

Foreign Broadcast Information Service, Tientsin Capital Construction Develops Rapidly, Peking NCNA in English, 1200 GMT, 20 11 1975 OW, accessed through Readex.

Foreign Broadcast Information Service, Tientsin First Secretary discusses Foreign Trade, Tientsin City Service in Mandarin, 2330 GMT, 23 08 1978 SK, accessed through Readex.

Foreign Broadcast Information Service, Tientsin plant takes on new look by following Mao, Peking NCNA International Service in English, 1310 GMT, 24 03 1970 B, accessed through Readex.

Foreign Broadcast Information Service, Tokyo Kyodo on Chou Meeting, Tokyo Kyodo in English, 0040 GMT, 19 01 1973, accessed through Readex.

Foreign Broadcast Information Service, Trade Official Assesses Debts of Socialist Countries, Cologne Deutschlandfunk Domestic Service in German, 1600 GMT, 28 10 1975 DW.

Foreign Broadcast Information Service, Tseng Shao-Chan Report at Liaoning People's Congress, Summary of Liaoning Provincial Revolutionary Committee work report presented by Tseng Shao-shan, chairman of Liaoning Provincial Revolutionary Committee at fifth Liaoning Provincial People's Congress on 23 December 1977, Shenyang Liaoning Provincial Service in Mandarin, 1100 GMT, 30 12 1977 SK, accessed through Readex.

Foreign Broadcast Information Service, Vice Premier Yu Chiu-Li Speaks at Taching Conference, Peking NCNA in English, 2105 GMT, 07 05 1977 OW.

Foreign Broadcast Information Service, Visits Austrian Industrial Fair, Peking NCNA in English, 1554 GMT 05 04 1974 B, accessed through Readex.

Foreign Broadcast Information Service, Wang Huai-hsiang 10 Feb Speech, Speech given by Comrade Wang Huai-hsiang, first secretary of the Kirin Provincial CCP Committee, on 0 February at the provincewide conference on learning from Tachai in agriculture: "Hold high the Great Banner of Chairman Mao and Strive Hard to Carry Out the Strategic Policy Decision of Chairman Hua and the Party Central Committee to grasp the Key Link in Running the Country" [Title read by announcer]. Changchun Kirin Provincial Service in Mandarin, 1100 GMT, 14 02 1977 OW, accessed through Readex.

Foreign Broadcast Information Service, Weekly International Observers Roundtable, Moscow International Service in Russian at 0730 GMT, 25 07 1976 LD, accessed through Readex.

Foreign Broadcast Information Service, Worker's Wages Increased 1 Oct, Peking NCNA in English, 1225 GMT, 10 11 1977 OW, accessed through Readex.

Foreign Broadcast Information Service, Wuhan Iron-Steel Complex, Peking NCNA in English, 1248 GMT, 30 12 1973 B, accessed through Readex.

Foreign Broadcast Information Service, Yu Chiu-Li Speech, Peking NCNA in English, 1922 GMT, 24 10 1977 OW, accessed through Readex.

Foreign Broadcast Information Service, Yuan Pao-hua Speech, Peking NCNA in English, 0700 GMT, 29 01 1978 OW, accessed through Readex.

Readex – Joint Publications Research Service (JPRS) reports

Joint Publications Research Service, Article by Chiang Huai: "Situation Regarding Communist China's Transportation and Communications", Taipei, Fei-Ch'ing Yueh-pao, Original in Mandarin, JPRS Report No. 89, 01 01 1970, accessed through Readex.

Joint Publications Research Service, Article explains how new teaching materials are written, excerpts from an article by the political economy department of Nankai University: "Write and compile new teaching material, using society as the factory", Peking Kuang-ming Jih-pao, Original in Mandarin, 12 08 1972, accessed through Readex.

Joint Publications Research Service, Chinese Communist Capital Construction Studied and Analyzed, Article by Ch'ien Yuan-heng, "Study and analysis of Chinese communist capital construction work", Taipei Chung-kung Yen-chiu, Vol. 7, No. 5, Original in Mandarin, 05 1973, accessed through Readex.

Joint Publications Research Service, Chinese Communist Industry in 1972, Article by Ch'ien Yüan-heng; Taipei Chung-kung Yen-chiu, Vol. 7, Original in Mandarin, 10 02 1973, pp. 15–26, accessed through Readex.

Joint Publications Research Service, Communist China's Industry in 1969, excerpts from an article by Ch'ien Yuan-heng, Taipei Chung-kung Yen-chiu, Vol. 4, No. 1, Original in Mandarin, 01 1970, pp. 18–28, accessed through Readex.

Joint Publications Research Service, Communist China's transportation and communications, Taipei Fei-ch'ing Yueh-pao, Original in Mandarin, 01 09 1970, accessed through Readex.

Joint Publications Research Service, Experts Downgraded, Worker's role stressed in planning, Article by Writing Group of State Construction Commission: "Relentlessly Pursue the Struggle of the Two Lines: Intently Inaugurate the Planning Revolution", Peking Jen-min Jih-Pao, Original in Mandarin, 19 04 1971, accessed through Readex.

Joint Publications Research Service, Overseas Chinese describes industrial agricultural projects, Article by Sun T'ien-chien: "Second visit to my motherland from England", Hong Kong Ta-kung Pao, Original in Mandarin, 08 06 1972, accessed through Readex.

Joint Publications Research Service, PRC regulations for waterway cargo transportation, Excerpts from a book by the Ministry of Communications, Peking Shui-lu Huo-wu Yun-shu Kuei-tse, Original in Mandarin, 02 1972, pp. 1–14, 23–27, 32, accessed through Readex.

Joint Publications Research Service, Problems of the Chinese communist State Council Reviewed, Article by Chin Ch'ien-li: "Longstanding, Big and Difficult Problems of the Chinese Communist State Council", Hong Kong Hsing-tao Juh-pao, Original in Mandarin, 21 01 1972, accessed through Readex.

Joint Publications Research Service, Provinicial Revolutionary Head reveals Agricultural Woes, T'an Fu-jen's Speech at the Province-Wide Agricultural Work Conference, Taipei Chung-kung Yen-chiu, Original in Mandarin, No. 9, 09 1970, pp. 118–132, accessed through Readex.

Joint Publications Research Service, Study and analysis of Chinese communist scientific and technical activities in agriculture, Article by Ch'iung Wen, Taipei Fei-ch'ing Yueh-pao, Original in Mandarin, 09 1972, pp. 56–63, accessed through Readex.

Joint Publications Research Service, The Red East – a long discussion with Chou En-lai, Cairo Al-Ahram, Original in Arabic, 23 02 1973, p. 4, accessed through Readex.

Joint Publications Research Service, 'High Official' discusses economic situation, Alain Jacob and Jean de la Gueriviere Peking dispatch, "It Appears That the Population Has Exceeded the 800 Million Mark", Paris Le Monde in French, 04 11 1976 LD, accessed through Readex.

Joint Publications Research Service, A Banner which is both Red and Expert – Learning from Comrade Li Ssu-Kuang, Peking Red Flag No. 11, Original in Mandarin, 07 11 1977, pp. 24–28, accessed through Readex.

Joint Publications Research Service, Article by Akio Akagi and Morihiko Sato of the Japan Broadcasting Corporation: "Tach'ing Oil Fields and China's Industrial Technology", Tokyo Shizen in Japanese, 05 1974, pp. 62–74, accessed through Readex.

Joint Publications Research Service, Article by Hansjörg Heinrich: "China Trade Shipping: No grounds for Euphoria", Germany DVZ Deutsche Verkehrszeitung, Original in German, 28 08 1973, p. 9, accessed through Readex.

Joint Publications Research Service, Bovin: Domestic Changes in PRC, No Change in Anti-Sovietism, Article by Aleksandr Bovin: "What has Changed?", Moscow Literaturnaya Gazeta, Original in Russian, 25 05 1977 LD, accessed through Readex.

Joint Publications Research Service, Brochure: The significance, mission, and requirements of the financial and accounting work of production teams, 01 01 1973, accessed through Readex.

Joint Publications Research Service, Ch'iao Kuan-Hua on World Situation and Foreign Policy, "Ch'iao Kuan-hua's Speech on the Current World Situation and Communist China's Foreign Policy", Taipei Fei-Ch'ing Yueh-Pao in Mandarin, Vol. 18, No. 3, 05 10 1975, accessed through Readex.

Joint Publications Research Service, Chiang Ch'ing's Address to Diplomatic Cadres, Taipei Fei-ch'ing Yueh-pao, Original in Chinese, 05 10 1975, accessed through Readex.

Joint Publications Research Service, Chinese Communist Capital Construction studied and analyzed, Article by Ch'ein Yuan-Heng: "Study and Analysis of Chinese Communist Capital Construction Work", Taipei Chung-Kung Yen-Chiu, Vol. 7, No. 5, 05 1973, pp. 62–72, accessed through Readex.

Joint Publications Research Service, Chinese Communists unfold all-encompassing campaign on Mainland for voluntary reduction of wages, Hong Kong Hsing-tao Jih-pao, Original in Mandarin, 22 06 1971, p. 4, accessed through Readex.

Joint Publications research Service, Communist China's 'Production-Construction Corps' studied, Article by Chang Yun-t'ien, "The Establishment and Expansion of Communist China's 'Production-Construction Corps': A Study of its Conditions and Functions", Taipei Chung-kung Yen-chiu, Original in Mandarin, 03 1970, pp. 31–40, accessed through Readex.

Joint Publications Research Service, Communist China's Industry in 1969, Excerpts from Article by Ch'ien Yuan-heng, Taipei Chung-kung Yen-chiu, Vol. 4, No. 1, Original in Mandarin, 01 1970, pp. 24 ff., accessed through Readex.

Joint Publications Research Service, Current Chinese Communist Trends, Article by Lin Pin, "Current Economic Trends of the Chinese Communists", Taipei Chung-kung Yen-chiu, Vol. 7, No. 5, Original in Mandarin, 05 1973, accessed through Readex.

Joint Publications Research Service, Developmental Phases of China's Iron and Steel Industry analyzed, Chapter 2 on "China's Iron and Steel Industry" from the book "The Developmental Phases of China's Industry and their Characteristics", Tokyo Chugoku Sangyo No Hatten Dankai To Sono Tokushitsu ni Tsuite, Original in Japanese, 03 1976, accessed through Readex.

Joint Publications Research Service, Haykal "Frankly Speaking" article: "The Red East – A Long Discussion with Chou En-lai", Cairo Al-Ahram, Original in Arabic, 23 02 1873, p. 4, accessed through Readex.

Joint Publications Research Service, Japanese Bankers Impressed by Tour of Mainland, Hong Kong Ta Kung Pao, Original in Mandarin, 18 10 1975, accessed through Readex.

Joint Publications Research Service, Kwangming Daily: Inequality still prevails in PRC under Socialism, Peking Kwangming Daily, Original in Mandarin, 18 02 1975, WA, accessed through Readex.

Joint Publications Research Service, Liang Hsiao scores Teng's 'Poisonous Weeds', Article by Liang Hsiao, "Grasp the Question of the Line and Deepen the Criticism of Teng Hsiao-ping", Peking Kwangming Daily, Original in Mandarin, 26 08 1976, HK/P, accessed through Readex.

Joint Publications Research Service, Liu Shao-ch'i's Confession at Chinese Communist Party Central Committee Work Conference (23 October 1966), Taipei Chung-kung Yen-chiu, Original in Mandarin, 01 1970, pp. 122–127.

Joint Publications Research Service, Mao's Teachings on Industrialization Praised, Article by Su Hsing: "The Beacon Shining on China's Road to industrialization – A Study of Volume V of the 'Selected Works of Mao Tsetung'", Peking Kwangming Daily, Original in Mandarin, 07 11 1977 HK, accessed through Readex.

Joint Publications Research Service, Material Incentives New Peking Slogan, Article by Harry Hamm, Original in German, Frankfurt Frankfurter Allgemeine No. 98, 28 04 1977, accessed through Readex.

Joint Publications Research Service, More Products Exported, Hong Kong Chung-kuo Hsin-wen, Original in Mandarin, 02 11 1976, accessed through Readex.

Joint Publications Research Service, Movement to clear all debts underway in Chinese Communes, Hong Kong Ming Pao, Original in Mandarin, 23 12 1974.

Joint Publications Research Service, Open Door Education Praised, Article by Educational Revolution Group of Shanghai Normal University: "Open-Door Education is Good", Shanghai Hsueh-His P'I-P'An, Original in Mandarin, No. 1, 1976, accessed through Readex.

Joint Publications Research Service, Opposition to Rectification means Opposition to Revolution, Article by Lo Yuan-cheng, Chang Cho-yuan and Liu Fu-jung, Peking Red Flag No. 10, Original in Mandarin, 08 10 1977, accessed through Readex.

Joint Publications Research Service, Peking's Electronics industry Develops Abundantly, Hong Kong Chung-kuo Hsin-wen, Original in Mandarin, 25 07 1975, accessed through Readex.

Joint Publications Research Service, People's Daily discusses 'Material Incentives', Article by Liu Yung-sen, "What kind of Question Is That About 'Tangible Means of Control'?", Peking People's Daily, Original in Mandarin, 19 07 1975, p. 3 WA, accessed through Readex.

Joint Publications Research Service, PRC use of Oil as Policy Tool Scored, Article by A. Karpenko, "The Maoists' 'Oil Diplomacy'", Moscow Economicheskaya Gazeta in Russian, No. 6, 02 02 1976, accessed through Readex.

Joint Publications Research Service, Provincial Revolutionary Head Reveals Agricultural Woes, Article: "T'an Fu-jen's Speech at the Province-Wide Agricultural Work Conference", Taipei Chung-kung Yen-chiu, Original in Mandarin, No. 9, 09 1970, pp. 128, accessed through Readex.

Joint Publications Research Service, Railroads in the People's Republic of China, Paris La vie du Rail Outre-Mer, Original in French, No. 249, 01 05 1975, accessed through Readex.

Joint Publications Research Service, Red Flag criticizes Gang's view of Bourgeois Rights, Article by Hsueh Mu-chiao: "Criticize the 'Gang of Four's' Reactionary Fallacies on the Question of Bourgeois Rights", Peking Red Flag No. 11, Original in Mandarin, 07 11 1977, pp. 35–42, accessed through Readex.

Joint Publications Research Service, Red Flag scores Teng on Enterprise Control, article by Chi Ping, "The Reactionary Nature of the Practice of 'Direct and Exclusive Control of Enterprise by the Ministry Concerned' Reemphasized by Teng Hsiao-ping", Peking Domestic Service in Mandarin, 0330 GMT, 09 09 1976 OW, accessed through Readex.

Joint Publications Research Service, Rural Credit Cooperatives Established, Article: "Monetary Network established in our country's rural areas", Hong Kong Wen Hui Pao, Original in Mandarin, 22 11 1974, accessed through Readex.

Joint Publications Research Service, Rural Market in Kwangsi, Article: "Rural Market in Kwangsi Presents Scene of Prosperity", Hong Kong Chung-kuo Hsin-wen, Original in Mandarin, 17 01 1976, accessed through Readex.

Joint Publications Research Service, Shanghai Instrument and Telecommunications Industry Doing Well, Article: "Shanghai Instrument and Telecommunications Industry

System Revolution, Production Situation Generally Good", Hong Kong Chung-kuo Hsin-wen, Original in Mandarin, 26 04 1976, accessed through Readex.

Joint Publications Research Service, Shanghai's Rubber Industry Overcomes Power Shortage, Peking Jen-min Jih-pao, Original in Mandarin, 11 03 1977, accessed through Readex.

Joint Publications Research Service, Situation of Chinese Communist communications sector, Article by Chiang Huai, Taipei Fei-ch'ing Yueh pao, No. 2, Original in Mandarin, 10 04 1973, p. 105, accessed through Readex.

Joint Publications Research Service, Speech at the Second Plenary Session of the eighth Central Committee of the Communist Party of China, 15 November 1956, Peking Mao Tse-Tung Hsuan-Chi, Original in Mandarin, 1977, accessed through Readex.

Joint Publications Research Service, State of PRC Communications Sector analysed, Article by Chiang Huai, Taipei Fei-ch'ing Yüeh-pao, Original in Mandarin, 10 03 1973, p. 109, accessed through Readex.

Joint Publications Research Service, Taiwan Reports on current status of PRC transportation, Article by Chiang Huai, Latest Chinese Communist Transportation, Taipei Fei-ch'ing Yueh-pao, Vol. 16, No. 5, Original in Mandarin, 10 07 1973, p. 104.

Joint Publications Research Service, Textile Industry Meets Needs of Nation's 800 Million People, Article by Ching Wen, "The Textile Industry of the New China", Hong Kong Ching-chu Tao-pao in Mandarin, 26 03 1975, accessed through Readex.

Joint Publications Research Service, Textile Industry propagates electronic technology, Hong Kong Ta Kung Pao, Original in Mandarin, 10 10 1975, p. 6, accessed through Readex.

Joint Publications Research Service, The Toast by Hua Kuo-Feng, Chairman of the CCP Central Committee and Premier of the State Council, at the Reception Marking the 28th National Day, Peking Red Flag No. 10, Original in Mandarin, 08 10 1977, accessed through Readex.

Joint Publications Research Service, Trade Negotiations between PRC, Common Market viewed, Unattributed 'Current Affairs Analysis' column: "The Trade Negotiations between China and the Common Market", Hong Kong Wen Wei Po, Original in Mandarin, 11 07 1977 HK, accessed through Readex.

Joint Publications Research Service, Translations on Communist China No. 90, Selections from Chairman Mao, Speech at Central Committee Political Work Report Meeting (24 October 1966), JPRS Document No. 49826, p. 12, 12 02 1970, accessed through Readex.

Joint Publications Research Service, Translations on Communist China No. 90, Selections from Chairman Mao, Talk at Hangchow Conference (21 December 1965), JPRS Document No. 4982, 12 02 1970, p. 2, accessed through Readex.

Joint Publications Research Service, Translations on Communist China No. 90, Selections from Chairman Mao, Speech at the 11th Plenary Session of 8th CCP Central Committee, Original in Mandarin, JPRS Document No. 49826, 12 02 1970, p. 7, accessed through Readex.

Joint Publications Research Service, Translations on Communist China No. 90, Selections from Chairman Mao, Comment on Comrade Ch'en Cheng-jen's Stay in a Primary Unit (29 January 1965), JPRS Document No. 4982, 12 02 1970, p. 23, accessed through Readex.

Joint Publications Research Service, Translations on Communist China No. 90, Selections from Chairman Mao, Talk at Hangchow Conference (21 December 1965), JPRS Document No. 49826, 12 02 1970, p. 5, accessed through Readex.

Joint Publications Research Service, Views expressed concerning implementation of directive, Article: "Views of the Chinese Communist X X X [anonymized] District Committee concerning the implementation of the CCP Central Committee Directive on the problem of distribution in the Rural People's Communes", Taipei Chung-kung Yen-chiu, No. 8, Original in Mandarin, 08 1972, pp. 101–110, accessed through Readex.

Archive of European Integration (AEI), University of Pittsburgh

Address by Jens Otto Krag, Head of the Delegation of the European Communities, Washington D.C., to the Conference on Trans-Atlantic Trade in an Era of Two Digit-Inflation at State University of New York at Albany. 7 February 1975, Archive of European Integration, Document No. 8315, available at: http://aei.pitt.edu/8315/, last accessed on 1 May 2020.

China and the European Community, 22 May 1974, AEI, Background note to Document No. 56842 of 22 May 1974, available at: http://aei.pitt.edu/56842/1/BN_9.74.pdf, last accessed on 1 May 2020.

China and the European Community. European Community Background Information No. 9, 22 May 1974, AEI, Document Nr. 56842, available at: http://aei.pitt.edu/id/eprint/56842, last accessed on 1 May 2020.

Commission of the European Communities, Proposal for a Council Decision provisionally extending in advance for 1977 the import quotas laid down for 1976 by Council Decision 75/788/EEC in respect of the People's Republic of China, COM (76) 496 final, 24 September 1976, AEI, Document No. 57880, available at: http://aei.pitt.edu/57880/, last accessed on 1 May 2020.

European Community Information Service, The United States and the European Community: Their Common Interests, second edition, New York 1973, p. 20, AEI, Document No. 9617, available at: http://aei.pitt.edu/9617/1/9617.pdf, last accessed on 1 May 2020.

The World Economy: Towards a New Consensus, Extract from a speech by the Rt. Hon. Sir Christopher Soames, Vice-President of the Commission of the European Communities, at a Luncheon given by the oil industries club at the Connaught Rooms, London, At 01:30 p.m., Tuesday, 1 July 1975, Archive of European Integration, Document No. 8493, available at: http://aei.pitt.edu/8493/1/8493.pdf, last accessed on 1 May 2020.

The World Economy: Towards a New Consensus, Tuesday, 1 July 1975, AEI, Document No. 8493, available at: http://aei.pitt.edu/8493/, last accessed on 1 May 2020.

Central Intelligence Agency (CIA), access under the *Freedom of Information Act*

Central Intelligence Agency, China: Demand for Foreign Grain, National Foreign Assessment Center, Research Paper, ER 79–10073, pp. 1f. and 4, available at: https://www.cia.gov/library/readingroom/document/cia-rdp83b00551r000100060009-4, last accessed on 1 May 2020.

Central Intelligence Agency, China: Foreign Trade Policy in the 1970s, National Foreign Assessment Center, Research Paper, ER 78–10455, pp. 4–6., available at: https://www.cia.gov/library/readingroom/docs/CIA-RDP80T00702A000200060012-0.pdf, last accessed on 1 May 2020.

Central Intelligence Agency, Report, USSR: The Role of Foreign Trade in the Economy, 1 July 1985, General CIA Records Collection, Document Nr. CIA-RDP08S01350R000200500001-0, available at: https://www.cia.gov/library/readingroom/document/cia-rdp08s01350r000200500001-0, last accessed on 1 May 2020.

China Foreign Languages Press (FLP) and related publications

Foreign Languages Press, *"On the Revolutionary 'Three-in-One' Combination"*, Editorial of Hongqi, No. 5, 1967, in: On the Revolutionary "Three-In-One" Combination [brochure published by FLP], Beijing 1968

Foreign Languages Press, A Glance at China's Economy, Beijing 1974.

Foreign Languages Press, First Five-year Plan for Development of the National Economy of the People's Republic of China in 1953–1957, Beijing 1953.

Foreign Languages Press, Speech by chairman of the delegation of the People's Republic of China, Teng Hsiao-ping , at the special session of the U.N. General Assembly, April 10, 1974, Beijing 1974.

Foreign Languages Press, The General Condition of China's Seaports, Beijing 1974.

Li Qiao, China's oil drilling champions take 'Iron Man' spirit to foreign fields, in: Global Times, 13 October 2019, Available at: https://www.globaltimes.cn/content/1166688.shtml, last accessed on 1 May 2020.

Speech by Chiao Kuan-hua, Chairman of Delegation of People's Republic of China, Peking Review, No. 47, 19 November 1971, p. 6, available at: https://www.marxists.org/subject/china/peking-review/1971/PR1971-47.pdf, last accessed on 1 May 2020.

Zedong Mao, Quotations from Chairman Mao Tse-tung (The Little Red Book) & Other Works, published independently.

Propaganda posters – The Stephan Landsberger Collection, Amsterdam

Propaganda Poster, *Chang xiao zhiqi gao, zhengzuo da gongxian*, 54x77 cm, Stephan Landsberger Collection at the Institute for International Social History (IISH), Call number BG E12/738.

Propaganda Poster, *Fengshou changshang pi xinzhuang, hanghai renmin chubanshe*, 53x77 cm, Stephan Landsberger Collection at the Institute for International Social History (IISH), Call number BG E13/49.

Propaganda Poster, *Gongye xue Daqing*, Jiangxi Renmin Chubanshe, 76.5x53 cm, Stephan Landsberger Collection at the Institute for International Social History (IISH), Call number BG E13/915.

Propaganda Poster, *Xuexi daqing jingshen, jianchi duli zizhu*, zili gengshengde weida fangzhen, Renmin meishu chubanshe, 77x106 cm, Stephan Landsberger Collection at the Institute for International Social History (IISH), Call number BG E13/620.

Diplomatic Documents of Switzerland (dodis)

Ambassade de Suisse en Chine, China 1967–1972, Politischer Bericht Nr. 5, Peking 22 Februar 1972, Ref: 382.1 – RO/hw. Available on Diplomatic Documents of Switzerland (dodis): dodis.ch/35819, last accessed on 1 May 2020.

Ambassade de Suisse en Chine, China 1967–1972, Politischer Bericht Nr. 5, Peking 22 Februar 1972, Ref: 382.1 – RO/hw. Available at dodis: dodis.ch/35819. Last accessed 1 May 2020.

Ambassade de Suisse en Chine, Die Schweiz und China, Peking, den 24. Oktober 1975, Ref. PB Nr. 36 / LB / we, pp. 5–6. Available at dodis: dodis.ch/37717. Last accessed on 12 August 2022.

Ambassade de Suisse en Chine, Lettre à Ernesto Thalmann, Pékin, ke 3 janvier 1973, Réf. 12.21.Cha. Available at dodis : dodis.ch/37712. Last accessed on 12 August 2022.

Ambassade de Suisse en Chine, Lettre à Peter Bettschart, Pékin, le 29 décembre 1977, Ref. 613.2 – DY/jg. Available at dodis : dodis.ch/49050. Last accessed on 12 August 2022.

Ambassade de Suisse en Chine, Rapport de fin de mission, 24 juin 1975, Réf : 004.5 – NT/PI/vi, p. 2. Available at dodis : dodis.ch/37707. Last accessed on 12 August 2022.

Ambassade de Suisse en Chine, Visite de M. Petitpierre à Pékin, Pékin, le 16 mai 1973, RéPf. 101.0, 712.0 – NT/hw. Available at dodis : dodis.ch/37713. Last accessed on 12 August 2022.

Ambassade de Suisse en Chine, Visite de M. Petitpierre à Pékin, Pékin le 16 mai 1973, Réf. 101.0, 712.0 – NT/hw, pp. 3–5. Available at dodis : dodis.ch/37713. Last accessed on 12 August 2022.

Ambassade de Suisse en Chine, Vol inaugural Swissair, les entretiens de M. Willy Ritschard, Conseiller fédéral, et de M. Thalmann, Secrétaire général, Pékin, le 14 avril 1975, Ref. p.B.15.21.Cha, pp. 9–10. Available at dodis : dodis.ch/37728. Last accessed on 12 August 2022.

Antwort Botschafter Probst aif Brief des Vereins schweiz. Textilindustrieller vom 18.10.74, 5. November 1974. Available at dodis: dodis.ch/37711. Last accessed on 12 August 2022.

Besuch Ku Mu, Bericht an Direktor Jolles, Bern, 18. Mai 1978. Available at dodis : dodis.ch/49051. Last accessed on 12 August 2022.

China – Reise 1974, Ergänzende Information von Botschafter Probst zum "volet économique" anlässlich der Botschafterkonferenz 1974 (4. September 1974), Beilage Nr. IV, p. 7. Available at dodis: dodis.ch/37654. Last accessed on 12 August 2022.

China – Reise 1974, Ergänzende Information von Botschafter Probst zum "volet économique" anlässlich der Botschafterkonferenz 1974 (4. September 1974), Beilage Nr. IV, p. 7. Available at dodis: dodix.ch/37654. Last accessed on 12 August 2022.

China als zukünftiger Handelspartner der Schweiz, Vortrag von Botschafter Raymond Probst, Delegierter des Bundesrates für handelsverträge, gehalten in Basel am 25. Februar 1975 vor dem hausverband der CIBA-GEIGY A. G., 20.2.1975, p. 14. Available at dodis: dodis.ch/37700. Last accessed on 12 August 2022.

China: Finanzprobleme, 13. September 1978, Ref. 821 AVA – vT/rf. Available at dodis: do dis.ch/49084. Last accessed on 12. August 2022.

Conference des Ambassadeurs 1974, Rapport de M. le Conseiller fédéral P. Graber, Chef du Département politique, sur son voyage en Chine, Bernerhof, mercredi 4 septembre 1974, 14.30 h, Annexe III, pp. 3–4. Available at dodis: dodis.ch/35124. Last accessed 12 August 2022.

Der Direktor der Eidgenössischen Handelsabteilung, Bericht über China-Mission (18. bis 29. September 1978), Bern, den 5. Oktober 1978, p. 7. Available at dodis: dodis.ch/49077. Last accessed on 12 August 2022.

Die erstaunlichen Chinesen, Notiz des Direktors der handelsabteilung des Volkswirtschaftsdepartements P. R. Jolles, Bern, den 29. November 1978. Available at dodis: dodis.ch/49088. Last accessed on 12 August 2022.

Eidgenössisches Luftamt, Bericht der Vorgespräche über ein Luftverkehrsabkommen Schweiz – Volksrepublik China vom 11.–16. Juni 1972 in Peking, 4. Juli 1972, Ref. 14/China-Ae, p. 2. Available at dodis: dodis.ch/35859. Last accessed on 12 August 2022.

Entretien du Conseiller fédéral Pierre Graber, Chef du Département politique, avec M. Li Chiang, Ministre chinois du Commerce extérieur, Grand Palais du Peuple, Minutes (PV), Beijing, 5 August 1974, dodis, document No. 37708, p. 16, available at: dodis.ch/37708, last accessed on 1 May 2020.

Entretien du Conseiller fédéral Pierre Graber, Chef du Département politique, avec M. Li Chiang, Ministre chinois du Commerce extérieur, Grand Palais du Peuple, Minutes (PV), Beijing, 5 August 1974, dodis, document No. 37708, p. 16, available at: dodis.ch/37708. Last accessed 1 May 2020.

Handelsabteilung EVD, Besuch Ku Mu, Bern, 25. Mai 1978, Ref. vT/Ze – China 821.AVA. Available at dodis : dodis.ch/49054. Last accessed on 12 August 2022.

Minister von Tscharner Chinareise Dir. Jolles: Bankgeschäfte, Peking, 12.9.1978, 13:00, Ref. 5.6.41.Cha.152.0. Available at dodis: dodis.ch/49076. Last accessed on 12 August 2022.

Notiz an Herrn Direktor Jolles, Volksrepublik China, Bern, den 7. November 1978, Ref. China 877.3 – Ro/ne. Available at dodis: dodis.ch/52802. Last accessed on 12 August 2022.

Notiz an Herrn Minister Zwahlen, China Gelder, Bern, den 14. September 1978, Ref. S.C.41.Cha.731.1. – PF/dem. Available at dodis: dodis.ch/49086. Last accessed on 12 August 2022.

Schweizerische Botschaft in China, VR China: Besuch der Volksbank, Peking, den 11. September 1978, Ref. 101.0, 512.0 – SC/em. Available at dodis: dodis.ch/49083. Last accessed on 12 August 2022.

Schweizerische Zentrale für Handelsförderung, Interner Bericht über den Besuch in der Volksrepublik China vom 20. bis 31. Oktober 1972 betreffend die Durchführung einer Schweizerischen Industrie-Ausstellung in Peking 1974, verfasst von Dr. H. J. Halbheer, Stellv. Direktor und Leiter des Sitzes Zürich der OSEC. Available at dodis: dodis.ch/35904. Last accessed on 12 August 2022.

Schweizerische Zentrale für Handelsförderung, Interner Bericht über den Besuch in der Volksrepublik China vom 20. bis 31. Oktober 1972 betreffend die Durchführung einer Schweizerischen Industrie-Ausstellung in Peking 1974, verfasst von Dr. H. J. Halbheer, Stellv. Direktor und Leiter des Sitzes Zürich der OSEC. Available at dodis: dodis.ch/35904. Last accessed on 12 August 2022.

Edited sources and travel accounts by foreign visitors to China

Bowie Robert R., Fairbank John King, Communist China 1955–1959: Policy Documents with Analysis, Cambridge 1971, pp. 540–549.

Chiang Ching's Address to Diplomatic Cadres, March 1975, Classified Chinese Communist Documents: A Selection, Taipei Institute of International Relations, 1978, pp. 537–545, available in: Chinese Law & Government, Vol. 9, No. 1–2, 1976, pp. 49–61.

Classified Chinese Communist Documents: A Selection, Taipei 1978.

Cortesi Mario, Meyer Frank A., Notizen aus China, Zürich 1972.

Economic Information & Agency, China's Foreign Trade and its Management, Hong Kong 1978.

Excerpts of Chiang Ch'ing's Address at the National Conference on Learning from Tachai in Agriculture, in: Classified Chinese Communist Documents: A Selection, Taipei 1978, p. 639, available at: https://www.marxists.org/archive/jiang-qing/1975/september/15.htm, last accessed on 1 May 2020.

Howe Christopher, Walker Kenneth R. (ed.), The Foundations of the Chinese Planned Economy: A Documentary Survey, 1953–65, London 1989.

Jiang Zilong, All the Colours of the Rainbow, Beijing 1983.

Joint Statement issued by the governments of Japan and the People's Republic of China at Peking, September 28 1972 in: Hsiao 1977, Appendix D, pp. 196–198.

Joseph Allan, Masked Intentions, Navigating a Computer Embargo on China, Bloomington 2010.

Krott Martin (ed.), Programm für Chinas Zukunft, Deng Xiaopings Dokumente zur Lage der Nation auf dem Höhepunkt des Machtkampfes 1975, Übersetzung und Kommentar, Hamburg 1978.

Lagercrantz Olof, China Report, Bericht einer Reise, Frankfurt am Main 1971.

Mao Zedong, *'There Are Two Intermediate Zones'*, September, 1963, History and Public Policy Program Digital Archive, Mao Zedong on Diplomacy (Beijing 1998), pp. 387–389. Available at: http://digitalarchive.wilsoncenter.org/document/121207, last accessed on 15 April 2020.

Martin Helmut (ed.), Mao Tse-tung, Das machen wir anders als Moskau!, Kritik an der sowjetischen Politökonomie, Hamburg 1975.

Schoenhals Michael, New Texts: Speeches at the Ninth National Congress of the Chinese Communist Party, in: The Stockholm Journal of East Asian Studies, No. 2, 1990.

Zhang Chunqiao, Report on the Revision of the Constitution, 13 January 1975, in: Documents of the First Session of the Fourth National People's Congress of the People's

Republic of China, paragraph 3, available at: https://www.marxists.org/reference/archive/zhang/1975/01/13.htm, last accessed on 1 May 2020.

Non-Chinese government publications

Bureau de l'Intégration du DPF et du DFEP, Rapport de synthèse no 2/79, Les Relations entre la CEE et la Chine, Mars 1979, Universitätsbibliothek Basel UB Wirtschaft, Magazin, SWA Vo H XI 1b CHN.
Central Intelligence Agency, People's Republic of China, International Trade Handbook, Washington D.C. October 1976.
Ministry of Commerce of The People's Republic Of China, The History, available at: http://english.mofcom.gov.cn/column/history.shtml, last accessed on 1 May 2020.
National Bureau of Statistics of China, China Statistical Yearbook, Beijing 1982.
Regulations for Taxation on the Transportation Income of Vessels of Foreign Nationality [expired], Peking University Law Repository, Regulation No. CLI.2.378(EN), available at: https://en.pkulaw.cn/Search/SearchLaw.aspx [no permalink available], last accessed on 1 May 2020.
Speech given by President Jiang Zemin at the Sanders Theatre, Harvard University, on 1 November 1997, in: China: President Jiang Zemin Handbook, Strategic Information and Materials, Washington D.C. 2015, pp. 94–98.
Swiss Confederation, Accord de commerce entre la Confédération suisse et la République populaire de Chine, Conclu le 20 décembre 1974, Recueil systématique (RS) 0.946.292.491, available at : https ://www.admin.ch/opc/fr/classified-compilation/19740367/index.html, last accessed on 1 May 2020.
US Department of Agriculture, The Agricultural Situation in the People's Republic of China and Other Communist Asian Countries, Review of 1975 and Outlook for 1976, Foreign Agricultural Economic Report No. 124, Washington D.C. 1976.
US Department of the Interior, Minerals Yearbook 1973, Volume III, Area Reports: International, Washington D.C. 1976, p. 232, available at: https://pubs.er.usgs.gov/publication/70048196, last accessed on 1 May 2020
US Government Printing Office, China: A Reassessment of the Economy, A Compendium of Papers submitted to the Joint Economic Committee, Congress of the United States, 94th Congress, first Session, 10 July 1975, Washington D.C. 1975.
US Government Printing Office, Chinese Economy Post-Mao, A Compendium of Papers submitted to the Joint Economic Committee Congress of the United States, Volume 1: Policy and Performance, 95th Congress, second session, November 9 1978, Washington D.C. 1978.
US Government Printing Office, People's Republic of China: An Economic Assessment, A Compendium of Papers submitted to the Joint Economic Committee of the Congress of the United States, 18 May 1972, Washington D.C. 1972.
US Government Printing Office, Sales of Grain to the Soviet Union, Hearing before the Permanent Subcommittee on Investigations of the Committee on Government Operations, United States Senate, Ninety-Third Congress, second session, 8 October 1974, Washington D.C. 1974.

US Government Printing Office, United States-China Trade Agreement, Hearings before the Subcommittee on Trade of the Committee on Ways and Means, House of Representatives, 96th Congress, First Session on Agreement on Trade Relations between the United States and the People's Republic of China, November 1, 2, and 29 1979, Washington D.C. 1980.

Washenko Steve, Better Harvests in People's Republic of China, Strengthen Push for Economic Development, in: US Department of Agriculture, Foreign Agriculture, October 11, Washington D.C. 1971, p. 4.

Other sources

Commodity.com, China Commodity Imports & Exports, 8 June 2020: How China Continues to Dominate World Trade, available at: https://commodity.com/china/, last accessed on 10 June 2020.

General Agreement on Tariffs and Trade, Article XIX – Proposed Action by the United States, High-Carbon Ferro-Chromium, 3 October 1978, Document L/4702, available at: https://www.wto.org/gatt_docs/English/SULPDF/90950256.pdf, last accessed on 10 May 2020.

Lelyveld Joseph, Chinese Oil-Output Figures Are a Puzzle, *The New York Times*, 9 January 1974, p. 2, available at: https://www.nytimes.com/1974/01/09/archives/chinese-oiloutput-figures-are-a-puzzle-assess-french-revolution.html, last accessed on 1 May 2020.

Malcolm Andrew H., Chinese Disclose That 1976 Quake Was Deadliest in Four Centuries, New York Times of 2 June 1977, p. 1, available at: https://www.nytimes.com/1977/06/02/archives/chinese-disclose-that-1976-quake-was-deadliest-in-four-centuries.html, last accessed on 10 May 2020.

OECD, "Trade openness, in: OECD Science, Technology and Industry Scoreboard 2011, Paris 2011.

OECD, Chinese Economic Performance in the Long Run: The Maoist Transformation and its Impact, Available at https://www.oecd.org/dev/chineseeconomicperformanceinthelongrunthemaoisttransformationanditsimpact.htm, last accessed on 10 May 2020.

Organisation for Economic Cooperation and Development (OECD), Statistics of Foreign Trade, Paris 1977.

Reagan Ronald, "Evil Empire Speech", Voices of Democracy, The U.S. Oratory Project, available at: https://voicesofdemocracy.umd.edu/reagan-evil-empire-speech-text/, last accessed on 15 May 2020.

Ronall Joachim O., China as an Oil-Exporting Nation, *The New York Times*, 5 January 1975, Section F, p. 3, available at: https://www.nytimes.com/1975/01/05/archives/china-as-an-oilexporting-nation-reserves-stir-wide-range-of.html, last accessed on 1 May 2020.

Roser May, Ritchie Hannah, Our World in Data, Long-term price index in food commodities, 1850–2015, World, 1960 to 1989; https://ourworldindata.org/food-prices, last accessed on 15 May 2020.

Shiphub, Shipping ports in China, available at: https://www.shiphub.co/the-biggest-ports-in-china/, last accessed on 1 May 2020.
The China Media Project at the Journalism and Media Studies Centre at Hong Kong University available at: https://chinamediaproject.org/~/views-analysis/, last accessed on 5 May 2020.
The General Agreement on Tariffs and Trade (GATT 1947), available at: https://www.wto.org/english/docs_e/legal_e/gatt47_01_e.htm, last accessed on 1 May 2020.
The World Bank, GDP growth (annual%) – China, available at: https://data.worldbank.org/indicator/NY.GDP.MKTP.KD.ZG?locations=CN, last accessed on 1 April 2020.
U.S. Energy Information Administration, Petroleum & Other Liquids, available at: https://www.eia.gov/dnav/pet/hist/LeafHandler.ashx?n=PET&s=F000000__3&f=A, last accessed on 15 May 2020.
United Nations General Assembly, Third Committee, 73rd Session, 25th and 26th Meetings, 19 October 2018, UN Document No. GA/SHC/4239, Available at: https://www.un.org/press/en/2018/gashc4239.doc.htm, last accessed on 1 April 2020.
Wikipedia in English, Four Modernizations, https://en.wikipedia.org/wiki/Four_Modernizations, last accessed on 15 May 2020.
World Bank national accounts data, https://data.worldbank.org/indicator/NE.TRD.GNFS.ZS?end=1990&start=1960, last accessed on 15 May 2020.
World Bank Statistics, Exports of goods and service (% of GDP) – China, available at: https://data.worldbank.org/indicator/NE.EXP.GNFS.ZS?end=1978&locations=CN&start=1970, last accessed on 1 May 2020.

Literature

Adam Jan, Economic Reforms in the Soviet Union and Eastern Europe since the 1960s, London 1989.
Aiguo L., China and the Global Economy Since 1840, London 2000.
Alexander Robert Jackson, Maoism in the Developed World, Westport 2001.
Allen Robert C., Farm to Factory, A Reinterpretation of the Soviet Industrial Revolution, Princeton and Oxford 2003.
Bahl Raghav, Superpower?: The Amazing Race Between China's Hare and India's Tortoise, Allen Lane 2010.
Bai Liang, Economic Legacies of the Cultural Revolution, Berkeley 2014.
Baldwin Richard, The Great Convergence: Information Technology and the New Globalization, Cambridge and London 2016.
Banister Judith, China's Changing Population, Stanford 1987.
Bartke Wolfgang, Oil in the People's Republic of China, Industry, Structure, Production, Exports, Hamburg 1977.
Berend Ivan T., Central and Eastern Europe, 1944–1993, Detour from the periphery to the periphery, New York 1996.
Bian Yanjie, Work and Inequality in Urban China, New York 1994.
Bicker Robert, The Scramble for China, Foreign Devils in the Qing Empire 1832–1914, London 2011.

BICKERS ROBERT, JACKSON ISABELLA (eds.), Treaty Ports in Modern China, Law, Land and Power, London 2016.

BIEBRICHER THOMAS, Neoliberalismus, Hamburg 2012.

BOCKMAN JOHANNA, Markets in the Name of Socialism, The Left-Wing Origins of Neoliberalism, Stanford 2011.

BRAMALL CHRIS, Chinese Economic Development, London and New York 2009.

BRAMALL CHRIS, The Industrialization of Rural China, Oxford and New York 2007.

BRANDT LOREN, RAWSKI THOMAS G. (eds.), China's Great Economic Transformation, New York 2008.

BRAUDEL FERNAND, Civilization and Capitalism: The Limits of the Possible: The Structures of Everyday, New York 1981.

BRODSGAARD KJELD ERIK (ed.), Critical Readings on the Chinese Communist Party, Leiden and Boston 2017.

BRUN ELLEN, HERSH JACQUES, Soviet-Third World Relations in a Capitalist World: The Political Economy of Broken Promises, New York 1990.

BURNAY MATTHIEU, Chinese Perspectives on the International Rule of Law, Cheltenham and Northampton 2018.

CHANG JUNG, HALLIDAY JON, Mao, The Unknown Story, New York 2005.

CHAURASIA RADHEY SHYAM, History of Modern China, New Delhi 2004.

CHAVANCE BERNARD, HAUSS CHARLES, SELDEN MARK, The Transformation of Communist Systems, New York 2019.

CHEN LUNG-CHU (ed.), The U.S.-Taiwan-China Relationship in International Law and Policy, New York 2016.

CHEN NAI-RUENN, GALENSON WALTER, The Chinese Economy under Maoism, The Early Years, 1949–1969, New Brunswick and London 1969.

CHENG CHU-YUAN, China's Economic Development, 1950–2014, London 2014.

CHENG CHU-YÜAN, Scientific and Engineering Manpower in Communist China, 1949–1963, Washington D.C. 1965.

CHENG, CHU-YUAN, China's Economic Development 1950–2015, London 2014.

CHOSSUDOVSKY MICHEL, Towards Capitalist Restoration? Chinese Socialism After Mao, New York 1986.

CHOW GREGORY C., China's Economic Transformation, third edition, Chichester 2015.

CHUNG HWA, China's Foreign Trade and Management, Hongkong 1978.

COASE RONALD, WANG NING, How China became Capitalist, Houndmills 2012.

CONQUEST ROBERT, The Great Terror, New York 1968.

CORRIGAN PHILIP, RAMSAY HARVIE, SAYER DEREK, Socialist Construction and Marxist Theory: Bolshevism and its Critique, London and Basingstoke 1978.

CUSHING LINCOLN, TOMPKINS ANN, Chinese Posters, Art from the Great Proletarian Cultural Revolution, San Francisco 2007, p. 12.

DANIELS ROBERT VINCENT, The Stalin Revolution: Foundations of Soviet Totalitarianism, Lexington 1972.

DAVIES ROBERT WILLIAM, The industrialization of Soviet Russia, Volume 1: The Socialist Offensive: The Collectivization of Soviet Agriculture, 1929–1930, Cambridge 1980.

DAVIS JOHN, WANG LIMING, China's Grain Economy, The Challenge of Feeding more than a Billion, Oxon and New York 2018.

DAY ALEXANDER F., The Peasant in Postsocialist China, History, Politics and Capitalism, New York 2013.

DELEYNE JAN, Die Chinesische Wirtschaftsrevolution, Eine Analyse der sozialistischen Volkswirtschaft Pekings, Reinbek bei Hamburg 1972.

DENG KENT G., China's Political Economy in Modern Times: Changes and Economic Consequences 1800–2000, New York 2012.

DEUTSCHER ISAAC, Stalin: A Political Biography, Harmondsworth 1966.

DIKÖTTER FRANK, The Cultural Revolution, A People's History 1962–1976, Croydon 2016.

DIKÖTTER FRANK, The Cultural Revolution, A People's History, 1962–1976, London 2016.

DILLON MICHAEL, China, A Modern History, New York 2012.

DITTMER LOWELL, Liu Shao-Chi and the Chinese Cultural Revolution: The Politics of Mass Criticism, London 1974.

DITTMER LOWELL, Liu Shaoqi and the Chinese Cultural Revolution, second revised edition, New York 1998.

DONNITHORNE AUDREY, China's Economic System, Abingdon 1967.

DOUGAN MARK, A Political Economy Analysis of China's Civil Aviation Industry, Oxon and New York 2002.

ECKSTEIN ALEXANDER, China's Economic Revolution, Cambridge 1977.

EGLI ESTHER, Die wirtschaftlichen Veränderungen zwischen 1972–1978 in China, Politische und wirtschaftliche Vorbereitungen auf die Reformen von 1978, Master's thesis at the Institute of History, University of Bern, 2011 (unpublished).

EICHENGREEN BARRY, The European Economy since 1945, Coordinated Capitalism and beyond, Princeton and Oxford 2007.

EISENMANN JOSHUA, Red China's Green Revolution, New York 2018.

EISENMANN JOSHUA, Red China's Green Revolution: Technological Innovation, Institutional Change, and Economic Development Under the Commune, New York, Chichester and West Sussex 2018.

ELLEMAN BRUCE A., PAINE S. C. M., Modern China: Continuity and Change, 1644 to the Present, second edition, Lanham, Boulder, New York and London 2019.

ENGELS FRIEDRICH, Herr Eugen Dühring's Umwälzung der Wissenschaft, third edition, Moscow 1969.

EVANS RICHARD, Deng Xiaoping and the Making of Modern China, London 1993.

FAIRBROTHER MALCOLM, Elites, Democracy, and the Rise of Globalization, New York 2020.

FARBER SAMUEL, Before Stalinism, The Rise and Fall of Soviet Democracy, New York 1990.

FEI XIAOTONG, Rural Development in China: Prospect and Retrospect, Chicago and London 1989.

FENBY JONATHAN, Tiger Head, Snake Tails, New York 2012.

FERGUSON NIALL, MAIER CHARLES S., MANELA EREZ, SARGENT DANIEL J. (eds.), The Shock of the Global, The 1970s in Perspective, Harvard 2011.

FIGES ORLANDO, A People's Tragedy: The Russian Revolution 1891–1924, London 2014.

FRANK RÜDIGER, BURGHART SABINE (eds.), Driving Forces of Socialist Transformation, North Korea and the Experience of Europe and East Asia, Vienna 2009.

FRIEDMAN JEREMY, Shadow Cold War: The Sino-Soviet Competition for the Third World, Chapel Hill 2015.

GADDIS JOHN LEWIS, The Cold War: A New History, New York 2005.

GAO WENQIAN, Zhou Enlai, The Last Perfect Revolutionary, New York 2007.

GARVER JOHN M., China's Quest, The History of the Foreign Relations of the People's Republic of China, New York 2016.

GERTH KARL, Unending Capitalism, How Consumerism Negated China's Communist Revolution, Cambridge 2020.

GEWIRTZ JULIAN B., Unlikely Partners, Chinese Reformers, Western Economists, and the Making of Global China, Cambridge 2017.

GHOSH ARUNABH, Making it Count: Statistics and Statecraft in the Early People's Republic of China, Princeton and Woodstock 2020.

GILL GRAEME J., Stalinism, London 1990.

GOH EVELYN, Constructing the U.S. Rapprochement with China 1961–1974, New York 2005.

GOH EVELYN, Meeting the China Challenge: The U.S. in southeast Asian Regional Security Strategies, Policy Studies No. 16, Washington D.C. 2005.

GOODMAN DAVID S., Centre and Province in the People's Republic of China: Sichuan and Guizhou, 1955–1965, London, New York and La Rochelle 1986.

GREENHALGH SUSAN, WINCKLER EDWIN, Governing China's Population: From Leninist to Neoliberal Biopolitics, Berkeley 2005.

GREGOR ANTHONY JAMES, Marxism and the Making of China, New York 2014.

GRZYBOWSKI KAZIMIERZ, Soviet International Law and the World Economic Order, Durham and London 1987.

GUO RONGXING, An Introduction to the Chinese Economy, The Driving Forces behind Modern Day China, Singapore 2010.

GURLEY JOHN G., China's Economy and the Maoist Strategy, New York and London 1976.

HAN ZHEN, ZHANG WEIWEN, Contemporary Value Systems in China, Beijing 2018.

HARRISON SELIG S., China, Oil and Asia, Conflict Ahead?, New York 1977.

HARVEY DAVID, A Brief History of Neoliberalism, New York 2005.

HARVEY DAVID, Spaces of Capitalism, A Theory of Uneven Geographical Development, London 2019.

HEILMANN SEBASTIAN, Red Swan, How Unorthodox Policy Making Facilitated China's Rise, Hong Kong 2018

HEINRICH MICHAEL, Kritik der politischen Ökonomie, fifth edition, Stuttgart 2007.

HERRMANN ULRIKE, Kein Kapitalismus ist auch keine Lösung, second edition, Frankfurt am Main 2019.

HINTON HAROLD C., The People's Republic of China: A Handbook, Dawson 1979.

HOBSBAWM ERIC, How to Change the World: Reflections on Marx and Marxism, New Haven 2011.

HOFFMANN, CHARLES, Work Incentive Practices and Policies in the People's Republic of China, 1953–1965, New York 1967.

HONG ZHOU, JUN ZHANG, Towards a Society with Social Protection for All: A Concise History of Social Security Transformation in Modern China, Singapore 2017.

HOWE CHRISTOPHER, Wage Patterns and Wage Policy in Modern China, 1919–1972, New York 1973.

HSIAO GENE T., The Foreign Trade of China: Policy, Law and Practice, Berkeley, Los Angeles and London 1977.
HSU IMMANUEL C. Y., China Without Mao, second edition, New York and Oxford 1990.
HUA SHIPING, Chinese Legal Culture and Constitutional Order, New York 2019.
HUDSON CHRISTOPHER (ed.), The China Handbook, Oxon 1997.
IKEDA SANFORD, Dynamics of the Mixed Economy: Toward a Theory of Interventionism, London 1997.
JENCKS HARLAN W., Politics and Professionalism in the Chinese Army, 1945–1981, New York 1982.
JONES DAVID M. (ed.), Basic Principles of Civil Law in China, New York 1989.
KAPLE DEBORAH A., Dream of a Red Factory: The Legacy of High Stalinism in China, New York and Oxford 1994.
KATZ ALYSSA, The Influence of the Machine: The U.S. Chamber of Commerce and the Corporate Capture of American Life, New York 2015.
KAVEN CARSTEN, Die Durchsetzung der Reformpolitik in China: Analyse eines Ereignisses, Berlin 2008.
KEAY JOHN, China: A History, London 2009.
KEITH RONALD C., Deng Xiaoping and China's Foreign Policy, New York 2018.
KEITH RONALD C., Diplomacy of Zhou Enlai, New York 1989.
KIM SAMUEL S., China, the United Nations and World Order, Princeton 1979.
KISSINGER HENRY, Years of Upheaval, New York, London, Toronto, Sydney, 2011.
KONDRATIEFF NIKOLAI, HÄNDELER ERIK (ed.), Die langen Wellen der Konjunktur, second edition, Moers 2016.
KORNAI JÁNOS, The Socialist System, The Political Economy of Communism, Princeton 1992.
KORT MICHAEL, The Soviet Colossus, History and Aftermath, seventh edition, Armonk and London 2010.
KOTZ DAVID, WEIR FRED, Revolution from Above: The Demise of the Soviet System, London 1997.
KOTZ DAVID, WEIR FRED, Russia's Path: From Gorbachev to Putin, The Demise of the Soviet System and the New Russia, London 2007.
KRISTOF NICHOLAS D., Rise of China, New York 1993.
KROEBER ARTHUR R., China's Economy, What everyone needs to know, Oxford 2016.
KUEH Y. Y., Agricultural Instability in China, 1931–1990: Weather, Technology, and Institutions, Oxford 1995.
KUNTZE PETER, China nach Mao: Rechtsputsch in der Volksrepublik, Munich and Vienna 1978.
LAFEBER WALTER, America, Russia, and the Cold War, 1945–2006, tenth edition, Boston 2008.
LAMB MALCOLM L., Directory of Officials and Organizations in China, Volume 1, third edition, New York 2003.
LARDY NICHOLAS, Markets over Mao: The Rise of Private Business in China, Washington D.C. 2014.
LAVIGNE MARIE, The Economics of Transition: From Socialist Economy to Market Economy, second edition, London 1999.

LEE CHAE-JIN, China and Japan: New Economic Diplomacy, Stanford 1984.

LEE KUAN YEW, From Third World to First, The Singapore Story: 1965–2000, Singapore 2000.

LEIPOLD HELMUT (ed.), Sozialistische Marktwirtschaften, Munich 1975.

LENIN VLADIMIR, Der Imperialismus als höchstes Stadium des Kapitalismus, Munich 2001.

LENIN VLADIMIR, Our Foreign and Domestic Position and Party Tasks, in: Collected Works, fourth edition, Moscow 1965.

LENIN VLADIMIR, The State and Revolution, Class Society and the State, Collected Works, Volume 25, Moscow 1964.

LEUNG LAIFONG (ed.), The Writings of Mao Zedong, 1949–1976, Volume II: January 1956-December 1957, Armonk 1992.

LEVINE STEVEN I., PANTSOV ALEXANDER V., Mao: The Real Story, New York 2012.

LEVINSON MARC, The Box: How the Shipping Container Made the World Smaller and the World Economy Bigger, Princeton 2010.

LI CHEN, China's Centralized Industrial Order: Industrial reform and the rise of centrally controlled big business, New York 2015.

LI DANHUI, SHEN ZHIHUA, After Leaning to One Side: China and Its Allies in the Cold War, Stanford 2011.

LI HUA-YU, Mao and the Economic Stalinization of China, 1948–1953, Oxford 2006.

LI KWOK-SING (ed.), A Glossary of Political Terms of the People's Republic of China, Hong Kong 1995.

LI ZHISUI, The Private Life of Chairman Mao, New York 1996.

LIBRACH JAN, The Rise of the Soviet Empire: A Study of Soviet Foreign Policy, New York 1964.

LIM TAI WEI, Oil in China: From Self-reliance to Internationalization, Singapore 2010.

LOVELL JULIA, Maoism: A Global History, London 2019.

LOVELL JULIA, The Opium War, Drugs, Dreams and the making of China, Oxford 2011.

LÜTHI LORENZ, Cold Wars, Asia, the Middle East, Europe, Cambridge 2020.

LÜTHI LORENZ, The Sino-Soviet Split, Cold War in the Communist World, Woodstock 2008.

MACKAY DEMERJIAN LOUISA (ed.), The Age of Dystopia: One Genre, Our Fears and Our Future, Newcastle upon Tyne 2016.

MANDEL ERNEST, Die Krise, Weltwirtschaft 1974–1986, Hamburg 1987.

MAO YUSHI, ZHAO NONG, YANG XIAOJING, Food Security and Farm Land Protection in China, Singapore 2013.

MARCUSE HERBERT, Die Gesellschaftslehre des sowjetischen Marxismus, second edition, Neuwied and Berlin 1969.

MARSH JOHN, Liberal Delusion: The roots of our current moral crisis, Bury St. Edmunds 2012.

MARX KARL, Das Kapital, Kritik der politischen Ökonomie, Cologne 2009.

MARX KARL, ENGELS FRIEDRICH, ADORATSKIJ VLADIMIR VIKTOROVIC (ed.), Die Deutsche Ideologie, Vienna and Berlin 1932.

MAXWELL NEVILLE (ed.), China's Road to Development, second edition, Amsterdam 1979.

McAloon David William, Leon Trotsky and the struggle for power in communist Russia, 1921–1923, University of Richmond Scholarship Repository Honors Theses, Richmond 2001.

McDermott Kevin, Agnew Jeremy, The Comintern, A History of International Communism from Lenin to Stalin, Houndmills and London 1996.

McGregor Richard, The Party: The Secret World of China's Communist Rulers, London 2010.

Meadows Donella H., Meadows Dennis L., Randers Jorgen, Behrens William W. III., The Limits to Growth, A Report for the Club of Rome's Project on the Predicament of Mankind, New York 1972.

Medvedev Roy, On Stalin and Stalinism, Oxford 1979.

Meisner Maurice, Mao's China and After, third edition, New York 1999.

Metzler Mark, Capital as Will and Imagination: Schumpeter's Guide to the Postwar Japanese Miracle, Ithaca and London 2013.

Meyer Jan, Kosta Jiri, Volksrepublik China, Ökonomisches System und wirtschaftliche Entwicklung, Frankfurt am Main and Cologne 1976.

Mitcham Chad J., China's Economic Relations with the West and Japan, 1949–79: grain, trade and diplomacy, Oxon 2005

Mühlhahn Klaus, Making China Modern: From the Great Qing to Xi Jinping, London 2019.

Mulder Nicholas, The Economic Weapon, The Rise of Sanctions as a Tool of Modern War, New Haven and London 2022.

Näth Marie L., Chinas Weg in die Weltpolitik, Berlin and New York 1976.

Nathan Andrew James, Scobell Andrew, China's Search for Security, New York and Chichester 2014.

Naughton Barry, Growing Out of the Plan: Chinese Economic Reform, 1978–1993, Cambridge 1995.

Ogden Chris, China and India: Asia's Emergent Great Powers, Cambridge 2017

On Kit Tam, China's Agricultural Modernization, The Socialist Mechanization Scheme, London, Sydney, Dover and New Hampshire 1985.

Osterhammel Jürgen, China und die Weltgesellschaft, Vom 18. Jahrhundert bis in unsere Zeit, Munich 1989.

Palmer James, The Death of Mao: The Tangshan Earthquake and the Birth of the New China, London 2012.

Paloczi-Horvath George, Mao Tse-Tung, Emperor of the Blue Ants, London 1962.

Pantsov, Alexander V., Levine Steven I., Mao: The Real Story, New York 2012.

Paxton John (ed.), The Statesman's Year-Book, Statistical and Historical Annual of the States of the World for the Year 1975–1976, London and Basingstoke 1975.

Péan Pierre, Après Mao les managers, Paris 1977.

Pei Minxin, From Reform to Revolution The Demise of Communism in China and the Soviet Union, Harvard 1998.

Perkins Dwight D., China's Modern Economy in Historical Perspective, Stanford 1975.

Perkins Dwight D., Rural Small-Scale Industry in the People's Republic of China, Berkeley, Los Angeles and London 1977.

Perkins Dwight D., The Economic Transformation of China, Singapore 2015.

Pfister Christian, Das 1950er Syndrom, Der Weg in die Konsumgesellschaft, second edition, Bern, Stuttgart und Wien 1996.

Pinker Steven, The Blank Slate: The Modern Denial of Human Nature, New York 2016.

Pomeranz Kenneth, The Great Divergence: China, Europe and the Making of the Modern World Economy, Princeton and Oxford 2000.

Potter Pitman B., From Leninist Discipline to Socialist Legalism, Peng Zhen on Law and Political Authority in the PRC, Stanford 2003.

Pribram Karl, A History of Economic Reasoning, Baltimore 1983.

Price Victoria Curzon, Industrial Policies in the European Community, London 1981.

Priestland David, Weltgeschichte des Kommunismus, Munich 2009.

Prybyla Jan S., Market and Plan under Socialism: The Bird in the Cage, Stanford 1987.

Putterman Louis, Continuity and Change in China's Rural Development: Collective and Reform Eras in Perspective, New York and Oxford 1993.

Qu Jingdong, Fu Chunhui, Wen Xiang, Organizational Transition and Systematic Governance, Labor Relations in Enterprises, Singapore 2018.

Reardon Lawrence C., The Reluctant Dragon: Crisis Cycles in Chinese Foreign Economic Policy, Washington D.C. 2002.

Rosas João Cardoso and Ferreira Ana Rita (eds.), Left and Right: The Great Dichotomy Revisited, Newcastle upon Tyne, 2013.

Ross Robert S. (ed.), China, the United States and the Soviet Union: Tripolarity and Policy Making in the Cold War, London 1993.

Rozman Gilbert, The Chinese Debate on Soviet Socialism, 1978–1985, Princeton 1987.

Rudolf Joachim, Tester Elisabeth, China – der nächste Horizont, Ein Kompass für Anleger und Unternehmer, Zürich 2016.

Sah Raaj K., Stiglitz Joseph E., Peasants versus City-Dwellers: Taxation and the Burden of Economic Development, Oxford 2002.

Scharping Thomas, Birth Control in China, 1949–2000: Population Policy and Demographic Development. London 2003.

Schell Orville, Delury John, Wealth and Power, China's Long March to the Twenty-First Century, New York 2013.

Schenkel Elmar, Unterwegs nach Xanadu, Begegnungen zwischen Ost und West, Frankfurt am Main 2021.

Schneider Eberhard, SED – Programm und Statut von 1976: Text, Kommentar, Didaktische Hilfen, Opladen 1977.

Schoenenhals Martin, The paradox of Power in a People's Republic of China Middle School, New York 1993.

Schram Stuart (ed.), Zedong Mao, Mao's Road to Power: Revolutionary Writings, 1912–49, Volume IV, The Rise and Fall of the Chinese Soviet Republic 1931–1934, New York 2015.

Schumpeter Joseph A., Kapitalismus, Sozialismus und Demokratie, Stuttgart 2005

Scranton Philip, Enterprise, Organization and Technology in China: A Socialist Experiment, 1950–1971, Cham 2019.

Seitz Konrad, China, Eine Weltmacht kehrt zurück, fifth edition, Munich 2006.

Sharma Shalendra D., China and India in the Age of Globalization, Cambridge 2009.

Sik Ota, Plan and Market Under Socialism, New York 2018.

SING LAM LAI, The International Environment and China's Twin Models of Development, Bern 2007.
SNOW EDGAR, Red Star over China, first revised and enlarged edition, New York 1968.
SOLINGER DOROTHY J., Chinese Business under Socialism: The Politics of Domestic Commerce, 1949–1980, Berkeley, Los Angeles and London 1984.
SOLOMOU SOLOMOS, Phases of Economic Growth 1850–1973: Kondratieff Waves and Kuznets Swings, Cambridge, New York and Melbourne 1990.
SONG LIGANG, WOO WING THYE (eds.), China's Dilemma: Economic Growth, the Environment and Climate Change, Canberra 2008.
SPENCE JONATHAN D., The Search for Modern China, New York 1990.
SPUFFORD FRANCIS, Red Plenty: Inside the Fifties' Soviet dream, London 2010.
STALIN JOSEPH, Economic Problems of Socialism in the USSR, New York 1952.
STEWART FRANCES, Technology and Underdevelopment, second edition, London and Basingstoke 1982.
STRAUSS JULIA (ed.), The History of the People's Republic of China, 1949–1976, Cambridge 2007.
STROHM HOLGER, Umweltschutz in der VR China, Hamburg 1978.
SUTELA PEKKA, Economic Thought and Economic Reform in the Soviet Union, Cambridge 1991.
SWAIN NIGEL, Hungary, The Rise and Fall of Feasible Socialism, New York 1992.
TALAS BARNA, Economic Reforms and Political Attempts in China 1979–1989, Budapest 1991.
TALEB NASSIM NICHOLAS, The Black Swan: The Impact of the Highly Improbable, New York 2007.
TALLEY CHRISTIAN, Forgotten Vanguard: Informal Diplomacy and the Rise of United States-China Trade, Notre Dame 2018.
TANG TSOU, The Cultural Revolution and Post-Mao Reforms, A Historical Perspective, Chicago and London 1986.
TAO YITAO, LU ZHIGUO (eds.), China's Economic Zones, Design Implementation and Impact, Reading 2012.
TEIWES FREDERICK C., SUN WARREN, Paradoxes of Post-Mao Rural Reform: Initial Steps Toward a New Chinese Countryside, 1976–1981, New York 2016.
TEIWES FREDERICK C., SUN WARREN, The End of the Maoist Era, Chinese Politics During the Twilight of the Cultural Revolution, 1972–1976, Armonk and London 2008.
TEIWES FREDERICK C., SUN WARREN, The Tragedy of Lin Biao: Riding the Tiger During the Cultural Revolution, London 1996.
TEN BRINK TOBIAS, China's Kapitalismus, Entstehung, Verlauf, Paradoxien, Frankfurt and New York 2013.
TERRILL ROSS, Mao, A Biography, Stanford 1980.
TIEN H. YUAN, China's Strategic Demographic Initiative, New York 1991.
TOFFLER ALVIN, The Third Wave, New York 1980; and Toffler Alvin, Future Shock, New York 1970.
TROTSKY LEON, EASTMAN MAX (ed.), The Revolution Betrayed, Mineola 2004.
VILLAUME POUL, MARIAGER RASMUS, PORSDAM HELLE (eds.), The "Long 1970s": Human Rights, East-West Détente and Transnational Relations, New York 2016.

VOGEL EZRA F., China and Japan: Facing History, London 2019.

VOGEL EZRA F., Deng Xiaoping and the Transformation of China, Cambridge and London 2013.

WANG GABE T., China's Population: Problems, Thoughts and Policies, New York 1999.

WANG JOSEPH EN-PAO (ed.), Selected Legal Documents of the People's Republic of China, Arlington 1976.

WANG LIMING, DAVIS JOHN, China's Grain Economy: The Challenge of Feeding More Than a Billion, New York 2000.

WANG NING, Rise of the Consumer in Modern China, Reading 2012.

WEATHERLEY ROBERT, Mao's Forgotten Successor: The Political Career of Hua Guofeng, Houndmills 2010.

WEGGEL, OSKAR, Das Aussenhandelsrecht der Volksrepublik China, Hamburg 1976.

WEIL ROBERT, Red Cat, White Cat, China and the Contradictions of "Market Socialism", New York 1996.

Wemheuer Felix (ed.), Jahrbuch für Historische Kommunismusforschung 2020, Berlin 2020.

WEMHEUER FELIX, A Social History of Maoist China, Conflict and Change, 1949–1976, Singapore 2019.

WEMHEUER FELIX, Famine Politics in Maoist China and the Soviet Union, New Haven 2014.

WEMHEUER FELIX, Mao Zedong, Reinbek bei Hamburg 2009.

WESTAD ODD ARNE, The Global Cold War: Third World Interventions and the Making of our Times, Cambridge 2007.

WHITAKER DONALD P, SHINN RINN-SUP et al., Area Handbook for the People's Republic of China, Washington D.C. 1972.

WHITE TYRENE, China's Longest Campaign: Birth Planning in the People's Republic, 1949–2005, Ithaca 2007.

WOLF MICHAEL, Chinese Propaganda Posters, Cologne 2011.

WU YICHING, The Cultural Revolution at the Margins, Cambridge and London 2014.

XUE MUQIAO, Sozialismus in China, Erfolge, Fehlschläge, Reformperspektiven, Hamburg 1982.

YANG CHI-JEN, Energy Policy in China, New York 2017.

YASHENG HUANG, Capitalism with Chinese characteristics, Cambridge 2008.

ZHANG JUN, Wages in China: An Economic Analysis, Hong Kong 2012.

ZHAO SUISHENG (ed.), Chinese Foreign Policy: Pragmatism and Strategic Behaviour, New York 2004.

ZUBOK VLADISLAV M., A Failed Empire: The Soviet Union in the Cold War from Stalin to Gorbachev, Chapel Hill 1964.

ZWEIG DAVID, Agrarian Radicalism in China, 1968–1981, Cambridge 1989.

Articles in journals and edited volumes

ABRAHAMSON PETER, European Welfare States: Neoliberal Retrenchment, Developmental Reinforcement or Plural Evolutions, in: KYUNG-SUP C., FINE B., WEISS L. (eds.),

Developmental Politics in Transition, International political Economy Series, London 2012, pp. 92–113.

Adamiak Richard, The "Withering Away" of the State: A Reconsideration, in: The Journal of Politics, Vol. 32, No. 1, February 1970, pp. 3–18.

Aghion Philippe, Burgess Robin, Redding Stephen, Zilibotti Fabrizio, The Unequal Effects of Liberalization: Evidence from Dismantling the License Raj in India, Swiss National Centre of Competence in Research on Financial Valuation and Risk Management (Finrisk), Working Paper No. 426, September 2007.

Ahn Byung-Joon, The Cultural Revolution and China's Search for Political Order, in: The China Quarterly, No. 58, April-June 1974, pp. 249–285.

Altehenger Jennifer, Social Imperialism and Mao's Three Worlds: Deng Xiaoping's Speech at the UN General Assembly, 1974, in: Hammersley Rachel (ed.), Revolutionary Moments: Reading Revolutionary Texts, London 2015, pp. 175–182.

Andors Stephen P., China's Industrialization in Historical Perspective, in: Maxwell (ed.) 1979, pp. 27–39.

Ash Robert, Squeezing the Peasants: Grain Extraction, Food Consumption and Rural Living Standards in Mao's China, in: The China Quarterly, No. 188, The History of the PRC (1949–1976), December 2006, pp. 959–998.

Bachman David, Differing Visions of China's Post-Mao Economy: The Ideas of Chen Yun, Deng Xiaoping, and Zhao Ziyang, in: Asian Survey, Vol. 26, No. 3, March 1986, pp. 292–321.

Bajt Alexander, Investment Cycles in European Socialist Economies, A Review Article, in: Jounral of Economic Literature, Vol. 9, No. 1, March 1971, pp. 53–63.

Balasubramanyam Vudayagi, Fu Xiaolan, Township and Village Enterprises in China, in: Journal of Development Studies, Vol. 39, No. 4, pp. 27–46.

Baudelle Guy, Peyrony Jean, Striving for Equity: Polycentric Development Policies in France, in: Built Environment, Vol. 31, No. 2, 2005, pp. 103–111.

Bauer Tamás, Investment Cycles in Planned Economies, in: Acta Oeconomica, Vol. 21, No. 3, 1978, p. 243–260.

Beaulac Stephane, The Westphalian Model in Defining International Law: Challenging the Myth, in: Australian Journal of Legal History, No. 8, 2004, pp. 181–213.

Bendix Reinhard, Reflections on Charismatic Leadership, in: Asian Survey, No. 6, Vol. 7, June 1967, p. 341–352.

Berger Roland, Economic Planning in China, in: Maxwell (ed.) 1979, pp. 169–203.

Birney Mayling, Decentralization and Veiled Corruption Under China's "Rule of Mandates", in: World Development, Draft Paper March 2013, available at: http://dx.doi.org/10.2139/ssrn.2279059, last accessed on 1 May 2020.

Bogdan Nina, October of 1917 Revisited – Revolution or Coup d'état?, in: Footnotes: A Journal of History, Vol. 1, 2017. Available at https://journals.uair.arizona.edu/index.php/UAHISTJRNL/article/view/20152, last accessed on 1 May 2020.

Bramall Chris, A Late Maoist Industrial Revolution? Economic Growth in Jiangsu Province (1966–1978), in: The China Quarterly, Vol. 240, December 2019, pp. 1039–1065.

Bramall Chris, The Last of the Romantics? Maoist Economic Development in Retrospect, in: The China Quarterly, No. 187, September 2006, pp. 686–692.

BRASS TOM, The Agrarian Myth, the "new" populism and the "new right", in: The Journal of Peasant Studies, Vol. 24, No. 4, pp. 201–245.

BRUNNER JAMES A., TAOKA GEORGE M., Marketing and Negotiating in the People's Republic of China: Perceptions of American Businessmen Who Attended the 1975 Fair, in: Journal of International Business Studies, Vol. 8, No. 2, Autumn/Winter 1977, pp. 69–82.

BURDEKIN RICHARD C.K., Preobrazhensky's Theory of Primitive Socialist Accumulation, in: Journal of Contemporary Asia, Vol. 19, No. 3, 1989, pp. 297–307.

Cambridge Dictionary, Economy, available at https://dictionary.cambridge.org/dictionary/english/economy, last accessed on 1 April 2020.

CAMERON GREGORY, Oikos and Economy: The Greek Legacy in Economic Thought, in: PhaenEx, Vol. 3, No. 1, Spring/Summer 2008, pp. 112–133.

CAMILLERI JOSEPH, Southeast Asia in China's Foreign Policy, Institute of Southeast Asian Studies of Singapore ISEAS, Occasional Paper No. 29, April 1975.

CARNEIRO CORRÊA VIEIRA, From Third World Theory to Belt and Road Initiative: International Aid as a Chinese Foreign Policy Tool, in: Contexto Internacional, Vol. 41, No. 3, September/December 2019, pp. pp.529-551.

CHAI TRONG R., The Chinese Academy of Sciences in the Cultural Revolution: A Test of the "Red and Expert" Concept, in: The Journal of Politics, Vol. 43, No. 4, November 1981, pp. 1215–1229.

CHAN KAM WING and ZHANG LI, The Hukou System and Rural-Urban Migration in China: Processes and Changes, in: The China Quarterly, No. 160, December 1990, pp. 818–855.

CHANG C.M., Communism and Nationalism in China, in: Foreign Affairs, Vol. 28, No. 4, July 1950, pp. 548–565.

CHANG GENE, YANG SHENKE, CHANG KATHRYN, The Immiserizing Growth During the Period of China's Cultural Revolution, in: The Chinese Economy, Vol. 51, No. 5, pp. 387–196.

CHANG PARRIS H., The Anti-Lin Piao and Confucius Campaign: Its Meaning and Purposes, in: Asian Survey, Vol. 14, No. 10, October 1974, pp. 871–886.

CHANG PARRIS H., The Cultural Revolution and Chinese higher education: Change and Controversy, in: The Journal of General Education, Vol. 26, No. 3, Fall 1974, pp. 187–194.

CHEN JOHN-REN, China's Way of Economic Transition, in: Transition Studies Review, Vol. 21, September 2005, pp. 315–333.

CHEN LEIN-LEIN, DEVEREUX JOHN, The Iron Rice Bowl: Chinese Living Standards 1952–1978, in: Comparative Economic Studies, No. 3, Vol. 2 2017, pp. 261–310.

CHEN NAI-RUENN, Industrial Development in Mainland China, in: Asian Affairs, Vol. 2, No. 5, 1975, pp. 276–294.

CHEN XIN-ZHU J., China and the US Trade Embargo, 1950–1972, Vol. 13, No. 2, October 2006, pp. 169–186.

CHENG JOSEPH Y. S., Mao Zedong's Perception of the World in 1968–1972: Rationale for the Sino-American Rapprochement, in: The Journal of American-East Asian Relations, Vol. 7, No. 2/4, Fall-Winter 1998, pp. 241–261.

CHUNG YEN-LIN, The Unknown Standard-Bearer of the Three Red Banners: Peng Zhen's Roles in the Great Leap Forward, in: The China Journal, No. 74, July 2015, pp. 129–143.

CIAO RICHARD, ZAGORIA DONALD, The Nature of Mainland Chinese Economic Structure, Leadership and Policy (1949–1969), in U.S. Arms Controls and Disarmament Agency, February 1972, pp. 181–182.

CLARK COLIN, Economic Development in Communist China, in: Journal of Political Economy, Vol. 84, No. 2, April 1976, pp. 239–264.

CLARKE SIMON, The Marxist Theory of Overaccumulation and Crisis, in: Science & Society, Vol. 54, No. 4, Winter 1990/1991, pp. 442–467.

ČOBELJÍC N., STOJANOVIĆ R., The theory of investment cycles in a socialist economy, in: Eastern European Economics, Vol. 7, No. 1–2, 1968 und 1969.

COHEN JEROME ALAN, China's Changing Constitution, in: The China Quarterly, No. 76, December 1978, pp. 794–841.

COHEN, JEROME ALAN, PARK, CHOON-HO, The Politics of China's Oil Weapon, in: Foreign Policy, No. 20, 1975, pp. 28–49.

CRAFTS NICHOLAS and TONIOLO GIANNI, A Restructured Economy: From the Oil Crisis to the Financial Crisis, 1973–2009, in: CRAFTS NICHOLAS and TONIOLO GIANNI (eds.), The Oxford Handbook of postwar European History, Oxford 2012, pp. 406–422.

DAI WUSAN, Communication Technology, in: LU YONGXIANG (ed.), A History of Chinese Science and Technology, Volume 3, Heidelberg, New York, Dordrecht and London 2015, pp. 405–513.

DAY RICHARD B., REVIEW: On "Primitive" and Other Forms of Socialist Accumulation: A Review of Preobrazhensky, Bukharin and Trotsky, in: Labor / Le Travail, Vol 10, Autumn 1982, pp. 165–174.

DE SILVA, S.B.D., The Region: Economic Trends – Inflation, Industrialization, and Growth, in: Southeast Asian Affairs, 1975, pp. 5–14.

DERNBERGER ROBERT F., Radical Ideology and Economic Development in China: The Cultural Revolution and its Impact on the Economy, in: Asian Survey, Vol. 12, No. 12, The Cultural Revolution and its Aftermath, December 1972, pp. 1048–1065.

DERNBERGER ROBERT F., The Role of the Foreigner in China's Economic Development, in: PERKINS DWIGHT H. (ed.), China's Modern Economy in Historical Perspective, Stanford 1975, pp. 19–48.

DESHINGKAR GIRI, Mao Zedong's Military Thought: A Perspective, in: China Report, No. 31, Vol. 1, February 1995, pp. 101–107.

DIAO RICHARD K., The Impact of the Cultural Revolution on China's Economic Elite, in: The China Quarterly, Vol. 42, June 1970, pp. 65–87.

DINGXIN ZHAO, The Han Bureaucracy: Its Origin, Nature and Development, in: SCHEIDEL WALTER (ed.), State Power in Ancient China and Rome, New York 2015, pp. 56–89.

DIRLIK ARIF, The New Culture Movement Revisited: Anarchism and the Idea of Social Revolution in New Culture Thinking, in: Modern China, Vol. 11, No. 3, July 1985, pp. 251–300.

DITTMER LOWELL, On China's Rise, in: BRANTLY (ed.) 2010, pp. 39–60.

DITTMER LOWELL, WU YU-SHAN, The Modernization of Factionalism in Chinese Politics, in: World Politics, Vol. 47, No. 4, July 1995, pp. 467–494.

ECKLUND GEORGE, Protracted Expropriation of Private Business in Communist China, in: Pacific Affairs, No. 3, 1963, pp. 238–249.

ECKSTEIN ALEXANDER, Economic Development Prospects and Problems in China, in: The Annals of the American Academy of Political and Social Science, Vol. 402, No. 1, 1972, pp. 107–116.

ECKSTEIN ALEXANDER, Sino-American Trade Prospects and Policy, in: The American Economic Review, Vol. 64, No. 2, May 1974, pp. 294–299.

EICH PETER, The Common Denominator: Late Roman Imperial Bureaucracy from a Comparative Perspective, in: SCHEIDEL WALTER (ed.), State Power in Ancient China and Rome, New York 2015, pp. 90–149.

EILAND MICHAEL D., Military Modernization and China's Economy, in: Asian Survey, Vol. 17, No. 12, December 1977, pp. 1143–1157.

ELLIOTT JOHN E., Marx's "Grundrisse": Vision of Capitalism's Creative Destruction, in: Journal of Post Keynesian Economics, Vol. 1, No. 2, Winter 1978–1979, pp. 148–169.

ELLMAN MICHAEL, Economic Reform in China, in: International Affairs, Vol. 62, No. 3, Summer 1986, pp. 423–442.

ERB GUY F., The Trade Reform Act of 1974, in: Challenge, Vol. 18, No. 1, 1975, pp. 60–61.

ERSHOVA IRINA, ERSHOV ALEKSEI, Development of a strategy of import substitution, in: Procedia Economics and Finance, No. 39, 2016, pp. 620–624.

ESTRIN SAUL, Yugoslavia: The Case of Self-Managing Market Socialism, in: Journal of Economic Perspectives, Vol. 5, No. 4, Fall 1991, pp. 187–194.

FAN LIANG-SHING, The Economy and Foreign Trade of China, in: Law and Contemporary Problems, Vol. 38, No. 2, Trade with China, Summer-Autumn 1973, pp. 249–259.

FARR JASON, Point: The Westphalia Legacy and the Modern Nation-State, in: International Social Science Review, Vol. 80, No. 3/4, 2005, pp. 156–159.

FEN SING-NAN, The May 7 Cadre Schools in the People's Republic of China: 1968–1976, in: Administration & Society, Vol. 18, No. 1, May 1986, pp. 29–43.

FITZPATRICK SHEILA, The Great Departure, Rural-Urban Migration in the Soviet Union, 1929–1933, in: WILLIAM G., ROSENBERG, SIEGELBAUM LEWIS H. (eds.), Social Dimensions of Soviet Industrialization, Bloomington and Indianapolis 1993, pp. 15–40.

FOLLY MARTIN H., Cold War Dichotomies, in: Journal of American Studies, Vol. 34, No. 3, 2000, pp. 503–508.

FROLIC, B. MICHAEL, Reflections on the Chinese Model of Development, in: Social Forces, Vol. 57, No. 2, December 1978, pp. 384–418.

GABRISCH HUBERT, HÖLSCHER JENS (eds.), The Successes and Failures of Economic Transition, The European Experience, London 2006.

GALLAGHER JOHN, ROBINSON RONALD, The Imperialism of Free Trade, in: The Economic History Review, Vol. 6, No. 1, 1953, pp. 1–15.

GAO X.M., WAILES ERIC J., CRAMER GAIL L., Partial Rationing and Chinese Urban Household Food Demand Analysis, in: Journal of Comparative Economics, No. 22, 1996, pp. 43–62.

GARDNER JOHN, Liu Shaoqi and the Cultural Revolution: The Rise and Fall of a Chosen Successor, in: GARDNER JOHN (ed.), Chinese Politics and the Succession to Mao, London 1982, pp. 9–39.

GARNAUT ANTHONY, Hard Facts and Half-Truths: The New Archival History of China's Great Famine, in: China Information, Vol. 27, No. 2, 2013, pp. 223–246.

GARVER JOHN W., The Indian Factor in Recent Sino-Soviet Relations, in: The China Quarterly, No. 125, March 1991, pp. 55–85.

GELB ALAN, JEFFERSON GARY, SINGH INDERJIT, Can Communist Economies Transform Incrementally? The Experience of China, in: NBER Macroeconomics Annual, Vol. 8, 1993, pp. 87–150.

GERLACH CHRISTIAN, Die Welternährungskrise 1972–1975, in: Geschichte und Gesellschaft, Vol. 31, Nr. 4, October-December 2005, pp. 546–585.

GOLDMAN MERLE, China's Anti-Confucian Campaign, in: The China Quarterly, No. 63, September 1975, pp. 435–462.

GOLDMANN JOSEF, Fluctuations and Trend in the Rate of Economic Growth in Some Socialist Countries, in: Economics of Planning, Vol. IV, 1964.

GRAY JACK, The Economics of Maoism, in: Bulletin of the Atomic Scientists, Vol. 25, No. 2, 1969, pp. 42–51.

GREGOR JAMES A., CHANG MARIA HSIA, Maoism and Marxism in Comparative Perspective, in: The Review of Politics, Vol. 40, No. 3, July 1978, pp. 307–327.

GREGOR JAMES A., CHANG MARIA XIA, Anti-Confucianism: Mao's Last Campaign, in: Asian Survey, Vol. 19, No. 11, November 1979, pp. 1073–1092.

GUEULLETTE AGOTA, Soviet Concepts of Foreign Trade 1917–1945, in: Soviet and Eastern European Foreign Trade, Vol. 27, No. 3, Fall 1991, pp. 3–23.

GURLEY JOHN G., Rural Development in China 1949–75, and the Lessons to be Learned from it, in: Maxwell (ed.) 1979, pp. 5–25.

HAAPANEN JARKKO, Adaptation to World Trends, A Rereading of the May Fourth Movement Radicalization, in: Jyväskylä Studies in Education, Psychology and Social Research, No. 463, 2013.

HAMEL HANNELORE, Sozialistische Marktwirtschaft in der DDR, Hinwendung und Abkehr, in: LEIPOLD HELMUT (ed.), Sozialistische Marktwirtschaften, Munich 1975, pp 72–103.

HAO YENPING, A "New Class" in China's Treaty Ports: The Rise of the Comprador-Merchants, in: The Business History Review, Vol. 44, No. 4, Winter 1970, pp. 446–459.

HARDING NEIL, Leninism and Stalinism, in: HARDING NEIL (ed.), Leninism, London 1996, pp. 243–263.

HARRISON MARK, Trends in Soviet labor productivity, 1928–85: War, postwar recovery, and slowdown, in: European Review of Economic History, Vol. 2, No. 2, August 1998, pp. 171–200.

HAYFORD CHARLES W., Mao's Journeys to the West, in: CHEEK TIMOTHY (ed.), A Critical Introduction to Mao, New York 2010, pp. 313–331.

HE YIMIN, ZHOU MINGCHANG, The 156 Projects and New China's Industrial and Urban Development, in: ZHANG XINGXING (ed.), Selected Essays on the History of Contemporary China, Leiden and Boston 2015, pp. 54–70.

HERMANN FELIX, Technology Gap, transnationale Integrationsbemühungen und nationale Egoismen: Der Aufbruch des Rats für gegenseitige Wirtschaftshilfe in das digitale Zeitalter, in: WEMHEUER FELIX (ed.) 2020, pp.209-223.

HEUSER ROBERT, Chinese Law of Foreign Trade: An Interview, in: The China Quarterly, No. 73, March 1973, pp. 159–165.

HEWETT EDBERT ANSGAR, Economic Reform in the Soviet Union, in: The Brookings Review, Vol. 2, No. 3, Spring 1984, pp. 8–11.

HIDASI GABOR, China's Economy in the early 1970s, in: Acta Oeconomica, Vol. 9, No. 1, 1972, pp. 81–94.

HIDASI GABOR, China's Economy in the mid-1970s and its Development Perspective, in: Acta Oeconomica, Vol. 14, No. 4, 1975, pp. 355–381.

HOEFFDING OLEG, Sino-Soviet Economic Relations, 1959–1962, in: The Annals of the American Academy of Political and Social Science, Vol. 349, September 1963, pp. 94–105.

HOFFMAN LISA, Autonomous choices and patriotic professionalism: On governmentality in late-socialist China, in: Economy and Society, Vol. 35, No. 4, 2006, pp. 550–570.

HOFFMAN LISA, Urban Modeling and Contemporary Technologies of City-Building in China: The Production of Regimes of Green Urbanism, in: ROY ANANYA, ONG AIHWA, Worlding Cities: Asian Experiments and the Art of being Global, Hoboken 2011, pp. 55–76.

HOFFMANN CHARLES, The Maoist Economic Model, in: Journal of Economic Issues, Vol. 5, No. 3, September 1971, pp. 12–27.

HÖHME HANS-JOACHIM, Charakter und Besonderheiten der gegenwärtigen kapitalistischen Wirtschaftskrise, in: Krise der kapitalistischen Weltwirtschaft 1974/76, IPW-Forschungshefte, Vol. 11, No. 2, 1976, pp. 7–40.

HOOK BRIAN, WILSON DICK AND YAHUDA MICHAEL (eds.), Quarterly Chronicle and Documentation, in: The China Quarterly, No. 61, June 1975, pp. 338–406.

HOWE CHRISTOPHER, Labor Organization and Incentives in Industry, before and after the Cultural Revolution, in: SCHRAM STUART (ed.), Authority, Participation, and Cultural Change in China, Cambridge 1974, pp. 233–256.

HSU ROBERT, Grain Procurement and Distribution in China's Rural Areas: Post-Mao Policies and Problems, in: Asian Survey, Vol. 24, No. 12, December 1984, pp. 1229–1246.

HU XUETAO, The Physical Properties of Reservoir Fluids, in: HU XUETAO, HU SHUYONG, JIN FAYANG, HUANG SU, Physics of Petroleum Reservoirs, second edition, Beijing 2017, pp. 165–324.

HUANG JIKUN, OTSUKA KEIJIRO, ROZELLE SCOTT, Agriculture in China's Development, Past Disappointments, Recent Successes and Future Challenges, in: BRANDT LOREN, RAWSKI THOMAS G. (eds.), China's Great Economic Transformation, New York 2008, pp. 467–505.

HUBBELL BRAM, Eurocentrism and the Myth of East Asian Isolation, Decolonizing the teaching of world history, 25 January 2016. Available at: https://www.liberatingnarratives.com/eurocentrism-and-the-myth-of-east-asian-isolation/, accessed on 1 October 2022.

HUENEMANN RALPH W., Urban Rationing in Communist China, in: The China Quarterly, No. 26, April-June 1966, pp. 44–57.

HYER ERIC, China's Policy of Conciliation and Reduction and its Impact on Boundary Negotiations and Settlements in the Early 1960s, CWIHP Working Paper 85, December 2017, available at: https://www.wilsoncenter.org/publication/chinas-policy-con

ciliation-and-reduction-and-its-impact-boundary-negotiations-and, last accessed on 10 May 2020.

ICKES BARRY W., Cyclical Fluctuations in Centrally Planned Economies: A Critique of the Literature, in: Soviet Studies, Vol. 38, No. 1, January 1986, pp. 36–52.

JESSOP ROBERT, Mode of Production, in: EATWELL JOHN, MILGATE MURRAY, NEWMAN PETER, Marxian Economics, London 1990, pp. 289–296.

JOFFE ELLIS, The Chinese Army after the Cultural Revolution: The Effects of Intervention, in: The China Quarterly, Vol. 55, September 1977, pp. 450–477.

JOHNSON HARRY G., The International Monetary Crisis of 1971, in: The Journal of Business, Vol. 46, No. 1, January 1973, pp. 11–23.

JOSEPH WILLIAM A., A Tragedy of Good Intentions: Post-Mao Views of the Great Leap Forward, in: Modern China, Vol. 12, No. 4, October 1986, pp. 419–457.

JUPE ROBERT, FUNNELL WARWICK, Neoliberalism, consultants and the privatization of public policy formulation: The case of Britain's rail industry, in: Critical Perspectives on Accounting, Vol. 29, June 2015, pp. 65–85.

KA-KUI TSE, Agricultural Collectivization and Socialist Construction: The Soviet Union and China, in: Dialectical Anthropology, Vol. 2, No. 3, August 1977, pp. 199–221.

KANG CHAO, The Growth of a Modern Cotton Textile Industry and the Competition with Handicrafts, in: PERKINS (ed.) 1975, pp. 167–202.

KAUFMAN ALISON, The "Century of Humiliation", then and now: Changing Chinese Perceptions of the International Order, APSA Toronto Meeting Paper 2009.

KAUPPINEN MARKO, Canon vs. Charisma, "Maoism" as an Ideological Construction, Jyväskylä Studies in Education, Psychology and Social Research, No. 296, Jyväskylä 2006.

KAY JOHN ANDERSON, MORRIS CHARLES NICHOLAS, POOLE KENYON EDWARDS, LINDBECK ASSSAR, DUE JOHN F., Encyclopedia Britannica, Government economic policy, available at https://www.britannica.com/topic/government-economic-policy , last accessed on 1 April 2020.

KELLER WOLFGANG, LI BEN, SHIUE CAROL H., China's foreign trade: Perspectives from the past 150 years, in: The World Economy, No. 36, Vol. 6, 2011, pp. 853–892.

KEYFITZ NATHAN, Alfred Sauvy, in: Population and Development Review, Vol. 16, No. 4, December 1990, pp. 727–733.

KING WHYTE MARTIN, Bureaucracy and Modernization in China: The Maoist Critique, in: American Sociological Review, Vol. 38, No. 2, April 1973, pp. 149–163.

KIRBY WILLIAM C., Technocratic Organization and Technological Development in China: The Nationalist Experience and Legacy, 1928–1953, in: SIMON DENIS FRED, GOLDMAN MERLE (eds.), Science and Technology in Post-Mao China, Harvard 1989, pp. 23–44.

KLEIN DONALD W., The Foreign Trade Apparatus, in: LI VICTOR H. (ed.), Law and Politics in China's Foreign Trade, Hong Kong 1977, pp. 308–329.

KLINGHOFFER, ARTHUR JAY, Sino-Soviet Relations and the Politics of Oil, in: Asian Survey, Vol. 16, No. 6, 1976, pp. 540–552.

KODITSCHEK THEODORE, How to Change History, in: History and Theory, Vol. 52, October 2013, pp. 433–450.

KOLLER JOHN M., Philosophical Aspects of Maoist Thought, in: Studies in Soviet Thought, Vol. 14, No. 1/2, March-June 1974, pp. 47–59.

KONG HANBING, The Transplantation and Entrenchment of the Soviet Economic Model in China, in: BERNSTEIN THOMAS P., LI HUA-YU, China Learns from the Soviet Union, 1949-present, Plymouth 2010, pp. 153–166.

KONTOROVICH VLADIMIR, The Military Origins of Soviet Industrialization, in: Comparative Economic Studies, April 2015, pp. 1–24.

KOSTA JIRI, Die tschechoslowakische Wirtschaftsreform der sechziger Jahre, in: LEIPOLD (ed.) 1975.

KOTKIN, STEPHEN, The Kiss of Debt: The East Bloc goes Borrowing, in: FERGUSON et al. 2010, pp. 80–93.

KRANCBERG SIGMUND, The Socialist World System: Alliance or Instrument of Domination?, in: Studies in Soviet Thought, Vol. 30, No. 1, July 1985, pp. 55–63.

KRASNER STEPHEN D., Compromising Westphalia, in: International Security, Vol. 20, No. 3, Winter 1995/1996, pp. 115–151.

KRAUS RICHARD CURT, The Limits of Maoist Egalitarianism, in: Asian Survey, Vol. 16, No. 11, November 1976, pp. 1081–1096.

KRAUS WILLY, The Policy of the Three Red Banners. The Second Five-Year Plan, 1958–1962, and the Consolidation Phase, 1963–1965, in: Economic Development and Social Change in the People's Republic of China, New York 1982, pp. 107–167.

KRISTOF NICHOLAS D., The Rise of China, in: Foreign Affairs, November/December 1993, available at: https://www.foreignaffairs.com/articles/asia/1993-12-01/rise-china, last accessed on 1 April 2020.

KUEH Y. Y., Mao and Agriculture in China's Industrialization: Three Antitheses in a 50-Year Perspective, in: The China Quarterly, No. 187, September 2006, pp. 700–723.

LEE GREGORY, Chinese Migrants and the "Infundation" Metaphor: Risk, Representation, Repression: Constructing and Manipulating Fear of the Chinese Other, Framing Risk: Hazard Perceptions as a Crucial Factor in Imagining East Asia, East Asia Net Workshop Paper, June 2007.

LEE HONG YUNG, The Politics of Cadre Rehabilitation since the Cultural Revolution, in: Asian Survey, Vol. 18, No. 9, September 1978, pp. 934–955.

LEE RENSSELAER W. III, Ideology and Technical Innovation in Chinese Industry, 1949–1971, in: Asian Survey, Vol. 12, No. 8, August 1972, pp. 647–661.

LEE THOMAS H.C., Review: Imagining the Chinese Examination System: Historical Nature and Modern Usefulness, in: China Review International, Vol. 13, No. 1, Spring 2006, pp. 1–12.

LENG SHAO-CHUANG, The Role of Law in the People's Republic of China as Reflecting Mao Tse-Tung's Influence, in: Journal of Criminal Law and Criminology, Vol. 68, No. 3, September 1977, pp. 356–373.

LEOGRANDE WILLIAM M., An Investigation into the "Young Marx" Controversy, in: Science & Society, Vol. 41, No. 2, Summer 1977, pp. 129–151.

LEUNG CYNTHIA B., WANG YIPING, Influences of the Cultural Revolution on Chinese Literacy Instruction, in: LEUNG CYNTHIA B., RUAN JIENING (eds.), Perspectives on Teaching and Learning Chinese Literacy in China, New York and London 2012, pp. 49–60.

LEVY RICHARD, His views on the Soviet Union's Political Economy, New Light on Mao Chapter 2, in: The China Quarterly, Vol. 61, Special issue, pp. 95–117.

LI CHOH MING, China's Industrial Development, 1958–1963, in: The China Quarterly, No. 17, January-March 1964, pp. 3–38.

LI XING, The Chinese Cultural Revolution Revisited, in: The China Review, Vol. 1, No. 1, Fall 2001, pp. 137–165.

LIONNET PHILIPPE, Anpassungen der Wirtschaftspolitik in der Volksrepublik China: die Scharnierjahre 1974/1975, in: WEMHEUER FELIX (ed.), Jahrbuch für historische Kommunismusforschung, Berlin 2020, pp. 155–172.

LOVBRAEK ASBJORN, The Chinese Model of Development, in: Journal of Peace Research, Vol. 13, No. 3, 1976, pp. 207–226.

LOVELL DAVID, Marx's Utopian legacy, in: The European Legacy, Vol. 9, No. 5, 2004, pp. 629–640.

LYNN MARTIN, British Policy, Trade, and Informal Empire in the Mid-Nineteenth Century, in: PORTER ANDREW (ed.), The Oxford History of the British Empire Volume III, The 19th century, Oxford 1999, pp. 101–121.

MARANGOS JOHN, Consistency and Viability of the Liberman-Kosygin Reforms: The Limited Market Relations Socialist Model, in: MARANGOS JOHN (ed.), Consistency and Viability of Socialist Economic Systems, New York 2013, pp. 93–105.

MAROT JOHN, The New Economic Policy Was the Alternative to Stalinism, Jacobin Magazine, 12 August 2019, available at: https://jacobinmag.com/2019/12/new-economic-policy-stalinism-nep-bolsheviks-october-revolution, last accessed on 5 May 2020.

MARTIN JOHN, An Attempt to Define Socialism, in: The American Economic Review, Vol. 1, No. 2, April 1911, pp. 347–354.

MARX KARL, Critique of the Gotha Program as abridged in: Die Neue Zeit, Vol. 1, No. 18, 1890/1891, available at: https://www.marxists.org/archive/marx/works/1875/gotha/ch01.htm, accessed on 5 May 2020.

MCMULLEN DAVID L., The Chinese Examination System in Dynastic China: Did it select the brightest and best?, in: Sunway Academic Journal, Vol. 8, 2011, pp. 1–11.

MEAD ROBERT W., China's agricultural reforms: The importance of private plots, in: China Economic Review, No. 11, 2000, pp. 54–78.

MEIER KENNETH J., Bureaucracy and Democracy: The Case for More Bureaucracy and Less Democracy, in: Public Administration Review, Vol. 57, No. 3, May/June 1997, pp. 193–199.

MELBY, JOHN F., Maoism as a World Force, in: The Annals of the American Academy of Political and Social Science, Vol. 402, July 1972, pp. 26–39.

MEYSKENS COVELL, Third Front Railroads and Industrial Modernity in Late Maoist China, in: Twentieth-Century China, Vol. 40, No. 3, October 2015, p. 238–260.

MILONAKIS DIMITRIS, New market socialism: a case for rejuvenation or inspired alchemy?, in: Cambridge Journal of Economics, Vol. 27, No. 1, January 2003, pp. 97–121.

MODONGAL SHAMEER, Development of nationalism in China, in: Cogent Social Sciences, Vol. 2, No. 1, 2016, available at: http://dx.doi.org/10.1080/23311886.2016.1235749, last accessed on 1 April 2020.

MORGAN JOHN W., Marxism-Leninism: The ideology of 20th Century communism, in: International Encyclopedia of the Social and Behavioral Sciences, second edition, Vol. 14, pp. 656–662.

MORRISON KENT, Domestic Politics and Industrialization in China: The Foreign Trade Factor, in: Asian Survey, Vol. 18, No. 7, July 1978, pp. 687–705.

NAKAJIMA MINEO, Foreign relations: from the Korean War to the Bandung Line, in: MACFARQUHAR RODERICK, FAIRBANK JOHN K. (eds.), The Cambridge History of China, Volume 14: The People's Republic, Part 1: The Emergence of Revolutionary China 1949–1965, Cambridge 1987, pp. 259–290.

NAUGHTON BARRY, Deng Xiaoping, The Economist, in: The China Quarterly, No. 135, Special Issue: Deng Xiaoping: An Assessment, September 1993, pp. 491–514.

NAUGHTON BARRY, The Socialist Era, 1949–1978: Big Push Industrialization and Policy Instability, in: NAUGHTON BARRY (ed.), The Chinese economy, transitions and growth, Cambridge Mass and London 2007, pp. 55–84.

NAUGHTON BARRY, The Third Front: Defense Industrialization in the Chinese interior, in: The China Quarterly, No. 115, September 1988, pp. 351–386.

NAYYAR DEEPAK, Globalization, history and development: a tale of two centuries, in: Cambridge Journal of Economics, Vol. 30, No. 1, January 2006, pp. 137–159.

NEE VICTOR, Organizational Dynamics of Market Transition: Hybrid Forms, Property Rights, and Mixed Economy in China, in: Administrative Science Quarterly, Vol. 37, No. 1, March 1992, pp. 1–27.

NEU AXEL D., Die Entfaltung der internationalen Erdölwirtschaft seit 1950, in: PFISTER CHRISTIAN (ed.), Das 1950er Syndrom, Der Weg in die Konsumgesellschaft, second edition, Bern, Stuttgart and Vienna 1996, pp.179-200.

NEVELING PATRICK, Export Processing Zones and Global Class Formation, in: Carrier James, Kalb Don (eds.), Anthropologies of Class: Power, Practice and Inequality, Cambridge 2015, pp. 164–182.

NEVELING PATRICK, Export Processing Zones/Special Economic Zones, in: Callan H. (ed.), The International Encyclopaedia of Anthropology, Hoboken 2018, pp. 2179–2185.

NOLAN PETER, ASH ROBERT, China's Economy on the Eve of Reform, in: The China Quarterly, No. 144, 1995, pp. 980–998.

NOLAN PETER, Collectivization in China: Some comparisons with the USSR, in: The Journal of Peasant Studies, Vol. 3, No. 2, 1976, pp. 192–220.

NONINI DONALD M., Is China Becoming Neoliberal, in: Critique of Anthropology, Vol. 28, No. 2, 2008, pp. 145–176.

Ó GRÁDA CORMAC, Great Leap into Famine: A Review Essay, in: Population and Development Review, Vol. 37, No. 1, 2011, pp. 191–202.

OLDHAM C.H.G., The challenge of China, in: The Business Quarterly, Vol. 32, No. 2, 1967, pp. 48–50.

OLIVEIRA G., Cyclical Growth Under Collectivism, Kyklos, Vol. 13, No. 2, 1960, pp. 229–255.

OLLÉ MANEL, China in the World: Historiographical Reflection, in: ELIZALDE MARÍA DOLORES, WANG JIANLANG, China's Development from a Global Perspective, Newcastle upon Tyne 2017, pp. 7–11.

PAINE SUZANNE, Balanced development: Maoist conception and Chinese practice, in: World Development, Vol. 4, No. 4, April 1976, pp. 277–304.

Palgrave McMillan, History of Economic Thought, available at: https://www.palgrave.com/gp/blogs/business-economics-finance-management/exploring-economic-history/history-of-economic-thought, last accessed on 1 April 2020.

Patnaik Utsa, The Economic Ideas of Mao Zedong on Agricultural Transformation and its Relation to Capital Formation and Industrialization, in: China Report, Vol. 31, No. 1, 1995, pp. 87–100.

Paying for the grey, The Economist, 5 April 2014, available at: https://www.economist.com/china/2014/04/05/paying-for-the-grey, last accessed on 1 May 2020.

Perelman Michael, Natural Resources and Agriculture under Capitalism: Marx's Economic Model, in: American Journal of Agricultural Economics, Vol. 57, No. 4, November 1975, pp. 701–704.

Perkins Dwight H., A Conference on Agriculture, in: The China Quarterly, No. 67, September 1976, pp. 596–610.

Perkins Dwight H., China's Prereform Economy in World Perspective, in: Womack Brantly (ed.), China's Rise in Historical Perspective, Plymouth 2010, pp. 109–128.

Perotti Enrico C., Sun Laixiang, Zou Liang, State-Owned versus Township and Village Enterprises in China, in: Brada Josef C., Wachtel Paul, Tao Yang Dennis, China's Economic Development, London 2014, pp. 33–59

Peters Florian, "Rette sich, wer kann", Die wirtschaftlichen Reformanläufe der polnischen Kommunisten in den 1980er-Jahren, in: Wemheuer (ed.) 2020, pp. 105–119.

Pfeffer Richard M., Mao and Marx in the Marxist-Leninist Tradition: A Critique of "The China Field" and a Contribution to a Preliminary Reappraisal, in: Modern China, Vol. 2, No. 4, October 1976, pp. 421–460.

Powell Ralph L., Soldiers in the Chinese Economy, in: Asian Survey, Vol. 11, No. 8, August 1971, pp. 742–760.

Prybyla Jan S., Industrial Development in China: 1967–76 and 1976–78, in: Challenge, Vol. 21, September/October 1978, pp. 7–13.

Prybyla, Jan S., Work Incentives in the People's Republic of China, in: Weltwirtschaftliches Archiv, Vol. 112, No. 4, 1976, pp. 761–791.

Qiang Zha, "Walking on Two Legs", A Policy Analysis of China's Move to Mass Higher Education, in: State and Market in Higher Education Reforms, Comparative and International Education book series Vol. 13, 2012, pp. 167–180.

Qin Yaqing, Why is There No Chinese International Relations Theory?, in: International Relations of the Asia-Pacific, Vol. 7, No. 3, 2007, pp. 313–340.

Radice Hugo, The Developmental State under Global Neoliberalism, in: Third World Quarterly, Vol. 29, No. 6, 2008, pp. 1153–1174.

Rawski Thomas G., China's Economy after Fifty Years: Retrospect and Prospect, in: International Journal, Vol. 55, No. 1, Winter 1999/2000, pp. 62–79.

Rawski Thomas G., The Growth of Producer Industries, 1900–1971, in: Perkins Dwight H. (ed.), China's Modern Economy in Historical Perspective, Stanford 1975, pp. 203–234.

Reuland James M., GATT and State-Trading Countries, in: Journal of World Trade Law, No. 3, 1975, pp.318-339.

Reynolds Lloyd G., China as a Less Developed Economy, in: The American Economic Review, Vol. 65, No. 3, June 1975, pp. 418–428.

ROBERTS ANDREW, The State of Socialism: A Note on Terminology, in: Slavic Review, Vol. 63, No. 2, Summer 2004, pp. 349–366.

ROBERTS PAUL CRAIG, "War Communism": A Re-examination, in: Slavic Review, Vol. 29, No. 2, June 1970, pp. 238–261.

ROBERTSON JAMES M., The Socialist World in the Second Age of Globalization: An Alternative History?, in Markets, Globalization & Development Review, Vol. 3, No, 2, Article 5.

ROGOFF KENNETH, SIBERT ANNE, Elections and Macroeconomic Policy Cycles, in: The Review of Economic Studies, Vol. 55, No. 1, January 1988, pp. 1–16.

ROSTOW WALT WITHMAN, Kondratieff, Schumpeter, and Kuznets: Trend Periods Revisited, in: The Journal of Economic History, Vol. 35, No. 4, December 1975, pp. 719–753.

ROTHBARD MURRAY N., The End of Socialism and the Calculation Debate Revisited, in: Review of Austrian Economics, Vol. 5, No. 2, 1991, pp. 51–76.

RUBIN SEYMOUR J., Most-Favored-Nation Treatment and the Multilateral Trade Negotiations: A Quiet Revolution, in: Maryland Journal of International Law, Vol. 6, No. 2, 1981, pp. 221–241.

RUSSO ALESSANDRO, How Did the Cultural Revolution End? The Last Dispute between Mao Zedong and Deng Xiaoping, 1975, in: Modern China, Vol. 39, No. 3, May 2013, pp. 239–279.

SANCHEZ-SIBONY OSCAR, Energie, die Sowjetunion und der Kampf um Kapital nach dem Zusammenbruch des Bretton-Woods-Systems, in: WEMHEUER 2020, pp. 193–208.

SARTORI GIOVANNI, Will Democracy Kill Democracy? Decision-Making by Majorities and by Committees, in: Government and Opposition, Vol. 10, No. 2, 1 April 1975, pp. 131–158.

SCHMIDT SEBASTIAN, To Order the Minds of Scholars: The Discourse of the Peace of Westphalia in International Relations Literature, in: International Studies Quarterly, Vol. 55, No. 3, September 2011, pp. 601–623.

SCHRAM STUART R., Mao Zedong a Hundred Years On: The Legacy of a Ruler, in: The China Quarterly, No. 137, March 1994, pp. 125–143.

SCHRAN PETER, China's price stability: Its meaning and distributive consequences, in: Journal of Comparative Economics, Vol. 1, No. 4, December 1977, pp. 367–388.

SCHURMANN FRANZ, China's „New Economic Policy" – Transition of Beginning, in: The China Quarterly, Vol. 17, March 1964, pp. 65–91.

SHAMBAUGH DAVID, Deng Xiaoping: The Politician, in: The China Quarterly, No. 135, Special Issue: Deng Xiaoping: An Assessment, September 1993, pp. 457–490.

SHIXIU BAO, Deterrence Revisited: Outer Space, in: China Security, Winter 2007, pp. 2–11.

SICULAR TERRY, Grain Pricing: A Key Link in Chinese Economic Policy, in: Modern China, Vol. 14, No. 4, October 1988, pp. 451–486.

SIDEL R., Self-help and mutual aid in the People's Republic of China, in: KATZ ALFRED H., BENDER EUGENE I. (eds.), The Strength in Us: Self-Help Groups in the Modern World, New York 1976, pp. 216–228.

SIGEL LOUIS T., On the "Two Roads" and Following Our Own Path: The Myth of the "Capitalist Road", in: The Australian Journal of Chinese Affairs, No. 7, 1982, pp. 55–83.

SINGER BABIARZ KIMBERLY, EGGLESTON KAREN, MILLER GRANT, ZHANG QIONG, An exploration of China's mortality decline under Mao: A provincial analysis, 1950–80, in: Population Studies, Vol. 69, No. 1, 2015, pp. 39–56.

SINGH AJIT, Die politische Ökonomie der sozialistischen Entwicklung in China seit 1949, in: HENNICKE PETER (ed.), Probleme des Sozialismus und der Übergangsgesellschaften, Frankfurt am Main 1973, pp. 392–433.

SOCHOR ZENOVIA A., Soviet Taylorism Revisited, Soviet Studies, Vol. 33, No. 2, April 1981, pp. 246–264.

SOMMER DEBORAH A., Images for Iconoclasts: Images of Confucius in the Cultural Revolution, in: JONES DAVID (ed.), East-West Connections: Review of Asian Studies, Vol. 7, No. 1, 2007, pp. 1–23.

SOO FRANCIS, China and Modernization: Past and Present, A Discussion, in: Studies in Soviet Thought, Vol. 38, No. 1, Modernization in China, July 1989, pp. 3–54.

STIGLITZ JOSEPH E., Beggar-Thyself versus Beggar-Thy-Neighbour Policies: The Dangers of Intellectual Incoherence in Addressing the Global Financial Crisis, in: Southern Economic Journal, Vol. 66, No. 1, July 1999, pp. 1–38.

STRAUSS JULIA, Morality, Coercion and State Building by Campaign in the Early PRC: Regime Consolidation and After, 1949–1956, in: The China Quarterly, No. 188, December 2006, pp. 891–912.

SUISHENG ZHAO, Beijing's Perception of the International System and Foreign Policy Adjustment after the Tiananmen Incident, in: SUISHENG ZHAO (ed.), Chinese Foreign Policy, Pragmatism and Strategic Behavior, New York 2016, chapter 8.

SULLIVAN MICHAEL, Louis T. Sigel and "Two Line Struggle Analysis": The Myth of the Objective Standard of Socialism, in: The Australian Journal of Chinese Affairs, Vol. 8, July 1982, pp. 65–74.

TANG TSOU, Mao Tse-tung Thought, the last Struggle for Succession, and the Post-Mao Era, in: The China Quarterly, No. 71, September 1977, pp. 498–527.

TANG ZAIFU, Land and Property Taxation and Fiscal Reform and Land Market Control, in: NI PENGFEI, ZOU LINHUA, GAO GUANGCHUN, JIANG XUEMEI (eds.), Housing Reform and China's Real Estate Industry, Singapore 2020, pp. 117–159.

TEIWES FREDERICK C., SUN WARREN, China's New Economic Policy under Hua Guofeng: Party Consensus and Party Myths, in: The China Journal, Vol. 66, July 2011, pp. 1–23.

TEIWES FREDERICK C., SUN WARREN, The First Tiananmen Incident Revisited: Elite Politics and Crisis Management at the End of the Maoist Era, in: Pacific Affairs, Vol. 77, No. 2, Summer 2004, pp. 211–235.

TEIWES FREDERICK C., The Origins of Rectification: Inner-Party Purges and Education before liberation, in: The China Quarterly, No. 65, March 1976, pp. 15–53.

TERRILL ROSS, China and the World: Self-Reliance or Interdependence?, in: Foreign Affairs, Vol. 55, No. 2, January 1977, p. 298.

TIDRICK GENE, China: Socialism and Reform, 1950–1990, in: GRILLI ENZO, SALVATORE DOMINICK (eds.), Handbook of Comparative Economic Policies, Vol. 4, 1994.

TIMMER PETER, Reflections on food crises past, in: Food Policy, Nr. 35, 2010, pp. 1–11.

TRETIAK DANIEL, The Canton Fair: An Academic Perspective, in: The China Quarterly, No. 56, October-December 1973, pp. 740–748.

TRUMAN EDWIN M., The End of the Bretton Woods International Monetary System, Peterson Institute for International Economics Working Paper, October 2017.

TSAI WEN-HUI, Mass Mobilization Campaigns in Mao's China, in: American Journal of Chinese Studies, Vol. 6, No. 1, April 1999, pp. 21–48.

TYSON LAURA D'ANDREA, The debt crisis and adjustment responses in Eastern Europe: a comparative perspective, in: International Organization, Vol. 40, No. 2, Spring 1986, pp. 239–285.

U EDDY, Dangerous Privilege: The United Front and the Rectification Campaign of the Early Mao Years, in: The China Journal, No. 68, July 2012, pp. 32–57.

UHALLEY STEPHEN, QIU JIN, The Lin Biao Incident: More Than Twenty Years Later, in: Pacific Affairs, Vol. 66, No. 3, Autumn 1993, pp. 386–398.

URBINA DANTE A., RUIZ-VILLAVERDE ALBERTO, A Critical Review of Homo Economicus from Five Approaches, in: American Journal of Economics and Sociology, Vol. 78, No. 1, 2019, pp. 63–93.

WAKE CHRISTOPHER, The Myth of Zheng He's Great Treasure Ships, in: International Journal of Maritime History, Vol. 16, No. 1, June 2004, pp. 59–75.

WALLERSTEIN IMMANUEL, The Rise and Future Demise of the World Capitalist System: Concepts for Comparative Analysis, in: Comparative Studies in Society and History, Vol. 16, No. 4, September 1974, pp. 387–415.

WANG RUOSHUI, The maid of Chinese politics, Mao Zedong and his philosophy of struggle, in: Journal of Contemporary China, Vol. 4, No. 10, pp. 66–80.

WANG YAN, YAO YUDONG, Sources of China's Economic Growth, 1952–99, Incorporating Human Capital Accumulation, The World Bank, Policy Research Working Paper 2650, July 2001.

WATANABE SHINO, Implementation System: Tools and Institutions, in: OHASHI HIDEO, SHIMOMURA YASUTAMI (eds.), A Study of China's Foreign Aid, an Asian Perspective, New York 2013, pp. 58–81.

WATSON, ANDREW, Agricultural Reform and China's Foreign Trade, in: The Australian Journal of Chinese Affairs No. 14, August 1985, pp. 39–63.

WEI CHUNJUAN NANCY, Barefoot Doctors: The Legacy of Chairman Mao's Healthcare, in: WEI CHUNJUAN NANCY, BROCK DARRYL E., (eds.), Mr. Science and Chairman Mao's Cultural Revolution, Plymouth 2013, pp. 251–280.

WEIGELIN-SCHWIEDRZIK SUSANNE, LIU HONG, Vergessene Partner im Reformprozess: Der Dialog der VR China mit reform-kommunistischen Strömungen in Osteuropa (1977–1987), in: WEMHEUER (ed.) 2020, pp. 37–54.

WEMHEUER FELIX, Dealing with Responsibility for the Great Leap Famine in the People's Republic of China, in: The China Quarterly, No. 201, March 2010, pp. 176–194.

WEMHEUER FELIX, Great Leap Famine in the People's Republic of China, in: The China Quarterly, No. 201, March 2010, pp. 176–194.

WEMHEUER FELIX, Sites of Horror: Mao's Great Famine, in: The China Journal No. 66, 2011, pp. 155–162.

WEMHEUER FELIX, Über den "Marktsozialismus" hinaus: Ein Vergleich der chinesischen Reform und Öffnung mit den Reformzyklen in Osteuropa seit den 1960er-Jahren, in: WEMHEUER (ed.) 2020, pp. 15–36.

WESTAD ODD ARNE, The Great Transformation, China in the Long 1970s, in: FERGUSON NIALL, MAIER CHARLES S., MANELA EREZ, SARGENT DANIEL J. (eds.), The Shock of the Global, The 1970s in Perspective, Harvard 2011, pp. 65–79.

WHEELER SNOW, LOIS, China's Foreign Trade and Aid, in: Journal of World Trade Law, Vol. 11, Issue 2, 1977, pp. 101–120.

WHYTE MARTIN K., Sub-optimal Institutions but Superior Growth: The Puzzle of China's Economic Boom, in: China's Economic Dynamics: A Beijing Consensus in the Making?, London 2014, pp. 15–47.

WILSON DICK, China's trading prospects, in: Far Eastern Economic Review, Vol. 45, No. 8, 1964, pp. 309–311.

WU FULONG, How neoliberal is China's Reform: The Origins of Change during transition, in: Eurasian Geography and Economics, Vol. 51, No. 5, 2010, pp. 619–631.

XI LINA, CORTESE CORINNE, ZHANG EAGLE, Exploring hegemonic change in China: a case of accounting evolution, in: Asian Review of Accounting, Vol. 21, No. 2, pp. 113–127.

XIUNG JAMES C. (ed.), Symposium: The trial of the "Gang of Four" and its implications in China, Occasional Papers in Asian Studies, Vol. 40, No. 3, 1981.

YAN HAIRONG, Neoliberal Governmentality and Neohumanism: Organizing Suzhi/Value Flow through Labor Recruitment Networks, in: Cultural Anthropology, Vol. 18, No. 4, pp. 493–523.

YANG DAN, LIU ZIMIN, Study on the Chinese farmer cooperative economy organizations and agricultural specialization, in: Agricultural Economy, No. 58, Vol 3, 2012, pp. 135–146.

YEH WEN-HSIN, Middle County Radicalism: The May Fourth Movement in Hangzhou, in: The China Quarterly, Vol. 140, December 1994, pp. 903–925.

YOUNG GRAHAM, On the Mass Line, in: Modern China, Vol. 6, No. 2, April 1980, pp. 225–240.

ZHANG LI, Urbanization, farm dependence and population change in China, in: GREEN GARY PAUL (ed.), Handbook of Rural Development, Cheltenham and Northampton 2013, pp. 294–314.

ZHENG SONG, STORESLETTEN KJETIL, ZILIBOTTI FABRIZIO, Growing Like China, in: American Economic Review, Vol. 101, February 2011, pp. 196–233.

ZHOU QINGSHENG, Capital Construction Investment and its Regional Distribution in China, in: International Journal of Urban and Regional Research, Vol. 17, No. 2, June 1993, pp. 159–177.

ZHOU YUN, Question of ethnic group formulation in the Chinese census, in: China Population and Development Studies, No. 3, 2019, pp. 67–83.

ZHU HONGWEN, PETERS MICHAEL A., Social governance, education and socialist rule of law in China, Educational Philosophy and Theory, Vol. 51 No. 7, 2019, pp. 670–673.

ZHU XIAODONG, Understanding China´s Growth: Past, Present, and Future, in: Journal of Economic Perspectives, Vol. 26, No. 4, Fall 2012, pp. 103–124.

ZOLOTAREV VLADIMIR IVANOVICH, Main Stages of Development of USSR Foreign Trade 1917–1967, in: Soviet and Eastern European Foreign Trade, Vol. 4, No. 2, Summer 1968, pp. 3–34.

Zweig David, "Developmental Communities" on China's Coast: The Impact of Trade, Investment, and Transnational Alliances, in: Comparative Politics, Vol. 27, No. 3, April 1995, pp. 253–274.

Historical Sciences

Aurora G. Morcillo
(In)visible Acts of Resistance in the Twilight of the Franco Regime
A Historical Narration

January 2022, 332 p., pb., ill.
50,00 € (DE), 978-3-8376-5257-4
E-Book: available as free open access publication
PDF: ISBN 978-3-8394-5257-8

Jesús Muñoz Morcillo, Caroline Y. Robertson-von Trotha (eds.)
Genealogy of Popular Science
From Ancient Ecphrasis to Virtual Reality

2020, 586 p., pb., col. ill.
49,00 € (DE), 978-3-8376-4835-5
E-Book:
PDF: 48,99 € (DE), ISBN 978-3-8394-4835-9

Monika Ankele, Benoît Majerus (eds.)
Material Cultures of Psychiatry

2020, 416 p., pb., col. ill.
40,00 € (DE), 978-3-8376-4788-4
E-Book: available as free open access publication
PDF: ISBN 978-3-8394-4788-8

All print, e-book and open access versions of the titles in our list are available in our online shop www.transcript-publishing.com!